T5-BAO-457

Official Wireless Application Protocol

Official Wireless Application Protocol: The Complete Standard with Searchable CD-ROM

Wireless Application Protocol Forum, Ltd.

Wiley Computer Publishing

John Wiley & Sons, Inc.

NEW YORK • CHICHESTER • WEINHEIM • BRISBANE • SINGAPORE • TORONTO

This book is printed on acid-free paper. ♾

Published by John Wiley & Sons, Inc.

Published simultaneously in Canada.

Library of Congress Cataloging-in-Publication Data:

Wireless Application Protocol Forum, Ltd.
Wireless application protocol / Wireless Applications Protocol Forum, Ltd.
p. cm.
Includes bibliographical references and index.
ISBN 0-471-32755-7 (cloth/CD-ROM : alk. paper)
1. Computer network protocols. 2. Wireless communication systems.
I. Title.
TK5105.55.W57 1999
004.6'2—dc21 98-53458
CIP

Printed in the United States of America.

10 9 8 7 6 5 4

Contents

Introduction

1. Scope

The Wireless Application Protocol (WAP) is a result of continuous work to define an industrywide specification for developing applications that operate over wireless communication networks. The scope for the WAP Forum is to define a set of specifications to be used by service applications. The wireless market is growing very quickly, and reaching new customers and services. To enable operators and manufacturers to meet the challenges in advanced services, differentiation, and fast/flexible service creation, WAP Forum defines a set of protocols in Transport, Security, Transaction, Session and application layers. For additional information on the WAP architecture, please refer to *Wireless Application Protocol Architecture Specification* [WAPARCH].

The Session layer protocol family in the WAP architecture is called the Wireless Session Protocol (WSP). WSP provides the upper-level application layer of WAP with a consistent interface for two session services. The first is a connection-mode service that operates above a Transaction layer protocol WTP, and the second is a connectionless service that operates above a secure or nonsecure datagram transport service. For more information on the transaction and transport services, please refer to *Wireless Application Protocol: Wireless Transaction Protocol Specification* [WAPWTP], and *Wireless Application Protocol: Wireless Datagram Protocol Specification* [WAPWDP].

The Wireless Session Protocols currently offer services most suited for browsing applications (WSP/B). WSP/B provides HTTP 1.1 functionality and incorporates new features such as long-lived sessions, a common facility for data push, capability negotiation, and session suspend/resume. The protocols in the WSP family are optimized for low-bandwidth bearer networks with relatively long latency.

2. WSP Architectural Overview

Wireless Session Protocol is a session-level protocol family for remote operations between a client and proxy or server.

2.1 Reference Model

A model of layering the protocols in WAP is illustrated in Figure I.1. WAP protocols and their functions are layered in a style resembling that of the ISO OSI Reference Model [ISO7498]. Layer management entities handle protocol initialization, configuration, and error conditions (such as loss of connectivity due to the mobile station roaming out of coverage) that are not handled by the protocol itself.

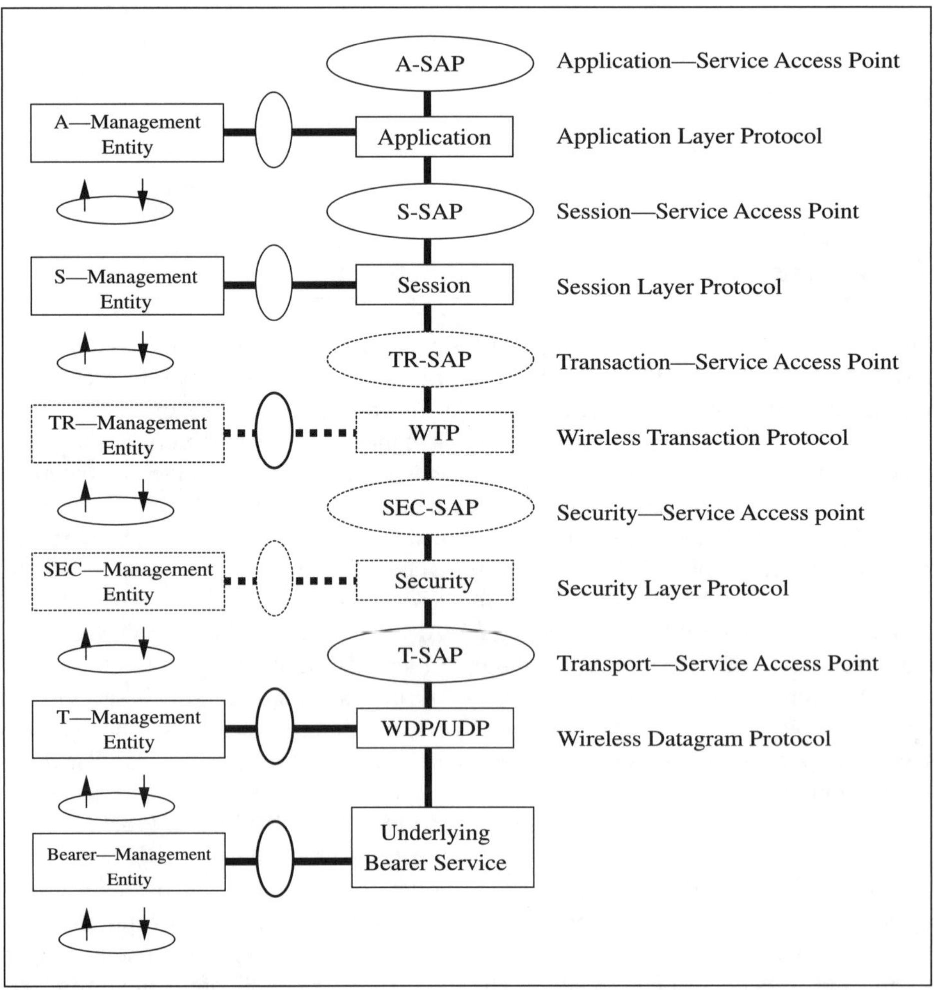

Figure I.1 Wireless Application Protocol reference model.

WSP is designed to function on the transaction and datagram services. Security is assumed to be an optional layer above the Transport layer. The Security layer preserves the Transport service interfaces. The transaction, session, or application management entities are assumed to provide the additional support that is required to establish security contexts and secure connections. This support is not provided by the WSP protocols directly. In this regard, the Security layer is modular. WSP itself does not require a Security layer; however, applications that use WSP may require it.

2.2 WSP/B Features

WSP provides a means for organized exchange of content between cooperating client/server applications. Specifically, it provides the applications means to:

- Establish a reliable session from client to server and release that session in an orderly manner
- Agree on a common level of protocol functionality using capability negotiation
- Exchange content between client and server using compact encoding
- Suspend and resume the session

The currently defined services and protocols (WSP/B) are most suited for browsing-type applications. WSP/B defines actually two protocols: One provides connection-mode session services over a transaction service, and another provides nonconfirmed, connectionless services over a datagram transport service. The connectionless service is most suitable when applications do not need reliable delivery of data and do not care about confirmation. It can be used without actually having to establish a session.

In addition to the general features, WSP/B offers means to:

- Provide HTTP/1.1 functionality:
  - Extensible request-reply methods
  - Composite objects
  - Content type negotiation
- Exchange client and server session headers
- Interrupt transactions in process
- Push content from server to client in an unsynchronized manner
- Negotiate support for multiple, simultaneous asynchronous transactions

2.2.1 Basic Functionality

The core of the WSP/B design is a binary form of HTTP. Consequently, the requests sent to a server and responses going to a client may include both headers (meta-information) and data. All the methods defined by HTTP/1.1 are supported. In addition, capability negotiation can be used to agree on a set of extended request methods, so that full compatibility to HTTP/1.1 applications can be retained.

WSP/B provides typed data transfer for the Application layer. The HTTP/1.1 content headers are used to define content type, character set encoding, languages, and so forth, in an extensible manner. However, compact binary encodings are defined for the well-known headers to reduce protocol overhead. WSP/B also specifies a compact composite data format that provides content headers for each component within the composite data object. This is a semantically equivalent binary form of the MIME "multipart/mixed" format used by HTTP/1.1.

WSP/B itself does not interpret the header information in requests and replies. As part of the session creation process, request and reply headers that remain constant over the life of the session can be exchanged between service users in the client and the server. These may include acceptable content types, character sets, languages, device capabilities, and other static parameters. WSP/B will pass through client and server session headers as well as request and response headers without additions or removals.

The life cycle of a WSP/B session is not tied to the underlying transport. A session can be suspended while the session is idle to free up network resources or save battery. A lightweight session reestablishment protocol allows the session to be resumed without the overhead of full-blown session establishment. A session may be resumed over a different bearer network.

2.2.2 Extended Functionality

WSP/B allows extended capabilities to be negotiated between the peers. This allows for both high-performance, feature-full implementation as well as simple, basic, and small implementations.

WSP/B provides an optional mechanism for attaching header information (metadata) to the acknowledgment of a transaction. This allows the client application to communicate specific information about the completed transaction back to the server.

WSP/B provides both push and pull data transfer. Pull is done using the request/response mechanism from HTTP/1.1. In addition, WSP/B provides three push mechanisms for data transfer:

- Confirmed data push within an existing session context
- Nonconfirmed data push within an existing session context
- Nonconfirmed data push without an existing session

The confirmed data push mechanism allows the server to push data to the client at any time during a session. The server receives confirmation that the push was delivered.

The nonconfirmed data push within an existing session provides a similar function as reliable data push, but without confirmation. The nonconfirmed data push can also occur without an existing session. In this case, a default session context is assumed. Nonconfirmed out-of-session data push can be used to send one-way messages over an unreliable transport.

WSP/B optionally supports asynchronous requests so that a client can submit multiple requests to the server simultaneously. This improves utilization of airtime in that multiple requests and replies can be coalesced into fewer messages. This also improves latency as the results of each request can be sent to the client when it becomes available.

WSP/B partitions the space of well-known header field names into *header code pages*. Each code page can define only a fairly limited number of encodings for well-known field names, which permits them to be represented more compactly. Running out of identities for well-known field names on a certain code page is still not a problem, since WSP/B specifies a mechanism for shifting from one header code page to another.

3. Definitions

For the purposes of this specification the following definitions apply.

Bearer Network. A bearer network is used to carry the messages of a Transport layer protocol—and ultimately also of the Session layer protocols—between physical devices. During the lifetime of a session, several bearer networks may be used.

Capability. Capability is a term to refer to the Session layer protocol facilities and configuration parameters that a client or server supports.

Capability Negotiation. Capability negotiation is the mechanism for agreeing on session functionality and protocol options. Session capabilities are negotiated during session establishment. Capability negotiation allows a server application to determine whether a client can support certain protocol facilities and configurations.

Client and Server. The terms *client* and *server* are used in order to map WSP to well-known and existing systems. A client is a device (or application) that initiates a request for a session. The server is a device that passively waits for session requests from client devices. The server can either accept the request or reject it.

An implementation of the WSP protocol may include only client or server functions in order to minimize the footprint. A client or server may only support a subset of the protocol facilities, indicating this during protocol capability negotiation.

Connectionless Session Service. Connectionless session service is an unreliable session service. In this mode, only the request primitive is available to service users, and only the indication primitive is available to the service provider.

Connection-Mode Session Service. Connection-mode session service is a reliable session service. In this mode, both request and response primitives are available to service users, and both indication and confirm primitives are available to the service provider.

Content. The entity body sent with a request or response is referred to as *content*. It is encoded in a format and encoding is defined by the entity-header fields.

Content Negotiation. Content negotiation is the mechanism the server uses to select the appropriate type and encoding of content when servicing a request. The type and encoding of content in any response can be negotiated. Content negotiation allows a server application to decide whether a client can support a certain form of content.

Entity. An entity is the information transferred as the payload of a request or response. An entity consists of meta-information in the form of entity-header fields and content in the form of an entity-body.

Header. A header contains meta-information. Specifically, a session header contains general information about a session that remains constant over the lifetime of a session; an entity-header contains meta-information about a particular request, response, or entity body (content).

Layer Entity. In the OSI architecture, the active elements within a layer that participate in providing layer service are called *layer entities*.

Method. Method is the *type* of client request as defined by HTTP/1.1 (e.g., Get, Post, etc.). A WSP client uses methods and extended methods to invoke services on the server.

Null Terminated String. A sequence of non-zero octets followed by a zero octet.

Peer Address Quadruplet. Sessions are associated with a particular client address, client port, server address, and server port. This combination of four values is called the *peer address quadruplet* in the specification.

Proxy. An intermediary program that acts both as a server and as a client for the purpose of making requests on behalf of other clients. Requests are serviced internally or by passing them on, with possible translation, to other server.

Pull and Push Data Transfer. Push and pull are common vernacular in the Internet world to describe push transactions and method transactions, respectively. A server "pushes" data to a client by invoking the WSP/B push service, whereas a client "pulls" data from a server by invoking the WSP/B method service.

Session. A long-lived communication context established between two programs for the purpose of transactions and typed data transfer.

Session Service Access Point (S-SAP). Session Service Access Point is a conceptual point at which session service is provided to the upper layer.

Session Service Provider. A Session Service Provider is a layer entity that actively participates in providing the session service via an S-SAP.

Session Service User. A Session Service User is a layer entity that requests services from a Session Service Provider via an S-SAP.

Transaction. Three forms of transactions are specified herein. We do not use the term *transaction* to imply the semantics often associated with database transactions.

- A *method transaction* is a three-way request-response-acknowledge communication initiated by the client to invoke a method on the server.
- A *push transaction* is a two-way request-acknowledge communication initiated by the server to push data to the client.
- A *transport transaction* is a lower-level transaction primitive provided by a Transaction Service Provider.

4. Abbreviations

For the purposes of this specification, the following abbreviations apply.

API	Application Programming Interface
A-SAP	Application Service Access Point
HTTP	Hypertext Transfer Protocol
ISO	International Organization for Standardization
MOM	Maximum Outstanding Method requests
MOP	Maximum Outstanding Push requests
MRU	Maximum Receive Unit
OSI	Open System Interconnection
PDU	Protocol Data Unit
S-SAP	Session Service Access Point
SDU	Service Data Unit
SEC-SAP	Security Service Access Point
T-SAP	Transport Service Access Point
TID	Transaction Identifier
TR-SAP	Transaction Service Access Point
WDP	Wireless Datagram Protocol
WSP	Wireless Session Protocol
WSP/B	Wireless Session Protocol—Browsing
WTP	Wireless Transaction Protocol

5. Documentation Conventions

This specification uses the same keywords as specified in RFC 2119 [RFC2119] for defining the significance of each particular requirement. These words are:

MUST. This word, or the terms "REQUIRED" or "SHALL," means that the definition is an absolute requirement of the specification.

MUST NOT. This phrase, or the phrase "SHALL NOT," means that the definition is an absolute prohibition of the specification.

SHOULD. This word, or the adjective "RECOMMENDED," means that there may exist valid reasons in particular circumstances to ignore a particular item, but the full implications must be understood and carefully weighed before choosing a different course.

SHOULD NOT. This phrase, or the phrase "NOT RECOMMENDED," means that there may exist valid reasons in particular circumstances when the particular behavior is acceptable or even useful, but the full implications should be understood and the case carefully weighed before implementing any behavior described with this label.

MAY. This word, or the adjective "OPTIONAL," means that an item is truly optional. One vendor may choose to include the item because a particular marketplace requires it or because the vendor feels that it enhances the product, while another vendor may omit the same item. An implementation that does not include a particular option MUST be prepared to interoperate with another implementation that does include the option, though perhaps with reduced functionality. In the same vein, an implementation that does include a particular option MUST be prepared to interoperate with another implementation that does not include the option (except, of course, for the feature the option provides).

6. Normative References

[WAPARCH] "WAP Architecture Specification," WAP Forum, 30-April-1998. URL: http://www.wapforum.org/

[WAPWDP] "Wireless Datagram Protocol Specification," WAP Forum, 30-April-1998. URL: http://www.wapforum.org/

[WAPWTP] "Wireless Transaction Protocol Specification," WAP Forum, 30-April-1998. URL: http://www.wapforum.org/

[RFC2119] "Key Words for Use in RFCs to Indicate Requirement Levels," Bradner, S., March 1997. URL: ftp://ftp.isi.edu/in-notes/rfc2119.txt

[RFC2068] "Hypertext Transfer Protocol—HTTP/1.1," Fielding, R., et. al., January 1997. URL: ftp://ftp.isi.edu/in-notes/rfc2068.txt

[RFC1521] "MIME (Multipurpose Internet Mail Extensions) Part One: Mechanisms for Specifying and Describing the Format of Internet Message Bodies," Borenstein, N., et. al., September 1993. URL: ftp://ftp.isi.edu/in-notes/rfc1521.txt

[RFC2047] "MIME (Multipurpose Internet Mail Extensions) Part Three: Message Header Extensions for Non-ASCII Text," Moore, K., November 1996. URL: ftp://ftp.isi.edu/in-notes/rfc2047.txt

[RFC822] "Standard for the Format of ARPA Internet Text Messages," Crocker, D., August 1982. URL: ftp://ftp.isi.edu/in-notes/rfc822.txt

7. Informative References

[ISO7498] "Information Technology—Open Systems Interconnection—Basic Reference Model: The Basic Model," ISO/IEC 7498-1:1994.

[ISO10731] "Information Technology—Open Systems Interconnection—Basic Reference Model—Conventions for the Definition of OSI Services," ISO/IEC 10731:1994.

[RFC1630] "Universal Resource Identifiers in WWW, A Unifying Syntax for the Expression of Names and Addresses of Objects on the Network as used in the World Wide Web," Berners-Lee, T., June 1994. URL: ftp://ftp.isi.edu/in-notes/rfc1630.txt

[RFC1738] "Uniform Resource Locators (URL)," Berners-Lee, T., et. al., December 1994.
URL: ftp://ftp.isi.edu/in-notes/rfc1738.txt

[RFC1808] "Relative Uniform Resource Locators," Fielding, R., June 1995.
URL: ftp://ftp.isi.edu/in-notes/rfc1808.txt

[RFC1864] "The Content-MD5 Header Field," Meyers, J. and Rose, M., October 1995.
URL: ftp://ftp.isi.edu/in-notes/rfc1864.txt

Part

One

The Architecture

CHAPTER

1

Wireless Application Protocol Architecture Specification

1. Scope

The Wireless Application Protocol (WAP) is a result of the WAP Forum's efforts to promote industrywide specifications for technology useful in developing applications and services that operate over wireless communication networks. WAP specifies an application framework and network protocols for wireless devices such as mobile telephones, pagers, and Personal Digital Assistants (PDAs). The specifications extend and leverage mobile networking technologies (such as digital data networking standards) and Internet technologies (such as XML, URLs, scripting, and various content formats). The effort is aimed at enabling operators, manufacturers, and content developers to meet the challenges in building advanced differentiated services and implementations in a fast and flexible manner.

The objectives of the WAP Forum are:

- To bring Internet content and advanced data services to digital cellular phones and other wireless terminals.
- To create a global wireless protocol specification that will work across differing wireless network technologies.
- To enable the creation of content and applications that scale across a very wide range of bearer networks and device types.
- To embrace and extend existing standards and technology wherever appropriate.

The WAP Architecture Specification is intended to present the system and protocol architectures essential to achieving the objectives of the WAP Forum. The WAP

Architecture Specification acts as the starting point for understanding the WAP technologies and resulting specifications. As such, it provides an overview of the different technologies and references the appropriate specifications for further details.

2. Background

2.1 Motivation

WAP is positioned at the convergence of two rapidly evolving network technologies, wireless data and the Internet. Both the wireless data market and the Internet are growing very quickly and are continuously reaching new customers. The explosive growth of the Internet has fueled the creation of new and exciting information services.

Most of the technology developed for the Internet has been designed for desktop and larger computers, and medium-to-high bandwidth, generally reliable data networks. Mass-market, handheld wireless devices present a more constrained computing environment compared to desktop computers. Because of fundamental limitations of power and form-factor, mass-market handheld devices tend to have:

- Less powerful CPUs
- Less memory (ROM and RAM)
- Restricted power consumption
- Smaller displays
- Different input devices (e.g., a phone keypad)

Similarly, wireless data networks present a more constrained communication environment compared to wired networks. Because of fundamental limitations of power, available spectrum, and mobility, wireless data networks tend to have:

- Less bandwidth
- More latency
- Less connection stability
- Less predictable availability

Mobile networks are growing in complexity, and the cost of all aspects for provisioning of more value-added services is increasing. In order to meet the requirements of mobile network operators, solutions must be:

Interoperable: Terminals from different manufacturers communicate with services in the mobile network.

Scaleable: Mobile network operators are able to scale services to customer needs.

Efficient: Provides quality of service suited to the behavior and characteristics of the mobile network.

Reliable: Provides a consistent and predictable platform for deploying services.

Secure: Enables services to be extended over potentially unprotected mobile networks while still preserving the integrity of user data; protects the devices and services from security problems such as denial of service.

Many of the current mobile networks include advanced services that can be offered to end users. Mobile network operators strive to provide advanced services in a useable and attractive way in order to promote increased usage of the mobile network services and to decrease the turnover rate of subscribers. Standard features, like call control, can be enhanced by using WAP technology to provide customized user interfaces. For example, services such as call forwarding may provide a user interface that prompts the user to make a choice of accepting a call, forwarding it to another person, forwarding it to voice mail, and so forth.

The WAP specifications address mobile network characteristics and operator needs by adapting existing network technology to the special requirements of mass-market, handheld wireless data devices, and by introducing new technology where appropriate.

2.2 Requirements

The requirements of the WAP Forum architecture are to:

- Leverage existing standards where possible
- Define a layered, scaleable, and extensible architecture
- Support as many wireless networks as possible
- Optimize for narrowband bearers with potentially high latency
- Optimize for efficient use of device resources (low memory/CPU usage/power consumption)
- Provide support for secure applications and communication
- Enable the creation of Man Machine Interfaces (MMIs) with maximum flexibility and vendor control
- Provide access to local handset functionality, such as logical indication for incoming call
- Facilitate network-operator and third-party service provisioning
- Support multivendor interoperability by defining the optional and mandatory components of the specifications
- Provide a programming model for telephony services and integration

3. Architecture Overview

3.1 The World Wide Web Model

The Internet World Wide Web (WWW) architecture provides a very flexible and powerful programming model (Figure 1.1). Applications and content are presented in standard data formats, and are *browsed* by applications known as *Web browsers*. The Web browser is a networked application; in other words, it sends requests for named data objects to a network server and the network server responds with the data encoded using the standard formats.

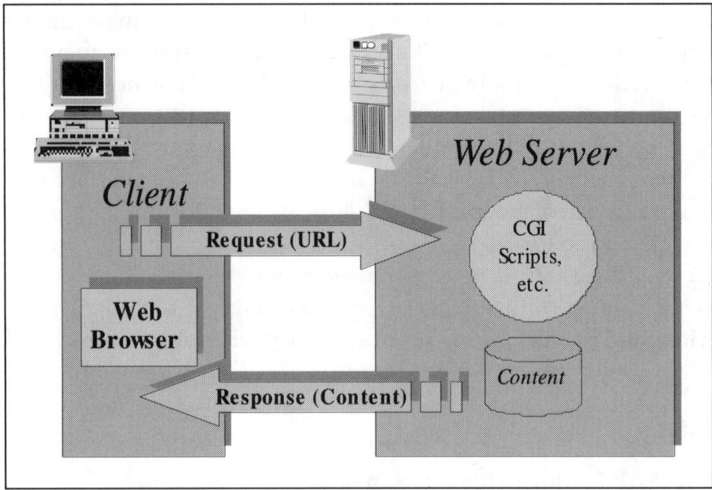

Figure 1.1 World Wide Web programming model.

The WWW standards specify many of the mechanisms necessary to build a general-purpose application environment, including:

Standard naming model. All servers and content on the WWW are named with an Internet-standard *Uniform Resource Locator* (URL) [RFC1738, RFC1808].

Content typing. All content on the WWW is given a specific type, thereby allowing Web browsers to correctly process the content based on its type [RFC2045, RFC2048].

Standard content formats. All Web browsers support a set of standard content formats. These include the HyperText Markup Language (HTML) [HTML4], the JavaScript scripting language [ECMAScript, JavaScript], and a large number of other formats.

Standard protocols. Standard networking protocols allow any Web browser to communicate with any Web server. The most commonly used protocol on the WWW is the HyperText Transport Protocol (HTTP) [RFC2068].

This infrastructure allows users to easily reach a large number of third-party applications and content services. It also allows application developers to easily create applications and content services for a large community of clients.

The WWW protocols define three classes of servers:

Origin server. The server on which a given resource (content) resides or is to be created.

Proxy. An intermediary program that acts as both a server and a client for the purpose of making requests on behalf of other clients. The proxy typically resides between clients and servers that have no means of direct communication; for example, across a firewall. Requests are either serviced by the proxy program or passed on, with possible translation, to other servers. A proxy must implement both the client and server requirements of the WWW specifications.

Gateway. A server that acts as an intermediary for some other server. Unlike a proxy, a gateway receives requests as if it were the origin server for the requested resource. The requesting client may not be aware that it is communicating with a gateway.

3.2 The WAP Model

The WAP programming model (Figure 1.2) is similar to the WWW programming model. This provides several benefits to the application developer community, including a familiar programming model, a proven architecture, and the ability to leverage existing tools (e.g., Web servers, XML tools, etc.). Optimizations and extensions have been made in order to match the characteristics of the wireless environment. Wherever possible, existing standards have been adopted or have been used as the starting point for the WAP technology.

WAP content and applications are specified in a set of well-known content formats based on the familiar WWW content formats. Content is transported using a set of standard communication protocols based on the WWW communication protocols. A *micro browser* in the wireless terminal coordinates the user interface and is analogous to a standard Web browser.

WAP defines a set of standard components that enable communication between mobile terminals and network servers, including:

Standard naming model. WWW-standard URLs are used to identify WAP content on origin servers. WWW-standard URIs are used to identify local resources in a device; for example, call control functions.

Content typing. All WAP content is given a specific type consistent with WWW typing. This allows WAP user agents to correctly process the content based on its type.

Standard content formats. WAP content formats are based on WWW technology and include display markup, calendar information, electronic business card objects, images and scripting language.

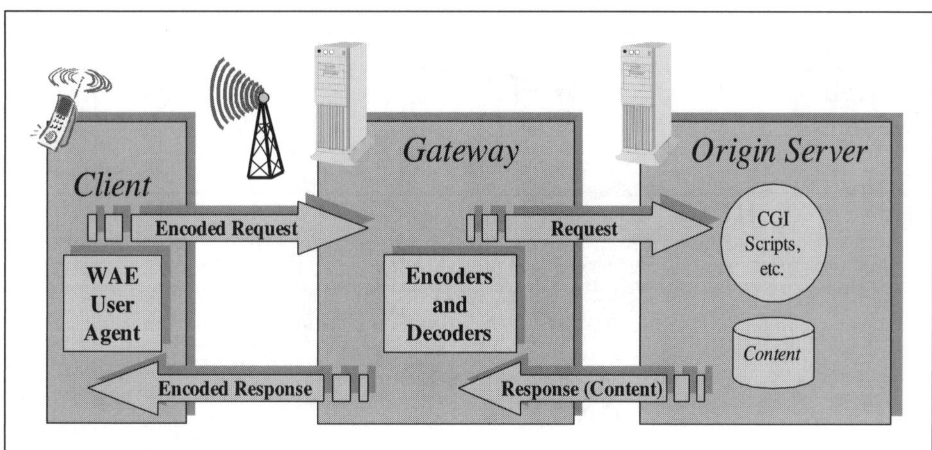

Figure 1.2 WAP programming model.

Standard communication protocols. WAP communication protocols enable the communication of browser requests from the mobile terminal to the network Web server.

The WAP content types and protocols have been optimized for mass-market, handheld wireless devices. WAP utilizes proxy technology to connect between the wireless domain and the WWW. The WAP proxy typically is comprised of the following functionality:

Protocol gateway. The protocol gateway translates requests from the WAP protocol stack (WSP, WTP, WTLS, and WDP) to the WWW protocol stack (HTTP and TCP/IP).

Content encoders and decoders. The content encoders translate WAP content into compact encoded formats to reduce the size of data over the network.

This infrastructure ensures that mobile terminal users can browse a wide variety of WAP content and applications, and that the application author is able to build content services and applications that run on a large base of mobile terminals. The WAP proxy allows content and applications to be hosted on standard WWW servers and to be developed using proven WWW technologies such as CGI scripting.

While the nominal use of WAP will include a Web server, WAP proxy and WAP client, the WAP architecture can easily support other configurations. It is possible to create an origin server that includes the WAP proxy functionality. Such a server might be used to facilitate end-to-end security solutions or applications that require better access control or a guarantee of responsiveness, (e.g., WTA).

3.3 Example WAP Network

The following is for illustrative purposes only. An example WAP network is shown in Figure 1.3.

In the example, the WAP client communicates with two servers in the wireless network. The WAP proxy translates WAP requests to WWW requests, thereby allowing the

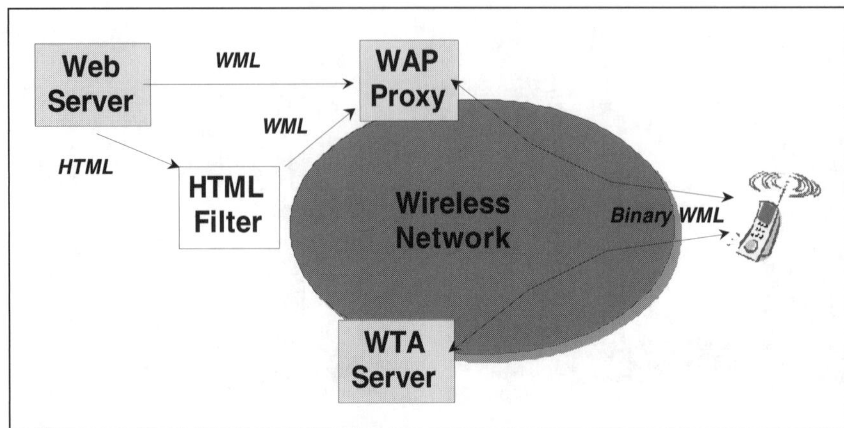

Figure 1.3 Example WAP network.

WAP client to submit requests to the Web server. The proxy also encodes the responses from the Web server into the compact binary format understood by the client.

If the Web server provides WAP content (e.g., WML), the WAP proxy retrieves it directly from the Web server. However, if the Web server provides WWW content (such as HTML), a filter is used to translate the WWW content into WAP content. For example, the HTML filter would translate HTML into WML.

The Wireless Telephony Application (WTA) server is an example origin or gateway server that responds to requests from the WAP client directly. The WTA server is used to provide WAP access to features of the wireless network provider's telecommunications infrastructure.

3.4 Security Model

WAP enables a flexible security infrastructure that focuses on providing connection security between a WAP client and server.

WAP can provide end-to-end security between WAP protocol endpoints. If a browser and origin server desire end-to-end security, they must communicate directly using the WAP protocols. End-to-end security may also be achieved if the WAP proxy is trusted or, for example, located at the same physically secure place as the origin server.

4. Components of the WAP Architecture

The WAP architecture provides a scaleable and extensible environment for application development for mobile communication devices. This is achieved through a layered design of the entire protocol stack (Figure 1.4). Each of the layers of the architecture is accessible by the layers above, as well as by other services and applications.

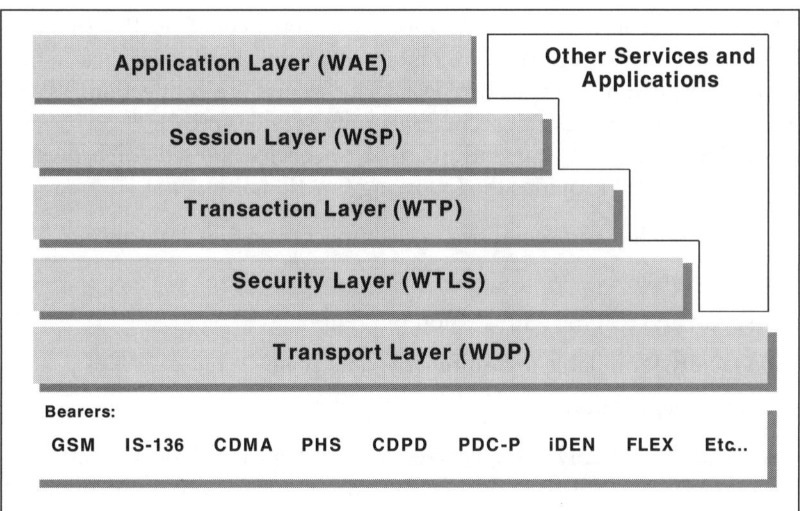

Figure 1.4 WAP architecture.

The WAP layered architecture enables other services and applications to utilize the features of the WAP stack through a set of well-defined interfaces. External applications may access the Session, Transaction, Security, and Transport layers directly. The following sections provide a description of the various elements of the protocol stack architecture.

4.1 Wireless Application Environment (WAE)

The Wireless Application Environment (WAE) is a general-purpose application environment based on a combination of World Wide Web and mobile telephony technologies. The primary objective of the WAE effort is to establish an interoperable environment that will allow operators and service providers to build applications and services that can reach a wide variety of different wireless platforms in an efficient and useful manner. WAE includes a micro-browser environment containing the following functionality:

Wireless Markup Language (WML). A lightweight markup language, similar to HTML, but optimized for use in handheld mobile terminals.

WMLScript. A lightweight scripting language, similar to JavaScript.

Wireless Telephony Application (WTA, WTAI). Telephony services and programming interfaces.

Content formats. A set of well-defined data formats, including images, phone book records, and calendar information.

A much more detailed description of the WAE architecture is provided in [WAE-oview].

4.2 Wireless Session Protocol (WSP)

The Wireless Session Protocol (WSP) provides the application layer of WAP with a consistent interface for two session services. The first is a connection-oriented service that operates above the transaction layer protocol WTP. The second is a connectionless service that operates above a secure or nonsecure datagram service (WDP).

The Wireless Session Protocols currently consist of services suited for browsing applications (WSP/B). WSP/B provides the following functionality:

- HTTP/1.1 functionality and semantics in a compact over-the-air encoding
- Long-lived session state
- Session suspend and resume with session migration
- A common facility for reliable and unreliable data push
- Protocol feature negotiation

The protocols in the WSP family are optimized for low-bandwidth bearer networks with relatively long latency. WSP/B is designed to allow a WAP proxy to connect a WSP/B client to a standard HTTP server. See [WSP] for more information.

4.3 Wireless Transaction Protocol (WTP)

The Wireless Transaction Protocol (WTP) runs on top of a datagram service and provides a lightweight transaction-oriented protocol that is suitable for implementation in "thin" clients (mobile stations). WTP operates efficiently over secure or nonsecure wireless datagram networks and provides the following features:

- Three classes of transaction service:

  Unreliable one-way requests

  Reliable one-way requests

  Reliable two-way request-reply transactions
- Optional user-to-user reliability: WTP user triggers the confirmation of each received message
- Optional out-of-band data on acknowledgments
- PDU concatenation and delayed acknowledgment to reduce the number of messages sent
- Asynchronous transactions

See [WTP] for more information.

4.4 Wireless Transport Layer Security (WTLS)

WTLS is a security protocol based upon the industry-standard Transport Layer Security (TLS) protocol, formerly known as Secure Sockets Layer (SSL). WTLS is intended for use with the WAP transport protocols and has been optimized for use over narrowband communication channels. WTLS provides the following features:

Data integrity. WTLS contains facilities to ensure that data sent between the terminal and an application server is unchanged and uncorrupted.

Privacy. WTLS contains facilities to ensure that data transmitted between the terminal and an application server is private and cannot be understood by any intermediate parties that may have intercepted the data stream.

Authentication. WTLS contains facilities to establish the authenticity of the terminal and application server.

Denial-of-service protection. WTLS contains facilities for detecting and rejecting data that is replayed or not successfully verified. WTLS makes many typical denial-of-service attacks harder to accomplish and protects the upper protocol layers.

WTLS may also be used for secure communication between terminals, such as for authentication of electronic business card exchange.

Applications are able to selectively enable or disable WTLS features depending on their security requirements and the characteristics of the underlying network (e.g., privacy may be disabled on networks already providing this service at a lower layer).

See [WTLS] for more information.

4.5 Wireless Datagram Protocol (WDP)

The Transport layer protocol in the WAP architecture is referred to as the Wireless Datagram Protocol (WDP). The WDP layer operates above the data-capable bearer services supported by the various network types. As a general transport service, WDP offers a consistent service to the upper-layer protocols of WAP and communicates transparently over one of the available bearer services.

Since the WDP protocols provide a common interface to the upper-layer protocols, the Security, Session, and Application layers are able to function independently of the underlying wireless network. This is accomplished by adapting the Transport layer to specific features of the underlying bearer. By keeping the Transport layer interface and the basic features consistent, global interoperability can be achieved using mediating gateways.

See [WDP] for more information.

4.6 Bearers

The WAP protocols are designed to operate over a variety of different bearer services, including short message, circuit-switched data, and packet data. The bearers offer differing levels of quality of service with respect to throughput, error rate, and delays. The WAP protocols are designed to compensate for or tolerate these varying levels of service.

Since the WDP layer provides the convergence between the bearer service and the rest of the WAP stack, the WDP specification [WDP] lists the bearers that are supported and the techniques used to allow WAP protocols to run over each bearer. The list of supported bearers will change over time, with new bearers being added as the wireless market evolves.

4.7 Other Services and Applications

The WAP layered architecture enables other services and applications to utilize the features of the WAP stack through a set of well-defined interfaces. External applications may access the Session, Transaction, Security, and Transport layers directly. This allows the WAP stack to be used for applications and services not currently specified by WAP but deemed to be valuable for the wireless market. For example, applications (e.g., electronic mail, calendar, phone book, notepad, and electronic commerce) or services (e.g., white and yellow pages) may be developed to use the WAP protocols.

4.8 Sample Configurations of WAP Technology

WAP technology is expected to be useful for applications and services beyond those specified by the WAP Forum. Figure 1.5 depicts several possible protocol stacks using WAP technology. These are for illustrative purposes only and do not constitute a statement of conformance or interoperability.

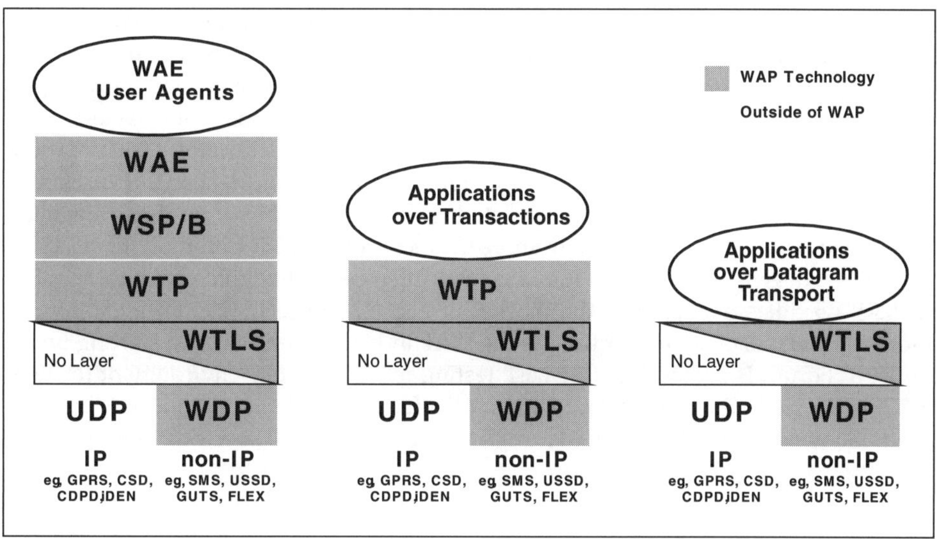

Figure 1.5 Sample WAP stacks.

The leftmost stack represents a typical example of a WAP application (i.e., WAE user agent) running over the complete portfolio of WAP technology. The middle stack is intended for applications and services that require transaction services with or without security. The rightmost stack is intended for applications and services that only require datagram transport with or without security.

5. Compliance and Interoperability

The WAP Forum views multivendor interoperability as an important element to the success of WAP products. In order to provide as high a probability as is technically possible that two WAP products developed independently by two different vendors will successfully interoperate, a rigorous definition of conformance, compliance, and testing must be developed. To this end the WAP Forum has created a WAP Conformance Specification [WAPConf] and is working to maintain current information relating to all issues of WAP interoperability.

Successful interoperability can only be achieved by testing products. Testing can be divided into two broad categories of *static testing* and *dynamic testing*. Static testing is a manufacturer's statement of the capabilities and functions of a product. Static testing will identify obvious areas of incompatibility between two products; in other words, where one implements a feature that the other does not support. All WAP specifications will provide a means for static testing in the form of a Protocol Implementation Conformance Statement (PICS). See [WAPConf] for more details on static testing.

Dynamic testing is the real form of testing that leads to a high degree of confidence that two products will successfully interoperate. Dynamic testing involves the execution or exercising of a product in a live environment, ultimately proving that the product meets the stated claims given in the static test (i.e., PICS). There are three general approaches to dynamic testing: pair-wise testing or bake-offs; use of a reference implementation against which all products are measured; and definition of formal test suites containing test cases to be run against a product in a testing laboratory. Each of these approaches to dynamic testing has cost trade-offs and some technical pluses and minuses. The cost of each approach is related to the total number of products that need to be tested. The WAP Forum will promote the most cost-effective method that leads to the greatest degree of confidence for successful interoperability given the total number of WAP products available in the market at a given time. This is an evolutionary approach that will change over time as the WAP industry matures. As a starting point, the WAP Forum is promoting pair-wise testing in a laboratory environment for new WAP products. As the WAP industry evolves, reference implementations may be identified, followed by the definition of formal test suites for WAP specifications.

6. Future Work Items

The Future Work Items list is a collection of areas that warrant further consideration in order to determine whether or not any working groups should be chartered with developing recommendations or specifications. The list is neither prescriptive nor exhaustive. This list is not prioritized in any way; in other words, no importance can be attached to the numbering scheme. Areas for consideration can be added or deleted at any time. The list currently contains the following items:

1. Connection-oriented data transport
2. Integration of SIM Toolkit, smartcard and WAP
3. Integration of MExE (ETSI) and WAP
4. Additional integration with the telephony network
5. Downloadable WMLScript libraries
6. Compression (WTLS or other layers)
7. Application levels security; e.g., crypto scripting libraries
8. Wider scope of security architecture, including smart card support, improved handling of end-to-end security, certificate authority hierarchies, etc.
9. Support for streaming multimedia content for higher-bandwidth bearers; e.g., GPRS
10. Support for multicast data
11. Support for location-dependent mobile services; e.g., positioning functions and features
12. Downloadable applications
13. Speech API
14. Management Entity Definitions for each layer and across all layers of the WAP

15. Quality of Service for the WAP stack with respect to each bearer service
16. Application Programming Interfaces for each layer of the WAP stack
17. Interoperability Testing (see previous section on compliance and interoperability testing)

7. Definitions

The following are terms and conventions used throughout this specification.

The key words "MUST", "MUST NOT", "REQUIRED", "SHALL", "SHALL NOT", "SHOULD", "SHOULD NOT", "RECOMMENDED", "MAY", and "OPTIONAL" in this document are to be interpreted as described in [RFC2119].

Author. An author is a person or program that writes or generates WML, WML-Script, or other content.

Client. A device (or application) that initiates a request for a connection with a server.

Content. Subject matter (data) stored or generated at an origin server. Content is typically displayed or interpreted by a user agent in response to a user request.

Content Encoding. When used as a verb, content encoding indicates the act of converting content from one format to another. Typically the resulting format requires less physical space than the original, is easier to process or store, and/or is encrypted. When used as a noun, *content encoding* specifies a particular format or encoding standard or process.

Content Format. Actual representation of content.

Device. A network entity that is capable of sending and receiving packets of information and has a unique device address. A device can act as both a client or a server within a given context or across multiple contexts. For example, a device can service a number of clients (as a server) while being a client to another server.

JavaScript. A *de facto* standard language that can be used to add dynamic behavior to HTML documents. JavaScript is one of the originating technologies of ECMA-Script.

Man-Machine Interface. A synonym for *user interface.*

Origin Server. The server on which a given resource resides or is to be created. Often referred to as a *Web server* or an *HTTP server*.

Resource. A network data object or service that can be identified by a URL. Resources may be available in multiple representations (e.g., multiple languages, data formats, size, and resolutions) or vary in other ways.

Server. A device (or application) that passively waits for connection requests from one or more clients. A server may accept or reject a connection request from a client.

Terminal. A device providing the user with user agent capabilities, including the ability to request and receive information. Also called a *mobile terminal* or *mobile station*.

User. A user is a person who interacts with a user agent to view, hear, or otherwise use a resource.

User Agent. A user agent is any software or device that interprets WML, WML-Script, WTAI, or other resources. This may include textual browsers, voice browsers, search engines, etc.

WMLScript. A scripting language used to program the mobile device. WMLScript is an extended subset of the JavaScript scripting language.

8. Abbreviations

For the purposes of this specification, the following abbreviations apply.

HTML	HyperText Markup Language [HTML4]
HTTP	HyperText Transfer Protocol [RFC2068]
MMI	Man-Machine Interface
PDA	Personal Digital Assistant
PICS	Protocol Implementation Conformance Statement
RFC	Request For Comments
SSL	Secure Sockets Layer
TLS	Transport Layer Security
URL	Uniform Resource Locator [RFC1738]
W3C	World Wide Web Consortium
WAE	Wireless Application Environment [WAE]
WAP	Wireless Application Protocol [WAP]
WDP	Wireless Datagram Protocol [WDP]
WML	Wireless Markup Language [WML]
WSP	Wireless Session Protocol [WSP]
WTA	Wireless Telephony Application [WTA]
WTLS	Wireless Transport Layer Security [WTLS]
WTP	Wireless Transaction Protocol [WTP]
WWW	World Wide Web

9. Normative References

[RFC2119] "Key words for use in RFCs to Indicate Requirement Levels," S. Bradner, March 1997.
URL: ftp://ftp.isi.edu/in-notes/rfc2119.txt

[WAEoview] "Wireless Application Environment Overview," WAP Forum, April 30, 1998.
URL: http://www.wapforum.org/

[WAE] "Wireless Application Environment Specification," WAP Forum, April 30, 1998.
URL: http://www.wapforum.org/

[WAP] "Wireless Application Protocol Architecture Specification," WAP Forum, April 30, 1998.
URL: http://www.wapforum.org/

[WAPConf] "Wireless Application Protocol Conformance Statement, Compliance Profile, and Release List," WAP Forum, April 30, 1998.
URL: http://www.wapforum.org/

[WDP] "Wireless Datagram Protocol Specification," WAP Forum, April 30, 1998.
URL: http://www.wapforum.org/

[WML] "Wireless Markup Language," WAP Forum, April 30, 1998.
URL: http://www.wapforum.org/

[WMLScript] "Wireless Markup Language Script," WAP Forum, April 30, 1998.
URL: http://www.wapforum.org/

[WMLSStdLib] "Wireless Markup Language Script Standard Libraries," WAP Forum, April 30, 1998.
URL: http://www.wapforum.org/

[WSP] "Wireless Session Protocol," WAP Forum, April 30, 1998.
URL: http://www.wapforum.org/

[WTA] "Wireless Telephony Application Specification," WAP Forum, April 30, 1998.
URL: http://www.wapforum.org/

[WTAI] "Wireless Telephony Application Interface," WAP Forum, April 30, 1998.
URL: http://www.wapforum.org/

[WTLS] "Wireless Transport Layer Security Protocol," WAP Forum, April 30, 1998.
URL: http://www.wapforum.org/

[WTP] "Wireless Transaction Protocol Specification," WAP Forum, April 30, 1998.
URL: http://www.wapforum.org/

10. Informative References

[ECMAScript] Standard ECMA-262: "ECMAScript Language Specification," ECMA, June 1997.

[HTML4] "HTML 4.0 Specification, W3C Recommendation 18-December-1997, REC-HTML40-971218," D. Raggett, et al., September 17, 1997.
URL: http://www.w3.org/TR/REC-html40

[JavaScript] "JavaScript: The Definitive Guide," David Flanagan. O'Reilly & Associates, Inc. 1997.

[RFC1738] "Uniform Resource Locators (URL)," T. Berners-Lee, et al., December 1994.
URL: ftp://ftp.isi.edu/in-notes/rfc1738.txt

[RFC1808] "Relative Uniform Resource Locators," R. Fielding, June 1995.
URL: ftp://ftp.isi.edu/in-notes/rfc1808.txt

[RFC2045] "Multipurpose Internet Mail Extensions (MIME) Part One: Format of Internet Message Bodies," N. Freed, et al., November 1996.
URL: ftp://ftp.isi.edu/in-notes/rfc2045.txt

[RFC2048] "Multipurpose Internet Mail Extensions (MIME) Part Four: Registration Procedures," N. Freed, et al., November 1996.
URL: ftp://ftp.isi.edu/in-notes/rfc2048.txt

[RFC2068] "Hypertext Transfer Protocol—HTTP/1.1," R. Fielding, et al., January 1997.
URL: ftp://ftp.isi.edu/in-notes/rfc2068.txt

Part

Two

The Application Layer

CHAPTER

2

Wireless Application Environment Overview

1. Scope

Wireless Application Environment (WAE) is a result of the Wireless Application Protocol (WAP) efforts to promote industrywide standards and specifications for developing applications and services that operate over wireless communication networks. WAE specifies an application framework for wireless devices such as mobile telephones, pagers, and PDAs. The framework extends and leverages other WAP technologies, including Wireless Transaction Protocol (WTP) and Wireless Session Protocol (WSP), as well as other Internet technologies such as XML, URLs, scripting, and various content formats. The effort is aimed at enabling operators, manufacturers, and content developers to meet the challenges of implementing advanced differentiating services and applications in a fast and flexible manner.

This document provides a general overview of the overall WAE architecture. Available WAE specifications are outlined and described in a subsequent section, *The WAE Document Suite*. For additional information on the WAP architecture, refer to *Wireless Application Protocol Architecture Specification* [WAP].

2. WAE Documentation

The following section outlines the set of WAE documentation available.

2.1 The WAE Document Suite

Several documents specify WAE:

Wireless Application Environment Specification [WAE]. The Wireless Application Environment specification is the root document in the WAE normative document hierarchy. The document specifies and references core WAE elements.

Wireless Markup Language Specification [WML]. The Wireless Markup Language specification describes the markup language, WML, including its semantics, its Document Type Definition (DTD), and its encoding extensions.

WAP Binary XML Format Specification [WBXML]. The WAP Binary XML Forum specification describes the XML document encoding and transfer framework used by WAE.

WMLScript Specification [WMLScript]. The WMLScript specification describes the scripting language, WMLScript, including its lexical and syntactic grammar, its transfer format, and a reference bytecode interpreter.

WMLScript Standard Libraries Specification [WAEStdLib]. The WMLScript Standard Libraries specification describes standard libraries available to WMLScript programs including a language library, a string library, a dialog library, a floating-point library, a browser library, and a URL library.

Wireless Telephony Application Specification [WTA]. The Wireless Telephony Application Specification specifies the technologies included in the Wireless Telephony Application reference architecture.

Wireless Telephony Application Interface [WTAI]. The Wireless Telephony Application Interface specification describes standard telephony-specific extensions to WAE, including WML and WMLScript interfaces to such items as call control features, address book and phonebook services.

2.2 Document Organization

The remaining sections of this document present an overview of:

- WAE's history, goals, initial accomplishments, and future plans
- The major components of the WAE architecture (see the various WAE specifications for more details)
- The major components of the WTA architecture (see [WTA] and [WTAI] for more details)

3. WAE Effort

The following section outlines the WAE effort including its background, and its initial and expected future directions.

3.1 Background

The WAE effort is an undertaking to build a general-purpose application environment based fundamentally on World Wide Web (WWW) technologies and philosophies. It is part of the overall WAP effort. The primary objective of the WAE effort is to establish an interoperable environment that will allow operators and service providers to build applications and services that can reach a wide variety of different wireless platforms in an efficient and useful manner.

The output of the WAE effort is a collection of technical specifications that are either new or based on existing and proven technologies. Among the existing technologies leveraged by the WAE effort are:

- Unwired Planet's Hand Held Mark-up Language (HDML)
- World Wide Web's Consortium's (W3C) Hypertext Mark-up Language (HTML)
- ECMA-262 Standard "ECMAScript Language Specification" [ECMASCRIPT] that is based on JavaScript
- IMC's calendar data exchange format (vCalendar) [VCAL] and phonebook data exchange format (vCard) [VCARD]
- A wide range of WWW technologies such as URLs and HTTP [RFC2068]
- A wide range of mobile network technologies such as GSM call control services, and generic IS-136 services such as send flash

The resulting WAE technologies are not fully compliant to all of the motivating technologies. Where necessary, modifications were made to better integrate the elements into a cohesive environment and better optimize the interaction and user interface for small-screen, limited-capability terminals that communicate over wireless networks.

3.2 Direction

The main objectives of the WAE effort are:

1. To define an application architecture model:
   - That fits within the WAP architecture and meets WAP's overall objectives.
   - That is suitable for building interactive applications that function well on devices with limited capabilities including limited memory, small screen size, limited battery life, and restricted input mechanisms.
   - That is suitable for building interactive applications that function well in narrowband environments with medium-to-high latencies.
   - That employs appropriate security and access control features to allow safe execution of anonymous and third-party content.
   - That leverages established and common standards and technologies that make WAE implementation simpler, as well as allow third-party developers to create and deploy applications inexpensively.

- That is global and supports established internationalization technologies and practices.

2. To define a general-purpose application programming model:
   - That is rich and enables interactive applications on current and future wireless devices.
   - That is based on the Internet's World Wide Web programming model including both browsing and scripting services.
   - That provides access to common mobile device functionality and services such as phonebooks, messaging services, and call control services.
   - That enables applications to be accessible to a wide range of devices.
   - That enables creation of applications that behave well on all WAP-compliant devices.
   - That allows developers to leverage specific functionality of specific devices.
3. To provide network operators the means to enhance and extend network services.
4. To enable multivendor interoperability.

3.2.1 Initial Phase Accomplishments

The initial focus of the WAE effort was the client. The following areas were established by the effort:

- A reference architecture definition
- Lightweight mark-up and scripting language specifications
- Encoding schemes for various content data such as mark-up documents, scripting programs, images, phonebook data, and calendar data
- Secure access mechanisms that third-party content can use to access services local to the device
- Generic interfaces to common local services such as messaging, phonebook, and calendar services
- Generic telephony-based interfaces to local services such as call control services
- Network-specific extensions to telephony-based services

3.2.2 Future Direction

While not formally established, future WAE efforts are expected in the following areas; the list is neither exhaustive nor prescriptive:

- Extensions to the defined languages as well as their encoding and transfer schemes (e.g., vCard and vCalendar encoding, dynamic client-side content building, additional intrinsic events, user input validation, etc.)
- Advanced internationalization issues (e.g., multilingual and bidirectional text)

- New media types
- Integration with other existing and emerging technologies (e.g., Smart cards, SIM cards, Java environments, etc.)
- Caching semantics
- Document structure for capturing user agent capabilities
- End-to-end security
- Additional session schemes
- Additional network-specific telephony interface extensions such as IS-95
- Server-side application level constructs
- Integration and interfacing to intelligent networks and switching networks

3.3 Goals and Requirements

The following list summarizes the requirements of the Wireless Application Environment (WAE):

WAE must enable simple yet efficient, meaningful, and powerful application development and execution environments.

WAE must provide a general framework. WAE cannot assume that a browser is the controlling agent in the device, nor can it assume that a browser is running at all times. Other applications may exist in the device; in which case, WAE must not prevent such applications from coexisting or even integrating with a browser. In addition, those other applications should be able to access and leverage common WAE services on the device where appropriate.

WAE must not dictate or assume any particular Man-Machine-Interface (MMI) model. WAE implementations must be able to introduce new MMI models or use existing MMI models. Implementers must be able to present end users with a consistent and meaningful MMI suitable to the targeted device.

WAE must be suited for a wide variety of limited-capability devices. WAE must have a small memory footprint and limited computational power requirement. WAE must be suitable for the current generation of wireless devices without jeopardizing its ability to evolve and support future generations of those devices.

WAE must promote as well as incorporate efficient means to reduce the amount and frequency of over-the-air data exchanges with origin servers. WAE must provide the means to communicate device capabilities to origin servers, which would enable origin server-side optimizations and further minimize over-the-air resource consumption. In addition, WAE network services must be based on WAP's network protocol stack.

WAE must support internationalization and localization using standard or well-accepted practices and methods.

WAE must not compromise WAP's security model. WAE must include meaningful access control mechanisms that ensure secure processing of network accessed content.

WAE must promote and enable interoperable implementation between various manufacturers and content or service providers.

WAE must include extensions to allow means for call control and messaging, as well as enabling a standard set of value-added call and feature control capabilities.

WAE must allow network operators to introduce new operator-specific features to their implementations.

4. WAE Architecture Overview

The WAE architecture includes all elements of the WAP architecture related to application specification and execution. At this point, the WAE architecture is predominately focused on the client-side aspects of WAP's system architecture; namely, items relating to user agents. Specifically, the WAE architecture is defined primarily in terms of networking schemes, content formats, programming languages, and shared services. Interfaces are not standardized and are specific to a particular implementation. This approach allows WAE to be implemented in a variety of ways without compromising interoperability or portability. This approach has worked particularly well with a browser (a class of user agents) model such as that used in the World Wide Web. The Internet and the WWW are the inspiration and motivation behind significant parts of the WAE specification, and consequently, a similar approach is used within WAE.

4.1 The WWW Model

The Internet's World Wide Web provides a very flexible and powerful logical model. Applications present content to a client in a set of standard data formats that are *browsed* by client-side user agents known as *Web browsers* (or simply *browsers*). Typically, a user agent sends requests for one or more named data objects (or content) to an origin server. An origin server responds with the requested data expressed in one of the standard formats known to the user agent (e.g., HTML). See Figure 2.1.

The WWW standards include all of the mechanisms necessary to build a general-purpose environment:

- All resources on the WWW are named with Internet-standard *Uniform Resource Locators* (URLs).
- All classes of data on the WWW are given a specific type allowing the user agent to correctly distinguish and present them appropriately. Furthermore, the WWW defines a variety of standard content formats supported by most browser user agents. These include the Hypertext Mark-up Language (HTML), the JavaScript scripting language, and a large number of other formats (e.g., bitmap image formats).

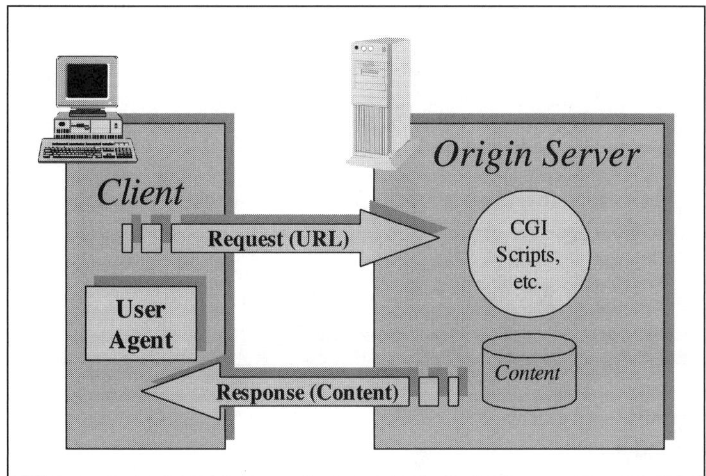

Figure 2.1 WWW logical model.

- The WWW also defines a set of standard networking protocols allowing any browser to communicate with any origin server. One of the most commonly used protocols on the WWW today is the Hypertext Transport Protocol (HTTP).

The WWW infrastructure and model has allowed users to easily reach a large number of third-party content and applications. It has allowed authors to easily deliver content and services to a large community of clients using various user agents (e.g., Netscape Navigator and Microsoft Internet Explorer).

4.2 The WAE Model

WAE adopts a model that closely follows the WWW model. All content is specified in formats that are similar to the standard Internet formats. Content is transported using standard protocols in the WWW domain and an optimized HTTP-like protocol in the wireless domain. WAE has borrowed from WWW standards, including authoring and publishing methods wherever possible. The WAE architecture allows all content and services to be hosted on standard Web origin servers that can incorporate proven technologies (e.g., CGI). All content is located using WWW standard URLs.

WAE enhances some of the WWW standards in ways that reflect the device and network characteristics. WAE extensions are added to support mobile network services such as call control and messaging. Careful attention is paid to the memory and CPU processing constraints that are found in mobile terminals. Support for low bandwidth and high-latency networks is included in the architecture as well.

WAE assumes the existence of *gateway* functionality responsible for encoding and decoding data transferred from and to the mobile client. The purpose of encoding content delivered to the client is to minimize the size of data sent to the client over-the-air as well as to minimize the computational energy required by the client to process that data. The gateway functionality can be added to origin servers or placed in dedicated gateways as illustrated in Figure 2.2.

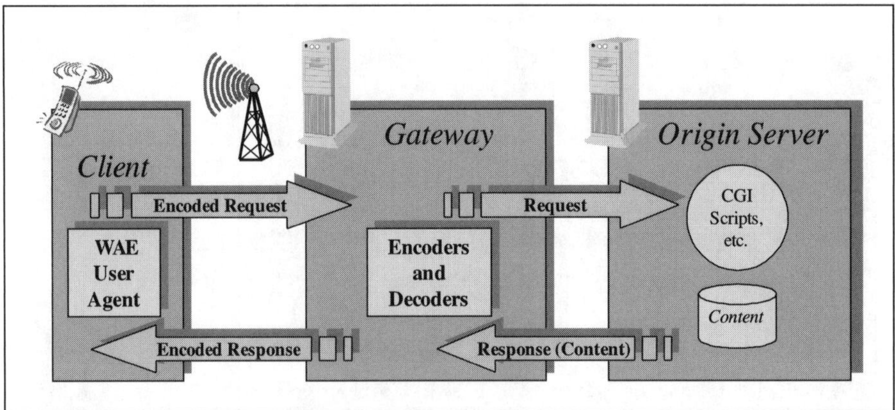

Figure 2.2 WAE logical model.

The major elements of the WAE model include:

WAE User Agents[1]. Client-side in-device software that provides specific functionality (e.g., display content) to the end user. User agents (such as browsers) are integrated into the WAP architecture. They interpret network content referenced by a URL. WAE includes user agents for the two primary standard contents: encoded Wireless Markup Language (WML) and compiled Wireless Markup Language Script (WMLScript).

Content Generators. Applications (or services) on origin servers (e.g., CGI scripts) that produce standard content formats in response to requests from user agents in the mobile terminal. WAE does not specify any standard content generators but expects that there will be a great variety available running on typical HTTP origin servers commonly used in WWW today.

Standard Content Encoding. A set of well-defined content encoding, allowing a WAE user agent (e.g., a browser) to conveniently navigate Web content. Standard content encoding includes compressed encoding for WML, bytecode encoding for WMLScript, standard image formats, a multipart container format, and adopted business and calendar data formats.

Wireless Telephony Applications (WTA). A collection of telephony-specific extensions for call and feature control mechanisms that provide authors (and ultimately, end users) advanced mobile network services.

The resulting WAE architecture fits within a model:

- That leverages the Internet (i.e., the model takes advantage of standards, technology, and infrastructure developed for the Internet)

[1]Except where noted, throughout this document, the term *WAE user agent* is used as a general term to denote any user agent that incorporates some or all of WAE's defined services. The document distinguishes types of user agents only where needed or appropriate.

- That leverages thin-client architecture advantages (e.g., service deployment has significantly lower cost per device due to the device-independent nature of WAE and the centralized management of the services at the origin servers)
- That provides end-user advanced mobile network services through network operator-controlled telephony value-added services
- That provides the means for vendors to build differentiating user-friendly services that can take advantage of WWW and mobile network services
- That provides an open extensible framework for building wireless services

Typically, a user agent on the terminal initiates a request for content. However, not all content delivered to the terminal will result from a terminal-side request. For example, WTA includes mechanisms that allow origin servers to deliver generated content to the terminal without a terminal's request, as illustrated in Figure 2.3.

In some cases, what the origin server delivers to the device may depend on the characteristics of the device. The user agent characteristics are communicated to the server via standard capability negotiation mechanisms that allow applications on the origin server to determine characteristics of the mobile terminal device. WAE defines a set of user agent capabilities that will be exchanged using WSP mechanisms. These capabilities include such global device characteristics as WML version supported, WMLScript version supported, floating-point support, image formats supported, and so on.

4.3 URL Naming

WAE architecture relies heavily on WWW's URL and HTTP semantics. WAE assumes:

- The existence of a generalized architecture for describing gateway behavior for different types of URLs
- Support for connection to at least one WAP gateway

In particular, the URL naming mechanisms used in WAE are motivated by the following scenarios:

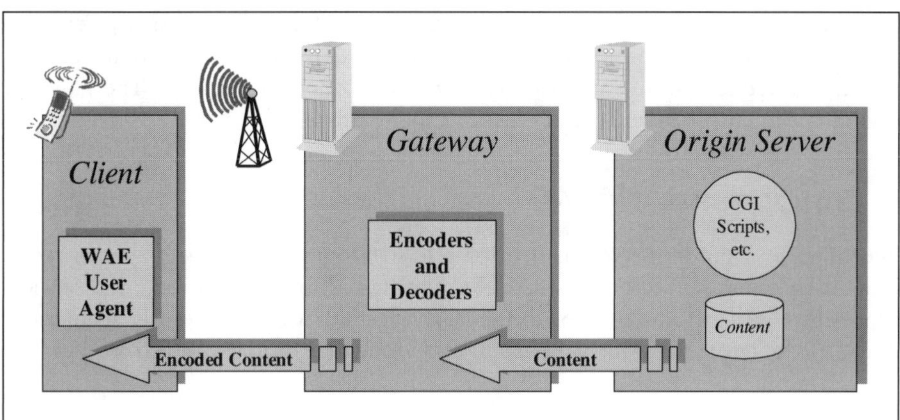

Figure 2.3 WAE push-based model.

- A secure service (e.g., banking or brokerage) where an end-to-end secure connection using WTLS [WTLS] is necessary, mandating a secure gateway controlled by the content provider.
- A content provider who wants to provide a caching gateway that will cache the encoded content in order to improve performance.
- A specialized service with a built-in server that will be accessible only to WAP devices and, therefore, wants to use WSP natively rather than incur the higher overhead of processing HTTP sessions.

WAE is based on the architecture used for WWW proxy servers. The situation in which a user agent (e.g., a browser) must connect through a proxy to reach an origin server (i.e., the server that contains the desired content) is very similar to the case of a wireless device accessing a server through a gateway.

Most connections between the browser and the gateway use WSP, regardless of the protocol of the destination server. The URL, used to distinguish the desired content, always specifies the protocol used by the destination server regardless of the protocol used by the browser to connect to the gateway. In other words, the URL refers only to the destination server's protocol and has no bearing on what protocols may be used in intervening connections.

In addition to performing protocol conversion by translating requests from WSP into other protocols and the responses back into WSP, the gateway also performs content conversion. This is analogous to HTML/HTTP proxies available on the Web today. For example, when an HTTP proxy receives an FTP or Gopher directory list, it converts the list into an HTML document that presents the information in a form acceptable to the browser. This conversion is analogous to the encoding of content destined to WAE user agents on mobile devices.

Currently, only one scheme is expected to be supported by WAE user agents: HTTP. The browser, in this case, communicates with the gateway using WSP. The gateway in turn would provide protocol conversion functions to connect to an HTTP origin server.

As an example, a user, with a WAP-compliant telephone, requests content using a specific URL. The telephone browser connects to the operator-controlled gateway with WSP and sends a GET request with that URL. The gateway resolves the host address specified by the URL and creates an HTTP session to that host. The gateway performs a request for the content specified by the URL. The HTTP server at the contacted host processes the request and sends a reply (e.g., the requested content). The gateway receives the content, encodes it, and returns it to the browser.[2]

4.4 Components of WAE

As illustrated in Figure 2.4, WAE is divided into two logical layers: user agents, which includes such items as browsers, phonebooks, message editors, and so forth; and services and formats, which include common elements and formats accessible to user agents such as WML, WMLScript, image formats, vCard and vCalendar formats, and so on.

[2]Encoding may not be necessary at the gateway in all cases. WAP architecture supports other scenarios. See [WSP] for additional information.

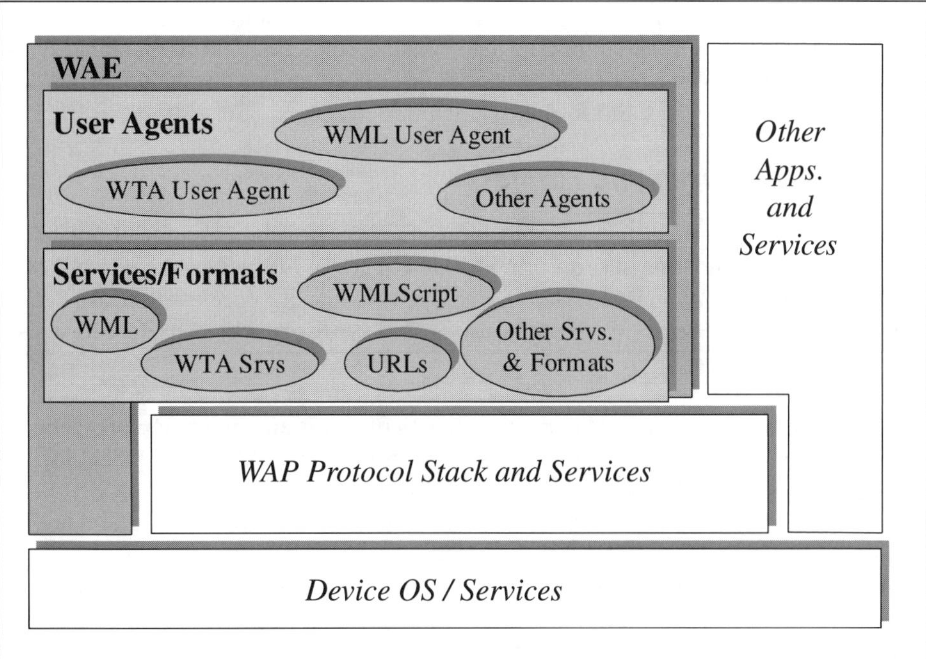

Figure 2.4 WAE client components.

WAE separates services from user agents and assumes an environment with multiple user agents. This logical view, however, does not imply or suggest an implementation. For example, WAE implementations may choose to combine all the services into a single user agent. Others may choose to distribute the services among several user agents. The resulting structure of a WAE implementation is determined by the design decisions of its implementers and should be guided by the specific constraints and objectives of the target environment.

4.4.1 WAE User Agents

The WML user agent[3] is a fundamental user agent of the WAE; however, WAE is not limited to a WML user agent. WAE allows the integration of domain-specific user agents with varying architectures and environments. In particular, a Wireless Telephony Application (WTA) user agent has been specified as an extension to the WAE specification for the mobile telephony environments. The WTA extensions allow authors to access and interact with mobile telephone features (e.g., call control) as well as other applications assumed on the telephones, such as phonebooks and calendar applications[4]. An overview of the WTA architecture is presented in Section 5.

[3]Except where noted, throughout this document, a WML user agent (or WML browser) refers to a basic user agent that supports WML, WMLScript, or both. It does not necessarily indicate if the user agent supports both WML and WMLScript or only one of them.

[4]Such applications (e.g., phonebook and calendar applications) are not specified by WAE.

WAE does not formally specify any user agent. Features and capabilities of a user agent are left to the implementers. Instead, WAE only defines fundamental services and formats that are needed to ensure interoperability among implementations. An overview of those services and formats is included in subsequent sections.

4.4.2 WAE Services and Formats

The WAE Services and Formats layer includes the bulk of technical contribution of the WAE effort. The following section provides an overview of the major components of WAE, including the Wireless Markup Language (WML), the Wireless Markup Scripting language (WMLScript), WAE applications, and WAE-supported content formats.

4.4.2.1 WML

WML is a tag-based document language; in particular, it is an application of a generalized mark-up language. WML shares a heritage with the WWW's HTML[HTML4] and Handheld Device Markup Language [HDML2]. WML is specified as an XML [XML] document type. It is optimized for specifying presentation and user interaction on limited capability devices such as telephones and other wireless mobile terminals.

WML and its supporting environment were designed with certain small narrowband device constraints in mind, including small displays, limited user-input facilities, narrowband network connections, limited memory resources, and limited computational resources. Given the wide and varying range of terminals targeted by WAP, considerable effort was put into the proper distribution of presentation responsibility between the author and the browser implementation.

WML is based on a subset of HDML version 2.0 [HDML2]. WML changes some elements adopted from HDML and introduces new elements, some of which have been modeled on similar elements in HTML. The resulting WML implements a card-and-deck metaphor. It contains constructs allowing the application to specify documents made up of multiple *cards*. An interaction with the user is described in a set of cards, which can be grouped together into a document (commonly referred to as a *deck*). Logically, a user navigates through a set of WML cards. The user navigates to a card, reviews its contents, may enter requested information, may make choices, and then moves on to another card. Instructions embedded within cards may invoke services on origin servers as needed by the particular interaction. Decks are fetched from origin servers as needed. WML decks can be stored in "static" files on an origin server, or they can be dynamically generated by a content generator running on an origin server. Each card in a deck contains a specification for a particular user interaction.

WML is specified in a way that allows presentation on a wide variety of devices, yet allows for vendors to incorporate their own MMIs. For example, WML does not specify *how* implementations request input from a user. Instead, WML specifies the *intent* in an abstract manner. This allows WML to be implemented on a wide variety of input devices and mechanisms. Implementations may, for example, choose to solicit user input visually like many WWW user agents, or it may choose to use a voice-based interface. The user agent must decide how to best present all elements within a card depending on the device capabilities. For example, certain user agents on devices with larger displays may choose to present all the information in a single card at once. Others with smaller displays may break the content up across several units of displays.

WML has a wide variety of features, including:

Support for text and images. WML provides the authors with means to specify text and images to be presented to the user. This may include layout and presentation hints. As with other mark-up languages, WML requires the author to specify the presentation in very general terms and gives the user agent a great deal of freedom to determine exactly how the information is presented to the end user. WML provides a set of text mark-up elements including various *emphasis* elements (e.g., bold, italic, big, etc.); various *line breaks* models (e.g., line wrapping, line wrapping suppression, etc.); and *tab columns* that support simple tabbing alignment.

Support for user input. WML supports several elements to solicit user input. The elements can be combined into one or more cards. All requests for user input are made in abstract terms, allowing the user agent the freedom to optimize features for the particular device. WML includes a small set of input controls. For example, WML includes a *text entry* control that supports text and password entry. Text entry fields can be masked, preventing the end user from entering incorrect character types. WML also supports client-side validation by allowing the author to invoke scripts at appropriate times to check the user's input. WML includes an *option selection* control that allows the author to present the user with a list of options that can set data, navigate among cards, or invoke scripts. WML supports both single and multiple option selections. WML also includes *task invocation* controls. When activated, these controls initiate a navigation or a history management task such as traversing a link to another card (or script), or popping the current card off of the history stack. The user agent is free to choose how to present these controls. It may, for example, bind them to physical keys on the device, render button controls in a particular region of the screen (or inline within the text), bind them to voice commands, and so on.

Navigation and history stack. WML allows several navigation mechanisms using URLs. It also exposes a first-class history mechanism. Navigation includes HTML-style hyperlinks, inter-card navigation elements, as well as history navigation elements.

International support. WML's document character set is Unicode [UNICODE]. This enables the presentation of most languages and dialects.

MMI independence. WML's abstract specification of layout and presentation enables terminal and device vendors to control the MMI design for their particular products.

Narrowband optimization. WML includes a variety of technologies to optimize communication on a narrowband device. This includes the ability to specify multiple user interactions (cards) in one network transfer (a deck). It also includes a variety of state management facilities that minimize the need for origin server requests. WML includes other mechanisms to help improve response time and minimize the amount of data exchanged over-the-air. For example, WML allows the author to parameterize (or pass variables to) a subsequent context. It supports variable substitution and provides out-of-band mechanisms for client-side variable passing without having to alter URLs. The out-of-band passing of variables without changing the way URLs appear attempts to improve client-side cache hits.

State and context management. WML exposes a flat context (i.e., a linear, non-nested context) to the author. Each WML input control can introduce variables. The state of the variables can be used to modify the contents of a parameterized card without having to communicate with the server. Furthermore, the lifetime of a variable state can last longer than a single deck and can be shared across multiple decks without having to use a server to save intermediate state between deck invocations.

4.4.2.2 WMLScript

WMLScript is a lightweight procedural scripting language. It enhances the standard browsing and presentation facilities of WML with behavioral capabilities, supports more advanced UI behavior, adds intelligence to the client, provides a convenient mechanism to access the device and its peripherals, and reduces the need for round-trips to the origin server.

WMLScript is loosely based on a subset of the JavaScript WWW scripting language. It is an extended subset of JavaScript and forms a standard means for adding procedural logic to WML decks. WMLScript refines JavaScript for the narrowband device, integrates it with WML, and provides hooks for integrating future services and in-device applications.

WMLScript provides the application programmer with a variety of interesting capabilities:

- Check the validity of user input before it is sent to the content server
- Access device facilities and peripherals
- Interact with the user without introducing round-trips to the origin server (e.g., display an error message)

Key WMLScript features include:

JavaScript-based scripting language. WMLScript starts with an industry-standard solution and adapts it to the narrowband environment. This makes WMLScript very easy for a developer to learn and use.

Procedural logic. WMLScript adds the power of procedural logic to WAE.

Event-based. WMLScript may be invoked in response to certain user or environmental events.

Compiled implementation. WMLScript can be compiled down to a more space-efficient bytecode that is transported to the client.

Integrated into WAE. WMLScript is fully integrated with the WML browser. This allows authors to construct their services using both technologies, using the most appropriate solution for the task at hand.[5] WMLScript has access to the WML state model and can set and get WML variables. This enables a variety of functionality (e.g., validation of user input collected by a WML card).

[5]A WAE user agent does not have to use both WML and WMLScript. Both are loosely coupled and can be used independently.

International support. WMLScript character set is Unicode [UNICODE]. This enables the presentation of most languages and dialects.

Efficient extensible library support. WMLScript can be used to expose and extend device functionality without changes to the device software.

One objective in designing the WMLScript language was to be close to core JavaScript. In particular, WMLScript was based on the ECMA-262 Standard "ECMAScript Language Specification." The originating technologies for the ECMA Standard include many technologies, most notably JavaScript and JScript. WMLScript is not fully compliant with ECMAScript. The standard has been used only as the basis for defining WMLScript language. The resulting WMLScript is a weakly typed language. Variables in the language are not formally typed in that a variable's type may change throughout the life cycle of the variable depending on the data it contains. The following basic data types are supported: *boolean*, *integer*, *floating-point*, *string*, and *invalid*. WMLScript attempts to automatically convert between the different types as needed. In addition, support for floating-point data types may vary depending on the capabilities of the target device.

WMLScript supports several categories of operations such as assignment operations, arithmetic operations, logical operations, and comparison operations. WMLScript supports several categories of functions, including *Local script functions* (i.e., script functions defined inside the same script that the calling expression is in), *External script functions* (i.e., script functions defined in another script not containing the calling expression), and *Standard library functions* (i.e., functions defined in a library that is part of the WAE specification). WMLScript defines several standard libraries, including a language library, a string library, a browser library, a floating-point library, and a dialog library.

4.4.2.3 URLs

WAE assumes a rich set of URL services that user agents can use; in particular, WAE relies heavily on HTTP and HTML URL semantics. In some cases, WAE components extend the URL semantics, such as in WML, where URL fragments has been extended to allow linking to particular WMLScript functions.

4.4.2.4 WAE Content Formats

WAE includes a set of agreed-upon content formats that facilitate interoperable data exchange. The method of exchange depends on the data and the targeted WAE user agents. The two most important formats defined in WAE are the encoded WML and the WMLScript bytecode formats. WAE defines WML and WMLScript encoding formats that make transmission of WML and WMLScript more efficient as well as minimize the computational efforts needed on the client.

In addition, WAE defines and adopts other formats for data types, including:

Images. WAE assumes visual environments that support images will support several image formats. The selection of formats was an attempt to meet several competing requirements, including support of multiple choices of pixel depth, support of colorspace tables, small encoding, very low CPU and RAM decoding and presentation demands, and availability of common tools and other developer support.

Multipart messages. WAE leverages a multipart-encoding scheme optimized for exchanging multiple typed content over WSP. See [WSP] for additional details.

User agent-specific formats. WAE adopts two additional content formats specific to exchanging data among user agents suitable for both client-server communication and peer-to-peer communication: *electronic business cards* (vCard.2.1) and *electronic calendaring and scheduling exchange format* (vCalendar 1.0) specified by the IMC. See [WAE].

WAE also defines WTA-specific formats that are previewed in subsequent sections and defined in [WTA].

4.5 WML and WMLScript Exchanges

Figure 2.5 presents the different parts of the logical architecture assumed by a WML user agent.

Origin servers provide application services to the end user. The service interaction between the end user and the origin server is packaged as standard WML decks and scripts. Services may rely on decks and scripts that are statically stored on the origin server, or they may rely on content produced dynamically by an application on the origin servers.

Several stages are involved when origin servers and WML user agents exchange WML and WMLScript. In particular, a user, wishing to access a particular service from an origin server, submits a request to the origin server using a WML user agent. The user agent requests the service from the origin server on behalf of the user using some URL scheme operation (e.g., HTTP GET request method).

The origin server honoring the user's request replies by sending back a single deck. Presumably, this deck is initially in a textual format. On their way back to the client, textual decks are expected to pass through a gateway where they are converted into formats better suited for over-the-air transmission and limited device processing. In principle, once the gateway receives the deck from the origin server, the gateway does

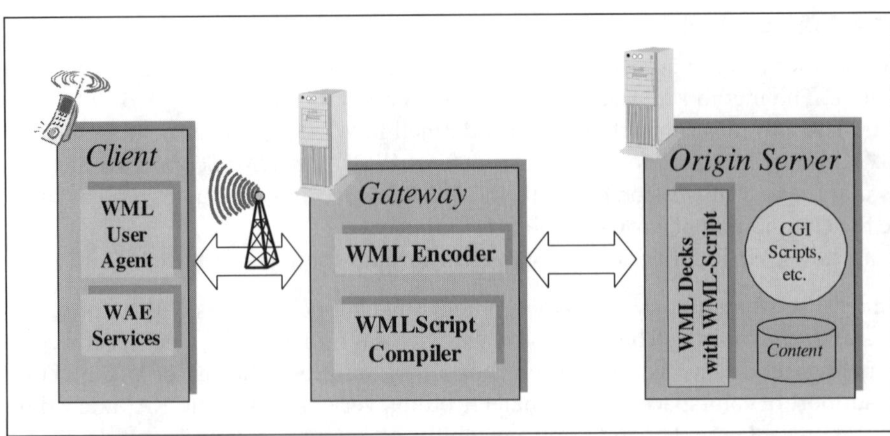

Figure 2.5 WML user agent logical architecture.

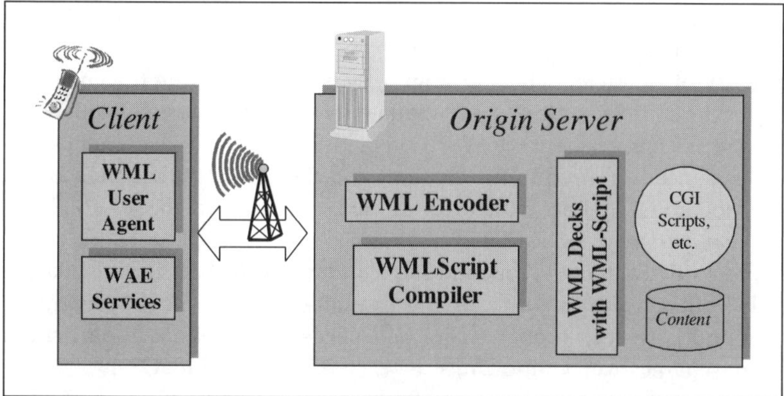

Figure 2.6 WML user agent logical architecture (without a gateway).

all the necessary conversions between the textual and binary formats. A WML encoder (or tokenizer) in the gateway converts each WML deck into its binary format. Encoded content is then sent to the client to be displayed and interpreted. Some optimization may be done at the gateway based on any negotiated features with the client.

The user agent may submit one or more additional requests (using some URL scheme) for WMLScript as the user agent encounters references to them in a WML deck. On its way back, a WMLScript compiler takes the script as input and compiles it into bytecode that is designed for low bandwidth and thin mobile clients. The compiled bytecode is then sent to the client for interpretation and execution.

The existence of a gateway is not mandatory, as illustrated in Figure 2.6. In particular, the location where the actual encoding and compilation is done is not of particular concern to WAE. It is conceivable that some origin servers will have built-in WML encoders and WMLScript compilers. It may also be possible, in certain cases, to statically store (or cache) particular services in tokenized WML and WMLScript bytecode formats, thereby eliminating the need to perform any on-the-fly conversion of the deck.

4.6 Internationalization

The WAE architecture is designed to support mobile terminals and network applications using a variety of languages and character sets. This work is collectively described as *internationalization* (referred to as I18N). It is a design goal of WAE to be fully global in its nature in that it supports any language.

WAE models a significant amount of its I18N architecture based on WWW and, in particular, on SGML and HTTP technologies. For example, it is assumed that HTTP headers are used to specify the current character encoding and language of any content delivered to the user agent.

The WAE architecture makes the following assumption regarding I18N:

- WAE user agents will have a current language and will accept content in a set of well-known character encoding sets.

Origin server-side applications can emit content in one or more encoding sets and can accept input from the user agent in one or more encoding sets.

The IANA registry of character sets and languages is used to define the encoding and language characteristics (see http://www.iana.org/iana/ for more information). Content fetched by a WAE user agent via WSP will be described by two attributes: the *Character set* (i.e., the encoding used in the content) and the *Language* (i.e., the default language for the document). These attributes are encapsulated in the WSP/HTTP *Content-Type* and *Content-Language* headers.

WAE has adopted the [ISO10646] (Unicode 2.0) standard as the basis for all character data. Unicode contains the majority of the characters and symbols present in human languages and is widely supported in the Internet community. In particular, WAE supports three character-encoding Unicode: UTF-8, UCS-2, and UCS-4.

Most components of WAE contain I18N-specific support. For example:

- WML contains additional support allowing the user agent and the origin server to negotiate the transmission encoding of user input sent from the user agent to the server (e.g., the *Accept-Charset* attribute).
- WMLScript defines string manipulation functionality to use Unicode collation order.
- All content and data types are transmitted via protocols, which support the declaration of language and encoding, or they include such information in the data format itself.

4.7 Security and Access Control

WAE leverages WTLS where services require authenticated and/or secure exchanges. In addition, both WML and WMLScript include access control constructs that communicate to the client URL-based access restrictions. In particular, the constructs allow the authors of WML decks and WMLScript to grant public access to the content (i.e., the deck or script can be referenced from other content), or restrict access to the content to a set of "trusted" decks or scripts.

5. WTA Architecture Overview

WTA is a collection of telephony-specific extensions for call and feature control mechanisms that make advanced mobile network services available to authors and end users.[6] WTA merges the features and services of data networks with the services of voice networks. It introduces mechanisms that ensure secure access to important resources within mobile devices. The WTA framework allows real-time processing of events important to the end user while browsing. Within the WTA framework, the client and server coordinate the set of rules that govern event handling via an event table. WTA origin servers can adjust the client's rules by pushing (or updating) a client's event table if required as defined in [WTA].

[6]Mobile network features, like "roaming," are transparent to application developers and not exposed by WTA.

The Wireless Telephony Application Framework has four main goals:

- Enable network operators to provide advanced telephony services that are well integrated and have consistent user interfaces.
- Enable network operators to create customized content to increase demands and accessibility for various services in their networks.
- Enable network operators to reach a wider range of devices by leveraging generic WAE features that allow the operator to create content independent of device-specific characteristics and environments.
- Enable third-party developers to create network-independent content that accesses basic features (i.e., nonprivileged).

Most of the WTA functionality is reserved for the network operators, as in-depth knowledge and access to the mobile network are needed to fully take advantage of the mobile network's features. Nevertheless, a limited set of basic WTA functions, such as initiating phone calls, is available to all WTA authors.[7]

5.1 WTA Framework Components

The following sections describe the key components of the WTA framework.

5.1.1 WTA Libraries

WTA exposes its services to content authors as a set of libraries and interfaces. WTA functionality is divided across several libraries according to its sensitivity and applicability. WTA defines three classes of WTA services[8]:

Common Network Services. WTA services that are available independent of network type. They are common to all networks (e.g., answering an incoming call). Access to these services is restricted to content running within a WTA user agent.

Network-Specific Services. WTA services that target a specific type of network. These services are extensions to Common Network Services that expose unique and common features of a particular type of network (e.g., IS-136 includes a *Send Flash* service). Like Common Network Services, these services are restricted to content running in a WTA user agent.

Public Services. WTA services are available to any anonymous or third-party content (e.g., initiate call setup.) There are no access restrictions on such services. Any user agent is free to access Public Services.

[7]For the most part, WTA functionality extends typical WML and WMLScript functionality by introducing library extensions. Some of these library extensions (in particular, nonprivileged functions) can be included in any WAE user agent. User agents announce their support of such features using standard capability negotiation mechanisms. See [WAE] for additional information.

[8]Operator-specific services may be added in any implementation. These services, however, are out of the scope of the WAP effort.

Classifying and separating services enables secure and reliable execution of content. It limits functions available to authors and developers at large.

Access to WTA services can be done directly from either the WML language, using the WTAI URL scheme, or from WMLScript functions by calling WTAI library functions.

5.1.2 WTA URL Scheme

WTA introduces a URL scheme that allows authors to invoke library services. The services may reside on the device or may be delegated[9] to a server. Using this scheme, authors can pass data to a service and receive data back from the services without having to leave the current browsing context. See [WTA] for a complete specification.

5.1.3 WTA Event Handling

The WTA framework provides a variety of means for authors to deal with telephony-based events in real-time and pseudo-real-time[10] manners. Fundamentally, telephony-based events can be sent to the WTA agent along with any required event-specific parameters and content. This allows a network operator to deploy content (e.g., decks) with call control and network event handling aspects. Clients can maintain event tables that describe how a user agent should deal with incoming events. This event table is coordinated with a WTA origin server controlled by the network operator.

For the most part, content sent with the event (or content already residing on the client) will be sufficient to handle most events. However, the framework does not prevent more advanced scenarios that require additional content to be retrieved from an origin server based on end-user demand. How a network operator chooses to handle events depends largely on the type of events, reliability and latency requirements, and quality desired.

5.1.4 WTA Network Security

The operator is assumed to have control as to what resources are be made accessible to any anonymous or third-party content in both the mobile network and the client. The integrity of the mobile network and the client are enforced because of a restricted WTA content delivery. In particular, content with privileged WTA services can only be executed when it is delivered to the WTA user agent through a dedicated WTA port running WTLS protocols. This allows network operators to use standard network security elements to protect their networks. For example, origin servers, delivering content, can be identified by the operator as either trusted WTA content servers that are under the control of the device's operator, or as untrusted third-party content servers, which may

[9]How a service request is handled is hidden from the author. The author does not know at the time of the request where the request will be resolved.

[10]Developers need to be aware of the constraints of handling real-time scenarios in the particular network when authoring content that relies on the communication between the server and the client.

include any public origin server on the Internet. Network operators can then use standard firewall technologies to regulate access to a mobile's ports. Port access can then be used to determine the credentials given to content, which determines its access privileges to WTA services in both the network and the client.

5.2 Telephony-Specific Exchanges

WTA user agents, defined by WAE as telephony-specific extensions, use similar exchange constructs as a WML user agent. However, WTA user agents rely on additional and extended interactions needed to deliver meaningful telephony-based services.

The elements of the logical WTA network, presented in Figure 2.7, are:

- Content and content generators
- Firewalls (optional)
- Mobile switching framework

The WTA user agent is connected to the mobile network using dedicated signaling connections. The WTA server (an origin server) communicates with the client using the WAP protocol stack. The WTA server may be connected to the mobile network and is responsible for deploying content to its clients. In the case of call handling, for example, the mobile network sets up the call to the client, the server delivers the event-

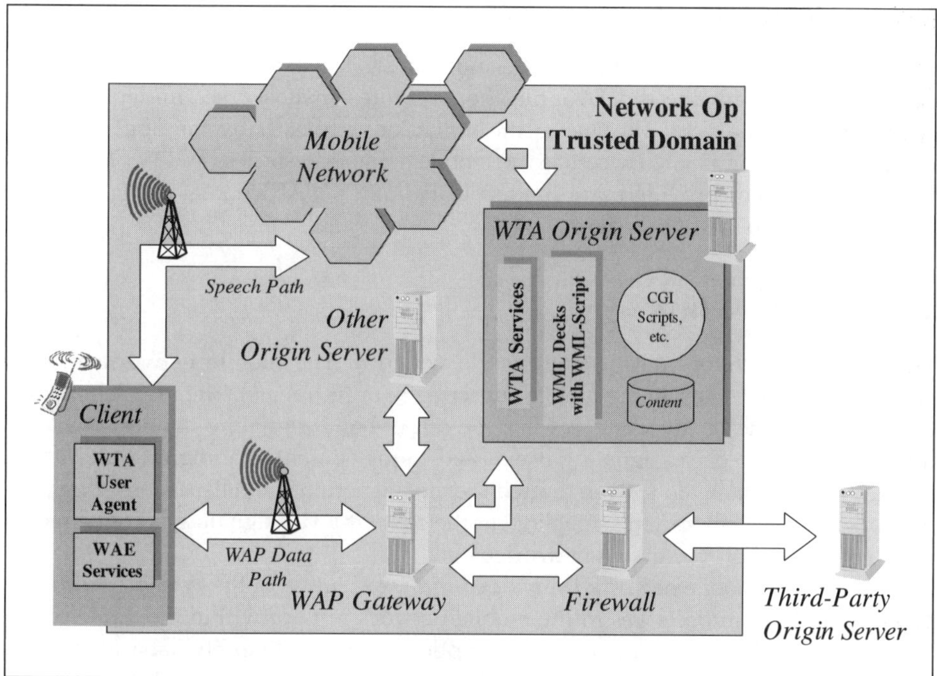

Figure 2.7 WTA logical architecture.

handling content, and the user agent invokes the event-handler content and manages the presentation of the call-handling service to the user.

The WTA user agent is a content interpreter that extends a typical WML user agent. It supports extended libraries and executes WML decks and WMLScript similar to a WML user agent. However, unlike a typical WML user agent, the WTA user agent has a very rigid and real-time context management component. For example, the user agent drops outdated (or stale) events, does not place intermediate results on the history stack, and typically terminates after the event is handled.

5.2.1 WTA Origin Servers

The WTA origin server is assumed to be under the control of the network operator and is therefore to be regarded as a "trusted content server." The operator's server is assumed to *control*, in varying degrees, the mobile network switch. The success of the WTA content (e.g., handling call control) is, to some extent, dependent on the operator's ability to access and control the features and characteristics of the mobile network.

The operator has information about latency, capacity, and reliability for the different bearers in the mobile network. Since the operator is able to provide the WTA services without needing to rely on the Internet, the operator can have more control over the behavior of the services than a third-party service provider can, and can better optimize its services to achieve good, real-time characteristics.

5.2.2 Third-Party Origin Servers

Content from third-party providers does not handle any extensive set of WTA functions. Developing advanced WTA applications requires, in most cases, in-depth knowledge of the mobile network. Due to the limitations imposed by the operator as to which third party is granted access to the mobile network resources and WTA services, third-party content providers are limited to handling WAE content using the subscriber's standard WML user agent.

5.2.3 Mobile Network

The network operator controls the mobile network. The mobile network handles switching and call setup to the mobile subscribers (or terminals). The mobile network connects with the client using in-band or out-of-band signaling connections. The mobile network-to-client signaling is exposed to the content running in a user agent using WTA network events. Even though the mobile network-to-client messaging uses network-level system-specific signaling, at the content level, signaling is converted to more generic and abstract WTA network events.

Although the mobile network is involved in the execution of the WTA network services, operations and services in the mobile network are not within the scope of the WAP effort. WTA services only make assumptions on the availability of basic network features like call setup, call accept, and so forth. Call control features in the mobile network are made available to the WTA user agent through the device's WTA interface.

6. Definitions

The following are terms and conventions used throughout this specification.

Author. An author is a person or program that writes or generates WML, WMLScript, or other content.

Bytecode. Content encoding where the content is typically a set of low-level opcodes (i.e., instructions) and operands for a targeted hardware (or virtual) machine.

Card. A single WML unit of navigation and user interface. May contain information to present to the user, instructions for gathering user input, etc.

Client. A device (or application) that initiates a request for connection with a server.

Client Server Communication. Communication between a client and a server. Typically, the server performs a task (such as generating content) on behalf of the client. Results of the task are usually sent back to the client (e.g., generated content).

Content. Synonym for *data objects*.

Content Encoding. When used as a verb, *content encoding* indicates the act of converting a data object from one format to another. Typically, the resulting format requires less physical space than the original, is easier to process or store, and/or is encrypted. When used as a noun, *content encoding* specifies a particular format or encoding standard or process.

Content Format. Actual representation of content.

Content Generator. A service that generates or formats content. Typically, content generators are on origin servers.

Deck. A collection of WML cards. A WML deck is also an XML document. May contain WMLScript.

Device. A network entity that is capable of sending and receiving packets of information and has a unique device address. A device can act as both a client and a server within a given context or across multiple contexts. For example, a device can service a number of clients (as a server) while being a client to another server.

JavaScript. A *de facto* standard language that can be used to add dynamic behavior to HTML documents. JavaScript is one of the originating technologies of ECMAScript.

Origin Server. The server on which a given resource resides or is to be created. Often referred to as a *Web server* or an *HTTP server*.

Peer-to-peer. Direct communication between two terminals typically thought of as clients without involving an intermediate server. Also known as *client-to-client communication*.

Resource. A network data object or service that can be identified by a URL. Resources may be available in multiple representations (e.g., multiple languages, data formats, size, and resolutions) or vary in other ways.

Server. A device (or application) that passively waits for connection requests from one or more clients. A server may accept or reject a connection request from a client.

SGML. The Standardized Generalized Markup Language (defined in [ISO8879]) is a general-purpose language for domain-specific markup languages.

Terminal. A device typically used by a user to request and receive information. Also called a *mobile terminal* or *mobile station*.

Transcode. The act of converting from one character set to another (e.g., conversion from UCS-2 to UTF-8).

User. A user is a person who interacts with a user agent to view, hear, or otherwise use a resource.

User Agent. A user agent is any software or device that interprets content (e.g., WML). This may include textual browsers, voice browsers, search engines, etc.

WMLScript. A scripting language used to program the mobile device. WMLScript is an extended subset of the JavaScript scripting language.

XML. The Extensible Markup Language is a World Wide Web Consortium (W3C) proposed standard for Internet markup languages, of which WML is one such language. XML is a restricted subset of SGML.

7. Abbreviations

For the purposes of this specification, the following abbreviations apply:

API	Application Programming Interface
BNF	Backus-Naur Form
CGI	Common Gateway Interface
ECMA	European Computer Manufacturers Association
ETSI	European Telecommunication Standardization Institute
GSM	Global System for Mobile Communication
HDML	Handheld Markup Language [HDML2]
HTML	HyperText Markup Language [HTML4]
HTTP	HyperText Transfer Protocol [RFC2068]
IANA	Internet Assigned Number Authority
IMC	Internet Mail Consortium
LSB	Least Significant Bits
MMI	Man-Machine-Interface
MSB	Most Significant Bits
MSC	Mobile Switch Centre
PDA	Personal Digital Assistant
RFC	Request For Comments
SAP	Service Access Point
SGML	Standardized Generalized Markup Language [ISO8879]

SSL	Secure Socket Layer
TLS	Transport Layer Security
URI	Uniform Resource Identifier
URL	Uniform Resource Locator [RFC1738]
URN	Uniform Resource Name
W3C	World Wide Web Consortium
WAE	Wireless Application Environment
WAP	Wireless Application Protocol [WAP]
WBMP	Wireless BitMaP
WSP	Wireless Session Protocol [WSP]
WTA	Wireless Telephony Applications
WTAI	Wireless Telephony Applications Interface
WTLS	Wireless Transport Layer Security
WTP	Wireless Transaction Protocol
WWW	World Wide Web
XML	Extensible Markup Language

8. Normative References

[ISO10646] "Information Technology—Universal Multiple-Octet Coded Character Set (UCS)—Part 1: Architecture and Basic Multilingual Plane," ISO/IEC 10646-1:1993.

[RFC1738] "Uniform Resource Locators (URL)," T. Berners-Lee, et al., December 1994.
URL: ftp://ftp.isi.edu/in-notes/rfc1738.txt

[RFC2068] "Hypertext Transfer Protocol—HTTP/1.1," R. Fielding, et al., January 1997.
URL: ftp://ftp.isi.edu/in-notes/rfc2068.txt

[UNICODE] "The Unicode Standard: Version 2.0," The Unicode Consortium, Addison-Wesley Developers Press, 1996.
URL: http://www.unicode.org/

[VCARD] vCard—The Electronic Business Card; version 2.1; The Internet Mail Consortium (IMC), September 18, 1996.
URL: http://www.imc.org/pdi/vcard-21.doc

[VCAL] vCalendar—the Electronic Calendaring and Scheduling Format; version 1.0; The Internet Mail Consortium (IMC), September 18, 1996.
URL: http://www.imc.org/pdi/vcal-10.doc

[WAE] "Wireless Application Environment Specification," WAP Forum, April 30, 1998.
URL: http://www.wapforum.org/

[WAP] "Wireless Application Protocol Architecture Specification," Wireless Application WAP Forum, April 30, 1998.
URL: http://www.wapforum.org/

[WBXML] "WAP Binary XML Content Format," WAP Forum, April 30, 1998.
URL: http://www.wapforum.org/

[WML] "Wireless Markup Language Specification," WAP Forum, April 30, 1998.
URL: http://www.wapforum.org/

[WMLScript] "WMLScript Language Specification," WAP Forum, April 30, 1998.
URL: http://www.wapforum.org/

[WMLStdLib] "WMLScript Standard Libraries Specification," WAP Forum, April 30, 1998.
URL: http://www.wapforum.org/

[WSP] "Wireless Session Protocol," WAP Forum, April 30, 1998.
URL: http://www.wapforum.org/

[WTA] "Wireless Telephony Application Specification," WAP Forum, April 30, 1998.
URL: http://www.wapforum.org/

[WTAI] "Wireless Telephony Application Interface Specification," WAP Forum, April 30, 1998.
URL: http://www.wapforum.org/

[WTLS] "Wireless Transport Layer Security Specification," WAP Forum, April 30, 1998.
URL: http://www.wapforum.org/

[WTP] "Wireless Transaction Protocol," WAP Forum, April 30, 1998.
URL: http://www.wapforum.org/

[XML] "Extensible Markup Language (XML), W3C Proposed Recommendation 8-December-1997, PR-xml-971208," T. Bray, et al., December 8, 1997.
URL: http://www.w3.org/TR/PR-xml

9. Informative References

[HDML2] "Handheld Device Markup Language Specification," P. King, et al., April 11, 1997.
URL: http://www.uplanet.com/pub/hdml_w3c/hdml20-1.html

[HTML4] "HTML 4.0 Specification, W3C Recommendation 18-December-1997, REC-HTML40-971218," D. Raggett, et al., September 17, 1997.
URL: http://www.w3.org/TR/REC-html40

[ISO8879] "Information Processing—Text and Office Systems—Standard Generalized Markup Language (SGML)," ISO 8879:1986.

[ECMASCRIPT] Standard ECMA-262: "ECMAScript Language Specification," ECMA, June 1997.

[JAVASCRIPT] "JavaScript: The Definitive Guide," David Flanagan. O'Reilly & Associates, Inc. 1997.

CHAPTER

3

Wireless Application Environment Specification

1. Scope

Wireless Application Protocol (WAP) is a result of continuous work to define an industrywide specification for developing applications that operate over wireless communication networks. The scope for the WAP Forum is to define a set of specifications to be used by service applications. The wireless market is growing very quickly and reaching new customers and services. To enable operators and manufacturers to meet the challenges in advanced services, differentiation, and fast/flexible service creation, WAP defines a set of protocols in Transport, Session, and Application layers.

Wireless Application Environment (WAE) is part of the WAP Forum's effort to specify an application framework for wireless terminals such as mobile phones, pagers, and PDAs (Personal Digital Assistants). The framework extends and leverages other WAP technologies, including WTP and WSP, as well as other Internet technologies such as XML, URLs, scripting, and various media types. The effort enables operators, manufacturers, and content developers to meet the challenges in building advanced and differentiating services and implementations in a fast and flexible manner.

This specification represents the root document of the WAE specification hierarchy; in other words, the normative document hierarchy. The document represents the core of the WAE specifications, from which additional WAE specification documents have evolved. For this reason, chapters or sections in this document reference all other WAE specifications and certain sections may be moved to other specifications in the future. For a general overview of the overall WAE architecture, please refer to [WAEOVER]. For additional information on the WAP architecture, refer to *"Wireless Application Protocol Architecture Specification"* [WAPARCH].

2. WAE Specification

The following sections provide a specification for the core components of WAE, including the Wireless Markup Language (WML), the Wireless Markup Scripting language (WMLScript), WAE user agents, and WAE supported media types.

2.1 General WAE Features

2.1.1 Session Layer Interface

The WML and the Wireless Telephony Application (WTA) user agents communicate using the Wireless Session Protocol (WSP) over one or more WSP sessions per user agent. This network communication is in the form of WSP/HTTP 1.1 headers and content. The WSP session is created and controlled by the Session Management Entity. The Session Management Entity is not defined within the WAP specification framework and is implementation specific.

2.1.2 Basic Authentication Scheme

WAE user agents should implement Basic Authentication as specified in the HTTP 1.1 specification [RFC2068].

2.1.3 URL Schemes

The following standard URL scheme is defined for WAP user agents:

http: This scheme identifies a particular URL syntax suitable for naming resources stored on HTTP origin servers (see [RFC1738]). The specification of an `http` scheme does not imply the use of a particular communication protocol between a phone and network gateway. The origin server specified by the URL may be accessed via a WSP-to-HTTP gateway (or proxy). Alternatively, the URL may specify a network server, which combines the function of WSP gateway and origin server into one entity. In this case, the resource is accessed directly across the WSP protocol.

Additional, nonstandard URL schemes are defined to access client/terminal-specific content within the WTAI specification (see [WTAI]). Since these schemes are specific to a particular WAE user agent, they are not included in this section.

2.1.4 User Agent Characteristics

In order to optimize the WAE client-server model, a number of characteristics are sent from the user agent to the WAP origin server. These characteristics allow the origin server to avoid sending inappropriate content to the user agent. They also provide the server and gateway with a means of customizing the response for a particular user agent.

The WSP layer provides typed data transfer for the WAE layer (see reference [WSP]). The WSP/HTTP 1.1 content headers are used to perform content negotiation and define character set encoding and language settings.

The origin server or WAP gateway may need or want to modify responses based on characteristics of the user agent. For each WAP-defined media type included in the WSP/HTTP `Accept` header, the user agent should include a parameter, named `uaprof`, specifying the URI for a profile specifying the user agent characteristics. The syntax and semantics of this profile will be specified in a separate document.

An example of an `Accept` header would be

```
Accept:    application/x-wap.wmlc;uaprof=http://www.vendor.com/phone1,
           application/x-wap.wmlscriptc;uaprof=http://www.vendor.com/phone1,
           text/x-vcard,
           text/x-vcal
```

For WAP-defined media types, the `uaprof` parameter, combined with the WSP/HTTP `Accept`, `Accept-Language`, and `Accept-Charset` headers, should completely describe all negotiable characteristics of the content. The combination of these three items henceforth is collectively referred to as the "characteristic headers."

Gateways that receive a request using characteristic headers must preserve the headers in any requests to origin servers on behalf of that user agent, and also insert the `uaprof` parameter on any media types that will be converted into a type specified with the parameter. For example, if the user agent's `Accept` header specifies that it accepts `application/x-wap.wmlc` and a gateway requests media of type `text/x-wap.wml` from an origin server, then the gateway must copy the user agent's `uaprof` parameter to its `Accept` header.

Some gateways may cache content received from origin servers. If a user agent requests content that a gateway has cached and the request contains characteristic headers, the gateway must not provide cached content to a user agent unless at least one of the three following conditions is true:

- The characteristic headers specified in the request are identical to the ones used when the gateway initially retrieved the content.
- The characteristic headers specified in the request are identical to the ones used when the gateway initially retrieved the content except for the `uaprof` parameter, and the profile specified by the URI in the `uaprof` header is semantically equivalent to the profile specified by the URI in the `uaprof` header of the request when the gateway initially retrieved the content.
- The gateway was able to guarantee through other mechanisms (e.g., analysis of HTTP metadata) that a new request to the origin server using the user agent's `Accept` header would result in the same content that the gateway has cached.

The use of WSP/HTTP headers is summarized in Table 3.1.

2.1.5 Wireless Markup Language

The specification of the WML language is available in [WML].

Table 3.1 User Agent Characteristics

ID	USER AGENT CHARACTERISTIC	CHARACTERISTIC DATA TYPE	DESCRIPTION/EXAMPLE	METHOD FOR TRANSMISSION
1	Character set/ encoding	IANA character set name	Character set(s)/encoding scheme(s) supported by the client.	Accept-Charset WSP/HTTP header as defined by [RFC2068]
2	Language	IANA country code	Languages supported by the client.	Accept-Language WSP/HTTP header as defined by [RFC2068]
3	Media type	IANA media type	Content formats/encoding supported by the client.	Accept WSP/HTTP header as defined by [RFC2068]
4	WML version	Version number	Refers to WML language supported. The current version of WML is 1.0.	Defined with user agent characteristics (see `uaprof` description in Section 2.1.4)
5	WMLScript version	Version number	Refers to WMLScript language supported. The current version of WMLScript is 1.0.	Defined with user agent characteristics (see `uaprof` description in Section 2.1.4)
	WMLScript support		If a version is reported, then the client supports scripting; otherwise, the origin server must assume it doesn't support/want scripts.	
	Floating-point support		Augment version number. The current version of WMLScript with floating-point support is 1.1F.	
6	Standard libraries supported	Version number	Refers to WMLScript standard libraries supported.	Defined with user agent characteristics (see `uaprof` description in Section 2.1.4)

Table 3.1 *(Continued)*

ID	USER AGENT CHARACTERISTIC	CHARACTERISTIC DATA TYPE	DESCRIPTION/EXAMPLE	METHOD FOR TRANSMISSION
7	WTA version	Version number	Refers to WTA user agent version supported. The current version of the WTA user agent is 1.0.	Defined with user agent characteristics (see `uaprof` description in Section 2.1.4)
	Event tables used		Augment version number. The current version of a WTA user agent supporting event tables (support for both server- and client-centric mode, see [WTA]) is 1.0C.	
8	WTAI basic version	Version number	Refers to WTAI basic library supported. The current WTAI basic library version is 1.0.	Defined with user agent characteristics (see `uaprof` description in Section 2.1.4)
9	WTAI public version	Version number	Refers to WTAI public lib supported. The current WTAI public lib version is 1.0.	Defined with user agent characteristics (see `uaprof` description in Section 2.1.4)
10	List WTAI Net-spec versions	List of version numbers	Refers to WTAI net-spec lib supported. The possible values are: 1.0GSM, 1.0IS-136, 1.0IS-95, 1.0PDC.	Defined with user agent characteristics (see `uaprof` description in Section 2.1.4)
	List WTAI network specific libraries		Any network-specific version must build on top of basic library.	

2.1.6 WMLScript

The specification of the WMLScript language is available in [WMLScript].

2.1.7 WAE User Agents

The WML user agent is a fundamental component of the WAE; however, WAE is not limited to WML user agents. WAE allows the integration of domain-specific user agents with varying architectures and environments. In particular, a WTA user agent and a WTAI (Wireless Telephony Application Interface) programming interface has been specified as part of the WAE specification for the mobile telephony environment. The WTAI functions allow authors to access and interact with mobile phone features (e.g., call control) as well as other user agents such as phone book and calendar user agents not specified by WAE.

2.1.7.1 WTA User Agent

The WTA user agent is not fully specified as part of the WAP Standards specification. A number of requirements and guidelines are specified in [WTA]. A specification of the WTAI, which is the WAP Telephony Value Added Service API, is available in [WTAI].

2.1.7.2 WML User Agent

The WML user agent is not fully specified as part of the WAP Standards specification. A number of requirements and guidelines are provided as part of the WML language specification (see Section 2.1.5) and the WMLScript language specification (see Section 2.1.6).

2.1.8 WAE Media Types

WAE specifies or adopts a number of content formats that facilitate interoperable exchange of data. The most important formats are the encoded WML and the WMLScript bytecode formats. The encoding of WML and WMLScript makes transmission of WML and WMLScript more efficient and minimizes the computational efforts needed to execute them on the client.

WAE adopts an additional class of media types to facilitate the exchange of data objects between client and server or between two clients. These are currently limited to electronic business cards and electronic calendar objects (see Sections 2.1.8.3 and 2.1.8.4). Such objects may be exchanged using WDP datagrams or through a WSP session. In case of exchange over datagrams, a set of well-defined ports has been reserved for the exchange to allow interoperability between different implementations (see [WTP]).

Other content formats include the WAE image exchange format and application-specific formats. In general, the method of data exchange depends on the data type and the user agent involved.

2.1.8.1 Encoded WML Format

The WML content format is defined in [WML] and [WBXML].

2.1.8.2 Encoded WMLScript Format

The WMLScript content format is defined in [WMLScript].

2.1.8.3 The Electronic Business Card Format (vCard 2.1)

The vCard format was defined by the Versit Consortium and is currently administered by the IMC.

WAP support for vCard is specified in Section 4.

2.1.8.4 The Electronic Calendar and Scheduling Exchange Format (vCalendar 1.0)

The vCalendar format was specified by the Versit Consortium and is currently administered by the IMC.

WAP support for vCalendar is specified in Section 4.

2.1.8.5 Images

WAE provides a visual environment that is designed to address several competing requirements, including support for multiple pixels depths, support for colorspace tables, small encoding, very low CPU and RAM decoding and presentation demands, and allowance for commonly available tools and support.

WAE meets these unique requirements by

- Supporting standard WSP/HTTP media types for commonly used image formats (e.g., *image/png*)
- Introducing an optimized bitmap format, the Wireless BitMaP (WBMP) (WSP/HTTP media type image/x-wap.wbmp)

WBMP is an encapsulation format; in other words, a WBMP object is a wrapper object that maps the verbose headers of the full image format to an identification (or typing) of the contents. The actual image contents contain all other information (e.g., color table (if any), image bit planes, etc.).

The WBMP specification is divided into two parts:

The **generic header** contains the following information, which is common to all image formats:

Type

Width and height

WBMP version number

The `type` identifier denotes the format of the embedded image. Type `0` is currently specified (see Appendix A, and Section 3.1).

The **type-specific formats specification**, indicating the data format for a particular WBMP `type`.

The WBMP format supports the definition of compact image formats suitable for encoding a wide variety of image formats and provides the means for optimization steps such as stripping of superfluous headers and special-purpose compression schemes. This leads to efficient communication to and from the client, and efficient presentation in the client display.

A WBMP image has the following characteristics:

- Compact binary encoding
- Scaleability; i.e., future support for all image qualities and types (color depths, animations, stream data, etc.)
- Extensibility (unlimited type definition space)
- Optimized for low computational costs in the client

2.1.8.6 Multipart Messages

WAE includes a multipart encoding specification suitable for exchanging multiple typed entities over WSP. WSP translates the MIME multipart entity (see [RFC2045]) into a compact binary form, which is optimized for narrowband environments. See [WSP].

2.1.8.7 WTA Events

WAE defines a separate content type and encoding for delivering events from the WTA server/gateway to the WTA user agent. See [WTA] for details on the event content type.

3. Wireless Bitmap Format

The WBMP format enables graphical information to be sent to a variety of handsets. The WBMP format is terminal independent and describes only graphical information.

3.1 WBMP Type Identifiers

The WBMP format is configured according to a type field value (TypeField below), which maps to all relevant image encoding information, such as:

- Pixel organization and encoding
- Palette organization and encoding
- Compression characteristics
- Animation encoding

For each TypeField value, all relevant image characteristics are fully specified as part of the WAP documentation. Currently, a simple, compact, monochrome image format is defined within the WBMP type space. See Table 3.2 for the type identifiers.

When initializing a session with a WAP server, the user agent reports all supported WBMP types. These are communicated using standard `Accept:` or `Content-Type:` WSP/HTTP headers. For example:

Table 3.2 WBMP Image Type Identifier Assignments

IMAGE TYPE IDENTIFIER, MULTI-BYTE INTEGER	IMAGE FORMAT DESCRIPTION
0	B/W, no compression

```
Accept: image/x-wap.wbmp; type=0
```

or

```
Content-Type: image/x-wap.wbmp; type=0
```

The type parameter refers to the WBMP types described in Table 3.2. In the current version of the specification, only `type=0` is supported.

The specification of WBMP type 0 is given in Appendix A.

3.2 WBMP Syntax

The following is a BNF-like description of the tokenized structure. The description uses the conventions established in [RFC822], except that the "|" character is used to designate alternatives and capitalized words indicate single-byte tokens, which are defined later. Briefly, "(" and ")" are used to group elements; optional elements are enclosed in "[" and "]". Elements may be preceded with <N>* to specify N or more repetitions of the following element (N defaults to zero when unspecified).

```
W-Bitmap = Header Image-data
Header = TypeField FixHeaderField [ExtFields] Width Height
TypeField  = 'Type of image which is defined in Section 3.1'
FixHeaderField = 'Octet which is defined in Table 3-3'
ExtFields = *ExtFieldType00 | ExtFieldType01  | ExtFieldType10 |
                                                  *ExtFieldType11
ExtFieldType00 = 'Octet which is defined in Section 3.3'
ExtFieldType01 = 'Octet which is defined in Section 3.3'
ExtFieldType10 = 'Octet which is defined in Section 3.3'
ExtFieldType11 = ParameterHeader ParameterIdentifier ParameterValue
ParameterHeader = 'Octet which is defined in Table 3-4'
ParameterIdentifier = 'Parameter identifier (US-ASCII string), length ≤
                                  8 bytes defined in ParameterHeader'
ParameterValue = 'Parameter value (alphanumeric string), length ≤ 16 bytes
defined in ParameterHeader'
Width  = 'Horizontal width of the bitmap in pixels (Multi-byte integer)'
Height  = 'Vertical height of the bitmap in pixels (Multi-byte integer)'
Image-data  = Main-image *Animated-image ;'There can be 0 to 15 animated
                                                             images'
Main-image  = 'Bitmap formed according to image data structure specified by
                                                      the TypeField'
Animated-image  = 'Bitmap formed according to image data structure
                                                  description below'
```

3.3 Header Data Structure

3.3.1 Multibyte Integer Format

The WBMP image encoding uses a multibyte representation for integer values. A multibyte integer consists of a series of octets, where the most significant bit is the continuation flag, and the remaining 7 bits are a scalar value. The continuation flag is used to indicate that an octet is not the end of the multibyte sequence. A single-integer value is encoded into a sequence of N octets. The first N–1 octets have the continuation flag set to a value of 1. The final octet in the series has a continuation flag value of 0. The remaining 7 bits in each octet are encoded in a big-endian order; in other words, most significant bit first. The octets are arranged in a big-endian order; the most significant 7 bits are transmitted first. In the situation where the initial octet has less than 7 bits of value, all unused bits must be set to 0.

For example, the integer value 0xA0 would be encoded with the 2-byte sequence 0x81 0x20. The integer value 0x60 would be encoded with the 1-byte sequence 0x60.

3.3.2 Header Formats

The header field contains an image type identifier of multibyte length (`TypeField`), an octet of general header information (`FixHeaderFiled`), zero or more extension header fields (`ExtField`), a multibyte width field (`Width`), and a multibyte height field (`Height`). (See Tables 3.3 and 3.4.)

The extension headers may be of type binary *00* through binary *11*, defined as follows (see Table 3.5):

- Type 00 indicates a multibyte bitfield used to specify additional header information. The first bit is set if a type 00 extension header is set if more data follows. The other bits are reserved for future use.
- Type 01—reserved for future use.
- Type 10—reserved for future use.
- Type 11 indicates a sequence of parameter/value pairs. These can be used for optimizations and special-purpose extensions (e.g., animation image formats). The "parameter size" tells the length (1–8 bytes) of the following parameter

Table 3.3 Length of Header Parts

DATA TYPE	LENGTH IN BITS (H, K, M, AND N ARE ARBITRARY INTEGERS)
TypeField(s)	8..8*h
FixHeaderField	8
ExtHeaderField(s)	0..8*k
Width	8..8*m
Height	8..8*n

Table 3.4 FixHeaderField Description

DESCRIPTION	BIT
Ext Headers flag, 1 = More will follow, 0 = Last octet	7
Extension Header Type, msb (See Section 3.3)	6
Extension Header Type, lsb	5
Reserved	4
Reserved	3
Reserved	2
Reserved	1
Reserved	0

name. The "value size" gives the length (1–16 bytes) of the following parameter value. The concatenation flag indicates whether another parameter/value pair will follow after reading the specified bytes of data.

The actual organization of the image data depends on the image type.

3.4 Image Data Structure

The data structure of the image data is dependent on the image type. Appendix A defines or references all image types supported by WAP.

3.5 Minimal Required Implementation

If a WAP device supports display of graphical images, it must support WBMP type 0 as defined in Appendix A.

4. Calendar and Phone Book

WAE includes support for the exchange of calendar and phone book data objects.

4.1 Data Formats

WAE has adopted the vCard and vCalendar data formats (see [VCARD] and [VCAL] for more information). These data formats are industry-standard means of exchanging phone book, electronic business card and calendar information, and are in use in a wide variety of devices and software. In this specification, the terms *electronic business cards*, *phone book information*, and *phone book data* are used to represent data encoded in the vCard format.

4.2 Data Transmission

There are currently two available methods for exchanging vCard and vCalendar data:

Using WDP datagrams: Enables clients to communicate using vCard and vCalendar without the use of a WAP gateway or other network proxy.

Issuing WSP-based requests to a network server: Enables clients to communicate with applications and servers using vCard and vCalendar.

4.2.1 WDP Datagram Data Exchange

To accurately identify data exchanged in a WDP datagram packet, a well-known port number is used. This allows the user agent to presume that any data received on the port is in a particular format. All data must be sent to the correct port number, and data received on that port should be assumed to be of the associated type.

For the vCard and vCalendar port number assignments, please refer to the [RFC2068] specification.

When datagrams are received at the given WDP port, the information can be provided to a standard vCard or vCard reader, or it can be accessed by another application, such as the WML user agent. The method of display is implementation dependent.

4.2.2 WSP Data Exchange

The WSP Content-Type header identifies data exchanged in a WSP request. This header contains a MIME media type, indicating the data type in the associated WSP payload (see Table 3.6).

In the situation where the Content-Type header is missing or unavailable, the user agent may use other methods of determining the type of the data. The file extension in the data name may provide an indication of the type as defined in Table 3.7.

Table 3.5 Extension Field Type 11

EXTFIELD TYPE 11, DESCRIPTION	BIT
Concatenation flag, 1 = More parameters follow, 0 = Last parameter assignment	7
Size of parameter identifier in bytes, msb	6
Size of parameter identifier in bytes	5
Size of parameter identifier in bytes, lsb	4
Size of parameter value in bytes, msb	3
Size of parameter value in bytes	2
Size of parameter value in bytes	1
Size of parameter value in bytes, lsb	0

Table 3.6 MIME Media Types

DATA TYPE	MIME MEDIA TYPE
vCard (phone book and business card data)	text/x-vcard
vCalendar (calendar data)	text/x-vcal

Table 3.7 File Extension Names

DATA TYPE	FILE EXTENSION NAME
vCard (phone book and business card data)	.vcf
vCalendar (calendar data)	.vcs

4.3 Required Terminal Behavior

The following behavior is defined independent of the data transmission method. The exchange of calendar, phone book, or electronic business card data over WDP as described in Section 4.2.1 must use the vCalendar and vCard data formats, respectively.

The following additional requirements apply to any terminal supporting phone book data exchange:

- Upon receipt of a vCard, the terminal must be able to display the vCard 'Name' and 'Telephone Number' properties to the user.
- Transmitted vCards must include the 'Name' and 'Telephone Number' properties.

The following additional requirements apply to any terminal supporting calendar data exchange:

- Upon receipt of a vCalendar data object, the terminal must at least be able to display the vEvent object to the user.

5. Definitions

All nontrivial abbreviations and definitions used in this document are listed in the following sections. The Definitions section includes description of general concepts and issues that may be fully defined in other documents. The purpose of this section is merely to advise the reader on the terminology used in the document.

The notation used in the specification part of this document uses the common elements defined here.

The key words "MUST", "MUST NOT", "REQUIRED", "SHALL", "SHALL NOT", "SHOULD", "SHOULD NOT", "RECOMMENDED", "MAY," and "OPTIONAL" in this document are to be interpreted as described in [RFC2119].

Author. An author is a person or program that writes or generates WML, WMLScript, or other content.

Bytecode. Content encoding where the content is typically a set of low-level opcodes (i.e., instructions) and operands for a targeted hardware (or virtual) machine.

Client. A device (or application) that initiates a request for connection with a server.

Client Server Communication. Communication between a client and a server. Typically, the server performs a task (such as generating content) on behalf of the client. Results of the task are usually sent back to the client (e.g., generated content).

Content. Synonym for *data objects*.

Content Encoding. When used as a verb, *content encoding* indicates the act of converting a data object from one format to another. Typically, the resulting format requires less physical space than the original, is easier to process or store, and/or is encrypted. When used as a noun, *content encoding* specifies a particular format or encoding standard or process.

Content Format. Actual representation of content.

Content Generator. A service that generates or formats content. Typically, content generators are on origin servers.

Device. A network entity that is capable of sending and receiving packets of information and has a unique device address. A device can act as both a client or a server within a given context or across multiple contexts. For example, a device can service a number of clients (as a server) while being a client to another server.

Origin Server. The server on which a given resource resides or is to be created. Often referred to as a *Web server* or an *HTTP server*.

Resource. A network data object or service that can be identified by a URL. Resources may be available in multiple representations (e.g., multiple languages, data formats, size, and resolutions) or vary in other ways.

Server. A device (or application) that passively waits for connection requests from one or more clients. A server may accept or reject a connection request from a client.

Terminal. A device typically used by a user to request and receiving information. Also called a *mobile terminal* or *mobile station*.

User. A user is a person who interacts with a user agent to view, hear, or otherwise use a resource.

User Agent. A user agent is any software or device that interprets WML, WML-Script, or other content. This may include textual browsers, voice browsers, search engines, etc.

WML. The Wireless Markup Language is a hypertext markup language used to represent information for delivery to a narrowband device, (e.g., a phone).

WMLScript. A scripting language used to program the mobile device. WMLScript is an extended subset of the JavaScript scripting language.

XML. The Extensible Markup Language is a World Wide Web Consortium (W3C) proposed standard for Internet markup languages, of which WML is one such language. XML is a restricted subset of SGML.

vCalendar. Internet Mail Consortium (IMC) electronic calendar record.

vCard. Internet Mail Consortium (IMC) electronic business card.

6. Abbreviations

The following abbreviations apply to this document:

API	Application Programming Interface
BNF	Backus-Naur Form
CGI	Common Gateway Interface
HTML	HyperText Markup Language
HTTP	HyperText Transfer Protocol [RFC2068]
IANA	Internet Assigned Numbers Authority
IMC	Internet Mail Consortium
LSB	Least Significant Bit
MSB	Most Significant Bit
PDA	Personal Digital Assistant
RFC	Request For Comments
URI	Uniform Resource Identifier
URL	Uniform Resource Locator
W3C	World Wide Web Consortium
WWW	World Wide Web
WSP	Wireless Session Protocol
WTP	Wireless Transaction Protocol
WDP	Wireless Datagram Protocol
WAP	Wireless Application Protocol
WAE	Wireless Application Environment
WTA	Wireless Telephony Application
WTAI	Wireless Telephony Application Interface
WBMP	Wireless BitMaP
XML	Extensible Markup Language

7. Normative References

[RFC822] "Standard for the Format of ARPA Internet Text Messages," STD 11, RFC 822, D. Crocker, August 1982.
URL: http://info.internet.isi.edu/in-notes/rfc/files/rfc822.txt

[RFC2045] "Multipurpose Internet Mail Extensions (MIME) Part One: Format of Internet Message Bodies," N. Freed, et al., November 1996.
URL: http://info.internet.isi.edu/in-notes/rfc/files/rfc2045.txt

[RFC2068] "Hypertext Transfer Protocol—HTTP/1.1," R. Fielding, et al., January 1997.
URL: http://info.internet.isi.edu/in-notes/rfc/files/rfc2068.txt

[RFC2119] "Key words for use in RFCs to Indicate Requirement Levels," S. Bradner, March 1997.
URL: http://info.internet.isi.edu/in-notes/rfc/files/rfc2119.txt

[VCARD] "vCard—The Electronic Business Card," version 2.1, The Internet Mail Consortium (IMC), September 18, 1996.
URL: http://www.imc.org/pdi/vcard-21.doc

[VCAL] "vCalendar—the Electronic Calendaring and Scheduling Format," version 1.0, The Internet Mail Consortium (IMC), September 18, 1996.
URL: http://www.imc.org/pdi/vcal-10.doc

[WSP] "Wireless Session Protocol," WAP Forum, January 30, 1998.
URL: http://www.wapforum.org/

[WAEOVER] "Wireless Application Environment Overview," WAP Forum, 30-April 30, 1998.
URL: http://www.wapforum.org/

[WAPARCH] "Wireless Application Protocol Architecture Specification," WAP Forum, April 30, 1998.
URL: http://www.wapforum.org/

[WBXML] "WAP Binary XML Content Format," WAP Forum, April 30, 1998.
URL: http://www.wapforum.org/

[WDP] "Wireless Datagram Protocol," WAP Forum, April 30, 1998.
URL: http://www.wapforum.org/

[WML] "Wireless Markup Language Specification," WAP Forum, April 30, 1998.
URL: http://www.wapforum.org/

[WMLScript] "WMLScript Specification," WAP Forum, April 30, 1998.
URL: http://www.wapforum.org/

[WTA] "Wireless Telephony Application Specification," WAP Forum, February 5, 1998.
URL: http://www.wapforum.org/

[WTAI] "Wireless Telephony Application Interface Specification," WAP Forum, April 30, 1998.
URL: http://www.wapforum.org/

8. Informative References

[RFC1738] "Uniform Resource Locators (URL)," T. Berners-Lee, et al., December 1994.
URL: ftp://ds.internic.net/rfc/rfc1738.txt

[RFC1808] "Relative Uniform Resource Locators," R. Fielding, June 1995.
URL: ftp://ds.internic.net/rfc/rfc1808.txt

[UNICODE] "The Unicode Standard: Version 2.0," The Unicode Consortium, Addison-Wesley Developers Press, 1996.
URL: http://www.unicode.org/

[XML] "Extensible Markup Language (XML), W3C Proposed Recommendation 10-February-1998, REC-xml-19980210," T. Bray, et al., February 10, 1998.
URL: http://www.w3.org/TR/REC-xml

Appendix A: Specification of Well-Defined WBMP Types

A.1 WBMP Type 0: B/W, Uncompressed Bitmap

WBMP type 0 has the following characteristics:

- No compression.
- Color: 1 bit with white=1, black=0.
- Depth: 1 bit deep (monochrome).
- The high bit of each byte is the rightmost pixel of the byte.
- The first row in the data is the upper row of the image.

The WBMP header encoding is shown in the Tables 3.8 and 3.9.

No extension headers are required for this format.

The WBMP image data is organized in pixel rows, which are represented by a sequence of octets. One bit represents 1-pixel intensity with value white=1 and value black=0. In the situation where the row length is not divisible by 8, the encoding of the next row must start at the beginning of the next octet, and all unused bits must be set to 0. The data bits are encoded in a big-endian order: most significant bit first. The octets are arranged in a big-endian order: The most significant octet is transmitted first. The most significant bit in a row represents the intensity of the leftmost pixel. The first row in the image data is the top row of the image.

Table 3.8 Length of Header Parts

DATA TYPE	LENGTH IN BITS, H AND K ARE ARBITRARY INTEGERS
TypeField	8
FixHeaderField	8
ExtHeaderField(s)	0
Width	8..8*h
Height	8..8*k

Table 3.9 FixHeaderField Description

FIXHEADERFIELD, DESCRIPTION	BIT VALUE
Ext Headers flag, 1 = More will follow, 0 = Last octet	0
Extension Header Type, msb (See Table 3.5)	any value
Reserved	0
Reserved	0
Reserved	0
Reserved	0
Reserved	0

CHAPTER

4

Wireless Markup Language Specification

1. Scope

Wireless Application Protocol (WAP) is a result of continuous work to define an industrywide specification for developing applications that operate over wireless communication networks. The scope for the WAP Forum is to define a set of specifications to be used by service applications. The wireless market is growing very quickly and reaching new customers and services. To enable operators and manufacturers to meet the challenges in advanced services, differentiation, and fast/flexible service creation, WAP defines a set of protocols in Transport, Session, and Application layers. For additional information on the WAP architecture, refer to *"Wireless Application Protocol Architecture Specification"* [WAP].

This specification defines the Wireless Markup Language (WML). WML is a markup language based on [XML] and is intended for use in specifying content and user interface for narrowband devices, including cellular phones and pagers.

WML is designed with the constraints of small narrowband devices in mind. These constraints include:

- Small display and limited user input facilities
- Narrowband network connection
- Limited memory and computational resources

WML includes four major functional areas:

Text presentation and layout. WML includes text and image support, including a variety of formatting and layout commands. For example, boldfaced text may be specified.

Deck/card organizational metaphor. All information in WML is organized into a collection of *cards* and *decks*. Cards specify one or more units of user interaction (e.g., a choice menu, a screen of text, or a text entry field). Logically, a user navigates through a series of WML cards, reviews the contents of each, enters requested information, makes choices, and moves on to another card.

Cards are grouped together into decks. A WML deck is similar to an HTML page in that it is identified by a URL [RFC1738] and is the unit of content transmission.

Intercard navigation and linking. WML includes support for explicitly managing the navigation between cards and decks. WML also includes provisions for event handling in the device, which may be used for navigational purposes or to execute scripts. WML also supports anchored links, similar to those found in [HTML4].

String parameterization and state management. All WML decks can be parameterized using a state model. Variables can be used in the place of strings and are substituted at runtime. This parameterization allows for more efficient use of network resources.

1.1 Device Types

WML is designed to meet the constraints of a wide range of small, narrowband devices. These devices are primarily characterized in four ways:

Display size: Smaller screen size and resolution. A small mobile device such as a phone may only have a few lines of textual display, each line containing 8–12 characters.

Input devices: A limited, or special-purpose input device. A phone typically has a numeric keypad and a few additional function-specific keys. A more sophisticated device may have software-programmable buttons but may not have a mouse or other pointing device.

Computational resources: Low-power CPU and small memory size; often limited by power constraints.

Narrowband network connectivity: Low bandwidth and high latency. Devices with 300bps to 10kbps network connections and 5–10 second round-trip latency are not uncommon.

This document uses the following terms to define broad classes of device functionality:

Phone: The typical display size ranges from 2 to 10 lines. Input is usually accomplished with a combination of a numeric keypad and a few additional function keys. Computational resources and network throughput is typically limited, especially when compared with more general-purpose computer equipment.

PDA: A Personal Digital Assistant is a device with a broader range of capabilities. When used in this document, it specifically refers to devices with additional display and input characteristics. A PDA display often supports resolution in the range of 160x100 pixels. A PDA may support a pointing device, handwriting recognition, and a variety of other advanced features.

These terms are meant to define very broad descriptive guidelines and to clarify certain examples in the document.

2. WML and URLs

The World Wide Web is a network of information and devices. Three areas of specification ensure widespread interoperability:

- A unified naming model. Naming is implemented with Uniform Resource Locators (URLs), which provide standard way to name any network resource. See [RFC1738].
- Standard protocols to transport information (e.g., HTTP).
- Standard content types (e.g., HTML, WML).

WML assumes the same reference architecture as HTML and the World Wide Web. Content is named using URLs and is fetched over standard protocols that have HTTP semantics, such as [WSP]. URLs are defined in [RFC1738]. The character set used to specify URLs is also defined in [RFC1738].

In WML, URLs are used in the following situations:

- When specifying navigation (e.g., hyperlinking)
- When specifying external resources (e.g., an image or a script).

2.1 URL Schemes

WML browsers must implement the URL schemes specified in [WAE].

2.2 Fragment Anchors

WML has adopted the HTML *de facto* standard of naming locations within a resource. A WML fragment anchor is specified by the document URL, followed by a hash mark (#), followed by a fragment identifier. WML uses fragment anchors to identify individual WML cards within a WML deck. If no fragment is specified, a URL names an entire deck. In some contexts, the deck URL also implicitly identifies the first card in a deck.

2.3 Relative URLs

WML has adopted the use of relative URLs, as specified in [RFC1808]. [RFC1808] specifies the method used to resolve relative URLs in the context of a WML deck. The base URL of a WML deck is the URL that identifies the deck.

3. WML Character Set

WML is an XML language and inherits the XML document character set. In SGML nomenclature, a document character set is the set of all logical characters that a document type may contain (e.g., the letter 'T' and a fixed integer identifying that letter). An SGML or XML document is simply a sequence of these integer tokens, which taken together form a document.

The document character set for XML and WML is the Universal Character Set of ISO/IEC-10646 ([ISO10646]). Currently, this character set is identical to Unicode 2.0 ([UNICODE]). WML will adopt future changes and enhancements to the [XML] and [ISO10646] specifications. Within this document, the terms *ISO10646* and *Unicode* are used interchangeably and indicate the same document character set.

There is no requirement that WML decks be encoded using the full Unicode encoding (e.g., UCS-4). Any character encoding ("charset") that contains a proper subset of the characters in Unicode may be used (e.g., US-ASCII, ISO-8859-1, UTF-8, etc.). Documents not encoded using UTF-8 or UTF-16 must declare their encoding as specified in the XML specification.

3.1 Reference Processing Model

The WML reference processing model is as follows. User agents must implement this processing model, or a model that is indistinguishable from it.

- The user agent must correctly map the external character encoding of the document to Unicode before processing the document in any way.
- Any processing of entities is done in the document character set.

A given implementation may choose any internal representation (or representations) that is convenient.

3.2 Character Entities

WML supports both named and numeric character entities. An important consequence of the reference processing model is that all numeric character entities are referenced with respect to the document character set (Unicode) and not to the current document encoding (charset).

This means that `Į` always refers to the same logical character, independent of the current character encoding.

WML supports the following character entity formats:

- Named character entities, such as `&` and `<`
- Decimal numeric character entities, such as ` `
- Hexadecimal numeric character entities, such as ` `

Seven named character entities are particularly important in the processing of WML:

```
<!ENTITY quot  "&#34;">      <!— quotation mark —>
<!ENTITY amp   "&#38;#38;"> <!— ampersand —>
<!ENTITY apos  "&#39;">      <!— apostrophe —>
<!ENTITY lt    "&#38;#60;"> <!— less than —>
<!ENTITY gt    "&#62;">      <!— greater than —>
<!ENTITY nbsp  " ">     <!— non-breaking space —>
<!ENTITY shy   "&#173;">     <!— soft hyphen (discretionary hyphen) —>
```

4. WML Syntax

WML inherits most of its syntactic constructs from XML. Refer to [XML] for in-depth information on syntactical issues.

4.1 Entities

WML text can contain numeric or named character entities. These entities specify specific characters in the document character set. Entities are used to specify characters in the document character set which either must be escaped in WML, or which may be difficult to enter in a text editor. For example, the ampersand (&) is represented by the named entity `&`. All entities begin with an ampersand and end with a semicolon.

WML is an XML language. This implies that the ampersand and less-than characters must be escaped when they are used in textual data (i.e., these characters may appear in their literal form only when used as markup delimiters, within a comment, etc.). See [XML] for more details.

4.2 Elements

Elements specify all markup and structural information about a WML deck. Elements may contain a start tag, content, and an end tag. Elements have one of two structures:

```
<tag> content </tag>
```

or

```
<tag/>
```

Elements containing content are identified by a start tag (`<tag>`) and an end tag (`</tag>`). An empty-element tag (`<tag/>`) identifies elements with no content.

4.3 Attributes

WML attributes specify additional information about an element. More specifically, attributes specify information about an element that is not part of the element's content. Attributes are always specified in the start tag of an element. For example:

```
<tag attr="abcd"/>
```

Attribute names are an XML NAME and are case sensitive.

XML requires that all attribute values be quoted using either double quotation marks (") or single quotation marks ('). Single quote marks can be included within the attribute value when the value is delimited by double quote marks and vice versa. Character entities may be included in an attribute value.

4.4 Comments

WML comments follow the XML commenting style and have the following syntax:

```
<!— a comment —>
```

Comments are intended for use by the WML author and should not be displayed by the user agent. WML comments cannot be nested.

4.5 Variables

WML cards and decks can be parameterized using variables. To substitute a variable into a card or deck, the following syntaxes are used:

```
$identifier
$(identifier)
$(identifier:conversion)
```

Parentheses are required if whitespace does not indicate the end of a variable. Variable syntax has the highest priority in WML; anywhere the variable syntax is legal, an unescaped '$' character indicates a variable substitution. Variable references are legal in any PCDATA and in any attribute value identified by the vdata entity type (see Section 5.3).

A sequence of two dollar signs ($$) represents a single dollar sign character.

See Section 7.3 for more information on variable syntax and semantics.

4.6 Case Sensitivity

XML is a case-sensitive language; WML inherits this characteristic. No case folding is performed when parsing a WML deck. This implies that all WML tags and attributes are case sensitive. In addition, any enumerated attribute values are case sensitive.

4.7 CDATA Section

CDATA sections are used to escape blocks of text and are legal in any PCDATA; for example, inside an element. CDATA sections begin with the string "<![CDATA[" and end with the string "]]>". For example:

```
<![CDATA[ this is <B> a test ]]>
```

Any text inside a CDATA section is treated as literal text and will not be parsed for markup. CDATA sections are useful anywhere literal text is convenient.

Refer to the [XML] specification for more information on CDATA sections.

4.8 Processing Instructions

WML makes no use of XML processing instructions beyond those explicitly defined in the XML specification.

4.9 Errors

The [XML] specification defines the concept of a well-formed XML document. WML decks that violate the definition of a well-formed document are in error. See Section 11.2.2 for related information.

5. Core WML Data Types

5.1 Character Data

All character data in WML is defined in terms of XML data types. In summary:

CDATA: Text which may contain numeric or named character entities. `CDATA` is used only in attribute values.

PCDATA: Text which may contain numeric or named character entities. This text may contain tags (`PCDATA` is "Parsed `CDATA`"). `PCDATA` is used only in elements.

NMTOKEN: A name token, containing any mixture of name characters, as defined by the XML specification.

See [XML] for more details.

5.2 Length

```
<!ENTITY % length  "CDATA">    <!— [0-9]+ for pixels or [0-9]+"%" for
                                                  percentage length —>
```

The `length` type may either be specified as an integer representing the number of pixels of the canvas (screen, paper) or as a percentage of the available horizontal or vertical space. Thus, the value "50" means 50 pixels. For widths, the value "50%" means half of the available horizontal space (between margins, within a canvas, etc.). For heights, the value "50%" means half of the available vertical space (in the current window, the current canvas, etc.).

The integer value consists of one or more decimal digits ([0–9]) followed by an optional percent character (%). The `length` type is only used in attribute values.

5.3 Vdata

```
<!ENTITY % vdata   "CDATA">    <!— attribute value possibly containing
                                                 variable references —>
```

The `vdata` type represents a string that may contain variable references (see Section 7.3). This type is only used in attribute values.

5.4 Flow and Inline

```
<!ENTITY % layout  "BR">
<!ENTITY % inline   "%text; | %layout;">
<!ENTITY % flow     "%inline; | IMG | A">
```

The `flow` type represents "card-level" information. The `inline` type represents "text-level" information. In general, `flow` is used anywhere general markup can be included. The `inline` type indicates areas that only handle pure text or variable references.

5.5 URL

```
<!ENTITY % URL      "%vdata;">  <!— URL or URN designating a hypertext
                                  node. May contain variable references —>
```

The `URL` type refers to either a relative or an absolute Uniform Resource Locator [RFC1738]. See Section 2 for more information.

5.6 Boolean

```
<!ENTITY % boolean "(TRUE|FALSE)">
```

The `boolean` type refers to a logical value of TRUE or FALSE.

5.7 Number

```
<!ENTITY % number  "NMTOKEN">  <!— a number, with format [0-9]+ —>
```

The `number` type represents an integer value greater than or equal to zero.

6. Events and Navigation

6.1 Navigation and Event Handling

WML includes navigation and event handling models. The associated elements allow the author to specify the processing of user agent events. Events may be bound to *tasks* by the author; when an event occurs, the bound task is executed. A variety of tasks may be specified, such as navigation to an author-specified URL. Event bindings are declared by several elements, including `DO` and `ONEVENT`.

6.2 History

WML includes a simple navigational history model that allows the author to manage backward navigation in a convenient and efficient manner. The user agent history is modeled as a stack of URLs that represent the navigational path the user traversed to arrive at the current card. Three operations may be performed on the history stack:

Reset: The history stack may be reset to a state where it only contains the current card. See the NEWCONTEXT attribute (Section 7.2) for more information.

Push: A new URL is pushed onto the history stack as an effect of navigation to a new card.

Pop: The current card's URL (top of the stack) is popped as a result of backward navigation.

The user agent must implement a navigation history. As each card is accessed via an explicitly specified URL (e.g., a URL attribute in GO), the card URL is added to the history stack. The user agent must provide a means for the user to navigate back to the previous card in the history. Authors can depend on the existence of a user interface construct allowing the user to navigate backwards in the history. The user agent must return the user to the previous card in the history if a PREV task is executed (see Section 6.3). The execution of PREV pops the current card URL from the history stack. Refer to Section 9.5.2 for more information on the semantics of PREV.

6.3 The VAR Element

```
<!ELEMENT VAR EMPTY>
<!ATTLIST VAR
  NAME          %vdata;             #REQUIRED
  VALUE         %vdata;             #REQUIRED
  >
```

The VAR element specifies the variable to set in the current browser context as a side effect of executing a task. The element must be ignored if the NAME attribute does not evaluate to a legal variable name at runtime (see Section 7.3). See Section 7.3.4 for more information on setting variables.

Attributes

NAME=*vdata*

The NAME attribute specifies the variable name.

VALUE=*vdata*

The VALUE attribute specifies the value to be assigned to the variable.

6.4 Tasks

```
<!ENTITY % task    "GO | PREV | NOOP | REFRESH">
```

Tasks specify processing that is performed in response to an event. Tasks are bound to events in the DO, ONEVENT, and A elements.

6.4.1 The GO Element

```
<!ELEMENT GO (VAR)*>
<!ATTLIST GO
  URL             %URL;           #REQUIRED
  SENDREFERER     %boolean;       "FALSE"
  METHOD          (POST|GET)      "GET"
  ACCEPT-CHARSET  CDATA           #IMPLIED
  POSTDATA        %vdata;         #IMPLIED
  >
```

The GO element declares a GO task, indicating navigation to a URL. If the URL names a WML card or deck, it is displayed. A GO executes a "push" operation on the history stack (see Section 6.2).

Refer to Section 9.5.1 for more information on the semantics of GO.

Attributes

URL=*URL*

The URL attribute specifies the destination URL (e.g., the URL of the card to display).

SENDREFERER=*boolean*

If this attribute is TRUE, the user agent must specify, for the server's benefit, the URL of the deck containing this task (i.e., the referring deck). This allows a server to perform a form of access control on URLs, based on which decks are linking to them. The URL must be the smallest relative URL possible if it can be relative at all. For example, if SENDREFERER=TRUE, an HTTP-based user agent shall indicate the URL of the current deck in the HTTP "Referer" request header [RFC2068].

METHOD=*(POST|GET)*

This attribute specifies the HTTP submission method. Currently, the values of GET and POST are accepted and cause the user agent to perform an HTTP GET or POST, respectively. If METHOD is not specified, the user agent must use the GET method, unless the POSTDATA attribute is present, in which case the user agent must use the POST method.

ACCEPT-CHARSET=*cdata*

This attribute specifies the list of character encodings for data that the origin server must accept when processing input. The value of this attribute is a comma- or space-separated list of character encoding names (charset) as specified in [RFC2045] and [RFC2068]. The IANA Character Set registry defines the public registry for charset values. This list is an exclusive-OR list; in other words, the server must accept any one of the acceptable character encodings.

The default value for this attribute is the reserved string UNKNOWN. User agents should interpret this value as the character encoding that was used to transmit the WML deck containing this attribute.

POSTDATA=*vdata*

This attribute specifies data to be posted to the server. The data is sent to the server as an application/x-www-form-urlencoded entity. The data is formatted as a stream of octets encoded using the URL-escaping mechanism specified in [RFC1738].

Specifically, the following occurs:

1. The user agent should transcode the input data to the correct character set, as specified explicitly by ACCEPT-CHARSET, or implicitly by the document encoding.
2. The data is escaped using URL-escaping. Any characters outside the legal URL character set will be converted into the sequence %XX, where XX is the octet represented as a hexadecimal number.
3. The resulting string is transmitted to the server in an application/x-www-form-urlencoded entity, with a charset parameter indicating the character encoding.

This attribute is ignored if the METHOD attribute has a value of GET.

6.4.2 The PREV Element

```
<!ELEMENT PREV (VAR)*>
```

The PREV element declares a PREV task, indicating navigation to the previous URL on the history stack. A PREV performs a "pop" operation on the history stack (see Section 6.2).

Refer to Section 9.5.2 for more information on the semantics of PREV.

6.4.3 The REFRESH Element

```
<!ELEMENT REFRESH (VAR)+>
```

The REFRESH element declares a REFRESH task, indicating an update of the user agent context as specified by the VAR elements. User-visible side effects of the state changes (e.g., a change in the screen display) occur during the processing of the REFRESH task.

Refer to Section 9.5.4 for more information on the semantics of REFRESH.

6.4.4 The NOOP Element

```
<!ELEMENT NOOP EMPTY>
```

This NOOP element specifies that nothing should be done; in other words, "no operation".

Refer to Section 9.5.3 for more information on the semantics of NOOP.

6.5 Card/Deck Task Shadowing

A variety of elements can be used to create an event binding for a card. These bindings may also be declared at the deck level:

Card-level: The event handling element may appear inside a CARD element and specify event processing behavior for that particular card.

Deck-level: The event handling element may appear inside a TEMPLATE element and specify event processing behavior for all cards in the deck. A deck-level event handling element is equivalent to specifying the event handling element in each card.

A card-level event handling element overrides (or "shadows") a deck-level event handling element if they both specify the same event. A card-level ONEVENT element will shadow a deck-level ONEVENT element if they both have the same TYPE. A card-level DO element will shadow a deck-level DO element if they have the same NAME.

If a card-level element shadows a deck-level element and the card-level element specifies the NOOP task, the event binding for that event will be completely masked. In this situation, the card- and deck-level element will be ignored and no side effects will occur on delivery of the event. In this case, user agents should not expose the element to the user (e.g., render a UI control). In effect, the NOOP removes the element from the card.

In the following example, a deck-level DO element indicates that a PREV task should execute on receipt of a particular user action. The first card inherits the DO element specified in the TEMPLATE element and will display the DO to the user. The second card shadows the deck-level DO element with a NOOP. The user agent will not display the DO element when displaying the second card. The third card shadows the deck-level DO element, causing the user agent to display the alternative label and to perform the GO task if the DO is selected.

```
<WML>
  <TEMPLATE>
    <DO TYPE="OPTIONS" NAME="do1" LABEL="default">
      <PREV/>
    </DO>
  </TEMPLATE>
  <CARD NAME="first">
    <!— deck-level DO not shadowed. The card exposes the
          deck-level DO as part of the current card —>
    <!— rest of card —>
    ...
  </CARD>
  <CARD NAME="second">
    <!— deck-level DO is shadowed with NOOP.
          It is not exposed to the user —>
    <DO TYPE="OPTIONS" NAME="do1">
      <NOOP/>
    </DO>
    <!— rest of card —>
    ...
  </CARD>
  <CARD NAME="third">
    <!— deck-level DO is shadowed. It is replaced by a card-level DO —>
    <DO TYPE="OPTIONS" NAME="do1" LABEL="options">
```

```
      <GO URL="/options"/>
    </DO>
    <!— rest of card —>
    ...
  </CARD>
</WML>
```

6.6 The DO Element

```
<!ENTITY % task   "GO | PREV | NOOP | REFRESH">
<!ELEMENT DO (%task;)>
<!ATTLIST DO
  TYPE          CDATA         #REQUIRED
  LABEL         %vdata;       #IMPLIED
  NAME          NMTOKEN       #IMPLIED
  OPTIONAL      %boolean;     "FALSE"
  >
```

The DO element provides a general mechanism for the user to act upon the current card; in other words, a card-level user interface element. The representation of the DO element is user agent dependent and the author must only assume that the element is mapped to a unique user interface *widget* that the user can activate. For example, the widget mapping may be to a graphically rendered button, a soft or function key, a voice-activated command sequence, or any other interface that has a simple "activate" operation with no interoperation persistent state.

The TYPE attribute is provided as a hint to the user agent about the author's intended use of the element and should be used by the user agent to provide a suitable mapping onto a physical user interface construct. WML authors must not rely on the semantics or behavior of an individual TYPE value, or on the mapping of TYPE to a particular physical construct.

The DO element may appear at both the card- and deck-level:

Card-level: The DO element may appear inside a CARD element and may be located anywhere in the text flow. If the user agent intends to render the DO element inline (i.e., in the text flow), it should use the element's anchor point as the rendering point. WML authors must not rely on the inline rendering of the DO element and must not rely on the correct positioning of an inline rendering of the element.

Deck-level: The DO element may appear inside a TEMPLATE element, indicating a deck-level DO element. A deck-level DO element applies to all cards in the deck (i.e., is equivalent to having specified the DO within each card). For the purposes of inline rendering, the user agent must behave as if deck-level DO elements are located at the end of the card's text flow.

A card-level DO element overrides (or "shadows") a deck-level DO element if they have the same NAME (see Section 6.5 for more details). For a single card, the *active* DO elements are defined as the DO elements specified in the card, plus any DO elements specified in the deck's TEMPLATE and not overridden in the card. All active DO elements with a NOOP task must not be presented to the user. All DO elements that are not active must not be presented to the user. All DO elements with a task other than NOOP must be made accessible to the user in some manner. In other words, it must be possible for the user to activate these user interface items when viewing the card containing the active DO elements. When the user activates the DO element, the associated task is executed.

Attributes

TYPE=*cdata*

The DO element type. This attribute provides a hint to the user agent about the author's intended use of the element and how the element should be mapped to a physical user interface construct. All types are reserved, except for those marked as experimental.

User agents must accept any TYPE, but may treat any unrecognized type as the equivalent of UNKNOWN.

In Table 4.1, the * character represents any string; for example, Test* indicates any string starting with the word Test.

LABEL=*vdata*

If the user agent is able to dynamically label the user interface widget, this attribute specifies a textual string suitable for such labeling. The user agent must make a best-effort attempt to label the UI widget and should adapt the label to the constraints of the

Table 4.1 Predefined DO Types

TYPE	DESCRIPTION
ACCEPT	Positive acknowledgment (acceptance)
PREV	Backward history navigation
HELP	Request for help. May be context-sensitive.
RESET	Clearing or resetting state.
OPTIONS	Context-sensitive request for options or additional operations.
DELETE	Delete item or choice.
UNKNOWN	A generic DO element. Equivalent to an empty string (e.g., TYPE="").
X-*, x-*	Experimental types. This set is not reserved.
vnd.*, VND.* and any combination of [Vv] [Nn] [Dd].*	Vendor-specific or user-agent-specific types. This set is not reserved. Vendors should allocate names with the format VND.CO-TYPE, where CO is a company name abbreviation and TYPE is the DO element type. See [RFC2045] for more information.

widget (e.g., truncate the string). If an element can not be dynamically labeled, this attribute may be ignored.

To work well on a variety of user agents, labels should be six characters or shorter in length.

NAME=*nmtoken*

This attribute specifies the name of the DO event binding. If two DO elements are specified with the same name, they refer to the same binding. If DO elements are specified both at the card level (in a CARD element) and at the deck level (in a TEMPLATE element) and both elements have the same NAME, the deck-level DO element is ignored. It is an error to specify two or more DO elements with the same NAME in a single card or in the TEMPLATE element. A NAME with an empty value is equivalent to an unspecified NAME attribute. An unspecified NAME defaults to the value of the TYPE attribute.

OPTIONAL=*boolean*

If this attribute has a value of TRUE, the user agent may ignore this element.

6.7 The A Element

```
<!ELEMENT A ( %inline; | GO | PREV | REFRESH )*>
<!ATTLIST A
  TITLE         %vdata;       #IMPLIED
  >
```

The A element specifies the head of a link. The tail of a link is specified as part of other elements (e.g., a card name attribute). It is an error to nest anchored links.

Anchors may be present in any text flow, excluding the text in OPTION elements (i.e., anywhere formatted text is legal, except for OPTION elements). Anchored links have an associated *task* that specifies the behavior when the anchor is selected. It is an error to specify more than one task element (e.g., GO, PREV, or REFRESH) in an A element.

Attributes

TITLE=*vdata*

This attribute specifies a brief text string identifying the link. The user agent may display it in a variety of ways, including dynamic labeling of a button or key, a *tool tip*, a voice prompt, and so forth. The user agent may truncate or ignore this attribute depending on the characteristics of the navigational user interface. To work well on a broad range of user agents, the author should limit all labels to six characters in length.

6.8 Intrinsic Events

Several WML elements are capable of generating events when the user interacts with them. These so-called "intrinsic events" indicate state transitions inside the user agent. Individual elements specify the events they can generate. WML defines the intrinsic events listed in Table 4.2.

Table 4.2 WML Intrinsic Events

EVENT	ELEMENT(S)	DESCRIPTION
ONTIMER	CARD, TEMPLATE	The ONTIMER event occurs when a timer expires. Timers are specified using the TIMER element (see Section 8.7).
ONENTERFORWARD	CARD, TEMPLATE	The ONENTERFORWARD event occurs when the user causes the user agent to enter a card using a GO task or any method with identical semantics. This includes card entry caused by a script function or user-agent-specific mechanisms, such as a means to directly enter and navigate to a URL. The ONENTERFORWARD intrinsic event may be specified at both the card and deck levels. Event bindings specified in the TEMPLATE element apply to all cards in the deck and may be overridden as specified in Section 6.5.
ONENTERBACKWARD	CARD, TEMPLATE	The ONENTERBACKWARD event occurs when the user causes the user agent to navigate into a card using a PREV task or any method with identical semantics. In other words, the ONENTERBACKWARD event occurs when the user causes the user agent to navigate into a card by using a URL retrieved from the history stack. This includes navigation caused by a script function or user-agent-specific mechanisms. The ONENTERBACKWARD intrinsic event may be specified at both the card and deck levels. Event bindings specified in the TEMPLATE element apply to all cards in the deck and may be overridden as specified in Section 6.5.
ONCLICK	OPTION	The ONCLICK event occurs when the user selects or deselects this item.

The author may specify that certain tasks are to be executed when an intrinsic event occurs. This specification may take one of two forms. The first form specifies a URL to be navigated to when the event occurs. This event binding is specified in a well-defined, element-specific attribute and is the equivalent of a GO task. For example:

```
<CARD ONENTERFORWARD="/url"> Hello </CARD>
```

This attribute value may only specify a URL.

The second form is an expanded version of the previous, allowing the author more control over user agent behavior. An ONEVENT element is declared within a parent element, specifying the full event binding for a particular intrinsic event. For example, the following is identical to the previous example:

```
<CARD>
  <ONEVENT TYPE="ONENTERFORWARD">
    <GO URL="/url"/>
  </ONEVENT>
  Hello
</CARD>
```

The user agent must treat the attribute syntax as an abbreviated form of the ONEVENT element where the attribute name is mapped to the ONEVENT type.

An intrinsic event binding is scoped to the element in which it is declared; for example, an event binding declared in a card is local to that card. Any event binding declared in an element is active only within that element. Event bindings specified in subelements take precedence over any conflicting event bindings declared in a parent element. Conflicting event bindings within an element are an error.

6.8.1 The ONEVENT Element

```
<!ENTITY % task   "GO | PREV | NOOP | REFRESH">
<!ELEMENT ONEVENT (%task;)>
<!ATTLIST ONEVENT
  TYPE         CDATA        #REQUIRED
  >
```

The ONEVENT element binds a task to a particular intrinsic event for the immediately enclosing element; in other words, specifying an ONEVENT element inside an "XYZ" element associates an intrinsic event binding with the "XYZ" element.

The user agent must ignore any ONEVENT element specifying a TYPE that does not correspond to a legal intrinsic event for the immediately enclosing element.

Attributes

TYPE=*cdata*

The TYPE attribute indicates the name of the intrinsic event.

6.8.2 Card/Deck Intrinsic Events

The ONENTERFORWARD and ONENTERBACKWARD intrinsic events may be specified at both the card and deck levels and have the shadowing semantics defined in Section 6.5. Intrinsic events may be overridden regardless of the syntax used to specify them. A deck-level event handler specified with the ONEVENT element may be overridden by the ONEVENTFORWARD attribute, and vice versa.

7. The State Model

WML includes support for managing user agent state, including:

Variables: Parameters used to change the characteristics and content of a WML card or deck.

History: Navigational history, which may be used to facilitate efficient backward navigation.

Implementation-dependent state: Other state relating to the particulars of the user agent implementation and behavior.

7.1 The Browser Context

WML state is stored in a single scope, known as a *browser context*. The browser context is used to manage all parameters and user agent state, including variables, the navigation history, and other implementation-dependent information related to the current state of the user agent.

7.2 The NEWCONTEXT Attribute

The browser context may be initialized to a well-defined state by the `NEWCONTEXT` attribute of the `CARD` element (see Section 8.5). This attribute indicates that the browser context should be reinitialized and must perform the following operations:

- Unset (remove) all variables defined in the current browser context
- Clear the navigational history state
- Reset implementation-specific state to a well-known value

`NEWCONTEXT` is only performed as part of the GO task. See Section 9.5 for more information on the processing of state during navigation.

7.3 Variables

All WML content can be parameterized, allowing the author a great deal of flexibility in creating cards and decks with improved caching behavior and better perceived interactivity. WML variables can be used in the place of strings and are substituted at runtime with their current value.

A variable is said to be *set* if it has a value not equal to the empty string. A value is *not set* if it has a value equal to the empty string, or is otherwise unknown or undefined in the current browser context.

7.3.1 Variable Substitution

The values of variables can be substituted into both the text (`#PCDATA`) of a card and into `%vdata` and `%URL` attribute values in WML elements. Only textual information can be substituted; no substitution of elements or attributes is possible. The substitution of variable values happens at runtime in the user agent. Substitution does not affect the current value of the variable and is defined as a string substitution operation. If an undefined variable is referenced, it results in the substitution of the empty string.

WML variable names consist of an US-ASCII letter or underscore followed by zero or more letters, digits, or underscores. Any other characters are illegal. Variable names are case sensitive.

The following is a BNF-like description of the variable substitution syntax. The description uses the conventions established in [RFC822], except that the "|" character is used to designate alternatives. Briefly, "(" and ")" are used to group elements, while optional elements are enclosed in "[" and "]". Elements may be preceded with <N>* to specify N or more repetitions of the following element (N defaults to zero when unspecified).

```
var      = ( "$" varname ) |
           ( "$(" varname [ conv ] ")" )
conv     = ":" ( escape | noesc | unesc )
escape   = ("E" | "e") [ ( "S" | "s" ) ( "C" | "c" )
                         ( "A" | "a" ) ( "P" | "p" )
                         ( "E" | "e" ) ]
noesc    = ( "N" | "n" ) [ ( "O" | "o" ) ("E" | "e")
                           ( "S" | "s" ) ( "C" | "c" ) ]
unesc    = ( "U" | "u" ) [ ( "N" | "n" ) ("E" | "e")
                           ( "S" | "s" ) ( "C" | "c" ) ]
varname = ( "_" | alpha ) *[ "_" | alpha | digit ]
alpha    = lalpha | halpha
lalpha   = "a" | "b" | "c" | "d" | "e" | "f" | "g" | "h" | "i" |
           "j" | "k" | "l" | "m" | "n" | "o" | "p" | "q" | "r" |
           "s" | "t" | "u" | "v" | "w" | "x" | "y" | "z"
halpha   = "A" | "B" | "C" | "D" | "E" | "F" | "G" | "H" | "I" |
           "J" | "K" | "L" | "M" | "N" | "O" | "P" | "Q" | "R" |
           "S" | "T" | "U" | "V" | "W" | "X" | "Y" | "Z"
digit    = "0" | "1" | "2" | "3" | "4" | "5" | "6" | "7" |
           "8" | "9"
```

Parentheses are required anywhere the end of a variable cannot be inferred from the surrounding context (e.g., an illegal character such as whitespace).

For example:

```
This is a $var
This is another $(var).
This is an escaped $(var:e).
Long form of escaped $(var:escape).
Long form of unescape $(var:unesc).
Short form of no-escape $(var:N).
Other legal variable forms: $_X $X32 $Test_9A
```

The value of variables can be converted into a different form as they are substituted. A conversion can be specified in the variable reference following the colon. Table 4.3 summarizes the current conversions and their legal abbreviations:

Table 4.3 Variable Escaping Methods

CONVERSION	EFFECT
noesc	No change to the value of the variable
escape	URL-escape the value of the variable
unesc	URL-unescape the value of the variable

The use of a conversion during variable substitution does not affect the actual value of the variable.

URL-escaping is detailed in [RFC1738]. All lexically sensitive characters defined in WML must be escaped, including all `reserved` and `unsafe` URL characters, as specified by [RFC1738].

If no conversion is specified, the variable is substituted using the conversion format appropriate for the context. The `ONENTERBACKWARD`, `ONENTERFORWARD`, `URL`, and `SRC` attributes default to escape conversion, elsewhere no conversion is done. Specifying the `noesc` conversion disables context sensitive escaping of a variable.

7.3.2 Parsing the Variable Substitution Syntax

The variable substitution syntax (e.g., `$X`) is parsed after all XML parsing is complete. In XML terminology, variable substitution is parsed after the *XML processor* has parsed the document and provided the resulting parsed form to the *XML application*. In the context of this specification, the WML parser and user agent is the *XML application*.

This implies that all variable syntax is parsed *after* the XML constructs, such as tags and entities, have been parsed. In the context of variable parsing, all XML syntax has a higher precedence than the variable syntax; for example, entity substitution occurs before the variable substitution syntax is parsed. The following examples are identical references to the variable named `X`:

```
$X
&#x24;X
$&#x58;
&#36;&#x58;
```

7.3.3 The Dollar-Sign Character

A side effect of the parsing rules is that the literal dollar sign must be encoded with a pair of dollar-sign entities. A single dollar-sign entity, even specified as `$`, results in a variable substitution.

In order to include a $ character in a WML deck, it must be explicitly escaped. This can be accomplished with the following syntax:

```
$$
```

Two dollar signs in a row are replaced with a single $ character. For example:

```
This is a $$ character.
```

This would be displayed as:

```
This is a $ character.
```

To include the $ character in URL-escaped strings, specify it with the URL-escaped form:

```
%24
```

7.3.4 Setting Variables

There are a number of ways to set the value of a variable. When a variable is set and it is already defined in the browser context, the current value is updated.

The `VAR` element allows the author to set variable state as a side effect of navigation. `VAR` may be specified in task elements, including `GO`, `PREV`, and `REFRESH`. The `VAR` element specifies a variable name and value; for example:

```
<VAR NAME="location" VALUE="$(X)"/>
```

The variable specified in the `NAME` attribute (e.g., `location`) is set as a side effect of navigation. See the discussion of event handling (Section 6 and Section 9.5) for more information on the processing of the `VAR` element.

Input elements set the variable identified by the `KEY` attribute to any information entered by the user. For example, an `INPUT` element assigns the entered text to the variable, and the `SELECT` element assigns the value present in the `VALUE` attribute of the chosen `OPTION` element.

User input is written to variables when the user commits the input to the `INPUT` or `SELECT` element. Committing input is an MMI-dependent concept, and the WML author must not rely on a particular user interface. For example, some implementations will update the variable with each character entered into an `INPUT` element, and others will defer the variable update until the `INPUT` element has lost focus. The user agent must update all variables prior to the execution of any task. The user agent may redisplay the current card when variables are set, but the author must not assume that this action will occur.

8. The Structure of WML Decks

WML data are structured as a collection of *cards*. A single collection of cards is referred to as a WML *deck*. Each card contains structured content and navigation specifications. Logically, a user navigates through a series of cards, reviews the contents of each, enters requested information, makes choices and navigates to another card, or returns to a previously visited card.

8.1 Document Prologue

A valid WML deck is a valid XML document and therefore must contain an XML declaration and a document type declaration (see [XML] for more detail about the definition of a valid document). A typical document prologue contains:

```
<?xml version="1.0"?>
<!DOCTYPE WML PUBLIC "-//WAPFORUM//DTD WML 1.0//EN"
                    "http://www.wapforum.org/DTD/wml.xml">
```

It is an error to omit the prologue.

8.2 The WML Element

```
<!ELEMENT WML ( HEAD?, TEMPLATE?, CARD+ )>
<!ATTLIST WML
  xml:lang        NMTOKEN        #IMPLIED
  >
```

The WML element defines a deck and encloses all information and cards in the deck.

Attributes

`xml:lang=`*`nmtoken`*

The `xml:lang` attribute specifies the natural or formal language in which the document is written. See [XML] for details on the syntax and specification of the attribute values. If the `xml:lang` attribute is specified, it takes precedence over any other specification of the document language (e.g., transport metadata).

8.2.1 A WML Example

The following is a deck containing two cards, each represented by a `CARD` element (see Section 8.5 for information on cards). After loading the deck, a user agent displays the first card. If the user activates the DO element, the user agent displays the second card.

```
<WML>
  <CARD>
    <DO TYPE="ACCEPT">
      <GO URL="#card2"/>
    </DO>
    Hello world!
    This is the first card...
  </CARD>
  <CARD NAME="card2">
    This is the second card.
    Goodbye.
  </CARD>
</WML>
```

8.3 The HEAD Element

```
<!ELEMENT HEAD ( ACCESS | META )+>
```

The HEAD element contains information relating to the deck as a whole, including metadata and access control elements.

8.3.1 The ACCESS Element

```
<!ELEMENT ACCESS EMPTY>
<!ATTLIST ACCESS
  DOMAIN       CDATA       #IMPLIED
  PATH         CDATA       #IMPLIED
  PUBLIC       %boolean;   "FALSE"
  >
```

The ACCESS element specifies access control information for the entire deck. It is an error for a deck to contain more than one ACCESS element.

Attributes

DOMAIN=*cdata*

PATH=*cdata*

A deck's DOMAIN and PATH attributes specify which other decks may access it. As the user agent navigates from one deck to another, it performs access control checks to determine whether the destination deck allows access from the current deck.

If a deck has a DOMAIN and/or PATH attribute, the referring deck's URL must match the values of the attributes. Matching is done as follows: The access domain is suffix-matched against the domain name portion of the referring URL, and the access path is prefix-matched against the path portion of the referring URL.

DOMAIN suffix matching is done using the entire element of each subdomain and must match each element exactly (e.g., www.wapforum.org shall match wapforum.org, but shall not match forum.org). PATH prefix matching is done using entire path elements and must match each element exactly (e.g., /X/Y matches /X but does not match /XZ).

The DOMAIN attribute defaults to the current deck's domain. The PATH attribute defaults to the value "/".

To simplify the development of applications that may not know the absolute path to the current deck, the PATH attribute accepts relative URLs. The user agent converts the relative path to an absolute path and then performs prefix matching against the PATH attribute.

For example, given the following access control attributes:

```
DOMAIN="wapforum.org"
PATH="/cbb"
```

the following referring URLs would be allowed to go to the deck:

```
http://wapforum.org/cbb/stocks.cgi
https://www.wapforum.org/cbb/bonds.cgi
http://www.wapforum.org/cbb/demos/alpha/packages.cgi?x=123&y=456
```

The following referring URLs would not be allowed to go to the deck:

```
http://www.test.net/cbb
http://www.wapforum.org/internal/foo.wml
```

DOMAIN and PATH follow URL capitalization rules.

PUBLIC=*boolean*

This attribute indicates whether deck access control has been disabled for this deck. If disabled (i.e., PUBLIC="TRUE" is specified), cards in any deck can access this deck. If enabled, then the DOMAIN and PATH attributes are used to determine which cards or decks can access the deck. By default, access control is enabled.

8.3.2 The META Element

```
<!ELEMENT META EMPTY>
<!ATTLIST META
  HTTP-EQUIV     CDATA     #IMPLIED
  NAME           CDATA     #IMPLIED
  USER-AGENT     CDATA     #IMPLIED
  CONTENT        CDATA     #REQUIRED
  SCHEME         CDATA     #IMPLIED
  >
```

The META element contains generic meta-information relating to the WML deck. Meta-information is specified with property names and values. This specification does not define any properties, nor does it define how user agents must interpret metadata. User agents are not required to support the metadata mechanism.

It is an error for a META element to contain more than one attribute specifying a property name; in other words, more than one attribute from the following set: NAME, HTTP-EQUIV, and USER-AGENT.

Attributes

NAME=*cdata*

This attribute specifies the property name. The user agent must ignore any metadata named with this attribute. Network servers should not emit WML content containing metadata named with this attribute.

HTTP-EQUIV=*cdata*

This attribute may be used in place of NAME and indicates that the property should be interpreted as an HTTP header (see [RFC2068]). Metadata named with this attribute should be converted to a WSP or HTTP response header if the content is tokenized before it arrives at the user agent.

USER-AGENT=*cdata*

This attribute may be used in place of NAME. This metadata must be delivered to the user agent and may not be removed by any network intermediary.

CONTENT=*cdata*

This attribute specifies the property value.

SCHEME=*cdata*

This attribute specifies a form or structure that may be used to interpret the property value. Scheme values vary depending on the type of metadata.

8.4 The TEMPLATE Element

```
<!ENTITY % navelmts "DO | ONEVENT">
<!ELEMENT TEMPLATE (%navelmts;)*>
<!ATTLIST TEMPLATE
  %cardev;
  >
```

The TEMPLATE element declares a template for cards in the deck. Event bindings specified in the TEMPLATE element (e.g., DO or ONEVENT) apply to all cards in the deck. Specifying an event binding in the TEMPLATE element is equivalent to specifying it in every card element. A card element may override the behavior specified in the TEMPLATE element. In particular:

- DO elements specified in the TEMPLATE element may be overridden in individual cards if both elements have the same NAME attribute value. See Section 6.5 for more information.
- Intrinsic event bindings specified in the TEMPLATE element may be overridden by the specification of an event binding in a card element. See Section 6.8 for more information.

See Section 8.5 for the definition of the card-level intrinsic events (the cardev entity).

Attributes Defined Elsewhere

The following task attributes are defined in Section 8.5.1:

%cardev

8.5 The Card Element

A WML deck contains a collection of cards. There is a variety of card types, each specifying a different mode of user interaction.

8.5.1 Card Intrinsic Events

```
<!ENTITY % cardev
 "ONENTERFORWARD  %URL;        #IMPLIED
```

```
ONENTERBACKWARD %URL;         #IMPLIED
ONTIMER         %URL;         #IMPLIED"
>
```

The following attributes are available in the CARD and TEMPLATE elements.

Attributes

ONENTERFORWARD=*URL*

The ONENTERFORWARD event occurs when the user causes the user agent to navigate into a card using a GO task.

ONENTERBACKWARD=*URL*

The ONENTERBACKWARD event occurs when the user causes the user agent to navigate into a card using a PREV task.

ONTIMER=*URL*

The ONTIMER event occurs when a TIMER expires.

8.5.2 The CARD Element

```
<!ENTITY % fields "%flow; | INPUT | SELECT | FIELDSET">
<!ELEMENT CARD (%fields; | %navelmts; | TIMER)*>
<!ATTLIST CARD
  NAME          NMTOKEN       #IMPLIED
  TITLE         %vdata;       #IMPLIED
  NEWCONTEXT    %boolean;     "FALSE"
  STYLE         (LIST|SET)    "LIST"
  %cardev;
  >
```

The CARD element is a container of text and input elements that is sufficiently flexible to allow presentation and layout in a wide variety of devices, with a wide variety of display and input characteristics. The CARD element indicates the general layout and required input fields but does not overly constrain the user agent implementation in the areas of layout or user input. For example, a CARD can be presented as a single page on a large-screen device, and as a series of smaller pages on a small-screen device.

A CARD can contain markup, input fields, and elements indicating the structure of the card. The order of elements in the card is significant and should be respected by the user agent.

Attributes

NAME=*nmtoken*

This attribute gives a name to the card. A card's name may be used as a fragment anchor. See Section 2.2 for more information.

TITLE=*vdata*

The `TITLE` attribute specifies advisory information about the card. The title may be rendered in a variety of ways by the user agent (e.g., suggested bookmark name, popup *tooltip*, etc.).

`NEWCONTEXT=`*`boolean`*

This attribute indicates that the current browser context should be reinitialized upon entry to this card. See Section 7.2 for more information.

`STYLE=`*`(LIST|SET)`*

This attribute specifies a hint to the user agent about the organization of the `CARD` content. This hint may be used to organize the content presentation or to otherwise influence layout of the card.

`LIST`: The card is naturally organized as a linear sequence of field elements; for example, a set of questions or fields which are naturally handled by the user in the order in which they are specified in the group. This style is best for short forms in which no fields are optional (e.g., sending an e-mail message requires a `To:` address, a subject, and a message, and they are logically specified in this order).

It is expected that in small-screen devices, `LIST` groups may be presented as a sequence of screens, with a screen flip in between each field or fieldset. Other user agents may elect to present all fields simultaneously.

`SET`: The card is a collection of field elements without a natural order. This is useful for collections of fields containing optional or unordered components or simple record data where the user is updating individual input fields. It is expected that in small-screen devices, `SET` groups may be presented by using a hierarchical or tree organization. In these types of presentation, the `TITLE` attribute of each field and fieldset may be used to define the name presented to the user in the top-level summary card.

The user agent may interpret the style attribute in a manner appropriate to its device capabilities (e.g., screen size or input device). In addition, the user agent should adopt user interface conventions for handling the editing of input elements in a manner that best suits the device's input model.

For example, a phone-class device displaying a `CARD` with `STYLE=SET` may use a softkey or button to select individual fields for editing or viewing. A PDA-class device might create soft buttons on demand, or simply present all fields on the screen for direct manipulation.

On devices with limited display capabilities, it is often necessary to insert screen flips or other user-interface transitions between fields. When this is done, the user agent needs to decide on the proper boundary between fields. User agents may use the following heuristic for determining the choice of a screen flip location:

- `FIELDSET` defines a logical boundary between fields.
- Fields (e.g., `INPUT`) may be individually displayed. When this is done, the line of markup (`flow`) immediately preceding the field should be treated as a field prompt and displayed with the input element.

Attributes Defined Elsewhere

The following task attributes are defined in Section 8.5.1:

```
%cardev
```

8.5.2.1 A CARD Example

The following is an example of a simple `CARD` element embedded within a WML deck. The card contains text, which is displayed by the user agent. In addition, the example demonstrates the use of a simple `DO` element, defined at the deck level.

```
<WML>
  <TEMPLATE>
    <DO TYPE="ACCEPT" LABEL="Exit">
      <PREV/>
    </DO>
  </TEMPLATE>
  <CARD>
    Hello World!
  </CARD>
</WML>
```

8.6 Control Elements

8.6.1 The TABINDEX Attribute

Attributes

`TABINDEX=`*`number`*

This attribute specifies the tabbing position of the current element. The tabbing position indicates the relative order in which elements are traversed when tabbing within a single WML card. A numerically greater `TABINDEX` value indicates an element that is later in the tab sequence than an element with a numerically lesser `TABINDEX` value.

Each input element (i.e., `INPUT` and `SELECT`) in a card is assigned a position in the card's tab sequence. In addition, the user agent may assign a tab position to other elements. The `TABINDEX` attribute indicates the tab position of a given element. Elements that are not designated with an author-specified tab position may be assigned one by the user agent. User agent-specified tab positions must be later in the tab sequence than any author-specified tab positions.

Tabbing is a navigational accelerator and is optional for all user agents. Authors must not assume that a user agent implements tabbing.

8.6.2 Select Lists

Select lists are an input element that specifies a list of options for the user to choose from. Single and multiple choice lists are supported.

8.6.2.1 The SELECT Element

```
<!ELEMENT SELECT (OPTGROUP|OPTION)+>
<!ATTLIST SELECT
  TITLE         %vdata;            #IMPLIED
  KEY           NMTOKEN            #IMPLIED
  DEFAULT       %vdata;            #IMPLIED
  IKEY          NMTOKEN            #IMPLIED
  IDEFAULT      %vdata;            #IMPLIED
  MULTIPLE      %boolean;          "FALSE"
  TABINDEX      %number;           #IMPLIED
  >
```

The `SELECT` element lets users pick from a list of options. Each option is specified by an `OPTION` element. Each `OPTION` element may have one line of formatted text (which may be wrapped or truncated by the user agent if too long). `OPTION` elements may be organized into hierarchical groups using the `OPTGROUP` element.

Attributes

`MULTIPLE=`*`boolean`*

This attribute indicates that the select list should accept multiple selections. When not set, the select list should only accept a single selected option.

`KEY=`*`nmtoken`*

`DEFAULT=`*`vdata`*

This `KEY` attribute indicates the name of the variable to set with the result of the selection. The variable is set to the string value of the chosen `OPTION` element, which is specified with the `VALUE` attribute. The `KEY` variable's value is used to preselect options in the select list.

The `DEFAULT` attribute indicates the default value of the variable named in the `KEY` attribute. When the element is displayed, and the variable named in the `KEY` attribute is not set, the `KEY` variable is assigned the value specified in the `DEFAULT` attribute. If the `KEY` variable already contains a value, the `DEFAULT` attribute is ignored. Any application of the default value is done before the list is preselected with the value of the `KEY` variable.

If this element allows the selection of multiple options, the result of the user's choice is a list of all selected values, separated by the semicolon character. The `KEY` variable is set with this result. In addition, the `DEFAULT` attribute is interpreted as a semicolon-separated list of preselected options.

`IKEY=`*`nmtoken`*

`IDEFAULT=`*`vdata`*

The `IKEY` attribute indicates the name of the variable to be set with the index result of the selection. The index result is the position of the currently selected `OPTION` in the select list. An index of 0 indicates that no `OPTION` is selected. Index numbering begins at 1 and increases monotonically.

The IDEFAULT attribute indicates the default-selected OPTION element. When the element is displayed, if the variable named in the IKEY attribute is not set, it is assigned the default-selected entry. If the variable already contains a value, the IDEFAULT attribute is ignored. If the IKEY attribute is not specified, the IDEFAULT value is applied every time the element is displayed.

If this element allows the selection of multiple options, the index result of the user's choice is a list of the indices of all the selected options, separated by the semicolon character (e.g., "1;2"). The IKEY variable is set with this result. In addition, the IDEFAULT attribute is interpreted as a semicolon-separated list of preselected options (e.g., "1;4").

TITLE=*vdata*

This attribute specifies a title for this element, which may be used in the presentation of this object.

Attributes Defined Elsewhere

The following attribute is defined in Section 8.6.1:

TABINDEX

On entry into a card containing a SELECT element, the user agent must select the initial options in the following way:

- If the IKEY attribute exists, the indices in the variable named by IKEY are used to select the option. If the specified variable is not set, the index is assumed to be 1. If any index is larger than the number of options in the select list, the last entry is selected.
- If the IKEY attribute does not exist and the KEY attribute exists, the value of the variable specified by KEY is used to select options. If the variable specified by KEY is not set, or no OPTION has a VALUE attribute matching the value, the first option is selected.

Once an OPTION is selected, the variable named by KEY is updated to the value of the option.

Both KEY and IKEY, or DEFAULT and IDEFAULT, may be specified. IDEFAULT takes precedence over DEFAULT, and IKEY takes precedence over KEY.

8.6.2.2 The OPTION Element

```
<!ELEMENT OPTION (%text; | ONEVENT)*>
<!ATTLIST OPTION
  VALUE      %vdata;    #IMPLIED
  TITLE      %vdata;    #IMPLIED
  ONCLICK    %URL;      #IMPLIED
  >
```

This element specifies a single choice option in a SELECT element.

Attributes

`VALUE=`*vdata*

The VALUE attribute specifies the value to be used when setting the KEY variable. When the user selects this option, the resulting value specified in the VALUE attribute is used to set the SELECT element's KEY variable.

The VALUE attribute may contain variable references, which are evaluated before the KEY variable is set.

`TITLE=`*vdata*

This attribute specifies a title for this element, which may be used in the presentation of this object.

`ONCLICK=`*URL*

The ONCLICK event occurs when the user selects or deselects this option. A multiple-selection option list generates an ONCLICK event whenever the user selects or deselects this option. A single-selection option list generates an ONCLICK event when the user selects this option; in other words, no event is generated for the deselection of any previously selected option.

8.6.2.3 The OPTGROUP Element

```
<!ELEMENT OPTGROUP (OPTGROUP|OPTION)+ >
<!ATTLIST OPTGROUP
  TITLE      %vdata;    #IMPLIED
  >
```

The OPTGROUP element allows the author to group related OPTION elements into a hierarchy. The user agent may use this hierarchy to facilitate layout and presentation on a wide variety of devices.

Attributes

`TITLE=`*vdata*

This attribute specifies a title for this element, which may be used in the presentation of this object.

8.6.2.4 Select list examples

In this example, a simple single-choice select list is specified. If the user were to choose the "Dog" option, the variable "X" would be set to a value of "D".

```
<WML>
  <CARD>
    Please choose your favourite animal:
    <SELECT KEY="X">
      <OPTION VALUE="D">Dog</OPTION>
      <OPTION VALUE="C">Cat</OPTION>
    </SELECT>
```

```
  </CARD>
</WML>
```

In this example, a single choice select list is specified. If the user were to choose the "Cat" option, the variable "I" would be set to a value of "2". In addition, the "Dog" option would be preselected if the "I" variable had not been previously set.

```
<WML>
  <CARD>
    Please choose your favourite animal:
    <SELECT IKEY="I" IDEFAULT="1">
      <OPTION VALUE="D">Dog</OPTION>
      <OPTION VALUE="C">Cat</OPTION>
    </SELECT>
  </CARD>
</WML>
```

In this example, a multiple-choice list is specified. If the user were to choose the "Cat" and "Horse" options, the variable "X" would be set to "C;H" and the variable "I" would be set to "1;3". In addition, the "Dog" and "Cat" options would be preselected if the variable "I" had not been previously set.

```
<WML>
  <CARD>
    Please choose <I>all</I> of your favourite animals:
    <SELECT KEY="X" IKEY="I" IDEFAULT="1;2" MULTIPLE="TRUE">
      <OPTION VALUE="D">Dog</OPTION>
      <OPTION VALUE="C">Cat</OPTION>
      <OPTION VALUE="H">Horse</OPTION>
    </SELECT>
  </CARD>
</WML>
```

8.6.3 The INPUT Element

```
<!ELEMENT INPUT EMPTY>
<!ATTLIST INPUT
  KEY         NMTOKEN            #REQUIRED
  TYPE        (TEXT|PASSWORD)    "TEXT"
  VALUE       %vdata;            #IMPLIED
  DEFAULT     %vdata;            #IMPLIED
  FORMAT      CDATA              #IMPLIED
  EMPTYOK     %boolean;          "FALSE"
  SIZE        %number;           #IMPLIED
  MAXLENGTH   %number;           #IMPLIED
  TABINDEX    %number;           #IMPLIED
  TITLE       %vdata;            #IMPLIED
  >
```

The `INPUT` element specifies a text entry object. The user input is constrained by the optional `FORMAT` attribute.

Attributes

`KEY=`*`nmtoken`*

`DEFAULT=`*`vdata`*

`VALUE=`*`vdata`*

The `KEY` attribute specifies the name of the variable to set with the result of the user's text input. The `KEY` variable's value is used to preload the text entry object.

The `DEFAULT` attribute indicates the default value of the variable named in the `KEY` attribute. When the element is displayed and the variable named in the `KEY` attribute is not set, the `KEY` variable is assigned the value specified in the `DEFAULT` attribute. If the `KEY` variable already contains a value, the `DEFAULT` attribute is ignored. If the `DEFAULT` attribute specifies a value that does not conform to the input mask specified by the `FORMAT` attribute, the user agent must ignore the `DEFAULT` attribute.

The `DEFAULT` and `VALUE` attributes are identical in their behavior and syntax.

`TYPE=`*`(TEXT|PASSWORD)`*

This attribute specifies the type of text-input area. The default type is `TEXT`. The following values are allowed:

- `TEXT`: A text entry box. Input should be displayed to the user in a readable form, and each character should be echoed in a manner appropriate to the user agent.
- `PASSWORD`: A text entry box. Input of each character should be echoed in an obscured or illegible form. For example, user agents may elect to display an asterisk in place of a character entered by the user. Typically, the `PASSWORD` input mode is indicated for password entry or other private data. Note that `PASSWORD` input is not secure and should not be depended on for critical applications.

In both cases, the user's input is applied to the `KEY` variable.

`FORMAT=`*`cdata`*

The `FORMAT` attribute specifies an input mask for user input entries. The string consists of mask control characters and static text that is displayed in the input area. The user agent may use the format mask to facilitate accelerated data input.

The format control characters specify the data format expected to be entered by the user. The default format is "*M". The format codes are:

A Entry of any uppercase alphabetic or punctuation character (i.e., uppercase nonnumeric character).

a Entry of any lowercase alphabetic or punctuation character (i.e., lowercase nonnumeric character).

N Entry of any numeric character.

X Entry of any uppercase character.

x Entry of any lowercase character.

M Entry of any character; the user agent may choose to assume that the character is uppercase for the purposes of simple data entry, but must allow entry of any character.

m Entry of any character; the user agent may choose to assume that the character is lowercase for the purposes of simple data entry, but must allow entry of any character.

***f** Entry of any number of characters; f is one of the preceding format codes and specifies what kind of characters can be entered. *Note: This format may only be specified once and must appear at the end of the format string.*

nf Entry of n characters where n is from 1 to 9; f is one of the preceding format codes and specifies what kind of characters can be entered. *Note: This format may only be specified once and must appear at the end of the format string.*

c Display the next character, c, in the entry field; allows quoting of the format codes so they can be displayed in the entry area.

User agents must implement the format codes to the best of their ability given the constraints of the input language and character set. If the input language and character set have a clear definition of numbers and character case, they must be followed. Authors must not rely on the interpretation of a particular format code in a given language.

`EMPTYOK=`*`boolean`*

The `EMPTYOK` attribute indicates that this `INPUT` element accepts empty input although a nonempty format string has been specified. Typically, the `EMPTYOK` attribute is indicated for formatted entry fields that are optional. By default, `INPUT` elements specifying a `FORMAT` require the user to input data matching the `FORMAT` specification.

`SIZE=`*`number`*

This attribute specifies the width, in characters, of the text-input area. The user agent may ignore this attribute.

`MAXLENGTH=`*`number`*

This attribute specifies the maximum number of characters that can be entered by the user in the text-entry area. The default value for this attribute is an unlimited number of characters.

`TITLE=`*`vdata`*

This attribute specifies a title for this element, which may be used in the presentation of this object.

Attributes Defined Elsewhere

The following attribute is defined in Section 8.6.1:

`TABINDEX`

8.6.3.1 INPUT Element Examples

In this example, an `INPUT` element is specified. This element accepts any characters and displays the input to the user in a human-readable form. The maximum number of characters entered is 32, and the resulting input is assigned to the variable named `X`.

```
<INPUT KEY="X" TYPE="TEXT" MAXLENGTH="32"/>
```

The following example requests input from the user and assigns the resulting input to the variable NAME. The text field has a default value of "Robert".

```
<INPUT KEY="NAME" TYPE="TEXT" DEFAULT="Robert"/>
```

The following example is a card that prompts the user for a first name, last name, and age.

```
<CARD>
  First name: <INPUT TYPE="TEXT" KEY="first"/><BR/>
  Last name: <INPUT TYPE="TEXT" KEY="last"/><BR/>
  Age: <INPUT TYPE="TEXT" KEY="age" FORMAT="*N"/>
</CARD>
```

8.6.4 The FIELDSET Element

```
<!ELEMENT FIELDSET (%fields;)* >
<!ATTLIST FIELDSET
  TITLE          %vdata;       #IMPLIED
  >
```

The FIELDSET element allows the grouping of related fields and text. This grouping provides information to the user agent, allowing the optimizing of layout and navigation. FIELDSET elements may nest, providing the user with a means of specifying behavior across a wide variety of devices. See Section 8.5.2 for information on how the FIELDSET element may influence layout and navigation.

Attributes

TITLE=*vdata*

This attribute specifies a title for this element, which may be used in the presentation of this object.

8.6.4.1 FIELDSET Element Examples

The following example specifies a WML deck that requests basic identity and personal information from the user. It is separated into multiple field sets, indicating the preferred field grouping to the user agent.

```
<WML>
  <CARD>
    <DO TYPE="ACCEPT">
      <GO URL="/submit?f=$(fname)&amp;l=$(lname)&amp;s=$(sex)&amp;a=$(age)"/>
    </DO>
    <FIELDSET TITLE="Name">
      First name: <INPUT TYPE="TEXT" KEY="fname" MAXLENGTH="32"/><BR/>
      Last name: <INPUT TYPE="TEXT" KEY="lname" MAXLENGTH="32"/><BR/>
    </FIELDSET>
```

```
    <FIELDSET TITLE="Info">
      <SELECT KEY="sex">
        <OPTION VALUE="F">Female</OPTION>
        <OPTION VALUE="M">Male</OPTION>
      </SELECT>
      <BR/>
      Age: <INPUT TYPE="TEXT" KEY="age" FORMAT="*N"/>
    </FIELDSET>
  </CARD>
</WML>
```

8.7 The TIMER Element

```
<!ELEMENT TIMER EMPTY>
<!ATTLIST TIMER
  KEY         NMTOKEN           #IMPLIED
  DEFAULT     %vdata;           #REQUIRED
  >
```

The TIMER element declares a card timer, which exposes a means of processing inactivity or idle time. The timer is initialized and started at card entry and is stopped when the card is exited. Card entry is any task or user action that results in the card being activated; for example, navigating into the card. Card exit is defined as the execution of any task (see Sections 6.3 and 9.5). The value of a timer will decrement from the initial value, triggering the delivery of an ONTIMER intrinsic event on transition from a value of 1 to 0. If the user has not exited the card at the time of timer expiration, an ONTIMER intrinsic event is delivered to the card.

Timer resolution is implementation dependent. The interaction of the timer with the user agent's user interface and other time-based or asynchronous device functionality is implementation dependent. It is an error to have more than one TIMER element in a card.

The TIMER timeout value is specified in units of one-tenth (1/10) of a second. The author should not expect a particular timer resolution and should provide the user with another means to invoke a timer's task. If the value of the timeout is not a positive integral number, the user agent must ignore the TIMER element. A timeout value of 0 disables the timer.

Attributes

KEY=*nmtoken*

The KEY attribute specifies the name of the variable to be set with the value of the timer. The KEY variable's value is used to set the timeout period upon timer initialization. The variable named by the KEY attribute will be set with the current timer value when the card is exited or when the timer expires. For example, if the timer expires, the KEY variable is set to a value of "0".

DEFAULT=*vdata*

The DEFAULT attribute indicates the default value of the variable named in the KEY attribute. When the timer is initialized and the variable named in the KEY attribute is not set, the KEY variable is assigned the value specified in the DEFAULT attribute. If the KEY variable already contains a value, the DEFAULT attribute is ignored. If the KEY attribute is not specified, the timeout is always initialized to the value specified in the DEFAULT attribute.

8.7.1 TIMER Example

The following deck will display a text message for approximately 10 seconds and will then go to the URL /next:

```
<WML>
  <CARD ONTIMER="/next">
       <TIMER DEFAULT="100"/>
       Hello World!
  </CARD>
</WML>
```

The same example could be implemented as:

```
<WML>
  <CARD>
    <ONEVENT TYPE="ONTIMER">
      <GO URL="/next"/>
    </ONEVENT>
    <TIMER DEFAULT="100"/>
    Hello World!
  </CARD>
</WML>
```

The following example illustrates how a timer can initialize and reuse a counter. Each time the card is entered, the timer is reset to value of the variable t. If t is not set, the timer is set to a value of 5 seconds.

```
<WML>
  <CARD ONTIMER="/next">
    <TIMER KEY="t" DEFAULT="50"/>
    Hello World!
  </CARD>
</WML>
```

8.8 Text

This section defines the elements and constructs related to text.

8.8.1 Whitespace

WML whitespace and line break handling is based on [XML] and assumes the default whitespace handling rules. The WML user agent ignores all *insignificant* whitespace, as defined by the XML specification. In addition, all other sequences of whitespace must be compressed into a single interword space.

User agents should treat interword spaces in a locale-dependent manner, as different written languages treat interword spacing in different ways.

8.8.2 Emphasis

```
<!ELEMENT EM     (%flow;)*>
<!ELEMENT STRONG (%flow;)*>
<!ELEMENT B      (%flow;)*>
<!ELEMENT I      (%flow;)*>
<!ELEMENT U      (%flow;)*>
<!ELEMENT BIG    (%flow;)*>
<!ELEMENT SMALL  (%flow;)*>
```

The emphasis elements specify text emphasis markup information.

EM: Render with emphasis.

STRONG: Render with strong emphasis.

B: Render with a bold font.

I: Render with an italic font.

U: Render with underline.

BIG: Render with a large font.

SMALL: Render with a small font.

Authors should use the STRONG and EM elements where possible. B, I, and U elements should not be used except where explicit control over text presentation is required.

8.8.3 Line Breaks

```
<!ENTITY % TAlign    "(LEFT|RIGHT|CENTER)" >
<!ENTITY % BRMode     "(WRAP|NOWRAP)" >
<!ELEMENT BR EMPTY>
<!ATTLIST BR
  ALIGN    %TAlign;     "LEFT"
  MODE     %BRMode;     #IMPLIED
>
```

WML has two line-wrapping modes: breaking and nonbreaking. In breaking mode, line breaks should be inserted into a text flow as appropriate for presentation on an individual device, and any interword space is a legal line break point. In nonbreaking mode, a line of text must not be automatically wrapped.

The nonbreaking space entity (or) indicates a space that must not be treated as an interword space by the user agent. Authors should use   to prevent undesired line breaks. The soft-hyphen character entity (or) indicates a location that may be used by the user agent for a line break. If a line break occurs at a soft hyphen, the user agent must insert a hyphen character (-) at the end of the line. In all other operations, the soft-hyphen entity should be ignored. A user agent may choose to entirely ignore soft hyphens when formatting text lines.

The BR element establishes the beginning of a new line and specifies the line break and alignment parameters for the new line. If the line break mode is not specified, it is identical to the line break mode of the previous line in the current card. If the text alignment is not specified, it defaults to LEFT.

A WML card has a line break and alignment mode. The initial line break mode for a card is MODE="WRAP" (breaking mode) and the initial text alignment is ALIGN="LEFT" (left alignment). If the first nonwhitespace markup in a card is a BR element, the BR begins the first line in the card. If the first nonwhitespace markup in a card is not a BR element, a new line is implicitly started with the default line break and alignment modes.

The treatment of a line too long to fit on the screen is specified by the current line break mode. If MODE="WRAP" is specified, the line is word-wrapped onto multiple lines. If MODE="LINE" is specified, the line is not wrapped. The user agent must provide a mechanism with which to view entire nonwrapped lines (e.g., horizontal scrolling or some other user-agent-specific mechanism).

Attributes

ALIGN= *(LEFT|RIGHT|CENTER)*

This attribute specifies the text alignment mode for the line. Text can be center aligned, left aligned, or right aligned when it is displayed to the user. Left alignment is the default alignment mode. If not explicitly specified, the text alignment is set to the default alignment. For example, a simple <BR/> element starts a new line and sets the alignment to LEFT.

MODE= *(WRAP|NOWRAP)*

This attribute specifies the line breaking mode for the subsequent text line. WRAP specifies breaking text mode and NOWRAP specifies nonbreaking text mode. If not explicitly specified, the line break mode is identical to the line break mode of the previous line in the text flow. For example, a simple <BR/> element starts a new line, but does not change the current line break mode.

8.8.3.1 Line Break Examples

The following example demonstrates how the BR element affects text alignment and line break mode:

```
<WML>
  <CARD>
    line 1, three-line card        <!— left alignment, breaking mode —>
    <BR ALIGN="RIGHT"/>line 2     <!— right alignment, breaking mode —>
    <BR MODE="NOWRAP"/>line 3     <!— left alignment, non-breaking mode —>
  </CARD>
  <CARD>
    <BR ALIGN="CENTER"/>
    line 1, one-line card          <!— centre alignment, breaking mode —>
  </CARD>
  <CARD>
    <BR MODE="NOWRAP"/>
    <BR ALIGN="CENTER"/>
```

```
    line 2, two-line card       <!— centre alignment, non-breaking mode —>
  </CARD>
</WML>
```

The following example demonstrates a more complex card and the interaction text alignment and line break modes:

```
<WML>
  <CARD>
    <FIELDSET>
      line 1                      <!— left alignment, breaking mode —>
      <BR ALIGN="NOWRAP"/>line 2  <!— left alignment, non-breaking mode —>
      <BR MODE="RIGHT"/>line 3    <!— right alignment, non-breaking mode —>
    </FIELDSET>
    <FIELDSET>
      Choose:                     <!— right alignment, non-breaking mode —>
      <SELECT KEY="X">
        <OPTION VALUE="1">One</OPTION>
        <OPTION VALUE="2">Two</OPTION>
      </SELECT>
      continuation of line 3      <!— right alignment, non-breaking mode —>
    </FIELDSET>
    <FIELDSET>
      still on line 3             <!— right alignment, non-breaking mode —>
      <INPUT KEY="Y"/>
      <BR MODE="WRAP"/>line 4     <!— left alignment, breaking mode —>
    </FIELDSET>
  </CARD>
</WML>
```

8.8.4 The TAB Element

The following elements specify tab columns:

```
<!ENTITY % tab      "TAB">
<!ENTITY % TAlign   "(LEFT|RIGHT|CENTER)" >
<!ELEMENT TAB EMPTY>
<!ATTLIST TAB
  ALIGN   %TAlign;  "LEFT"
  >
```

The `TAB` element is used to create aligned columns in a line. `TAB` elements separate markup into columns but do not specify column widths. Columns are specified in row order, and a given row is terminated by a `BR` or any other non-`%text;` element that terminates a line.

A column group is defined as the largest set of contiguous lines containing `TAB` elements that can be formed at any given point in the text flow. Depending on the display characteristics, the user agent may create aligned columns for each column group, or may use a single set of aligned columns for all column groups in a card. To ensure the narrowest display width, the user agent should determine the width of each column from the maximum width of the text and images in that column. A nonzero width gutter must be used to separate each nonempty column.

Columns empty in all lines of a column group may be ignored. A given line may have fewer TAB elements than other lines in its column group, in which case its right-hand columns are assumed empty.

Attributes

ALIGN= *(LEFT|RIGHT|CENTER)*

This attribute specifies the text layout within a column. Text can be center aligned, left aligned, or right aligned when it is displayed to the user. Left alignment is the default.

8.8.5 TAB Examples

The following example contains a card with a single column group, containing two columns and three rows:

```
<WML>
  <CARD>
    One <TAB/> Two <BR/>
    1   <TAB/>     <BR/>
    A   <TAB/> B   <BR/>
  </CARD>
</WML>
```

An acceptable layout for this card is:

```
One   Two
1
A     B
```

The following example contains a card with two column groups, separated by a line of text. This example demonstrates that multiple column groups may be rendered with separate column widths.

```
<WML>
  <CARD>
    alpha <TAB/> beta <BR/>
    gamma <TAB/> epsilon <BR/>

    this is a test<BR/>

    1 <TAB/> 2 <BR/>
    3 <TAB/> 4 <BR/>
  </CARD>
</WML>
```

An acceptable layout for this card is

```
alpha  beta
gamma  epsilon
```

```
this is a test…
1  2
3  4
```

The following example contains a card with one column group, a variety of column alignments, and an empty initial column:

```
<WML>
  <CARD>
    <TAB/>                  alpha <TAB/>                 beta    <BR/>
    <TAB/>                  gamma <TAB/>                 epsilon <BR/>
    <TAB/>                        <TAB ALIGN="RIGHT"/>  2       <BR/>
    <TAB ALIGN="CENTER"/> 3      <TAB ALIGN="CENTER"/> 4       <BR/>
  </CARD>
</WML>
```

An acceptable layout for this card is:

```
alpha    beta
gamma    epsilon
               2
  3         4
```

8.9 Images

```
<!ENTITY % IAlign "(TOP|MIDDLE|BOTTOM)" >
<!ELEMENT IMG EMPTY>
<!ATTLIST IMG
  ALT         %vdata;       #IMPLIED
  SRC         %URL;         #IMPLIED
  LOCALSRC    %vdata;       #IMPLIED
  VSPACE      %length;      "0"
  HSPACE      %length;      "0"
  ALIGN       %IAlign;      "BOTTOM"
  HEIGHT      %length;      #IMPLIED
  WIDTH       %length;      #IMPLIED
  >
```

The IMG element indicates that an image is to be included in the text flow. Image layout is done within the context of normal text layout.

Attributes

ALT=*vdata*

This attribute specifies an alternative textual representation for the image. This representation is used when the image cannot be displayed using any other method (i.e., the user agent does not support images, or the image contents can not be found).

SRC=*URL*

This attribute specifies the URL for the image. If the browser supports images, it downloads the image from the specified URL and renders it when the text is being displayed.

`LOCALSRC=`*`vdata`*

This attribute specifies an alternative internal representation for the image. This representation is used if it exists; otherwise, the image is downloaded from the URL specified in the `SRC` attribute. Any `LOCALSRC` parameter specified takes precedence over the image specified in the `SRC` parameter.

`VSPACE=`*`length`*

`HSPACE=`*`length`*

These attributes specify the amount of whitespace to be inserted to the left and right (`HSPACE`) and above and below (`VSPACE`) an image or object. The default value for this attribute is not specified but is generally a small, nonzero length. If `length` is specified as a percentage value, the resulting size is based on the available horizontal or vertical space, not on the natural size of the image. These attributes are hints to the user agent and may be ignored.

`ALIGN=`*`(TOP|MIDDLE|BOTTOM)`*

This attribute specifies image alignment within the text flow and with respect to the current insertion point. `ALIGN` has three possible values:

`BOTTOM`: The bottom of the image should be vertically aligned with the current baseline. This is the default value.

`MIDDLE`: The center of the image should be vertically aligned with the center of the current text line.

`TOP`: The top of the image should be vertically aligned with the top of the current text line.

`HEIGHT=`*`length`*

`WIDTH=`*`length`*

These attributes give user agents an idea of the size of an image or object so that they may reserve space for it and continue rendering the card while waiting for the image data. User agents may scale objects and images to match these values if appropriate. If `length` is specified as a percentage value, the resulting size is based on the available horizontal or vertical space, not on the natural size of the image. These attributes are a hint to the user agent and may be ignored.

9. User Agent Semantics

9.1 Deck Access Control

The introduction of variables into WML exposes potential security issues that do not exist in other markup languages such as HTML. In particular, certain variable states may be considered private by the user. While the user may be willing to send a private information to a secure service, an insecure or malicious service should not be able to retrieve that information from the user agent by other means.

A conforming WML user agent must implement deck-level access control, including the ACCESS element and the PUBLIC, SENDREFERER, DOMAIN, and PATH attributes.

A WML author should remove private or sensitive information from the browser context by clearing the variables containing this information.

9.2 Low-Memory Behavior

WML is targeted at devices with limited hardware resources, including significant restrictions on memory size. It is important that the author have a clear expectation of device behavior in error situations, including those caused by lack of memory.

9.2.1 Limited History

The user agent may limit the size of the history stack (i.e., the depth of the historical navigation information). In the case of history size exhaustion, the user agent should delete the least recently used history information.

It is recommended that all user agents implement a minimum history stack size of 10 entries.

9.2.2 Limited Browser Context Size

In some situations, it is possible that the author has defined an excessive number of variables in the browser context, leading to memory exhaustion.

In this situation, the user agent should attempt to acquire additional memory by reclaiming cache and history memory as described in Section 9.2.1. If this fails and the user agent has exhausted all memory, the user should be notified of the error, and the user agent should be reset to a predictable user state. For example, the browser may be terminated, or the context may be cleared and the browser reset to a well-known state.

9.3 Error Handling

Conforming user agents must enforce error conditions defined in this specification and must not hide errors by attempting to infer author or origin server intent.

9.4 Unknown DTD

A WML deck encoded with an alternate DTD may include elements or attributes that are not recognized by certain user agents. In this situation, a user agent should render the deck as if the unrecognized tags and attributes were not present. Content contained in unrecognized elements should be rendered.

9.5 Reference Processing Behavior—Intercard Navigation

The following process describes the reference model for intercard traversal in WML. All user agents must implement this process, or one that is indistinguishable from it.

9.5.1 The GO Task

The process of executing a GO task comprises the following steps:

1. If the originating task contains VAR elements, the variable name and value in each VAR element is converted into a simple string by substituting all referenced variables. The resulting collection of variable names and values is stored in temporary memory for later processing. See Section 7.3 for more information on variable substitution.
2. The target URL is identified and fetched by the user agent. The URL attribute value is converted into a simple string by substituting all referenced variables.
3. The access control parameters for the fetched deck are processed as specified in Section 8.3.1.
4. The destination card is located using the fragment name specified in the URL.
   a) If no fragment name was specified as part of the URL, the first card in the deck is the destination card.
   b) If a fragment name was identified and a card has a NAME attribute that is identical to the fragment name, then that card is the destination card.
   c) If the fragment name cannot be associated with a specific card, the first card in the deck is the destination card.
5. If the destination card contains a NEWCONTEXT attribute, the current browser context is reinitialized as described in Section 7.2.
6. The variable assignments resulting from the processing done in step #1 (the VAR element) are applied to the current browser context.
7. The destination card is pushed onto the history stack.
8. If the destination card specifies an ONENTERFORWARD intrinsic event binding, the task associated with the event binding is executed and processing stops. See Section 6.8 for more information.
9. If the destination card contains a TIMER element, the timer is started as specified in Section 8.7.
10. The destination card is displayed using the current variable state and processing stops.

9.5.2 The PREV Task

The process of executing a PREV task comprises the following steps:

1. If the originating task contains VAR elements, the variable name and value in each VAR element is converted into a simple string by substituting all referenced variables. The resulting collection of variable names and values is stored in temporary memory for later processing. See Section 7.3 for more information on variable substitution.
2. The target URL is identified and fetched by the user agent. The history stack is popped and the target URL is the top of the history stack. If there is no previous card in the history stack, processing stops.

3. The access control parameters for the fetched deck are processed as specified in Section 8.3.1.
4. The destination card is located using the fragment name specified in the URL.
   a) If no fragment name was specified as part of the URL, the first card in the deck is the destination card.
   b) If a fragment name was identified and a card has a `NAME` attribute that is identical to the fragment name, then that card is the destination card.
5. The variable assignments resulting from the processing done in step #1 (the `VAR` element) are applied to the current browser context.
6. If the destination card specifies an `ONENTERBACKWARD` intrinsic event binding, the task associated with the event binding is executed and processing stops. See Section 6.8 for more information.
7. If the destination card contains a `TIMER` element, the timer is started as specified in Section 8.7.
8. The destination card is displayed using the current variable state and processing stops.

9.5.3 The NOOP Task

No processing is done for a `NOOP` task.

9.5.4 The REFRESH Task

The process of executing a `REFRESH` task comprises the following steps:

1. For each `VAR` element, the variable name and value in each `VAR` element is converted into a simple string by substituting all referenced variables. The resulting collection of variable names and values is stored in temporary memory for later processing. See Section 7.3 for more information on variable substitution.
2. The variable assignments resulting from the processing done in step #1 (the `VAR` element) are applied to the current browser context.
3. The current card is redisplayed using the current variable state and processing stops.

9.5.5 Task Execution Failure

If a task fails to fetch its target URL, or the access control restrictions prevent a successful intercard transition, the user agent must notify the user and take the following actions:

- The invoking card remains the current card.
- No changes are made to the browser context, including any pending variable assignments or NEWCONTEXT processing.
- No intrinsic event bindings are executed.

10. WML Reference Information

WML is an application of [XML] version 1.0.

10.1 Document Identifiers

These identifiers have not yet been registered with the IANA or ISO 9070 Registrar.

10.1.1 SGML Public Identifier

```
-//WAPFORUM//DTD WML 1.0//EN
```

10.1.2 WML Media Type

Textual form:

```
text/x-wap.wml
```

Tokenized form:

```
application/x-wap.wmlc
```

These types are not yet registered with the IANA and are consequently *experimental* media types.

10.2 Document Type Definition (DTD)

```
<!—
Wireless Markup Language (WML) Document Type Definition.
WML is an XML language. Typical usage:
   <?xml version="1.0"?>
   <!DOCTYPE WML PUBLIC "-//WAPFORUM//DTD WML 1.0//EN"
                        "http://www.wapforum.org/DTD/wml.xml">
   <WML>
   ...
   </WML>
—>
<!ENTITY % length  "CDATA">    <!— [0-9]+ for pixels or [0-9]+"%" for
                                   percentage length —>
<!ENTITY % vdata   "CDATA">    <!— attribute value possibly containing
                                   variable references —>
<!ENTITY % URL     "%vdata;">  <!— URL or URN designating a hypertext
                                   node. May contain variable
                                   references —>
<!ENTITY % boolean "(TRUE|FALSE)">
<!ENTITY % number  "NMTOKEN">  <!— a number, with format [0-9]+ —>
<!ENTITY % emph    "EM | STRONG | B | I | U | BIG | SMALL">
```

```
<!ENTITY % tab      "TAB">
<!ENTITY % layout   "BR">
<!ENTITY % text      "#PCDATA | %emph; | %tab;">
<!ENTITY % inline    "%text; | %layout;">
<!— flow covers "card-level" elements, such as text and images —>
<!ENTITY % flow      "%inline; | IMG | A">
<!— Task types —>
<!ENTITY % task    "GO | PREV | NOOP | REFRESH">
<!— Navigation and event elements —>
<!ENTITY % navelmts "DO | ONEVENT">
<!—================ Decks and Cards ================—>
<!ELEMENT WML ( HEAD?, TEMPLATE?, CARD+ )>
<!ATTLIST WML
  xml:lang        NMTOKEN        #IMPLIED
  >
<!— card intrinsic events —>
<!ENTITY % cardev
 "ONENTERFORWARD  %URL;          #IMPLIED
  ONENTERBACKWARD %URL;          #IMPLIED
  ONTIMER         %URL;          #IMPLIED"
  >
<!— CARD field types —>
<!ENTITY % fields  "%flow; | INPUT | SELECT | FIELDSET">
<!ELEMENT CARD (%fields; | %navelmts; | TIMER)*>
<!ATTLIST CARD
  NAME            NMTOKEN       #IMPLIED
  TITLE           %vdata;       #IMPLIED
  NEWCONTEXT      %boolean;     "FALSE"
  STYLE           (LIST|SET)    "LIST"
  %cardev;
  >
<!—================ Event Bindings ================—>
<!ELEMENT DO (%task;)>
<!ATTLIST DO
  TYPE         CDATA       #REQUIRED
  LABEL        %vdata;     #IMPLIED
  NAME         NMTOKEN     #IMPLIED
  OPTIONAL     %boolean;   "FALSE"
  >
<!ELEMENT ONEVENT (%task;)>
<!ATTLIST ONEVENT
  TYPE         CDATA       #REQUIRED
  >
<!—================ Deck-level declarations ================—>
<!ELEMENT HEAD ( ACCESS | META )+>
<!ELEMENT TEMPLATE (%navelmts;)*>
<!ATTLIST TEMPLATE
  %cardev;
  >
<!ELEMENT ACCESS EMPTY>
<!ATTLIST ACCESS
```

```
  DOMAIN       CDATA       #IMPLIED
  PATH         CDATA       #IMPLIED
  PUBLIC       %boolean;   "FALSE"
  >
<!ELEMENT META EMPTY>
<!ATTLIST META
  HTTP-EQUIV     CDATA      #IMPLIED
  NAME           CDATA      #IMPLIED
  USER-AGENT     CDATA      #IMPLIED
  CONTENT        CDATA      #REQUIRED
  SCHEME         CDATA      #IMPLIED
  >
<!—=============== Tasks ================—>
<!ELEMENT GO (VAR)*>
<!ATTLIST GO
  URL              %URL;            #REQUIRED
  SENDREFERER      %boolean;        "FALSE"
  METHOD           (POST|GET)       "GET"
  ACCEPT-CHARSET  CDATA            #IMPLIED
  POSTDATA         %vdata;          #IMPLIED
  >
<!ELEMENT PREV (VAR)*>
<!ELEMENT REFRESH (VAR)+>
<!ELEMENT NOOP EMPTY>
<!—=============== VAR ================—>
<!ELEMENT VAR EMPTY>
<!ATTLIST VAR
  NAME         %vdata;            #REQUIRED
  VALUE        %vdata;            #REQUIRED
  >
<!—=============== CARD Fields ================—>
<!ELEMENT SELECT (OPTGROUP|OPTION)+>
<!ATTLIST SELECT
  TITLE        %vdata;            #IMPLIED
  KEY          NMTOKEN            #IMPLIED
  DEFAULT      %vdata;            #IMPLIED
  IKEY         NMTOKEN            #IMPLIED
  IDEFAULT     %vdata;            #IMPLIED
  MULTIPLE     %boolean;          "FALSE"
  TABINDEX     %number;           #IMPLIED
  >
<!ELEMENT OPTGROUP (OPTGROUP|OPTION)+ >
<!ATTLIST OPTGROUP
  TITLE      %vdata;     #IMPLIED
  >
<!ELEMENT OPTION (%text; | ONEVENT)*>
<!ATTLIST OPTION
  VALUE      %vdata;     #IMPLIED
  TITLE      %vdata;     #IMPLIED
  ONCLICK    %URL;       #IMPLIED
  >
```

```
<!ELEMENT INPUT EMPTY>
<!ATTLIST INPUT
  KEY        NMTOKEN           #REQUIRED
  TYPE       (TEXT|PASSWORD)   "TEXT"
  VALUE      %vdata;           #IMPLIED
  DEFAULT    %vdata;           #IMPLIED
  FORMAT     CDATA             #IMPLIED
  EMPTYOK    %boolean;         "FALSE"
  SIZE       %number;          #IMPLIED
  MAXLENGTH  %number;          #IMPLIED
  TABINDEX   %number;          #IMPLIED
  TITLE      %vdata;           #IMPLIED
  >
<!ELEMENT FIELDSET (%fields;)* >
<!ATTLIST FIELDSET
  TITLE           %vdata;      #IMPLIED
  >
<!ELEMENT TIMER EMPTY>
<!ATTLIST TIMER
  KEY        NMTOKEN           #IMPLIED
  DEFAULT    %vdata;           #REQUIRED
  >
<!-================ Images ================->
<!ENTITY % IAlign "(TOP|MIDDLE|BOTTOM)" >
<!ELEMENT IMG EMPTY>
<!ATTLIST IMG
  ALT        %vdata;      #IMPLIED
  SRC        %URL;        #IMPLIED
  LOCALSRC   %vdata;      #IMPLIED
  VSPACE     %length;     "0"
  HSPACE     %length;     "0"
  ALIGN      %IAlign;     "BOTTOM"
  HEIGHT     %length;     #IMPLIED
  WIDTH      %length;     #IMPLIED
  >
<!-================ Anchor ================->
<!ELEMENT A ( %inline; | GO | PREV | REFRESH )*>
<!ATTLIST A
  TITLE          %vdata;      #IMPLIED
  >
<!-================ Text layout and line breaks ================->
<!- Text alignment attributes ->
<!ENTITY % TAlign   "(LEFT|RIGHT|CENTER)" >
<!ELEMENT TAB EMPTY>
<!ATTLIST TAB
  ALIGN   %TAlign;   "LEFT"
  >
<!ELEMENT EM     (%flow;)*>
<!ELEMENT STRONG (%flow;)*>
<!ELEMENT B      (%flow;)*>
```

```
<!ELEMENT I       (%flow;)*>
<!ELEMENT U       (%flow;)*>
<!ELEMENT BIG     (%flow;)*>
<!ELEMENT SMALL   (%flow;)*>
<!ENTITY % BRMode     "(WRAP|NOWRAP)" >
<!ELEMENT BR EMPTY>
<!ATTLIST BR
  ALIGN   %TAlign;    "LEFT"
  MODE    %BRMode;    #IMPLIED
  >
<!ENTITY quot  "&#34;">      <!— quotation mark —>
<!ENTITY amp   "&#38;#38;"> <!— ampersand —>
<!ENTITY apos  "&#39;">      <!— apostrophe —>
<!ENTITY lt    "&#38;#60;"> <!— less than —>
<!ENTITY gt    "&#62;">      <!— greater than —>
<!ENTITY nbsp  " ">     <!— non-breaking space —>
<!ENTITY shy   "&#173;">     <!— soft hyphen (discretionary hyphen) —>
```

11. A Compact Binary Representation of WML

WML may be encoded using a compact binary representation. This content format is based upon the WAP Binary XML Content Format [WBXML].

11.1 Extension Tokens

11.1.1 Global Extension Tokens

The [WBXML] global extension tokens are used to represent WML variables. Variable references may occur in a variety of places in a WML deck (see Section 7.3). There are several codes that indicate variable substitution. Each code has different escaping semantics (e.g., direct substitution, escaped substitution, and unescaped substitution). The variable name is encoded in the current document character encoding and must be encoded as specified in the source document (e.g., variable names may not be shortened, mapped, or otherwise changed). For example, the global extension token EXT_I_0 represents an escaped variable substitution, with the variable name inline.

11.1.2 Tag Tokens

WML defines a set of single-byte tokens corresponding to the tags defined in the DTD. All of these tokens are defined within code page zero.

11.1.3 Attribute Tokens

WML defines a set of single-byte tokens corresponding to the attribute names and values defined in the DTD. All of these tokens are defined within code page zero.

11.2 Encoding Semantics

11.2.1 Encoding Variables

All variable references must be converted to variable reference tokens (e.g., `EXT_I_0`).

11.2.2 Document Validation

XML document validation (see [XML]) should occur during the process of tokenizing a WML deck and must be based on the DOCTYPE declared in the WML deck. When validating the source text, the tokenization process must accept any DOCTYPE or public identifier if the document is identified as a WML media type (see Section 10.1.2).

The tokenization process should notify the user of any well-formedness or validity errors detected in the source deck.

11.2.2.1 Validate %length;

The WML tokenization process should validate that attribute values defined as `%length;` contain either a `NMTOKEN` or a `NMTOKEN` followed by a percentage sign character. For example, the following attributes are legal:

```
VSPACE="100%"
HSPACE="123"
```

`%length;` data is encoded using normal attribute value encoding methods.

11.2.2.2 Validate %vdata;

The WML tokenization process should validate that attribute values defined as `%vdata;` contain variables and that other `CDATA` attribute values do not. Attribute values not defined in the DTD must allow variable references.

11.3 Numeric Constants

11.3.1 WML Extension Token Assignment

The global extension tokens in Table 4.4 are used in WML and occupy document-type-specific token slots in the global token range. As with all tokens in the global range, these codes must be reserved in every code page. All numbers are in hexadecimal.

11.3.2 Tag Tokens

The token codes in Table 4.5 represent tags in code page zero (0). All numbers are in hexadecimal.

11.3.3 Attribute Start Tokens

The token codes in Table 4.6 represent the start of an attribute in code page zero (0). All numbers are in hexadecimal.

Table 4.4 Global Extension Token Assignments

TOKEN NAME	TOKEN	DESCRIPTION
EXT_I_0	40	Variable substitution—escaped. Name of the variable is inline and follows the token as a `termstr`.
EXT_I_1	41	Variable substitution—unescaped. Name of the variable is inline and follows the token as a `termstr`.
EXT_I_2	42	Variable substitution—no transformation. Name of the variable is inline and follows the token as a `termstr`.
EXT_T_0	80	Variable substitution—escaped. Variable name encoded as a reference into the string table.
EXT_T_1	81	Variable substitution—unescaped. Variable name encoded as a reference into the string table.
EXT_T_2	82	Variable substitution—no transformation. Variable name encoded as a reference into the string table.
EXT_0	C0	Reserved for future use.
EXT_1	C1	Reserved for future use.
EXT_2	C2	Reserved for future use.

Table 4.5 Tag Tokens

TAG NAME	TOKEN	TAG NAME	TOKEN
A	22	NOOP	31
ACCESS	23	PREV	32
B	24	ONEVENT	33
BIG	25	OPTGROUP	34
BR	26	OPTION	35
CARD	27	REFRESH	36
DO	28	SELECT	37
EM	29	SMALL	38
FIELDSET	2A	STRONG	39
GO	2B	TAB	3A
HEAD	2C	TEMPLATE	3B
I	2D	TIMER	3C
IMG	2E	U	3D
INPUT	2F	VAR	3E
META	30	WML	3F

Table 4.6 Attribute Start Tokens

ATTRIBUTE NAME	ATTRIBUTE VALUE PREFIX	TOKEN
ACCEPT-CHARSET		5
ALIGN	BOTTOM	6
ALIGN	CENTER	7
ALIGN	LEFT	8
ALIGN	MIDDLE	9
ALIGN	RIGHT	A
ALIGN	TOP	B
ALT		C
CONTENT		D
DEFAULT		E
DOMAIN		F
EMPTYOK	FALSE	10
EMPTYOK	TRUE	11
FORMAT		12
HEIGHT		13
HSPACE		14
IDEFAULT		15
IKEY		16
KEY		17
LABEL		18
LOCALSRC		19
MAXLENGTH		1A
METHOD	GET	1B
METHOD	POST	1C
MODE	NOWRAP	1D
MODE	WRAP	1E
MULTIPLE	FALSE	1F
MULTIPLE	TRUE	20
NAME		21

Table 4.6 *(Continued)*

ATTRIBUTE NAME	ATTRIBUTE VALUE PREFIX	TOKEN
NEWCONTEXT	FALSE	22
NEWCONTEXT	TRUE	23
ONCLICK		24
ONENTERBACKWARD		25
ONENTERFORWARD		26
ONTIMER		27
OPTIONAL	FALSE	28
OPTIONAL	TRUE	29
PATH		2A
POSTDATA		2B
PUBLIC	FALSE	2C
PUBLIC	TRUE	2D
SCHEME		2E
SENDREFERER	FALSE	2F
SENDREFERER	TRUE	30
SIZE		31
SRC		32
STYLE	LIST	33
STYLE	SET	34
TABINDEX		35
TITLE		36
TYPE		37
TYPE	ACCEPT	38
TYPE	DELETE	39
TYPE	HELP	3A
TYPE	PASSWORD	3B
TYPE	ONCLICK	3C
TYPE	ONENTERBACKWARD	3D
TYPE	ONENTERFORWARD	3E

(continues)

Table 4.6 *(Continued)*

ATTRIBUTE NAME	ATTRIBUTE VALUE PREFIX	TOKEN
TYPE	ONTIMER	3F
TYPE	OPTIONS	45
TYPE	PREV	46
TYPE	RESET	47
TYPE	TEXT	48
TYPE	vnd.	49
URL		4A
URL	http://	4B
URL	https://	4C
USER-AGENT		4D
VALUE		4E
VSPACE		4F
WIDTH		50
xml:lang		51

11.3.4 Attribute Value Tokens

The token codes in Table 4.7 represent attribute values in code page zero (0). All numbers are in hexadecimal.

11.4 WML Encoding Examples

Refer to [WBXML] for additional examples.

The following is another example of a tokenized WML deck. It demonstrates variable encoding, attribute encoding, and the use of the string table. Source deck:

```
<WML>
  <CARD NAME="abc" STYLE="LIST">
    <DO TYPE="ACCEPT">
      <GO URL="http://xyz.org/s"/>
    </DO>
    X: $(X)<BR/>
```

```
    Y: $(&#x59;)<BR MODE="NOWRAP"/>
    Enter name: <INPUT TYPE="TEXT" KEY="N"/>
  </CARD>
</WML>
```

Tokenized form (numbers in hexadecimal) follows. This example only uses inline strings and assumes that the character encoding uses a NULL terminated string format. It also assumes that the character encoding is UTF-8.

```
00   02   04   'X'  00   'Y'  00   7F   E8   21   03   'a'  'b'  'c'  00
33   01   E9   38   01   AD   4B   03   'x'  'y'  'z'  00   88   03   's'
00   01   03   ' '  'X'  ':'  ' '  00   82   00   27   03   ' '  'Y'  ':'
' '  00   82   02   A7   1D   01   03   ' '  'E'  'n'  't'  'e'  'r'  ' '
'n'  'a'  'm'  'e'  ':'  ' '  00   B1   48   18   03   'N'  00   01   01
01
```

For an expanded and annotated form, see Table 4.8.

Table 4.7 Attribute Value Tokens

ATTRIBUTE VALUE	TOKEN	ATTRIBUTE VALUE	TOKEN
.com/	85	NOWRAP	94
.edu/	86	ONCLICK	95
.net/	87	ONENTERBACKWARD	96
.org/	88	ONENTERFORWARD	97
ACCEPT	89	ONTIMER	98
BOTTOM	8A	OPTIONS	99
CLEAR	8B	PASSWORD	9A
DELETE	8C	RESET	9B
HELP	8D	SET	9C
http://	8E	TEXT	9D
http://www.	8F	TOP	9E
https://	90	UNKNOWN	9F
https://www.	91	WRAP	A0
LIST	92	www.	A1
MIDDLE	93		

Table 4.8 Example Tokenized Deck

TOKEN STREAM	DESCRIPTION
00	WBXML Version number
02	WML Public ID
04	String table length
'X',00,'Y',00	String table
7F	WML, with content
E9	CARD, with content and attributes
21	NAME=
03	Inline string follows
'a','b','c',00	string
33	STYLE="LIST"
01	END (of CARD attribute list)
EA	DO, with content and attributes
38	TYPE=ACCEPT
01	END (of DO attribute list)
AD	GO, with attributes
4B	URL="http://"
03	Inline string follows
'x','y','z',0	string
88	".org/"
03	Inline string follows
's',0	string
01	END (of DO element)
03	Inline string follows
' ','X',':',' ',00	String
82	Direct variable reference (EXT_T_2)
00	Variable offset 0
28	BR
03	Inline string follows

Table 4.8 *(Continued)*

TOKEN STREAM	DESCRIPTION
`' ','Y',':',' ',00`	String
82	Direct variable reference (EXT_T_2)
02	Variable offset 2
A7	BR, with attributes
1D	MODE="NOWRAP"
01	END (of BR attribute list)
03	Inline string follows
`' ','E','n','t','e','r', '','n','a','m','e',':',' ',00`	String
B1	INPUT, with attributes
48	TYPE="TEXT"
18	KEY=
03	Inline string follows
`'N',00`	String
01	END (of INPUT attribute list)
01	END (of CARD element)
01	END (of WML element)

12. Definitions

The following are terms and conventions used throughout this specification.

The key words "MUST", "MUST NOT", "REQUIRED", "SHALL", "SHALL NOT", "SHOULD", "SHOULD NOT", "RECOMMENDED", "MAY", and "OPTIONAL" in this document are to be interpreted as described in [RFC2119].

Author. An author is a person or program that writes or generates WML, WMLScript, or other content.

Card. A single WML unit of navigation and user interface. May contain information to present to the user, instructions for gathering user input, etc.

Client. A device (or application) that initiates a request for connection with a server.

Content. Subject matter (data) stored or generated at an origin server. Content is typically displayed or interpreted by a user agent in response to a user request.

Content Encoding. When used as a verb, *content encoding* indicates the act of converting content from one format to another. Typically, the resulting format requires less physical space than the original, is easier to process or store, and/or is encrypted. When used as a noun, *content encoding* specifies a particular format or encoding standard or process.

Content Format. Actual representation of content.

Deck. A collection of WML cards. A WML deck is also an XML document.

Device. A network entity that is capable of sending and receiving packets of information and has a unique device address. A device can act as both a client or a server within a given context or across multiple contexts. For example, a device can service a number of clients (as a server) while being a client to another server.

JavaScript. A *de facto* standard language that can be used to add dynamic behavior to HTML documents. JavaScript is one of the originating technologies of ECMAScript.

Man-Machine Interface. A synonym for user interface.

Origin Server. The server on which a given resource resides or is to be created. Often referred to as a *Web server* or an *HTTP server*.

Resource. A network data object or service that can be identified by a URL. Resources may be available in multiple representations (e.g., multiple languages, data formats, size, and resolutions) or vary in other ways.

Server. A device (or application) that passively waits for connection requests from one or more clients. A server may accept or reject a connection request from a client.

SGML. The Standardized Generalized Markup Language (defined in [ISO8879]) is a general-purpose language for domain-specific markup languages.

Terminal. A device providing the user with user agent capabilities, including the ability to request and receive information. Also called a *mobile terminal* or *mobile station*.

Transcode. The act of converting from one character set to another; for example, conversion from UCS-2 to UTF-8.

User. A user is a person who interacts with a user agent to view, hear, or otherwise use a resource.

User Agent. A user agent is any software or device that interprets WML, WMLScript, WTAI, or other resources. This may include textual browsers, voice browsers, search engines, etc.

WMLScript. A scripting language used to program the mobile device. WMLScript is an extended subset of the JavaScript scripting language.

XML. The Extensible Markup Language is a World Wide Web Consortium (W3C) standard for Internet markup languages, of which WML is one such language. XML is a restricted subset of SGML.

13. Abbreviations

For the purposes of this specification, the following abbreviations apply:

BNF	Backus-Naur Form
HDML	Handheld Markup Language [HDML2]
HTML	HyperText Markup Language [HTML4]
HTTP	HyperText Transfer Protocol [RFC2068]
IANA	Internet Assigned Number Authority
MMI	Man-Machine Interface
PDA	Personal Digital Assistant
RFC	Request For Comments
SGML	Standardized Generalized Markup Language [ISO8879]
UI	User Interface
URL	Uniform Resource Locator [RFC1738]
URN	Uniform Resource Name
W3C	World Wide Web Consortium
WAE	Wireless Application Environment [WAE]
WAP	Wireless Application Protocol [WAP]
WSP	Wireless Session Protocol [WSP]
XML	Extensible Markup Language [XML]

14. Normative References

[ISO10646] "Information Technology—Universal Multiple-Octet Coded Character Set (UCS)—Part 1: Architecture and Basic Multilingual Plane," ISO/IEC 10646-1:1993.

[RFC822] "Standard for the Format of ARPA Internet Text Messages," STD 11, RFC 822, D. Crocker, August 1982.
URL: ftp://ds.internic.net/rfc/rfc822.txt

[RFC1738] "Uniform Resource Locators (URL)," T. Berners-Lee, et al., December 1994.
URL: ftp://ds.internic.net/rfc/rfc1738.txt

[RFC1808] "Relative Uniform Resource Locators," R. Fielding, June 1995.
URL: ftp://ds.internic.net/rfc/rfc1808.txt

[RFC2045] "Multipurpose Internet Mail Extensions (MIME) Part One: Format of Internet Message Bodies," N. Freed, et al., November 1996.
URL: ftp://ds.internic.net/rfc/rfc2045.txt

[RFC2048] "Multipurpose Internet Mail Extensions (MIME) Part Four: Registration Procedures," N. Freed, et al., November 1996.
URL: ftp://ds.internic.net/rfc/rfc2048.txt

[RFC2068] "Hypertext Transfer Protocol—HTTP/1.1," R. Fielding, et al., January 1997.
URL: ftp://ds.internic.net/rfc/rfc2068.txt

[RFC2119] "Key Words for Use in RFCs to Indicate Requirement Levels," S. Bradner, March 1997.
URL: ftp://ds.internic.net/rfc/rfc2119.txt

[UNICODE] "The Unicode Standard: Version 2.0," The Unicode Consortium, Addison-Wesley Developers Press, 1996.
URL: http://www.unicode.org/

[WAE] "Wireless Application Environment Specification," WAP Forum, 30-April-1998.
URL: http://www.wapforum.org/

[WAP] "Wireless Application Protocol Architecture Specification," WAP Forum, 30-April-1998.
URL: http://www.wapforum.org/

[WBXML] "WAP Binary XML Content Format," WAP Forum, 30-April-1998.
URL: http://www.wapforum.org/

[WSP] "Wireless Session Protocol," WAP Forum, 30-April-1998.
URL: http://www.wapforum.org/

[XML] "Extensible Markup Language (XML), W3C Proposed Recommendation 10-February-1998, REC-xml-19980210," T. Bray, et al., February 10, 1998.
URL: http://www.w3.org/TR/REC-xml

15. Informative References

[HDML2] "Handheld Device Markup Language Specification," P. King, et al., April 11, 1997.
URL: http://www.uplanet.com/pub/hdml_w3c/hdml20-1.html

[HTML4] "HTML 4.0 Specification, W3C Recommendation 18-December-1997, REC-HTML40-971218," D. Raggett, et al., September 17, 1997.
URL: http://www.w3.org/TR/REC-html40

[ISO8879] "Information Processing—Text and Office Systems—Standard Generalized Markup Language (SGML)," ISO 8879:1986.

CHAPTER

5

Binary XML Content Format Specification

1. Scope

Wireless Application Protocol (WAP) is a result of continuous work to define an industrywide specification for developing applications that operate over wireless communication networks. The scope of the WAP Forum is to define a set of specifications to be used by service applications. The wireless market is growing very quickly and reaching new customers and services. To enable operators and manufacturers to meet the challenges in advanced services, differentiation, and fast/flexible service creation, WAP defines a set of protocols in Transport, Session, and Application layers. For additional information on the WAP architecture, refer to *"Wireless Application Protocol Architecture Specification"* [WAP].

This specification defines a compact binary representation of the Extensible Markup Language [XML]. The binary XML content format is designed to reduce the transmission size of XML documents, allowing more effective use of XML data on narrowband communication channels. Refer to the [WML] specification for one example use of the binary XML content format.

The binary format was designed to allow for compact transmission with no loss of functionality or semantic information. The format is designed to preserve the element structure of XML, allowing a browser to skip unknown elements or attributes. The binary format encodes the parsed physical form of an XML document; in other words, the structure and content of the document entities. Meta-information, including the document type definition and conditional sections, is removed when the document is converted to the binary format.

2. Binary XML Content Structure

The data types listed in Table 5.1 are used in the specification of the XML tokenized format.

Network byte order is big-endian; in other words, the most significant byte is transmitted on the network first, followed by the less significant bytes. Network bit ordering within a byte is big-endian; in other words, bit fields described first are placed in the most significant bits of the byte.

2.1 Multibyte Integers

This encoding uses a multibyte representation for integer values. A multibyte integer consists of a series of octets, where the most significant bit is the *continuation* flag and the remaining 7 bits are a scalar value. The continuation flag indicates that an octet is not the end of the multibyte sequence. A single integer value is encoded into a sequence of `N` octets. The first `N–1` octets have the continuation flag set to a value of 1. The final octet in the series has a continuation flag value of 0.

The remaining 7 bits in each octet are encoded in a big-endian order, e.g., most significant bit first. The octets are arranged in a big-endian order; in other words, the most significant 7 bits are transmitted first. In the situation where the initial octet has less than 7 bits of value, all unused bits must be set to 0.

For example, the integer value `0xA0` would be encoded with the 2-byte sequence `0x81 0x20`. The integer value `0x60` would be encoded with the 1-byte sequence `0x60`.

2.2 Character Encoding

The encoding of all strings in the XML binary content format is specified by transport or container meta-information. Specifically, it is assumed that a *charset* declaration accompanies the binary XML content and indicates the encoding of all strings. The XML binary representation can support any string encoding but requires that all strings include an encoding-specific termination character (e.g., a `NULL` terminator), which can be reliably used to detect the end of a string. If a character encoding includes a `NULL` (e.g., Unicode, ASCII, ISO-8859-1, etc.), the `NULL` character must be used as the termination character. As with the textual format of XML, it is also assumed that all tag and attribute names can be represented in the target character encoding.

Table 5.1 Data Types Used in Tokenized Format

DATA TYPE	DEFINITION
bit	1 bit of data
byte	8 bits of opaque data
u_int8	8 bit unsigned integer
mb_u_int32	32-bit unsigned integer, encoded in multibyte integer format

2.3 BNF for Document Structure

A binary XML document is composed of a sequence of elements. Each element may have zero or more attributes and may contain embedded content. This structure is very general and does not have explicit knowledge of XML element structure or semantics. This generality allows user agents and other consumers of the binary format to skip elements and data that are not understood.

The following is a BNF-like description of the tokenized structure. The description uses the conventions established in [RFC822], except that the "|" character is used to designate alternatives and capitalized words indicate single-byte tokens, which are defined later. Briefly, "(" and ")" are used to group elements, while optional elements are enclosed in "[" and "]". Elements may be preceded with <N>* to specify N or more repetitions of the following element (N defaults to zero when unspecified).

```
start     = version publicid strtbl 1*content
strtbl    = length *byte
content   = element | string | extension | entity | pi

element   = stag [ 1*attribute END ] [ *content END ]
stag      = TAG | ( LITERAL index )
attribute = attrStart *attrValue
attrStart = ATTRSTART | ( LITERAL index )
attrValue = ATTRVALUE | string | extension | entity

extension = ( EXT_I termstr ) | ( EXT_T index ) | EXT

string    = inline | tableref
inline    = STR_I termstr
tableref  = STR_T index

entity    = ENTITY entcode
entcode   = mb_u_int32     // UCS-4 character code

pi        = PI attrStart *attrValue END

version   = u_int8 containing WBXML version number
publicid  = mb_u_int32 | ( zero index )
termstr   = charset-dependent string with termination
index     = mb_u_int32       // integer index into string table.
length    = mb_u_int32    // integer length.
zero      = u_int8       // containing the value zero (0)
```

2.4 Version Number

```
version   = u_int8 containing WBXML version number
```

All WBXML documents contain a version number in their initial byte. This version specifies the WBXML version. The version byte contains the major version minus 1 in the upper 4 bits and the minor version in the lower 4 bits. For example, the version number 2.7 would be encoded as 0x17. This document specifies WBXML version 1.0.

2.5 Document Public Identifier

```
publicid  = mb_u_int32 | ( zero index )
zero      = u_int8       // containing the value zero (0)
```

The binary XML format contains a representation of the XML document public identifier. This `publicid` is used to identify the well-known document type contained within the WBXML entity.

The first form of `publicid` is a multibyte positive integer value, greater than 0, representing a well-known XML document type (e.g., `-//WAPFORUM//DTD WML 1.0//EN`).

mb_u_int32

Public identifiers may also be encoded as strings, in the situation where a predefined numeric identifier is not available.

0	index

See Section 4.2 for numeric constants related to public identifiers.

2.6 String Table

```
strtbl    = length *byte
```

A binary XML document must include a string table immediately after the public identifier. Minimally, the string table consists of a `mb_u_int32` encoding the string table length in bytes, not including the length field (e.g., a string table containing a 2-byte string is encoded with a length of 2). If the length is nonzero, one or more strings follow. The encoding of the strings follows the current *charset* specified by transport meta-information.

Various tokens encode references to the contents of the string table. These references are encoded as scalar byte offsets from the first byte of the first string in the string table. For example, the offset of the first string is 0.

2.7 Token Structure

Tokens are split into a set of overlapping *code spaces*. The meaning of a particular token is dependent on the context in which it is used. Tokens are organized in the following manner:

- There are two classifications of tokens: global tokens and application tokens.
- Global tokens are assigned a fixed set of codes in all contexts and are unambiguous in all situations. Global codes are used to encode inline data (e.g., strings, entities, opaque data, etc.) and to encode a variety of miscellaneous control functions.
- Application tokens have a context-dependent meaning and are split into two overlapping *code spaces*. These two code spaces are the *tag code space* and the *attribute code space*. A given token value (e.g., `0x99`) will have a different meaning depending on whether it represents a token in the tag or attribute code space.

- The tag code space represents specific tag names. Each tag token is a single-byte code and represents a specific tag name (e.g., `CARD`).
- The attribute code space is split into two numeric ranges representing attribute prefixes and attribute values, respectively.

Each code space is further split into a series of 256 *code pages*. Code pages allow for future expansion of the well-known codes. A single token (`SWITCH_PAGE`) switches between the code pages.

The definition of tag and attribute codes is document-type-specific. Global codes are divided between a generic set of codes common to all document types and a set reserved for document-type-specific extensions.

2.7.1 Parser State Machine

The tokenized format has two states, each of which has an associated code space. The states are traversed according to the syntax described in Section 2.3. Code spaces are associated with parser states in the following manner (see Table 5.2):

Any occurrence of code page switch tokens (`SWITCH_PAGE`) while in a given state changes the current code page for that state. This new code page remains as the current code page until another `SWITCH_PAGE` is encountered in the same state or the document end is reached. Each parser state maintains a separate "current code page." The initial code page for both parser states is 0.

Figure 5.1 illustrates an alternative representation of the state transitions and is provided as a reference model.

2.7.2 Tag Code Space

Tag tokens are a single `u_int8` and are structured as shown in Table 5.3:

For example:

- Tag value `0xC6`: indicates tag six (`6`), with both attributes and content following the tag; e.g.,

  ```
  <TAG arg="1">foo</TAG>
  ```

- Tag value `0x46`: indicates tag six (`6`), with content following the start tag. This element contains no attributes; e.g.,

  ```
  <TAG>test</TAG>
  ```

- Tag value `0x06`: indicates tag six (`6`). This element contains no content and has no attributes; e.g.,

  ```
  <TAG/>
  ```

Table 5.2 Parser States

PARSER STATE	CODE SPACE
`stag`	Tags
`attribute`	Attributes

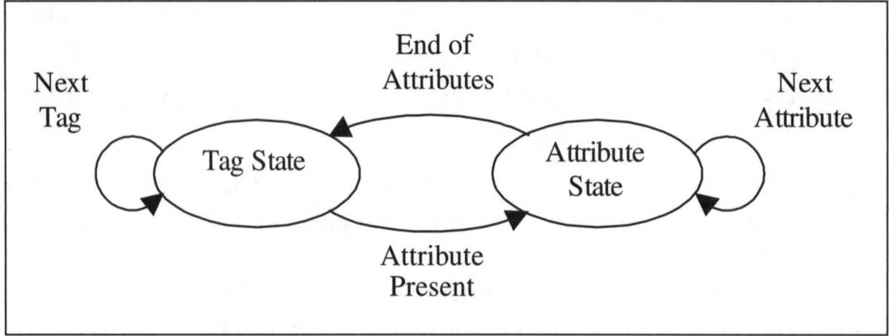

Figure 5.1 Alternative representation of state transitions.

Table 5.3 Tag Format

BIT(S)	DESCRIPTION
7 (most significant)	Indicates whether attributes follow the tag code. If this bit is 0, the tag contains no attributes. If this bit is 1, the tag is followed immediately by one or more attributes. The attribute list is terminated by an END token.
6	Indicates whether this tag begins an element containing content. If this bit is 0, the tag contains no content and no end tag. If this bit is 1, the tag is followed by any content it contains and is terminated by an END token.
5 - 0	Indicates the tag identity.

The globally unique code `LITERAL` (see Section 2.7.4.5) represents unknown tag names. An XML tokenizer should avoid the use of the `LITERAL` or string representations of a tag when a more compact form is available.

Tags containing both attributes and content always encode the attributes before the content.

2.7.3 Attribute Code Space (ATTRSTART and ATTRVALUE)

Attribute tokens are a encoded as a single `u_int8`. The attribute code space is split into two ranges (in addition to the global range present in all code spaces):

Attribute Start. Tokens with a value less than `128` indicate the start of an attribute. The attribute start token fully identifies the attribute name (e.g., `URL=`) and may optionally specify the beginning of the attribute value (e.g., `PUBLIC="TRUE"`). Unknown attribute names are encoded with the globally unique code `LITERAL` (see Section 2.7.4.4). `LITERAL` must not be used to encode any portion of an attribute value.

Attribute Value. Tokens with a value of `128` or greater represent a well-known string present in an attribute value. These tokens may only be used to represent attribute values. Unknown attribute values are encoded with string, entity, or extension codes (see Section 2.7.4).

All tokenized attributes must begin with a single attribute start token and may be followed by zero or more attribute value, string, entity, or extension tokens. An attribute start token, a `LITERAL` token, or the `END` token indicates the end of an attribute value. This allows a compact encoding of strings containing well-known substrings and entities.

For example, if the attribute start token `TOKEN_URL` represents the attribute name `"URL"`, the attribute value token `TOKEN_COM` represents the string `".com"`, and the attribute value token `TOKEN_HTTP` represents the string `"http://"`, the attribute `URL="http://foo.com/x"` might be encoded with the following sequence:

```
TOKEN_URL TOKEN_HTTP STR_I "foo" TOKEN_COM STR_I "/x"
```

In another example, if the attribute start token `TOKEN_PUBLIC_TRUE` represents the attribute name `"PUBLIC"` and the value prefix `"TRUE"`, the attribute `PUBLIC="TRUE"` might be encoded with the following sequence:

```
TOKEN_PUBLIC_TRUE
```

An XML tokenizer should avoid the use of the `LITERAL` or string representations of an attribute name when a more compact form is available. An XML tokenizer should avoid the use of string representations of a value when a more compact form is available.

2.7.4 Global Tokens

Global tokens have the same meaning and structure in all code spaces and in all code pages. The classes of global tokens are:

Strings: Inline and table string references

Extension: Document-type-specific extension tokens

Opaque: Inline opaque data

Entity: Character entities

Processing Instruction: XML PIs

Literal: Unknown tag or attribute name

Control codes: Miscellaneous global control tokens

2.7.4.1 Strings

```
string    = inline | tableref
inline    = STR_I termstr
tableref  = STR_T index
```

Strings encode inline character data or references into a string table. The string table is a concatenation of individual strings. String termination is dependent on the character document encoding and should not be presumed to include NULL termination. References to each string include an offset into the table, indicating the string being referenced.

Inline string references have the following format:

STR_I	... char data ...

String table references have the following format:

STR_T	mb_u_int32

The string table offset is from the first byte of the first string in the table (i.e., not a character offset).

2.7.4.2 Global Extension Tokens

```
extension = ( EXT_I termstr ) | ( EXT_T index ) | EXT
```

The global extension tokens are available for document-specific use. The semantics of the tokens are defined only within the context of a particular document type, but the format is well defined across all documents. There are three classes of global extension tokens: single-byte extension tokens, inline string extension tokens, and inline integer extension tokens.

Inline string extension tokens (`EXT_I*`) have the following format:

EXT_I*	... char data ...

Inline integer extension tokens (`EXT_T*`) have the following format:

EXT_T*	mb_u_int32

Single-byte extension tokens (`EXT*`) have the following format:

EXT*

2.7.4.3 Character Entity

```
entity     = ENTITY entcode
entcode    = mb_u_int32      // UCS-4 character code
```

The character entity token (`ENTITY`) encodes a numeric character entity. This has the same semantics as an XML numeric character entity (e.g., ` `). The `mb_u_int32` refers to a character in the UCS-4 character encoding. All entities in the source XML document must be represented using either a string token (e.g., `STR_I`) or the `ENTITY` token.

The format of the character entity is:

ENTITY	mb_u_int32

2.7.4.4 Processing Instruction

```
pi        = PI attrStart *attrValue END
```

The processing instruction (PI) token encodes an XML processing instruction. The encoded PI has semantics identical to an XML PI. The `attrStart` encodes the `PITarget` and the `attrValue` encodes the PI's optional value. For more details on processing instructions, see [XML].

The format of the PI tag is:

PI	attrStart	attrValue	END

PIs without a value are encoded as:

PI	attrStart	END

2.7.4.5 Literal Tag or Attribute Name

The literal token encodes a tag or attribute name that does not have a well-known token code. The actual meaning of the token (i.e., tag versus attribute name) is determined by the token parsing state. All literal tokens indicate a reference into the string table, which contains the actual name.

The format of the LITERAL tag is:

LITERAL	mb_u_int32

2.7.4.6 Miscellaneous Control Codes

2.7.4.6.1 END Token The END token is used to terminate attribute lists and elements. END is a single-byte token.

2.7.4.6.2 Code Page Switch Token The code-page switch token (`SWITCH_PAGE`) indicates a switch in the current code page for the current token state. The code-page switch is encoded as a 2-byte sequence:

2.7.4.7 Reserved Tokens

There are several reserved global tokens. These must not be emitted by a tokenizer and should be treated as a single-byte token by a user agent.

The code page 255 is reserved for implementation-specific or experimental use. The tokens in this code page will never be used to represent standard XML document constructs.

3. Encoding Semantics

3.1 Document Tokenization

The process of tokenizing an XML document must convert all markup and XML syntax (i.e., entities, tags, attributes, etc.) into their corresponding tokenized format. All comments must be removed. Processing directives intended for the tokenizer may be removed. Other meta-information, such as the document type definition and unnecessary conditional sections must be removed. All text and entities must be converted to string (e.g., `STR_I`) or entity (`ENTITY`) tokens. Entities in the textual markup (e.g., `&`) must be converted to string form when tokenized, if the target character encoding can represent the entity. Characters present in the textual form may be encoded using the `ENTITY` token when they can not be represented in the target character encoding. Attribute names must be converted to an attribute start token or must be represented by a single `LITERAL` token. Attribute values may not be represented by a `LITERAL` token.

It is illegal to encode markup constructs as strings. The user agent must treat all text tokens (e.g., `STR_I` and `ENTITY`) as CDATA (i.e., text with no embedded markup).

3.2 Document Structure Conformance

The tokenized XML document must accurately represent the structure and semantics of the textual source document. This implies that the source document must be well-formed, as defined in [XML]. Document tokenization may validate the document as specified in [XML], but this is not required. If the semantics of a particular DOCTYPE are well known, additional semantic checks may be applied during the tokenization process.

3.3 Encoding Default Attribute Values

The tokenized representation of a XML document may omit any attributes that are implied in the DTD or are specified with their default value. This implies that a user agent implementation must be aware of the attribute defaults of a given version of the DTD. This information can be inferred from the version number in the tokenized data format.

4. Numeric Constants

4.1 Global Tokens

The token codes listed in Table 5.4 are common across all document types and are present in all code spaces and all code pages. All numbers are in hexadecimal.

4.2 Public Identifiers

The values listed in Table 5.5 represent well-known document-type public identifiers. The first 128 values are reserved for use in future WAP specifications. All numbers are in hexadecimal.

Table 5.4 Global Tokens

TOKEN NAME	TOKEN	DESCRIPTION
SWITCH_PAGE	0	Change the code page for the current token state. Followed by a single u_int8 indicating the new code page number.
END	1	Indicates the end of an attribute list or the end of an element.
ENTITY	2	A character entity. Followed by a `mb_u_int32` encoding the character entity number.
STR_I	3	Inline string. Followed by a `termstr`.
LITERAL	4	An unknown tag or attribute name. Followed by an `mb_u_int32` that encodes an offset into the string table.
EXT_I_0	40	Inline string document-type-specific extension token. Token is followed by a `termstr`.
EXT_I_1	41	Inline string document-type-specific extension token. Token is followed by a `termstr`.
EXT_I_2	42	Inline string document-type-specific extension token. Token is followed by a `termstr`.
PI	43	Processing instruction.
LITERAL_C	44	Unknown tag, with content.
EXT_T_0	80	Inline integer document-type-specific extension token. Token is followed by a `mb_uint_32`.
EXT_T_1	81	Inline integer document-type-specific extension token. Token is followed by a `mb_uint_32`.
EXT_T_2	82	Inline integer document-type-specific extension token. Token is followed by a `mb_uint_32`.
STR_T	83	String table reference. Followed by a `mb_u_int32` encoding a byte offset from the beginning of the string table.
LITERAL_A	84	Unknown tag, with attributes.
EXT_0	C0	Single-byte document-type-specific extension token.
EXT_1	C1	Single-byte document-type-specific extension token.
EXT_2	C2	Single-byte document-type-specific extension token.
RESERVED_2	C3	Reserved for future use.
LITERAL_AC	C4	Unknown tag, with content and attributes.

Table 5.5 Public Identifiers

VALUE	PUBLIC IDENTIFIER
0	String table index follows; public identifier is encoded as a literal in the string table.
1	Unknown or missing public identifier.
2	"-//WAPFORUM//DTD WML 1.0//EN" (WML 1.0)
3	"-//WAPFORUM//DTD WTA 1.0//EN" (WTA Event 1.0)
4 - 7F	Reserved

5. Encoding Examples

5.1 A Simple XML Document

The following is an example of a simple tokenized XML document. It demonstrates basic element, string, and entity encoding. Source document:

```
<?xml version="1.0"?>
<!DOCTYPE XYZ [
<!ELEMENT XYZ (CARD)+>
<!ELEMENT CARD (#PCDATA | BR)*>
<!ELEMENT BR EMPTY>
<!ENTITY nbsp " ">
]>
<XYZ>
  <CARD>
    X &amp; Y<BR/>
    X = 1
  </CARD>
</XYZ>
```

The following tokens are defined for the tag code space:

TAG NAME	TOKEN
BR	5
CARD	6
XYZ	7

Tokenized form (numbers in hexadecimal) follows. This example uses only inline strings and assumes that the character encoding uses a NULL terminated string format. It also assumes that the transport character encoding is US-ASCII. This encoding is incapable of supporting some of the characters in the deck (e.g., ` `), forcing the use of the `ENTITY` token.

```
00  01  00  47  46  03  ' ' 'X' ' ' '&' ' ' 'Y' 00  05  03  ' '
'X' 00  02  81  20  03  '=' 00  02  81  20  03  '1' ' ' 00  01 01
```

For an expanded and annotated form, see Table 5.6.

Table 5.6 Example Tokenized Deck

TOKEN STREAM	DESCRIPTION
`00`	Version number–WBXML version 1.0.
`01`	Unknown public identifier
`00`	String table length
`47`	`XYZ`, with content
`46`	`CARD`, with content
`03`	Inline string follows
`' ','X',' ','&',' ','Y',00`	String
`05`	`BR`
`03`	Inline string follows
`' ','X',00`	String
`02`	`ENTITY`
`81 20`	Entity value (`0x160`)
`03`	Inline string follows
`'=',00`	String
`02`	`ENTITY`
`81 20`	Entity value (`0x160`)
`03`	Inline string follows
`'1',' ',00`	String
`01`	`END` (of `CARD` element)
`01`	`END` (of `XYZ` element)

5.2 An Expanded Example

The following is another example of a tokenized XML document. It demonstrates attribute encoding and the use of the string table. Source document:

```
<?xml version="1.0"?>
<!DOCTYPE XYZ [
<!ELEMENT XYZ ( CARD )+ >
<!ELEMENT CARD (#PCDATA | INPUT | DO)*>
<!ATTLIST CARD NAME NMTOKEN #IMPLIED>
<!ATTLIST CARD STYLE (LIST|SET) 'LIST'>
<!ELEMENT DO EMPTY>
<!ATTLIST DO TYPE CDATA #REQUIRED>
<!ATTLIST DO URL CDATA #IMPLIED>
<!ELEMENT INPUT EMPTY>
<!ATTLIST INPUT TYPE (TEXT|PASSWORD)'TEXT'>
<!ATTLIST INPUT KEY NMTOKEN #IMPLIED>
<!ENTITY nbsp " ">
]>
<!– This is a comment –>
<XYZ>
  <CARD NAME="abc" STYLE="LIST">
    <DO TYPE="ACCEPT" URL="http://xyz.org/s"/>
    Enter name: <INPUT TYPE="TEXT" KEY="N"/>
  </CARD>
</XYZ>
```

The following tokens are defined for the tag code space:

TAG NAME	TOKEN
CARD	5
INPUT	6
XYZ	7
DO	8

The following attribute start tokens are defined:

ATTRIBUTE NAME	ATTRIBUTE VALUE PREFIX	TOKEN
STYLE	LIST	5
TYPE		6
TYPE	TEXT	7
URL	http://	8
NAME		9
KEY		B

The following attribute value tokens are defined:

ATTRIBUTE VALUE	TOKEN
.org	85
ACCEPT	86

Tokenized form (numbers in hexadecimal) follows. This example assumes an UTF-8 character encoding and NULL terminated strings.

```
00  01  12  'a' 'b' 'c' 00 ' ' 'E' 'n' 't' 'e' 'r' ' ' 'n'
'a' 'm' 'e' ':' ' ' 00 47  C5  09  03  00  05  01  88  06
86  08  03  'x' 'y' 'z' 00  85  03  '/' 's' 00  01 83  04
01  83  04  86  07  0A  03  'N' 00  01  01  01
```

For an expanded and annotated form, see Table 5.7.

Table 5.7 Example Tokenized Deck

TOKEN STREAM	DESCRIPTION
00	Version number—WBXML version 1.0
01	Unknown public identifier
12	String table length
'a','b','c',00,' ','E','n', 't','e','r',' ','n','a', 'm','e',':',' ',00	String table
47	XYZ, with content
C5	CARD, with content and attributes
09	NAME=
83	String table reference follows
00	String table index
05	STYLE="LIST"
01	END (of CARD attribute list)
88	DO, with attributes
06	TYPE=
86	ACCEPT
08	URL="http://"
03	Inline string follows

(Continues)

Table 5.7 *(Continued)*

TOKEN STREAM	DESCRIPTION
'x','y','z',00	string
85	".org"
03	Inline string follows
'/','s',00	string
01	END (of DO attribute list)
83	String table reference follows
04	String table index
86	INPUT, with attributes
07	TYPE="TEXT"
0A	KEY=
03	Inline string follows
'N',00	String
01	END (of INPUT attribute list)
01	END (of CARD element)
01	END (of XYZ element)

6. Definitions

The following are terms and conventions used throughout this specification:

The key words "MUST", "MUST NOT", "REQUIRED", "SHALL", "SHALL NOT", "SHOULD", "SHOULD NOT", "RECOMMENDED", "MAY", and "OPTIONAL" in this document are to be interpreted as described in [RFC2119].

Author. An author is a person or program that writes or generates WML, WMLScript, or other content.

Content. Subject matter (data) stored or generated at an origin server. Content is typically displayed or interpreted by a user agent in response to a user request.

Resource. A network data object or service that can be identified by a URL. Resources may be available in multiple representations (e.g., multiple languages, data formats, size, and resolutions) or vary in other ways.

SGML. The Standardized Generalized Markup Language (defined in [ISO8879]) is a general-purpose language for domain-specific markup languages.

User. A user is a person who interacts with a user agent to view, hear, or otherwise use a resource.

User Agent. A user agent is any software or device that interprets the binary XML content format or other resources. This may include textual browsers, voice browsers, search engines, etc.

XML. The Extensible Markup Language is a World Wide Web Consortium (W3C) standard for Internet markup languages, of which WML is one such language. XML is a restricted subset of SGML.

7. Abbreviations

For the purposes of this specification, the following abbreviations apply:

API	Application Programming Interface
BNF	Backus-Naur Form
LSB	Least Significant Bits
MSB	Most Significant Bits
MSC	Mobile Switch Center
RFC	Request For Comments
SGML	Standardized Generalized Markup Language [ISO8879]
UCS-4	Universal Character Set—4 byte [ISO10646]
URL	Universal Resource Locator
UTF-8	UCS Transformation Format 8 [ISO10646]
W3C	World Wide Web Consortium
WAP	Wireless Application Protocol [WAP]
WML	Wireless Markup Language [WML]
XML	Extensible Markup Language [XML]

8. Normative References

[ISO10646] "Information Technology—Universal Multiple-Octet Coded Character Set (UCS)—Part 1: Architecture and Basic Multilingual Plane," ISO/IEC 10646-1:1993.

[RFC822] "Standard for the Format of ARPA Internet Text Messages," STD 11, RFC 822, D. Crocker, August 1982.
URL: ftp://ds.internic.net/rfc/rfc822.txt

[RFC2119] "Key words for Use in RFCs to Indicate Requirement Levels," S. Bradner, March 1997.
URL: ftp://ds.internic.net/rfc/rfc2119.txt

[WAP] "Wireless Application Protocol Architecture Specification," WAP Forum, 30-April-1998.
URL: http://www.wapforum.org/

[XML] "Extensible Markup Language (XML), W3C Proposed Recommendation 10-February-1998, REC-xml-19980210," T. Bray, et al., February 10, 1998.
URL: http://www.w3.org/TR/REC-xml

9. Informative References

[ISO8879] "Information Processing—Text and Office Systems—Standard Generalized Markup Language (SGML)," ISO 8879:1986.

[UNICODE] "The Unicode Standard: Version 2.0," The Unicode Consortium, Addison-Wesley Developers Press, 1996.
URL: http://www.unicode.org/

[WML] "Wireless Markup Language," WAP Forum, 30-April-1998.
URL: http://www.wapforum.org/

CHAPTER

6

WMLScript Language Specification

1. Scope

Wireless Application Protocol (WAP) is a result of continuous work to define an industrywide specification for developing applications that operate over wireless communication networks. The scope for the WAP Forum is to define a set of standards to be used by service applications. The wireless market is growing very quickly and reaching new customers and services. To enable operators and manufacturers to meet the challenges in advanced services, differentiation, and fast/flexible service creation, WAP defines a set of protocols in Transport, Session, and Application layers. For additional information on the WAP architecture, refer to *Wireless Application Protocol Architecture Specification* [WAP].

This paper is a specification of the WMLScript language. It is part of the WAP Application layer and it can be used to add client-side procedural logic. The language is based on ECMAScript [ECMA262], but it has been modified to better support low-bandwidth communication and thin clients. WMLScript can be used together with Wireless Markup Language [WML] to provide intelligence to the clients, but it has also been designed so that it can be used as a standalone tool.

One of the main differences between ECMAScript and WMLScript is the fact that WMLScript has a defined bytecode and an interpreter reference architecture. This way, the narrowband communication channels available today can be optimally utilized and the memory requirements for the client kept to the minimum. Many of the advanced features of the ECMAScript language have been dropped to make the language smaller, easier to compile into bytecode, and easier to learn. For example, WMLScript is a procedural language and it supports locally installed standard libraries.

2. Overview

2.1 Why Scripting?

WMLScript is designed to provide general scripting capabilities to the WAP architecture. Specifically, WMLScript can be used to complement the Wireless Markup Language [WML]. WML is a markup language based on Extensible Markup Language [XML]. It is designed to be used to specify application content for narrowband devices like cellular phones and pagers. This content can be represented with text, images, selection lists, and so forth. Simple formatting can be used to make the user interfaces more readable as long as the client device used to display the content can support it. However, all this content is *static* and there is no way to extend the language without modifying WML itself. The following list contains some capabilities that are not supported by WML:

- Check the validity of user input (validity checks for the user input):
- Access to facilities of the device; for example, on a phone, allow the programmer to make phone calls, send messages, add phone numbers to the address book, access the SIM card, etc.
- Generate messages and dialogs locally, thus reducing the need for expensive round-trip to show alerts, error messages, confirmations, etc.
- Allow extensions to the device software and configuring a device after it has been deployed.

WMLScript was designed to overcome these limitations and to provide programmable functionality that can be used over narrowband communication links in clients with limited capabilities.

2.2 Benefits of Using WMLScript

Many of the services that can be used with thin mobile clients can be implemented with WML. Scripting enhances the standard browsing and presentation facilities of WML with behavioral capabilities. They can be used to support more advanced UI functions, add intelligence to the client, provide access to the device and its peripheral functionality, and reduce the amount of bandwidth needed to send data between the server and the client.

WMLScript is loosely based on ECMAScript [ECMA262] and does not require the developers to learn new concepts to be able to generate advanced mobile services.

3. WMLScript Core

One objective for the WMLScript language is to be close to the core of the ECMAScript Language specification [ECMA262]. The part in the ECMAScript Language specification that defines basic types, variables, expressions, and statements is called *core* and can almost be used "as is" for the WMLScript specification. This section gives an overview of the core parts of WMLScript.

See Chapter 5, "WMLScript Grammar," for syntax conventions and precise language grammar.

3.1 Lexical Structure

This section describes the set of elementary rules that specify how you write programs in WMLScript.

3.1.1 Case Sensitivity

WMLScript is a case-sensitive language. All language keywords, variables, and function names must use the proper capitalization of letters.

3.1.2 Whitespace and Line Breaks

WMLScript ignores spaces, tabs, newlines, and so forth that appear between tokens in programs, except those that are part of string constants.

Syntax:

WhiteSpace ::

<TAB>

<VT>

<FF>

<SP>

<LF>

<CR>

LineTerminator ::

<LF>

<CR>

<CR><LF>

3.1.3 Usage of Semicolons

The following statements in WMLScript have to be followed by a semicolon:[1]

- Empty statement (see Section 3.5.1)
- Expression statement (see Section 3.5.2)
- Variable statement (see Section 3.5.4)
- Break statement (see Section 3.5.8)
- Continue statement (see Section 3.5.9)
- Return statement (see Section 3.5.10)

[1]Compatibility note: ECMAScript supports optional semicolons.

3.1.4 Comments

The language defines two comment constructs: *line comments* (i.e., start with // and end in the end of the line) and *block comments* (i.e., consisting of multiple lines starting with /* and ending with */). It is illegal to have nested block comments.[2]

Syntax:

Comment ::

MultiLineComment

SingleLineComment

MultiLineComment ::

/* $MultiLineCommentChars_{opt}$ */

SingleLineComment ::

// $SingleLineCommentChars_{opt}$

3.1.5 Literals

3.1.5.1 Integer Literals

Integer literals can be represented in three different ways: decimal, octal, and hexadecimal integers.

Syntax:

DecimalIntegerLiteral ::

0

NonZeroDigit $DecimalDigits_{opt}$

NonZeroDigit :: **one of**

1 2 3 4 5 6 7 8 9

DecimalDigits ::

DecimalDigit

DecimalDigits DecimalDigit

DecimalDigit :: **one of**

1 2 3 4 5 6 7 8 9

HexIntegerLiteral ::

0x *HexDigit*

0X *HexDigit*

HexIntegerLiteral HexDigit

HexDigit :: **one of**

0 1 2 3 4 5 6 7 8 9 a b c d e f A B C D E F

[2]Compatibility note: ECMAScript also supports HTML comments.

OctalIntegerLiteral ::

  `0` *OctalDigit*

  OctalIntegerLiteral OctalDigit

OctalDigit :: **one of**

  `0 1 2 3 4 5 6 7`

The minimum and maximum sizes for integer literals and values are specified in Section 3.2.7.1. An integer literal that is not within the specified value range must result in a compile time error.

3.1.5.2 Floating-Point Literals

Floating-point literals can contain a decimal point as well as an exponent.

Syntax:

DecimalFloatLiteral ::

  DecimalIntegerLiteral . *DecimalDigits*$_{opt}$ *ExponentPart*$_{opt}$

  . *DecimalDigits ExponentPart*$_{opt}$

  DecimalIntegerLiteral ExponentPart

DecimalDigits ::

  DecimalDigit

  DecimalDigits DecimalDigit

ExponentPart ::

  ExponentIndicator SignedInteger

ExponentIndicator :: **one of**

  `e E`

SignedInteger ::

  DecimalDigits

  + *DecimalDigits*

  - *DecimalDigits*

The minimum and maximum sizes for floating-point literals and values are specified in Section 3.2.7.2. A floating-point literal that is not within the specified value range must result in a compile time error. A floating-point literal underflow results in a floating-point literal zero (`0.0`).

3.1.5.3 String Literals

Strings are any sequence of zero or more characters enclosed within double (") or single quotes (').

Syntax:

StringLiteral ::

  " *DoubleStringCharacters*$_{opt}$ "

  ' *SingleStringCharacters*$_{opt}$ '

Examples of valid strings are:

```
"Example"     'Specials: \x00 \' \b'     "Quote: \""
```

Since some characters are not representable within strings, WMLScript supports special escape sequences by which these characters can be represented:

SEQUENCE	CHARACTER REPRESENTED[3]	UNICODE	SYMBOL
\'	Apostrophe or single quote	\u0027	'
\"	Double quote	\u0022	"
\\	Backslash	\u005C	\
\/	Slash	\u002F	/
\b	Backspace	\u0008	
\f	Form feed	\u000C	
\n	Newline	\u000A	
\r	Carriage return	\u000D	
\t	Horizontal tab	\u0009	
\x*hh*	The character with the encoding specified by two hexadecimal digits *hh* (Latin-1 ISO8859-1)		
ooo	The character with the encoding specified by the three octal digits *ooo* (Latin-1 ISO8859-1)		
\u*hhhh*	The Unicode character with the encoding specified by the four hexadecimal digits *hhhh*.		

An escape sequence occurring within a string literal always contributes a character to the string value of the literal and is never interpreted as a line terminator or as a quote mark that might terminate the string literal.

3.1.5.4 Boolean Literals

A "truth value" in WMLScript is represented by a Boolean literal. The two Boolean literals are `true` and `false`.

Syntax:

BooleanLiteral ::

```
true
false
```

[3]Compatibility note: ECMAScript also supports nonescape characters preceded by a backslash.

3.1.5.5 Invalid Literal

WMLScript supports a special *invalid* literal to denote an invalid value.

Syntax:

InvalidLiteral ::

```
invalid
```

3.1.6 Identifiers

Identifiers are used to name and refer to three different elements of WMLScript: variables (see Section 3.2), functions (see Section 3.4), and pragmas (see Section 3.7). Identifiers[4] cannot start with a digit but can start with an underscore (_).

Syntax:

Identifier ::

IdentifierName **but not** *ReservedWord*

IdentifierName ::

IdentifierLetter

IdentifierName IdentifierLetter

IdentifierName DecimalDigit

IdentifierLetter :: **one of**

```
a b c d e f g h i j k l m n o p q r s t u v w x y z
A B C D E F G H I J K L M N O P Q R S T U V W X Y Z
_
```

DecimalDigit :: **one of**

```
0 1 2 3 4 5 6 7 8 9
```

Examples of legal identifiers are:

```
timeOfDay  speed  quality  HOME_ADDRESS  var0  _myName  ____
```

The compiler looks for the longest string of characters that make up a valid identifier. Identifiers cannot contain any special characters except underscore (_). WMLScript keywords and reserved words cannot be used as identifiers. Examples of illegal identifiers are:

```
while  for  if  my~name  $sys  123  3pieces  take.this
```

Uppercase and lowercase letters are distinct, which means that the identifiers `speed` and `Speed` are different.

[4]Compatibility note: ECMAScript supports the use of $ character in any position of the name, too.

3.1.7 Reserved Words

WMLScript specifies a set of reserved words that have a special meaning in programs and they cannot be used as identifiers. Examples of such words are:

```
break  continue  false  true  while
```

3.1.8 Namespaces

WMLScript supports namespaces for identifiers that are used for different purposes. The following namespaces are supported:

- Function names (see Section 3.4)
- Function parameters (see Section 3.4) and variables (see Section 3.2)
- Pragmas (see Section 3.7)

Thus, the same identifiers can be used to specify a function name, variable/parameter name, or a name for a pragma within the same compilation unit:

```
use url myTes¡t "http://www.host.com/script"

function myTest(myTest) {
  var value = myTest#myTest(myTest)
  return value;
};
```

3.2 Variables and Data Types

This section describes the two important concepts of WMLScript language: *variables* and *internal data types*. A variable is a name associated with a data value. Variables can be used to store and manipulate program data. WMLScript supports local variables[5] only declared inside functions or passed as function parameters (see Section 3.4).

3.2.1 Variable Declaration

Variable declaration is compulsory[6] in WMLScript. Variable declaration is done simply by using the *var* keyword and a variable name (see Section 3.5.4 for information about variable statements). Variable names follow the syntax defined for all identifiers (see Section 3.1.6):

```
var x;
var price;
var x,y;
var size = 3;
```

[5]Compatibility note: ECMAScript supports global variables, too.

[6]Compatibility note: ECMAScript supports automatic declaration, too.

Variables must be declared before they can be used. Initialization of variables is optional. Uninitialized variables are automatically initialized to contain an empty string ("").

3.2.2 Variable Scope and Lifetime

The scope of WMLScript variables is the remainder of the function (see Section 3.4) in which they have been declared. All variable names within a function must be unique. Block statements (see 3.5.3) are not used for scoping.

```
function priceCheck(givenPrice) {
  if (givenPrice > 100) {
    var newPrice = givenPrice;
  } else {
    newPrice = 100;
  };
  return newPrice;
};
```

The lifetime of a variable is the time between the variable declaration and the end of the function.

```
function foo()  {
  x = 1;            // Error: usage before declaration
  var x,y;
  if (x) {
    var y;          // Error: redeclaration
  };
};
```

3.2.3 Variable Access

Variables are accessible only within the function in which they have been declared. Accessing the content of a variable is done by using the variable name:

```
var myAge   = 37;
var yourAge = 63;
var ourAge  = myAge + yourAge;
```

3.2.4 Variable Type

WMLScript is a weakly typed language. The variables are not typed, but internally the following basic data types are supported: *boolean*, *integer*, *floating-point*, and *string*. In addition to these, a fifth data type, *invalid*, is specified to be used in cases an invalid data type is needed to separate it from the other internal data types. Since these data types are supported only internally, the programmer does not have to specify variable types, and any variable can contain any type of data at any given time. WMLScript will attempt to automatically convert between the different types as needed.

```
var flag        = true;        // Boolean
var number      = 12;          // Integer
var temperature = 37.7;        // Float
number          = "XII";       // String
var except      = invalid;     // Invalid
```

3.2.5 L-Values

Some operators (see Section 3.3.1 for more information about assignment operators) require that the left operand is a reference to a variable (L-value) and not the variable value. Thus, in addition to the five data types supported by WMLScript, a sixth type, *variable*, is used to specify that a variable name must be provided.

```
result += 111;   // += operator requires a variable
```

3.2.6 Type Equivalency

WMLScript supports operations on different data types. All operators (see Section 3.3) specify the accepted data types for their operands. Automatic data type conversions (see Section 4) are used to convert operand values to required data types.

3.2.7 Numeric Values

WMLScript supports two different numeric variable values: *integer* and *floating-point* values.[7] Variables can be initialized with integer and floating-point literals, and several operators can be used to modify their values during runtime. Conversion rules between integer and floating-point values are specified in Section 4.

```
var pi     = 3.14;
var length = 0;
var radius = 2.5;
length     = 2*pi*radius;
```

3.2.7.1 Integer Size

The size of the integer is 32 bits (2's complement). This means that the supported value range[8] for integer values is –2147483648 and 2147483647. *Lang* [WMLSLibs] library functions can be used to get these values during runtime:

[7]Convention: In cases where the value can be either an integer or a floating-point, a more generic term, *number*, is used instead.

[8]Compatibility note: ECMAScript does not specify maximum and minimum values for integers. All numbers are represented as floating-point values.

`Lang.maxInt()`	Maximum representable integer value
`Lang.minInt()`	Minimum representable integer value

3.2.7.2 Floating-Point Size

The minimum/maximum values[9] and precision for floating-point values are specified by [IEEE754]. WMLScript supports 32-bit single precision floating-point format:

- Maximum value: 3.40282347E+38
- Minimum positive nonzero value (at least the normalized precision must be supported): 1.17549435E-38 or smaller

The *Float* [WMLSLibs] library can be used to get these values during runtime:

`Lang.maxFloat()`	Maximum representable floating-point value supported
`Lang.minFloat()`	Smallest positive nonzero floating-point value supported

The special floating-point number types are handled by using the following rules:

- If an operation results in a floating-point number that is not part of the set of finite real numbers (not a number, positive infinity, etc.) supported by the single precision floating-point format, then the result is an `invalid` value.
- If an operation results in a floating-point *underflow*, the result is zero (0.0).
- *Negative* and *positive zero* are equal and undistinguishable.

3.2.8 String Values

WMLScript supports *strings* that can contain letters, digits, special characters, and so forth. Variables can be initialized with string literals, and string values can be manipulated both with WMLScript operators and functions specified in the standard *String* library [WMLSLibs].

```
var msg = "Hello";
var len = String.length(msg);
msg     = msg + ' Worlds!';
```

3.2.9 Boolean Values

Boolean values can be used to initialize or assign a value to a variable or in statements which require a Boolean value as one of the parameters. Boolean value can be a literal or the result of a logical expression evaluation (see Section 3.3.3 for more information).

```
var truth = true;
var lie   = !truth;
```

[9]Compatibility note: ECMAScript uses double-precision 64-bit format [IEEE754] floating-point values for all numbers.

3.3 Operators and Expressions

The following sections describe the operators supported by WMLScript and how they can be used to form complex expressions.

3.3.1 Assignment Operators

WMLScript supports several ways to assign a value to a variable. The simplest one is the regular assignment (=), but assignments with operation are also supported.

OPERATOR	OPERATION
=	Assign
+=	Add (numbers)/concatenate (strings) and assign
-=	Subtract and assign
*=	Multiply and assign
/=	Divide and assign
div=	Divide (integer division) and assign
%=	Remainder (the sign of the result equals the sign of the dividend) and assign
<<=	Bitwise left shift and assign
>>=	Bitwise right shift with sign and assign
>>>=	Bitwise right shift zero fill and assign
&=	Bitwise AND and assign
^=	Bitwise XOR and assign
|=	Bitwise OR and assign

Assignment does not necessarily imply sharing of structure, nor does assignment of one variable change the binding of any other variable.

```
var a = "abc";
var b = a;
b     = "def";  // Value of a is "abc"
```

3.3.2 Arithmetic Operators

WMLScript supports all the basic binary arithmetic operations.

OPERATOR	OPERATION
+	Add (numbers)/concatenation (strings)
-	Subtract
*	Multiply
/	Divide
div	Integer division

In addition to these, a set of more complex binary operations are supported, too:

OPERATOR	OPERATION
%	Remainder, the sign of the result equals the sign of the dividend
<<	Bitwise left shift
>>	Bitwise right shift with sign
>>>	Bitwise shift right with zero fill
&	Bitwise AND
|	Bitwise OR
^	Bitwise XOR

The basic unary operations supported are:

OPERATOR	OPERATION
+	Plus
-	Minus
—	Pre-or-post decrement
++	Pre-or-post increment
~	Bitwise NOT

Examples:

```
var y = 1/3;
var x = y*3+(++b);
```

3.3.3 Logical Operators

WMLScript supports the basic logical operations:

OPERATOR	OPERATION
&&	Logical AND
||	Logical OR
!	Logical NOT (unary)

Logical AND operator evaluates the first operand and tests the result. If the result is `false`, the result of the operation is `false` and the second operand is not evaluated. If the first operand evaluates to `true`, the result of the operation is the result of the evaluation of the second operand. If the first operand evaluates to `invalid`, the second operand is not evaluated and the result of the operation is `invalid`.

Similarly, the logical OR evaluates the first operand and tests the result. If the result is `true`, the result of the operation is `true` and the second operand is not evaluated. If the first operand evaluates to `false`, the result of the operation is the result of the evaluation of the second operand. If the first operand evaluates to `invalid`, the second operand is not evaluated and the result of the operation is `invalid`.

```
weAgree = (iAmRight && yourAreRight) ||
          (!iAmRight && !youAreRight);
```

WMLScript requires a value of Boolean type for logical operations. Automatic conversions from other types to Boolean type and *vice versa* are supported (see 4).

Notice: If the value of the first operand for logical AND or OR is `invalid`, the second operand is not evaluated and the result of the operand is `invalid`:

```
var a = (1/0) || foo(); // result: invalid, no call to foo()
var b = true  || (1/0); // true
var c = false || (1/0); // invalid
```

3.3.4 String Operators

WMLScript supports string concatenation as a built-in operation. The + and += operators used with strings perform a concatenation on the strings. Other string operations[10] are supported by a standard *String* library (see [WMLSLibs]).

```
var str = "Beginning" + "End";
var chr = String.charAt(str,10); // chr = "E"
```

3.3.5 Comparison Operators

WMLScript supports all the basic comparison operations:

OPERATOR	OPERATION
<	Less than
<=	Less than or equal
==	Equal
>=	Greater or equal
>	Greater than
!=	Inequality

Comparison operators use the following rules:

- *Boolean*: `true` is larger than `false`.
- *Integer*: Comparison is based on the given integer values.
- *Floating-point*: Comparison is based on the given floating-point values.
- *String*: Comparison is based on the order of [UNICODE] character codes of the given string values.
- *Invalid*: If at least one of the operands is `invalid`, then the result of the comparison is `invalid`.

[10]Compatibility note: ECMAScript supports String objects and a length attribute for each string. WMLScript does not support objects. However, similar functionality is provided by WMLScript libraries.

Examples:

```
var res = (myAmount > yourAmount);
var val = ((1/0) == invalid);       // val = invalid
```

3.3.6 Array Operators

WMLScript does not support arrays[11] as such. However, the standard *String* library (see [WMLSLibs]) supports functions by which array-like behavior can be implemented by using strings. A string can contain elements that are separated by a separator specified by the application programmer. For this purpose, the *String* library contains functions by which creation and management of string arrays can be done.

```
function dummy() {
  var str  = "Mary had a little lamb";
  var word = String.elementAt(str,4," ");
};
```

3.3.7 Comma Operator

WMLScript supports the comma (,) operator by which multiple evaluations can be combined into one expression. The result of the comma operator is the value of the second operand.

```
for (a=1, b=100; a < 10; a++,b++) {
  … do something …
};
```

Commas used in the function call to separate parameters and in the variable declarations to separate multiple variable declarations are not comma operators. In these cases, the comma operator must be placed inside the parentheses.

```
var a=2;
var b=3, c=(a,3);
myFunction("Name", 3*(b*a,c)); // Two parameters: "Name",9
```

3.3.8 Conditional Operator

WMLScript supports the conditional (?:) operator, which takes three operands. The operator selectively evaluates one of the given two operands based on the Boolean value of the first operand. If the value of the first operand (condition) is `true`, then the result of the operation is the result of the evaluation of the second operand. If the value of the first operand is `false` or `invalid`, then the result of the operation is the result of the evaluation of the third operand.

```
myResult = flag ? "Off" : "On (value=" + level + ")";
```

[11]Compatibility note: ECMAScript supports arrays.

Notice: This operator behaves like an *if* statement (see 3.5.5). The third operand is evaluated if the evaluation of the condition results in `false` or `invalid`.

3.3.9 typeof Operator

Although WMLScript is a weakly typed language, internally the following basic data types are supported: *boolean, integer, floating-point, string,* and *invalid*. Typeof (*typeof*) operator returns an integer value[12] that describes the type of the given expression. The possible results are:

TYPE	CODE
Integer:	0
Floating-point:	1
String:	2
Boolean:	3
Invalid:	4

Typeof operator does not try to convert the result from one type to another, but returns the type as it is after the evaluation of the expression.

```
var str    = "123";
var myType = typeof str; // myType = 2
```

3.3.10 isvalid Operator

This operator can be used to check the type of the given expression. It returns a Boolean value `false` if the type of the expression is invalid; otherwise, `true` is returned. *isvalid* operator does not try to convert the result from one type to another, but returns the type as it is after the evaluation of the expression.

```
var str = "123";
var ok  = isvalid str;    // true
var tst = isvalid (1/0); // false
```

3.3.11 Expressions

WMLScript supports most of the expressions supported by other programming languages. The simplest expressions are constants and variable names, which simply evaluate to either the value of the constant or the variable.

```
567
66.77
"This is too simple"
```

[12]Compatibility note: ECMAScript specifies that the *typeof* operator returns a string representing the variable type.

```
'This works too'
true
myAccount
```

Expressions that are more complex can be defined by using simple expressions together with operators and function calls.

```
myAccount + 3
(a + b)/3
initialValue + nextValue(myValues);
```

3.3.12 Expression Bindings

The following table contains all operators supported by WMLScript. The table also contains information about operator precedence (the order of evaluation) and the operator associativity (left-to-right (L) or right-to-left (R)).

PRECE-DENCE[13]	ASSOCIA-TIVITY	OPERATOR	OPERAND TYPES	RESULT TYPE	OPERATION PERFORMED
1	R	++	Number	Number*	Pre- or post-increment (unary)
1	R	—	Number	Number*	Pre- or post-decrement (unary)
1	R	+	Number	Number*	Unary plus
1	R	-	Number	Number*	Unary minus (negation)
1	R	~	Integer	Integer*	Bitwise NOT (unary)
1	R	!	Boolean	Boolean*	Logical NOT (unary)
1	R	typeof	Any	Integer	Return internal data type (unary)
1	R	isvalid	Any	Boolean	Check for validity (unary)
2	L	*	Numbers	Number*	Multiplication
2	L	/	Numbers	Floating-point*	Division
2	L	div	Integers	Integer*	Integer division
2	L	%	Integers	Integer*	Remainder
3	L	-	Numbers	Number*	Subtraction
3	L	+	Numbers or strings	Numbers or string*	Addition (numbers) or string concatenation
4	L	<<	Integers	Integer*	Bitwise left shift
4	L	>>	Integers	Integer*	Bitwise right shift with sign
4	L	>>>	Integers	Integer*	Bitwise right shift with zero fill
5	L	<, <=	Numbers or strings	Boolean*	Less than, less than or equal

(Continues)

[13]Binding: 0 binds tightest

<table>
<tr><th>PRECE-
DENCE</th><th>ASSOCIA-
TIVITY</th><th>OPERATOR</th><th>OPERAND
TYPES</th><th>RESULT
TYPE</th><th>OPERATION PERFORMED</th></tr>
<tr><td>5</td><td>L</td><td>>, >=</td><td>Numbers or strings</td><td>Boolean*</td><td>Greater than, greater or equal</td></tr>
<tr><td>6</td><td>L</td><td>==</td><td>Numbers or strings</td><td>Boolean*</td><td>Equal (identical values)</td></tr>
<tr><td>6</td><td>L</td><td>!=</td><td>Numbers or strings</td><td>Boolean*</td><td>Not equal (different values)</td></tr>
<tr><td>7</td><td>L</td><td>&</td><td>Integers</td><td>Integer*</td><td>Bitwise AND</td></tr>
<tr><td>8</td><td>L</td><td>^</td><td>Integers</td><td>Integer*</td><td>Bitwise XOR</td></tr>
<tr><td>9</td><td>L</td><td>|</td><td>Integers</td><td>Integer*</td><td>Bitwise OR</td></tr>
<tr><td>10</td><td>L</td><td>&&</td><td>Booleans</td><td>Boolean*</td><td>Logical AND</td></tr>
<tr><td>11</td><td>L</td><td>||</td><td>Booleans</td><td>Boolean*</td><td>Logical OR</td></tr>
<tr><td>12</td><td>L</td><td>? :</td><td>Boolean, any, any</td><td>Any*</td><td>Conditional expression</td></tr>
<tr><td>13</td><td>R</td><td>=</td><td>Variable, any</td><td>Any</td><td>Assignment</td></tr>
<tr><td>13</td><td>R</td><td>*=, /=, %=, -=, div=</td><td>Variable, number</td><td>Number*</td><td>Assignment with numeric operation</td></tr>
<tr><td>13</td><td>R</td><td>+=</td><td>Variable, number or string</td><td>Number or string*</td><td>Assignment with addition or concatenation</td></tr>
<tr><td>13</td><td>R</td><td><<=, >>=, >>>=, &=, ^=, |=</td><td>Variable, integer</td><td>Integer*</td><td>Assignment with bitwise operation</td></tr>
<tr><td>14</td><td>L</td><td>,</td><td>Any</td><td>Any</td><td>Multiple evaluation</td></tr>
</table>

***The operator can return an `invalid` value in case the data type conversions fail (see Chapter 4 for more information about conversion rules) or one of the operands is `invalid`.**

3.4 Functions

A WMLScript function is a named part of the WMLScript compilation unit that can be called to perform a specific set of statements and to return a value. The following sections describe how WMLScript functions can be declared and used.

3.4.1 Declaration

Function declaration can be used to declare a WMLScript function name (*Identifier*) with the optional parameters (*FormalParameterList*) and a block statement that is executed when the function is called. All functions have the following characteristics:

- Function declarations *cannot* be nested.
- Function names must be *unique* within one compilation unit.
- All parameters to functions are *passed by value.*

- Function calls must pass *exactly* the same number of arguments to the called function as specified in the function declaration.
- Function parameters behave like *local variables* that have been initialized before the function body (block of statements) is executed.
- A function *always* returns a value. By default, it is an empty string (""). However, a *return* statement can be used to specify other return values.

Functions in WMLScript are not data types[14] but a syntactical feature of the language.

Syntax:

FunctionDeclaration :

`extern`$_{opt}$ `function` *Identifier* (*FormalParameterList*$_{opt}$) *Block* ;$_{opt}$

FormalParameterList :

Identifier

FormalParameterList , *Identifier*

Arguments: The optional `extern` keyword can be used to specify a function to be externally accessible. External functions can be called from outside the compilation unit in which they are defined. *Identifier* is the name specified for the function. *FormalParameterList* (optional) is a comma-separated list of argument names. *Block* is the body of the function that is executed when the function is called and the parameters have been initialized by the passed arguments.

Examples:

```
function currencyConverter(currency, exchangeRate) {
  return currency*exchangeRate;
};

extern function testIt() {
  var UDS = 10;
  var FIM = currencyConverter(USD, 5.3);
};
```

3.4.2 Function Calls

The way a function is called depends on where the called (target) function is declared. The following sections describe the three function calls supported by WMLScript: local script function call, external function call, and library function call.

3.4.2.1 Local Script Functions

Local script functions (defined inside the same compilation unit) can be called simply by providing the function name and a comma-separated list of arguments (number of arguments must match the number of parameters[15] accepted by the function).

[14]Compatibility note: Functions in ECMAScript are actual data types.

[15]Compatibility note: ECMAScript supports a variable number of arguments in a function call.

Syntax:

LocalScriptFunctionCall :

FunctionName Arguments

FunctionName :

Identifier

Arguments :

( )

(*ArgumentList*)

ArgumentList :

AssignmentExpression

ArgumentList , *AssignmentExpression*

Functions inside the same compilation unit can be called before the function has been declared.

```
function test2(param) {
  return test1(param+1);
};

function test1(val) {
  return val*val;
};
```

3.4.2.2 External Functions

External function calls must be used when the called function is declared in an external compilation unit. The function call is similar to a local function call, but it must be prefixed with the name of the external compilation unit.

Syntax:

ExternalScriptFunctionCall :

ExternalScriptName # *FunctionName Arguments*

ExternalScriptName :

Identifier

Pragma `use url` (see Section 3.7) must be used to specify the external compilation unit. It defines the mapping between the external unit and a name that can be used within function declarations. This name and the hash symbol (#) are used to prefix the standard function call syntax.

```
use url OtherScript "http://www.host.com/script"

function test3(param) {
  return OtherScript#test2(param+1);
};
```

3.4.2.3 Library Functions

Library function calls must be used when the called function is a WMLScript standard library function [WMLSLibs].

Syntax:

LibraryFunctionCall :

LibraryName . *FunctionName Arguments*

LibraryName :

Identifier

A library function can be called by prefixing the function name with the name of the library (see Section 3.6 for more information) and the dot symbol (.).

```
function test4(param) {
  return Float.sqrt(Lang.abs(param)+1);
};
```

3.4.3 Default Return Value

The default return value for a function is an empty string (""). Return values of functions can be ignored (i.e., function call as a statement).

```
function test5() {
  test4(4);
};
```

3.5 Statements

WMLScript statements consist of expressions and keywords used with the appropriate syntax. A single statement may span multiple lines. Multiple statements may occur on a single line.

The following sections define the statements available in WMLScript[16]: empty statement, expression statement, block statement, break, continue, for, if...else, return, var, and while.

3.5.1 Empty Statement

Empty statement is a statement that can be used where a statement is needed but no operation is required.

Syntax:

EmptyStatement :

;

Examples:

```
while (!poll(device)) ; // Wait until poll() is true
```

[16] Compatibility note: ECMAScript supports also *for..in* and *with* statements.

3.5.2 Expression Statement

Expression statements are used to assign values to variables, calculate mathematical expressions, make function calls, and so forth.

Syntax:

ExpressionStatement :

Expression ;

Expression :

AssignmentExpression

Expression , *AssignmentExpression*

Examples:

```
str  = "Hey " + yourName;
val3 = prevVal + 4;
counter++;
myValue1 = counter, myValue2 = val3;
alert("Watch out!");
retVal = 16*Lang.max(val3,counter);
```

3.5.3 Block Statement

A set of statements enclosed in curly brackets is a block statement. It can be used anywhere a single statement is needed.

Syntax:

Block :

{ $StatementList_{opt}$ }

StatementList :

Statement

StatementList Statement

Example:

```
{
  var i = 0;
  var x = Lang.abs(b);
  popUp("Remember!");
}
```

3.5.4 Variable Statement

This statement declares variables with initialization (optional, variables are initialized to empty string ("") by default). The scope of the declared variable is the rest of the current function (see Section 3.2.2 for more information about variable scoping).

Syntax:

VariableStatement :

var *VariableDeclarationList* ;

VariableDeclarationList :

VariableDeclaration

VariableDeclarationList , *VariableDeclaration*

VariableDeclaration :

Identifier $VariableInitializer_{opt}$

VariableInitializer :

= *ConditionalExpression*

Arguments: *Identifier* is the variable name. It can be any legal identifier. *Conditional-Expression* is the initial value of the variable and can be any legal expression. This expression (or the default initialization to an empty string) is evaluated every time the variable statement is executed.

Variable names must be unique within a single function.

Examples:

```
function count(str) {
  var result = 0;       // Initialized once
  while (str != "") {
    var ind = 0;        // Initialized every time
    // modify string
  };
  return result
};

function example(param) {
  var a = 0;
  if (param > a) {
    var b = a+1;        // Variables a and b can be used
  } else {
    var c = a+2;        // Variables a, b and c can be used
  };
  return a;             // Variable a, b and c are accessible
};
```

3.5.5 If Statement

This statement is used to specify conditional execution of statements. It consists of a condition and one or two statements, and executes the first statement if the specified condition is *true*. If the condition is *false*, the second (optional) statement is executed.

Syntax:

IfStatement :

if (*Expression*) *Statement* else *Statement*

if (*Expression*) *Statement*

Arguments: *Expression* (condition) can be any WMLScript expression that evaluates (directly or after conversion) to a *boolean* or an *invalid* value. If condition evaluates to `true`, the first statement is executed. If condition evaluates to `false` or `invalid`, the second (optional) `else` statement is executed. *Statement* can be any WMLScript statement, including another (nested) `if` statement. `else` is always tied to the closest `if`.

Example:

```
if (sunShines) {
  myDay = "Good";
  goodDays++;
} else
  myDay = "Oh well...";
```

3.5.6 While Statement

This statement is used to create a loop that evaluates an expression and, if it is `true`, executes a statement. The loop repeats as long as the specified condition is `true`.

Syntax:

WhileStatement :

`while` (*Expression*) *Statement*

Arguments: *Expression* (condition) can be any WMLScript expression that evaluates (directly or after the conversion) to a *boolean* or an *invalid* value. The condition is evaluated before each execution of the loop statement. If this condition evaluates to `true`, the *Statement* is performed. When condition evaluates to `false` or `invalid`, execution continues with the statement following *Statement*. *Statement* is executed as long as the condition evaluates to `true`.

Example:

```
var counter = 0;
var total   = 0;
while (counter < 3) {
  counter++;
  total += c;
};
```

3.5.7 For Statement

This statement is used to create loops. The statement consists of three optional expressions enclosed in parentheses and separated by semicolons followed by a statement executed in the loop.

Syntax:

ForStatement :

`for` ($Expression_{opt}$; $Expression_{opt}$; $Expression_{opt}$) *Statement*

`for` (`var` *VariableDeclarationList* ; $Expression_{opt}$; $Expression_{opt}$) *Statement*

Arguments: The first *Expression* or *VariableDeclarationList* (initializer) is typically used to initialize a counter variable. This expression may optionally declare new variables with the *var* keyword. The scope of the defined variables is the rest of the function (see Section 3.2.2 for more information about variable scoping).

The second *Expression* (condition) can be any WMLScript expression that evaluates (directly or after the conversion) to a *boolean* or an *invalid* value. The condition is evaluated on each pass through the loop. If this condition evaluates to `true`, the *Statement* is performed. This conditional test is optional. If omitted, the condition always evaluates to `true`.

The third *Expression* (increment-expression) is generally used to update or increment the counter variable. *Statement* is executed as long as the condition evaluates to `true`.

Example:

```
for (var index = 0; index < 100; index++) {
  count += index;
  myFunc(count);
};
```

3.5.8 Break Statement

This statement is used to terminate the current *while* or *for* loop and continue the program execution from the statement following the terminated loop. It is an error to use a break statement outside a *while* or a *for* statement.

Syntax:

BreakStatement :

```
break ;
```

Example:

```
function testBreak(x) {
  var index = 0;
  while (index < 6) {
    if (index == 3) break;
    index++;
  };
  return index*x;
};
```

3.5.9 Continue Statement

This statement is used to terminate execution of a block of statements in a *while* or *for* loop and continue execution of the loop with the next iteration. The continue statement does not terminate the execution of the loop:

- In a *while* loop, it jumps back to the condition.
- In a *for* loop, it jumps to the update expression.

It is an error to use a continue statement outside a *while* or a *for* statement.

Syntax:

ContinueStatement :

```
continue ;
```

Example:

```
var index = 0;
var count = 0;
while (index < 5) {
   index++;
   if (index == 3)
      continue;
   count += index;
};
```

3.5.10 Return Statement

This statement can be used inside the function body to specify the function return value. If no return statement is specified, or none of the function return statements is executed, the function returns an empty string by default.

Syntax:

ReturnStatement :

return $Expression_{opt}$;

Example:

```
function square( x ) {
  if (!(Lang.isFloat(x))) return invalid;
  return x * x;
};
```

3.6 Libraries

WMLScript supports the usage of libraries.[17] Libraries are named collections of functions that belong logically together. These functions can be called by using a dot ('.') separator with the library name and the function name with parameters.

```
An example of a library function call:
function dummy(str) {
  var i = String.elementAt(str,3," ");
};
```

[17]Compatibility note: ECMAScript does not support libraries, it supports a set of predefined objects with attributes. WMLScript uses libraries to support similar functionality.

3.6.1 Standard Libraries

Standard libraries are specified in more detail in the *WMLScript Standard Libraries Specification* [WMLSLibs].

3.7 Pragmas

WMLScript supports the usage of *pragmas* that specify compilation unit level information. Pragmas are specified at the beginning of the compilation unit before any function declaration. All pragmas start with the keyword `use` and are followed by pragma specific attributes.

Syntax:

CompilationUnit :

Pragmas$_{opt}$ *FunctionDeclarations*

Pragmas :

Pragma

Pragmas Pragma

Pragma :

`use` *PragmaDeclaration* ;

PragmaDeclaration :

ExternalCompilationUnitPragma

AccessControlPragma

MetaPragma

The following sections contain more information about the supported pragmas.

3.7.1 External Compilation Units

WMLScript compilation units can be accessed by using a URL. Thus, each WMLScript function can be accessed by specifying the URL of the WMLScript resource and its name. A `use url` pragma must be used when calling a function in an external compilation unit.

Syntax:

ExternalCompilationUnitPragma :

`url` *Identifier StringLiteral*

The `use url` pragma specifies the location (URL) of the external WMLScript resource and gives it a local *name*. This name can then be used inside the function declarations to make external function calls (see Section 3.4.2.2).

```
use url OtherScript "http://www.host.com/app/script"

function test(par1, par2) {
  return OtherScript#check(par1-par2);
};
```

The behavior of the previous example is the following:

- The pragma specifies a URL to a WMLScript compilation unit.
- The function call loads the compilation unit by using the given URL (`http://www.host.com/app/script`).
- The content of the compilation unit is verified and the specified function (`check`) is executed.

The `use url` pragma has its own namespace for local names. However, the local names must be unique within one compilation unit. The following URLs are supported:

- Uniform Resource Locators [RFC1738] without a hash mark (#) or a fragment identifier. The schemes supported are specified in [WAE].
- Relative URLs [RFC1808] without a hash mark (#) or a fragment identifier. The base URL is the URL that identifies the current compilation unit.

The given URL must be escaped according to the URL escaping rules. No compile time automatic escaping, URL syntax, or URL validity checking is performed.

3.7.2 Access Control

A WMLScript compilation unit can protect its content by using an *access control* pragma. Access control must be performed before calling external functions. It is an error for a compilation unit to contain more than one access control pragma.

Syntax:

AccessControlPragma :

`access` *AccessControlSpecifier*

AccessControlSpecifier :

`public`

`domain` *StringLiteral*

`path` *StringLiteral*

`domain` *StringLiteral* `path` *StringLiteral*

Every time a script calls an external function, an access control check is performed to determine whether the destination compilation unit allows access from the caller. Access control pragma is used to specify *domain* and *path* attributes against which these access control checks are performed. If a compilation unit has a domain and/or path attribute, the referring compilation unit's URL must match the values of the attributes. Matching is done as follows: The access domain is suffix-matched against the domain name portion of the referring URL, and the access path is prefix-matched against the path portion of the referring URL. Domain and path attributes follow the URL capitalization rules.

Domain suffix matching is done using the entire element of each subdomain and must match each element exactly (e.g., `www.wapforum.org` shall match `wapforum.org`, but shall not match `forum.org`).

Path prefix matching is done using entire path elements and must match each element exactly (e.g., `/X/Y` matches `/X`, but does not match `/XZ`).

The domain attribute defaults to the current compilation unit's domain. The path attribute defaults to the value "/".

To simplify the development of applications that may not know the absolute path to the current compilation unit, the path attribute accepts relative URLs [RFC1808]. The user agent converts the relative path to an absolute path and then performs prefix matching against the path attribute.

Given the following access control attributes for a compilation unit:

```
use access domain "wapforum.org" path "/finance"
```

the following referring URLs would be allowed to call the external functions specified in this compilation unit:

```
http://wapforum.org/finance/money.cgi
https://www.wapforum.org/finance/markets.cgi
http://www.wapforum.org/finance/demos/packages.cgi?x=123&y=456
```

The following referring URLs would not be allowed to call the external functions:

```
http://www.test.net/finance
http://www.wapforum.org/internal/foo.wml
```

A compilation unit can specify that all external functions have public access (i.e., calls to external functions are accepted from any compilation unit) by using the `public` access control attribute:

```
use access public
```

By default, access control is enabled.

3.7.3 Meta-Information

Pragmas can also be used to specify compilation unit specific meta-information. Meta-information is specified with property names and values. This specification does not define any properties, nor does it define how user agents must interpret metadata. User agents are not required to act on the metadata.

Syntax:

MetaPragma :

`meta` *MetaSpecifier*

MetaSpecifier :

MetaName

MetaHttpEquiv

MetaUserAgent

MetaName :

`name` *MetaBody*

MetaHttpEquiv :

`http equiv` *MetaBody*

MetaUserAgent :

    `user agent` *MetaBody*

MetaBody :

    MetaPropertyName MetaContent $MetaScheme_{opt}$

Meta-pragmas have three attributes: *property name, content* (the value of the property), and optional *scheme* (specifies a form or structure that may be used to interpret the property value—the values vary depending on the type of metadata). The attribute values are string literals.

3.7.3.1 Name

Name meta-pragma is used to specify meta-information intended to be used by the origin servers. The user agent should ignore any metadata named with this attribute. Network servers should not emit WMLScript content containing meta-name pragmas.

```
use meta name "Created" "18-March-1998"
```

3.7.3.2 HTTP Equiv

HTTP equiv meta-pragma is used to specify meta-information that indicates that the property should be interpreted as an HTTP header (see [RFC2068]). Metadata named with this attribute should be converted to a WSP or HTTP response header if the compilation unit is compiled before it arrives at the user agent.

```
use meta http equiv "Keywords" "Script,Language"
```

3.7.3.3 User Agent

User agent meta-pragma is used to specify meta-information intended to be used by the user agents. This metadata must be delivered to the user agent and must not be removed by any network intermediary.

```
use meta user agent "Type" "Test"
```

4. Automatic Data Type Conversion Rules

In some cases, WMLScript operators require specific data types as their operands. WMLScript supports automatic data type conversions to meet the requirements of these operators. The following sections describe the different conversions in detail.

4.1 General Conversion Rules

WMLScript is a weakly typed language, and the variable declarations do not specify a type. However, internally, the language handles the following data types:

- *Boolean*: Represents a Boolean value of true or false.
- *Integer*: Represents an integer value.
- *Floating-point*: Represents a floating-point value.

- *String*: Represents a sequence of characters.
- *Invalid*: Represents a type with a single value `invalid`.

A variable at any given time can contain a value of one of these types. WMLScript provides an operator *typeof*, which can be used to determine what is the current type of a variable or any expression (no conversions are performed).

Each WMLScript operator accepts a predefined set of operand types. If the provided operands are not of the right data type, an automatic conversion must take place. The following sections specify the legal automatic conversions between two data types.

4.1.1 Conversions to String

Legal conversions from other data types to string are:

- Integer value must be converted to a string of decimal digits that follows the numeric string grammar rules for decimal integer literals. See Section 5.4 for more information about the numeric string grammar.
- Floating-point value must be converted to an implementation-dependent string representation that follows the numeric string grammar rules for decimal floating-point literals (see Section 5.4 for more information about the numeric string grammar). The resulting string representation must be equal to the original value (e.g., `.5` can be represented as `"0.5"`, `".5e0"`, etc.).
- The Boolean value `true` is converted to string `"true"`, and the value `false` is converted to string `"false"`.
- `Invalid` can not be converted to a string value.

4.1.2 Conversions to Integer

Legal conversions from other data types to integer are:

- A string can be converted into an integer value only if it contains a decimal representation of an integer number (see Section 5.4 for the numeric string grammar rules for a decimal integer literal).
- Floating-point value cannot be converted to an integer value.
- The Boolean value `true` is converted to integer value 1, `false` to 0.
- `Invalid` can not be converted to an integer value.

4.1.3 Conversions to Floating-Point

Legal conversions from other data types to floating-point are:

- A string can be converted into a floating-point value only if it contains a valid representation of a floating-point number (see Section 5.4 for the numeric string grammar rules for a decimal floating-point literal).
- An integer value is converted to a corresponding floating-point value.

- The Boolean value `true` is converted to a floating-point value 1.0, `false` to 0.0.
- `Invalid` cannot be converted to a floating-point value.

The conversions between a string and a floating-point type must be transitive within the ability of the data types to accurately represent the value. A conversion could result in loss of precision.

4.1.4 Conversions to Boolean

Legal conversions from other data types to Boolean are:

- The empty string ("") is converted to `false`. All other strings are converted to `true`.
- An integer value 0 is converted to `false`. All other integer numbers are converted to `true`.
- A floating-point value 0.0 is converted to `false`. All other floating-point numbers are converted to `true`.
- `Invalid` can not be converted to a Boolean value.

4.1.5 Conversions to Invalid

There are no legal conversion rules for converting any of the other data types to an invalid type. `Invalid` is either a result of an operation error or a literal value. In most cases, an operator that has an `invalid` value as an operand evaluates to `invalid` (see the operators in Sections 3.3.8, 3.3.9, and 3.3.10 for the exceptions to this rule).

4.1.6 Summary

The following table contains a summary of the legal conversions between data types:

GIVEN \ USED AS:	BOOLEAN	INTEGER	FLOATING-POINT	STRING
Boolean true	-	1	1.0	"true"
Boolean false	-	0	0.0	"false"
Integer 0	False	-	0.0	"0"
Any other integer	True	-	Floating-point Value of number	String representation of a decimal integer
Floating-point 0.0	False	Illegal	-	Implementation-dependent string representation of a floating-point value; e.g., "0.0"

GIVEN \ USED AS:	BOOLEAN	INTEGER	FLOATING-POINT	STRING
Any other floating-point	True	Illegal	-	Implementation-dependent string representation of a floating-point value
Empty string	False	Illegal	Illegal	-
Non-empty string	True	Integer value of its string representation (if valid—see Section 5.4 for numeric string grammar for decimal integer literals) or illegal	Floating-point value of its string representation (if valid—see Section 5.4 for numeric string grammar for decimal floating-point literals) or illegal	-
invalid	Illegal	Illegal	Illegal	Illegal

4.2 Operator Data Type Conversion Rules

The previous conversion rules specify when a legal conversion is possible between two data types. WMLScript operators use these rules, the operand data type and values, to select the operation to be performed (in case the type is used to specify the operation) and to perform the data type conversions needed for the selected operation. The rules are specified in the following way:

- The additional conversion rules are specified in steps. Each step is performed in the given order until the operation and the data types for its operands are specified and the return value defined.
- If the type of the operand value matches the required type, then the value is used as such.
- If the operand value does not match the required type, then a conversion from the current data type to the required one is attempted:
    - *Legal conversion*: Conversion can be done only if the general conversion rules (see Section 4.1) specify a *legal* conversion from the current operator data type to the required one.
    - *Illegal conversion*: Conversion cannot be done if the general conversion rules (see Section 4.1) do not specify a *legal* conversion from the current type to the required type.
- If a legal conversion rule is specified for the operand (unary) or for all operands, then the conversion is performed, the operation performed on the converted val-

ues, and the result returned as the value of the operation. If a legal conversion results in an `invalid` value, then the operation returns an `invalid` value.

- If no legal conversion is specified for one or more of the operands, then no conversion is performed and the next step in the additional conversion rules is performed.

The following table contains the operator data type conversion rules based on the given operand data types:

<table>
<tr><th>OPERAND TYPES</th><th>ADDITIONAL CONVERSION RULES</th><th>EXAMPLES</th></tr>
<tr><td>Boolean(s)</td><td>• If the operand is of type Boolean or can be converted into a Boolean value[18], then perform a Boolean operation and return its value; otherwise,
• Return invalid.</td><td>true && 3.4 => boolean
1 && 0 => boolean
"A" || "" => boolean
!42 => boolean
!invalid => invalid
3 && invalid => invalid</td></tr>
<tr><td>Integer(s)</td><td>• If the operand is of type integer or can be converted into an integer value[18], then perform an integer operation and return its value; otherwise,
• Return invalid.</td><td>"7" << 2 => integer
true << 2 => integer
7.2 >> 3 => invalid
2.1 div 4 => invalid</td></tr>
<tr><td>Floating-point(s)</td><td>• If the operand is of type floating-point or can be converted into a floating-point value[18], then perform a floating-point operation and return its value; otherwise,
• Return invalid.</td><td>-</td></tr>
<tr><td>String(s)</td><td>• If the operand is of type string or can be converted into a string value[18], then perform a string operation and return its value; otherwise,
• Return invalid.</td><td>-</td></tr>
<tr><td>Integer or floating-point (unary)</td><td>• If the operand is of type integer or can be converted into an integer value, then perform an integer operation and return its value; otherwise,
• If the operand is of type floating-point or can be converted into a floating-point value[18], then perform a floating-point operation and return its value; otherwise,
• Return invalid.</td><td>+10 => integer
-10.3 => float
-"33" => integer
+"47.3" => float
+true => integer 1
-false => integer 0
="ABC" => invalid
="9e9999" => invalid</td></tr>
</table>

OPERAND TYPES	ADDITIONAL CONVERSION RULES	EXAMPLES

Integers or floating-points	• If at least one of the operands is of type floating-points, then convert the remaining operand to a floating-point value, perform a floating-point operation, and return its value; otherwise,
	• If the operands are of type integer or can be converted into integer values[18], then perform an integer operation and return its value; otherwise,
	• If the operands can be converted into floating-point values[18], then perform a floating-point operation and return its value; otherwise,
	• Return `invalid`.
		`100/10.3 => float`
		`33*44 => integer`
		`"10"*3 => integer`
		`3.4*"4.3" => float`
		`"10"-"2" => integer`
		`"2.3"*"3" => float`
		`3.2*"A" => invalid`
		`.9*"9e999" => invalid`
		`invalid*1 => invalid`

Integers, floating-points, or strings	• If at least one of the operands is of type string, then convert the remaining operand to a string value, perform a string operation, and return its value; otherwise,
	• If at least one of the operands is of type floating-point, then convert the remaining operand to a floating-point value, perform a floating-point operation, and return its value; otherwise,
	• If the operands are of type integer or can be converted into integer values[18], then perform an integer operation and return its value; otherwise,
	• Return `invalid`.
		`12+3 => integer`
		`32.4+65 => float`
		`"12"+5.4 => string`
		`43.2<77 => float`
		`"Hey"<56 => string`
		`2.7+"4.2" => string`
		`9.9+true => float`
		`3<false => integer`
		`"A"+invalid => invalid`

Any	Any type is accepted.	`a = 37.3 => float` `b = typeof "s" => string`

[18]Conversion can be done if the general conversion rules (see Section 4.1) specify a legal conversion from the current type to the required type.

4.3 Summary of Operators and Conversions

The following sections contain a summary on how the conversion rules are applied to WMLScript operators and what are their possible return value types.

4.3.1 Single-Typed Operators

Operators that accept operands of one specific type use the general conversion rules directly. The following list contains all single type WMLScript operators:

<table>
<tr><th>OPERATOR</th><th>OPERAND TYPES</th><th>RESULT TYPE[19]</th><th>OPERATION PERFORMED</th></tr>
<tr><td>!</td><td>Boolean</td><td>Boolean</td><td>Logical NOT (unary)</td></tr>
<tr><td>&&</td><td>Booleans</td><td>Boolean</td><td>Logical AND</td></tr>
<tr><td>||</td><td>Booleans</td><td>Boolean</td><td>Logical OR</td></tr>
<tr><td>~</td><td>Integer</td><td>Integer</td><td>Bitwise NOT (unary)</td></tr>
<tr><td><<</td><td>Integers</td><td>Integer</td><td>Bitwise left shift</td></tr>
<tr><td>>></td><td>Integers</td><td>Integer</td><td>Bitwise right shift with sign</td></tr>
<tr><td>>>></td><td>Integers</td><td>Integer</td><td>Bitwise right shift with zero fill</td></tr>
<tr><td>&</td><td>Integers</td><td>Integer</td><td>Bitwise AND</td></tr>
<tr><td>^</td><td>Integers</td><td>Integer</td><td>Bitwise XOR</td></tr>
<tr><td>|</td><td>Integers</td><td>Integer</td><td>Bitwise OR</td></tr>
<tr><td>%</td><td>Integers</td><td>Integer</td><td>Remainder</td></tr>
<tr><td>div</td><td>Integers</td><td>Integer</td><td>Integer division</td></tr>
<tr><td><<=, >>=, >>>=, &=, ^=, |=</td><td>First operand: variable
Second operand: integer</td><td>Integer</td><td>Assignment with bitwise operation</td></tr>
<tr><td>%=, div=</td><td>First operand: variable
Second operand: integer</td><td>Integer</td><td>Assignment with numeric operation</td></tr>
</table>

4.3.2 Multi-Typed Operators

The following sections contain the operators that accept multi-typed operands:

[19]All operators may have an invalid result type.

OPERATOR	OPERAND TYPES	RESULT TYPE[20]	OPERATION PERFORMED
++	Integer or floating-point	Integer/floating-point	Pre- or post-increment (unary)
—	Integer or floating-point	Integer/floating-point	Pre- or post-decrement (unary)
+	Integer or floating-point	Integer/floating-point	Unary plus
-	Integer or floating-point	Integer/floating-point	Unary minus (negation)
*	Integers or floating-points	Integer/floating-point	Multiplication
/	Integers or floating-points	Integer-floating-point	Division
-	Integers or floating-points	Integer/floating point	Subtraction
+	Integers, floating-points, or strings	Integer/floating-point/ string	Addition or string concatenation
<, <=	Integers, floating-points, or strings	Boolean	Less than, less than or equal
>, >=	Integers, floating-points, or strings	Boolean	Greater than, greater or equal
==	Integers, floating-points, or strings	Boolean	Equal (identical values)
!=	Integers, floating-points, or strings	Boolean	Not equal (different values)
*=, /=, -=	First operand: variable Second operand: integer or floating-point	Integer/floating-point	Assignment with numeric operation
+=	First operand: variable Second operand: integer, floating-point, or string	Integer/floating-point/ string	Assignment with addition or concatenation
typeof	Any	Integer[21]	Return internal data type (unary)
isvalid	Any	Boolean[21]	Check for validity (unary)
? :	First operand: Boolean Second operand: any Third operand: any	Any	Conditional expression
=	First operand: variable Second operand: any	Any	Assignment
,	First operand: any Second operand: any	Any	Multiple evaluation

[20]All operators (unless otherwise stated) may have an invalid result type.

[21]Operator does not generate an invalid result type.

5. WMLScript Grammar

The grammars used in this specification are based on [ECMA262]. Since WMLScript is not compliant with ECMAScript, the standard has been used only as the basis for defining WMLScript language.

5.1 Context-Free Grammars

This section describes the context-free grammars used in this specification to define the lexical and syntactic structure of a WMLScript program.

5.1.1 General

A *context-free grammar* consists of a number of *productions*. Each production has an abstract symbol called a *nonterminal* as its *left-hand side* and a sequence of one or more nonterminal and *terminal* symbols as its *right-hand side*. For each grammar, the terminal symbols are drawn from a specified alphabet.

A given context-free grammar specifies a *language*. It begins with a production consisting of a single distinguished nonterminal called the *goal symbol* followed by a (perhaps infinite) set of possible sequences of terminal symbols. They are the result of repeatedly replacing any nonterminal in the sequence with a right-hand side of a production for which the nonterminal is the left-hand side.

5.1.2 Lexical Grammar

A *lexical grammar* for WMLScript is given in Section 5.2. This grammar has as its terminal symbols the characters of the Universal Character set of ISO/IEC-10646 ([ISO10646]). It defines a set of productions, starting from the goal symbol *Input* that describes how sequences of characters are translated into a sequence of input elements.

Input elements other than whitespace and comments form the terminal symbols for the syntactic grammar for WMLScript and are called WMLScript *tokens*. These tokens are the reserved words, identifiers, literals, and punctuators of the WMLScript language. Simple whitespace and single-line comments are simply discarded and do not appear in the stream of input elements for the syntactic grammar. Likewise, a multiline comment is simply discarded if it contains no line terminator. But if a multiline comment contains one or more line terminators, then it is replaced by a single-line terminator, which becomes part of the stream of input elements for the syntactic grammar.

Productions of the lexical grammar are distinguished by having two colons "::" as separating punctuation.

5.1.3 Syntactic Grammar

The *syntactic grammar* for WMLScript is given in Section 5.3. This grammar has WMLScript tokens defined by the lexical grammar as its terminal symbols. It defines a set of productions, starting from the goal symbol *CompilationUnit*, that describe how sequences of tokens can form syntactically correct WMLScript programs.

When a stream of Unicode characters is to be parsed as a WMLScript, it is first converted to a stream of input elements by repeated application of the lexical grammar; this stream of input elements is then parsed by a single application of the syntax grammar. The program is syntactically in error if the tokens in the stream of input elements cannot be parsed as a single instance of the goal nonterminal *CompilationUnit*, with no tokens left over.

Productions of the syntactic grammar are distinguished by having just one colon ":" as punctuation.

5.1.4 Numeric String Grammar

A third grammar is used for translating strings into numeric values. This grammar is similar to the part of the lexical grammar having to do with numeric literals and has as its terminal symbols the characters of the Unicode character set. This grammar appears in Section 5.4.

Productions of the numeric string grammar are distinguished by having three colons ":::" as punctuation.

5.1.5 Grammar Notation

Terminal symbols of the lexical and string grammars and some of the terminal symbols of the syntactic grammar are shown in `fixed width` font, both in the productions of the grammars and throughout this specification whenever the text directly refers to such a terminal symbol. These are to appear in a program exactly as written.

Nonterminal symbols are shown in *italic* type. The definition of a nonterminal is introduced by the name of the nonterminal being defined followed by one or more colons. (The number of colons indicates to which grammar the production belongs.) One or more alternative right-hand sides for the nonterminal then follow on succeeding lines. For example, the syntactic definition:

> *WhileStatement* :
>
> `while` (*Expression*) *Statement*

states that the nonterminal *WhileStatement* represents the token `while`, followed by a left parenthesis token, followed by an *Expression*, followed by a right parenthesis token, followed by a *Statement*. The occurrences of *Expression* and *Statement* are themselves nonterminals. As another example, the syntactic definition:

> *ArgumentList* :
>
> *AssignmentExpression*
>
> *ArgumentList* , *AssignmentExpression*

states that an *ArgumentList* may represent either a single *AssignmentExpression* or an *ArgumentList*, followed by a comma, followed by an *AssignmentExpression*. This definition of *ArgumentList* is *recursive*; that is to say, it is defined in terms of itself. The result is that an *ArgumentList* may contain any positive number of arguments, separated by commas, where each argument expression is an *AssignmentExpression*. Such recursive definitions of nonterminals are common.

The subscripted suffix "*opt*", which may appear after a terminal or nonterminal, indicates an *optional symbol*. The alternative containing the optional symbol actually specifies two right-hand sides, one that omits the optional element and one that includes it. This means that:

VariableDeclaration :

Identifier VariableInitializer$_{opt}$

is a convenient abbreviation for:

VariableDeclaration :

Identifier

Identifier VariableInitializer

and that:

IterationStatement :

`for` (*Expression*$_{opt}$; *Expression*$_{opt}$; *Expression*$_{opt}$) *Statement*

is a convenient abbreviation for:

IterationStatement :

`for` (; *Expression*$_{opt}$; *Expression*$_{opt}$) *Statement*

`for` (*Expression* ; *Expression*$_{opt}$; *Expression*$_{opt}$) *Statement*

which in turn is an abbreviation for:

IterationStatement :

`for` (; ; *Expression*$_{opt}$) *Statement*

`for` (; *Expression* ; *Expression*$_{opt}$) *Statement*

`for` (*Expression* ; ; *Expression*$_{opt}$) *Statement*

`for` (*Expression* ; *Expression* ; *Expression*$_{opt}$) *Statement*

which in turn is an abbreviation for:

IterationStatement :

`for` (; ;) *Statement*

`for` (; ; *Expression*) *Statement*

`for` (; *Expression* ;) *Statement*

`for` (; *Expression* ; *Expression*) *Statement*

`for` (*Expression* ; ;) *Statement*

`for` (*Expression* ; ; *Expression*) *Statement*

`for` (*Expression* ; *Expression* ;) *Statement*

`for` (*Expression* ; *Expression* ; *Expression*) *Statement*

Therefore, the nonterminal *IterationStatement* actually has eight alternative right-hand sides.

Any number of occurrences of *LineTerminator* may appear between any two consecutive tokens in the stream of input elements without affecting the syntactic acceptability of the program.

When the words "one of" follow the colon(s) in a grammar definition, they signify that each of the terminal symbols on the following line or lines is an alternative definition. For example, the lexical grammar for WMLScript contains the production:

ZeroToThree :: one of

```
0    1    2    3
```

which is merely a convenient abbreviation for:

ZeroToThree ::

```
0
1
2
3
```

When an alternative in a production of the lexical grammar or the numeric string grammar appears to be a multicharacter token, it represents the sequence of characters that would make up such a token.

The right-hand side of a production may specify that certain expansions are not permitted by using the phrase "but not" and then indicating the expansions to be excluded. For example, the production:

Identifier ::

IdentifierName but not *ReservedWord*

means that the nonterminal *Identifier* may be replaced by any sequence of characters that could replace *IdentifierName* provided that the same sequence of characters could not replace *ReservedWord*.

Finally, a few nonterminal symbols are described by a descriptive phrase in roman type in cases where it would be impractical to list all the alternatives.

SourceCharacter:

any Unicode character

5.1.6 Source Text

WMLScript source text is represented as a sequence of characters representable using the Universal Character set of ISO/IEC-10646 ([ISO10646]). Currently, this character set is identical to Unicode 2.0 ([UNICODE]). Within this document, the terms ISO10646 and Unicode are used interchangeably and will indicate the same document character set.

SourceCharacter ::

any Unicode character

There is no requirement that WMLScript documents be encoded using the full Unicode encoding (e.g., UCS-4). Any character encoding ("charset") that contains an inclusive subset of the characters in Unicode may be used (e.g., US-ASCII, ISO-8859-1, etc.).

Every WMLScript program can be represented using only ASCII characters (which are equivalent to the first 128 Unicode characters). Non-ASCII Unicode characters may appear only within comments and string literals. In string literals, any Unicode character may also be expressed as a Unicode escape sequence consisting of six ASCII characters, namely \u plus four hexadecimal digits. Within a comment, such an escape sequence is effectively ignored as part of the comment. Within a string literal, the Unicode escape sequence contributes one character to the string value of the literal.

5.2 WMLScript Lexical Grammar

The following contains the specification of the lexical grammar for WMLScript:

SourceCharacter ::

any Unicode character

WhiteSpace ::

<TAB>

<VT>

<FF>

<SP>

<LF>

<CR>

LineTerminator ::

<LF>

<CR>

<CR><LF>

Comment ::

MultiLineComment

SingleLineComment

MultiLineComment ::

/* *MultiLineCommentChars*$_{opt}$ */

MultiLineCommentChars ::

MultiLineNotAsteriskChar MultiLineCommentChars$_{opt}$

* *PostAsteriskCommentChars*$_{opt}$

PostAsteriskCommentChars ::

MultiLineNotForwardSlashOrAsteriskChar MultiLineCommentChars$_{opt}$

* *PostAsteriskCommentChars*$_{opt}$

MultiLineNotAsteriskChar ::

SourceCharacter but not *asterisk* *

MultiLineNotForwardSlashOrAsteriskChar ::

SourceCharacter but not *forward-slash* / or *asterisk* *

SingleLineComment ::

  // *SingleLineCommentChars*$_{opt}$

SingleLineCommentChars ::

  SingleLineCommentChar SingleLineCommentChars$_{opt}$

SingleLineCommentChar ::

  SourceCharacter but not *LineTerminator*

Token ::

  ReservedWord

  Identifier

  Punctuator

  Literal

ReservedWord ::

  Keyword

  KeywordNotUsedByWMLScript

  FutureReservedWord

Keyword :: one of

```
access      equiv       meta        var
agent       extern      name        while
break       for         path        url
continue    function    public
div         header      return
div=        http        typeof
domain      if          use
else        isvalid     user
```

KeywordNotUsedByWMLScript :: one of

```
delete      null
in          this
lib         void
new         with
```

FutureReservedWord :: one of

```
case        default     finally     super
catch       do          import      switch
class       enum        private     throw
const       export      sizeof      try
debugger    extends     struct
```

Identifier ::

  IdentifierName but not *ReservedWord*

IdentifierName ::

IdentifierLetter

IdentifierName IdentifierLetter

IdentifierName DecimalDigit

IdentifierLetter :: one of[22]

```
a b c d e f g h i j k l m n o p q r s t u v w x y z
A B C D E F G H I J K L M N O P Q R S T U V W X Y Z
_
```

DecimalDigit :: one of

```
0  1  2  3  4  5  6  7  8  9
```

Punctuator :: one of[23]

```
=      >      <      ==     <=     >=
!=     ,      !      ~      ?      :
.      &&     ||     ++     --     +
-      *      /      &      |      ^
%      <<     >>     >>>    +=     -=
*=     /=     &=     |=     ^=     %=
<<=    >>=    >>>=   (      )      {
}      ;      #
```

Literal ::[24]

InvalidLiteral

BooleanLiteral

NumericLiteral

StringLiteral

InvalidLiteral ::[25]

invalid

BooleanLiteral ::[26]

true

false

NumericLiteral ::

DecimalIntegerLiteral

[22]Compatibility note: ECMAScript supports the use of dollar sign ($) in identifier names, too.

[23]Compatibility note: ECMAScript supports arrays and square brackets ([ ]), too.

[24]Compatibility note: ECMAScript supports *Null* literal, too.

[25]Compatibility note: ECMAScript does not support *invalid*.

[26]Compatibility note: ECMAScript supports both lower and uppercase Boolean literals.

HexIntegerLiteral

OctalIntegerLiteral

DecimalFloatLiteral

DecimalIntegerLiteral ::

`0`

NonZeroDigit $DecimalDigits_{opt}$

NonZeroDigit :: one of

`1 2 3 4 5 6 7 8 9`

HexIntegerLiteral ::

`0x` *HexDigit*

`0X` *HexDigit*

HexIntegerLiteral HexDigit

HexDigit :: one of

`0 1 2 3 4 5 6 7 8 9 a b c d e f A B C D E F`

OctalIntegerLiteral ::

0 *OctalDigit*

OctalIntegerLiteral OctalDigit

OctalDigit :: one of

`0 1 2 3 4 5 6 7`

DecimalFloatLiteral ::

DecimalIntegerLiteral . $DecimalDigits_{opt}$ $ExponentPart_{opt}$

. *DecimalDigits* $ExponentPart_{opt}$

DecimalIntegerLiteral ExponentPart

DecimalDigits ::

DecimalDigit

DecimalDigits DecimalDigit

ExponentPart ::

ExponentIndicator SignedInteger

ExponentIndicator :: one of

`e E`

SignedInteger ::

DecimalDigits

\+ *DecimalDigits*

\- *DecimalDigits*

StringLiteral ::

" $DoubleStringCharacters_{opt}$ "

' $SingleStringCharacters_{opt}$ '

DoubleStringCharacters ::

DoubleStringCharacter DoubleStringCharacters$_{opt}$

SingleStringCharacters ::

SingleStringCharacter SingleStringCharacters$_{opt}$

DoubleStringCharacter ::

SourceCharacter but not *double-quote* "or *backslash* \ or *LineTerminator*

EscapeSequence

SingleStringCharacter ::

SourceCharacter but not *single-quote* 'or *backslash* \ or *LineTerminator*

EscapeSequence

EscapeSequence ::

CharacterEscapeSequence

OctalEscapeSequence

HexEscapeSequence

UnicodeEscapeSequence

CharacterEscapeSequence ::

\ *SingleEscapeCharacter*

SingleEscapeCharacter :: one of

`'    "    \    /    b    f    n    r    t`

HexEscapeSequence ::

\x *HexDigit HexDigit*

OctalEscapeSequence ::

\ *OctalDigit*

\ *OctalDigit OctalDigit*

\ *ZeroToThree OctalDigit OctalDigit*

ZeroToThree :: one of

`0    1    2    3`

UnicodeEscapeSequence ::

\u *HexDigit HexDigit HexDigit HexDigit*

5.3 WMLScript Syntactic Grammar

The following contains the specification of the syntactic grammar for WMLScript:

PrimaryExpression :[27]

Identifier

Literal

(*Expression*)

[27]Compatibility note: ECMAScript supports objects and *this*, too.

CallExpression :[28]

  PrimaryExpression

  LocalScriptFunctionCall

  ExternalScriptFunctionCall

  LibraryFunctionCall

LocalScriptFunctionCall :

  FunctionName Arguments

ExternalScriptFunctionCall :

  ExternalScriptName # *FunctionName Arguments*

LibraryFunctionCall :

  LibraryName . *FunctionName Arguments*

FunctionName :

  Identifier

ExternalScriptName :

  Identifier

LibraryName :

  Identifier

Arguments :

  ( )

  (*ArgumentList*)

ArgumentList :

  AssignmentExpression

  ArgumentList , *AssignmentExpression*

PostfixExpression :

  CallExpression

  Identifier ++

  Identifier –

UnaryExpression :[29]

  PostfixExpression

  `typeof` *UnaryExpression*

[28]Compatibility note: ECMAScript support for arrays ([]) and object allocation (*new*) removed. *MemberExpression* is used for specifying library functions; e.g., `String.length("abc")`, not for accessing members of an object.

[29]Compatibility note: ECMAScript operators *delete* and *void* are not supported. *parseInt* and *parseFloat* are supported as library functions. ECMAScript does not support operator *isvalid*.

isvalid *UnaryExpression*

++ *Identifier*

– *Identifier*

+ *UnaryExpression*

- *UnaryExpression*

~ *UnaryExpression*

! *UnaryExpression*

MultiplicativeExpression :[30]

UnaryExpression

MultiplicativeExpression * *UnaryExpression*

MultiplicativeExpression / *UnaryExpression*

MultiplicativeExpression div *UnaryExpression*

MultiplicativeExpression % *UnaryExpression*

AdditiveExpression :

MultiplicativeExpression

AdditiveExpression + *MultiplicativeExpression*

AdditiveExpression - *MultiplicativeExpression*

ShiftExpression :

AdditiveExpression

ShiftExpression << *AdditiveExpression*

ShiftExpression >> *AdditiveExpression*

ShiftExpression >>> *AdditiveExpression*

RelationalExpression :

ShiftExpression

RelationalExpression < *ShiftExpression*

RelationalExpression > *ShiftExpression*

RelationalExpression <= *ShiftExpression*

RelationalExpression >= *ShiftExpression*

EqualityExpression :

RelationalExpression

EqualityExpression == *RelationalExpression*

EqualityExpression != *RelationalExpression*

BitwiseANDExpression :

EqualityExpression

BitwiseANDExpression & *EqualityExpression*

[30]Compatibility note: Integer division (*div*) is not supported by ECMAScript.

BitwiseXORExpression :

BitwiseANDExpression

BitwiseXORExpression ^ *BitwiseANDExpression*

BitwiseORExpression :

BitwiseXORExpression

BitwiseORExpression | *BitwiseXORExpression*

LogicalANDExpression :

BitwiseORExpression

LogicalANDExpression && *BitwiseORExpression*

LogicalORExpression :

LogicalANDExpression

LogicalORExpression || *LogicalANDExpression*

ConditionalExpression :

LogicalORExpression

LogicalORExpression ? *AssignmentExpression* : *AssignmentExpression*

AssignmentExpression :

ConditionalExpression

Identifier AssignmentOperator AssignmentExpression

AssignmentOperator :: `one of`

`= *= /= %= += -= <<= >>= >>>= &= ^= |= div=`

Expression :

AssignmentExpression

Expression , *AssignmentExpression*

Statement :[31]

Block

VariableStatement

EmptyStatement

ExpressionStatement

IfStatement

IterationStatement

ContinueStatement

BreakStatement

ReturnStatement

Block :

{ $StatementList_{opt}$ }

[31]Compatibility note: ECMAScript *with* statement is not supported.

StatementList :

Statement

StatementList Statement

VariableStatement :

`var` *VariableDeclarationList* ;

VariableDeclarationList :

VariableDeclaration

VariableDeclarationList , *VariableDeclaration*

VariableDeclaration :

Identifier $VariableInitializer_{opt}$

VariableInitializer :

= *ConditionalExpression*

EmptyStatement :

;

ExpressionStatement :

Expression ;

IfStatement :[32]

`if` (*Expression*) *Statement* else *Statement*

`if` (*Expression*) *Statement*

IterationStatement :[33]

WhileStatement

ForStatement

WhileStatement :

`while` (*Expression*) *Statement*

ForStatement :

`for` ($Expression_{opt}$; $Expression_{opt}$; $Expression_{opt}$) *Statement*

`for` (var *VariableDeclarationList* ; $Expression_{opt}$; $Expression_{opt}$) *Statement*

ContinueStatement :[34]

`continue ;`

BreakStatement :[35]

`break ;`

ReturnStatement :

`return` $Expression_{opt}$;

[32]*else* is always tied to the closest *if*.

[33]Compatibility note: ECMAScript *for in* statement is not supported.

[34]Continue statement can only be used inside a *while* or a *for* statement.

[35]Break statement can only be used inside a *while* or a *for* statement.

FunctionDeclaration :[36]

  `extern`$_{opt}$ `function` *Identifier* (*FormalParameterList*$_{opt}$) *Block* ;$_{opt}$

FormalParameterList :

  Identifier

  FormalParameterList , *Identifier*

CompilationUnit :

  Pragmas$_{opt}$ *FunctionDeclarations*

Pragmas :[37]

  Pragma

  Pragmas Pragma

Pragma :

  `use` *PragmaDeclaration* ;

PragmaDeclaration :

  ExternalCompilationUnitPragma

  AccessControlPragma

  MetaPragma

ExternalCompilationUnitPragma :

  `url` *Identifier StringLiteral*

AccessControlPragma :[38]

  `access` *AccessControlSpecifier*

AccessControlSpecifier :

  `public`

  `domain` *StringLiteral*

  `path` *StringLiteral*

  `domain` *StringLiteral* path *StringLiteral*

MetaPragma :

  `meta` *MetaSpecifier*

MetaSpecifier :

  MetaName

  MetaHttpEquiv

  MetaUserAgent

MetaName :

  `name` *MetaBody*

[36]Compatibility note: ECMAScript does not support keyword *extern*.

[37]Compatibility note: ECMAScript does not support *pragmas*.

[38]Compilation unit can contain only one *access control* pragma.

MetaHttpEquiv :

`http equiv` *MetaBody*

MetaUserAgent :

`user agent` *MetaBody*

MetaBody :

MetaPropertyName MetaContent $MetaScheme_{opt}$

MetaPropertyName :

StringLiteral

MetaContent :

StringLiteral

MetaScheme :

StringLiteral

FunctionDeclarations :

FunctionDeclaration

FunctionDeclarations FunctionDeclaration

5.4 Numeric String Grammar

The following contains the specification of the numeric string grammar for WMLScript. This grammar is used for translating strings into numeric values. This grammar is similar to the part of the lexical grammar having to do with numeric literals and has as its terminal symbols the characters of the Unicode character set.

The following grammar can be used to convert strings into the following numeric literal values:

- *Decimal Integer Literal*: Use the following productions starting from the goal symbol *StringDecimalIntegerLiteral*.
- *Decimal Floating-Point Literal*: Use the following productions starting from the goal symbol *StringDecimalFloatingPointLiteral*.

StringDecimalIntegerLiteral :::

$StrWhiteSpace_{opt}$ *StrDecimalIntegerLiteral* $StrWhiteSpace_{opt}$

StringDecimalFloatingPointLiteral :::

$StrWhiteSpace_{opt}$ *StrDecimalIntegerLiteral* $StrWhiteSpace_{opt}$

$StrWhiteSpace_{opt}$ *StrDecimalFloatingPointLiteral* $StrWhiteSpace_{opt}$

StrWhiteSpace :::

StrWhiteSpaceChar $StrWhiteSpace_{opt}$

StrWhiteSpaceChar :::

any Unicode character with character code less than or equal to 32

StrDecimalIntegerLiteral :::

StrDecimalDigits

+ *StrDecimalDigits*

- *StrDecimalDigits*

StrDecimalFloatingPointLiteral :::

StrDecimalDigits . $StrDecimalDigits_{opt}$ $StrExponentPart_{opt}$

. *StrDecimalDigits* $StrExponentPart_{opt}$

StrDecimalDigits StrExponentPart

StrDecimalDigits :::

StrDecimalDigit

StrDecimalDigits StrDecimalDigit

StrDecimalDigit ::: `one of`

`0 1 2 3 4 5 6 7 8 9`

StrExponentPart :::

StrExponentIndicator StrSignedInteger

StrExponentIndicator ::: `one of`

`e E`

StrSignedInteger :::

StrDecimalDigits

+ *StrDecimalDigits*

– *StrDecimalDigits*

6. WMLScript Bytecode Interpreter

The textual format of WMLScript language must be compiled into a binary format before it can be interpreted by the WMLScript bytecode interpreter. *WMLScript compiler* encodes one WMLScript compilation unit into WMLScript bytecode using the encoding format presented in Chapter 7, "WMLScript Standard Libraries Specification." A WMLScript *compilation unit* (see Section 5.1.3) is a unit containing pragmas and any number of WMLScript functions. WMLScript compiler takes one compilation unit as input and generates the WMLScript bytecode as its output.

6.1 Interpreter Architecture

WMLScript interpreter takes WMLScript bytecode as its input and executes encoded functions as they are called. Figure 6.1 contains the main parts related to WMLScript bytecode interpretation.

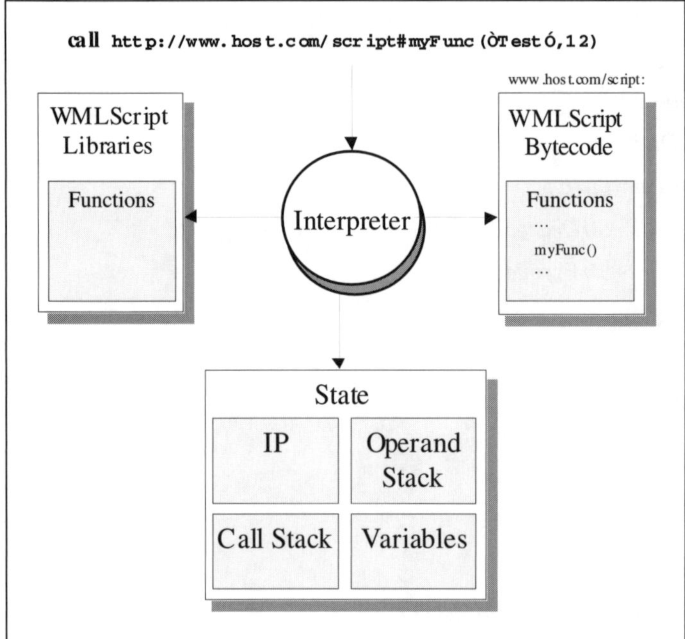

Figure 6.1 General architecture of the WMLScript interpreter.

The WMLScript interpreter can be used to call and execute functions in a compilation unit encoded as WMLScript bytecode. Each function specifies the number of *parameters* it accepts and the *instructions* used to express its behavior. Thus, a call to a WMLScript function must specify the function, the function call arguments, and the compilation unit in which the function is declared. Once the execution completes normally, the WMLScript interpreter returns the *control* and the *return value* back to the caller.

Execution of a WMLScript function means interpreting the instructions residing in the WMLScript bytecode. While a function is being interpreted, the WMLScript interpreter maintains the following *state* information:

- *IP (Instruction Pointer)*: This points to an instruction in the bytecode that is being interpreted.
- *Variables*: Maintenance of function parameters and variables.
- *Operand stack*: It is used for expression evaluation and passing arguments to called functions and back to the caller.
- *Function call stack*: WMLScript function can call other functions in the current or separate compilation unit or make calls to library functions. The function call stack maintains the information about functions and their return addresses.

6.2 WMLScript and URLs

The World Wide Web is a network of information and devices. Three areas of specification ensure widespread interoperability:

- A *unified naming model*. Naming is implemented with Uniform Resource Locators (URLs), which provide a standard way to name any network resource. See [RFC1738].
- Standard *protocols* to transport information (e.g., HTTP).
- Standard *content types* (e.g., HTML, WMLScript).

WMLScript assumes the same reference architecture as HTML and the World Wide Web. WMLScript compilation unit is named using URLs and can be fetched over standard protocols that have HTTP semantics, such as [WSP]. URLs are defined in [RFC1738]. The character set used to specify URLs is also defined in [RFC1738].

In WMLScript, URLs are used in the following situations:

- When a user agent wants to make a WMLScript call (see Section 6.2.4)
- When specifying *external compilation units* (see Section 3.7.1)
- When specifying *access control information* (see Section 3.7.2)

6.2.1 URL Schemes

A WMLScript interpreter must implement the URL schemes specified in [WAE].

6.2.2 Fragment Anchors

WMLScript has adopted the HTML *de facto* standard of naming locations within a resource. A WMLScript fragment anchor is specified by the document URL, followed by a hash mark (#), followed by a fragment identifier. WMLScript uses fragment anchors to identify individual WMLScript functions within a WMLScript compilation unit. The syntax of the fragment anchor is specified in the following section.

6.2.3 URL Call Syntax

This section contains the grammar for specifying the syntactic structure of the URL call. This grammar is similar to the part of the WMLScript lexical and syntactic grammars having to do with function calls and literals, and has as its terminal symbols the characters of the US-ASCII character set.

```
http://www.host.com/scr#foo(1,-3,'hello')          // OK
http://www.host.com/scr#bar(1,-3+1,'good')         // Error
http://www.host.com/scr#test(foo(1,-3,'hello'))    // Error
```

Only the syntax for the fragment anchor (#) is specified (see [RFC1808] for more information about URL syntax).

URLCallFragmentAnchor :::

FunctionName( )

FunctionName(*ArgumentList*)

FunctionName :::

FunctionNameLetter

FunctionName FunctionNameLetter

FunctionName DecimalDigit

FunctionNameLetter ::: `one of`

`a b c d e f g h i j k l m n o p q r s t u v w x y z`

`A B C D E F G H I J K L M N O P Q R S T U V W X Y Z`

`_`

DecimalDigit ::: `one of`

`0 1 2 3 4 5 6 7 8 9`

ArgumentList :

Argument

ArgumentList , Argument

Argument :::

$WhiteSpace_{opt}$ *Literal* $WhiteSpace_{opt}$

WhiteSpace :::

any US-ASCII character with character code less than or equal to 32

Literal :::

InvalidLiteral

BooleanLiteral

NumericLiteral

StringLiteral

InvalidLiteral :::

`invalid`

BooleanLiteral :::

`true`

`false`

NumericLiteral :::

SignedDecimalIntegerLiteral

SignedDecimalFloatLiteral

SignedDecimalIntegerLiteral :::

DecimalIntegerLiteral

+ *DecimalIntegerLiteral*

- *DecimalIntegerLiteral*

DecimalIntegerLiteral :::

DecimalDigit $DecimalDigits_{opt}$

SignedDecimalFloatLiteral :::

DecimalFloatLiteral

+ *DecimalFloatLiteral*

- *DecimalFloatLiteral*

DecimalFloatLiteral :::

DecimalIntegerLiteral . $DecimalDigits_{opt}$ $ExponentPart_{opt}$

. *DecimalDigits* $ExponentPart_{opt}$

DecimalIntegerLiteral ExponentPart

DecimalDigits :::

DecimalDigit

DecimalDigits DecimalDigit

ExponentPart :::

ExponentIndicator SignedInteger

ExponentIndicator ::: `one of`

`e E`

SignedInteger :::

DecimalDigits

+ *DecimalDigits*

- *DecimalDigits*

StringLiteral :::

" $DoubleStringCharacters_{opt}$ "

' $SingleStringCharacters_{opt}$ '

DoubleStringCharacters :::

DoubleStringCharacter $DoubleStringCharacters_{opt}$

SingleStringCharacters :::

SingleStringCharacter $SingleStringCharacters_{opt}$

DoubleStringCharacter :::

SourceCharacter `but not` *double-quote* " `or` *backslash* \

EscapeSequence

SingleStringCharacter :::

SourceCharacter `but not` *single-quote* ' `or` *backslash* \

EscapeSequence

EscapeSequence :::

CharacterEscapeSequence

OctalEscapeSequence

HexEscapeSequence

UnicodeEscapeSequence

CharacterEscapeSequence :::

\ *SingleEscapeCharacter*

SingleEscapeCharacter ::: one of

' " \ / b f n r t

HexEscapeSequence :::

\x *HexDigit HexDigit*

OctalEscapeSequence :::

\ *OctalDigit*

\ *OctalDigit OctalDigit*

\ *ZeroToThree OctalDigit OctalDigit*

ZeroToThree ::: one of

0 1 2 3

UnicodeEscapeSequence :::

\u *HexDigit HexDigit HexDigit HexDigit*

6.2.4 URL Calls and Parameter Passing

A user agent can make a call to an external WMLScript function by providing the following information using URLs and fragment anchors:

- URL of the compilation unit (e.g., `http://www.x.com/myScripts.scr`)
- Function name and parameters as the fragment anchor (e.g., `testFunc('Test%20argument',-8)`)

The final URL with the fragment is:

```
http://www.x.com/myScripts.scr#testFunc('Test%20argument',-8)
```

If the given URL denotes a valid WMLScript compilation unit, then:

- Access control checks are performed (see Section 3.7.2). The call fails if the caller does not have rights to call the compilation unit.
- The function name specified in the fragment anchor is matched against the external functions in the compilation unit. The call fails if no match is found.
- The parameter list in the fragment anchor (see Section 6.2.2) is parsed and the given arguments with their appropriate types (string literals as string data types, integer literals as integer data types, etc.) are passed to the function. The call fails if the parameter list has an invalid syntax.

6.2.5 Character Escaping

URL calls can use both URL escaping [RFC1738] to specify the URL and WMLScript string escaping (see Section 3.1.5.3) for any Unicode characters inside string literals. A URL is unescaped by first applying the URL escaping rules and then WMLScript string literal escaping rules for each string literal passed as a function parameter.

6.2.6 Relative URLs

WMLScript has adopted the use of relative URLs, as specified in [RFC1808]. [RFC1808] specifies the method used to resolve relative URLs in the context of a WMLScript compilation unit. The base URL of a WMLScript compilation unit is the URL that identifies the compilation unit.

6.3 Bytecode Semantics

The following sections describe the general encoding rules that must be used to generate WMLScript bytecode. These rules specify what the WMLScript compiler can assume from the behavior of the WMLScript interpreter.

6.3.1 Passing of Function Arguments

Arguments must be present in the operand stack in the same order as they are presented in a WMLScript function declaration at the time of a WMLScript or library function call. Thus, the first argument is pushed into the operand stack first, the second argument is pushed next, and so on.

6.3.2 Automatic Function Return Value

WMLScript function must return an empty string in case the end of the function is encountered without a return statement. The compiler can rely on the WMLScript interpreter to automatically return an empty string every time the interpreter reaches the end of the function without encountering a return instruction.

6.3.3 Initialization of Variables

The WMLScript compiler should rely on the WMLScript interpreter to initialize all function local variables initially to an empty string. Thus, the compiler does not have to generate initialization code for variables declared without initialization.

6.4 Access Control

WMLScript provides two mechanisms for controlling the access to the functions in the WMLScript compilation unit: *external* keyword and a specific *access control* pragma. Thus, the WMLScript interpreter must support the following behavior:

- *External functions*: Only functions specified as *external* can be called from other compilation units (see Section 3.4).
- *Access control*: Access to the external functions defined inside a compilation unit is allowed from other compilation units that match the given access domain and access path definitions (see Section 3.7.2).

7. WMLScript Binary Format

The following sections contain the specifications for the WMLScript bytecode, a compact binary representation for compiled WMLScript functions. The format was designed to allow for compact transmission over narrowband channels, with no loss of functionality or semantic information.

7.1 Conventions

The following sections describe the general encoding conventions and data types used to generate WMLScript bytecode.

7.1.1 Used Data Types

The following data types are used in the specification of the WMLScript bytecode:

DATA TYPE	DEFINITION
bit	1 bit of data.
byte	8 bits of opaque data.
int8	8-bit signed integer (2's complement encoding).
u_int8	8-bit unsigned integer.
int16	16-bit signed integer (2's complement encoding).
u_int16	16-bit unsigned integer.
mb_u_int16	16-bit unsigned integer, in multibyte integer format. See Section 7.1.2 for more information.
int32	32-bit signed integer (2's complement encoding).
u_int32	32-bit unsigned integer.
mb_u_int32	32-bit unsigned integer, in multibyte integer format. See Section 7.1.2 for more information.
float32	32-bit signed floating-point value in ANSI/IEEE Std 754-1985 [IEEE754] format.

Network byte order for multibyte integer values is big-endian; in other words, the most significant byte is transmitted on the network first, followed subsequently by the less significant bytes. Network bit ordering for bit fields within a byte is big-endian; in other words, bit fields described first are placed in the most significant bits of the byte.

7.1.2 Multibyte Integer Format

This encoding uses a multibyte representation for integer values. A multibyte integer consists of a series of octets, where the most significant bit is the *continuation flag* and the remaining 7 bits are a scalar value. The continuation flag is used to indicate that an octet is not the end of the multibyte sequence. A single integer value is encoded into a sequence of N octets. The first N–1 octets have the continuation flag set to a value of 1. The final octet in the series has a continuation flag value of 0.

The remaining 7 bits in each octet are encoded in a big-endian order; in other words, most significant bit first. The octets are arranged in a big-endian order; the most significant 7 bits are transmitted first. In the situation where the initial octet has less than 7 bits of value, all unused bits must be set to 0.

For example, the integer value `0xA0` would be encoded with the 2-byte sequence `0x81 0x20`. The integer value `0x60` would be encoded with the 1-byte sequence `0x60`.

7.1.3 Character Encoding

WMLScript character strings use the Unicode [UNICODE] character set. WMLScript bytecode supports the following Unicode character encodings:

- UTF-8 (see [RFC2279])
- UCS-2 (see [ISO10646])
- UCS-4 (see [ISO10646])

The compiler must select one of these encodings to encode character strings in the WMLScript bytecode.

WMLScript language constructs, such as *function names* in WMLScript, are written by using only a subset of Unicode character set; in other words, a subset of US-ASCII characters. Thus, function names in the WMLScript bytecode must use a fixed UTF-8 encoding.

7.1.4 Notational Conventions

WMLScript bytecode is a set of bytes that represent WMLScript functions in a binary format. It contains all the information needed by the WMLScript interpreter to execute the encoded functions as specified. The bytecode can be divided into sections and subsections, each of which contains a binary representation of a logical WMLScript unit.

The WMLScript bytecode structure and content is presented using the following table-based notation:

NAME	DATA TYPE AND SIZE	COMMENT
This is a *name* of a section inside the bytecode.	This specifies a *data type* and its *size* reserved for a section in case it cannot be divided into smaller subsections. Subsection specification is given in a separate table. Reference to the table is provided.	This gives a general overview of the meaning of this section.
The name of the next section. Any number of sections can be presented in one table.		
...		

The following conventions apply:

- Sections of bytecode are represented as rows in a table.
- Each section may be divided into subsections and represented in separate tables. In such a case, a reference to the subsection table is provided.
- Repetitive sections are denoted by section name followed by three dots (...).

7.2 WMLScript Bytecode

The WMLScript encoding contains two major elements: constant literals and the constructs needed to describe the behavior of each WMLScript function. Thus, the WMLScript bytecode consists of the following sections:

NAME	DATA TYPE AND SIZE	COMMENT
HeaderInfo	See Section 7.3	Contains general information related to the bytecode
ConstantPool	See Section 7.4	Contains the information of all constants specified as part of the WMLScript compilation unit that are encoded into bytecode
PragmaPool	See Section 7.5	Contains the information related to pragmas specified as part of the WMLScript compilation unit that are encoded into bytecode
FunctionPool	See Section 7.6	Contains all the information related to the encoding of functions and their behavior

The following sections define the encoding of these sections and their subsections in detail.

7.3 Bytecode Header

The header of the WMLScript bytecode contains the following information:

NAME	DATA TYPE AND SIZE	COMMENT
VersionNumber	byte	Version number of the WMLScript bytecode. The version byte contains the *major version* minus 1 in the upper 4 bits and the *minor version* in the lower 4 bits. The current version is 1.0. Thus, the version number must be encoded as `0x00`.
CodeSize	mb_u_int32	The size of the rest of the bytecode (not including the version number and this variable) in bytes.

7.4 Constant Pool

Constant pool contains all the constants used by the WMLScript functions. Each of the constants has an index number starting from zero that is defined by its position in the list of constants. The instructions use this index to refer to specific constants.

NAME	DATA TYPE AND SIZE	COMMENT
NumberOfConstants	mb_u_int16	Specifies how many constants are encoded in this pool.
Constants...	See Section 7.4.1	Contains the definitions for each constant in the constant pool. The number of constants is specified by NumberOfConstants.

7.4.1 Constants

Constants are stored into the bytecode one after each other. Encoding of each constant starts with the definition of its type (integer, floating-point, string, etc.). It is being followed by constant type-specific data that represents the actual value of the constant.

NAME	DATA TYPE AND SIZE	COMMENT
ConstantType	u_int8	The type of the constant.
ConstantValue	See Sections 7.4.1.1, 7.4.1.2 and 7.4.1.3	Type-specific value definition.

The following encoding for constant types is used:

CODE	TYPE	ENCODING
0	8-bit signed integer	7.4.1.1.1
1	16-bit signed integer	7.4.1.1.2
2	32-bit signed integer	7.4.1.1.3
3	32-bit signed floating-point	7.4.1.2
4	UTF-8 String	7.4.1.3.1
5	UCS-2 String	7.4.1.3.2
6	UCS-4 String	7.4.1.3.3
7	Empty String	7.4.1.3.4
8–255	Reserved for future use	

7.4.1.1 Integers

WMLScript bytecode supports 8-bit, 16-bit, and 32-bit signed integer constants. The compiler can optimize the WMLScript bytecode size by selecting the smallest integer constant type that can still hold the integer constant value.

7.4.1.1.1 8-Bit Signed Integer 8-bit signed integer constants are represented in the following format:

NAME	DATA TYPE AND SIZE	COMMENT
ConstantInteger8	int8	The value of the 8-bit signed integer constant.

7.4.1.1.2 16-Bit Signed Integer 16-bit signed integer constants are represented in the following format:

NAME	DATA TYPE AND SIZE	COMMENT
ConstantInteger16	int16	The value of the 16-bit signed integer constant.

7.4.1.1.3 32-Bit Signed Integer 32-bit signed integer constants are represented in the following format:

NAME	DATA TYPE AND SIZE	COMMENT
ConstantInteger32	int32	The value of the 32-bit signed integer constant.

7.4.1.2 Floats

Floating-point constants are represented in 32-bit ANSI/IEEE Std 754-1985 [IEEE754] format:

NAME	DATA TYPE AND SIZE	COMMENT
ConstantFloat32	float32	The value of the 32-bit floating-point constant.

7.4.1.3 Strings

WMLScript bytecode supports several ways to encode Unicode string constants[39] into the constant pool. The compiler can optimize the WMLScript bytecode size by selecting the smallest string constant type that can still hold the string constant value.

7.4.1.3.1 UTF-8 Strings Strings that use UTF-8 encoding are encoded into the bytecode by first specifying their length and then the content:

NAME	DATA TYPE AND SIZE	COMMENT
StringSizeUTF8	mb_u_int32	The size of the following string in bytes (not containing this variable).
ConstantStringUTF8	StringSize UTF8 bytes	The value of the Unicode string (non-null terminated) constant encoded using UTF-8. See Section 7.1.3 for more information about transfer encoding of strings.

[39]Note that string constants can contain embedded null characters.

7.4.1.3.2 UCS-2 Strings Strings that use UCS-2 encoding are encoded into the bytecode by first specifying their length and then the content:

NAME	DATA TYPE AND SIZE	COMMENT
StringSizeUCS2	mb_u_int32	The size of the following string in bytes (not containing this variable).
ConstantStringUCS2	StringSizeUCS2 bytes	The value of the Unicode string (nonnull terminated) constant encoded using UCS-2. See Section 7.1.3 for more information about transfer encoding of strings.

7.4.1.3.3 UCS-4 Strings Strings that use UCS-4 encoding are encoded into the bytecode by first specifying their length and then the content:

NAME	DATA TYPE AND SIZE	COMMENT
StringSizeUCS4	mb_u_int32	The size of the following string in bytes (not containing this variable).
ConstantStringUCS4	StringSizeUCS4 bytes	The value of the Unicode string (nonnull terminated) constant encoded using UCS-4. See Section 7.1.3 for more information about transfer encoding of strings.

7.4.1.3.4 Empty Strings Empty strings do not need any additional encoding for their value.

7.5 Pragma Pool

The pragma pool contains the information for pragmas defined in the compiled compilation unit.

NAME	DATA TYPE AND SIZE	COMMENT
NumberOfPragmas	mb_u_int16	The number of pragmas (not containing this variable).
Pragmas...	See Section 7.5.1	Contains the definitions for each pragma in the pragma pool. The number of pragmas is specified by NumberOfPragmas.

7.5.1 Pragmas

Pragmas are stored into the bytecode one after another. Encoding of each pragma starts with the definition of its type. It is being followed by pragma type-specific data that represents the actual value of the pragma:

NAME	DATA TYPE AND SIZE	COMMENT
PragmaType	u_int8	The type of the pragma following pragma value.
PragmaValue	See Sections 7.5.1.1 and 7.5.1.2	Pragma type-specific value definition.

The following encoding for pragma types is used:

CODE	TYPE	ENCODING
0	Access Control Disabled	7.5.1.1.1
1	Access Domain	7.5.1.1.2
2	Access Path	7.5.1.1.3
3	User Agent Property	7.5.1.2.1
4	User Agent Property and Scheme	7.5.1.2.2
5–255	Reserved for future use	

7.5.1.1 Access Control Pragmas

Access control information is encoded into the bytecode using three different pragma types: *access control disabled*, *access domain*, and *access path*. The pragma pool can contain only one entry for each access control pragma type.

7.5.1.1.1 Access Control Disabled This pragma specifies that access control for the compilation unit is disabled. If pragma pool contains entries for *access domain* and *access path*, their values are ignored. No additional encoding is needed.

7.5.1.1.2 Access Domain This pragma specifies the access domain to be used for the access control.

NAME	DATA TYPE AND SIZE	COMMENT
AccessDomainIndex	mb_u_int16	Constant pool index to a string constant containing the value of the access domain. The referred constant type must be between 4 and 7.

7.5.1.1.3 Access Path This pragma specifies the access path to be used for access control.

NAME	DATA TYPE AND SIZE	COMMENT
AccessPathIndex	mb_u_int16	Constant pool index to a string constant containing the value of the access path. The referred constant type must be between 4 and 7.

7.5.1.2 Meta-Information Pragmas

These pragmas contain meta-information that is meant for the WMLScript interpreter. Meta-information contains the following entities: name, content, and scheme (optional).

7.5.1.2.1 User Agent Property User agent properties are encoded by first specifying their name and then their value as indexes to the constant pool.

NAME	DATA TYPE AND SIZE	COMMENT
PropertyNameIndex	mb_u_int16	Constant pool index to a string constant (constant types 4 to 7) containing the property name.
ContentIndex	mb_u_int16	Constant pool index to a string constant (constant types 4 to 7) containing the property value.

7.5.1.2.2 User Agent Property and Scheme This pragma is encoded by specifying the property name, the value, and the additional scheme:

NAME	DATA TYPE AND SIZE	COMMENT
PropertyNameIndex	mb_u_int16	Constant pool index to a string constant (constant types 4 to 7) containing the property name.
ContentIndex	mb_u_int16	Constant pool index to a string constant (constant types 4 to 7) containing the property value.
SchemeIndex	mb_u_int16	Constant pool index to a string constant (constant types 4 to 7) containing the property schema.

7.6 Function Pool

The function pool contains the function definitions. Each of the functions has an index number starting from zero that is defined by its position in the list of functions. The instructions use this index to refer to specific functions.

NAME	DATA TYPE AND SIZE	COMMENT
NumberOfFunctions	u_int8	The number of functions specified in this function pool.
FunctionNameTable	See Section 7.6.1	Function name table contains the names of all external functions present in the bytecode.
Functions...	See Section 7.6.2	Contains the bytecode for each function.

7.6.1 Function Name Table

The names of the functions that are specified as *external* (`extern`) are stored into a function name table. The names must be presented in the same order as the functions are represented in the function pool. Functions that are not specified as external are not represented in the function name table. The format of the table is the following:

NAME	DATA TYPE AND SIZE	COMMENT
NumberOfFunctionNames	u_int8	The number of function names stored into the following table.
FunctionNames...	See Section 7.6.1.1	Each external function name represented in the same order as the functions are stored into the function pool.

7.6.1.1 Function Names

Function name is provided only for functions that are specified as *external* in WML-Script. Each name is represented in the following manner:

NAME	DATA TYPE AND SIZE	COMMENT
FunctionIndex	u_int8	The index of the function for which the following name is provided.
FunctionNameSize	u_int8	The size of the following function name in bytes (not including this variable).
FunctionName	FunctionNameSize bytes	The characters of the function name encoded by using UTF-8. See Section 7.1.3 for more information about function name encoding.

7.6.2 Functions

Each function is defined by its prologue and code array:

NAME	DATA TYPE AND SIZE	COMMENT
NumberOfArguments	u_int8	The number of arguments accepted by the function.
NumberOfLocalVariables	u_int8	The number of local variables used by the function (not including arguments).
FunctionSize	mb_u_int32	Size of the following CodeArray (not including this variable) in bytes.
CodeArray	See Section 7.6.2.1	Contains the code of the function.

7.6.2.1 Code Array

Code array contains all instructions that are needed to implement the behavior of a WMLScript function. See Section 8 for more information about the WMLScript instruction set.

NAME	DATA TYPE AND SIZE	COMMENT
Instructions...	See Section 8	The encoded instructions.

7.7 Limitations

The following table contains the limitations inherent in the selected bytecode format and instructions:

Maximum size of the bytecode	4294967295 bytes
Maximum number of constants in the constant pool	65535
Maximum number of different constant types	256
Maximum size of a constant string	4294967295 bytes
Maximum size of a constant URL	4294967295 bytes
Maximum length of function name	255
Maximum number of different pragma types	256
Maximum number of pragmas in the pragma pool	65536
Maximum number of functions in the function pool	255
Maximum number of function parameters	255
Maximum number of local variables / function	255
Maximum number of local variables and function parameters	256
Maximum number of libraries	65536
Maximum number of functions / library	256

8. WMLScript Instruction Set

The WMLScript instruction set specifies a set of assembly-level instructions that must be used to encode all WMLScript language constructs and operations. These instructions are defined in such a way that they are easy to implement efficiently on a variety of platforms.

8.1 Conversion Rules

The following table contains a summary of the conversion rules specified for the WMLScript interpreter:

RULE—OPERAND TYPE(S)	CONVERSIONS
1—Boolean(s)	See the conversion rules for *Boolean(s)* in Section 4.2, *Operator Data Type* Conversion Rules.
2—Integer(s)	See the conversion rules for *Integer(s)* in Section 4.2, *Operator Data Type* Conversion Rules.
3—Floating-point(s)	See the conversion rules for *Floating-point(s)* in Section 4.2, *Operator Data Type* Conversion Rules.
4—String(s)	See the conversion rules for *String(s)* in Section 4.2, *Operator Data Type* Conversion Rules.
5—Integer or floating-point (unary)	See the conversion rules for *Integer or floating-point (unary)* in Section 4.2, *Operator Data Type* Conversion Rules.
6—Integers or floating-points	See the conversion rules for *Integers or floating-points* in Section 4.2, *Operator Data Type* Conversion Rules.
7—Integers, floating-points, or strings	See the conversion rules for *Integers, floating-points, or strings* in Section 4.2, *Operator Data Type* Conversion Rules.
8—Any	See the conversion rules for *Any* in Section 4.2, *Operator Data Type* Conversion Rules.

8.2 Fatal Errors

The following table contains a summary of the fatal errors specified for the WMLScript interpreter:

ERROR CODE:	FATAL ERROR:
1 (Verification Failed)	See Section 10.3.1.1, *Verification Failed*, for details.
2 (Fatal Library Function Error)	See Section 10.3.1.2, *Fatal Library Function Error*, for details.
3 (Invalid Function Arguments)	See Section 10.3.1.3, *Invalid Function Arguments*, for details.
4 (External Function Not Found)	See Section 10.3.1.4, *External Function Not Found*, for details.
5 (Unable to Load Compilation Unit)	See Section 10.3.1.5, *Unable to Load Compilation Unit*, for details.
6 (Access Violation)	See Section 10.3.1.6, *Access Violation*, for details.
7 (Stack Underflow)	See Section 10.3.1.7, *Stack Underflow*, for details.
8 (Programmed Abort)	See Section 10.3.2.1, *Programmed Abort*, for details.
9 (Stack Overflow)	See Section 10.3.3.1, *Stack Overflow*, for details*.
10 (Out of Memory)	See Section 10.3.3.2, *Out of Memory*, for details*.
11 (User Initiated)	See Section 10.3.4.1, *User Initiated*, for details*.
12 (System Initiated)	See Section 10.3.4.2, *System Initiated*, for details*.

*These fatal errors are not related to computation but can be generated as a result of memory exhaustion or external signals.

8.3 Optimizations

WMLScript instruction set has been defined so that it provides at least the minimal set of instructions by which WMLScript language operations can be presented. Since the WMLScript bytecode is being transferred from the gateway to the client through a narrowband connection, the selected instructions have been optimized so that the compilers can generate code of minimal size. In some cases, this has meant that several instructions with different parameters have been introduced to perform the same operation. The compiler should use the one that generates optimal code.

Inline parameters have been used to optimally pack information into as few bytes as possible. The following inline parameter optimizations have been introduced:

SIGNATURE	AVAILABLE INSTRUCTIONS	USED FOR
1XXPPPPP	4	JUMP_FW_S, JUMP_BW_S, TJUMP_FW_S, LOAD_VAR_S
010XPPPP	2	STORE_VAR_S, LOAD_CONST_S
011XXPPP	4	CALL_S, CALL_LIB_S, INCR_VAR_S
00XXXXXX	63	The rest of the instructions

8.4 Notational Conventions

The following sections contain the definitions of instructions in the WMLScript instruction set. For each instruction, the following information is provided:

- *Instruction*: A symbolic name given to the instruction and its parameters.
- *Opcode*: The 8-bit encoding of the instruction.
- *Parameters*: Parameter description specifying their ranges and semantics. Some instructions are optimized and can contain an *implicit parameter* as part of the encoding; in other words, a set of bits from the 8-bit encoding is reserved for a parameter value.
- *Operation*: Description of the operation of the instruction, its parameters, and the effects they have on the execution and the operand stack.
- *Operands*: Specifies the number of operands required by the instruction and all acceptable operand types.
- *Conversion*: Specifies the used conversion rule (see Section 8.1).
- *Result*: Specifies the result and its type.
- *Operand stack*: Specifies the effect on the operand stack. It is described by using notation where the part before the arrow (=>) represents the stack before the instruction has been executed, and the part after the arrow the stack after the execution.
- *Errors*: Specifies the possible fatal errors that can occur during the execution of the instruction (see Section 8.2).

All instructions except the control flow instructions continue the execution at the following instruction. Control flow instructions specify the next instruction explicitly.

Fatal errors that can be encountered at any time (see Section 10.3.4, *External Exceptions*, and Section 10.3.3, *Memory Exhaustion Errors*) are assumed to be possible with every instruction.

The result of the instruction can be an `invalid` value. This is not explicitly stated with each instruction, but is assumed to be the result of the used conversion rule, a load of an invalid or unsupported floating-point constant, or a result of an operation with an `invalid` operand.

8.5 Instructions

The following sections contain the descriptions of each instruction divided into subcategories.

8.5.1 Control Flow Instructions

Instruction:	**JUMP_FW_S**
Opcode:	100iiiii (*iiiii* is the implicit unsigned *offset*)
Parameter:	*Offset* is an unsigned 5-bit integer in the range of 0–31.
Operation:	Jumps forward to an offset. Execution proceeds at the given *offset* from the address of the first byte following this instruction.
Operands:	-
Conversion:	-
Result:	-
Operand stack:	No change
Errors:	1 (Verification Failed)

Instruction:	**JUMP_FW** *offset*
Opcode:	00000001
Parameter:	*Offset* is an unsigned 8-bit integer in the range of 0–255.
Operation:	Jumps forward to an offset. Execution proceeds at the given *offset* from the address of the first byte following this instruction.
Operands:	-
Conversion:	-
Operand stack:	No change
Errors:	1 (Verification Failed)

Instruction:	**JUMP_FW_W** <*offset1,offset2*>
Opcode:	00000010
Parameter:	*Offset* is an unsigned 16-bit integer <*offset1, offset2*> in the range of 0–65535.
Operation:	Jumps forward to an offset. Execution proceeds at the given *offset* from the address of the first byte following this instruction.
Operands:	-
Conversion:	-
Result:	-
Operand stack:	No change
Errors:	1 (Verification Failed)

Instruction:	**JUMP_BW_S**
Opcode:	101iiiii (*iiiii* is the implicit unsigned *offset*)
Parameter:	*Offset* is an unsigned 5-bit integer in the range of 0–31.
Operation:	Jumps backward to an offset. Execution proceeds at the given *offset* from the address of this instruction.
Operands:	-
Conversion:	-
Result:	-
Operand stack:	No change
Errors:	1 (Verification Failed)

Instruction:	**JUMP_BW** *offset*
Opcode:	00000011
Parameter:	*Offset* is an unsigned 8-bit integer in the range of 0–255.
Operation:	Jumps backward to an offset. Execution proceeds at the given *offset* from the address of this instruction.
Operands:	-
Conversion:	-
Result:	-
Operand stack:	No change
Errors:	1 (Verification Failed)

Instruction:	**JUMP_BW_W** <*offset1,offset2*>
Opcode:	00000100
Parameter:	*Offset* is an unsigned 16-bit integer <*offset1, offset2*> in the range of 0–65535.
Operation:	Jumps backward to an offset. Execution proceeds at the given *offset* from the address of this instruction.
Operands:	-
Conversion:	-
Result:	-
Operand stack:	No change
Errors:	1 (Verification Failed)

Instruction:	**TJUMP_FW_S**
Opcode:	110iiiii (*iiiii* is the implicit unsigned *offset*)
Parameter:	*Offset* is an unsigned 5-bit integer in the range of 0–31.

Operation: Pops a value from the operand stack and jumps forward to an *offset* if the value is either `false` or `invalid`. Execution proceeds at the given *offset* from the address of the first byte following this instruction. Otherwise, the execution continues at the next instruction.

Operand: Boolean

Conversion: 1 – Boolean(s)

Result: -

Operand stack: ..., value => ...

Errors: 1 (Verification Failed), 7 (Stack Underflow)

Instruction: **TJUMP_FW** *offset*

Opcode: 00000101

Parameter: *Offset* is an unsigned 8-bit integer in the range of 0–255.

Operation: Pops a value from the operand stack and jumps forward to an *offset* if the value is either `false` or `invalid`. Execution proceeds at the given *offset* from the address of the first byte following this instruction. Otherwise, the execution continues at the next instruction.

Operand: Boolean

Conversion: 1 – Boolean(s)

Result: -

Operand stack: ..., value => ...

Errors: 1 (Verification Failed), 7 (Stack Underflow)

Instruction: **TJUMP_FW_W** <*offset1,offset2*>

Opcode: 00000110

Parameter: *Offset* is an unsigned 16-bit integer <*offset1*, *offset2*> in the range of 0–65535.

Operation: Pops a value from the operand stack and jumps forward to an *offset* if the value is either `false` or `invalid`. Execution proceeds at the given *offset* from the address of the first byte following this instruction. Otherwise, the execution continues at the next instruction.

Operand: Boolean

Conversion: 1 – Boolean(s)

Result: -

Operand stack: ..., value => ...

Errors: 1 (Verification Failed), 7 (Stack Underflow)

Instruction: **TJUMP_BW** *offset*

Opcode: 00000111

Parameter: *Offset* is an unsigned 8-bit integer in the range of 0–255.

Operation: Pops a value from the operand stack and jumps backward to an *offset* if the value is either `false` or `invalid`. Execution proceeds at the given *offset* from the address of this instruction. Otherwise, the execution continues at the next instruction.

Operand: Boolean

Conversion: 1 – Boolean(s)

Result: -

Operand stack: …, value => …

Errors: 1 (Verification Failed), 7 (Stack Underflow)

Instruction: **TJUMP_BW_W** *<offset1,offset2>*

Opcode: 00001000

Parameter: *Offset* is an unsigned 16-bit integer *<offset1, offset2>* in the range of 0–65535.

Operation: Pops a value from the operand stack and jumps backward to an *offset* if the value is either `false` or `invalid`. Execution proceeds at the given *offset* from the address of this instruction. Otherwise, the execution continues at the next instruction.

Operand: Boolean

Conversion: 1 – Boolean(s)

Result: -

Operand stack: …, value => …

Errors: 1 (Verification Failed), 7 (Stack Underflow)

8.5.2 Function Call Instructions

Instruction: **CALL_S**

Opcode: 01100iii (*iii* is the implicit *findex*)

Parameter: *Findex* is an unsigned 3-bit integer in the range of 0–7.

Operation: Calls a local function defined in the same function pool. Execution proceeds from the first instruction of the function *findex*.

Operands: Variable number, any type

Conversion: -

Result: Any (function return value)

Operand stack: …, [arg1, [arg2 …]] => …, ret-value

Errors: 1 (Verification Failed), 7 (Stack Underflow)

Instruction: **CALL** *findex*

Opcode: 00001001

Parameter: *Findex* is an unsigned 8-bit integer in the range of 0–255.

Operation: Calls a local function defined in the same function pool. Execution proceeds from the first instruction of the function *findex*.

Operands: Variable number, any type

Conversion: -

Result: Any (function return value)

Operand stack: ..., [arg1, [arg2 ...]] => ..., ret-value

Errors: 1 (Verification Failed), 7 (Stack Underflow)

Instruction: **CALL_LIB_S** *lindex*

Opcode: 01101iii (*iii* is the implicit *findex*)

Parameters: *Findex* is an unsigned 3-bit integer in the range of 0–7.

Lindex is an unsigned 8-bit integer in the range of 0–255.

Operation: Calls a library function *findex* defined in the specified library *lindex*.

Operands: Variable number (specified by the called library function), any type

Conversion: -

Result: Any (function return value)

Operand stack: ..., [arg1, [arg2 ...]] => ..., ret-value

Errors: 1 (Verification Failed), 2 (Fatal Library Function Error), 7 (Stack Underflow), 8 (Programmed Abort)

Instruction: **CALL_LIB** *findex lindex*

Opcode: 00001010

Parameters: *Findex* is an unsigned 8-bit integer in the range of 0–255.

Lindex is an unsigned 8-bit integer in the range of 0–255.

Operation: Calls a library function *findex* defined in the specified library *lindex*.

Operands: Variable number (specified by the called library function), any type

Conversion: -

Result: Any (function return value)

Operand stack: ..., [arg1, [arg2 ...]] => ..., ret-value

Errors: 1 (Verification Failed), 2 (Fatal Library Function Error), 7 (Stack Underflow), 8 (Programmed Abort)

Instruction: **CALL_LIB_W** *findex* <*lindex1*, *lindex2*>

Opcode: 00001011

Parameters: *Findex* is an unsigned 8-bit integer in the range of 0–255.

Lindex is an unsigned 16-bit integer <*lindex1*,*lindex2*> in the range of 0–65535.

Operation: Calls a library function *findex* defined in the specified library *lindex*.

Operands: Variable number (specified by the called library function), any type

Conversion: -

Result: Any (function return value)

Operand stack: …, [arg1, [arg2 …]] => …, ret-value

Errors: 1 (Verification Failed), 2 (Fatal Library Function Error), 7 (Stack Underflow), 8 (Programmed Abort)

Instruction: **CALL_URL** *urlindex findex args*

Opcode: 00001100

Parameters: *Urlindex* is an unsigned 8-bit integer in the range of 0–255 that must point to the constant pool containing a valid URL. The referred constant type must be between 4 and 7.

Findex is an unsigned 8-bit integer in the range of 0–255 that must point to the constant pool containing a valid function name. The referred constant type must be 4.

Args is an unsigned 8-bit integer in the range of 0–255 that must contain the number of function arguments pushed on the operand stack.

Operation: Calls a function specified by *findex* defined in the specified URL address *urlindex*.

Operands: Variable number (specified by *args*), any type

Conversion: -

Result: Any (function return value)

Operand stack: …, [arg1, [arg2 …]] => …, ret-value

Errors: 1 (Verification Failed), 3 (Invalid Function Arguments), 4 (External Function Not Found), 5 (Unable to Load Compilation Unit), 6 (Access Violation), 7 (Stack Underflow)

Instruction: **CALL_URL_W** *<urlindex1,urlindex2> <findex1,findex2> args*

Opcode: 00001101

Parameters: *Urlindex* is an unsigned 16-bit integer *<urlindex1,urlindex2>* in the range of 0–65535 that must point to the constant pool containing a valid URL. The referred constant type must be between 4 and 7.

Findex is an unsigned 16-bit integer *<findex1,findex2>* in the range of 0–65535 that must point to the constant pool containing a valid function name. The referred constant type must be 4.

Args is an unsigned integer in the range of 0–255 that must contain the number of function arguments pushed on the operand stack.

Operation: Calls a function specified by *findex* defined in the specified URL address *urlindex*.

Operands: Variable number (specified by *args*), any type

Conversion: -

Result: Any (function return value)

Operand stack: …, [arg1, [arg2 …]] => …, ret-value

Errors: 1 (Verification Failed), 3 (Invalid Function Arguments), 4 (External Function Not Found), 5 (Unable to Load Compilation Unit), 6 (Access Violation), 7 (Stack Underflow)

8.5.3 Variable Access and Manipulation

Instruction: **LOAD_VAR_S**
Opcode: 111iiiii (*iiiii* is the implicit *vindex*)
Parameter: *Vindex* is an unsigned 5-bit integer in the range of 0–31.
Operation: Pushes the value of the variable *vindex* on the operand stack.
Operands: -
Conversion: -
Result: Any (content of the variable)
Operand stack: … => …, value
Errors: 1 (Verification Failed)

Instruction: **LOAD_VAR** *vindex*
Opcode: 00001110
Parameter: *Vindex* is an unsigned 8-bit integer in the range of 0–255.
Operation: Pushes the value of the variable *vindex* on the operand stack.
Operands: -
Conversion: -
Result: Any (content of the variable)
Operand stack: … => …, value
Errors: 1 (Verification Failed)

Instruction: **STORE_VAR_S**
Opcode: 0100iiii (*iiii* is the implicit *vindex*)
Parameter: *Vindex* is an unsigned 4-bit integer in the range of 0–15.
Operation: Pops the value from the operand stack and stores it into the variable *vindex*.
Operand: Any
Conversion: 8 - Any
Result: -
Operand stack: …, value => …
Errors: 1 (Verification Failed), 7 (Stack Underflow)

Instruction: **STORE_VAR** *vindex*
Opcode: 00001111
Parameter: *Vindex* is an unsigned 8-bit integer in the range of 0–255.

Operation: Pops the value from the operand stack and stores it into the variable *vindex*.

Operand: Any

Conversion: 8 - Any

Result: -

Operand stack: …, value => …

Errors: 1 (Verification Failed), 7 (Stack Underflow)

Instruction: **INCR_VAR_S**

Opcode: 01110iii (*iii* is the implicit *vindex*)

Parameter: *Vindex* is an unsigned 3-bit integer in the range of 0–7.

Operation: Increments the value of a variable *vindex* by 1.

Operands: -

Conversion: 5 – Integer or floating-point (unary)

Result: -

Operand stack: No change

Errors: 1 (Verification Failed)

Instruction: **INCR_VAR** *vindex*

Opcode: 00010000

Parameter: *Vindex* is an unsigned 8-bit integer in the range of 0–255.

Operation: Increments the value of a variable *vindex* by one.

Operands: -

Conversion: 5 – Integer or floating-point (unary)

Result: -

Operand stack: No change

Errors: 1 (Verification Failed)

Instruction: **DECR_VAR** *vindex*

Opcode: 00010001

Operation: Decrements the value of a variable *vindex* by 1.

Parameter: *Vindex* is an unsigned 8-bit integer in the range of 0–255.

Operands: -

Conversion: 5 – Integer or floating-point (unary)

Result: -

Operand stack: No change

Errors: 1 (Verification Failed)

8.5.4 Access to Constants

Instruction: **LOAD_CONST_S**

Opcode: 0101iiii (*iiii* is the implicit *cindex*)

Parameter: *Cindex* is an unsigned 4-bit integer in the range of 0–15 that points to the constant pool containing the actual constant. The referred constant type must be between 0 and 7.

Operation: Pushes the value of the constant denoted by *cindex* on the operand stack.

Operands: -

Conversion: -

Result: Any (content of the constant)

Operand stack: … => …, value

Errors: 1 (Verification Failed)

Instruction: **LOAD_CONST** *cindex*

Opcode: 00010010

Parameter: *Cindex* is an unsigned 8-bit integer in the range of 0–255 that points to the constant pool containing the actual constant. The referred constant type must be between 0 and 7.

Operation: Pushes the value of the constant denoted by *cindex* on the operand stack.

Operands: -

Conversion: -

Result: Any (content of the constant)

Operand stack: … => …, value

Errors: 1 (Verification Failed)

Instruction: **LOAD_CONST_W** *<cindex1,cindex2>*

Opcode: 00010011

Parameter: *Cindex* is an unsigned 16-bit integer *<cindex1,cindex2>* in the range of 0–65535 that points to the constant pool containing the actual constant. The referred constant type must be between 0 and 7.

Operation: Pushes the value of the constant *cindex* on the operand stack.

Operands: -

Conversion: -

Result: Any (content of the constant)

Operand stack: … => …, value

Errors: 1 (Verification Failed)

Instruction:	**CONST_0**
Opcode:	00010100
Parameters:	-
Operation:	Pushes an integer value 0 on the operand stack.
Operands:	-
Conversion:	-
Result:	Integer
Operand stack:	… => …, value_0
Errors:	-

Instruction:	**CONST_1**
Opcode:	00010101
Parameters:	-
Operation:	Pushes an integer value 1 on the operand stack.
Operands:	-
Conversion:	-
Result:	Integer
Operand stack:	… => …, value_1
Errors:	-

Instruction:	**CONST_M1**
Opcode:	00010110
Parameters:	-
Operation:	Pushes an integer value –1 on the operand stack.
Operands:	-
Conversion:	-
Result:	Integer
Operand stack:	… => …, value_-1
Errors:	-

Instruction:	**CONST_ES**
Opcode:	00010111
Parameters:	-
Operation:	Pushes an empty string on the operand stack.
Operands:	-
Conversion:	-
Result:	String
Operand stack:	… => …, value_""
Errors:	-

Instruction: **CONST_INVALID**
Opcode: 00011000
Parameters: -
Operation: Pushes an `invalid` value on the operand stack.
Operands: -
Conversion: -
Result: Invalid
Operand stack: … => …, invalid
Errors: -

Instruction: **CONST_TRUE**
Opcode: 00011001
Parameters: -
Operation: Pushes a Boolean value `true` on the operand stack.
Operands: -
Conversion: -
Result: Boolean
Operand stack: … => …, value_true
Errors: -

Instruction: **CONST_FALSE**
Opcode: 00011010
Parameters: -
Operation: Pushes a Boolean value `false` on the operand stack.
Operands: -
Conversion: -
Result: Boolean
Operand stack: … => …, value_false
Errors: -

8.5.5 Arithmetic Instructions

Instruction: **INCR**
Opcode: 00011011
Parameters: -
Operation: Increments the value on the top of the operand stack by 1.
Operand: Integer or floating-point
Conversion: 5 – Integer or floating-point (unary)
Result: Integer or floating-point (incremented by one)

Operand stack: ..., value => ..., value+1
Errors: 7 (Stack Underflow)

Instruction: **DECR**
Opcode: 00011100
Parameters: -
Operation: Decrements the value on the top of the operand stack by 1.
Operand: Integer or floating-point
Conversion: 5 – Integer or floating-point (unary)
Result: Integer or floating-point (decremented by 1)
Operand stack: ..., value => ..., value-1
Errors: 7 (Stack Underflow)

Instruction: **ADD_ASG** *vindex*
Opcode: 00011101
Parameter: *Vindex* is an unsigned 8-bit integer in the range of 0–255.
Operation: Pops a value from the operand stack and adds the value to the variable *vindex*.
Operands: Integers, floating-points, or strings
Conversion: 7 – Integers, floating-points, or strings
Result: *For integers or floating-points*: variable containing the result of the addition
For strings: variable containing the result of string concatenation
Operand stack: ..., value => ...
Errors: 1 (Verification Failed), 7 (Stack Underflow)

Instruction: **SUB_ASG** *vindex*
Opcode: 00011110
Parameter: *Vindex* is an unsigned 8-bit integer in the range of 0–255.
Operation: Pops a value (subtractor) from the operand stack and subtracts the value from the variable *vindex*.
Operands: Integers or floating-points
Conversion: 6 – Integers or floating-points
Result: Variable containing the result of the subtraction
Operand stack: ..., value => ...
Errors: 1 (Verification Failed), 7 (Stack Underflow)

Instruction: **UMINUS**
Opcode: 00011111
Parameters: -

Operation: Pops a value from the operand stack and performs a unary minus operation on it and pushes the result back on the operand stack.

Operand: Integer or floating-point

Conversion: 5 – Integer or floating-point (unary)

Result: Integer or floating-point (negated)

Operand stack: …, value => …, -value

Errors: 7 (Stack Underflow)

Instruction: **ADD**

Opcode: 00100000

Parameters: -

Operation: Pops two values from the operand stack and performs an add operation on them and pushes the result back on the operand stack.

Operands: Integers, floating-points, or strings

Conversion: 7 – Integers, floating-points, or strings

Result: *For integers or floating-points*: the result of the addition

For strings: the result of the concatenation

Operand stack: …, value1, value2 => …, value1 + value2

Errors: 7 (Stack Underflow)

Instruction: **SUB**

Opcode: 00100001

Parameters: -

Operation: Pops two values from the operand stack and performs a subtract operation on them and pushes the result back on the operand stack.

Operands: Integers or floating-points

Conversion: 6 – Integers or floating-points

Result: Integer or floating-point

Operand stack: …, value1, value2 => …, value1 - value2

Errors: 7 (Stack Underflow)

Instruction: **MUL**

Opcode: 00100010

Parameters: -

Operation: Pops two values from the operand stack, performs a multiplication operation on them, and pushes the result back on the operand stack.

Operands: Integers or floating-points

Conversion: 6 – Integers or floating-points

Result: Integer or floating-point

Operand stack: ..., value1, value2 => ..., value1 * value2

Errors: 7 (Stack Underflow)

Instruction: **DIV**

Opcode: 00100011

Parameters: -

Operation: Pops two values from the operand stack, performs a division operation on them, and pushes the result back on the operand stack.

Operands: Integers or floating-points

Conversion: 6 – Integers or floating-points

Result: Integer or floating-point

Operand stack: ..., value1, value2 => ..., value1 / value2

Errors: 7 (Stack Underflow)

Instruction: **IDIV**

Opcode: 00100100

Parameters: -

Operation: Pops two values from the operand stack, performs an integer division operation on them, and pushes the result back on the operand stack.

Operands: Integers

Conversion: 2 – Integer(s)

Result: Integer

Operand stack: ..., value1, value2 => ..., value1 IDIV value2

Errors: 7 (Stack Underflow)

Instruction: **REM**

Opcode: 00100101

Parameters: -

Operation: Pops two values from the operand stack, performs a reminder operation on them (the sign of the result equals the sign of the dividend), and pushes the result back on the operand stack.

Operands: Integers

Conversion: 6 – Integers or floating-points

Result: Integer

Operand stack: ..., value1, value2 => ..., value1 % value2

Errors: 7 (Stack Underflow)

8.5.6 Bitwise Instructions

Instruction: **B_AND**
Opcode: 00100110
Parameters: -
Operation: Pops two values from the operand stack and performs a bitwise *and* operation on them, and pushes the result back on the operand stack.
Operands: Integers
Conversion: 2 – Integer(s)
Result: Integer
Operand stack: …, value1, value2 => …, value1 & value2
Errors: 7 (Stack Underflow)

Instruction: **B_OR**
Opcode: 00100111
Parameters: -
Operation: Pops two values from the operand stack and performs a bitwise *or* operation on them, and pushes the result back on the operand stack.
Operands: Integers
Conversion: 2 – Integer(s)
Result: Integer
Operand stack: …, value1, value2 => …, value1 | value2
Errors: 7 (Stack Underflow)

Instruction: **B_XOR**
Opcode: 00101000
Parameters: -
Operation: Pops two values from the operand stack, performs a bitwise *xor* operation on them, and pushes the result back on the operand stack.
Operands: Integers
Conversion: 2 – Integer(s)
Result: Integer
Operand stack: …, value1, value2 => …, value1 ^ value2
Errors: 7 (Stack Underflow)

Instruction: **B_NOT**
Opcode: 00101001
Parameters: -

Operation: Pops a value from the operand stack and performs a bitwise *complement* operation on it, and pushes the result back on the operand stack.

Operands: Integer

Conversion: 2 – Integer(s)

Result: Integer

Operand stack: …, value => …, ~value

Errors: 7 (Stack Underflow)

Instruction: **B_LSHIFT**

Opcode: 00101010

Parameters: -

Operation: Pops two values from the operand stack, performs a bitwise left-shift operation on them, and pushes the result back on the operand stack.

Operands: Integers

Conversion: 2 – Integer(s)

Result: Integer

Operand stack: …, value, amount => …, value << amount

Errors: 7 (Stack Underflow)

Instruction: **B_RSSHIFT**

Opcode: 00101011

Parameters: -

Operation: Pops two values from the operand stack, performs a bitwise *signed right-shift* operation on them, and pushes the result back on the operand stack.

Operands: Integers

Conversion: 2 – Integer(s)

Result: Integer

Operand stack: …, value, amount => …, value >> amount

Errors: 7 (Stack Underflow)

Instruction: **B_RSZSHIFT**

Opcode: 00101100

Parameters: -

Operation: Pops two values from the operand stack and performs a bitwise *right-shift with zero* operation on them, and pushes the result back on the operand stack.

Operands: Integers

Conversion: 2 – Integer(s)

Result: Integer

Operand stack: ..., value, amount => ..., value >>> amount

Errors: 7 (Stack Underflow)

8.5.7 Comparison Instructions

Instruction: **EQ**

Opcode: 00101101

Parameters: -

Operation: Pops two values from the operand stack, performs a logical equality operation on them, and pushes the result back on the operand stack.

Operands: Integers, floating-points, or strings

Conversion: 7 – Integers, floating-points, or strings

Result: Boolean

Operand stack: ..., value1, value2 => ..., value1 EQ value2

Errors: 7 (Stack Underflow)

Instruction: **LE**

Opcode: 00101110

Parameters: -

Operation: Pops two values from the operand stack, performs a logical larger-or-equal operation on them, and pushes the result back on the operand stack.

Operands: Integers, floating-points, or strings

Conversion: 7 – Integers, floating-points, or strings

Result: Boolean

Operand stack: ..., value1, value2 => ..., value1 LE value2

Errors: 7 (Stack Underflow)

Instruction: **LT**

Opcode: 00101111

Parameters: -

Operation: Pops two values from the operand stack, performs a logical larger-than operation on them, and pushes the result back on the operand stack.

Operands: Integers, floating-points, or strings

Conversion: 7 – Integers, floating-points, or strings

Result: Boolean

Operand stack: ..., value1, value2 => ..., value1 LT value2

Errors: 7 (Stack Underflow)

Instruction: **GE**
Opcode: 00110000
Parameters: -
Operation: Pops two values from the operand stack, performs a logical greater-or-equal operation on them, and pushes the result back on the operand stack.
Operands: Integers, floating-points, or strings
Conversion: 7 – Integers, floating-points, or strings
Result: Boolean
Operand stack: …, value1, value2 => …, value1 GE value2
Errors: 7 (Stack Underflow)

Instruction: **GT**
Opcode: 00110001
Parameters: -
Operation: Pops two values from the operand stack, performs a greater-than operation on them, and pushes the result back on the operand stack.
Operands: Integers, floating-points, or strings
Conversion: 7 – Integers, floating-points, or strings
Result: Boolean
Operand stack: …, value1, value2 => …, value1 GT value2
Errors: 7 (Stack Underflow)

Instruction: **NE**
Opcode: 00110010
Parameters: -
Operation: Pops two values from the operand stack, performs a logical not-equal operation on them, and pushes the result back on the operand stack.
Operands: Integers, floating-points, or strings
Conversion: 7 – Integers, floating-points, or strings
Result: Boolean
Operand stack: …, value1, value2 => …, value1 NE value2
Errors: 7 (Stack Underflow)

8.5.8 Logical Instructions

Instruction: **NOT**
Opcode: 00110011
Parameters: -

Operation:	Pops a value from the operand stack, performs a logical complement operation on it, and pushes the result back on the operand stack.
Operands:	Boolean
Conversion:	1 – Boolean(s)
Result:	Boolean
Operand stack:	..., value => ..., !value
Errors:	7 (Stack Underflow)

Instruction:	**SCAND**
Opcode:	00110100
Parameters:	-
Operation:	Pops a value from the operand stack and converts it to a Boolean value. If the converted value is `false` or `invalid`, then the converted value itself is pushed on the operand stack and the Boolean value `false` is pushed on the operand stack. If the converted value is `true`, then the converted value itself is pushed on the operand stack.
Operands:	Any
Conversion:	1 – Boolean(s)
Result:	Boolean
Operand stack:	..., value => ..., false, false (in case the value is `false`) ..., value => ..., true (in case the value is `true`) ..., value => ..., invalid, false (in case the value is `invalid`)
Errors:	7 (Stack Underflow)

Instruction:	**SCOR**
Opcode:	00110101
Parameters:	-
Operation:	Pops a value from the operand stack and converts it to a Boolean value. If the converted value is `false`, then the Boolean value `true` is pushed on the operand stack. If the converted value is `true` or `invalid`, then the converted value itself is pushed on the operand stack and the Boolean value `false` is pushed on the operand stack.
Operands:	Any
Conversion:	1 – Boolean(s)
Result:	Boolean
Operand stack:	..., value => ..., true (in case the value is `false`) ..., value => ..., true, false (in case the value is `true`) ..., value => ..., invalid, false (in case the value is `invalid`)
Errors:	7 (Stack Underflow)

Instruction: **TOBOOL**

Opcode: 00110110

Parameters: -

Operation: Pops a value from the operand stack, converts the value to a Boolean value, and pushes the converted value on the operand stack. If the popped value is `invalid`, then an `invalid` value is pushed back on the operand stack.

Operands: Any

Conversion: 1 – Boolean(s)

Result: Boolean

Operand stack: ..., value => ..., tobool

Errors: 7 (Stack Underflow)

8.5.9 Stack Instructions

Instruction: **POP**

Opcode: 00110111

Parameters: -

Operation: Pops a value from the operand stack.

Operands: Any

Conversion: -

Result: -

Operand stack: ..., value => ...

Errors: 7 (Stack Underflow)

8.5.10 Access to Operand Type

Instruction: **TYPEOF**

Opcode: 00111000

Parameters: -

Operation: Pops a value from the operand stack and checks its type. Pushes the result as an integer on the operand stack. The possible results are: 0 = Integer, 1 = Floating-point, 2 = String, 3 = Boolean, 4 = Invalid.

Operands: Any

Conversion: -

Result: Integer

Operand stack: ..., value => ..., typeof?

Errors: 7 (Stack Underflow)

Instruction:	**ISVALID**
Opcode:	00111001
Parameters:	-
Operation:	Pops a value from the operand stack and checks its type. If the type is *invalid*, a Boolean value `false` is pushed on the operand stack; otherwise, a Boolean value `true` is pushed on the operand stack.
Operands:	Any
Conversion:	-
Result:	Boolean
Operand stack:	…, value => …, valid?
Errors:	7 (Stack Underflow)

8.5.11 Function Return Instructions

Instruction:	**RETURN**
Opcode:	00111010
Parameters:	-
Operation:	Pops a return value from the operand stack and returns it to the caller. Any other values on the operand stack are discarded. The execution continues at the next instruction following the function call of the calling function.
Operands:	Any
Conversion:	-
Result:	-
Operand stack:	…, ret-value => …
Errors:	7 (Stack Underflow)

Instruction:	**RETURN_ES**
Opcode:	00111011
Parameters:	-
Operation:	Returns an empty string to the caller. Any other values on the operand stack are discarded. The execution continues at the next instruction following the function call of the calling function.
Operands:	-
Conversion:	-
Result:	-
Operand stack:	No change
Errors:	-

8.5.12 Miscellaneous Instructions

Instruction:	**DEBUG**
Opcode:	00111100
Parameters:	-
Operation:	No operation. Reserved for debugging and profiling purposes.
Operands:	-
Conversion:	-
Result:	-
Operand stack:	No change
Errors:	-

9. Bytecode Verification

Bytecode verification takes place before or while the bytecode is used for execution. The purpose of the verification is to make sure that the content follows the WMLScript bytecode specification. In case of verification failure, the failed bytecode should not be used for execution, or the execution must be aborted and failure signaled to the caller of the WMLScript interpreter.

The following checks are to be executed in the WMLScript Interpreter either before the execution is started or during the execution of WMLScript bytecode.

9.1 Integrity Check

The following list contains checks that must be used to verify the integrity of the WMLScript bytecode *before* it is executed:

- Check that the *version number* is correct: The bytecode version number must be compared with the bytecode version number supported by the WMLScript interpreter. The *major* version numbers must match. The *minor* version number of the bytecode must be less than or equal to the *minor* version number supported by the WMLScript interpreter.
- Check that the *size of the bytecode* is correct: The size specified in the bytecode must match exactly the byte size of the content.
- Check the *constant pool*:
  - The *number of constants* is correct: The number of constants specified in the constant pool must match the number of constants stored into the constant pool.
  - The *types of constants* are valid: The numbers used to specify the constant types in the constant pool must match the supported constant types. Reserved constant types (8–255) result in a verification failure.
  - The *sizes of constants* are valid: Each constant must allocate only the correct number of bytes specified by the WMLScript bytecode specification (fixed-

size constants such as integers) or the size parameter provided as part of the constant entity (constants of varying size such as strings).

- Check the *pragma pool*:
  - The *number of pragmas* is correct: The number of pragmas specified in the pragma pool must match the number of pragmas stored into the constant pool.
  - The *types of pragmas* are valid: The numbers used to specify the pragma types in the pragma pool must match the supported pragma types. Reserved pragma types (5–255) result in a verification failure.
  - The *constant pool indexes* are valid:
    - The access control domain and path must point to string constants.
    - The constant pool indexes used in meta-information pragmas must point to string constants.
- Check the *function pool*:
  - The *number of functions* is correct: The number of functions specified in the function pool must match the number of functions stored into the function pool.
  - The *function name table* is correct:
    - The *number of function names* is correct: The number of function names specified in the function name table must match the number of function names stored into the function name table.
    - The *function name indexes* are correct: The indexes must point to existing functions in the function pool.
    - The *function names* contain only valid function name characters: Function names must follow the WMLScript function name syntax.
  - The *function prologue* is correct:
  - The *number of arguments* and *local variables* is correct: The sum of the number of arguments and local variables must be less than or equal to 256.
  - The *size of the function* is correct: The size specified in the function prologue must match exactly the byte size of the function.

9.2 Runtime Validity Checks

The following list contains the checks that have to be done *during* the execution to verify that the used instructions are valid and they use valid parameter values:

- Check that the bytecode contains only valid *instructions*: Only instructions that are defined in Chapter 8 are valid.
- Check that *local variable references* are valid: The references must be within the boundaries specified by the number of function local variables in the function prologue.
- Check that *constant references* are valid:

  - The references must be within the boundaries specified by the number of constants in the constant pool.
  - The references must point to the valid constant types specified by each instruction.
  - In case of URL references, the referred constant strings must contain a valid URL (see [RFC1808]).
  - In case of Function Name references, the referred constant strings must contain a valid WMLScript function name.
- Check that the standard *library indexes* and *library function indexes* are valid: The indexes must be within the boundaries specified by the WMLScript Standard Libraries specification [WMLSLibs].
- Check that *local function call indexes* are valid: The function indexes must match with the number of functions specified in the function pool.
- Check that the *jumps* are within function boundaries: All jumps must have a target inside the function in which they are specified.
- Check that the targets of *jumps* are valid: The target of all jumps must be the beginning of an instruction.
- Check that the *ends* of the functions are valid: Functions must not *end* in the middle of an instruction.

10. Runtime Error Detection and Handling

Since WMLScript functions are used to implement services for users that expect the terminals (in particular mobile phones) to work properly in all situations, error handling is of utmost importance. This means that while the language does not provide, for example, an exception mechanism, it should provide tools to either prevent errors from happening or tools to notice them and take appropriate actions. Aborting a program execution should be the last resort used only in cases in which nothing else is possible.

The following section lists errors that can happen when downloading bytecode and executing it. It does not contain programming errors (such as infinite loop, etc.). For these cases, a user-controlled abortion mechanism is needed.

10.1 Error Detection

The goal of error detection is to give tools for the programmer to detect errors (if possible) that would lead to erroneous behavior. Since WMLScript is a weakly typed language, special functionality has been provided to detect errors that are caused by invalid data types.

- Check that the given variable contains the *right value*: WMLScript supports type validation library [WMLSLibs] functions such as *Lang.isInt()*, *Lang.isFloat()*, *Lang.parseInt()*, and *Lang.parseFloat()*.

- Check that the given variable contains a value that is of *right type*: WMLScript supports the operators *typeof* and *isvalid*, which can be used for this purpose.

10.2 Error Handling

Error handling takes place after an error has already happened. This is the case when the error could not be prevented by error detection (memory limits, external signals, etc.), or it would have been too difficult to do so (overflow, underflow, etc.). These cases can be divided into two classes:

Fatal errors: These are errors that cause the program to abort. Since WMLScript functions are always called from some other user agents, program abortion should always be signaled to the calling user agent. It is then its responsibility to take the appropriate actions to signal the user of errors.

Nonfatal errors: These are errors that can be signaled back to the program as special return values, and the program can decide on the appropriate action.

The following error descriptions are divided into sections based on their fatality.

10.3 Fatal Errors

10.3.1 Bytecode Errors

These errors are related to the bytecode and the instructions being executed by the WMLScript Bytecode Interpreter. They are indications of erroneous constant pool elements, invalid instructions, invalid arguments to instructions, or instructions that cannot be completed.

10.3.1.1 Verification Failed

Description: Reports that the specified bytecode for the called compilation unit did not pass the verification (see Section 9 for more information about bytecode verification).

Generated: At any time when a program attempts to call an external function.

Example: `var a = 3*OtherScript#doThis(param);`

Severity: Fatal.

Predictable: Is detected during the bytecode verification.

Solution: Abort program and signal an error to the caller of the WMLScript interpreter.

10.3.1.2 Fatal Library Function Error

Description: Reports that a call to a library function resulted in a fatal error.

Generated: At any time when a call to a library function is used (CALL_LIB). Typically, this is an unexpected error in the library function implementation.

Example: `var a = String.format(param);`

Severity: Fatal.

Predictable: No.

Solution: Abort program and signal an error to the caller of the WMLScript interpreter.

10.3.1.3 Invalid Function Arguments

Description: Reports that the number of arguments specified for a function call do not match with the number of arguments specified in the called function.

Generated: At any time a call to an external function is used (CALL_URL).

Example: Compiler generates an invalid parameter to an instruction, or the number of parameters in the called function has changed.

Severity: Fatal.

Predictable: No.

Solution: Abort program and signal an error to the caller of the WMLScript interpreter.

10.3.1.4 External Function Not Found

Description: Reports that a call to an external function could not be found from the specified compilation unit.

Generated: At any time when a program attempts to call an external function (CALL_URL).

Example: `var a = 3*OtherScript#doThis(param);`

Severity: Fatal.

Predictable: No.

Solution: Abort program and signal an error to the caller of the WMLScript interpreter.

10.3.1.5 Unable to Load Compilation Unit

Description: Reports that the specified compilation unit could not be loaded due to unrecoverable errors in accessing the compilation unit in the network server, or the specified compilation unit does not exist in the network server.

Generated: At any time when a program attempts to call an external function (CALL_URL).

Example: `var a = 3*OtherScript#doThis(param);`

Severity: Fatal.

Predictable: No.

Solution: Abort program and signal an error to the caller of the WMLScript interpreter.

10.3.1.6 Access Violation

Description: Reports an access violation. The called external function resides in a protected compilation unit.

Generated: At any time when a program attempts to call an external function (CALL_URL).

Example: `var a = 3*OtherScript#doThis(param);`

Severity: Fatal.

Predictable: No.

Solution: Abort program and signal an error to the caller of the WMLScript interpreter.

10.3.1.7 Stack Underflow

Description: Indicates a stack underflow because of a program error (compiler generated bad code).

Generated: At any time when a program attempts to pop an empty stack.

Example: Only generated if compiler generates bad code.

Severity: Fatal.

Predictable: No.

Solution: Abort program and signal an error to the caller of the WMLScript interpreter.

10.3.2 Program Specified Abortion

This error is generated when a WMLScript function calls the library function *Lang.abort()* (see [WMLSLibs]) to abort the execution.

10.3.2.1 Programmed Abort

Description: Reports that the execution of the bytecode was aborted by a call to *Lang.abort()* function.

Generated: At any time when a program makes a cal to *Lang.abort()* function.

Example: `Lang.abort("Unrecoverable error");`

Severity: Fatal.

Predictable: No.

Solution: Abort program and signal an error to the caller of the WMLScript interpreter.

10.3.3 Memory Exhaustion Errors

These errors are related to the dynamic behavior of the WMLScript interpreter (see Section 6.1 for more information) and its memory usage.

10.3.3.1 Stack Overflow

Description: Indicates a stack overflow.

Generated: At any time when a program recourses too deep or attempts to push too many variables onto the operand stack.

Example:

```
function f(x) { f(x+1); };
```

Severity: Fatal.

Predictable: No.

Solution: Abort program and signal an error to the caller of the WMLScript interpreter.

10.3.3.2 Out of Memory

Description: Indicates that no more memory resources are available to the interpreter.

Generated: At any time when the operating system fails to allocate more space for the interpreter.

Example:

```
function f(x) {
x=x+"abcdefghijklmnopqrstuvzyxy";
f(x);
};
```

Severity: Fatal.

Predictable: No.

Solution: Abort program and signal an error to the caller of the WMLScript interpreter.

10.3.4 External Exceptions

The following exceptions are initiated outside of the WMLScript Bytecode Interpreter.

10.3.4.1 User Initiated

Description: Indicates that the user wants to abort the execution of the program (reset button, etc.).

Generated: At any time.

Example: User presses reset button while an application is running.

Severity: Fatal.

Predictable: No.

Solution: Abort program and signal an error to the caller of the WMLScript interpreter.

10.3.4.2 System Initiated

Description: Indicates that an external fatal exception occurred while a program is running and it must be aborted. Exceptions can be originated from a low battery, power off, etc.

Generated: At any time.

Example: The system is automatically switching off due to a low battery.

Severity: Fatal.

Predictable: No.

Solution: Abort program and signal an error to the caller of the WMLScript interpreter.

10.4 Nonfatal Errors

10.4.1 Computational Errors

These errors are related to arithmetic operations supported by the WMLScript.

10.4.1.1 Divide by Zero

Description: Indicates a division by 0.

Generated: At any time when a program attempts to divide by 0 (integer or floating-point division or remainder).

Example:

```
var a = 10;
var b = 0;
var x = a / b;
var y = a div b;
var z = a % b;
a /= b;
```

Severity: Nonfatal.

Predictable: Yes.

Solution: The result is an `invalid` value.

10.4.1.2 Integer Overflow

Description: Reports an arithmetic integer overflow.

Generated: At any time when a program attempts to execute an integer operation.

Example:

```
var a = Lang.maxInt();
var b = Lang.maxInt();
```

```
var c = a + b;
```

Severity: Nonfatal.

Predictable: Yes (but difficult in certain cases).

Solution: The result is an `invalid` value.

10.4.1.3 Floating-Point Overflow

Description: Reports an arithmetic floating-point overflow.

Generated: At any time when a program attempts to execute a floating-point operation.

Example:

```
var a = 1.6e308;
var b = 1.6e308;
var c = a * b;
```

Severity: Nonfatal.

Predictable: Yes (but difficult in certain cases).

Solution: The result is an `invalid` value.

10.4.1.4 Floating-Point Underflow

Description: Reports an arithmetic underflow.

Generated: At any time when the result of a floating-point operation is smaller than what can be represented.

Example:

```
var a = Float.precision();
var b = Float.precision();
var c = a * b;
```

Severity: Nonfatal.

Predictable: Yes (but difficult in certain cases).

Solution: The result is a floating-point value `0.0`.

10.4.2 Constant Reference Errors

These errors are related to runtime references to constants in the constant pool.

10.4.2.1 Not a Number Floating-Point Constant

Description: Reports a reference to a floating-point literal in the constant pool that is *Not a Number* [IEEE754].

Generated: At any time when a program attempts to access a floating-point literal and the compiler has generated a *Not a Number* as a floating-point constant.

Example: A reference to a floating-point literal.

Severity: Nonfatal.

Predictable: Yes.

Solution: The result is an `invalid` value.

10.4.2.2 Infinite Floating-Point Constant

Description: Reports a reference to a floating-point literal in the constant pool that is either positive or negative infinity [IEEE754].

Generated: At any time when a program attempts to access a floating-point literal and the compiler has generated a floating-point constant with a value of positive or negative infinity.

Example: A reference to a floating-point literal.

Severity: Nonfatal.

Predictable: Yes.

Solution: The result is an `invalid` value.

10.4.2.3 Illegal Floating-Point Reference

Description: Reports an erroneous reference to a floating-point value in the constant pool.

Generated: At any time when a program attempts to use floating-point values and the environments supports only integer values.

Example: `var a = 3.14;`

Severity: Nonfatal.

Predictable: Can be detected during runtime.

Solution: The result is an `invalid` value.

10.4.3 Conversion Errors

These errors are related to automatic conversions supported by the WMLScript.

10.4.3.1 Integer Too Large

Description: Indicates a conversion to an integer value where the integer value is too large (positive/negative).

Generated: At any time when an application attempts to make an automatic conversion to an integer value.

Example:

```
var a = -"999999999999999999999999999999999999999999";
```

Severity: Nonfatal.

Predictable: No.

Solution: The result is an `invalid` value.

10.4.3.2 Floating-Point Too Large

Description: Indicates a conversion to a floating-point value where the floating-point value is too large (positive/negative).

Generated: At any time when an application attempts to make an automatic conversion to a floating-point value.

Example: `var a = -"9999999.9999999999e99999";`

Severity: Nonfatal.

Predictable: No.

Solution: The result is an `invalid` value.

10.4.3.3 Floating-Point Too Small

Description: Indicates a conversion to a floating-point value where the floating-point value is too small (positive/negative).

Generated: At any time when an application attempts to make an automatic conversion to a floating-point value.

Example: `var a = -"0.01e-99";`

Severity: Nonfatal.

Predictable: No.

Solution: The result is a floating-point value `0.0`.

10.5 Library Calls and Errors

Since WMLScript supports the usage of libraries, there is a possibility that errors take place inside the library functions. Design and the behavior of the library functions are not part of the WMLScript language specification. However, certain guidelines should be followed when designing libraries:

- Provide the library users mechanisms by which errors can be detected before they happen.
- Use the same error handling mechanisms as WMLScript operators in cases where error should be reported back to the caller.
- Minimize the possibility of fatal errors in all library functions.

11. Support for Integer-Only Devices

The WMLScript language has been designed to also run on devices that do not support floating-point operations. The following rules apply when WMLScript is used with such devices:

- Variables can only contain the following internal data types:
  - Boolean

  - Integer
  - String
  - Invalid
- Any LOAD_CONST bytecode that refers to a floating point constant in the constant pool will push an `invalid` value on the operand stack instead of the constant value.
- Division (/) operation returns always an `invalid` value.
- All conversion rules related to floating-points are ignored.
- URL call with a floating-point value as an argument results in a failure to execute the call due to an invalid URL syntax.

The programmer can use *Lang.float()* [WMLSLibs] to test (during runtime) if floating-point operations are supported.

12. Content Types

The content types specified for the WMLScript compilation unit and its textual and binary encoding are:

- Textual form: `text/x-wap.wmlscript`
- Binary form: `application/x-wap.wmlscriptc`

These types are not yet registered with the IANA and are consequently *experimental* content types.

13. Definitions

The following are terms and conventions used throughout this specification:

The key words "MUST", "MUST NOT", "REQUIRED", "SHALL", "SHALL NOT", "SHOULD", "SHOULD NOT", "RECOMMENDED", "MAY", and "OPTIONAL" in this document are to be interpreted as described in [RFC2119].

Bytecode. Content encoding where the content is typically a set of low-level opcodes (i.e., instructions) and operands for a targeted hardware (or virtual) machine.

Client. A device (or application) that initiates a request for connection with a server.

Content. Subject matter (data) stored or generated at an origin server. Content is typically displayed or interpreted by a user agent in response to a user request.

Content Encoding. When used as a verb, *content encoding* indicates the act of converting a data object from one format to another. Typically, the resulting format requires less physical space than the original, is easier to process or store, and/or is encrypted. When used as a noun, *content encoding* specifies a particular format or encoding standard or process.

Content Format. Actual representation of content.

Device. A network entity that is capable of sending and receiving packets of information and has a unique device address. A device can act as both a client or a server within a given context or across multiple contexts. For example, a device can service a number of clients (as a server) while being a client to another server.

JavaScript. A *de facto* standard language that can be used to add dynamic behavior to HTML documents. JavaScript is one of the originating technologies of ECMAScript.

Origin Server. The server on which a given resource resides or is to be created. Often referred to as a *Web server* or an *HTTP server*.

Resource. A network data object or service that can be identified by a URL. Resources may be available in multiple representations (e.g., multiple languages, data formats, size, and resolutions) or vary in other ways.

Server. A device (or application) that passively waits for connection requests from one or more clients. A server may accept or reject a connection request from a client.

User. A user is a person who interacts with a user agent to view, hear, or otherwise use a rendered content.

User Agent. A user agent (or content interpreter) is any software or device that interprets WML, WMLScript, or resources. This may include textual browsers, voice browsers, search engines, etc.

Web Server. A network host that acts as an HTTP server.

WML. The Wireless Markup Language is a hypertext markup language used to represent information for delivery to a narrowband device (e.g., a phone).

WMLScript. A scripting language used to program the mobile device. WMLScript is an extended subset of the JavaScript scripting language.

14. Abbreviations

For the purposes of this specification, the following abbreviations apply:

API	Application Programming Interface
BNF	Backus-Naur Form
ECMA	European Computer Manufacturer Association
HTML	HyperText Markup Language [HTML4]
HTTP	HyperText Transfer Protocol [RFC2068]
IANA	Internet Assigned Number Authority
LSB	Least Significant Bits
MSB	Most Significant Bits
RFC	Request For Comments
UI	User Interface

URL	Uniform Resource Locator [RFC1738]
UTF	UCS Transformation Format
UCS	Universal Multiple-Octet Coded Character Set
W3C	World Wide Web Consortium
WWW	World Wide Web
WSP	Wireless Session Protocol
WTP	Wireless Transport Protocol
WAP	Wireless Application Protocol
WAE	Wireless Application Environment
WTA	Wireless Telephony Applications
WTAI	Wireless Telephony Applications Interface
WBMP	Wireless BitMaP

15. Normative References

[ECMA262] Standard ECMA-262: "ECMAScript Language Specification," ECMA, June 1997.

[IEEE754] ANSI/IEEE Std 754-1985: "IEEE Standard for Binary Floating-Point Arithmetic." Institute of Electrical and Electronics Engineers, New York (1985).

[ISO10646] "Information Technology—Universal Multiple-Octet Coded Character Set (UCS)—Part 1: Architecture and Basic Multilingual Plane," ISO/IEC 10646-1:1993.

[RFC1738] "Uniform Resource Locators (URL)," T. Berners-Lee, et al., December 1994.
URL: ftp://ftp.isi.edu/in-notes/rfc1738.txt

[RFC1808] "Relative Uniform Resource Locators," R. Fielding, June 1995.
URL: ftp://ftp.isi.edu/in-notes/rfc1808.txt

[RFC2279] "UTF-8, a transformation format of Unicode and ISO 10646," F. Yergeau, January 1998.
URL: ftp://ftp.isi.edu/in-notes/rfc2279.txt

[RFC2068] "Hypertext Transfer Protocol—HTTP/1.1," R. Fielding, et al., January 1997.
URL: ftp://ftp.isi.edu/in-notes/rfc2068.txt

[RFC2119] "Key Words for Use in RFCs to Indicate Requirement Levels," S. Bradner, March 1997.
URL: ftp://ftp.isi.edu/in-notes/rfc2119.txt

[UNICODE] "The Unicode Standard: Version 2.0," The Unicode Consortium, Addison-Wesley Developers Press, 1996.
URL: http://www.unicode.org/

[WAP] "Wireless Application Protocol Architecture Specification," WAP Forum, 30-April-1998.
URL: http://www.wapforum.org/

[WML] "Wireless Markup Language Specification," WAP Forum, 30-April-1998. URL: http://www.wapforum.org/

[WMLSLibs] "WMLScript Standard Libraries Specification," WAP Forum, 30-April-1998. URL: http://www.wapforum.org/

[WSP] "Wireless Session Protocol," WAP Forum, 30-April-1998. URL: http://www.wapforum.org/

[XML] "Extensible Markup Language (XML), W3C Proposed Recommendation 10-February-1998, REC-xml-19980210," T. Bray, et al., February 10, 1998. URL: http://www.w3.org/TR/REC-xml

16. Informative References

[HTML4] "HTML 4.0 Specification, W3C Recommendation 18-December-1997, REC-HTML40-971218," D. Raggett, et al., September 17, 1997. URL: http://www.w3.org/TR/REC-html40

[JavaScript] "JavaScript: The Definitive Guide," David Flanagan. O'Reilly & Associates, Inc. 1997.

[WAE] "Wireless Application Environment Specification," WAP Forum, 30-April-1998. URL: http://www.wapforum.org/

CHAPTER

7

WMLScript Standard Libraries Specification

1. Scope

Wireless Application Protocol (WAP) is a result of continuous work to define an industrywide specification for developing applications that operate over wireless communication networks. The scope for the WAP Forum is to define a set of standards to be used by service applications. The wireless market is growing very quickly, and reaching new customers and services. To enable operators and manufacturers to meet the challenges in advanced services, differentiation, and fast/flexible service creation, WAP defines a set of protocols in Transport, Session, and Application layers. For additional information on the WAP architecture, refer to *Wireless Application Protocol Architecture Specification* [WAP].

This document specifies the library interfaces for the standard set of libraries supported by WMLScript [WMLScript] to provide access to the core functionality of a WAP client. WMLScript is a language that can be used to provide programmed functionality to WAP-based applications. It is part of the WAP platform and it can be used to add script support also to the client.

One of the main differences between ECMAScript [ECMA262] and WMLScript is the fact that WMLScript is compiled into bytecode *before* it is being sent to the client. This way, the narrowband communication channels available today can be optimally utilized and the memory requirements for the client kept to the minimum. For the same reasons, many of the advanced features of the JavaScript language have been removed to make the language optimal, easier to compile into bytecode, and easier to learn.

Library support has been added to the WMLScript to replace some of the functionality that has been removed from ECMAScript in order to make the WMLScript more efficient. This feature provides access to built-in functionality and a means for future expansion without unnecessary overhead.

The following chapters describe the set of libraries defined to provide access to core functionality of a WAP client. This means that all libraries, except *Float*, are present in the client's scripting environment. Float library is optional and only supported with clients that can support floating-point arithmetic operations.

2. Notational Conventions

The libraries in this document are represented by providing the following information:

Name: Library name. The syntax of the library name follows the syntax specified in the [WMLScript] specification. Library names are case sensitive.

Examples: `Lang`, `String`

Library ID: The numeric identifier reserved for the library to be used by the WMLScript Compiler. The range of values reserved for this identifier is divided into the following two categories:

0–32767 Reserved for standard libraries.

32768–65535 Reserved for future use.

Description: A short description of the library and used conventions.

Each function in the library is represented by providing the following information:

Function: Specifies the function name and the number of function parameters. The syntax of the function name follows the syntax specified in the [WMLScript] specification. Function names are case sensitive.

Example: abs(*value*)

Usage: `var a = 3*Lang.abs(length);`

Function ID: The numeric identifier reserved for the function to be used by the WMLScript Compiler. The range of values reserved for this identifier is: 0–255.

Description: Describes the function behavior and its parameters.

Parameters: Specifies the function parameter types.

Example: *value* = Number

Return value: Specifies the type(s) of the return value.

Example: String or invalid.

Exceptions: Describes the possible special exceptions and error codes and the corresponding return values. Standard errors, common to all functions, are not described here (see Section 3.3 for more information about error handling).

Example: If the *value1* <= 0 and *value2* < 0 and not an integer, then `invalid` is returned.

Example: Gives a few examples of how the function could be used.

```
var a = -3;
var b = Lang.abs(a);   // b = 3
```

3. WMLScript Compliance

WMLScript standard library functions provide a mechanism to extend the WMLScript language. Thus, the specified library functions must follow the WMLScript conventions and rules.

3.1 Supported Data Type

The following WMLScript types [WMLScript] are used in the function definitions to denote the type of both the function parameters and return values: *Boolean*, *Integer*, *Float*, *String*, and *Invalid*.

In addition to these, *number* can be used to denote a parameter type when both integer and floating-point parameter value types are accepted. *Any* can be used when the type can be any of the supported types.

3.2 Data Type Conversions

Since WMLScript is a weakly typed language, the conversions between the data types are done automatically if necessary (see [WMLScript] for more details about data type conversion rules). The library functions follow WMLScript operator data type conversion rules except where explicitly stated otherwise.

3.3 Error Handling

Error cases are handled in the same way as in the WMLScript language (see [WMLScript] for more details):

- An `invalid` function argument results in an `invalid` return value with no other side effects unless explicitly stated otherwise.
- A function argument that cannot be converted to the required parameter type results in an `invalid` return value with no side effects. See Section 3.2 for more information about data type conversions.
- Function-dependent error cases are handled by returning a suitable error code specified in each function definition. These errors are documented as part of the function specification (exceptions).

3.4 Support for Integer-Only Devices

The WMLScript language has been designed to run also on devices that do not support floating-point operations. The WMLScript standard libraries have operations that require floating-point support. Thus, the following rules apply when the libraries are implemented for an integer-only device:

- Library functions accept arguments of the following type only: *boolean*, *integer*, *string*, and *invalid*.
- All conversion rules related to floating-point data are ignored.
- *Lang.float()* function returns `false`.
- *Lang.parseFloat()* function returns `invalid`.
- All *Float* (see Section 5) library functions return `invalid`.

4. Lang

Name: Lang

Library ID: 0

Description: This library contains a set of functions that are closely related to the WMLScript language core.

4.1 abs

Function: abs(*value*)

Function ID: 0

Description: Returns the absolute value of the given number. If the given number is of type integer, then an integer value is returned. If the given number is of type floating-point, then a floating-point value is returned.

Parameters: *value* = Number

Return value: Number or invalid.

Exceptions: -

Example:

```
var a = -3;
var b = Lang.abs(a);   // b = 3
```

4.2 min

Function: min(*value1*, *value2*)

Function ID: 1

Description: Returns the minimum value of the given two numbers. The value and type returned is the same as the value and type of the selected number. The selection is done in the following way:

- WMLScript operator data type conversion rules for *integers* and *floating-points* (see [WMLScript]) must be used to specify the data type (integer or floating-point) for comparison.
- Compare the numbers to select the smaller one.
- If the values are equal, then the first value is selected.

Parameters: *value1* = Number
value2 = Number

Return value: Number or invalid.

Exceptions: -

Example:

```
var a = -3;
var b = Lang.abs(a);
var c = Lang.min(a,b);        // c = -3
var d = Lang.min(45, 76.3); // d = 45 (integer)
var e = Lang.min(45, 45.0); // e = 45 (integer)
```

4.3 max

Function: max(*value1*, *value2*)

Function ID: 2

Description: Returns the maximum value of the given two numbers. The value and type returned is the same as the value and type of the selected number. The selection is done in the following way:

- WMLScript operator data type conversion rules for *integers* and *floating-points* (see [WMLScript]) must be used to specify the data type (integer or floating-point) for comparison.
- Compare the numbers to select the larger one.
- If the values are equal, then the first value is selected.

Parameters: *value1* = Number
value2 = Number

Return value: Number or invalid.

Exceptions: -

Example:

```
var a = -3;
var b = Lang.abs(a);
var c = Lang.max(a,b);        // c = 3
var d = Lang.max(45.5, 76); // d = 76 (integer)
var e = Lang.max(45.0, 45); // e = 45.0 (float)
```

4.4 parseInt

Function: parseInt(*value*)

Function ID: 3

Description: Returns an integer value defined by the string *value*. The legal integer syntax is specified by the WMLScript (see [WMLScript]) numeric string grammar for *decimal integer literals* with the following additional parsing rule:

- Parsing ends when the first character is encountered that is not a leading '+' or '-' or a decimal digit.

The result is the parsed string converted to an integer value.

Parameters: *value* = String

Return value: Integer or invalid.

Exceptions: In case of a parsing error, an `invalid` value is returned.

Example:

```
var i = Lang.parseInt("1234");      // i = 1234
var j = Lang.parseInt(" 100 m/s"); // j = 100
```

4.5 parseFloat

Function: parseFloat(*value*)

Function ID: 4

Description: Returns a floating-point value defined by the string *value*. The legal floating-point syntax is specified by the WMLScript (see [WMLScript]) numeric string grammar for *decimal floating-point literals* with the following additional parsing rule:

- Parsing ends when the first character is encountered that cannot be parsed as being part of the floating-point representation.

The result is the parsed string converted to a floating-point value.

Parameters: *value* = String

Return value: Floating-point or invalid.

Exceptions: In case of a parsing error, an `invalid` value is returned.

If the system does not support floating-point operations, then an `invalid` value is returned.

Example:

```
var a = Lang.parseFloat("123.7");             // a = 123.7
var b = Lang.parseFloat("   +7.34e2 Hz");     // b = 7.34e2
var c = Lang.parseFloat(" 70e-2 F");          // c = 70.0e-2
var d = Lang.parseFloat("-.1 C");             // d = -0.1
var e = Lang.parseFloat(" 100 ");             // e = 100.0
var f = Lang.parseFloat("Number: 5.5");       // f = invalid
var g = Lang.parseFloat("7.3e meters");       // g = invalid
var h = Lang.parseFloat("7.3e- m/s");         // h = invalid
```

4.6 isInt

Function: isInt(*value*)

Function ID: 5

Description: Returns a Boolean value that is `true` if the given *value* can be converted into an integer number by using parseInt(*value*). Otherwise, `false` is returned.

Parameters: *value* = Any

Return value: Boolean or invalid.

Exceptions: -

Example:

```
var a = Lang.isInt(" -123");    // true
var b = Lang.isInt(" 123.33"); // true
var c = Lang.isInt("string");   // false
var d = Lang.isInt("#123");     // false
var e = Lang.isInt(invalid);    // invalid
```

4.7 isFloat

Function: isFloat(*value*)

Function ID: 6

Description: Returns a Boolean value that is `true` if the given *value* can be converted into a floating-point number using parseFloat(*value*). Otherwise, `false` is returned.

Parameters: *value* = Any

Return value: Boolean or invalid.

Exceptions: If the system does not support floating-point operations, then an `invalid` value is returned.

Example:

```
var a = Lang.isFloat(" -123");    // true
var b = Lang.isFloat(" 123.33"); // true
var c = Lang.isFloat("string");   // false
var d = Lang.isFloat("#123.33"); // false
var e = Lang.isFloat(invalid);    // invalid
```

4.8 maxInt

Function: maxInt()

Function ID: 7

Description: Returns the maximum integer value.

Parameters: -

Return value: Integer 2147483647.

Exceptions: -

Example: `var a = Lang.maxInt();`

4.9 minInt

Function: minInt()

Function ID: 8

Description: Returns the minimum integer value.

Parameters: -

Return value: Integer –2147483648.

Exceptions: -

Example: `var a = Lang.minInt();`

4.10 float

Function: float()

Function ID: 9

Description: Returns `true` if floating-points are supported and `false` if not.

Parameters: -

Return value: Boolean.

Exceptions: -

Example: `var floatsSupported = Lang.float();`

4.11 exit

Function: exit(*value*)

Function ID: 10

Description: Ends the interpretation of the WMLScript bytecode and returns the control back to the caller of the WMLScript interpreter with the given return *value*. This function can be used to perform a *normal* exit from a function in cases where the execution of the WMLScript bytecode should be discontinued.

Parameters: *value* = Any

Return value: None (this function ends the interpretation).

Exceptions: -

Example:

```
Lang.exit("Value: " + myVal); // Returns a string
Lang.exit(invalid);           // Returns invalid
```

4.12 abort

Function: abort(*errorDescription*)

Function ID: 11

Description: Aborts the interpretation of the WMLScript bytecode and returns the control back to the caller of the WMLScript interpreter with the return *errorDescription*. This function can be used to perform an *abnormal* exit in cases where the execution of the WMLScript should be discontinued due to serious errors detected by the calling function. If the type of the *errorDescription* is `invalid`, string `"invalid"` is used as the *errorDescription* instead.

Parameters: *errorDescription* = String

Return value: None (this function aborts the interpretation).

Exceptions: -

Example:

```
Lang.abort("Error: " + errVal);  // Error value is
a string
```

4.13 random

Function: random(*value*)

Function ID: 12

Description: Returns an integer value with positive sign that is greater than or equal to 0 but less than or equal to the given *value*. The return value is chosen randomly or pseudo-randomly with approximately uniform distribution over that range, using an implementation-dependent algorithm or strategy.

If the *value* is of type floating-point, *Float.int()* is first used to calculate the actual integer *value*.

Parameters: *value* = Integer

Return value: Integer or invalid.

Exceptions: If *value* is equal to 0, the function returns 0.

If *value* is less than 0, the function returns `invalid`.

Example:

```
var a = 10;
var b = Lang.random(5.1)*a;     // b = 0..50
var c = Lang.random("string"); // c = invalid
```

4.14 seed

Function: seed(*value*)

Function ID: 13

Description: Initializes the pseudo-random number sequence and returns an empty string. If the *value* is 0 or a positive integer, then the given *value* is used for initialization; otherwise, a random, system-dependent initialization value is used.

If the *value* is of type floating-point, *Float.int()* is first used to calculate the actual integer *value*.

Parameters: *value* = Integer

Return value: String or invalid.

Exceptions: -

Example:

```
var a = Lang.seed(123);     // a = ""
var b = Lang.random(20);    // b = 0..20
var c = Lang.seed("seed");  // c = invalid (random seed left
                            //              unchanged)
```

5. Float

Name: Float

Library ID: 1

Description: This library contains a set of typical arithmetic floating-point functions that are frequently used by applications.

The implementation of these library functions is *optional* and implemented only by devices that can support floating-point operations (see Section 3.4). If floating-point operations are not supported, all functions in this library must return `invalid`.

5.1 int

Function: int(*value*)

Function ID: 0

Description: Returns the integer part of the given value. If the *value* is already an integer, the result is the *value* itself.

Parameters: *value* = Number

Return value: Integer or invalid.

Exceptions: -

Example:

```
var a = 3.14;
var b = Float.int(a);     // b = 3
var c = Float.int(-2.8); // c = -2
```

5.2 floor

Function: floor(*value*)

Function ID: 1

Description: Returns the greatest integer value that is not greater than the given *value*. If the *value* is already an integer, the result is the *value* itself.

Parameters: *value* = Number

Return value: Integer or invalid.

Exceptions: -

Example:

```
var a = 3.14;
var b = Float.floor(a);     // b = 3
var c = Float.floor(-2.8); // c = -3
```

5.3 ceil

Function: ceil(*value*)

Function ID: 2

Description: Returns the smallest integer value that is not less than the given *value*. If the *value* is already an integer, the result is the *value* itself.

Parameters: *value* = Number

Return value: Integer or invalid.

Exceptions: -

Example:

```
var a = 3.14;
var b = Float.ceil(a);     // b = 4
var c = Float.ceil(-2.8); // c = -2
```

5.4 pow

Function: pow(*value1*, *value2*)

Function ID: 3

Description: Returns an implementation-dependent approximation to the result of raising *value1* to the power of *value2*. If *value1* is a negative number, then *value2* must be an integer.

Parameters: *value1* = Number
value2 = Number

Return value: Floating-point or invalid.

Exceptions: If *value1* == 0 and *value2* < 0, then `invalid` is returned.
If *value1* < 0 and *value2* is not an integer, then `invalid` is returned.

Example:

```
var a = 3;
var b = Float.pow(a,2); // b = 9
```

5.5 round

Function: round(*value*)

Function ID: 4

Description: Returns the number value that is closest to the given *value* and is equal to a mathematical integer. If two integer number values are equally close to the *value*, the result is the larger number value. If the *value* is already an integer, the result is the *value* itself.

Parameters: *value* = Number

Return value: Integer or invalid.

Exceptions: -

Example:

```
var a = Float.round(3.5);  // a = 4
var b = Float.round(-3.5); // b = -3
var c = Float.round(0.5);  // c = 1
var d = Float.round(-0.5); // b = 0
```

5.6 sqrt

Function: sqrt(*value*)

Function ID: 5

Description: Returns an implementation-dependent approximation to the square root of the given *value*.

Parameters: *value* = Floating-point

Return value: Floating-point or invalid.

Exceptions: If *value* is a negative number, then `invalid` is returned.

Example:

```
var a = 4;
var b = Float.sqrt(a); // b = 2.0
var c = Float.sqrt(5); // c = 2.2360679775
```

5.7 maxFloat

Function: maxFloat()

Function ID: 6

Description: Returns the maximum floating-point value supported by [IEEE754] single precision floating-point format.

Parameters: -

Return value: Floating-point 3.40282347E+38.

Exceptions: -

Example:

```
var a = Float.maxFloat();
```

5.8 minFloat

Function: minFloat()

Function ID: 7

Description: Returns the smallest nonzero floating-point value supported by [IEEE754] single precision floating-point format.

Parameters: -

Return value: Floating-point. Smaller than or equal to the normalized minimum single precision floating-point value: 1.17549435E-38.

Exceptions: -

Example:
```
var a = Float.minFloat();
```

6. String

Name: String

Library ID: 2

Description: This library contains a set of string functions. A string is an array of Unicode characters. Each of the characters has an index. The first character in a string has an index 0. The length of the string is the number of characters in the array.

The user of the String library can specify a special *separator* by which *elements* in a string can be separated. These elements can be accessed by specifying the separator and the element index. The first element in a string has an index 0. Each occurrence of the separator in the string separates two elements (no escaping of separators is allowed).

A *whitespace character* is any character with a Unicode 2.0 character code that is less than or equal to 32 (decimal).

6.1 length

Function: length(*string*)

Function ID: 0

Description: Returns the length (number of Unicode characters) of the given *string*.

Parameters: *string* = String

Return value: Integer or invalid.

Exceptions: -

Example:
```
var a = "ABC";
var b = String.length(a);    // b = 3
```

```
var c = String.length("");    // c = 0
var d = String.length(342);   // d = 3
```

6.2 isEmpty

Function: isEmpty(*string*)

Function ID: 1

Description: Returns a Boolean `true` if the string length is 0, and Boolean `false` otherwise.

Parameters: *string* = String

Return value: Boolean or invalid.

Exceptions: -

Example:

```
var a = "Hello";
var b = "";
var c = String.isEmpty(a);     // c = false;
var d = String.isEmpty(b);     // d = true
var e = String.isEmpty(true); // e = false
```

6.3 charAt

Function: charAt(*string*, *index*)

Function ID: 2

Description: Returns a new string of length 1 containing the character at the specified *index* of the given *string*.

If the *index* is of type floating-point, *Float.int()* is first used to calculate the actual integer *index*.

Parameters: *string* = String
index = Number (the index of the character to be returned)

Return value: String or invalid.

Exceptions: If *index* is out of range, then an empty string ("") is returned.

Example:

```
var a = "My name is Joe";
var b = String.charAt(a, 0);        // b = "M"
var c = String.charAt(a, 100);      // c = ""
var d = String.charAt(34, 0);       // d = "3"
var d = String.charAt(a, "first"); // e = invalid
```

6.4 subString

Function: subString(*string*, *startIndex*, *length*)

Function ID: 3

Description: Returns a new string that is a substring of the given *string*. The substring begins at the specified *startIndex* and its length (number of characters) is the given *length*. If the *startIndex* is less than 0, then 0 is used for the *startIndex*. If the *length* is larger than the remaining number of characters in the string, the *length* is replaced with the number of remaining characters.

If the *startIndex* or the *length* is of type floating-point, *Float.int()* is first used to calculate the actual integer value.

Parameters: *string* = String
startIndex = Number (the beginning index, inclusive)
length = Number (the length of the substring)

Return value: String or invalid.

Exceptions: If *startIndex* is larger than the last index, an empty string ("") is returned.

If *length* <= 0, an empty string ("") is returned.

Example:

```
var a = "ABCD";
var b = String.subString(a, 1, 2);     // b = "BC"
var c = String.subString(a, 2, 5);     // c = "CD"
var d = String.subString(1234, 0, 2); // d = "12"
```

6.5 find

Function: find(*string*, *subString*)

Function ID: 4

Description: Returns the index of the first character in the *string* that matches the requested *subString*. If no match is found, integer value `-1` is returned.

Two strings are defined to match when they are *identical*. Characters with multiple possible representations match only if they have the same representation in both strings. No case folding is performed.

Parameters: *string* = String
subString = String

Return value: Integer or invalid.

Exceptions: -

Example:

```
var a = "abcde";
var b = String.find(a, "cd");     // b = 2
var c = String.find(34.2, "de"); // c = -1
var d = String.find(a, "qz");     // d = -1
var e = String.find(34, "3");     // e = 0
```

6.6 replace

Function: replace(*string*, *oldSubString*, *newSubString*)

Function ID: 5

Description: Returns a new string resulting from replacing all occurrences of *old-SubString* in this string with *newSubString*.

Two strings are defined to match when they are *identical*. Characters with multiple possible representations match only if they have the same representation in both strings. No case folding is performed.

Parameters: *string* = String
oldSubString = String
newSubString = String

Return value: String or invalid.

Exceptions: -

Example:

```
var a = "Hello Joe. What is up Joe?";
var newName = "Don";
var oldName = "Joe";
var c = String.replace(a, oldName, newName);
//  c = "Hello Don.  What is up Don?";
var d = String.replace(a, newName, oldName);
//  d = "Hello Joe.  What is up Joe?"
```

6.7 elements

Function: elements(*string, separator*)

Function ID: 6

Description: Returns the number of elements in the given *string* separated by the given *separator*.

Parameters: *string* = String
separator = String (the first character of the string used as separator)

Return value: Integer or invalid.

Exceptions: Returns `invalid` if the *separator* is an empty string.

Example:

```
var a = "My name is Joe; Age 50;";
var b = String.elements(a, " ");        // b = 6
var c = String.elements(a, ";");        // c = 3
var d = String.elements("", ";");       // d = 0
var e = String.elements("a", ";");      // e = 1
var f = String.elements(";", ";");      // f = 2
var g = String.elements(";;,;", ";,"); // g = 4 separator = ;
```

6.8 elementAt

Function: elementAt(*string, index, separator*)

Function ID: 7

Description: Search *string* for *index*'th element, elements being separated by *separator*, and return the corresponding element. If the *index* is less than 0, then the first element is returned. If the *index* is larger than the number of elements, then the last element is returned. If the *string* is an empty string, then an empty string is returned.

If the *index* is of type floating-point, *Float.int()* is first used to calculate the actual *index* value.

Parameters: *string* = String
index = Number (the index of the element to be returned)
separator = String (the first character of the string used as separator)

Return value: String or invalid.

Exceptions: Returns `invalid` if the *separator* is an empty string.

Example:

```
var a = "My name is Joe; Age 50;";
var b = String.elementAt(a, 0, " ");  // b = "My"
var c = String.elementAt(a, 14, ";"); // c = ""
var d = String.elementAt(a, 1, ";");  // d = " Age 50"
```

6.9 removeAt

Function: removeAt(*string*, *index*, *separator*)

Function ID: 8

Description: Returns a new string where the element and the corresponding *separator* (if existing) with the given *index* are removed from the given *string*. If the *index* is less than 0, then the first element is removed. If the *index* is larger than the number of elements, then the last element is removed. If the *string* is empty, the function returns a new empty string.

If the *index* is of type floating-point, *Float.int()* is first used to calculate the actual *index* value.

Parameters: *string* = String
index = Number (the index of the element to be deleted)
separator = String (the first character of the string used as separator)

Return value: String or invalid.

Exceptions: Returns `invalid` if the *separator* is an empty string.

Example:

```
var a = "A A;  B C D";
var s = " ";
var b = String.removeAt(a, 1, s);
//  b = "A  B C D"
var c = String.removeAt(a, 0, ";");
//  c = "  B C D"
var d = String.removeAt(a, 14, ";");
//  d = "A A"
```

6.10 replaceAt

Function: replaceAt(*string*, *element*, *index*, *separator*)

Function ID: 9

Description: Returns a string with the current element at the specified *index* replaced with the given *element*. If the *index* is less than 0, then the first element is replaced. If the *index* is larger than the number of elements, then the last element is replaced. If the *string* is empty, the function returns a new string with the given *element*.

If the *index* is of type floating-point, *Float.int()* is first used to calculate the actual *index* value.

Parameters: *string* = String
element = String
index = Number (the index of the element to be replaced)
separator = String (the first character of the string used as separator)

Return value: String or invalid.

Exceptions: Returns `invalid` if the *separator* is an empty string.

Example:

```
var a = "B C; E";
var s = " ";
var b = String.replaceAt(a, "A", 0, s);
//  b = "A C; E"
var c = String.replaceAt(a, "F", 5, ";");
//  c = "B C;F"
```

6.11 insertAt

Function: insertAt(*string*, *element*, *index*, *separator*)

Function ID: 10

Description: Returns a string with the *element* and the corresponding *separator* (if needed) inserted at the specified element *index* of the original *string*. If the *index* is less than 0, then 0 is used as the *index*. If the *index* is larger than the number of elements, then the element is appended at the end of the *string*. If the *string* is empty, the function returns a new string with the given *element*.

If the *index* is of type floating-point, *Float.int()* is first used to calculate the actual *index* value.

Parameters: *string* = String (original string)
element = String (element to be inserted)
index = Number (the index of the element to be added)
separator = String (the first character of the string used as separator)

Return value: String or invalid.

Exceptions: Returns `invalid` if the *separator* is an empty string.

Example:

```
var a = "B C; E";
var s = " ";
var b = String.insertAt(a, "A", 0, s);
//  b = "A B C; E"
var c = String.insertAt(a, "X", 3, s);
//  c = "B C; E X"
var d = String.insertAt(a, "D", 1, ";");
//  d = "B C;D; E"
var e = String.insertAt(a, "F", 5, ";");
//  e = "B C; E;F"
```

6.12 squeeze

Function: squeeze(*string*)

Function ID: 11

Description: Returns a string where all consecutive series of whitespaces within the *string* are reduced to one.

Parameters: *String* = String

Return value: String or invalid.

Exceptions: -

Example:

```
var a = "Hello";
var b = " Bye    Jon .  See you!  ";
var c = String.squeeze(a); // c = "Hello";
var d = String.squeeze(b); // d = " Bye Jon . See you! ";
```

6.13 trim

Function: trim(*string*)

Function ID: 12

Description: Returns a string where all trailing and leading whitespaces in the given *string* have been trimmed.

Parameters: *String* = String

Return value: String or invalid.

Exceptions: -

Example:

```
var a = "Hello";
var b = " Bye    Jon .  See you! ";
var c = String.trim(a); // c = "Hello"
var d = String.trim(b); // d = "Bye   Jon . See you!"
```

6.14 compare

Function: compare(*string1, string2*)

Function ID: 13

Description: The return value indicates the lexicographic relation of *string1* to *string2*. The relation is based on the relation of the Unicode character codes. The return value is –1 if *string1* is less than *string2*, 0 if *string1* is identical to *string2*, or 1 if *string1* is greater than *string2*.

Parameters: *String1* = String
String2 = String

Return value: Integer or invalid.

Exceptions: -

Example:

```
var a = "Hello";
var b = "Hello";
var c = String.compare(a, b);          // c = 0
var d = String.compare("Bye", "Jon"); // d = -1
var e = String.compare("Jon", "Bye"); // e = 1
```

6.15 toString

Function: toString(*value*)

Function ID: 14

Description: Returns a string representation of the given *value*. This function performs exactly the same conversions as supported by the [WMLScript] language (automatic conversion from Boolean, integer, and floating-point values to strings), except that `invalid` value returns the string `"invalid"`.

Parameters: *value* = Any

Return value: String.

Exceptions: -

Example:

```
var a = String.toString(12);    // a = "12"
var b = String.toString(true); // b = "true"
```

6.16 format

Function: format(*format*, *value*)

Function ID: 15

Description: Converts the given *value* to a string by using the given formatting provided as a *format* string. The format string can contain only one format specifier, which can be located anywhere inside the string. If more than one is specified, only the first one (leftmost) is used and the remaining specifiers are replaced by an empty string. The format specifier has the following form:

```
% [width] [.precision] type
```

The `width` argument is a nonnegative decimal integer controlling the minimum number of characters printed. If the number of characters in the output value is less than the specified width, blanks are added to the left until the minimum width is reached. The `width` argument never causes the *value* to be truncated. If the number of characters in the output value is greater than the specified width, or if width is not given, all characters of the *value* are printed (subject to the precision argument).

The `precision` argument specifies a nonnegative decimal integer, preceded by a period (.), that can be used to set the precision of the output value. The interpretation of this value depends on the given `type`:

d Specifies the minimum number of digits to be printed. If the number of digits in the *value* is less than precision, the output value is padded on the left with 0s. The value is not truncated when the number of digits exceeds precision. Default precision is 1. If precision is specified as 0 and the value to be converted is 0, the result is an empty string.

f Specifies the number of digits after the decimal point. If a decimal point appears, at least one digit appears before it. The value is rounded to the appropriate number of digits. Default precision is 6; if precision is 0 or if the period (.) appears without a number following it, no decimal point is printed.

s Specifies the maximum number of characters to be printed. By default, all characters are printed.

Unlike the `width` argument, the `precision` argument can cause either truncation of the output value or rounding of a floating-point value.

The type argument is the only required format argument; it appears after any optional format fields. The type character determines whether the given value is interpreted as integer, floating-point or string. The supported type arguments are:

d Integer: The output value has the form [-]dddd, where dddd is one or more decimal digits.

f Floating-point: The output value has the form [-]dddd.dddd, where dddd is one or more decimal digits. The number of digits before the decimal point depends on the magnitude of the number and the number of digits after the decimal point depends on the requested precision.

s String: Characters are printed up to the end of the string or until the precision value is reached.

Percent character (%) in the format string can be presented by preceding it with another percent character (%%).

Parameters: *format* = String
value = Any

Return value: String or invalid.

Exceptions: Illegal format specifier results in an invalid return value.

Example:

```
var a = 45;
var b = -45;
var c = "now";
var d = 1.2345678;
var e = String.format("e: %6d", a);     // e = "e:    45"
var f = String.format("%6d", b);        // f = "   -45"
var g = String.format("%6.4d", a);      // g = "  0045"
var h = String.format("%6.4d", b);      // h = " -0045"
var i = String.format("Do it %s", c);   // i = "Do it now"
var j = String.format("%3f", d);        // j = "1.234567"
var k = String.format("%10.2f%%", d);   // k = "      1.23%"
var l = String.format("%3f %2f.", d);   // l = "1.234567 ."
var m = String.format("%.0d", 0);       // m = ""
var n = String.format("%7d", "Int");    // n = invalid
var o = String.format("%s", true);      // o = "true"
```

7. URL

Name: URL

Library ID: 3

Description: This library contains a set of functions for handling both absolute URLs and relative URLs. The general URL syntax supported is (see [RFC1808])

`<scheme>://<host>:<port>/<path>;<params>?<query>#<fragment>`

7.1 isValid

Function: isValid(*url*)

Function ID: 0

Description: Returns `true` if the given *url* has the right URL syntax; otherwise, returns `false`. Both absolute and relative URLs are supported. Relative URLs are not resolved into absolute URLs.

Parameters: *url* = String

Return value: Boolean or invalid.

Exceptions: -

Example:
```
var a = URL.isValid("http://w.hst.com/script#func()");
// a = true
var b = URL.isValid("../common#test()");
// b = true
var c = URL.isValid("experimental?://www.host.com/cont");
// c = false
```

7.2 getScheme

Function: getScheme(*url*)

Function ID: 1

Description: Returns the scheme used in the given *url*. Both absolute and relative URLs are supported. Relative URLs are not resolved into absolute URLs.

Parameters: *url* = String

Return value: String or invalid.

Exceptions: If an invalid URL syntax is encountered while extracting the scheme, an `invalid` value is returned.

Example:
```
var a = URL.getScheme("http://w.h.com/path#frag");
// a = "http"
var b = URL.getScheme("w.h.com/path#frag");
// b = ""
```

7.3 getHost

Function: getHost(*url*)

Function ID: 2

Description: Returns the host specified in the given *url*. Both absolute and relative URLs are supported. Relative URLs are not resolved into absolute URLs.

Parameters: *url* = String

Return value: String or invalid.

Exceptions: If an invalid URL syntax is encountered while extracting the host part, an `invalid` value is returned.

Example:
```
var a = URL.getHost("http://w.h.com/path#frag");
// a = "w.h.com"
var b = URL.getHost("path#frag");
// b = ""
```

7.4 getPort

Function: getPort(*url*)

Function ID: 3

Description: Returns the port number specified in the given *url*. If no port is specified, then an empty string is returned. Both absolute and relative URLs are supported. Relative URLs are not resolved into absolute URLs.

Parameters: *url* = String

Return value: String or invalid.

Exceptions: If an invalid URL syntax is encountered while extracting the port number, an `invalid` value is returned.

Example:

```
var a = URL.getPort("http://w.h.com:80/path#frag");
//  a = "80"
var b = URL.getPort("http://w.h.com/path#frag");
//  b = ""
```

7.5 getPath

Function: getPath(*url*)

Function ID: 4

Description: Returns the path specified in the given *url*. Both absolute and relative URLs are supported. Relative URLs are not resolved into absolute URLs.

Parameters: *url* = String

Return value: String or invalid.

Exceptions: If an invalid URL syntax is encountered while extracting the path, an `invalid` value is returned.

Example:

```
a = URL.getPath("http://w.h.com/home/sub/comp#frag");
//  a = "/home/sub/comp"
b = URL.getPath("../home/sub/comp#frag");
//  b = "../home/sub/comp"
```

7.6 getParameters

Function: getParameters(*url*)

Function ID: 5

Description: Returns the parameters used in the given *url*. If no parameters are specified, an empty string is returned. Both absolute and relative URLs are supported. Relative URLs are not resolved into absolute URLs.

Parameters: *url* = String

Return value: String or invalid.

Exceptions: If an invalid URL syntax is encountered while extracting the parameters, an `invalid` value is returned.

Example:

```
a = URL.getParameters("http://w.h.com/script;3;2?x=1&y=3");
//  a = "3;2"
b = URL.getParameters("../script;3;2?x=1&y=3");
//  b = "3;2"
```

7.7 getQuery

Function: getQuery(*url*)

Function ID: 6

Description: Returns the query part specified in the given *url*. If no query part is specified, an empty string is returned. Both absolute and relative URLs are supported. Relative URLs are not resolved into absolute URLs.

Parameters: *url* = String

Return value: String or invalid.

Exceptions: If an invalid URL syntax is encountered while extracting the query part, an `invalid` value is returned.

Example:

```
a = URL.getParameters("http://w.h.com/home;3;2?x=1&y=3");
//  a = "x=1&y=3"
```

7.8 getFragment

Function: getFragment(*url*)

Function ID: 7

Description: Returns the fragment used in the given *url*. If no fragment is specified, an empty string is returned. Both absolute and relative URLs are supported. Relative URLs are not resolved into absolute URLs.

Parameters: *url* = String

Return value: String or invalid.

Exceptions: If an invalid URL syntax is encountered while extracting the fragment, an `invalid` value is returned.

Example:

```
var a = URL.getFragment("http://w.h.com/cont#frag");
//  a = "frag"
```

7.9 getBase

Function: getBase()

Function ID: 8

Description: Returns an absolute URL (without the fragment) of the current WMLScript compilation unit.

Parameters: -

Return value: String.

Exceptions: -

Example:

```
var a = URL.getBase();
//  Result: "http://www.host.com/test.scr"
```

7.10 getReferer

Function: getReferer()

Function ID: 9

Description: Returns the smallest relative URL (relative to the base URL of the current compilation unit, see Section 7.9) to the resource that called the current compilation unit. Local function calls do not change the referer. If the current compilation unit does not have a referer, then an empty string is returned.

Parameters: -

Return value: String.

Exceptions: -

Example:

```
var base    = URL.getBase();
//  base    = "http://www.host.com/current.scr"
var referer = URL.getReferer();
//  referer = "app.wml"
```

7.11 resolve

Function: resolve(*baseUrl*, *embeddedUrl*)

Function ID: 10

Description: Returns an absolute URL from the given *baseUrl* and the *embeddedUrl* according to the rules specified in [RFC1808]. If the *embeddedUrl* is already an absolute URL, the function returns it without modification.

Parameters: *baseUrl* = String
embeddedUrl = String

Return value: String or invalid.

Exceptions: If an invalid URL syntax is encountered as part of the resolution, an `invalid` value is returned.

Example:
```
var a = URL.resolve("http://foo.com/","foo.vcf");
//  a = "http://foo.com/foo.vcf"
```

7.12 escape

Function: escape(*string*)

Function ID: 11

Description: This function computes a new version of a *string* value in which special characters specified by [RFC1738] have been replaced by a hexadecimal escape sequence. The result contains no special characters that might have special meaning within a URL.

For special characters, whose Unicode encoding is `0xFF` or less, a two-digit escape sequence of the form `%xx` is used in accordance with [RFC1738].

Both absolute and relative URLs are supported. Relative URLs are not resolved into absolute URLs.

Parameters: *string* = String

Return value: String or invalid.

Exceptions: If *string* contains characters that are not part of the US-ASCII character set, an `invalid` value is returned.

If an invalid URL syntax is encountered while escaping the given URL, an `invalid` value is returned.

Example:
```
var a = URL.escape("http://w.h.com/dck?x=\u00ef#crd");
//  a = "http://w.h.com/dck?x=%ef#crd"
```

7.13 unescape

Function: unescape(*string*)

Function ID: 12

Description: The unescape function computes a new version of a *string* value in which each escape sequence of the sort that might be introduced by the escape function (see Section 7.12) is replaced with the character that it represents.

Both absolute and relative URLs are supported. Relative URLs are not resolved into absolute URLs.

Parameters: *string* = String

Return value: String or invalid.

Exceptions: If *string* contains characters that are not part of the US-ASCII character set, an `invalid` value is returned.

If an invalid URL syntax is encountered while unescaping the given URL, an `invalid` value is returned.

Example:

```
var a = URL.unescape("http://w.h.com/dck?x=%31%32#crd");
//  a = "http://w.h.com/dck?x=12#crd"
```

7.14 escapeString

Function: escapeString(*string*)

Function ID: 13

Description: This function computes a new version of a *string* value in which special characters (unsafe, reserved, and unprintable characters) specified by [RFC1738] have been replaced by a hexadecimal escape sequence. The given string is escaped as such; no URL parsing is performed.

For special characters, whose Unicode encoding is `0xFF` or less, a two-digit escape sequence of the form `%xx` is used in accordance with [RFC1738].

Parameters: *string* = String

Return value: String or invalid.

Exceptions: If *string* contains characters that are not part of the US-ASCII character set, an `invalid` value is returned.

Example:

```
var a = URL.escapeString("http://w.h.com/dck?x=\u00ef#crd");
//  a = "http%3a%2f%2fw.h.com%2fdck%3fx%3d%ef%23crd"
```

7.15 unescapeString

Function: unescapeString(*string*)

Function ID: 14

Description: The unescape function computes a new version of a *string* value in which each escape sequence of the sort that might be introduced by the *URL.escapeString()* function (see Section 7.14) is replaced with the character that it represents. The given string is unescaped as such; no URL parsing is performed.

Parameters: *string* = String

Return value: String or invalid.

Exceptions: If *string* contains characters that are not part of the US-ASCII character set, an `invalid` value is returned.

Example:

```
var a = "http%3a%2f%2fw.h.com%2fdck%3fx%3d12%23crd";
var b = URL.unescapeString(a);
//  b = "http://w.h.com/dck?x=12#crd"
```

7.16 loadString

Function: loadString(*url, contentType*)

Function ID: 15

Description: Returns the content denoted by the given absolute *url* and the *content type*. The *content type* must specify only one content type; no wildcards are allowed.

The behavior of this function is the following:

- The content with the given *content type* and *url* is loaded. The rest of the attributes needed for the content load are specified by the default settings of the user agent.
- If the load is successful and the returned content type matches the given *content type*, then the content is converted to a Unicode string and returned.
- If the load is unsuccessful or the returned content is of wrong content type, then a scheme-specific error code is returned.

Parameters: *url* = String
contentType = String

Return value: String, integer, or invalid.

Exceptions: Returns an integer *error code* that depends on the used URL scheme in case the load fails. If HTTP [RFC2068] or WSP (see [WAE]) schemes are used, HTTP error codes are returned.

If *content type* specifies more than one content type or contains wildcards, then `invalid` value is returned.

Example:

```
var myUrl = "http://www.host.com/vcards/myaddr.vcf";
myCard = URL.loadString(myUrl,"text/x-vcard");
```

8. WMLBrowser

Name: WMLBrowser

Library ID: 4

Description: This library contains functions by which WMLScript can access the different WML Browser variables and attributes. If the system does not support WML Browser, then all following functions return `invalid` value.

8.1 getVar

Function: getVar(*name*)

Function ID: 0

Description: Returns the value of the variable with the given *name* in the current browser context. Returns an empty string if the given variable does not exist.

Parameters: *name* = String

Return value: String or invalid.

Exceptions: -

Example:

```
var a = WMLBrowser.getVar("name");
// a = "Jon" or whatever value the variable has.
```

8.2 setVar

Function: setVar(*name*, *value*)

Function ID: 1

Description: Returns `true` if the variable with the given *name* is successfully set to contain the given *value* in the current browser context; `false` otherwise.

Parameters: *name* = String
value = String

Return value: Boolean or invalid.

Exceptions: -

Example:

```
var a = WMLBrowser.setVar("name", Mary); // a = true
```

8.3 go

Function: go(*url*, *vars*)

Function ID: 2

Description: Specifies the content denoted by the given *url* and the variable mappings to be loaded. This function has the same semantics as the GO task in WML (see [WML] for more information). The content is loaded after the WMLScript interpreter returns the control back to the WML browser. No content is loaded if the given *url* is an empty string (""). This function returns an empty string.

go() and *prev()* (see Section 8.4) functions override each other. Both of these functions can be called multiple times before returning the control back to the WML browser; however, only the settings of the last call stay in effect. In particular, if the last call to *go()* or *prev()* sets the URL to an empty string (""), all requests are effectively cancelled.

Parameters: *url* = String
vars = String

Return value: String or invalid.

Exceptions: -

Example:

```
var card = "http://www.host.com/loc/app.dck#start";
var vars = "x=3&y=2";
WMLBrowser.go(card,vars);
```

8.4 prev

Function: prev(*vars*)

Function ID: 3

Description: Signals the WML browser to go back to the previous WML card with the given variable mappings. This function has the same semantics as the PREV task in WML (see [WML] for more information). The previous card is loaded after the WMLScript interpreter returns the control back to the WML browser. This function returns an empty string.

prev() and *go()* (see Section 8.3) functions override each other. Both of these functions can be called multiple times before returning the control back to the WML browser; however, only the settings of the last call stay in effect. In particular, if the last call to *go()* or *prev()* sets the URL to an empty string (""), all requests are effectively cancelled.

Parameters: *vars* = String

Return value: String or invalid.

Exceptions: -

Example:

```
WMLBrowser.prev("price=" + currentPrice);
```

8.5 newContext

Function: newContext()

Function ID: 4

Description: Clears the current WML Browser context and returns an empty string. This function has the same semantics as the NEWCONTEXT attribute in WML (see [WML] for more information).

Parameters: -

Return value: String or invalid.

Exceptions: -

Example:

```
WMLBrowser.newContext();
```

8.6 getCurrentCard

Function: getCurrentCard()

Function ID: 5

Description: Returns the smallest relative URL (relative to the base of the current compilation unit, see Section 7.9 for information about how to access the current base) specifying the card (if any) currently being processed by the WML Browser (see [WML] for more information). The function returns an absolute URL in case the WML deck containing the current card does not have the same base as the current compilation unit.

Parameters: -

Return value: String or invalid.

Exceptions: Returns `invalid` in case there is no current card.

Example:

```
var a = WMLBrowser.getCurrentCard();
//  a = "deck#input"
```

8.7 refresh

Function: refresh()

Function ID: 6

Description: Forces the WML Browser to update its context and returns an empty string. This function has the same semantics as the REFRESH task in WML (see [WML] for more information). As a result, the user interface is updated to reflect the updated context.

Parameters: -

Return value: String or invalid.

Exceptions: -

Example:

```
WMLBrowser.setVar("name","Zorro");
WMLBrowser.refresh();
```

9. Dialogs

Name: Dialogs

Library ID: 5

Description: This library contains a set of typical user interface functions.

9.1 prompt

Function: prompt(*message, defaultInput*)

Function ID: 0

Description: Displays the given *message* and prompts for user input. The *defaultInput* parameter contains the initial content for the user input. Returns the user input.

Parameters: *message* = String
defaultInput = String

Return value: String or invalid.

Exceptions: -

Example:

```
var a = "09-555 3456";
var b = Dialogs.prompt("Phone number: ",a);
```

9.2 confirm

Function: confirm(*message, ok, cancel*)

Function ID: 1

Description: Displays the given *message* and two reply alternatives: *ok* and *cancel*. Waits for the user to select one of the reply alternatives and returns `true` for *ok* and `false` for *cancel*.

Parameters: *message* = String
ok = String (text, empty string results in the default implementation-dependent text)
cancel = String (text, empty string results in the default implementation-dependent text)

Return value: Boolean or invalid.

Exceptions: -

Example:

```
function onAbort() {
return Dialogs.confirm("Are you sure?","Yes","Well...");
};
```

9.3 alert

Function: alert(*message*)

Function ID: 2

Description: Displays the given *message* to the user, waits for the user confirmation, and returns an empty string.

Parameters: *message* = String

Return value: String or invalid.

Exceptions: -

Example:

```
function testValue(textElement) {
  if (String.length(textElement) > 8) {
    Dialogs.alert("Enter name < 8 chars!");
  };
};
```

10. Definitions

The following are terms and conventions used throughout this specification.

The keywords "MUST", "MUST NOT", "REQUIRED", "SHALL", "SHALL NOT", "SHOULD", "SHOULD NOT", "RECOMMENDED", "MAY", and "OPTIONAL" in this document are to be interpreted as described in [RFC2119].

Bytecode. Content encoding where the content is typically a set of low-level opcodes (i.e., instructions) and operands for a targeted hardware (or virtual) machine.

Client. A device (or application) that initiates a request for connection with a server.

Content. Subject matter (data) stored or generated at an origin server. Content is typically displayed or interpreted by a user agent in response to a user request.

Content Encoding. When used as a verb, *content encoding* indicates the act of converting a data object from one format to another. Typically, the resulting format requires less physical space than the original, is easier to process or store, and/or is encrypted. When used as a noun, *content encoding* specifies a particular format or encoding standard or process.

Content Format. Actual representation of content.

Device. A network entity that is capable of sending and receiving packets of information and has a unique device address. A device can act as both a client or a server within a given context or across multiple contexts. For example, a device can service a number of clients (as a server) while being a client to another server.

JavaScript. A *de facto* standard language that can be used to add dynamic behavior to HTML documents. JavaScript is one of the originating technologies of ECMAScript.

Origin Server. The server on which a given resource resides or is to be created. Often referred to as a *Web server* or an *HTTP server*.

Resource. A network data object or service that can be identified by a URL. Resources may be available in multiple representations (e.g., multiple languages, data formats, size, and resolutions) or vary in other ways.

Server. A device (or application) that passively waits for connection requests from one or more clients. A server may accept or reject a connection request from a client.

User. A user is a person who interacts with a user agent to view, hear, or otherwise use a rendered content.

User Agent. A user agent (or content interpreter) is any software or device that interprets WML, WMLScript, or resources. This may include textual browsers, voice browsers, search engines, etc.

Web Server. A network host that acts as an HTTP server.

WML. The Wireless Markup Language is a hypertext markup language used to represent information for delivery to a narrowband device (e.g., a phone).

WMLScript A scripting language used to program the mobile device. WMLScript is an extended subset of the JavaScript scripting language.

11. Abbreviations

For the purposes of this specification, the following abbreviations apply:

API	Application Programming Interface
ECMA	European Computer Manufacturer Association
HTTP	HyperText Transfer Protocol [RFC2068]
LSB	Least Significant Bits
MSB	Most Significant Bits
RFC	Request For Comments
UI	User Interface
URL	Uniform Resource Locator [RFC1738]
W3C	World Wide Web Consortium
WWW	World Wide Web
WSP	Wireless Session Protocol
WTP	Wireless Transport Protocol
WAP	Wireless Application Protocol
WAE	Wireless Application Environment
WTA	Wireless Telephony Applications
WTAI	Wireless Telephony Applications Interface
WBMP	Wireless BitMaP

12. Normative References

[ECMA262] Standard ECMA-262: "ECMAScript Language Specification," ECMA, June 1997.

[IEEE754] ANSI/IEEE Std 754-1985: "IEEE Standard for Binary Floating-Point Arithmetic," Institute of Electrical and Electronics Engineers, New York, 1985.

[RFC1738] "Uniform Resource Locators (URL)," T. Berners-Lee, et al., December 1994.
URL: ftp://ftp.isi.edu/in-notes/rfc1738.txt

[RFC1808] "Relative Uniform Resource Locators," R. Fielding, June 1995.
URL: ftp://ftp.isi.edu/in-notes/rfc1808.txt

[RFC2119] "Key Words for Use in RFCs to Indicate Requirement Levels," S. Bradner, March 1997.
URL: ftp://ftp.isi.edu/in-notes/rfc2119.tx

[UNICODE] "The Unicode Standard: Version 2.0," The Unicode Consortium, Addison-Wesley Developers Press, 1996.
URL: http://www.unicode.org/

[WAP] "Wireless Application Protocol Architecture Specification," WAP Forum, 30-April-1998.

URL: http://www.wapforum.org/
[WML] "Wireless Markup Language Specification," WAP Forum, 30-April-1998. URL: http://www.wapforum.org/
[WMLScript] "WMLScript Language Specification," WAP Forum, 30-April-1998. URL: http://www.wapforum.org/

13. Informative References

[JavaScript] "JavaScript: The Definitive Guide," David Flanagan. O'Reilly & Associates, Inc. 1997.
[RFC2068] "Hypertext Transfer Protocol—HTTP/1.1," R. Fielding, et al., January 1997. URL: ftp://ftp.isi.edu/in-notes/rfc2068.txt
[WAE] "Wireless Application Environment Specification," WAP Forum, 30-April-1998. URL: http://www.wapforum.org/
[WSP] "Wireless Session Protocol," WAP Forum, 1998. URL: http://www.wapforum.org/
[XML] "Extensible Markup Language (XML), W3C Proposed Recommendation 10-February-1998, REC-xml-19980210," T. Bray, et al., February 10, 1998. URL: http://www.w3.org/TR/REC-xml

Appendix A: Library Summary

The libraries and their library identifiers:

LIBRARY NAME	LIBRARY ID	PAGE
Lang	0	7
Float	1	17
String	2	22
URL	3	38
WMLBrowser	4	50
Dialogs	5	56

The libraries and their functions:

LANG LIBRARY	FUNCTION ID
abs	0
min	1
max	2
parseInt	3
parseFloat	4

isInt	5
isFloat	6
maxInt	7
minInt	8
float	9
exit	10
abort	11
random	12
seed	13

FLOAT LIBRARY	FUNCTION ID
int	0
floor	1
ceil	2
pow	3
round	4
sqrt	5
maxFloat	6
minFloat	7

STRING LIBRARY	FUNCTION ID
length	0
isEmpty	1
charAt	2
subString	3
find	4
replace	5
elements	6
elementAt	7
removeAt	8
replaceAt	9
insertAt	10
squeeze	11
trim	12
compare	13
toString	14
format	15

URL LIBRARY	FUNCTION ID
isValid	0
getScheme	1
getHost	2
getPort	3
getPath	4
getParameters	5
getQuery	6
getFragment	7
getBase	8
getReferer	9
resolve	10
escape	11
unescape	12
escapeString	13
unescapeString	14
loadString	15

WMLBROWSER LIBRARY	FUNCTION ID
getVar	0
setVar	1
go	2
prev	3
newContext	4
getCurrentCard	5
refresh	6

DIALOGS LIBRARY	FUNCTION ID
prompt	0
confirm	1
alert	2

CHAPTER

8

WMLScript Statement of Intent

Statement of Intended Work

The WMLScript specification (version 30-Apr-1998) supports international content and scripts with the Unicode character encoding. Scripts are transported over the network using Unicode character sets, such as UTF-8 or UCS-2. Unicode provides a means of representing a very large number of languages and characters with predictable programming characteristics. However, Unicode may consume extra bandwidth and mobil terminal resources in certain markets.

The WAP Forum intends to pursue two tasks in the near future:

- The identification of character encodings with characteristics suited to individual markets and locales
- The enhancement of WMLScript to support character sets other than Unicode

Character sets to be studied include, but are not limited to:

- Japanese: JIS, Shift_JIS, EUC-JP
- Korean: iso-ir-149, EUC-KR
- Chinese: GB2312, Big5, EUC-TW
- Central European: ISO-8859-2

CHAPTER

9

Wireless Telephony Application Interface Specification

1. Scope

Wireless Application Protocol (WAP) is a result of continuous work to define an industry-wide specification for developing applications that operate over wireless communication networks. The scope for the WAP Forum is to define a set of specifications to be used by service applications. The wireless market is growing very quickly, and reaching new customers and services. To enable operators and manufacturers to meet the challenges in advanced services, differentiation, and fast/flexible service creation, WAP defines a set of protocols in Transport, Session, and Application layers. For additional information on the WAP architecture, refer to *"Wireless Application Protocol Architecture Specification"* [WAP].

This document outlines the extensions to the WAP Application Environment (WAE) to support Wireless Telephony Applications. The specifics of the Wireless Telephony Applications are introduced in the form of an interface. The acronym WTAI is used in the document to denote the Wireless Telephony Application Interface. For maximum benefit, the reader should be somewhat familiar with WML [WML] and WMLScript [WMLScript].

2. WTA Background

The WAP WTAI features provide the means to create Telephony Applications, using a WTA user agent with the appropriate WTAI function libraries. A typical example is to set up a mobile originated call using the WTAI functions accessible from either a WML deck/card or WMLScript.

The application model for WTA is based on a WTA user agent, executing WML and WMLScript. The WTA user agent uses the WTAI function libraries to make function calls related to network services. The WTA user agent is able to receive WTA events from the mobile network, and pushed content, like WML decks and WTA events, from the WTA server. WTA events and WTAI functions make it possible to interact and handle resources (e.g., call control) in the mobile network.

The WTA server can invoke applications dynamically using content push with WML and WMLScript.

2.1 WTAI Libraries

The WTAI features are partitioned into a collection of WTAI function libraries. The type of function and its availability determines where the different functions are specified. The WTAI function libraries are accessible from both WML, using URLs, or from WMLScript using the scripting function libraries.

Network Common WTA The most common features that are available in all networks. They are only accessible from the WTA user agent. Examples of functions are call setup and answer incoming call.

Network-Specific WTA Features that are only available in certain types of networks. Operator-specific features may also reside in this set.

Public WTA Simple features that are available to third-party applications executing using the standard WAE user agent.

2.2 Event Handling

WTA event is one method that can be used to convey the change of state in the WTA server or the mobile network. The WTA user agent can be set up to act on a WTA event. WTA events must be mapped into URLs indicating the content that must be loaded to handle the WTA event, either by using the WTA event table or being handled dynamically, from within the WTA user agent context using temporary event binding.

See more details on the event handling in the WTA Specification [WTA].

3. WTA Interface

3.1 WTAI Function Libraries

The WTAI functions are divided into libraries depending on type of function. A function library can also be specific to a certain type of network, and then a "well-known" network name is included in the name of the library. The WTAI specification defines the set of predefined WTA function libraries for public and network common WTA, listed in Tables 9.1 and 9.2. Network-specific WTA function libraries are specified as addenda to the WTAI specification.

Table 9.1 Public WTA Function Libraries

FUNCTION LIBRARY	NAME	DESCRIPTION OF LIBRARY
Public WTAI	"wp"	Public available WTAI functions.

Table 9.2 Network Common WTA Function Libraries

FUNCTION LIBRARY	NAME	DESCRIPTION OF LIBRARY
Call Control	"cc"	Call Control library. Handles call setup and control of device during an ongoing call.
Network Text	"nt"	Network Text library. Sending and retrieval of network text.
Phonebook	"pb"	Phonebook library. Manages the entries in the device phonebook.
Miscellaneous	"ms"	Handling of miscellaneous features. An example is logical indications.

3.2 WTAI API Delimiters

All parameters are assumed to be of type string, unless otherwise specified. In addition, all parameters are mandatory, unless marked as optional. The WTAI functions are accessed using the WTAI URI scheme, a CGI-like style parameter scheme, or by using the defined WMLScript calls.

Notations used for the WTAI syntax are:

- < > Angle brackets denote an enumerated parameter.
- [ ] Square brackets denote an optional section.
- | Vertical bar denotes a pair of mutually exclusive options.
- ( )* Repeat none or multiple times.
- *( ) Repeat one or multiple times.

Specification of parameters:

A general rule is to always specify all input and output parameters unless otherwise stated. The WTA user agent should not fail if a result parameter is not specified. The recommended procedure in this instance is to discard the result.

3.3 WTAI URI Scheme

Access to the WTAI function libraries from WML can be handled through URI "calls" using the dedicated WTAI URI encoding scheme (see Table 9.3). Using a predefined reference to the specific WTAI function library together with the actual function name

Table 9.3 WTAI URI Scheme

<library>	Name that identifies the type of function; e.g., Call Control uses the library name "cc".
<function>	Function identifier within a specific library. An example is "ac" for the function "Accept Call" residing in the library "Network Common WTA".
<parameter>	Zero or more parameters to be sent to the function. Delimiter between subsequent parameters must be a semicolon ";".
<result>	Start of the result data section is indicated by an exclamation mark "!". Result is zero or more names of variables that will be set in the WTA user agent context as a result from the function call. Delimiter between subsequent result data must be a semicolon ";".

forms the WTAI URI. The WTAI URI library identifier can be used to identify the library. An example of a predefined library is "WTACallCont", specifying the common call control features.

A set of "well-known" network library names will be used to specify the WTAI URIs for the network-specific features.

WTAI functions are named using URIs. URIs are defined in [RFC1630]. The character set used to specify URIs is also defined in [RFC1630]. Consequently, characters such as space, used in a WTAI URI, must be escaped (see [RFC1630] for more details on escaping).

```
wtai://<library>/<function> (; <parameter>)* [! <result> (; <result> )* ]
```

3.4 WTAI Function Definition Format

Description: This is where the function is described.

URI: The URI form of the function.

WMLScript: The WMLScript form for the function.

Function ID: The number of the function in its library.

Parameters: Describes the identified parameters.

Output: Describes the output of the function. See Appendix B of this chapter for WTAI predefined error codes.

Examples: Gives an example for function use as a URI Method.
And an example of the function as a Script.

Associated Events: This section lists WTA events that may occur after the function call has been initiated. An example is the function "accept call". An associated event in this case would be "disconnect indication".

Notes: Extra notes that may be helpful.

4. Public WTA

The Public WTA functions are available to applications not originating from the network WTA server (i.e., third-party server applications). The handling of public applications differs from the network WTA in that the user must be able to cancel any specific operation before it is carried out. An example of an application, from a third-party service provider, could be a "Phone Number Guide" to customer services. The listed numbers are in fact "identifiers," URIs, that call the "Public WTA" function "makeCall".

Name: WTAPublic

Library ID: 512

Description: This library contains a public function that presents a number that can be dialed.

4.1 Make Call

Description: This function is used to initiate a mobile originated call using the specified *number*. The user must explicitly acknowledge the operation.

The *Make Call* function can be used from within any application, not only WTA, to present the user with a number that can be dialed.

URI: wtai://wp/mc ; <number>

WMLScript: makeCall(*number*);

Function ID: 0

Parameters: <number> = String:

Destination number to call. May use any valid telephony number characters and digits.

Output: -

Examples: URI: wtai://wp/mc; 5554367
WMLScript: WTAPublic.makeCall("5554367");

Associated Events: -

Notes: The call must be terminated using the standard MMI.

5. Network Common WTA

Functions defined in this section apply to all types of mobile networks that WAP is intended to use. Network-specific functions are defined in addendums to this document.

5.1 Network Events

WTAI specifies the names of the WTA events that map to the mobile networks, native events (see Table 9.4). These mobile network events convey the state of services in the mobile network. They may be handled by the active context or can be used to start the WTA user agent with a new context.

Table 9.4 Predefined Call Control Events

EVENT	PARAMETERS	DESCRIPTION
cc/ic	id, callerID	Incoming call indication. An incoming call has reached the user agent and may be picked up from the application using the WTAI function "Accept Call". < id>: Identity generated by the user agent itself to be used with subsequent call control operations. <callerID>: Contains the number of the calling party if available to the user agent; otherwise, an empty string will be returned.
cc/di	id	Disconnect Indication. The network has disconnected the call. <id>: The identity of the call that has been disconnected.
cc/ca	id, callerID	Call Answered. The called party has lifted the handset. <id>: The identity of the call that has been answered. <callerID>: Contains the number of the answering party if available to the user agent; otherwise, an empty string will be returned.
cc/cn	id, result	Call Not Answered. The called party doesn't answer. <id>: The identity of the call that reported busy. <result>: The result indicates why the called party doesn't answer. See Appendix B - "WTAI Predefined Error Codes."

5.2 Call Control

During a call, the following WTA functions can be used, where applicable, to control the operation of available call control features such as accept call and release call.

Name: WTACallControl

Library ID: 513

Description: This library contains functions that are related to call control, common for all "well-known" networks.

5.2.1 Setup Call

Description: Set up a mobile originated call to the specified number. The *mode* parameter indicates how the call should be handled if the context in the WTA user agent terminates. There are two modes: "drop" and "keep". "Drop" means that the OS will release the call if the context should be restarted. "Keep" makes it possible to maintain the call even after the current context has terminated.

URI: wtai://cc/sc ; <number> ; <mode> [! <result>]

WMLScript: set-up(number, mode);

Function ID: 0

Parameters: <number> = String:
Destination number to call. May use any valid telephony number characters and digits
<mode>:
0 = drop, Drop Call when current context is removed.
1 = keep, Keep Call after current context is removed.

Output: <result> = String:
The return value is the identity of the created call or a negative number in case of failure, the WTAI error code.

Examples: URI: wtai://cc/sc; 5554367;1
WMLScript: WTACallCont.setup("5554367", 0);

Associated Events: cc/di, Call Disconnect
cc/ca, Call Answered
cc/cn, Call Not Answered

Notes: -

5.2.2 Accept Call

Description: Accepts an incoming call or waiting call and lifts the handset. The "id" is the ordinal number assigned by the indevice call handler and will be returned if the call is carried out. If the call, for some reason, cannot be carried out, the return value contains an error code.

Any party or the network can terminate a call. When a call is terminated, the disconnect Indication will be generated and may be detected by the application.

The *mode* parameter indicates how the call should be handled if the context in the WTA user agent terminates. There are two modes: "drop" and "keep". "Drop" means that the OS will release the call if the context should be restarted. "Keep" makes it possible to maintain the call even after the current context has terminated.

URI: wtai://cc/ac;<id>; <mode> [! <result>]

WMLScript: accept(id, mode);

Function ID: 1

Parameters: <id> = String:
The identity of the call to be accepted.
<mode> = String:
0 = drop, Drop Call when current context is removed.
1 = keep, Keep Call after current context is removed.

Output: <result> = String:
The return value is the identity of the created call or a negative number in case of failure, the WTAI error code.

Examples: URI: wtai://cc/ac; 1;1
WMLScript: WTACallCont.accept ("1", 0);

Associated Events: cc/di, Call Disconnect
cc/ca, Call Answered
cc/cn, Call Not Answered

Notes: -

5.2.3 Release Call

Description: Release the specified call. Calls involved in a multiparty group can be released using the call identity.

URI: wtai://cc/rc;<id> [! <result>]

WMLScript: release(id);

Function ID: 2

Parameters: <id> = String:
The identity of the call to be released.

Output: <result> = String:
The return value is the identity of the created call or a negative number in case of failure, the WTAI error code.

Examples: URI: wtai://cc/rc; 1
WMLScript: WTACallCont.release ("1");

Associated Events: cc/di, Call Disconnect

Notes: -

5.2.4 Send DTMF Tones

Description: Send DTMF tone sequence through an active voice connection. If the call succeeds, the integer value 0 is returned. In case of unsuccessful outcome, an error code will be returned.

URI: wtai://cc/sd;<dtmf> [! <result>]

WMLScript: sendDTMF(dtmf);

Function ID: 3

Parameters: <dtmf> = String:
Any valid sequence of standard DTMF characters.

Output: <result> = String:
Integer value below 0 indicates unsuccessful execution.

Examples: URI: wtai://cc/sd; 555*1234
WMLScript: WTACallCont.sendDTMF ("555*1234");

Associated Events: cc/di, Call Disconnect

Notes: -

5.3 Network Text

The Network Text WTA function library handles sending and retrieval of text messages from the network text application in the device. The available "network text" functions are send, read, delete, and getFieldValue.

Name: WTANetText

Library ID: 514

Description: This library contains functions that handle sending and retrieval of network text.

5.3.1 Send Text

Description: Sends a network text message, if feature is available in the network, to a destination identified by number.

URI: -

WMLScript: send (number, text);

Function ID: 0

Parameters: <number> = String:
Destination number. Any valid telephony characters and digits.
<text> = String:
Network text data structure. The text to send.

Output: <result> = String:
Integer value below 0 indicates unsuccessful execution.

Examples: WMLScript: WTANetText.send ("5554567", "WAP Forum");

Associated Events: -

Notes: -

5.3.2 Read Text

Description: Read the network text data that may be stored in the device. Data is retrieved in the form of a field-encoded character string. Use the GetFieldValue to extract values for any specific fields.

URI: -

WMLScript: read (id);

Function ID: 2

Parameters: <id> = String:
Identity of network text to read. If id is empty, the last unread message is returned.

Output: <struct> = String:
The name of variable to receive the network text data structure. Integer value below 0 indicates unsuccessful execution.

Examples: WMLScript: WTANetText.read (3);

Associated Events: -

Notes: -

5.3.3 Delete Text

Description: Deletes a network text message identified by id. If no record can be identified, an error code will be returned.

URI: -

WMLScript: delete (id);

Function ID: 3

Parameters: <id> = String:
Identity of network text message to be deleted.

Output: <result> = String:
Integer value below 0 indicates unsuccessful execution.

Examples: WMLScript: WTANetText.delete (3);

Associated Events: -

Notes: -

5.3.4 GetFieldValue

Description: Retrieves the value, from the string <struct>, identified by "field".

URI: -wtai://nt/gv;<struct>; <field> ! <result>

WMLScript: getFieldValue(struct,field);

Function ID: 4

Parameters: <struct> = String:
Formatted character string containing the fields with the associated data.
<field> = String:
Name of field containing the value that will be retrieved from <struct>.

Output: <result> = String:
String, Value associated with the requested field. Value below 0 indicates unsuccessful execution.

Examples: WMLScript: WTANetText.getFieldValue($struct,"name");

Associated Events: -

Notes: If the field does not exist in <struct>, then the result contains an empty string.

5.4 Phonebook

The Phonebook WTA function library handles requests for operations towards the phonebook application. The requested operations can be used for storage and retrieval of phonebook entries. It is also possible to search the phonebook for a certain number, name or identity. The Phonebook in general will be specified with an extensible format regarding available fields in order to facilitate "contacts," ("address info"), applications.

Using the *read* function, phonebook entries are retrieved as "*structs*," a formatted character string containing *fields* with associated data. Data from each field can then be retrieved using the *GetFieldValue* function. There are three types of "well-known" field names required for a minimal implementation:

- *name*: Contains the entry's name
- *number*: Contains the entry's telephone number
- *id*: Contains the entry's id

The Phonebook functions are write, read, delete, and GetFieldValue.

Name: WTAPhoneBook

Library ID: 515

Description: This library contains functions that handle operation towards the phonebook application[1], such as storage and retrieval of phonebook entries.

[1]Existence of a phonebook application is implementation dependent and is not within the scope of WAP to define.

5.4.1 Write Phonebook Entry

Description: Writes a new entry to the phonebook. Any previous phonebook entry with the same identity will be overwritten. If no identity is specified, the next available phonebook entry will be used and the new identity is returned.

In case of unsuccessful operation, the output contains a negative number identifying the WTAI error code.

URI: -

WMLScript: write(id, number, name);

Function ID: 0

Parameters: <id> = String:
Identity of the phonebook entry.
<number> = String:
Phone number to be stored.
<name> = String:
Name that will be associated with the phone number.

Output: <result> = String:
Phonebook entry identity. A value below 0 indicates an error.

Examples: WMLScript: WTAPhoneBook.write("2", "5554367", "EINSTEIN");

Associated Events: -

Notes: -

5.4.2 Read Phonebook Entry

Description: Returns the specified phonebook entry (matched using the identity, text, or phone number). The selection criterion is based on the identity (where to find the entry in the phonebook database), phone number, or any searchable text (e.g., a name). If the parameters are left blank (""), the last used criteria will be reused for "get next match." If the search criterions can't be found, an empty string is returned.

URI: -

WMLScript: read(id, criteria);
(Criteria are id, text, or number)

Function ID: 1

Parameters: No parameters:
The last search criterion is used again for the next match.
<mode> = String:
Search mode (I=id, t=text, n=number).
<id> = String:
Identity of the phonebook entry.

<text>= String:
Search text; e.g., name.
<number>= String:
Phone number.

Output: <struct> = String:
Encoded message structure.

Examples: WMLScript: WTAPhoneBook.read("t", "My MOM");

Associated Events: -

Notes: -

5.4.3 Delete Phonebook Entry

Description: Deletes a phonebook entry. If the call succeeds, then the result variables contain a 0. If the function fails, then a negative number will be returned indicating the WTAI error code.

URI: -

WMLScript: delete(id);

Function ID: 2

Parameters: <id> = String:
Identity of the phonebook entry.

Output: <result> = String:
0 if successful. Integer value below 0 indicates unsuccessful execution.

Examples: WMLScript: WTAPhoneBook.delete("2");

Associated Events: -

Notes: -

5.4.4 GetFieldValue

Description: Retrieves a value, from the string <struct>, identified by "field".

URI: -

WMLScript: getFieldValue(struct,field);

Function ID: 3

Parameters: <struct> = String:
Formatted character string containing the fields with the associated data.
<field> = String:
Name of field containing the value that will be retrieved from <struct>.

Output: <result> = String:
String ,value associated with the requested field.

Examples: WMLScript: WTAPhoneBook.getFieldValue($struct,"name");

Associated Events: -

Notes: If the field does not exist in <struct>, then the result contains an empty string.

5.5 Miscellaneous

Various utility functions are used with the WTA user agent.

Name: WTAMisc

Library ID: 516

Description: This library contains functions for controlling logical device features like indications.

5.5.1 Indication

Description: Turns logical indication on or off. The appearance in the MMI is implementation dependent. An example would be a logical indication that can be visual and/or audible. An indication can also be set to show, for example, the number of e-mail messages.

URI: -

WMLScript: indication(type, operation, count);

Function ID: 0

Parameters: <type> = String:

0 = Incoming speech call
1 = Incoming data call
2 = Incoming fax call
3 = Call waiting
4 = Received text
5 = Voice mail notification
6 = Fax notification
7 = E-mail notification
8–15 = Extra notifications

<operation> = String:

1 = Set.
Activates the selected indication (e.g., starts ringing, animating, etc.).
2 = Reset.
Changes the indicator back to the state it was before the set function was called, or in case there are no previous set operations the default status for the indication will be set instead.

<count> = String:
The number of new text, voice mails, etc.

Output: -

Examples: WMLScript: WTAMisc.indication(5, 1, 3);

Associated Events: -

Notes: Count is not mandatory to show by the WTA user agent. How count is used depends on the implementation.

5.5.2 Terminate WTA User Agent

Description: This function removes the content and terminates the context for the WTA user agent.

URI: wtai://ms/ec

WMLScript: endcontext;

Function ID: 1

Parameters: -

Output: -

Examples: URI: wtai://ms/ec
WMLScript: WTAMisc.endcontext;

Associated Events: -

Notes: The *newcontext* attribute defined in [WML] is used when the context only needs to be cleared.

Notice the capability of error checking and reporting in the Script example.

6. Definitions

The following are terms and conventions used throughout this specification.

The following section describes definitions and abbreviations common to this document.

The keywords "MUST", "MUST NOT", "REQUIRED", "SHALL", "SHALL NOT", "SHOULD", "SHOULD NOT", "RECOMMENDED", "MAY", and "OPTIONAL" in this document are to be interpreted as **Card**–a navigable part of a WML document (deck). May contain information to present on the screen, instructions for gathering user input, etc.

Client. A device (or application) that initiates a request for connection with a server.

Content. Synonym for resources.

Deck. A WML document. May contain WMLScript.

Device. A device is a network entity that is capable of sending and receiving packets of information and has a unique device address. A device can act as both a client and a server within a given context or across multiple contexts. For example, a device can service a number of clients (as a server) while being a client to another server.

Server. A device (or application) that passively waits for connection requests from one or more clients. A server may accept or reject a connection request from a client.

User. A user is a person who interacts with a user agent to view, hear, or otherwise use a rendered content.

User Agent. A user agent (or content interpreter) is any software or device that interprets WML, WMLScript, or resources. This may include textual browsers, voice browsers, search engines, etc.

WML. The Wireless Markup Language is a hypertext markup language used to represent information for delivery to a narrowband device, (e.g., a phone).

WMLScript. A scripting language used to program the mobile device. WMLScript is an extended subset of the JavaScript scripting language.

7. Abbreviations

For the purposes of this specification, the following abbreviations apply:

API	Application Programming Interface
CGI	Common Gateway Interface
DCS	Digital Communications System
GSM	Global System for Mobile Communication
OS	Operating System
PCS	Personal Communications System
PDC	Personal Digital Cellular
RFC	Request For Comments
URI	Uniform Resource Identifier [RFC1630]
URL	Uniform Resource Locator
W3C	World Wide Web Consortium
WAE	Wireless Application Environment [WAE]
WAP	Wireless Application Protocol [WAP]
WTA	Wireless Telephony Applications [WTA]
WTAI	Wireless Telephony Applications Interface [WTAI]
WWW	World Wide Web

8. Normative References

[RFC2119] "Key Words for Use in RFCs to Indicate Requirement Levels," S. Bradner, March 1997.
URL: ftp://ds.internic.net/rfc/rfc2119.txt

[RFC1630] "Uniform Resource Identifiers (URI)," T. Berners-Lee, et al., June 1994. URL: ftp://ds.internic.net/rfc/rfc1630.txt

[WAE] "Wireless Application Environment Specification," WAP Forum, 1998. URL: http://www.wapforum.org/

[WAP] "Wireless Application Protocol Architecture Specification, version 0.9," WAP Forum, 1997. URL: http://www.wapforum.org/

[WML] "Wireless Markup Language," WAP Forum, 1998. URL: http://www.wapforum.org/

[WMLScript] "WMLScript Language Specification," WAP Forum, 1998. URL: http://www.wapforum.org/

[WSP] "Wireless Session Protocol Specification," WAP Forum, 1998. URL: http://www.wapforum.org/

[WTA] "Wireless Telephony Application Specification," WAP Forum, 1998. URL: http://www.wapforum.org/

[XML] "Extensible Markup Language (XML), W3C Proposed Recommendation 10-February-1998, REC-xml-19980210," T. Bray, et al., February 10, 1998. URL: http://www.w3.org/TR/REC-xml

9. Informative References

[RFC1738] "Uniform Resource Locators (URL)," T. Berners-Lee, et al., December 1994. URL: ftp://ds.internic.net/rfc/rfc1738.txt described in [RFC2119].

Appendix A: WTA URI and WMLScript Function Libraries

In the tables shown next, the URI and WMLScript Function Libraries Calls are summarized. The arguments have been left out in order to increase readability. The figures in the column named "Lib/Func ID" denote the *Library* and *Function IDs*.

A.1 Public WTA

Public WTAI

LIB/FUNC ID	URI	SCRIPT CALL	DESCRIPTION
512.0	`wtai://wp/mc`	`WTAPublic.makeCall`	Make a call.

A.2 Network Common WTA

Call Control

LIB/FUNC ID	URI	WMLSCRIPT CALL	DESCRIPTION
513.0	`wtai://cc/sc`	`WTACallCont.setup`	Set up a new call.
513.1	`wtai://cc/ac`	`WTACallCont.accept`	Accept an incoming call.
513.2	`wtai://cc/rc`	`WTACallCont.release`	Release a call.
513.3	`wtai://cc/sd`	`WTACallCont.sendDTMF`	Send DTMF.

Network Text

LIB/FUNC ID	URI	WMLSCRIPT CALL	DESCRIPTION
514.0	-	`WTANetText.send`	Send network text.
514.1	-	`WTANetText.read`	Read network text.
514.2	-	`WTANetText.delete`	Delete network text.
514.3	-	`WTANetText.getFieldValue`	Get Field Value.

Phonebook

LIB/FUNC ID	URI	WMLSCRIPT CALL	DESCRIPTION
515.0	-	`WTAPhoneBook.write`	Write phonebook entry.
515.1	-	`WTAPhoneBook.read`	Read phonebook entry.
515.2	-	`WTAPhoneBook.delete`	Delete phonebook entry.
515.3	-	`WTAPhoneBook.getFieldValue`	Get Field Value.

Miscellaneous

LIB/FUNC ID	URI	WMLSCRIPT CALL	DESCRIPTION
516.1	-	`WTAMisc.indication`	Logical indications.
516.2	`wtai://ms/ec`	`WTAMisc.endcontext`	Terminates user agent context.

Appendix B: WTAI Predefined Error Codes

Functions in the WTA function library may return a result code indicating the outcome of a function call (see Table B.1). In most cases, a positive integer indicates a successful outcome. WTAI defines a set of error codes, nonpositive result codes, which can be returned by the WTAI functions. Note: Not all codes are used by all functions. Codes in the range –1 to –63 are reserved for WTA standard library functions. Network-specific WTA must use codes in the range –64 to –127.

Table B.1 WTAI Predefined Error Codes

ERROR CODE	DESCRIPTION
–1	Id not found. Function could not be completed.
–2	Illegal number of parameters. Function could not be resolved due to missing parameters.
–3	Service not available or nonexistent function.
–4	Service temporarily unavailable.
–5	Called party is busy.
–6	Network is busy.
–7	No answer; i.e., call setup timed out.
–8 to –63	Reserved for future use by WTA standard library functions.
–64 to –127	Network-specific error codes.

Appendix C: Examples Using WTAI

WTAI functions can be called in either two ways. First, a WTAI function can be called as a URL call. Second, a WTAI function can be performed via a Script. The two examples show how a simple problem could be solved using either WML or WMLScript.

Here is an example of a WTAI function as a URL call:

```
<WML>
  <CARD>
    <DO TYPE="ACCEPT" TASK="GO" URL="#eFood"/>
    Welcome!
  </CARD>
  <CARD NAME="eFood">
```

```
    <DO TYPE="ACCEPT" TASK="GO" URL="wtai://cc/mc;$FoodNum"/>
    Choose Food:
     <SELECT KEY="FoodNum">
      <OPTION VALUE="5556789">Pizza</OPTION>
      <OPTION VALUE="5551234">Chinese</OPTION>
      <OPTION VALUE="5553344">Sandwich</OPTION>
      <OPTION VALUE="5551122">Burger</OPTION>
     <SELECT>
  </CARD>

</WML>
```

Here is an example of a WTAI function as a Script call:

```
WMLSCRIPT:
  function CallFood(N) {
    var i = wtaCallControl.Setup(N;1);
    if (i >= 0) {
     // Call is good, show call is done
      Browser.setVar("Msg", "Called");
      Browser.setVar("Nmbr", N);
    }
    else {
  // Call failed, we could tell user why
  Browser.setVar("Msg", "Error");
      Browser.setVar("Nmbr", $i);
    }
    Browser.go("displayMsg");
  }
<WML>
  <CARD>
    <DO TYPE="ACCEPT" TASK="GO" URL="/script#CallFood($FoodNum)"/>
    Choose Food:
    <SELECT KEY="FoodNum">
      <OPTION VALUE="5556789">Pizza</OPTION>
      <OPTION VALUE="5551234">Chinese</OPTION>
      <OPTION VALUE="5553344">Sandwich</OPTION>
      <OPTION VALUE="5551122">Burger</OPTION>
    <SELECT>
  </CARD>
  <CARD NAME="displayMsg">
    Call Status: $Msg $Nmbr
  </CARD>
</WML>
```

CHAPTER

10

Wireless Telephony Application Interface Specification IS-136 Specific Addendum

1. Scope

Wireless Application Protocol (WAP) is a result of continuous work to define an industrywide specification for developing applications that operate over wireless communication networks. The scope for the WAP Forum is to define a set of specifications to be used by service applications. The wireless market is growing very quickly, and reaching new customers and services. To enable operators and manufacturers to meet the challenges in advanced services, differentiation, and fast/flexible service creation, WAP defines a set of protocols in Transport, Session, and Application layers. For additional information on the WAP architecture, refer to *Wireless Application Protocol Architecture Specification* [WAP].

This document is an addendum to the *Wireless Telephony Application Interface* (WTAI). While WTAI defines an API that is valid for all supported types of mobile networks, this document outlines functions that are specific to IS-136 networks.

2. IS-136 Specific Library

In addition to the WTA functions defined in [WTAI], IS-136 networks also supports the functions specified in this chapter.

2.1 Network Events

WTAI specifies the names of the WTA events that map to the IS-136 mobile network, native events. These mobile network events convey the state of services in the mobile

Table 10.1 Predefined Call Control Events

EVENT	PARAMETERS	DESCRIPTION
is136/ia	aseq	Incoming Alert Info. The device has received an Alert sequence. <aseq>: Alert sequence information
is136/if	fseq	Incoming Flash Info. The device has received a Flash sequence. <fseq>: Flash sequence information

network. They may be handled by the active context or can be used to start the WTA user agent with a new context (see Table 10.1).

2.2 Network Functions

The functions defined in this chapter follows the same function definition format as the one used in [WTAI]. Technical terms used in this chapter (e.g., events and error codes) are also explained in [WTAI].

Name: WTAIS136

Library ID: 517

Description: This library contains functions that are unique to IS-136 networks.

2.3 Send Flash Code

Description: Send a flash code sequence through an active voice connection. If the call succeeds, the integer value 0 is returned. In case of unsuccessful outcome, an error code will be returned.

URI: wtai://is136/sf; <flash> [! <result>]

WMLScript: sendFlash("123");

Function ID: 0

Parameters: <flash> = String:
Any valid sequence of flash codes.

Output: <result> = String:
Integer value below 0 indicates unsuccessful execution.

Examples: URI: wtai://is136/sf;123
WMLScript: WTAIS136.sendFlash ("123");

Associated Events: -

Notes: -

2.4 Send Alert Code

Description: Send an alert code sequence through an active voice connection. If the call succeeds, the integer value 0 is returned. In case of unsuccessful outcome, an error code will be returned.

URI: wtai://is136/sa; <alert> [! <result>]

WMLScript: sendAlert ("123");

Function ID: 1

Parameters: <alert> = String:
Any valid sequence of alert codes.

Output: <result> = String:
The return value is 0 on success or a negative number in case of failure, the WTAI error code.

Examples: URI: wtai://is136/sa;123
WMLScript: WTAIS136.sendAlert ("123");

Associated Events: -

Notes: -

3. Definitions

The following are terms and conventions used throughout this specification.

The following section describes definitions and abbreviations common to this document.

The keywords "MUST", "MUST NOT", "REQUIRED", "SHALL", "SHALL NOT", "SHOULD", "SHOULD NOT", "RECOMMENDED", "MAY", and "OPTIONAL" in this document are to be interpreted as described in [RFC2119].

WMLScript. A scripting language used to program the mobile device. WMLScript is an extended subset of the JavaScript scripting language.

4. Abbreviations

For the purposes of this specification, the following abbreviations apply:

API	Application Programming Interface
IS-136	TDMA Cellular/PCS—Radio Interface—Mobile Station—Base Station Compatibility Standard
RFC	Request For Comments
URI	Uniform Resource Identifier [RFC1630]
WAP	Wireless Application Protocol [WAP]
WTA	Wireless Telephony Applications [WTA]
WTAI	Wireless Telephony Applications Interface [WTAI]

5. Normative References

The following section describes references relevant to this document:

[RFC1630] "Uniform Resource Identifiers (URI)," T. Berners-Lee, et al., June 1994. URL: ftp://ds.internic.net/rfc/rfc1630.txt

[RFC2119] "Key Words for Use in RFCs to Indicate Requirement Levels," S. Bradner, March 1997. URL: ftp://ds.internic.net/rfc/rfc2119.txt

[WAP] "Wireless Application Protocol Architecture Specification, version 0.9," WAP Forum, 1997. URL: http://www.wapforum.org/

[WMLScript] "WMLScript Language Specification," WAP Forum, 1998. URL: http://www.wapforum.org/

[WTA] "Wireless Telephony Application Specification," WAP Forum, 1998. URL: http://www.wapforum.org/

[WTAI] "Wireless Telephony Application Interface Specification," WAP Forum, 1997. URL: http://www.wapforum.org/

Appendix A: WTA URI and WMLScript Function Libraries

In Table A.1, the URI and WMLScript function libraries calls valid for IS-136 networks are summarized. The arguments have been left out in order to increase readability. The figures in the column named "Lib/Func ID" denote the *Library* and *Function IDs*.

Table A.1 URI and WMLScript Functions

LIB/FUNC ID	URI	WMLSCRIPT CALL	DESCRIPTION
517.0	`wtai://is136/sf`	`WTAIS136.sendFlash`	Send a flash code.
517.1	`wtai://is136/sa`	`WTAIS136.sendAlert`	Send an alert code.

CHAPTER

11

Wireless Telephony Application Interface Specification GSM Specific Addendum

1. Scope

Wireless Application Protocol (WAP) is a result of continuous work to define an industrywide specification for developing applications that operate over wireless communication networks. The scope for the WAP Forum is to define a set of specifications to be used by service applications. The wireless market is growing very quickly, and reaching new customers and services. To enable operators and manufacturers to meet the challenges in advanced services, differentiation, and fast/flexible service creation, WAP defines a set of protocols in Transport, Session, and Application layers. For additional information on the WAP architecture, refer to *Wireless Application Protocol Architecture Specification* [WAP].

This document is an addendum to the *Wireless Telephony Application Interface* (WTAI). While WTAI defines an API that is valid for all supported types of mobile networks, this document outlines functions that are specific to networks using GSM technology. In this specification, the following networks are supported: GSM, DCS1800, and PCS1900.

2. GSM Specific Library

In addition to the WTA functions defined in [WTAI], GSM networks also supports the functions specified in this chapter. Since GSM is the predecessor, the function library is named using that abbreviation.

2.1 Network Functions

The functions defined in this chapter follows the same function definition format as the one used in [WTAI]. Technical terms used in this chapter (e.g., events and error codes) are also explained in [WTAI].

Name: WTAGSM

Library ID: 518

Description: This library contains functions that are unique to GSM networks.

2.2 Call Reject

Description: Rejects an unanswered call.

URI: wtai://gsm/cr;<id> [! <result>]

WMLScript: reject(id);

Function ID: 0

Parameters: <id> = String:
The identity of the call to be rejected.

Output: <result> = String:
The return value is the identity of the rejected call or a negative number in case of failure, the WTAI error code.

Examples: URI: wtai://gsm/cr; 1
WMLScript: WTAGSM.reject ("1");

Associated Events: -

Notes: -

2.3 Call Hold

Description: Puts an answered call on hold.

URI: wtai://gsm/ch;<id> [! <result>]

WMLScript: hold(id);

Function ID: 1

Parameters: <id> = String:
The identity of the call to be put on hold.

Output: <result> = String:
The return value is the identity of the held call or a negative number in case of failure, the WTAI error code.

Examples: URI: wtai://gsm/ch; 1

WMLScript: WTAGSM.hold ("1");

Associated Events: -

Notes: The call can be retrieved using the *Accept Call* function (wtai://cc/ac) or released using the *Release Call* function (wtai://cc/rc).

2.4 Call Transfer

Description: Transfers an unanswered call to another party.

URI: wtai://gsm/ct; <id> ; <dest> [! <result>]

WMLScript: transfer(id);

Function ID: 2

Parameters: <id> = String:
The identity of the call to be transferred.
<dest> = String:
The destination to where the call should be transferred (any valid phone number).

Output: <result> = String:
The return value is the identity of the transferred call or a negative number in case of failure, the WTAI error code.

Examples: URI: wtai://gsm/ct; 1;"+1 555 1234"
WMLScript: WTAGSM. transfer ("1" ,"+1 555 1234");

Associated Events: -

Notes: -

2.5 Join Multiparty

Description: This function is partly used for establishing a multiparty call and partly for joining new parties to an existing multiparty.
Establish a multiparty: Joins an active call with a call on hold. A multiparty call (with a unique "id") is established.
Add new party: Joins an active call with a multiparty on hold.
How a call is put on hold is described in [WTAI].

URI: wtai://gsm/jm [! <result>]

WMLScript: Multiparty;

Function ID: 3

Parameters: -

Output: <result> = String:
The return value is the identity of the multiparty call or a negative number in case of failure, the WTAI error code.

Examples: URI: wtai://gsm/jm
WMLScript: WTAGSM.multiparty;

Associated Events: -

Notes: -

2.6 Retrieve from Multiparty

Description: Separates a certain party from a multiparty call for a private conversation. The rest of the multiparty is put on hold.

URI: wtai://gsm/rm;<id> [! <result>]

WMLScript: retrieve("1");

Function ID: 4

Parameters: <id> = String:
The identity of the call to be retrieved from the multiparty.

Output: <result> = String:
The return value is the identity of the retrieved call or in case of failure, a negative number and the WTAI error code.

Examples: URI: wtai://gsm/rm;1
WMLScript: WTAGSM.retrieve ("1");

Associated Events: -

Notes: -

3. Definitions

The following section describes definitions and abbreviations common to this document.

The keywords "MUST", "MUST NOT", "REQUIRED", "SHALL", "SHALL NOT", "SHOULD", "SHOULD NOT", "RECOMMENDED", "MAY", and "OPTIONAL" in this document are to be interpreted as described in [RFC2119].

The following are terms and conventions used throughout this specification.

WMLScript. A scripting language used to program the mobile device. WMLScript is an extended subset of the JavaScript scripting language.

4. Abbreviations

For the purposes of this specification, the following abbreviations apply:

API Application Programming Interface
DCS Digital Communications System
GSM Global System for Mobile Communication
PCS Personal Communications System

RFC	Request For Comments
URI	Uniform Resource Identifier [RFC1630]
WAP	Wireless Application Protocol [WAP]
WTA	Wireless Telephony Applications [WTA]
WTAI	Wireless Telephony Applications Interface [WTAI]

5. Normative References

[RFC1630] "Uniform Resource Identifiers (URI)," T. Berners-Lee, et al., June 1994. URL: ftp://ds.internic.net/rfc/rfc1630.txt

[RFC2119] "Key Words for Use in RFCs to Indicate Requirement Levels," S. Bradner, March 1997. URL: ftp://ds.internic.net/rfc/rfc2119.txt

[WAP] "Wireless Application Protocol Architecture Specification, version 0.9," WAP Forum, 1997. URL: http://www.wapforum.org/

[WMLScript] "WMLScript Language Specification," WAP Forum, 1998. URL: http://www.wapforum.org/

[WTA] "Wireless Telephony Application Specification," WAP Forum, 1998. URL: http://www.wapforum.org/

[WTAI] "Wireless Telephony Application Interface Specification," WAP Forum, 1997. URL: http://www.wapforum.org/

Appendix A: WTA URI and WMLScript Function Libraries

In Table A.1, the URI and WMLScript Function Libraries Calls valid for GSM networks are summarized. The arguments have been left out in order to increase readability. The figures in the column named "Lib/Func ID" denote the *Library* and *Function IDs*.

Table A.1 URI and WMLScript Functions

LIB/FUNC ID	URI	WMLSCRIPT CALL	DESCRIPTION
518.0	`wtai://gsm/cr`	`WTAGSM.reject`	Reject an incoming call.
518.1	`wtai://gsm/ch`	`WTAGSM.hold`	Put a call on hold.
518.2	`wtai://gsm/ct`	`WTAGSM.transfer`	Transfer an unanswered call.
518.3	`wtai://gsm/jm`	`WTAGSM.multiparty`	Join/create a multiparty call.
518.4	`wtai://gsm/rm`	`WTAGSM.retrieve`	Retrieve a party from a multiparty call.

CHAPTER

12

Wireless Telephony Application Interface Specification PDC Specific Addendum

1. Scope

Wireless Application Protocol (WAP) is a result of continuous work to define an industrywide specification for developing applications that operate over wireless communication networks. The scope for the WAP Forum is to define a set of specifications to be used by service applications. The wireless market is growing very quickly, and reaching new customers and services. To enable operators and manufacturers to meet the challenges in advanced services, differentiation, and fast/flexible service creation, WAP defines a set of protocols in Transport, Session, and Application layers. For additional information on the WAP architecture, refer to *Wireless Application Protocol Architecture Specification* [WAP].

This document is an addendum to the *Wireless Telephony Application Interface* (WTAI). While WTAI defines an API that is valid for all supported types of mobile networks, this document outlines functions that are specific to PDC networks.

2. PDC Specific Library

In addition to the WTA functions defined in [WTAI], PDC networks also supports the functions specified in this chapter.

2.1 Network Functions

The functions defined in this chapter follows the same function definition format as the one used in [WTAI]. Technical terms used in this chapter (e.g., events and error codes) are also explained in [WTAI].

Name: WTAPDC

Library ID: 520

Description: This library contains functions that are unique to PDC networks.

2.2 Call Reject

Description: Rejects an unanswered call.

URI: wtai://pdc/cr;<id> [! <result>]

WMLScript: reject(id)

Function ID: 0

Parameters: <id> = String:
The identity of the call to be rejected.

Output: <result> = String:
The return value is the identity of the rejected call or a negative number in case of failure, the WTAI error code.

Examples: URI: wtai://pdc/cr; 1
WMLScript: WTAPDC.reject ("1");

Associated Events: -

Notes: -

2.3 Call Hold

Description: Puts an answered call on hold.

URI: wtai://pdc/ch;<id> [! <result>]

WMLScript: hold(id);

Function ID: 1

Parameters: <id> = String:
The identity of the call to be put on hold.

Output: <result> = String:
The return value is the identity of the held call or a negative number in case of failure, the WTAI error code.

Examples: URI: wtai://pdc/ch; 1
WMLScript: WTAPDC.hold ("1");

Associated Events: -

Notes: -

2.4 Call Transfer

Description: Transfers an unanswered call to another party.

URI: wtai://pdc/ct; <id> ; <dest> [! <result>]

WMLScript: transfer(id);

Function ID: 2

Parameters: <id> = String:
The identity of the call to be transferred.
<dest> = String:
The destination to where the call should be transferred (any valid phone number).

Output: <result> = String:
The return value is the identity of the transferred call or a negative number in case of failure, the WTAI error code.

Examples: URI: wtai://pdc/ct; 1;"+15551234"
WMLScript: WTAPDC. transfer ("1" ,"+15551234");

Associated Events: -

Notes: -

2.5 Join Multiparty

Description: This function is partly used for establishing a multiparty call, and partly for joining new parties to an existing multiparty.
Establish a multiparty: Joins an active call with a call on hold. A multiparty call (with a unique "id") is established.
Add new party: Joins an active call with a multiparty on hold.
How a call is put on hold is described in [WTAI].

URI: wtai://pdc/jm [! <result>]

WMLScript: Multiparty;

Function ID: 3

Parameters: -

Output: <result> = String:
The return value is the identity of the multiparty call or a negative number in case of failure, the WTAI error code.

Examples: URI: wtai://pdc/jm
WMLScript: WTAPDC.multiparty;

Associated Events: -

Notes: -

2.6 Retrieve from Multiparty

Description: Separates a certain party from a multiparty call for a private conversation. The rest of the multiparty is put on hold.

URI: wtai://pdc/rm;<id> [! <result>]

WMLScript: Retrieve("1");

Function ID: 4

Parameters: <id> = String:
The identity of the call to be retrieved from the multiparty.

Output: <result> = String:
The return value is the identity of the retrieved call or in case of failure a negative number, the WTAI error code.

Examples: URI: wtai://pdc/rm;1
WMLScript: WTAPDC.retrieve ("1");

Associated Events: -

Notes: -

3. Definitions

The following are terms and conventions used throughout this specification.

The following section describes definitions and abbreviations common to this document.

The keywords "MUST", "MUST NOT", "REQUIRED", "SHALL", "SHALL NOT", "SHOULD", "SHOULD NOT", "RECOMMENDED", "MAY", and "OPTIONAL" in this document are to be interpreted as described in [RFC2119].

WMLScript. A scripting language used to program the mobile device. WMLScript is an extended subset of the JavaScript scripting language.

4. Abbreviations

For the purposes of this specification, the following abbreviations apply:

API	Application Programming Interface
GSM	Global System for Mobile Communication
PDC	Pacific Digital Cellular System
RFC	Request For Comments
URI	Uniform Resource Identifier [RFC1630]
WAP	Wireless Application Protocol [WAP]
WTA	Wireless Telephony Applications [WTA]
WTAI	Wireless Telephony Applications Interface [WTAI]

5. Normative References

[RFC2119] "Key Words for Use in RFCs to Indicate Requirement Levels," S. Bradner, March 1997.
URL: ftp://ds.internic.net/rfc/rfc2119.txt

[RFC1630] "Uniform Resource Identifiers (URI)," T. Berners-Lee, et al., June 1994.
URL: ftp://ds.internic.net/rfc/rfc1630.txt

[WAP] "Wireless Application Protocol Architecture Specification, version 0.9," WAP Forum, 1997.
URL: http://www.wapforum.org/

[WMLScript] "WMLScript Language Specification," WAP Forum, 1998.
URL: http://www.wapforum.org/

[WTA] "Wireless Telephony Application Specification," WAP Forum, 1998.
URL: http://www.wapforum.org/

[WTAI] "Wireless Telephony Application Interface Specification," WAP Forum, 1997.
URL: http://www.wapforum.org/

Appendix A: WTA URI and WMLScript Function Libraries

In Table A.1, the URI and WMLScript Function Libraries Calls valid for PDC networks are summarized. The arguments have been left out in order to increase readability. The figures in the column named "Lib/Func ID" denote the *Library* and *Function IDs*.

Table A.1 URI and WMLScript Functions

LIB/FUNC ID	URI	WMLSCRIPT CALL	DESCRIPTION
520.0	`wtai://pdc/cr`	`WTAPDC.reject`	Reject an incoming call.
520.1	`wtai://pdc/ch`	`WTAPDC.hold`	Put a call on hold.
520.2	`wtai://pdc/ct`	`WTAPDC.transfer`	Transfer an unanswered call.
520.3	`wtai://pdc/jm`	`WTAPDC.multiparty`	Join/create a multiparty call.
520.4	`wtai://pdc/rm`	`WTAPDC.retrieve`	Retrieve a party from a multiparty call.

CHAPTER

13

Wireless Telephony Application Specification

1. Scope

Wireless Application Protocol (WAP) is a result of continuous work to define an industrywide specification for developing applications over wireless communication networks. The scope for the WAP working group is to define a set of specifications to be used by service applications. The wireless market is growing very quickly and reaching new customers and services. To enable operators and manufacturers to meet the challenges in advanced services, differentiation, and fast/flexible service creation, WAP defines a set of protocols in Transport, Session, and Application layers. For additional information on the WAP architecture, refer to *Wireless Application Protocol Architecture Specification* [WAP].

This specification defines the Wireless Telephony Application (WTA). The WTA user agent is an extension of the WAE user agent using WTA Interface [WTAI]. WTA is intended for use in specifying Wireless Telephony Applications that interface with local and network telephony infrastructure.

WTA interfaces can be broken down to three different types. The first two types, Network Common and Network Specific, are reserved for the network operators. This is because the mobile network operators control and maintain the services for users on their mobile network. The third type, Public, is a limited set of WTA functions, such as initiating a mobile phone call, available to content from any content developer [WTAI].

Wireless Telephony Applications have four main goals:

Advanced end-user services. WTA makes it possible for network operators to provide advanced services with a consistent interface towards the end users.

Increased utilization of network. Network operators can utilize WTA to increase the use of the network services.

Interoperability. WAP Applications written using the WTA interface can execute on a variety of telephony devices. Interoperability across Terminals!

Network-independent applications. WTA content developers write telephony applications that span various networks that use different protocols.

2. WTA Overview

WTA enables content written in WML and WMLScript to utilize telephony features in the device and the mobile network. The WTA server, the mobile network, and the WTA client can be thought of as a single application with parts in the client and the WTA server. The WTA server acts as the principal content generator. The WTA server may be connected to the mobile network where it could have the means to control the mobile network services. Content may be customized by the WTA server and downloaded to the client.

WTA extends the basic WAE application model in three ways:

- WTA provides a means for a WTA server to push content to the device.
- WTA provides a means for mobile network events to trigger the rendering of content in the device.
- WTA provides telephony functions on the device that can be accessed from WML or WMLScript.

The WSP push feature [WSP] is used by the WTA server to push down content to the WTA client. While content can be essentially anything, there are two fundamentally different types of content formats: standard WAE content formats, such as WML, WMLScript, or WBMP; and the specific WTA content format called *WTA event*. The WTA framework allows a flexible implementation for the client that allows it to support pushed standard content, WTA event, or both. The WTA server must decide what features to use based on the user agent characteristics and the profile specified for the specific WTA user agent [WAE].

2.1 Server-Centric and Client-Centric Mode

The fundamental differences between pushing a WTA event or content are illustrated in Figures 13.1 and 13.2. The coordinating network element has been used for naming the particular model. The two important network elements in this case are the WTA server and the WTA client. In both models, the WTA server acts as the content generator toward the WTA client.

Server-centric mode (Figure 13.1): The WTA server handles events, such as incoming calls, that occur in the mobile network and provides the WTA client with content that is used for handling the specific task. The WTA server deploys content customized for the occurring event.

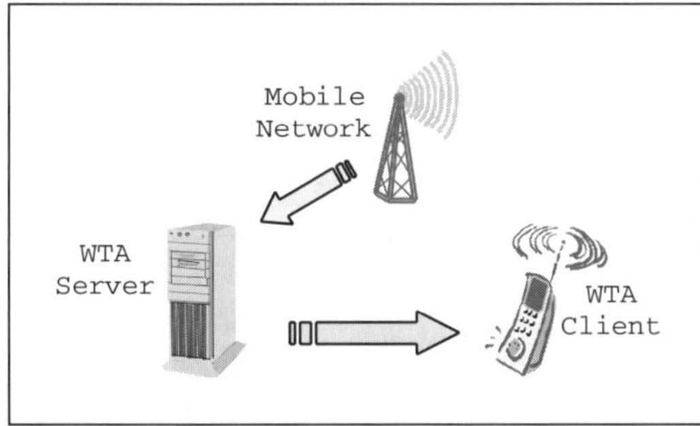

Figure 13.1 Server-centric mode.

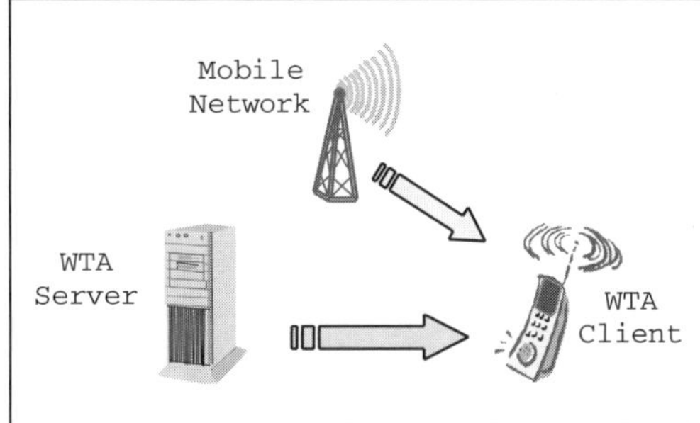

Figure 13.2 Client-centric mode.

Client-centric mode (Figure 13.2): The WTA client handles events, such as incoming calls, received from the mobile network. Event bindings in the WTA client can be used to associate the event to executable content that is used for handling the specific task.

By combining the server- and client-centric models in the same architecture, the operator can take advantage of the features that best fits the particular type of mobile network and type of applications.

2.2 User Agent Characteristics

The WAP proxy is informed of the available WTA features, such as available WTAI Libraries [WTAI], and the selected WTA network-programming model (i.e., server- or client-centric mode).

2.3 WTAI Function Calls

Provides access to features in the device and the mobile network [WTAI]. An example of local device features is logical indications for call control . Mobile network features include call control and network text.

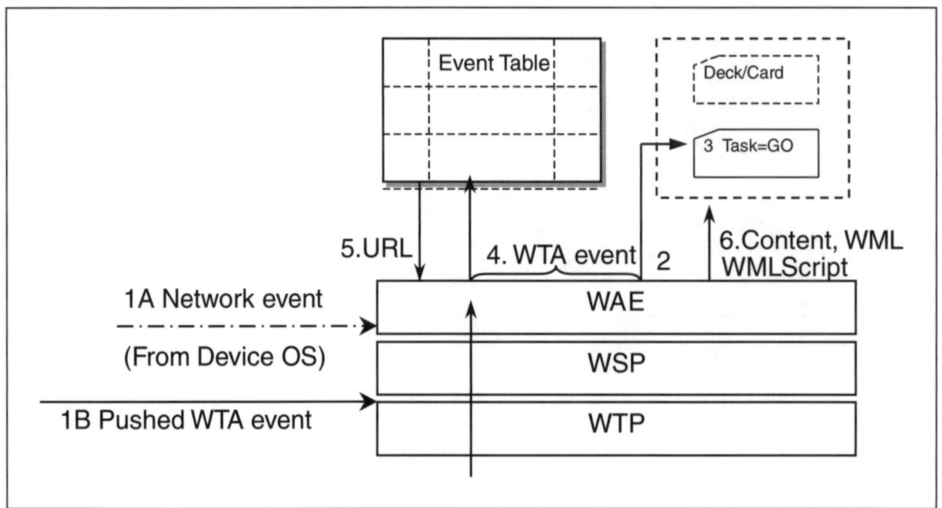

Figure 13.3 WTA event transformation.

2.4 WTA Events

Figure 13.3 illustrates WTA event transition. WTA event transition is the process used by the WTA user agent for handling the transformation of a network event to a WTA event and then to an appropriate action by the client (e.g., ringing on the event of an incoming call). WTA events are then matched to the appropriate WTA event handler depending on the state of the WTA user agent and the current WTA context, if any.

The two ways in which a client can receive a WTA event are illustrated in Figure 13.3. The first way is via the device operating system; the OS detects an event and then passes that event to the WAE basic services (denoted with an A as a suffix). The second way (denoted with a B as a suffix) is through a pushed WTA event that is received from the WTA server. Network events, as specified by [WTAI], are converted into the abstract WTA event form. See Table 13.1.

3. Supported Content Formats

This section describes the specific types of content formats that must be supported and the required behavior of the WTA client depending on the mode (client centric or server centric) when receiving the content.

The following three fundamental methods for content transfer are described:

Mobile network event: The representation of the network-specific signaling that can be handled [WTAI]. The WTA user agent encounters the network event in an abstract form of the WTA event (abstract as no physical WTA event content is needed).

Table 13.1 Event Flow Walkthrough

1A	The Device OS receives a network event and converts it to a WTA event, which is injected into WAE.
1B	The WTA event content format is received from the WTA server using the WSP push service [WSP].
2	In case of a user agent context, the WTA event must first be matched to any existing WML event bindings.
3	In case of a WML event binding with task=go, the URL locates the resource that must be loaded [WML].
4	No match with the WML event binding means the WTA event must be tested for a match with the event table.
5	A match must return the associated URL. The URL is extracted from the WTA event table binding.
6	The WTA user agent is restarted with a new context and then loads the content located by the URL[1]. Any values received, with the WTA event, must be stored in the variables identified by the parameters list.

Acknowledged content: Content that must be acknowledged to the sending party; an example is the event table.

Unacknowledged content: Content that does not require an acknowledge; an example is a WML deck.

Figure 13.4 shows the content formats that must be supported by the WTA client depending on the WTA client mode, server centric or client centric. The content formats supported in the server-centric mode must also be supported by the client-centric mode.

Figure 13.4 is constructed based on the domains of content formats for the client-centric and server-centric modes. The server-centric content formats are thus also contained in the client-centric domain. The opposite is not true; there is no support for event table or WTA event in the server-centric domain.

Methods for content transfer are rendered in a bold font. Arrows point to the content formats that could be transferred using the specified method. Italic font denotes the processing that will take place for content formats that originate from events (WTA events or mobile network events). This is only a logical diagram of network events; in reality, they must be converted to an abstraction of a WTA event prior to being processed by the user agent or the event table.

[1]A URL, stored in the event table, can be relative (e.g., a card name), in which case the base URL must be provided with the event table.

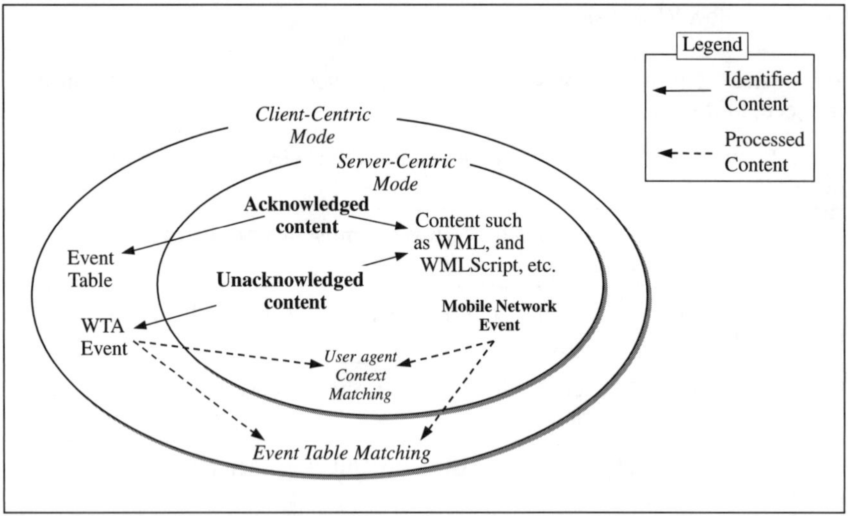

Figure 13.4 WTA content formats relational diagram.

3.1 Performance Requirements

The terms *immediately* and *unattended* in the following section are used to describe the expected response for a particular implementation in the WTA client and the WTA server. The term *immediately* means that the user agent must cancel the execution of any other content and start the processing of the new content. The term *unattended* means that from the WTA server's perspective there has been no "acknowledge" response from the WTA client during a predefined timeout period. The timeout period is dependent on the bearer used. Refer to the WAP architecture document [WAPARCH] for recommendations on bearer characteristics such as the timeout for acknowledged content to the WTA client.

3.2 Content Serialization

The model for handling content must apply an order of processing that ensures all content to be handled in the order of reception. No other content must be handled until the processing of the current content is concluded. A WTA event is considered concluded as soon as the event has been resolved into a URL or by other means, such as the WML event bindings, where it is bound to a specific task, to begin execution. Handling of content such as WML and WMLScript is considered concluded as soon as the content has been loaded into the context and the execution has started.

3.3 Server-Centric Mode

In this mode, WTA event and event table must not be sent to the WTA client from the WTA server. The following rules state the required behavior for a WTA user agent and WTA server in server-centric mode:

Required steps for handling a mobile network event:

1. The network event must be serviced immediately after reception and conversion to a WTA event.
2. If a user agent context exists, "Event matching" must be applied in order to find a matching WML event binding stored in the user agent context; e.g., a WML element "ONEVENT" with a matching event name.

Required steps for handling acknowledged content:

1. The content must be serviced immediately by the WTA user agent.
2. When the content has been identified by the WTA user agent, the result code indicating "success" must be acknowledged [WSP] to the WTA server.
3. For content that cannot be identified by the WTA user agent, the result code indicating "failure" must be acknowledged [WSP] to the WTA server.
4. For unattended content, the WTA server must apply the same rule as if the content was acknowledged with the result code indicating "failure".

Required steps for handling unacknowledged content:

1. The content must be indicated to the end user. There must be a possibility for the end user to detect content that eventually needs to be attended. What an end-user indication might look like is up to the implementation and is not specified by WAP.
2. The content must not be processed unless the context in the WTA user agent has been terminated. In other words, the new content must not be allowed to interrupt any other content that is executed by the user agent. The end user may decide to terminate any current content, and context, in the user agent and instead attend the new content.

3.4 Client-Centric Mode

The same rules apply for a WTA user agent in client-centric mode as for the server-centric mode with regard to handling a mobile network event and content such as WML and WMLScript. In addition, the client-centric mode also requires that the WTA user agent support WTA event and the event table.

The following rules state the required behavior for a WTA client in client-centric mode:

Required steps for handling event table:

1. The event table must be serviced immediately by the WTA user agent.
2. When the event table has been successfully set up by the WTA user agent, the result code indicating "success" must be acknowledged [WSP] to the WTA server. A successful setup means that the event table was possible to verify with regard to the required elements in the encoded form. Refer to Section 10. The new event table is effective at the same time an acknowledgment is sent back.

3. For an event table that cannot be set up by the WTA user agent due to reception of a mobile network event or a failure in the verification, the result code indicating "failure" must be acknowledged [WSP] to the WTA server.
4. For unattended event table content, the WTA server must apply the same internal rules as if the event table content was acknowledged with the result code indicating "failure." The internal rules are specific to any implementation of the WTA server.

Required steps for handling acknowledged WTA event:

1. The WTA event must be serviced immediately by the WTA user agent.
2. Event matching determines if a match can be found in an existing WTA user agent context. If a WTA event is verified to be correct with regard to the required elements in the encoded form (refer to Section 10), and there is a match to the event bindings, the result code indicating "success" must be acknowledged [WSP] to the WTA server.
3. If no match can be found for an existing WTA user agent context, or the WTA event was not possible to verify with regard to the required elements in the encoded form (refer to Section 10), event matching must be applied to the event table. If a match can be found, the result code indicating "success" must be acknowledged [WSP] to the WTA server.
4. If a match cannot be found in the event table, the result code indicating "failure" must be acknowledged [WSP] to the WTA server.
5. For a WTA event that cannot be handled by the WTA user agent due to reception of a mobile network event or a failure in the verification, the result code indicating "failure" must be acknowledged [WSP] to the WTA server.
6. For an unattended WTA event, the WTA server must apply the same rule as if the WTA event was acknowledged with the result code indicating "failure."

Required steps for handling unacknowledged WTA event:

1. The WTA event must be serviced immediately by the WTA user agent.
2. The WTA event is handled according to the procedures described in Section 6.

4. WTA URIs and URLs

Wireless devices come in many flavors with regard to available bearers and types of telephony features. There are many standards, such as GSM, that support device access to telephony features of the mobile network. URIs form a unifying naming model for how to identify features independently of the internal structure in the device and the mobile network.

In WTA, URIs are used in the following situations:

- When specifying the identity of local resources like logical indicators [WTAI]
- When specifying telephony features like the setup of mobile originated call [WTAI]

4.1 Use of URLs

The WTA user agent is based on the WAE standard user agent, and as such the same rule applies for specifying and using URLs [WML].

In WTA, the URLs can also occur in the following situations:

- When specifying URLs in the WTA event table
- When specifying well-known resources in the WTA server like the event table

5. The User Agent State Model

The WTA user agent includes the same basic support for managing user agent state as the standard WAE user agent [WML].

The WTA user agent also includes support for managing user agent state including:

Associated state of a specific call with the user agent context. WTAI functions such as accept or set up calls, must be associated with a behavior on how the call is handled in case the WTA user agent context is intentionally terminated [WTAI].

Implementation-dependent state. Other state relating to the particulars of the user agent implementation and its behavior. Examples are the current power save status, memory used and communication settings for SMS, etc.

5.1 The User Agent Context

WTA user agent is based on the WAE standard user agent, and as such the same principles apply for handling a user agent context. In addition, the WTA user agent also includes support for termination of the browser context and implicit creation of variables due to reception of WTA event parameters.

5.2 Termination of Context

The WTAI function "exit" [WTAI] indicates that the user agent context must be "terminated" and the following operations must be performed by the WTA user agent:

- Active calls are handled according to the mode of the call; i.e., the association with the life span of the context [WTAI].
- Any processing of content such as WML, WMLScript, is terminated.
- The browser context is removed and all data stored in the context is consequently discarded.

5.3 Variables

The WTA user agent is based on the WAE standard user agent [WAE], and as such the same rules apply for variables as used with the standard WAE user agent [WML].

The WTA user agent also includes support for implicit creation of variables in the following situations:

- Optional parameters received with a WTA event bound to the user agent context with a WTA event binding can be parameterized (see Section 6.3) and are accessible to the user agent context.
- Optional parameters received with a WTA event that is matched against the event table in the form of a WTA event table binding can be parameterized (see Section 6.2) and are accessible to the user agent context.

6. WTA Events and Navigation

The WTA event contains data to be stored in the current WTA context. The procedure for doing this is referred to as "WTA event binding." How the "WTA event binding" is performed depends on the state of the WTA user agent.

There are three distinct states when a WTA event can be handled:

The user agent context matches a WTA event: The user agent context contains an event binding matching with the WTA event.

No active user agent context or WTA event match: The WTA event table contains a WTA event binding that matches the WTA event.

No active user agent context or WTA event match with the event table bindings: If the WTA event originates from a mobile network event, the WTA event may be forwarded to the device OS.

6.1 Precedence of Event Handlers

The following steps must be carried out in the specified order:

1. **User agent context:** If there is a user agent context, then event matching must be used to determine if the WTA event matches with an event binding in the user agent context.
2. **Event table:** If there is a event table, then event matching must be used to determine if the WTA event matches with an event binding in the event table.
3. **Device OS:** WTA events, originating from the mobile network (i.e., converted from a network event into a WTA event) must be forwarded to the device OS. WAP does not, however, require the device OS to handle events.

6.2 WTA Event Table

6.2.1 Programming the Event Table

The client can be programmed, using the event table, to act on incoming events from the mobile network or the WTA server. WTA events that are received are transformed into URLs that can be executed by the WTA user agent. The WTA event table is programmed using the WTA event content format that must be pushed from the WTA server and requested during startup of a WTA session in client-centric mode (see Figure 13.5).

Example 1:
Server pushes an event table to be set up by the WTA client.

Example 2:
Network event/message occurs. In this case, the WTA client converts the actual network event to the more general WTA event. If the event binding exists in the event table, any optional parameters are stored in a new user agent context and the associated URL is called.

Example 3:
Server pushes a WTA event. The WTA event is handled in the same way as the converted network event.

6.2.2 WTA Event Table Binding

The WTA event table is consulted when there is no current WTA user agent context or if there was no match in the WTA user agent context for that particular WTA event. The following steps must be carried out:

1. Check the event table for a matching event binding with the WTA event.

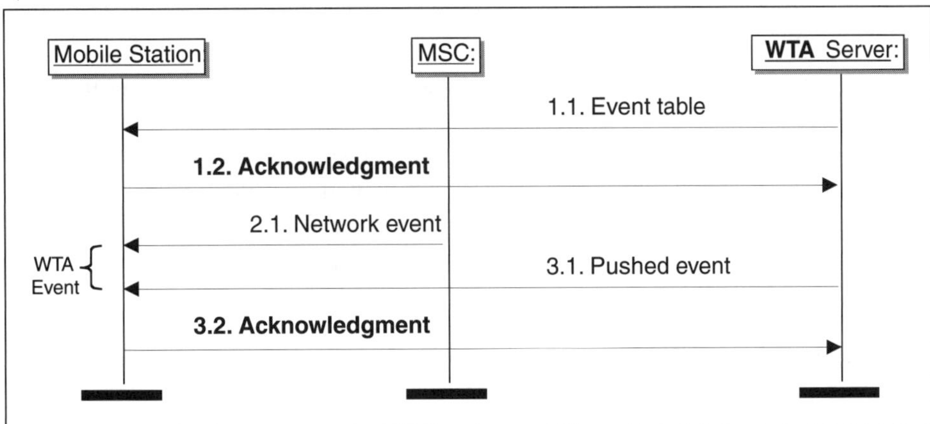

Figure 13.5 Event table programming.

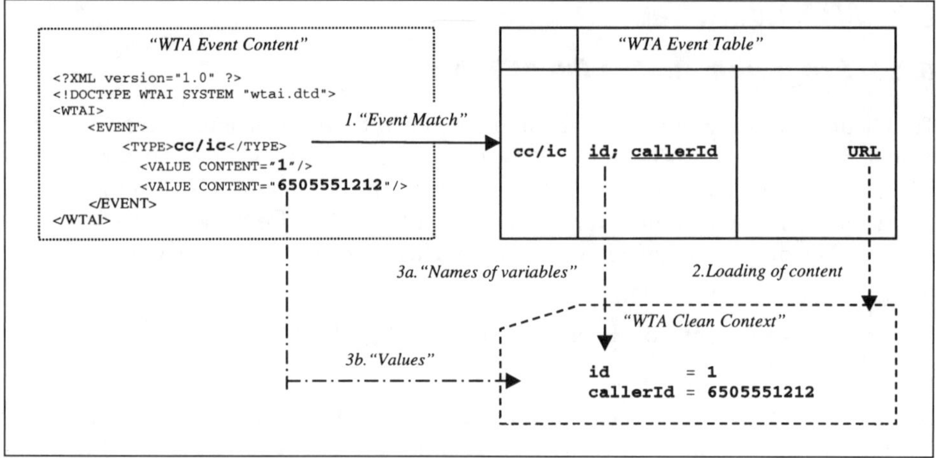

Figure 13.6 Binding event data to new user agent context.

2. In case of a match, the user agent calls the indicated URL stored in the event table. The WTA content is loaded into a clean context; i.e., no previous variables or state are associated with the user agent context (see Figure 13.6).
3. The WTA event table contains the names of the variables that must be assigned to the values of the parameters received with the WTA event.

6.3 WTA Event Bindings in User Agent Context

Data received with the WTA event can be stored in the user agent context. The WML construct for handling events defines the syntax how to specify the WTA event bindings using the WML markup. See details in [WML].

The following rules must be applied when using event bindings with the user agent context (see Figure 13.7):

1. The event bindings stored in the WTA user agent context must be consulted for a match with the particular WTA event.
2. Optional parameters received with the WTA event must be made available to the user agent context in the form of implicitly created variable names.
3. The WTA user agent context must assign the implicit variables to other variables or use the implicit variables as parameters when calling a URL.

7. User Agent Semantics

The WTA user agent is based on the standard WML user agent, using WML and WMLScript. WAE identifies content for the WTA user agent based on the fact that is was received through a dedicated WTP port in the device for WTA access. Content executed

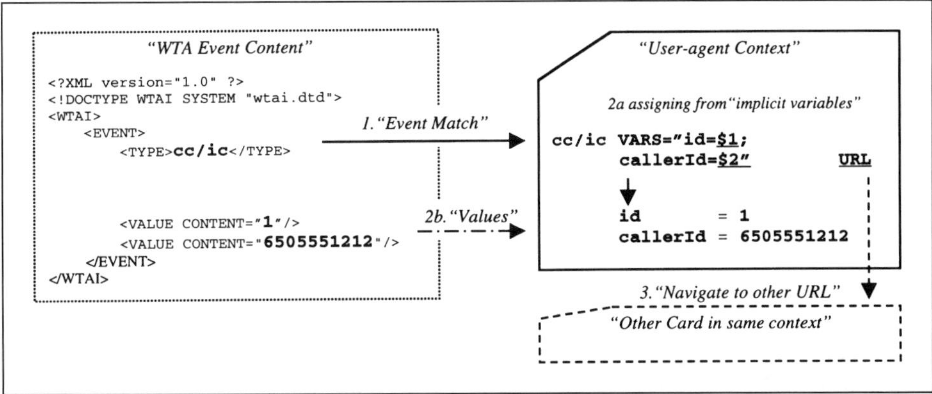

Figure 13.7 Binding event data to user agent context.

by the WTA user agent is fully qualified for access to telephony features in the device and the mobile network using the WTAI telephony functions Interface [WTAI].

WTA network events are the means for the WTA user agent to receive the response from the mobile network. WTA events or other content can also be received from the WTA server using the WTA content push feature. WTA network event is derived from the network-to-client signaling and is recast into the more generic and abstract WTA event.

A set of user agent characteristics define the required behavior for the WTA user agent:

- There must be only one WTA user agent context active at a specific time.
- Reception of "pushed" content [WSP] must be supported by the WTA user agent in either the server-centric or client-centric mode. WTA event only with the client-centric mode.
- Any existing WTA user agent context must be removed prior to processing any pushed content except for WTA event.
- The WTA user agent context must be terminated when instructed by the content.
- There is a predefined order of precedence that must be followed when handling WTA events.

7.1 Low-Memory Behavior

WTA is targeted at devices with limited hardware resources, including significant restrictions on memory size. It is important that the author have a clear expectation of device behavior in error situations, including those caused by lack of memory.

7.1.1 Limited History

The user agent may limit the size of the history stack (i.e., the depth of the historical navigation information). In the case of history size exhaustion, the user agent should delete the least recently used history information.

It is recommended that all user agents implement a minimum history stack size of 10 entries.

7.1.2 Limited User Agent Context Size

In some situations, it is possible that the author has defined an excessive number of variables in the browser context, leading to memory exhaustion.

In this situation, the user agent should attempt to acquire additional memory by reclaiming cache and history memory as described in Section 7.1.1. If this fails and the user agent has exhausted all memory, the user should be notified of the error.

7.2 Error Handling

Conforming user agents must enforce error conditions defined in this specification.

7.3 Unknown DTD

A WTA event content format encoded with an alternate DTD may include elements or attributes that are not recognized by certain user agents. In this situation, a user agent should handle the WTA event content format as if the unrecognized tags and attributes were not present.

8. WTA Session Management

This section describes the required behavior for setup and termination of a WTA session. A WTA session is used by the WTA user agent to facilitate interaction with the WTA server and the mobile network. The term *WTA session* is used in the following section to denote a WSP session [WSP] over a secure port [WTLS] connecting the WTA client with the WTA server [WAEARCH].

Setting up a WTA session also includes the setup procedure for the event table when the WTA client supports the client-centric mode. The WTA server must then use a reliable connection [WSP] for download of the event table. For additional information, see the WSP [WSP] and the WTLS [WTLS] specifications.

The following common WSP and WTLS services are used by the WTA client to start up a WTA session:

- Start up a new WSP session
- Request content (event table)
- Start up a WTLS, secure session
- Termination of a WSP session

8.1 Startup of a WTA Session

The startup makes it possible for a WTA server to gracefully detect that a WTA client can communicate with the WTA server and the mobile network.

The following rules apply for the WTA server when determining that the WTA session has been started:

- An indication from the WAP gateway that a WTA session to the WTA client has been established.
- A "successful" content exchange, pushed or pulled [WSP]; i.e., an old session was resumed.

For the startup of the WTA session, the following information must be provided by the implementation:

- Required bearer (based on preference or availability)
- Required level of security, bearer dependent [WAPARCH]
- The WTA server address (bearer specific; for example, MSISDN)
- The well-known WTA server port number [WSP]
- The WTA user agent characteristics [WAE]

Starting up a WTA user agent must includes the following steps:
(The keyword *conditional* used below denotes a step used when supporting the client-centric mode.)

1. **Request a new WTA session:** A request for a secure WSP session [WSP] to be used with WTA is sent to the WSP Session layer.
2. **Check for existing event table (conditional):** The WTA client must check for the presence of an existing WTA event table.

   Missing event table (i.e., due to memory loss or intentionally removed from device): Send a request for a new event table to the WTA server. The request must omit the http header "time of last modification" or include an empty "time of last modification" header.

   Existing event table: Send a request for a new event table to the WTA server. The request must include the http header "time of last modification," indicating the date when the current event table content was modified.
3. **Request the well-known resource WTA event table (conditional):** A request URL must be constructed using the well known resource name "wtatable.wtae" and the domain name of the WTA server.

   Example: http://www.operator.com/wtatable.wtae
4. **Reply from the WTA server (conditional):** The WTA server must reply with a new event table content or include a result code using HTTP headers [WSP] indicating that the requested content is the same as already stored in the client.
5. **Setting up the event table (conditional):** If the WTA server wants to remove any existing event table, an empty event table must be sent with the reply to the client.
6. **Acknowledge to the WTA server (conditional):** The outcome of the setup procedure for the event table in the WTA client is reported back to the WTA server using a result PDU with the acknowledge for the reply [WSP].

7. **Conclusion of the startup procedure (conditional):** The following rules must be applied when determining the state of the WTA client:
   1. Acknowledge "success"—The acknowledge indicating success means that there is now a new event table in the WTA client ready for service.
   2. Acknowledge "failure"—The acknowledge indicating failure means that the state of the event table in the WTA client is the same as indicated by the request from the WTA client for a new event table; i.e., existence of the "time of last modification" information.
   3. Acknowledge lost—If an acknowledge to the reply with a new event table cannot be received by the WTA server, then the same rules apply as if an acknowledge with a failure was received.
   4. The WTA server must assume the mode of the WTA client, server-centric or client-centric mode, based on the reported WTA user agent characteristics [WAE].

8.2 Termination of a WTA Session

The termination process makes it possible for a WTA server to gracefully detect that a WTA client has terminated the WTA session to the WTA server.

The following rules apply for determining that the WTA client has been terminated:

- The WTA server receives an indication from the WAP gateway that the WTA session has been terminated by the WTA client.
- A WTA server that cannot reach a WTA client due to *nonexistent session* must assume the same state as if the WTA session had been terminated by the WTA client.

8.3 Reliable Content Push

A WTA server can push content, decks, and events to the client's WTA port. The push services are provided by the WSP layer [WSP]. The reliable WSP service is generally referred to as *acknowledged content* in the WTA specification.

The WTA port is used for the reception of pushed content. The WTA server have the option to request an acknowledge message that the client actually received the pushed content. In order for the WTA server to determine how to proceed when there is no user response, it has to implement its own timeout handling. The WTA client must only receive one push at a time, which also has to be acknowledged back to the WTA server.

9. WTA Reference Information

This section defines the content format used to represent the WTA event and the WTA event table.

WTA Event is an application of [XML] version 1.0.

9.1 Document Identifiers

These identifiers have not yet been registered with the IANA or ISO 9070 Registrar.

9.1.1 SGML Public Identifier

```
-//WAPFORUM//DTD WTA 1.0//EN
```

9.1.2 WTA Event Media Type

Textual form:

```
text/x-wap.wtae
```

Tokenized form:

```
application/x-wap.wtaec
```

These types are not yet registered with the IANA and are consequently *experimental* media types.

9.2 Document Type Definition (DTD)

```
<!ELEMENT WTAI ( ( EVENTTABLE )+ | ( EVENT ) ) >
<!ELEMENT EVENTTABLE    ( TYPE | URL | VAR )* >
<!ELEMENT EVENT         ( TYPE | VAR | VALUE )* >
<!ELEMENT TYPE (#PCDATA) >          <!— Event type —>
<!ELEMENT URL (#PCDATA) >           <!— Event Table URL —>
<!— Variable declaration —>
<!ELEMENT VAR EMPTY>
<!ATTLIST VAR
  NAME ID #REQUIRED
  >
<!— Variable value —>
<!ELEMENT VALUE EMPTY>
<!ATTLIST VALUE
  NAME    IDREF #REQUIRED
  CONTENT CDATA #REQUIRED
  >
```

10. WTA Event Binary Encoding

The WTA event is encoded using a compact binary representation. This content format is based on the WAP Binary XML Content Format [WBXML].

10.1 Extension Tokens

10.1.1 Global Extension Tokens

The [WBXML] global extension tokens are used to represent WTA event table variables. Same rules apply for WTA event variables as for WML variables [WML].

10.1.2 Tag Tokens

WTA event defines a set of single-byte tokens corresponding to the tags defined in the DTD. All of these tokens are defined within code page 1.

10.1.3 Attribute Tokens

WTA event defines a set of single-byte tokens corresponding to the attribute names and values defined in the DTD. All of these tokens are defined within code page 1.

10.2 Encoding Semantics

10.2.1 Encoding Variables

All variable references must be converted to variable reference tokens (e.g., `EXT_I_0`).

10.2.2 Document Validation

XML document validation (see [XML]) should occur during the process of tokenizing a WTA event, and must be based on the DOCTYPE declared in the WTA event. The tokenization process should notify the user of any well-formedness or validity errors detected in the source deck.

10.3 Numeric Constants

10.3.1 Tag Tokens

The token codes in Table 13.1 represent tags in code page 0. All numbers are in hexadecimal.

Note: Token assignments may change before final publication.

10.3.2 Attribute Start Tokens

The token codes in Table 13.2 represent the start of an attribute in code page 0. All numbers are in hexadecimal.

Note: Token assignments may change before final publication.

10.3.3 Attribute Value Tokens

No additional attribute values have been defined for WTA events. Same rules apply as for WML [WML].

Table 13.1 Tag Tokens

TAG NAME	TOKEN
EVENT	5
EVENTTABLE	6
TYPE	7
URL	8
WTAI	9

Table 13.2 Attribute Start Tokens

ATTRIBUTE NAME	ATTRIBUTE VALUE PREFIX	TOKEN
NAME		5
VALUE		6

10.4 WTA Encoding Examples

10.4.1 WTA Event

The following is an example of a tokenized WTA event. It demonstrates variable encoding, attribute encoding, and the use of the string table. Source WTA event:

```
<WTAI>
    <EVENT>
        <TYPE>cc/ic</TYPE>
        <VALUE CONTENT="1"/>
        <VALUE CONTENT="6505551212"/>
    </EVENT>
</WTAI>
```

Tokenized form (numbers in hex) follows in Table 13.3. This example only uses inline strings and assumes that the character encoding uses a NULL terminated string format. It also assumes that the character encoding is UTF-8.

Table 13.3 Example Tokenized WTA Event

TOKEN STREAM	DESCRIPTION
`00`	WBXML version number
`01`	`END` (of `WTAI` element)

10.4.2 WTA Event Table

The following is an example of a tokenized WTA event table. It demonstrates variable encoding, attribute encoding, and the use of the string table. Source WTA event table:

```
<?XML version="1.0" ?>
<!DOCTYPE WTAI SYSTEM "wtai.dtd">
<WTAI>
    <EVENTTABLE>
        <TYPE>cc/ic</TYPE>
        <URL>http://foo.com/call</URL>
        <VAR NAME="id"/>
        <VAR NAME="callerID"/>
    </EVENTTABLE>
    <EVENTTABLE>
        <TYPE>cc/if</TYPE>
        <URL>http://foo.com/flash</URL>
        <VAR NAME="string"/>
    </EVENTTABLE>
</WTAI>
```

Tokenized form (numbers in hex) follows in Table 13.4. This example only uses inline strings and assumes that the character encoding uses a NULL terminated string format. It also assumes that the character encoding is UTF-8.

11. WTA Examples

There are probably several ways to create these services and the use cases must consequently only be considered as examples, not necessarily the easiest or the foolproof ways to handle them.

11.1 Provisioning

The example assumes a new WAP MS without any preloaded WTA content. The question would then be how to activate the WTA features. Figure 13.8 shows the sequence for the WAP transactions between the MS and the WTA server.

Table 13.4 Example Tokenized WTA Event

TOKEN STREAM	DESCRIPTION
00	WBXML version number
01	END (of WML element)

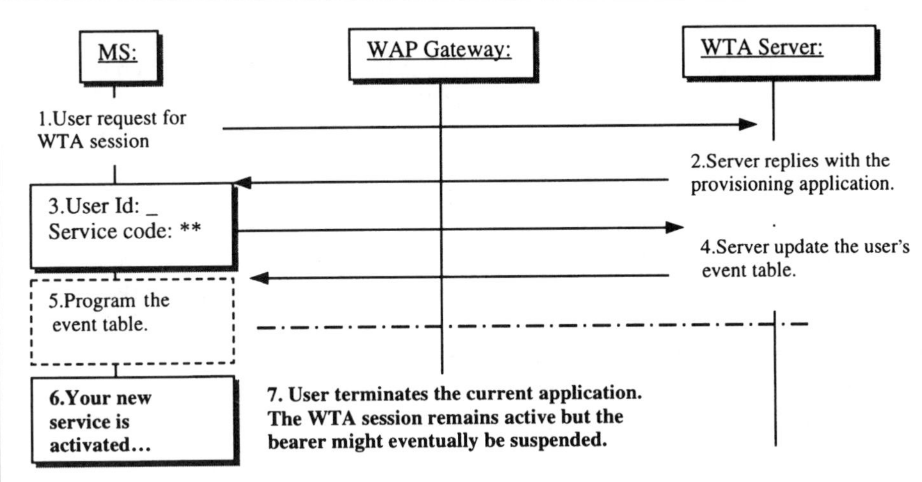

Walkthrough of the service "provisioning":

1) The network operator may have informed the user about the location of the "WTA" WAP Gateway.[2] Starting the WTA user agent, from the user perspective, also means that the WAP stack is initialized. The "preferred" Gateway is forwarded to WSP and consequently WTP. The user requests a new WTA session.
2) The WTA server replies with the "Provisioning Application."
3) The user enters his subscription id and "Requested Service Code."
4) The server checks the user and then sends down the updated appropriate event table.
5) The WTA client uses the downloaded content to "program" the new event table.
6) After the successful operation, the user is notified that the service is activated.
7) Assuming the handset is powered up and WAP is enabled, the user is now ready for WTA.

Figure 13.8 WTA service "provisioning."

[2]The information on the location of the WAP gateway or the WTA server is either manually entered into the device or can be part of the configuration.

11.2 Incoming Call

"Incoming Call" WTA use case is an example of how an application can be deployed using features in the client-centric mode of the WTA architecture. The example assumes that the content, in the form of WML and WMLScript, already is stored in the WAP client. The example shows how a "generic" application WTA event activates the handling of a call application and gives the called party value-added services like precall options in the form of a menu. The normal mobile network call handling must be overridden in order to handle the call and intercept the standard call handling in the mobile phone. Figure 13.9 shows the outline of the sample service network.

The example is concluded with the mobile network establishing the actual call between the two parts (Figure 13.10).

11.3 Voice Mail

Voice Mail interaction between the WTA server and WTA client gives an example of an application that starts up as a standard "browsing" use case and, with the help from the WTA server, eventually invokes a voice connection.

12. Definitions

All non-trivial abbreviations and definitions used in this document are listed in the following sections. The definitions section includes description of general concepts and issues that may be fully defined in other documents. The purpose of this section is merely to advise the reader on the terminology used in the document.

The following are terms and conventions used throughout this specification.

The key words "MUST", "MUST NOT", "REQUIRED", "SHALL", "SHALL NOT", "SHOULD", "SHOULD NOT", "RECOMMENDED", "MAY", and "OPTIONAL" in this document are to be interpreted as described by [RFC2119].

Author. An author is a person or program that writes or generates WML, WMLScript or other content.

Card. A single WML unit of navigation and user interface. May contain information to present on the screen, instructions for gathering user input, etc.

Clear. Used in conjunction with WTA context. Means that all variables stored in the WTA user context are removed.

Client. A device (or application) that initiates a request for connection with a server.

Client Centric. External events (e.g., network events) are processed by the client portion of the WTA application.

Content. Subject matter (data) stored or generated at an origin server. Content is typically displayed or interpreted by a user agent in response to a user request.

Content Encoding. When used as a verb, *content encoding* indicates the act of converting a data object from one format to another. Typically, the resulting format requires less physical space than the original, is easier to process or store, and/or is encrypted. When used as a noun, *content encoding* specifies a particular format or encoding standard or process.

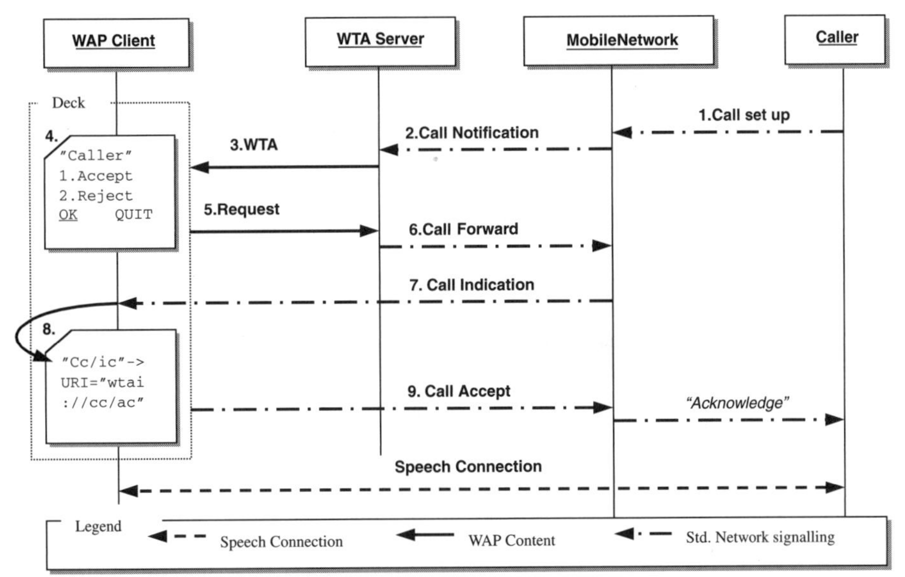

Walkthrough of the "Incoming Call" application:

1) A "Caller" intends to call the WAP client end user. The mobile network, configured to divert the calls to another entity, temporarily holds the Call setup request from the "Caller."

2) The mobile network sends a call notification to the WTA server about the pending call.

3) The WTA server pushes down a WTA event that is detected by the call control content.

4) The WAP client end user is presented with a menu that tells him about the incoming call and the different options for how to proceed (The WTAI "logical indication" function alerts the end user).

5) The WAP client end user decides to accept the call. A request for the "accept call" service is sent to the WTA server.

6) The WTA server instructs the mobile network to forward the held call to the WAP client.

7) The mobile network allocates the traffic channel and sends a "call indication" to the WAP client.

8) An "Incoming Call" WTA event is generated locally as a result of the network event "call indication."

9) As the content detects the preconfigured WTA event, the WTA-enabled WML/WMLScript content[3] answers the call using WTAI functions.

Figure 13.9 WTA "Incoming Call."

[3]The standard Mobile Phone MMI does not intervene or generate the standard "Incoming Call" notification.

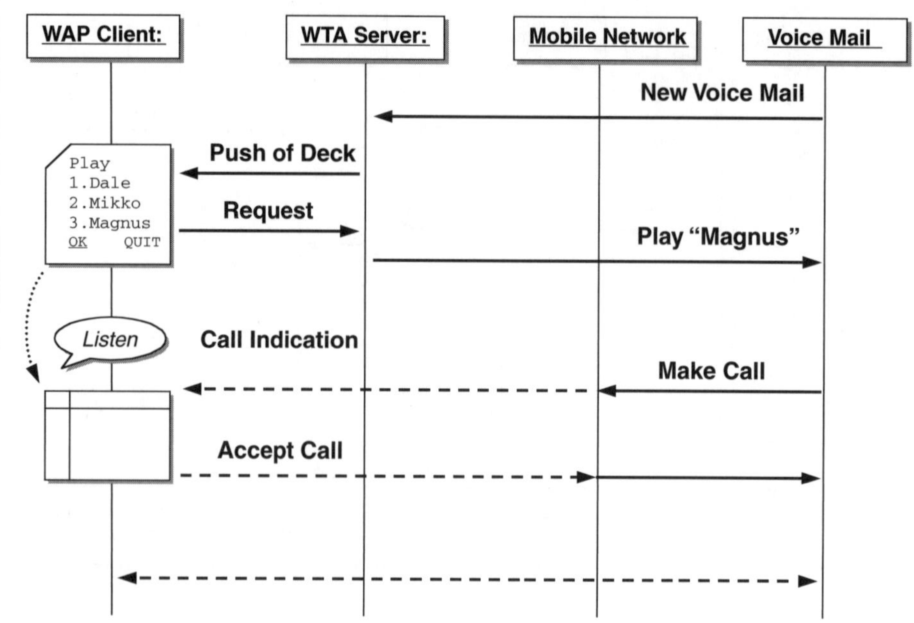

Walkthrough:

1) In the beginning there is a new voice mail in the voice mail system.
2) The voice mail system informs the WTA server about the voice mails.
3) WTA server creates a deck, which is pushed to the client.
4) The client shows a list of voice mails to the user and the user selects a voice mail to listen for.
5) A request is sent back to the WTA server.
6) At the same time a new card is shown to the user ("Listen") and the network event, "incoming call" is mapped using a WTA event binding in order to be answered automatically.
7) The WTA server sends information back to the voice mail system about which voice mail to play.
8) The voice mail system makes the call to the WTA client.
9) Since there is an event mapping, the incoming call is answered automatically and therefore the client can accept the call without the need for user interaction.
10) When the speech connection is established, the voice mail system starts playing the voice mail and the user can listen.

Figure 13.10 Voice mail sequence.

Content Format. Actual representation of content.

Content Generator. A service that generates or formats content. Typically, content generators are on origin servers.

Deck. A collection of WML cards. A WML deck is also an XML document. May contain WMLScript.

Device A network entity that is capable of sending and receiving packets of information and has a unique device address. A device can act as either a client or a server within a given context or across multiple contexts. For example, a device can service a number of clients (as a server) while being a client to another server.

Device OS. The standard operating system in a device. Not part of what is specified by WAP.

Implicit Variables. Variables that are created by the user agent itself because of an incoming WTA event.

Origin Server. The server on which a given resource resides or is to be created. Often referred to as a *Web server* or an *HTTP server*.

Resource. Network data object or service that can be identified by a URL. Resources may be available in multiple representations (e.g., multiple languages, data formats, size, and resolutions) or vary in other ways.

Reset. Used in conjunction with WTA context, meaning that the state of the WTA user agent is set to a state with an empty history stack. Implementation-specific state is set to a well-known state.

Server. A device (or application) that passively waits for connection requests from one or more clients. A server may accept or reject a connection request from a client.

Server Centric. Content from different sources is terminated in the server.

Terminal. A device typically used by a user to request and receive information. Also called a *mobile terminal* or *mobile station*.

User. A user is a person who interacts with a user agent to view, hear, or otherwise use a rendered content.

User Agent. A user agent (or content interpreter) is any software or device that interprets resources. This may include textual browsers, voice browsers, search engines, etc.

Web Server. A network host that acts as an HTTP server.

WML. The Wireless Markup Language is a hypertext markup language used to represent information for delivery to a narrowband device (e.g., a mobile phone).

WMLScript. A scripting language used to program the mobile device. WMLScript is an extended subset of the JavaScript scripting language.

WTA Context. The complete set of variables, with content and the state of the WTA user agent.

WTA Event Context Binding. A WTA event name specified using the type attribute in the WML "ONEVENT" construct [WML].

WTA Event. A notification, in the form of content, that conveys a change of state of the sender. A WTA event can be received from a WTA originating server or be generated from events occurring in the mobile network (e.g., incoming call).

WTA Event Table. A specific WTA content format with an ordered sequence of WTA event table bindings. The WTA event table is stored persistently in a device using a device-dependent format.

WTA Event Table Binding. A WTA event name with an associated URL and an optional list of parameter names.

WTA Event Handler. The entity that is used for the event matching. Can be the WTA context, the WTA event table, or the device OS.

WTA event matching. The process in which a WTA event name is compared with a WTA event name stored as a WTA event table binding or in the WTA context using WTA event context bindings. If the WTA event name is equal to the stored WTA event name, then there is a match.

XML. The Extensible Markup Language is a World Wide Web Consortium (W3C) proposed standard for Internet markup languages, of which WML is one such language. XML is a restricted subset of SGML.

13. Abbreviations

For the purposes of this specification, the following abbreviations apply:

API	Application Programming Interface
BNF	Backus-Naur Form
CGI	Common Gateway Interface
ECMA	European Computer Manufacturers Association
ETSI	European Telecommunication Standardization Institute
GSM	Global System for Mobile Communication
HTML	HyperText Markup Language
HTTP	HyperText Transfer Protocol
IANA	Internet Assigned Number Authority
MSC	Mobile Switching Centre
MSISDN	Mobile Station International Subscriber Device Number
RFC	Request For Comments
SGML	Standardized Generalized Markup Language
URI	Uniform Resource Identifier
URL	Uniform Resource Locator [RFC1738]
WAE	Wireless Application Environment
WAP	Wireless Application Protocol [WAP]
WSP	Wireless Session Protocol [WSP]

WTA	Wireless Telephony Applications
WTAI	Wireless Telephony Applications Interface
WTP	Wireless Transaction Protocol
WWW	World Wide Web
W3C	World Wide Web Consortium
XML	Extensible Markup Language [XML]

14. Normative References

[RFC2119] "Key Words for Use in RFCs to Indicate Requirement Levels," S. Bradner, March 1997.
URL: ftp://ds.internic.net/rfc/rfc2119.txt

[RFC1738] "Uniform Resource Locators (URL)," T. Berners-Lee, et al., December 1994.
URL: ftp://ds.internic.net/rfc/rfc1738.txt

[RFC1630] "Uniform Resource identifiers (URI)," T. Berners-Lee, et al., June 1994.
URL: ftp://ds.internic.net/rfc/rfc1630.txt

[WAE] "Wireless Application Environment Specification," WAP Forum, 1998.
URL: http://www.wapforum.org/

[WAEARCH] "Wireless Application Environment Architecture Overview," WAP Forum, 1998.
URL: http://www.wapforum.org/

[WAP] "Wireless Application Protocol Architecture Specification, version 0.9," WAP Forum, 1997.
URL: http://www.wapforum.org/

[WML] "Wireless Markup Language," WAP Forum, 1997.
URL: http://www.wapforum.org/

[WMLScript] "WMLScript Language Specification," WAP Forum, 1998.
URL: http://www.wapforum.org/

[WAEStdLib] "WMLScript Standard Libraries Specification," WAP Forum, 1997.
URL: http://www.wapforum.org/

[WSP] "Wireless Session Protocol Specification," WAP Forum, 1997.
URL: http://www.wapforum.org/

[WTAI] "Wireless Telephony Application Interface Specification," WAP Forum, 1997.
URL: http://www.wapforum.org/

[XML] "Extensible Markup Language (XML), W3C Proposed Recommendation 10-February-1998, REC-xml-19980210," T. Bray, et al., February 10, 1998.
URL: http://www.w3.org/TR/REC-xml

Part

Three

The Protocol Layer

CHAPTER

14

Wireless Session Protocol Specification

1. Scope

The Wireless Application Protocol (WAP) is a result of continuous work to define an industrywide specification for developing applications that operate over wireless communication networks. The scope for the WAP Forum is to define a set of specifications to be used by service applications. The wireless market is growing very quickly, and reaching new customers and services. To enable operators and manufacturers to meet the challenges in advanced services, differentiation, and fast/flexible service creation, WAP Forum defines a set of protocols in Transport, Security, Transaction, Session, and Application layers. For additional information on the WAP architecture, please refer to *Wireless Application Protocol Architecture Specification* [WAPARCH].

The Session layer protocol family in the WAP architecture is called the Wireless Session Protocol (WSP). WSP provides the upper-level Application layer of WAP with a consistent interface for two session services. The first is a connection-mode service that operates above a Transaction layer protocol WTP, and the second is a connectionless service that operates above a secure or nonsecure datagram transport service. For more information on the transaction and transport services, please refer to *Wireless Application Protocol: Wireless Transaction Protocol Specification* [WAPWTP] and *Wireless Application Protocol: Wireless Datagram Protocol Specification* [WAPWDP].

The Wireless Session Protocols currently offer services most suited for browsing applications (WSP/B). WSP/B provides HTTP 1.1 functionality and incorporates new features such as long-lived sessions, a common facility for data push, capability negotiation, and session suspend/resume. The protocols in the WSP family are optimized for low-bandwidth bearer networks with relatively long latency.

2. WSP Architectural Overview

Wireless Session Protocol is a session-level protocol family for remote operations between a client and proxy or server.

2.1 Reference Model

A model of layering the protocols in WAP is illustrated in Figure 14.1. WAP protocols and their functions are layered in a style resembling that of the ISO OSI Reference Model [ISO7498]. Layer Management Entities handle protocol initialization, configuration, and error conditions (such as loss of connectivity due to the mobile station roaming out of coverage) that are not handled by the protocol itself.

WSP is designed to function on the transaction and datagram services. Security is assumed to be an optional layer above the Transport layer. The Security layer preserves

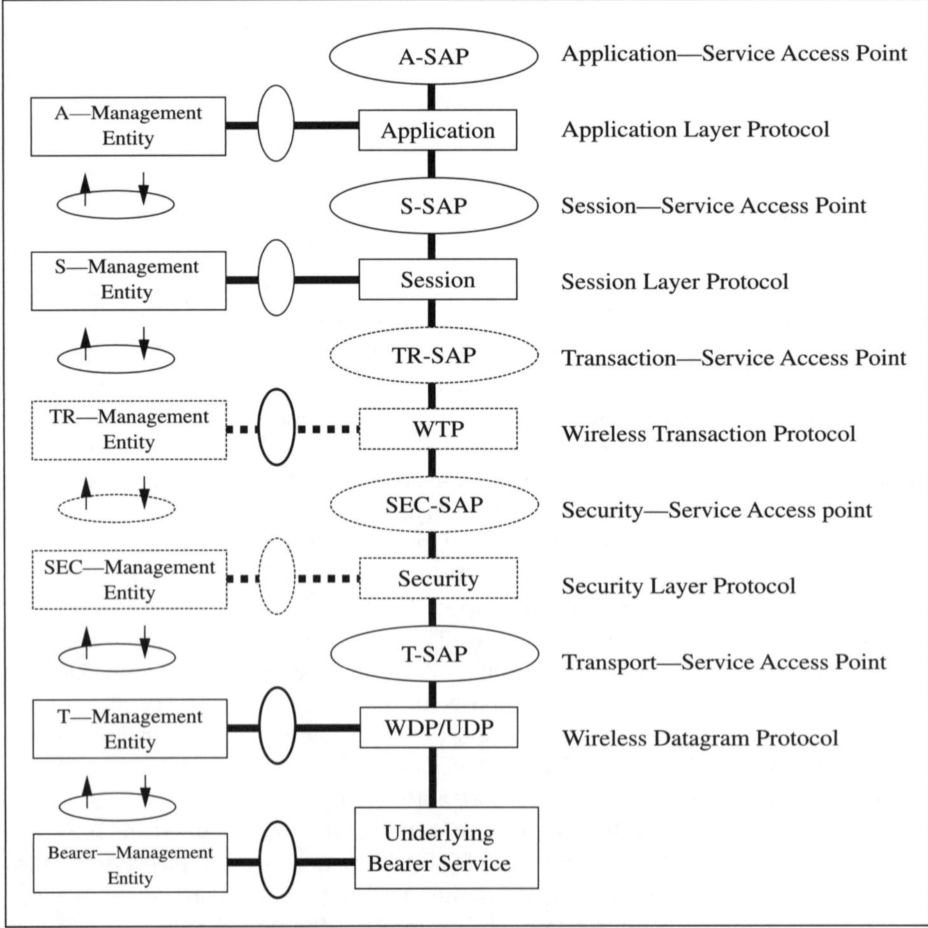

Figure 14.1 Wireless Application Protocol reference model.

the transport service interfaces. The transaction, session, or application management entities are assumed to provide the additional support that is required to establish security contexts and secure connections. This support is not provided by the WSP protocols directly. In this regard, the Security layer is modular. WSP itself does not require a security layer; however, applications that use WSP may require it.

2.2 WSP/B Features

WSP provides a means for organized exchange of content between cooperating client/server applications. Specifically, it provides the applications means to:

- Establish a reliable session from client to server and release that session in an orderly manner
- Agree on a common level of protocol functionality using capability negotiation
- Exchange content between client and server using compact encoding
- Suspend and resume the session

The currently defined services and protocols (WSP/B) are most suited for browsing-type applications. WSP/B actually defines two protocols: One provides connection-mode session services over a transaction service, and another provides nonconfirmed, connectionless services over a datagram transport service. The connectionless service is most suitable when applications do not need reliable delivery of data and do not care about confirmation. It can be used without actually having to establish a session.

In addition to the general features, WSP/B offers means to:

- Provide HTTP/1.1 functionality:
  - Extensible request-reply methods
  - Composite objects
  - Content type negotiation
- Exchange client and server session headers
- Interrupt transactions in process
- Push content from server to client in an unsynchronized manner
- Negotiate support for multiple, simultaneous asynchronous transactions

2.2.1 Basic Functionality

The core of the WSP/B design is a binary form of HTTP. Consequently, the requests sent to a server and responses going to a client may include both headers (meta-information) and data. All the methods defined by HTTP/1.1 are supported. In addition, capability negotiation can be used to agree on a set of extended request methods so that full compatibility to HTTP/1.1 applications can be retained.

WSP/B provides typed data transfer for the Application layer. The HTTP/1.1 content headers are used to define content type, character set encoding, languages, and so forth, in an extensible manner. However, compact binary encodings are defined for the well-known headers to reduce protocol overhead. WSP/B also specifies a compact composite data format that provides content headers for each component within the composite data object. This is a semantically equivalent binary form of the MIME "multipart/mixed" format used by HTTP/1.1.

WSP/B itself does not interpret the header information in requests and replies. As part of the session creation process, request and reply headers that remain constant over the life of the session can be exchanged between service users in the client and the server. These may include acceptable content types, character sets, languages, device capabilities, and other static parameters. WSP/B will pass through client and server session headers as well as request and response headers without additions or removals.

The life cycle of a WSP/B session is not tied to the underlying transport. A session can be suspended while the session is idle to free up network resources or save battery. A lightweight session reestablishment protocol allows the session to be resumed without the overhead of full-blown session establishment. A session may be resumed over a different bearer network.

2.2.2 Extended Functionality

WSP/B allows extended capabilities to be negotiated between the peers. This allows for both high-performance, feature-full implementation as well as simple, basic, and small implementations.

WSP/B provides an optional mechanism for attaching header information (metadata) to the acknowledgment of a transaction. This allows the client application to communicate specific information about the completed transaction back to the server.

WSP/B provides both push and pull data transfer. Pull is done using the request/response mechanism from HTTP/1.1. In addition, WSP/B provides three push mechanisms for data transfer:

- Confirmed data push within an existing session context
- Nonconfirmed data push within an existing session context
- Nonconfirmed data push without an existing session

The confirmed data push mechanism allows the server to push data to the client at any time during a session. The server receives confirmation that the push was delivered.

The nonconfirmed data push within an existing session provides a similar function as reliable data push but without confirmation. The nonconfirmed data push can also occur without an existing session. In this case, a default session context is assumed. Nonconfirmed out-of-session data push can be used to send one-way messages over an unreliable transport.

WSP/B optionally supports asynchronous requests so that a client can submit multiple requests to the server simultaneously. This improves utilization of airtime in that multiple requests and replies can be coalesced into fewer messages. This also improves latency as the results of each request can be sent to the client when it becomes available.

WSP/B partitions the space of well-known header field names into *header code pages*. Each code page can define only a fairly limited number of encodings for well-known field names, which permits them to be represented more compactly. Running out of identities for well-known field names on a certain code page is still not a problem, since WSP/B specifies a mechanism for shifting from one header code page to another.

3. WSP Elements of Layer-to-Layer Communication

The Session layer in WAP provides both connection-mode and connectionless services. They are defined using an abstract description technique based on service primitives, which is borrowed from [ISO10731]. Some of the terms and concepts used to describe the communication mechanisms are borrowed from [ISO7498], whereas the terminology used for operations and the manipulated data objects is based on [RFC2068].

This service definition specifies the minimum functionality that the WAP session must be able to provide to support its users. Since this definition is abstract, it does not specify or constrain programming interfaces or implementations. In fact, the same service could be delivered by different protocols.

3.1 Notations Used

3.1.1 Definition of Service Primitives and Parameters

Communications between layers and between entities within the Session layer are accomplished by means of service primitives. Service primitives represent, in an abstract way, the logical exchange of information and control between the Session layer and adjacent layers.

Service primitives consist of commands and their respective responses associated with the particular service provided. The general syntax of a primitive is:

X-Service.type (Parameters)

where *X* designates the layer providing the service. For this specification, *X* is "S" for the Session layer.

Service primitives are not the same as an application-programming interface (API) and are not meant to imply any specific method of implementing an API. Service primitives are an abstract means of illustrating the services provided by the Protocol layer to the layer above. In particular, the service primitives and their parameters are not intended to include the information that an implementation might need to route the primitives to each implementation object, which corresponds to some abstract user or service provider entity instance. The mapping of these concepts to a real API and the semantics associated with a real API is an implementation issue and beyond the scope of this specification.

3.1.2 Time Sequence Charts

The behavior of service primitives is illustrated using time sequence charts, which are described in [ISO10731].

Figure 14.2 illustrates a simple nonconfirmed service, which is invoked using a request primitive and results in an indication primitive in the peer. The dashed line represents propagation through the provider over a period of time indicated by the vertical difference between the two arrows representing the primitives. If the labels

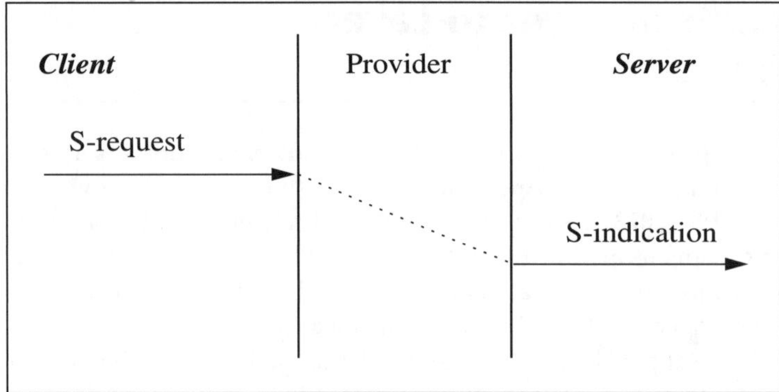

Figure 14.2 A nonconfirmed service.

Client and *Server* are included in the diagram, this indicates that both peers cannot originate a primitive; if the labels are omitted, either peer can originate the primitive.

3.1.3 Primitives Types

The primitives types defined in this specification are:

TYPE	ABBREVIATION	DESCRIPTION
Request	req	Used when a higher layer is requesting a service from the next lower layer.
Indication	ind	A layer providing a service uses this primitive type to notify the next higher layer of activities related to the peer (such as the invocation of the request primitive) or to the provider of the service (such as a protocol generated event).
Response	res	A layer uses the response primitive type to acknowledge receipt of the indication primitive type from the next lower layer.
Confirm	cnf	The layer providing the requested service uses the confirm primitive type to report that the activity has been completed successfully.

3.1.4 Primitive Parameter Tables

The service primitives are defined using tables indicating which parameters are possible and how they are used with the different primitive types. If some primitive type is not possible, the column for it will be omitted.

The entries used in the primitive type columns are defined in Table 14.1.

Table 14.1 Parameter Usage Legend

M	Presence of the parameter is mandatory—it MUST be present.
C	Presence of the parameter is conditional depending on values of other parameters.
O	Presence of the parameter is a user option—it MAY be omitted.
P	Presence of the parameter is a service provider option—an implementation MAY not provide it.
–	The parameter is absent.
*	Presence of the parameter is determined by the lower layer protocol.
(=)	The value of the parameter is identical to the value of the corresponding parameter of the preceding service primitive.

For example, a simple confirmed primitive might be defined using the following:

PRIMITIVE	S-PRIMITIVEX			
PARAMETER	***REQ***	***IND***	***RES***	***CNF***
Parameter 1	M	M(=)	–	–
Parameter 2	–	–	O	C(=)

In the preceding example definition, *Parameter 1* is always present in *S-PrimitiveX .request* and corresponding *S-PrimitiveX.indication*. *Parameter* 2 MAY be specified in *S-PrimitiveX.response,* and in that case it MUST be present and have the equivalent value also in the corresponding *S-PrimitiveX.confirm*; otherwise, it MUST NOT be present.

An example of a simpler primitive is:

PRIMITIVE	S-PRIMITIVEY	
PARAMETER	***REQ***	***IND***
Parameter 2	–	M

In this example, *S-PrimitiveY.request* has no parameters, but the corresponding *S-PrimitiveX.indication* MUST always have *Parameter* 2. *S-PrimitiveX.response* and *S-PrimitiveX.confirm* are not defined and so can never occur.

3.2 Service Parameter Types

This section describes the types of the abstract parameters used subsequently in the service primitive definition. The actual format and encoding of these types is an implementation issue not addressed by this service definition.

In the primitive descriptions the types are used in the names of parameters, and they often have an additional qualifier indicating where or how the parameter is being used. For example, parameter *Push Body* is of the type *Body*, and parameter *Client Address* of type *Address*.

3.2.1 Address

The Session layer uses directly the addressing scheme of the layer below. *Server Address* and *Client Address* together form the peer address quadruplet, which identifies the local lower-layer service access point to be used for communication. This access point has to be prepared for communication prior to invoking the session services; this is expected to be accomplished with interactions between the service user and management entities in a manner that is not a part of this specification.

3.2.2 Body and Headers

The *Body* type is equivalent to the HTTP entity-body [RFC2068]. The *Headers* type represents a list of attribute information items, which are equivalent to HTTP headers.

3.2.3 Capabilities

The *Capabilities* type represents a set of service facilities and parameter settings, which are related to the operation of the service provider. The predefined capabilities are described in Section 3.3.2.2, but the service providers may recognize additional capabilities.

3.2.4 Push Identifier (Push Id)

The *Push Identifier* type represents an abstract value, which can be used to uniquely distinguish among the push transactions of a session that are pending on the service interface.

3.2.5 Reason

The service provider uses the *Reason* type to report the cause of a particular indication primitive. Each provider MAY define additional *Reason* values, but the service user MUST be prepared for the following ones:

REASON VALUE	DESCRIPTION
PROTOERR	The rules of the protocol prevented the peer from performing the operation in its current state. For example, the used PDU was not allowed.
DISCONNECT	The session was disconnected while the operation was still in progress.
SUSPEND	The session was suspended while the operation was still in progress.

RESUME	The session was resumed while the operation was still in progress.
CONGESTION	The peer implementation could not process the request due to lack of resources.
CONNECTERR	An error prevented session creation.
MRUEXCEEDED	The SDU size in a request was larger than the Maximum Receive Unit negotiated with the peer.
MOREXCEEDED	The negotiated upper limit on the number of simultaneously outstanding method or push requests was exceeded.
PEERREQ	The service peer requested the operation to be aborted.
NETERR	An underlying network error prevented completion of a request.
USERREQ	An action of the local service user was the cause of the indication.

3.2.6 Request URI

The *Request URI* parameter type is intended to have a similar use as the Request-URI in HTTP method requests [RFC2068]. However, the session user MAY use it as it sees fit, even leaving it empty or including binary data not compatible with the URI syntax.

3.2.7 Status

The *Status* parameter type has values equivalent to the HTTP/1.1 status codes [RFC2068].

3.2.8 Transaction Identifier (Transaction Id)

The *Transaction Identifier* type represents an abstract value, which can be used to uniquely distinguish among the method invocation transactions of a session that are pending on the service interface.

3.3 Connection-Mode Session Service

3.3.1 Overview

The connection-mode session service is divided into facilities, some of which are optional. Most of the facilities are asymmetric so that the operations available for the client and the server connected by the session are different. The provided facilities are:

- Session Management facility
- Method Invocation facility
- Exception Reporting facility
- Push facility
- Confirmed Push facility
- Session Resume facility

The Session Management and Exception reporting facilities are always available. The others are controlled by capability negotiation during session establishment.

Session Management allows a client to connect with a server and to agree on the facilities and protocol options to be used. A server can refuse the connection attempt, optionally redirecting the client to another server. During session establishment the client and server can also exchange attribute information, which is expected to remain valid for the duration of the session. Both the server and the client service user can also terminate the session, so that the peer is eventually notified of the termination. The user is also notified if session termination occurs due to the action of the service provider or a management entity.

Method Invocation permits the client to ask the server to execute an operation and return the result. The available operations are the HTTP methods [RFC2068] or user-defined extension operations, which fit into the same request-reply or transaction pattern. The service users both in the client and the server are always notified about the completion of the transaction, whether it succeeds or fails. Failure can be caused by an abort initiated either by the service user or the service provider.

The *Exception Reporting* facility allows the service provider to notify the user about events that are related to no particular transaction and do not cause a change in the state of the session.

The *Push* facility permits the server to send unsolicited information to the client taking advantage of the session information shared by the client and the server. This facility is a nonconfirmed one, so delivery of the information MAY be unreliable.

The *Confirmed Push* facility is similar to the *Push* facility, but the client confirms the receipt of the information. The client may also choose to abort the push so that the server is notified.

The *Session Resume* facility includes means to suspend a session so that the state of the session is preserved, but both peers know that further communication is not possible until the client resumes the session. This mechanism is also used to handle the situations in which the service provider detects that further communication is no longer possible until some corrective action is taken by the service user or management entities. It can also be used to switch the session to use an alternate bearer network, which has more appropriate properties than the one being used. This facility SHOULD be implemented to ensure reasonable behavior in certain bearer network environments.

3.3.2 Capabilities

Information that is related to the operation of the session service provider is handled using *capabilities*. Capabilities are used for a wide variety of purposes, ranging from representing the selected set of service facilities and settings of particular protocol parameters, to establishing the code page and extension method names used by both peers.

3.3.2.1 Capability Negotiation

Capability negotiation is used between service peers to agree on a mutually acceptable level of service and to optimize the operation of the service provider according to the actual requirements of the service user. Capability negotiation is to be applied only to *negotiable* capabilities; *informational* capabilities are to be communicated to the peer service user without modifications.

The peer that starts the capability negotiation process is called the *initiator*, and the other peer is called the *responder*. Only a *one-way capability negotiation* is defined, in which the initiator proposes a set of capabilities, and the responder replies to these. The capability negotiation process is under the control of the initiator, so that the responder MUST NOT ever reply with any capability setting, which implies a higher level of functionality than the one proposed by the initiator and supported by the service provider peers. Capability negotiation applies always to all the known capabilities. If a particular capability is omitted from the set of capabilities carried by a service primitive, this must be interpreted to mean that the originator of the primitive wants to use the current capability setting, either the default or the value agreed upon during capability negotiation process. However, the responder may still reply with a different capability value, as long as this does not imply a higher level of functionality.

The one-way capability negotiation proceeds as follows:

1. Service user in initiator proposes a set of capability values.
2. The service provider in the initiator modifies the capabilities so that they do not imply a higher level of functionality than the provider actually can support.
3. The service provider in the responder further modifies the capabilities so that they do not imply a higher level of functionality than the provider in the responder actually can support.
4. The service user in the responder receives this modified set of capabilities and responds with a set of capabilities, which reflect the level of functionality it actually wishes to use. If a particular capability is omitted, this is interpreted to mean that the responding service user wants to use the proposed capability setting.
5. The capabilities selected by the service user in the responder are indicated to the service user in the initiator. They will become the default settings, which will be applicable in the next capability negotiation during the session.

If the operation implied by the service primitive that is used to convey the capability information fails, the capability settings that were in effect before the operation shall remain in effect.

If a negotiable capability value is a positive integer, the final capability setting shall be the minimum of the values, which the service users have proposed to use and which the service provider peers are capable of supporting.

If a negotiable capability value is a set, the final capability setting shall contain only those elements, which are all included in the subsets that the service users have proposed to use and which the service provider peers are capable of supporting.

3.3.2.2 Defined Capabilities

A service user and a service provider MUST recognize the following capabilities:

CAPABILITY NAME	CLASS	TYPE	DESCRIPTION
Aliases	I	List of addresses	A service user can use this capability to indicate which alternate addresses the peer may use to access the same service user instance that is using the current session. The addresses are listed in a preference order, with the most preferred alias first. This information can, for example, be used to facilitate a switch to a new bearer when a session is resumed.
Client SDU Size	N	Positive integer	The client and server use this capability to agree on the size of the largest transaction service data unit, which may be sent to the *client* during the session.
Extended Methods	N	Set of method names	This capability is used to agree on the set of extended methods (beyond those defined in HTTP/1.1), which are supported both by the client and the server peer, and may be used subsequently during the session.
Header Code Pages	N	Set of code page names	This capability is used to agree on the set of extension header code pages, which are supported both by the client and the server, and shall be used subsequently during the session.
Maximum Outstanding Method Requests	N	Positive integer	The client and server use this capability to agree on the maxiumum number of method invocations, which can be active at the same time during the session.
Maximum Outstanding Push Requests	N	Positive integer	The client and server use this capability to agree on the maximum number of confirmed push invocations, which can be active at the same time during the session.
Protocol Options	N	Set of facilities and features	This capability is used to enable the optional service facilities and features. It may contain elements from the list: Push, Confirmed Push, Session Resume, and Acknowledgment Headers. The presence of an element indicates that use of the specific facility or feature is enabled.
Server SDU Size	N	Positive integer	The client and server use this capability to agree on the size of the largest transaction service data unit, which may be sent to the *server* during the session.

In the *Class* column *N* stands for negotiable, *I* for informational.

3.3.3 Service Primitives

This section lists all the abstract service primitives provided by the service and defines their meaning.

3.3.3.1 S-Connect

This primitive is used to initiate session establishment and to notify of its success. It also provides one-way capability negotiation with the client being the initiator and the server being the responder. It is part of the *Session Management* facility.

PRIMITIVE	S-CONNECT			
PARAMETER	***REQ***	***IND***	***RES***	***CNF***
Server Address	M	M(=)	–	–
Client Address	M	M(=)	–	–
Client Headers	O	C(=)	–	–
Requested Capabilities	O	M	–	–
Server Headers	–	–	O	C(=)
Negotiated Capabilities	–	–	O	M(=)

Server Address identifies the peer with which the session is to be established.

Client Address identifies the originator of the session.

Client Headers and *Server Headers* represent attribute information compatible with HTTP message headers [RFC2068], which is communicated without modification between the service users. They can be used for application-level parameters or to cache request headers and response headers, respectively, that are constant throughout the session. However, the actual interpretation and use of this information are completely up to the service users. If these parameters are not provided, applications may rely on application-dependant default session headers to provide a static form of session-wide information.

Requested Capabilities and *Negotiated Capabilities* are used to implement the capability negotiation process described in Section 3.3.2.1, *Capability Negotiation*. If the rules for capability negotiation are violated, the appropriate action is to fail the session establishment.

The service user may during session establishment invoke some service primitives that will turn out not to be part of the finally selected session functionality. When session establishment and the associated capability negotiation completes, such service requests shall be aborted and the appropriate error shall be indicated to the service user. It is an error if such primitives are invoked after the session has been established, and the appropriate action is a local implementation matter.

Figure 14.3 illustrates the primitives used in a successful session establishment. The service user MAY request a method invocation already while the session is being established. Primitives related to this are shown with dashed lines.

A disconnect indication generated by the service provider can occur also at any time during the session establishment.

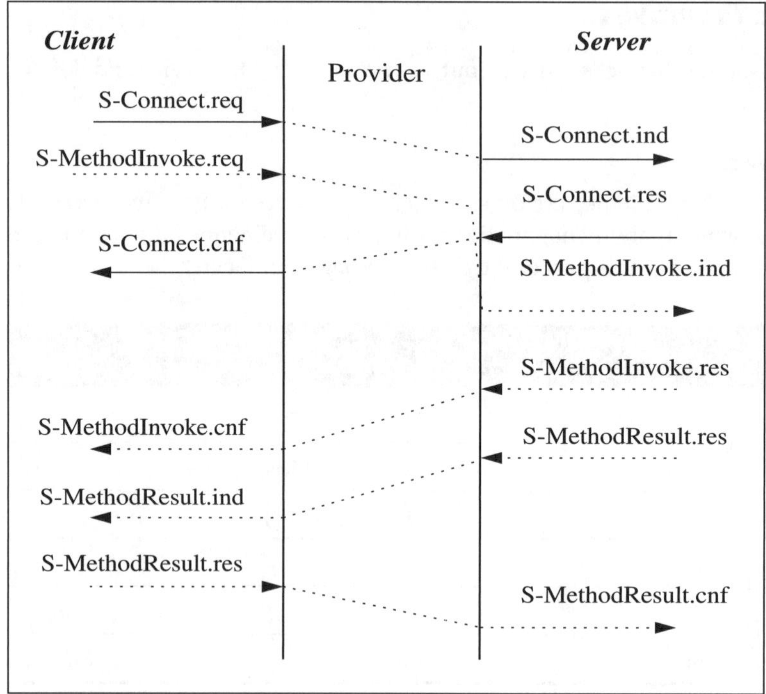

Figure 14.3 Successful session establishment.

3.3.3.2 S-Disconnect

This primitive is used to disconnect a session and to notify the session user that the session could not be established or has been disconnected. It is part of the *Session Management* facility. This primitive is always indicated when the session termination is detected, regardless of whether the disconnection was initiated by the local service user, the peer service user, or the service provider. Before the disconnect indication, the session service provider MUST abort all incomplete method and push transactions. After the indication, further primitives associated with the session MUST NOT occur.

PRIMITIVE	S-DISCONNECT	
PARAMETER	*REQ*	*IND*
Reason Code	M	M(=)
Redirect Security	C	C(=)
Redirect Addresses	C	C(=)
Error Headers	O	P(=)
Error Body	O	P(=)

The *Reason Code* parameter indicates the cause of disconnection. The possible values are a union of the values possible for the Reason and Status parameter types.

If *Reason Code* indicates that the client is being redirected to contact a new server address, the *Redirect Security* and *Redirect Addresses* parameters MUST be present.

Redirect Security indicates whether or not the client MAY reuse the current secure session when redirecting to the new server or whether it MUST use a different secure session.

Redirect Addresses are the alternate addresses, which the client at the moment MUST use to establish a session with the same service it initially tried to contact. If *Reason Code* indicates that the client is being redirected temporarily, it SHOULD use the original *Server Address* in future attempts to establish a session with the service, once the subsequent session with one of the redirect addresses has terminated. If *Reason* indicates that the client is being redirected permanently, it SHOULD use one of the *Redirect Addresses* in future attempts to establish a session with the service.

If *Reason Code* takes one of the values in the Status type, *Error Headers* and *Error Body* SHOULD be included to provide meaningful information about the error in addition to the *Reason Code*. The size of the headers and body MUST NOT cause the SDU to exceed the currently selected Maximum Receive Unit of the peer. The service provider MAY choose not to communicate the *Error Headers* and *Error Body* to the peer service user.

Figure 14.4 illustrates the primitives used when the server rejects or redirects the session. The service user MAY request a method invocation already while the session is being established. Primitives related to this are shown with dashed lines.

A disconnect indication generated by the service provider can occur at any time during the session.

The primitive sequence for session termination of an active session is shown in Figure 14.5. The S-Disconnect.indication indicates that the session has been torn down

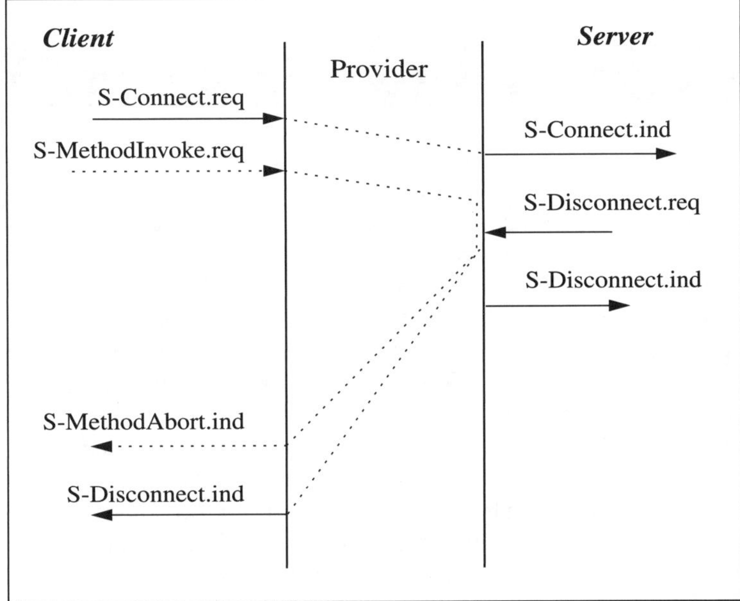

Figure 14.4 Refused session establishment.

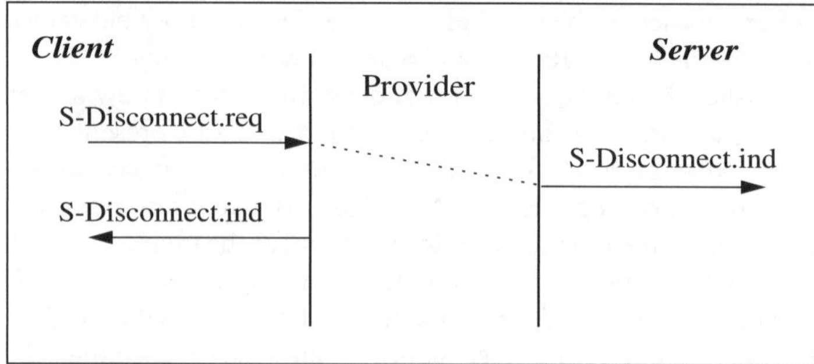

Figure 14.5 Active session termination.

and cannot generate any further indications. The service provider shall abort all outstanding transactions prior to the S-Disconnect.indication.

The service user must be prepared for the session being disconnected at any time. If it wishes to continue communication, it has to establish the session again and retry the method invocations that may have been aborted.

3.3.3.3 S-Suspend

This primitive is used to request the session to be suspended, so that no other activity can occur on it until it is either resumed or disconnected. Before the session becomes suspended, the session service provider MUST abort all incomplete method and push transactions. This primitive is part of the *Session Resume* facility.

PRIMITIVE / PARAMETER	S-SUSPEND REQ	S-SUSPEND IND
Reason	–	M

Reason provides the reason for the suspension. The service user may have requested it, or the service provider may have initiated it.

A possible flow of primitives is shown in Figure 14.6.

Typically, the client would suspend a session when it knows it will not be available to respond to data pushes, for example, because it will be closing a data circuit in the underlying bearer network. A side effect of S-Suspend.request is that all data transfer transactions are immediately aborted.

The service provider MAY also cause an established session to be suspended at any time; for example, if the bearer network becomes unavailable. Figure 14.7 shows a scenario in which only one of the peers—in this case, the client—is notified about the suspension. When the client tries to resume the session, the server refuses the attempt by disconnecting the session. For example, the server may consider the used bearer network to be unsuitable.

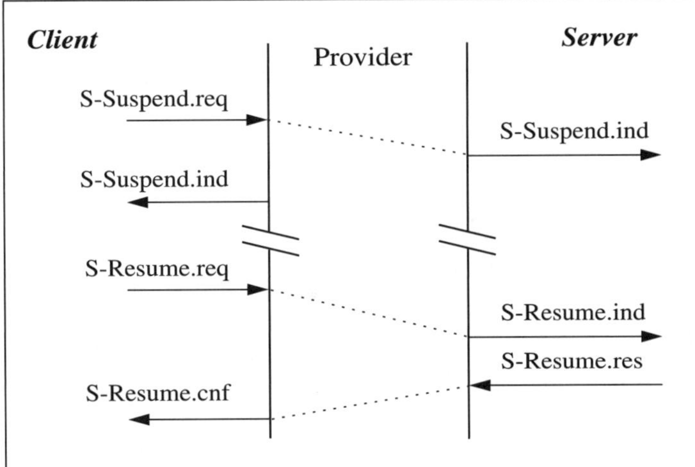

Figure 14.6 Session suspension and resume.

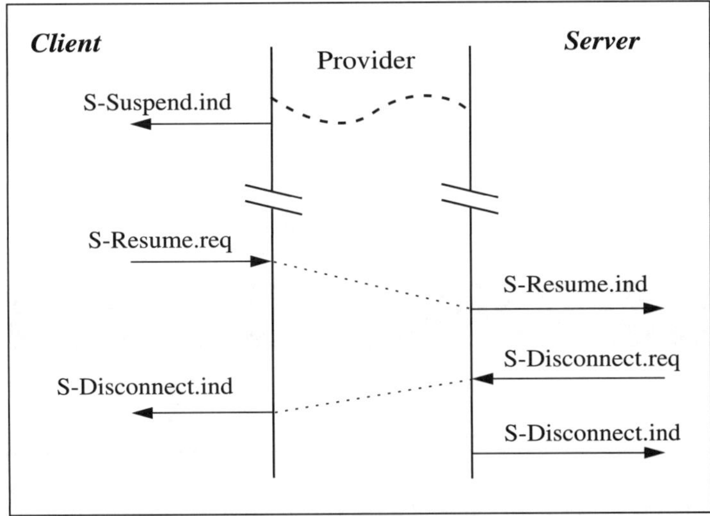

Figure 14.7 Suspend by provider and refused resume.

Figure 14.8 shows a sequence of events in which both service users happen to be notified about the suspended session. However, in this case one service user decides to disconnect instead of trying to resume the session. The service user may tear down one-half of the session at any time by invoking the S-Disconnect.request primitive. However, the other half of the session will not be notified of this, since the communication path between the service peers is not available. As shown in Figure 14.8, the service provider SHOULD eventually terminate a suspended session. The time a suspended session is retained is a local implementation matter.

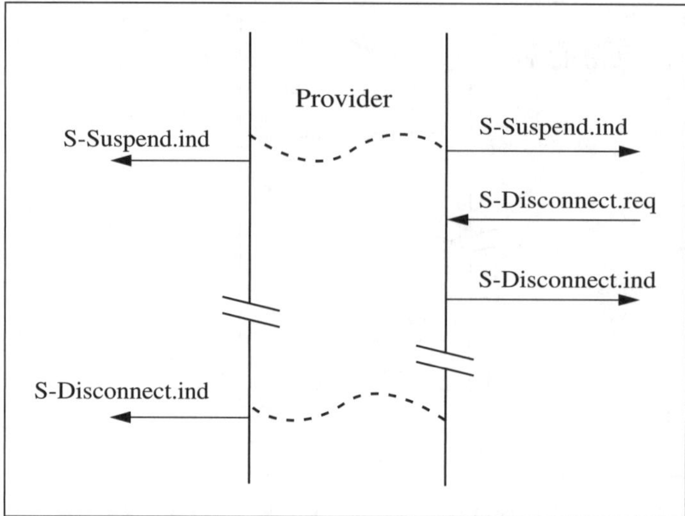

Figure 14.8 Suspended session termination.

3.3.3.4 S-Resume

This primitive is used to request the session to be resumed using the new service access point identified by the addresses. It is part of the *Session Resume* facility.

PRIMITIVE	S-RESUME			
PARAMETER	***REQ***	***IND***	***RES***	***CNF***
Server Address	M	M(=)	–	–
Client Address	M	M(=)	–	–

Server Address identifies the peer with which the session is to be resumed.

Client Address identifies the current origin of the session.

Both the *Server Address* and *Client Address* MAY be different than the one that was in effect before the session was suspended. If the *Server Address* is different than before suspension, the service user is responsible for providing an address, which will contact the same server instance that was previously in use.

3.3.3.5 S-Exception

This primitive is used to report events that neither are related to a particular transaction nor cause the session to be disconnected or suspended. It is part of the *Exception Reporting* facility.

PARAMETER	PRIMITIVE	S-EXCEPTION IND
Exception Data		M

Exception Data includes information from the service provider. Exceptions may occur for many reasons:

- Changes to the underlying transport (e.g., roaming out of coverage)
- Changes to quality of service
- Changes or problems in the Security layer

3.3.3.6 S-MethodInvoke

This primitive is used to request an operation to be executed by the server. It can be used only together with the S-MethodResult primitive. This primitive is part of the *Method Invocation* facility.

PRIMITIVE	S-METHODINVOKE			
PARAMETER	***REQ***	***IND***	***RES***	***CNF***
Client Transaction Id	M	–	–	M(=)
Server Transaction Id	–	M	M(=)	–
Method	M	M(=)	–	–
Request URI	M	M(=)	–	–
Request Headers	O	C(=)	–	–
Request Body	C	C(=)	–	–

The service user in the client can use *Client Transaction Id* to distinguish between pending transactions.

The service user in the server can use *Server Transaction Id* to distinguish between pending transactions.

Method identifies the requested operation: either an HTTP method [RFC2068] or one of the extension methods established during capability negotiation.

Request URI specifies the entity to which the operation applies.

Request Headers are a list of attribute information semantically equivalent to HTTP headers [RFC2068].

Request Body is the data associated with the request, which is semantically equivalent to HTTP entity body. If the request *Method* is not defined to allow an entity body, *Request Body* MUST NOT be provided [RFC2068].

3.3.3.7 S-MethodResult

This primitive is used to return a response to an operation request. It can be invoked only after a preceding S-MethodInvoke primitive has occurred. This primitive is part of the *Method Invocation* facility.

PRIMITIVE	S-METHODRESULT			
PARAMETER	***REQ***	***IND***	***RES***	***CNF***
Server Transaction Id	M	–	–	M(=)
Client Transaction Id	–	M	M(=)	–
Status	M	M(=)	–	–
Response Headers	O	C(=)	–	–
Response Body	C	C(=)	–	–
Acknowledgment Headers	–	–	O	P(=)

The service user in the client can use *Client Transaction Id* to distinguish between pending transactions. It MUST match the Client Transaction Id of a previous S-MethodInvoke.request for which S-MethodResult.indication has not yet occurred.

The service user in the server can use *Server Transaction Id* to distinguish between pending transactions. It MUST match the Server Transaction Id of a previous S-MethodInvoke.response for which S-MethodResult.request has not yet occurred.

Status is semantically equivalent to an HTTP status code [RFC2068].

Response Headers are a list of attribute information semantically equivalent to HTTP headers [RFC2068].

Response Body is the data associated with the response, which is semantically equivalent to an HTTP entity body. If *Status* indicates an error, *Response Body* SHOULD provide additional information about the error in a form, which can be shown to the human user.

Acknowledgment Headers MAY be used to return some information back to the server. However, the provider MAY ignore this parameter or support the transfer of a very limited amount of data.

Figure 14.9 illustrates the flow of primitives in a complete transaction.

If the transaction is aborted for any reason, an S-MethodAbort.indication will be delivered to the service user. It can occur instead of one of the shown indication or confirm primitives or after one of them. Once the abort indication is delivered, no further primitives related to the transaction can occur.

The Session layer does not provide any sequencing between multiple overlapping method invocations, so the indications may be delivered in a different order than the corresponding requests. The same applies to the responses and confirmations, as well as to the corresponding S-MethodResult primitives. The end result is that the results of method invocations may be delivered in an order different from the original order of the requests. Figure 14.10 illustrates this (omitting the responses and confirmations for clarity).

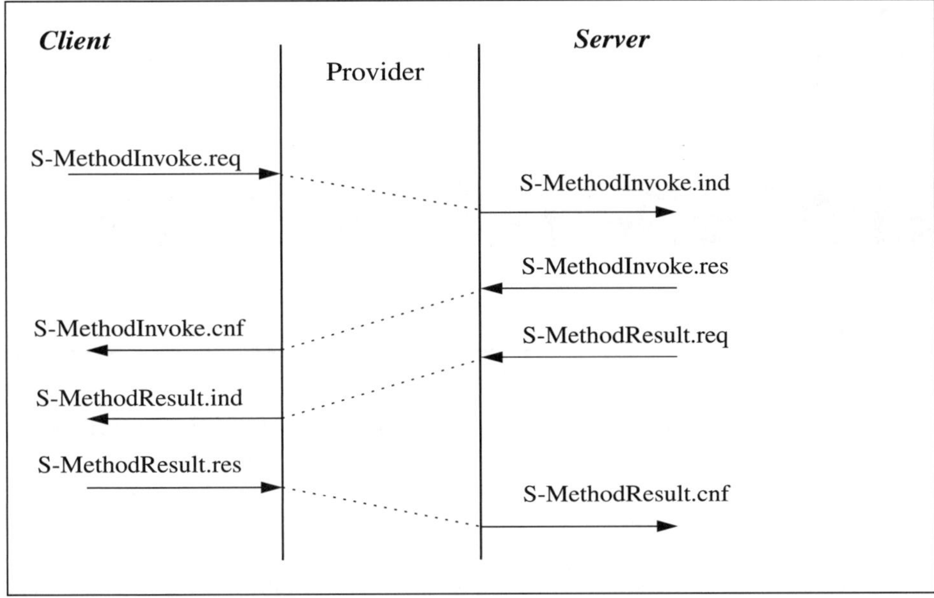

Figure 14.9 Completed transaction.

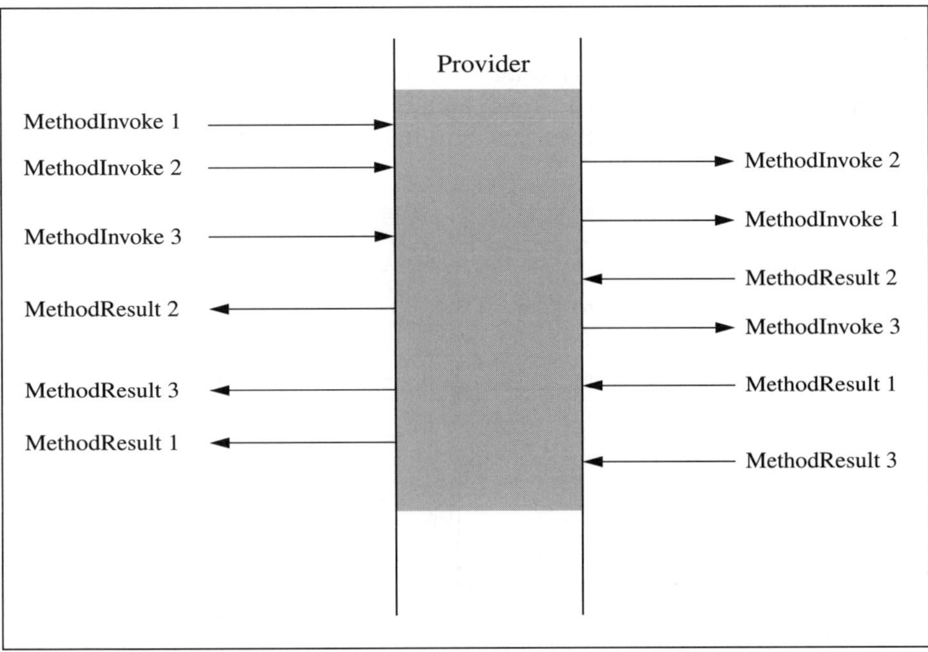

Figure 14.10 Unordered asynchronous requests.

3.3.3.8 S-MethodAbort

This primitive is used to abort an operation request that is not yet complete. It can be invoked only after a preceding S-MethodInvoke primitive has occurred. It is part of the *Method Invocation* facility.

PRIMITIVE PARAMETER	S-METHODABORT *REQ*	 *IND*
Transaction Id	M	M
Reason	–	M

The service user in the client uses *Transaction Id* to distinguish between pending transactions when invoking S-MethodAbort.request. It MUST match the *Client Transaction Id* of a previous S-MethodInvoke.request for which S-MethodResult.response has not yet occurred. The *Transaction Id* of the S-MethodAbort.indication in the server will in this case match the *Server Transaction Id* of that transaction.

The service user in the server uses *Transaction Id* to distinguish between pending transactions when invoking S-MethodAbort.request. It MUST match the *Server Transaction Id* of a previous S-MethodInvoke.indication for which S-MethodResult.confirm has not yet occurred. The *Transaction Id* of the S-MethodAbort.indication in the client will in this case match the *Client Transaction Id* of that transaction.

Reason is the reason for aborting the transaction. It will be PEERREQ, if the peer invoked S-MethodAbort.request.

There are two scenarios depending on the timing of the primitives.

The first scenario is shown in Figure 14.11. The abort request is submitted, while the method invocation is still being communicated to the provider peer, before the S-MethodInvoke.indication has occurred. In this case, the transaction is aborted without the peer user ever being notified about the transaction.

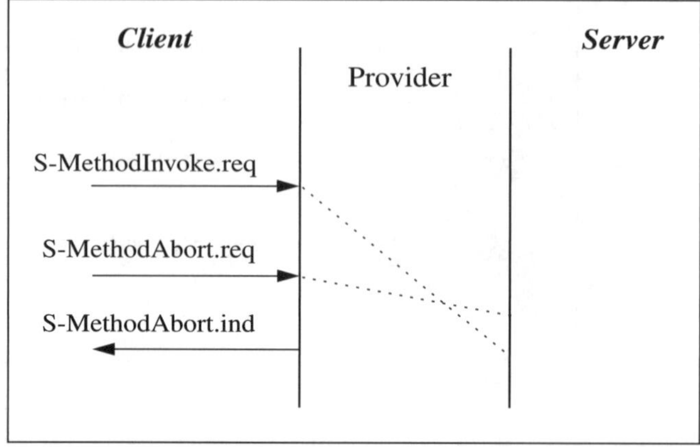

Figure 14.11 Abort before S-MethodInvoke.indication.

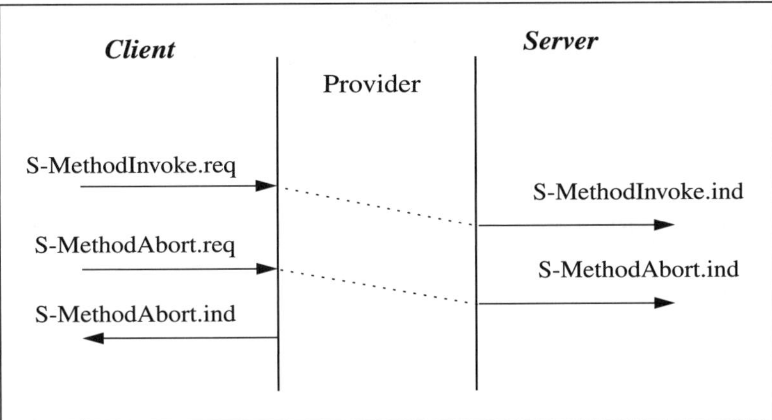

Figure 14.12 Abort after S-MethodInvoke.indication.

The second scenario is shown in Figure 14.12. The abort request is communicated to the provider peer *after* the S-MethodInvoke.indication has occurred. In this case, the S-MethodAbort.indication will occur as well, and the application MUST NOT invoke any further S-MethodInvoke or S-MethodResult primitives applying to the aborted transaction.

The S-MethodAbort primitive may be invoked in the client at any time between S-MethodInvoke.request and S-MethodResult.response for the transaction to be aborted. Likewise, S-MethodAbort may be invoked in the server at any time between S-MethodInvoke.indication and S-MethodResult.confirm.

3.3.3.9 S-Push

This primitive is used to send unsolicited information from the server within the session context in a nonconfirmed manner (see Figure 14.13). This primitive is part of the *Push* facility.

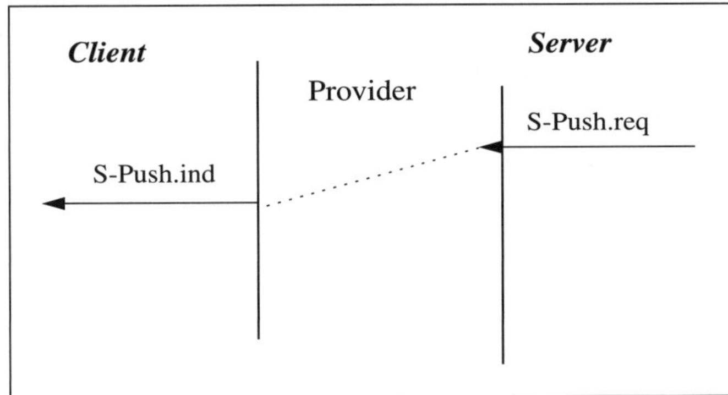

Figure 14.13 Nonconfirmed data push.

PARAMETER	S-PUSH REQ	S-PUSH IND
Push Headers	O	C(=)
Push Body	O	C(=)

If the location of the pushed entity needs to be indicated, the Content-Location header [RFC2068] SHOULD be included in *Push Headers* to ensure interoperability.

Delivery of information to the peer is not assured, so the scenario shown in Figure 14.14 is also permitted:

3.3.3.10 S-ConfirmedPush

This primitive is used to send unsolicited information from the server within the session context in a confirmed manner. It is part of the *Confirmed Push* facility.

PARAMETER	S-CONFIRMEDPUSH REQ	IND	RES	CNF
Server Push Id	M	–	–	M(=)
Client Push Id	–	M	M(=)	–
Push Headers	O	C(=)	–	–
Push Body	O	C(=)	–	–
Acknowledgment Headers	–	–	O	P(=)

The service user in the server can use *Server Push Id* to distinguish between pending pushes.

The service user in the client can use *Client Push Id* to distinguish between pending pushes.

If the location of the pushed entity needs to be indicated, the Content-Location header [RFC2068] SHOULD be included in *Push Headers* to ensure interoperability.

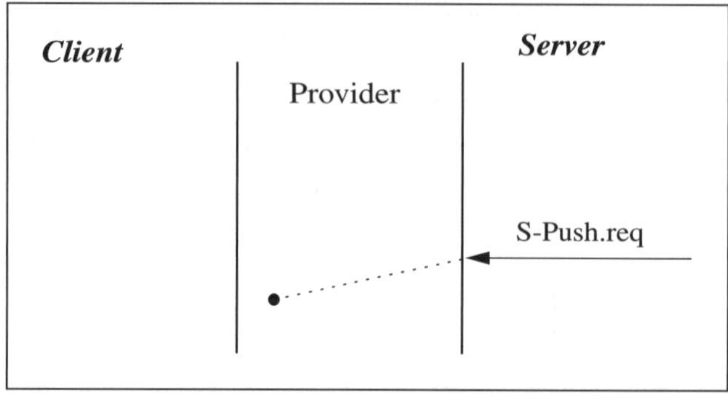

Figure 14.14 Failed nonconfirmed data push.

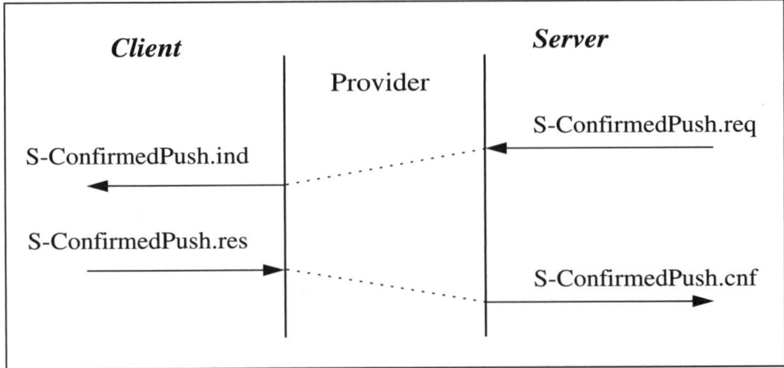

Figure 14.15 Confirmed data push.

Acknowledgment Headers MAY be used to return some information back to the server. However, the provider MAY ignore this parameter or support the transfer of a very limited amount of data.

3.3.3.11 S-PushAbort

This primitive is used to reject a push operation. It is part of the *Confirmed Push* facility (see Figure 14.15).

PRIMITIVE / PARAMETER	S-PUSHABORT REQ	S-PUSHABORT IND
Client Push Id	M	–
Server Push Id	–	M
Reason	M	M(=)

The service user in the client can use *Client Push Id* to distinguish between pending pushes. It must match the *Client Push Id* of a previous S-ConfirmedPush.indication.

The service user in the server can use *Server Push Id* to distinguish which push was aborted. It will match the *Server Push Id* of a previous S-ConfirmedPush.request, which has not yet been confirmed or indicated as aborted.

Reason is the reason for aborting the push. It will either be the value provided by the peer service user or a reason code from the service provider.

Figure 14.16 shows the behavior of S-PushAbort. It can be requested only after an S-ConfirmedPush.indication, replacing an S-ConfirmedPush.response.

S-PushAbort.indication can also occur without the user's request as the result of a provider-initiated abort.

3.3.4 Constraints on Using the Service Primitives

Tables 14.2–14.4 define the permitted primitive sequences on the service interface. The client and server have separate tables, since the service is asymmetric.

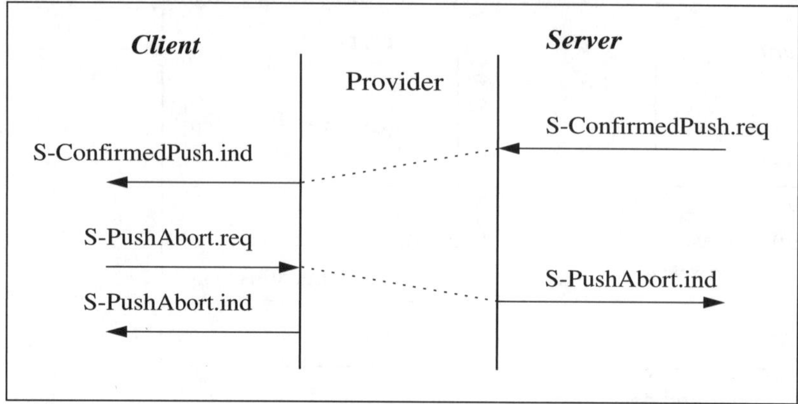

Figure 14.16 Aborted confirmed data push.

Only the permitted primitives are listed on the rows; the layer prefix is omitted for brevity. The table entries are interpreted as follows:

The life cycles of transactions in the client and the server are defined in Tables 14.5 and 14.6. Once again, only the permitted primitives are listed on the rows.

The life cycles of confirmed push transactions in the server and the client are defined in Tables 14.7 and 14.8. Once again, only the permitted primitives are listed on the rows.

3.3.5 Error Handling

The connection-mode session service provider uses a four-tier strategy in handling errors and other exceptional conditions:

1. If an exceptional condition is not related to any particular transaction, it is reported through the *Exception Reporting* facility without disturbing the overall state of the session.
2. Errors related to a particular transaction cause a method or push abort indication with the appropriate reason code without disturbing the overall state of the session.
3. Conditions which prevent the session peers from communicating with each other will cause suspend indications, if the *Session Resume* facility is selected. Otherwise, they will cause a disconnection to be indicated.
4. Other errors will cause a session disconnect to be indicated with the appropriate reason code.

Certain race conditions may cause the abort reason code of a method or push transaction to be reported as DISCONNECT, but this must not be interpreted as indicating that the session has been disconnected; session disconnection is always indicated using only the S-Disconnect primitive.

Table 14.2 Table Entry Legend

ENTRY	DESCRIPTION
–	The indication or confirm primitive cannot occur.
N/A	Invoking this primitive is an error. The appropriate action is a local implementation matter.
STATE_NAME	Primitive is permitted and moves the service interface view to the named state.
[1]	If the number of outstanding transactions is equal to the selected Maximum Outstanding Method Requests value, invoking this primitive is an error. The appropriate action is a local implementation matter; delivery of the primitive might be delayed until it is permitted.
[2]	If there is no outstanding transaction with a matching Transaction Id, invoking this primitive is an error. The appropriate action is a local implementation matter.
[3]	If the *Confirmed Push* facility has not been selected during capability negotiation, invoking this primitive is an error; likewise, if there is no outstanding push with a matching Push Id. The appropriate action is a local implementation matter.
[4]	Possible only if the *Push* facility has been selected during capability negotiation.
[5]	Possible only if the *Confirmed Push* facility has been selected during capability negotiation.
[6]	If the *Push* facility has not been selected during capability negotiation, invoking this primitive is an error. The appropriate action is a local implementation matter.
[7]	If the *Confirmed Push* facility has not been selected during capability negotiation, invoking this primitive is an error. The appropriate action is a local implementation matter.
[8]	If the *Confirmed Push* facility has not been selected during capability negotiation, invoking this primitive is an error. The appropriate action is a local implementation matter. Also, if the number of outstanding pushes is equal to the selected Maximum Outstanding Push Requests value, invoking this primitive is an error. The appropriate action is a local implementation matter; delivery of the primitive might be delayed until it is permitted.
[9]	If the *Session Resume* facility has not been selected during capability negotiation, invoking this primitive is an error. The appropriate action is a local implementation matter.
[10]	Possible only if the *Session Resume* facility has been selected during capability negotiation.

Table 14.3 Permitted Client Session Layer Primitives

CLIENT			***SESSION STATES***				
S-PRIMITIVE	**NULL**	**CONNECTING**	**CONNECTED**	**CLOSING**	**SUSPENDING**	**SUSPENDED**	**RESUMING**
Connect.req	CONNECTING	N/A	N/A	N/A	N/A	N/A	N/A
Disconnect.req	N/A	CLOSING	CLOSING	N/A	CLOSING	CLOSING	CLOSING
MethodInvoke.req	N/A	[1]	[1]	N/A	N/A	N/A	[1]
MethodResult.res	N/A	N/A	[2]	N/A	N/A	N/A	N/A
MethodAbort.req	N/A	[2]	[2]	N/A	N/A	N/A	[2]
ConfirmedPush.res	N/A	N/A	[3]	N/A	N/A	N/A	N/A
PushAbort.req	N/A	N/A	[3]	N/A	N/A	N/A	N/A
Suspend.req	N/A	N/A	SUSPENDING [9]	N/A	N/A	N/A	SUSPENDING [9]
Resume.req	N/A	N/A	RESUMING [9]	N/A	RESUMING [9]	RESUMING [9]	N/A
Connect.cnf	–	CONNECTED	–	–	–	–	–
Exception.ind	–	CONNECTING	CONNECTED	CLOSING	SUSPENDING	–	RESUMING
Disconnect.ind	–	NULL	NULL	NULL	NULL	NULL	NULL
MethodInvoke.cnf	–	–	CONNECTED	–	–	–	–
MethodResult.ind	–	–	CONNECTED	–	–	–	–
MethodAbort.ind	–	CONNECTING	CONNECTED	CLOSING	SUSPENDING	–	RESUMING
Push.ind	–	–	CONNECTED [4]	CLOSING [4]	SUSPENDING [4]	–	–
ConfirmedPush.ind	–	–	CONNECTED [5]	–	–	–	–
PushAbort.ind	–	–	CONNECTED [5]	–	SUSPENDING [5]	–	–
Suspend.ind	–	–	SUSPENDED [10]	–	SUSPENDED [10]	–	SUSPENDED [10]
Resume.cnf	–	–	–	–	–	–	CONNECTED [10]

Table 14.4 Permitted Server Session Layer Primitives

SERVER	*SESSION STATES*						
S-PRIMITIVE	**NULL**	**CONNECTING**	**CONNECTED**	**CLOSING**	**SUSPENDING**	**SUSPENDED**	**RESUMING**
Connect.res	N/A	CONNECTED	N/A	N/A	N/A	N/A	N/A
Disconnect.req	N/A	CLOSING	CLOSING	N/A	CLOSING	NULL	CLOSING
MethodInvoke.res	N/A	N/A	[2]	N/A	N/A	N/A	N/A
MethodResult.req	N/A	N/A	[2]	N/A	N/A	N/A	N/A
MethodAbort.req	N/A	N/A	[2]	N/A	N/A	N/A	N/A
Push.req	N/A	N/A	[6]	N/A	N/A	N/A	N/A
ConfirmedPush.req	N/A	N/A	[8]	N/A	N/A	N/A	N/A
Resume.res	N/A	N/A	N/A	N/A	N/A	N/A	CONNECTED [9]
Connect.ind	CONNECTING	–	–	–	–	–	–
Exception.ind	–	CONNECTING	CONNECTED	CLOSING	SUSPENDING	–	RESUMING
Disconnect.ind	–	NULL	NULL	NULL	NULL	NULL	NULL
MethodInvoke.ind	–	–	CONNECTED	–	–	–	–
MethodResult.cnf	–	–	CONNECTED	–	–	–	–
MethodAbort.ind	–	–	CONNECTED	CLOSING	SUSPENDING	–	–
ConfirmedPush.cnf	–	–	CONNECTED [5]	–	CONNECTED [5]	–	–
PushAbort.ind	–	–	CONNECTED [5]	CLOSING [5]	CONNECTED [5]	–	–
Suspend.ind	–	–	SUSPENDED [10]	–	SUSPENDED [10]	–	SUSPENDED [10]
Resume.ind	–	–	RESUMING [10]	–	RESUMING	RESUMING [10]	–

Table 14.5 Permitted Client Transaction Primitives

CLIENT S-PRIMITIVE	NULL	REQUESTING	WAITING	COMPLETING	ABORTING
			TRANSACTION STATES		
MethodInvoke.req	REQUESTING	N/A	N/A	N/A	N/A
MethodResult.res	N/A	N/A	N/A	NULL	N/A
MethodAbort.req	N/A	ABORTING	ABORTING	ABORTING	N/A
MethodInvoke.cnf	-	WAITING	-	-	-
MethodResult.ind	-	-	COMPLETING	-	-
MethodAbort.ind	-	NULL	NULL	NULL	NULL

Table 14.6 Permitted Server Transaction Primitives

SERVER S-PRIMITIVE	NULL	REQUESTING	PROCESSING	REPLYING	ABORTING
			TRANSACTION STATES		
MethodInvoke.res	N/A	PROCESSING	N/A	N/A	N/A
MethodResult.req	N/A	N/A	REPLYING	N/A	N/A
MethodAbort.req	N/A	ABORTING	ABORTING	ABORTING	N/A
MethodInvoke.ind	REQUESTING	-	-	-	-
MethodResult.cnf	-	-	-	NULL	-
MethodAbort.ind	-	NULL	NULL	NULL	NULL

Table 14.7 Permitted Server Confirmed Push Primitives

SERVER S-PRIMITIVE	NULL	PUSHING
	CONFIRMED PUSH STATES	
ConfirmedPush.req	PUSHING	N/A
ConfirmedPush.cnf	-	NULL
PushAbort.ind	-	NULL

Table 14.8 Permitted Client Confirmed Push Primitives

CLIENT S-PRIMITIVE	NULL	RECEIVING	ABORTING
		CONFIRMED PUSH STATES	
ConfirmedPush.res	N/A	NULL	N/A
PushAbort.req	N/A	ABORTING	N/A
ConfirmedPush.ind	RECEIVING	-	-
PushAbort.ind	-	NULL	NULL

3.4 Connectionless Session Service

3.4.1 Overview

The connectionless session service provides nonconfirmed facilities, which can be used to exchange content entities between layer users. The provided service is asymmetric in a manner similar to the connection-mode service.

Only the Method Invocation and Push facilities are available. The facilities are nonconfirmed, so the communication between the peer entities MAY be unreliable.

3.4.2 Service Primitives

The service primitives are defined using types from the *Service Parameter Types* section.

3.4.2.1 S-Unit-MethodInvoke

This primitive is used to invoke a method in the server in a nonconfirmed manner. It is part of the Method Invocation facility.

PRIMITIVE	S-UNIT-METHODINVOKE	
PARAMETER	*REQ*	*IND*
Server Address	M	M(=)
Client Address	M	M(=)
Transaction Id	M	M(=)
Method	M	M(=)
Request URI	M	M(=)
Request Headers	O	C(=)
Request Body	C	C(=)

Server Address identifies the peer to which the request is to be sent.

Client Address identifies the originator of the request.

The service users MAY use *Transaction Id* to distinguish between transactions. It is communicated transparently from service user to service user.

Method identifies the requested operation, which must be one of the HTTP methods [RFC2068].

Request URI specifies the entity to which the operation applies.

Request Headers are a list of attribute information semantically equivalent to HTTP headers [RFC2068].

Request Body is the data associated with the request, which is semantically equivalent to HTTP entity body. If the request *Method* is not defined to allow an entity body, *Request Body* MUST NOT be provided [RFC2068].

3.4.2.2 S-Unit-MethodResult

This primitive is used to return the result of a method invocation from the server in a nonconfirmed manner. It is part of the Method Invocation facility.

PRIMITIVE	S-UNIT-METHODRESULT	
PARAMETER	***REQ***	***IND***
Client Address	M	M(=)
Server Address	M	M(=)
Transaction Id	M	M(=)
Status	M	M(=)
Response Headers	O	C(=)
Response Body	C	C(=)

Client Address identifies the peer to which the result is to be sent.

Server Address identifies the originator of the result.

The service users MAY use *Transaction Id* to distinguish between transactions.

Status is semantically equivalent to an HTTP status code [RFC2068].

Response Headers are a list of attribute information semantically equivalent to HTTP headers [RFC2068].

Response Body is the data associated with the response, which is semantically equivalent to an HTTP entity body. If *Status* indicates an error, *Response Body* SHOULD provide additional information about the error in a form, which can be shown to the human user.

3.4.2.3 S-Unit-Push

This primitive is used to send unsolicited information from the server to the client in a nonconfirmed manner. It is part of the Push facility.

PRIMITIVE	S-UNIT-PUSH	
PARAMETER	***REQ***	***IND***
Client Address	M	M(=)
Server Address	M	M(=)
Push Id	M	M(=)
Push Headers	O	C(=)
Push Body	O	C(=)

Client Address identifies the peer to which the push is to be sent.

Server Address identifies the originator of the push.

The service users MAY use *Push Id* to distinguish between pushes.

Table 14.9 Connectionless Service Primitives

GENERIC NAME	TYPE REQ	IND	RES	CNF	DESCRIPTION
S-Unit-MethodInvoke	C	S	-	-	Invoke a method in the server with no confirmation
S-Unit-MethodResult	S	C	-	-	Return response from the server with no confirmation
S-Unit-Push	S	C	-	-	Push content with no confirmation

- – Primitive may not occur
C – Primitive may occur on the client
S – Primitive may occur on the server

If the location of the pushed entity needs to be indicated, the Content-Location header [RFC2068] SHOULD be included in *Push Headers* to ensure interoperability.

3.4.3 Constraints on Using the Service Primitives

The service user MAY invoke the permitted request primitives at any time, once the underlying layers have been prepared for communication. This is expected to occur through the appropriate interactions with management entities, which are not part of this specification. A failure to do so is an error, and the appropriate action is a local implementation matter.

The service provider SHOULD deliver an indication primitive when it is notified that the corresponding request primitive has been invoked by a peer user entity.

Table 14.9 defines the primitives, which the client and server entities are permitted to invoke.

A failure to conform to these restrictions is an error. The appropriate action is a local implementation matter.

3.4.4 Error Handling

If a request cannot be communicated to the provider peer, the connectionless session service provider will not generate any indication primitive. Detection of exceptional conditions and appropriate actions are a local implementation matter.

4. WSP/B Protocol Operations

This section describes the protocols used between session service peers to realize functions described in the abstract service interface definition.

4.1 Connection-Mode WSP/B

This section describes the operations of WSP/B over the WTP transaction service [WAPWTP].

4.1.1 Utilization of WTP

The WTP transaction classes utilized by each WSP facility is summarized in Table 14.10.

A connection-mode WSP/B client MUST support initiation of WTP Class 0 and Class 2 transactions. The client SHOULD accept Class 0 transaction invocations from the server, so that the server is able to disconnect the session explicitly. If the client is to support the push facilities, it MUST accept transactions in the class, which Table 14.10 defines to be used by each push facility.

4.1.2 Protocol Description

The following figures illustrate the use of a transaction service by the session facilities. The specific details of how the protocol works are expressed in the state tables in Section 4.1.6, *State Tables*, below. Any discrepancy between the diagrams and the state tables shall be decided in favor of the state tables.

The dashed arrows represent the WTP protocol messages carrying acknowledgments and WSP/B PDUs as their data; the messages indicated by parallel arrows are likely to be concatenated into a single transport datagram.

4.1.2.1 Session Management Facility

Normal session creation proceeds without any error or redirection as shown in Figure 14.17.

Session creation wherein the client is redirected to another server is shown in Figure 14.18.

Session creation wherein the server session user refuses to accept the session is shown in Figure 14.19.

Session termination is shown in Figure 14.20.

Table 14.10 Utilization of WTP

WSP FACILITY	WTP TRANSACTION CLASSES
Session Management	Class 0 and Class 2
Method Invocation	Class 2
Session Resume	Class 0 and Class 2
Push	Class 0
Confirmed Push	Class 1

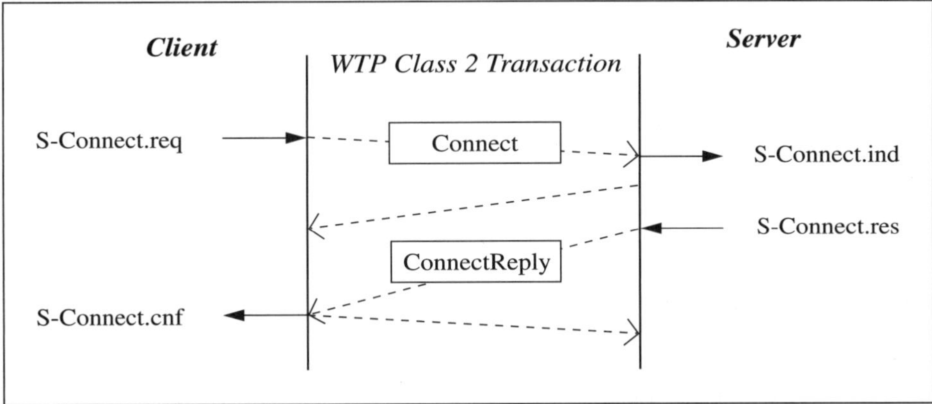

Figure 14.17 Normal session creation.

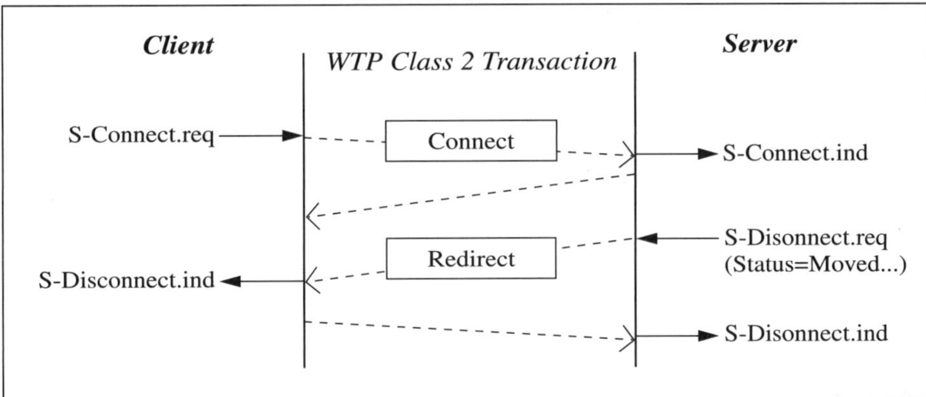

Figure 14.18 Session creation with redirect.

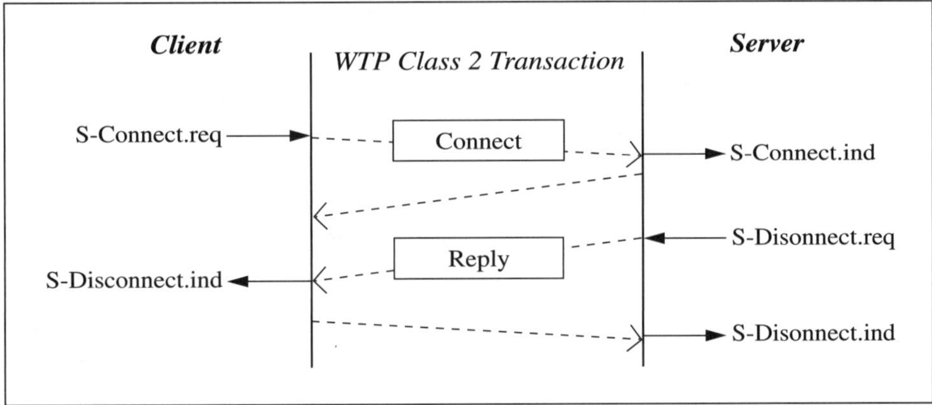

Figure 14.19 Session creation with server error.

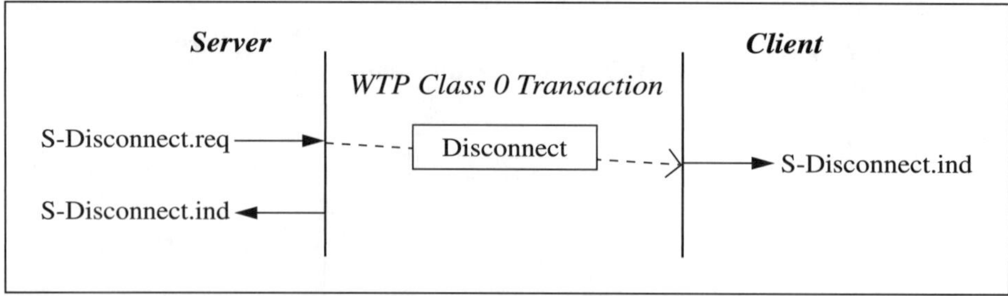

Figure 14.20 Session termination.

4.1.2.2 Session Resume Facility

Session suspend is shown in Figure 14.21.

When session resume succeeds, it proceeds as shown in Figure 14.22.

A session resume wherein the server session user refuses to resume the session is shown in Figure 14.23.

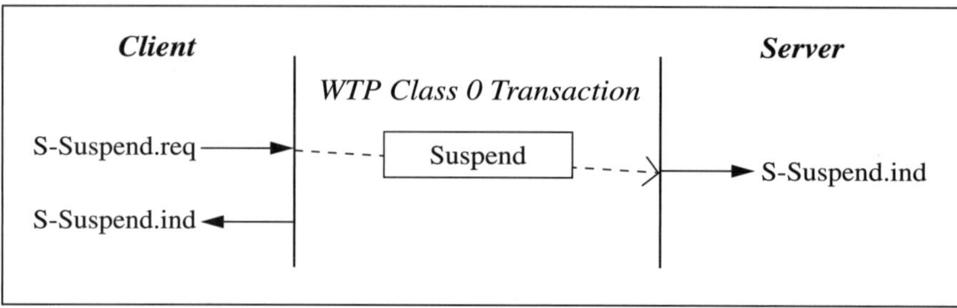

Figure 14.21 Session suspend.

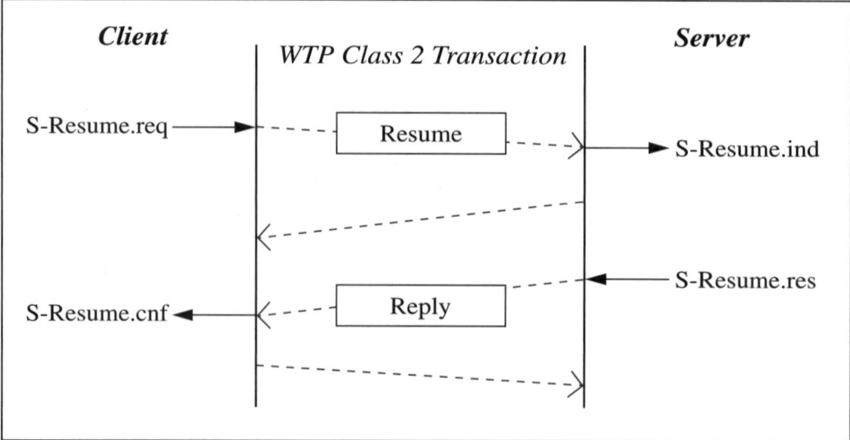

Figure 14.22 Normal session resume.

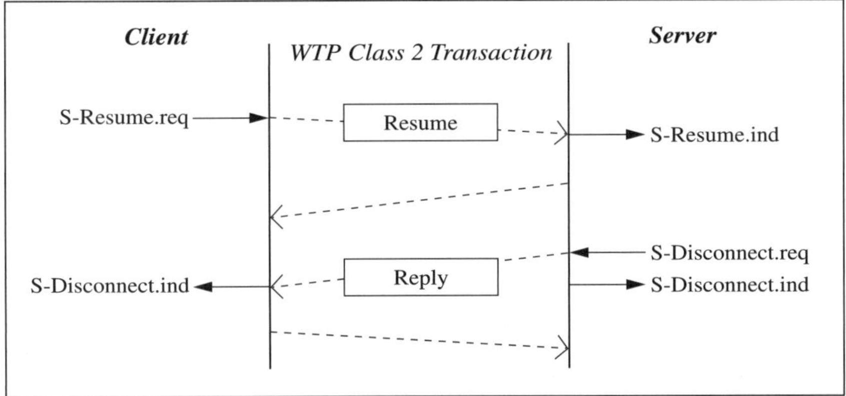

Figure 14.23 Session resume with server error.

4.1.2.3 Method Invocation Facility

A method invocation is shown in Figure 14.24.

4.1.2.4 Push Facility

An unconfirmed push is shown in Figure 14.25.

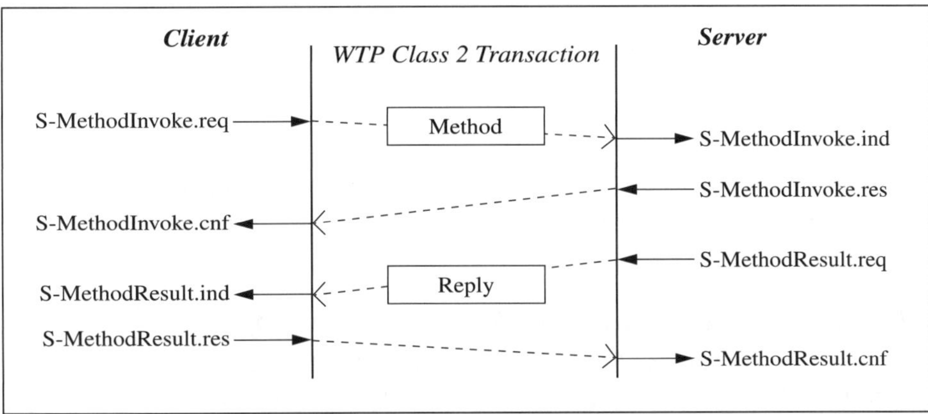

Figure 14.24 Normal method invocation.

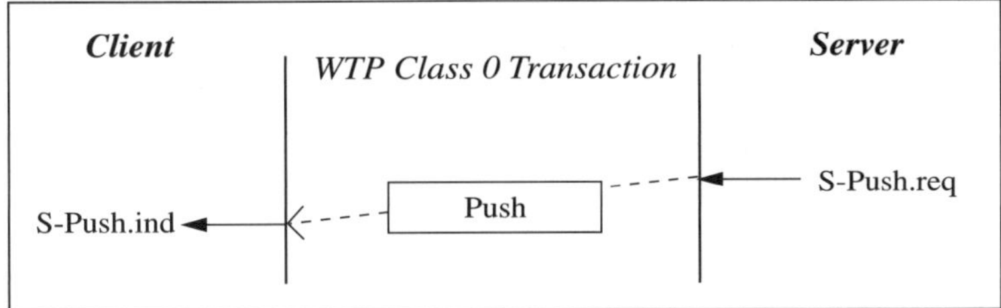

Figure 14.25 Push invocation.

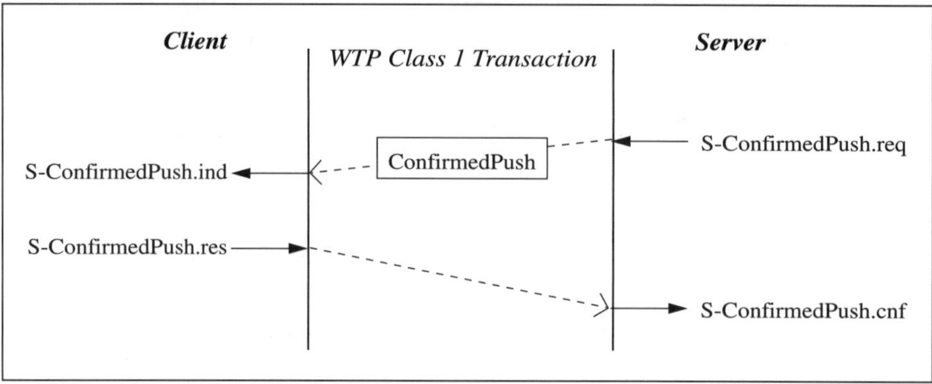

Figure 14.26 Confirmed push invocation.

4.1.2.5 Confirmed Push Facility

A confirmed push is shown in Figure 14.26.

4.1.3 Protocol Parameters

The protocol state machine uses the following parameters.

4.1.3.1 Maximum Receive Unit (MRU)

The Maximum Receive Unit (MRU) is the size of the largest SDU the Session layer can accept from the underlying service provider. The initial value is set to the default SDU sizes as specified in Section 5.3.3. The value can be modified during capability negotiation.

4.1.3.2 Maximum Outstanding Method Requests (MOM)

The Maximum Outstanding Method Requests (MOM) is the number of method transactions that can be outstanding at a given time. The initial value is set to the default MOM as specified in Section 5.3.3. The value can be modified during capability negotiation.

4.1.3.3 Maximum Outstanding Push Requests (MOP)

The Maximum Outstanding Push Requests (MOP) is the number of push transactions that can be outstanding at a given time. The initial value is set to the default MOP as specified in Section 5.3.3. The value can be modified during capability negotiation.

4.1.4 Variables

The protocol state machine uses the following variables.

4.1.4.1 N_Methods

N_Methods keeps track of the number of method transactions in process in the server.

4.1.4.2 N_Pushes

N_Pushes keeps track of the number of push transactions in process in the client.

4.1.4.3 Session_ID

Session_ID saves the session identifier assigned by the server in both the client and the server. The method used to assign the identifiers must be chosen so that a session identifier value cannot be repeated during the lifetime of a message in the used transport network; otherwise, the session management logic may be confused.

4.1.5 Event Processing

Sessions are associated with a peer address quadruplet: the client address, client port, server address, and server port. Incoming transactions are assigned to a particular session based on the peer address quadruplet. As a consequence, the peer address quadruplet is the true unique protocol-level identifier of a session. There can be only one session bound to a peer address quadruplet at a time.

In order to create a new session for a particular peer address quadruplet when one already appears to exist, the server session provider must allow for the creation of a *proto-session*. This is a second, constrained instance of a session that is used to process the session creation transaction on the server (i.e., the Connect and ConnectReply PDUs). This is detailed in the following table.

Indications and confirmations from the Transaction layer are termed *events*. Each event is validated and then processed according to the protocol state tables. The protocol state tables also use *pseudo-events* to trigger state changes within the protocol implementation itself. Pseudo-events are generated by the actions in protocol state machines or by the implementation itself, whenever this is considered appropriate. For instance, they may represent the effect of a management operation, which destroys a session that has been inactive for too long a period.

These pseudo-events are identified by names in *italics* and are defined as follows:

PSEUDO-EVENT	DESCRIPTION
Abort	Abort a method or push transaction.
Release	Allow a method transaction to proceed.
Suspend	Suspend the session.
Disconnect	Disconnect the session.

Incoming transaction invocations are validated before being processed according to the state tables. The following tests are performed; if no action is taken, the event is processed according to the state table.

TEST	ACTION
TR-Invoke.ind with SDU size > MRU	TR-Abort.req(MRUEXCEEDED) the TR-Invoke.
Class 2 TR-Invoke.ind, on server, Connect PDU	a) Create a new proto-session that is responsible for processing the remainder of the Connect transaction. b) The proto-session signals S-Connect.indication to the session user. c) If the session user accepts the new session by invoking S-Connect.response, the proto-session is turned into a new session for the peer address quadruplet. *Disconnect* is invoked on any old sessions bound to that quadruplet.
Class 2 TR-Invoke.ind, on server, Resume PDU	Pass to session identified by the SessionId in Resume PDU instead of the session identified by the peer address quadruplet. If the SessionId is not valid; i.e., the session does not exist, TR-Abort.req(DISCONNECT) the TR-Invoke.
Class 1-2 TR-Invoke.ind, no session matching the peer address quadruplet	TR-Abort.req(DISCONNECT) the TR-Invoke.
Class 1-2 TR-Invoke.ind PDU not handled by state tables	TR-Abort.req(PROTOERR) the TR-Invoke.
Class 0 TR-Invoke.ind PDU not handled by state tables	Ignore.
Any other event not handled by state tables	TR-Abort.req(PROTOERR) if it is some other transaction event than abort *Abort*(PROTOERR) all method and push transactions S-Disconnect.ind(PROTOERR).

The service provided by the underlying Transaction layer is such that a protocol entity cannot reliably detect that the peer has discarded the session state information, unless a method or push transaction is in progress. This may eventually result in a large number of sessions, which no longer have any peer protocol entity. The implementation SHOULD be able to *Disconnect* sessions, which are considered to be in such a state.

4.1.6 State Tables

The following state tables define the actions of connection-mode WSP/B. Because multiple methods and pushes can occur at the same time, there are three state tables defined for client and server: one for the session states, one for the states of a method, and one for the states of a push.

The state names used in the tables are logically completely separate from the states defined for the abstract service interface, although the names may be similar. Typically, a particular state at the service interface maps into a protocol state with the same name, but a state also may map into multiple or no protocol states at all.

A single *Event* may have several entries in the *Condition* column. In such a case, the conditions are expected to be evaluated row by row from top to bottom, with the most specific condition being the first one. A single *Condition* entry may contain several conditions separated with a comma ",". In this case, all of these have to be satisfied in order for the condition to be true.

4.1.6.1 Client Session State Tables

The following tables show the session states and event processing that occur on the client when using a transaction service:

CLIENT SESSION NULL			
EVENT	**CONDITIONS**	**ACTION**	**NEXT STATE**
S-Connect.req		*Disconnect* any other session for the peer address quadruplet TR-Invoke.req(Class 2, Connect) N_PUSHES = 0	CONNECTING

CLIENT SESSION CONNECTING			
EVENT	**CONDITIONS**	**ACTION**	**NEXT STATE**
S-Disconnect.req		TR-Abort.req(DISCONNECT) the Connect *Abort*(DISCONNECT) all outstanding method transactions S-Disconnect.ind(USERREQ)	NULL
Disconnect		TR-Abort.req(DISCONNECT) the Connect *Abort*(DISCONNECT) all outstanding method transactions S-Disconnect.ind(DISCONNECT)	NULL
S-MethodInvoke.req		Start a new method transaction with this event (see method state table)	
S-MethodAbort.req		See method state table	
Suspend		TR-Abort.req(SUSPEND) the Connect *Abort*(SUSPEND) all method transactions S-Disconnect.ind(SUSPEND)	NULL
TR-Invoke.ind	Class 1, ConfirmedPush PDU	TR-Abort.req(DISCONNECT) the TR-Invoke	

(*Continues*)

CLIENT SESSION CONNECTING (CONT.)			
EVENT	**CONDITIONS**	**ACTION**	**NEXT STATE**
TR-Result.ind	Connect transaction, SDU size > MRU	TR-Abort.req(MRUEXCEEDED) the Connect *Abort*(CONNECTERR) all outstanding method transactions S-Disconnect.ind(MRUEXCEEDED)	NULL
	Connect transaction, ConnectReply PDU	TR-Result.res Session_ID = SessionId from PDU S-Connect.cnf	CONNECTED
	Connect transaction, Redirect PDU	TR-Result.res *Abort*(CONNECTERR) all method transactions S-Disconnect.ind(Redirect parameters)	NULL
	Connect transaction, Reply PDU	TR-Result.res *Abort*(CONNECTERR) all method transactions S-Disconnect.ind(Reply parameters)	NULL
	Other	TR-Abort.req(PROTOERR) *Abort*(CONNECTERR) all outstanding method transactions S-Disconnect.ind(PROTOERR)	NULL
TR-Invoke.cnf	Connect transaction Method transaction	Ignore *Abort*(DISCONNECT) method transaction	
TR-Abort.ind	Connect transaction	*Abort*(CONNECTERR) all outstanding method transactions S-Disconnect.ind(abort reason)	NULL
	Method transaction	See method state table	

CLIENT SESSION CONNECTED			
EVENT	**CONDITIONS**	**ACTION**	**NEXT STATE**
S-Disconnect.req		*Abort*(DISCONNECT) all method and push transactions TR-Invoke.req(Class 0, Disconnect) S-Disconnect.ind(USERREQ)	NULL
Disconnect		*Abort*(DISCONNECT) all method and push transactions S-Disconnect.ind(DISCONNECT)	NULL
S-MethodInvoke.req		Start a new method transaction with this event	
S-MethodResult.res		See method state table	
S-MethodAbort.req		See method state table	

S-ConfirmedPush.res		See push state table	
S-PushAbort.req		See push state table	
S-Suspend.req		*Abort*(SUSPEND) all method and push transactions TR-Invoke.req(Class 0, Suspend) S-Suspend.ind(USERREQ)	SUSPENDED
Suspend	Session Resume facility disabled	*Abort*(SUSPEND) all method and push transactions S-Disconnect.ind(SUSPEND)	NULL
	Session Resume facility enabled	*Abort*(SUSPEND) all method and push transactions S-Suspend.ind(SUSPEND)	SUSPENDED
S-Resume.req		*Abort*(USERREQ) all method and push transactions Bind session to the new peer address quadruplet TR-Invoke(Class 2, Resume)	RESUMING
TR-Invoke.ind	Class 0, Disconnect PDU	*Abort*(DISCONNECT) all method and push transactions S-Disconnect.ind(DISCONNECT)	NULL
	Class 0, Push PDU, Push facility enabled	S-Push.ind	
	Class 1, ConfirmedPush PDU, Confirmed Push facility enabled	Start a new push transaction with this event	
TR-Result.ind	Method transaction	See method state table	
TR-Invoke.cnf	Method transaction	See method state table	
TR-Abort.ind	Method transaction	See method state table	
	Push transaction	See push state table	

CLIENT SESSION SUSPENDED			
EVENT	**CONDITIONS**	**ACTION**	**NEXT STATE**
S-Disconnect.req		S-Disconnect.ind(USERREQ)	NULL
Disconnect		S-Disconnect.ind(DISCONNECT)	NULL
S-Resume.req		TR-Invoke.req(Class 2, Resume)	RESUMING
TR-Invoke.ind	Class 0, Disconnect PDU Class 1, ConfirmedPush PDU, Confirmed Push facility enabled	S-Disconnect.ind(DISCONNECT) TR-Abort.req(SUSPEND) the TR-Invoke	NULL
TR-Invoke.cnf	Ignore		
TR-Abort.ind	Ignore		

CLIENT SESSION RESUMING			
EVENT	**CONDITIONS**	**ACTION**	**NEXT STATE**
S-Disconnect.req		TR-Abort.req(DISCONNECT) the Resume *Abort*(DISCONNECT) all outstanding method transactions. S-Disconnect.ind(USERREQ)	NULL
Disconnect		TR-Abort.req(DISCONNECT) the Resume *Abort*(DISCONNECT) all outstanding method transactions. S-Disconnect.ind(DISCONNECT)	NULL
S-MethodInvoke.req		Start a new method transaction with this event. (see method state table)	
S-MethodAbort.req		See method state table.	
S-Suspend.req		TR-Abort.req(SUSPEND) the Resume *Abort*(SUSPEND) all outstanding method transactions. TR-Invoke.req(Class 0, Suspend) S-Suspend.ind(USERREQ)	SUSPENDED
Suspend		TR-Abort.req(SUSPEND) the Resume *Abort*(SUSPEND) all outstanding method transactions. S-Suspend.ind(SUSPEND)	SUSPENDED
TR-Invoke.ind	Class 0, Disconnect PDU	TR-Abort.req(DISCONNECT) the Resume *Abort*(DISCONNECT) all outstanding method transactions. S-Disconnect.ind(DISCONNECT)	NULL
	Class 1, ConfirmedPush PDU, Confirmed Push facility enabled	TR-Abort.req(SUSPEND) the TR-Invoke	
TR-Result.ind	Resume transaction, SDU size > MRU	TR-Abort.req(MRUEXCEEDED) the TR-Result *Abort*(SUSPEND) all outstanding method transactions. S-Suspend.ind(MRUEXCEEDED)	NULL
	Resume transaction, Reply PDU (status == OK)	TR-Result.res S-Resume.cnf	CONNECTED
	Resume transaction, Reply PDU (status != OK)	TR-Result.res *Abort*(DISCONNECT) all outstanding method transactions. S-Disconnect.ind(Reply parameters)	NULL

	Other	TR-Abort.req(PROTOERR) the TR-Result *Abort*(SUSPEND) all outstanding method transactions. S-Suspend.ind(PROTOERR)	SUSPENDED
TR-Invoke.cnf	Resume transaction Method transaction	Ignore. *Abort*(SUSPEND) method transaction.	
TR-Abort.ind	Resume transaction, Reason == DISCONNECT	*Abort*(DISCONNECT) all outstanding method transactions. S-Disconnect.ind(DISCONNECT)	NULL
	Resume transaction	*Abort*(SUSPEND) all outstanding method transactions. S-Suspend.ind(abort reason)	SUSPENDED
	Method transaction	See method state table.	

4.1.6.2 Client Method State Table

The following tables show the method states and event processing that occur on the client when using a transaction service:

CLIENT METHOD NULL			
EVENT	**CONDITIONS**	**ACTION**	**NEXT STATE**
S-MethodInvoke.req		TR-Invoke.req(Class 2, Method)	REQUESTING
		Note: "Method" means either the Get or Post PDU using the PDU type assigned to the particular method.	

CLIENT METHOD REQUESTING			
EVENT	**CONDITIONS**	**ACTION**	**NEXT STATE**
S-MethodAbort.req		TR-Abort.req(PEERREQ) the Method S-MethodAbort.ind(USERREQ)	NULL
Abort		TR-Abort.req(abort reason) the Method S-MethodAbort.ind(USERREQ)	NULL
TR-Invoke.cnf		S-MethodInvoke.cnf	WAITING
TR-Abort.ind	Reason == DISCONNECT Reason == SUSPEND Other	*Disconnect* the session *Suspend* the session S-MethodAbort.ind(abort reason)	NULL NULL NULL

CLIENT METHOD WAITING			
EVENT	**CONDITIONS**	**ACTION**	**NEXT STATE**
S-MethodAbort.req		TR-Abort.req(PEERREQ) the Method S-MethodAbort.ind(USERREQ)	NULL
Abort		TR-Abort.req(abort reason) the Method S-MethodAbort.ind(abort reason)	NULL
TR-Result.ind	SDU size > MRU	TR-Abort.req(MRUEXCEEDED) S-MethodAbort.ind(MRUEXCEEDED)	NULL
	Reply PDU	S-MethodResult.ind	COMPLETING
	Other	TR-Abort.req(PROTOERR) S-MethodAbort.ind(PROTOERR)	NULL
TR-Abort.ind	Reason == DISCONNECT	*Disconnect* the session	NULL
	Reason == SUSPEND	*Suspend* the session	NULL
	Other	S-MethodAbort.ind(abort reason)	NULL

CLIENT METHOD COMPLETING			
EVENT	**CONDITIONS**	**ACTION**	**NEXT STATE**
S-MethodResult.res		TR-Result.res(Exit Info = Acknowledgment Headers) *Note:support for Acknowledgment Headers is optional*	NULL
S-MethodAbort.req		TR-Abort.req(PEERREQ) the Method S-MethodAbort.ind(USERREQ)	NULL
Abort		TR-Abort.req(abort reason) the Method S-MethodAbort.ind(abort reason)	NULL
TR-Abort.ind	Reason == DISCONNECT	*Disconnect* the session	NULL
	Reason == SUSPEND	*Suspend* the session	NULL
	Other	S-MethodAbort.ind(abort reason)	NULL

4.1.6.3 Client Push State Table

The following tables show the push states and event processing that occur on the client when using a transaction service:

CLIENT PUSH NULL			
EVENT	**CONDITIONS**	**ACTION**	**NEXT STATE**
TR-Invoke.ind	Class 1, ConfirmedPush PDU, N_PUSHES == MOP	TR-Abort.req(MOREXCEEDED) the TR-Invoke	NULL
	Class 1, ConfirmedPush PDU, N_PUSHES < MOP	Increment N_PUSHES S-ConfirmedPush.ind	RECEIVING

CLIENT PUSH RECEIVING			
EVENT	**CONDITIONS**	**ACTION**	**NEXT STATE**
S-ConfirmedPush.res		TR-Invoke.res(Exit Info = Acknowledgment Headers) *Note:support for Acknowledgment Headers is optional* Decrement N_PUSHES	NULL
S-PushAbort.req		TR-Abort.req(abort reason) the TR-Invoke Decrement N_PUSHES	NULL
Abort		TR-Abort.req(abort reason) the TR-Invoke Decrement N_PUSHES	NULL
TR-Abort.ind	Reason == DISCONNECT	*Disconnect* the session	NULL
	Reason == SUSPEND	*Suspend* the session	NULL
	Other	S-PushAbort.ind(abort reason) Decrement N_PUSHES	NULL

4.1.6.4 Server Session State Table

The following tables show the session states and event processing that occur on the server when using a transaction service:

SERVER SESSION NULL			
EVENT	**CONDITIONS**	**ACTION**	**NEXT STATE**
TR-Invoke.ind	Class 2, Connect	TR-Invoke.res N_Methods = 0 S-Connect.ind	CONNECTING

SERVER SESSION CONNECTING			
EVENT	**CONDITIONS**	**ACTION**	**NEXT STATE**
S-Connect.res		*Disconnect* any other session for this peer address quadruplet. Assign a Session_ID for this session. TR-Result.req(ConnectReply) *Release* all method transactions in HOLDING state	CONNECTING_2
S-Disconnect.req	Reason == Moved Permanently *or* Moved Temporarily	TR-Result.req(Redirect) *Abort*(DISCONNECT) all method transactions S-Disconnect.ind(USERREQ)	TERMINATING
	Other	TR-Result.req(Reply(status = reason)) *Abort*(DISCONNECT) all method transactions S-Disconnect.ind(USERREQ)	TERMINATING

(*Continues*)

SERVER SESSION CONNECTING (CONT.)			
EVENT	**CONDITIONS**	**ACTION**	**NEXT STATE**
Disconnect		TR-Abort.req(DISCONNECT) the Connect transaction *Abort*(DISCONNECT) all method transactions S-Disconnect.ind(DISCONNECT)	NULL
Suspend		TR-Abort.req(DISCONNECT) the Connect transaction *Abort*(DISCONNECT) all method transactions S-Disconnect.ind(SUSPEND)	NULL
TR-Invoke.ind	Class 2, Method	Start new method transaction (see method state table)	
	Class 2, Resume	TR-Abort.req(DISCONNECT) the TR-Invoke	
TR-Abort.ind		*Abort*(DISCONNECT) all method transactions S-Disconnect.ind(abort reason)	NULL

SERVER SESSION TERMINATING			
EVENT	**CONDITIONS**	**ACTION**	**NEXT STATE**
Disconnect		TR-Abort.req(DISCONNECT) remaining transport transaction	NULL
Suspend		TR-Abort.req(SUSPEND) remaining transport transaction	NULL
TR-Result.cnf		Ignore	NULL
TR-Abort.ind		Ignore	NULL

SERVER SESSION CONNECTING_2			
EVENT	**CONDITIONS**	**ACTION**	**NEXT STATE**
S-Disconnect.req		TR-Abort.req(DISCONNECT) the Connect transaction *Abort*(DISCONNECT) all method and push transactions TR-Invoke.req(Class 0, Disconnect) S-Disconnect.ind(USERREQ)	NULL
Disconnect		TR-Abort.req(DISCONNECT) the Connect transaction *Abort*(DISCONNECT) all method and push transactions S-Disconnect.ind(DISCONNECT)	NULL

S-MethodInvoke.res		See method state table	
S-MethodResult.req		See method state table	
S-Push.req		TR-Invoke.req(Class 0, Push)	
S-ConfirmedPush.req		Start new push transaction (see push state table)	
Suspend	Session Resume facility disabled	TR-Abort.req(DISCONNECT) the Connect transaction *Abort* (DISCONNECT) all method and push transactions S-Disconnect.ind(SUSPEND)	NULL
	Session Resume facility enabled	TR-Abort.req(SUSPEND) the Connect transaction *Abort*(SUSPEND) all method and push transactions S-Suspend.ind(SUSPEND)	SUSPENDED
TR-Invoke.ind	Class 2, Method	Start new method transaction (see method state table) *Release* the new method transaction	
	Class 2, Resume, Session Resume facility disabled	TR-Abort.req(DISCONNECT) the TR-Invoke	
	Class 2, Resume, Session Resume facility enabled	TR-Invoke.res TR-Abort.req(RESUME) the Connect transaction *Abort*(RESUME) all method and push transactions S-Suspend.ind(RESUME) S-Resume.ind	RESUMING
	Class 0, Disconnect	TR-Abort.req(DISCONNECT) the Connect transaction *Abort*(DISCONNECT) all method and push transactions S-Disconnect.ind(DISCONNECT)	NULL
	Class 0, Suspend, Session Resume facility enabled	TR-Abort.req(SUSPEND) the Connect transaction *Abort*(SUSPEND) all method and push transactions S-Suspend.ind(SUSPEND)	SUSPENDED
TR-Invoke.cnf	Push transaction	See push state table	
TR-Result.cnf	Connect transaction Method transaction	See method state table	CONNECTED
TR-Abort.ind	Connect transaction	*Abort*(DISCONNECT) all method and push transactions S-Disconnect.ind(abort reason)	NULL
	Push transaction	See push state table	
	Method transaction	See method state table	

SERVER SESSION CONNECTED			
EVENT	**CONDITIONS**	**ACTION**	**NEXT STATE**
S-Disconnect.req		*Abort*(DISCONNECT) all method and push transactions TR-Invoke.req(Class 0, Disconnect) S-Disconnect.ind(USERREQ)	NULL
Disconnect		*Abort*(DISCONNECT) all method and push transactions S-Disconnect.ind (DISCONNECT)	NULL
S-MethodInvoke.res		See method state table	
S-MethodResult.req		See method state table	
S-Push.req		TR-Invoke.req(Class 0, Push)	
S-ConfirmedPush.req		Start new push transaction (see push state table)	
Suspend	Session Resume facility disabled	*Abort*(SUSPEND) all method and push transactions S-Disconnect.ind(SUSPEND)	NULL
	Session Resume facility enabled	*Abort*(SUSPEND) all method and push transactions S-Suspend.ind(SUSPEND)	SUSPENDED
TR-Invoke.ind	Class 2, Method	Start new method transaction (see method state table) *Release* the new method transaction	
	Class 2, Resume, Session Resume facility disabled	TR-Abort.req(DISCONNECT) the TR-Invoke	RESUMING
	Class 2, Resume, Session Resume facility enabled	TR-Invoke.res *Abort*(RESUME) all method and push transactions S-Suspend.ind(RESUME) S-Resume.ind	RESUMING
	Class 0, Disconnect	*Abort*(DISCONNECT) all method and push transactions S-Disconnect.ind(DISCONNECT)	NULL
	Class 0, Suspend, Session Resume facility enabled	*Abort*(SUSPEND) all method and push transactions S-Suspend.ind(SUSPEND)	SUSPENDED
TR-Invoke.cnf	Push transaction	See push state table	
TR-Result.cnf	Method transaction	See method state table	
TR-Abort.ind	Push transaction Method transaction	See push state table See method state table	

SERVER SESSION SUSPENDED			
EVENT	**CONDITIONS**	**ACTION**	**NEXT STATE**
S-Disconnect.req		S-Disconnect.ind(USERREQ)	NULL
Disconnect		S-Disconnect.ind(DISCONNECT)	NULL
TR-Invoke.ind	Class 2, Method	TR-Abort.req(SUSPEND) the TR-Invoke	
	Class 2, Resume	TR-Invoke.res S-Resume.ind	RESUMING
	Class 0, Disconnect	S-Disconnect.ind(DISCONNECT)	NULL

SERVER SESSION RESUMING			
EVENT	**CONDITIONS**	**ACTION**	**NEXT STATE**
S-Disconnect.req		TR-Abort.req(DISCONNECT) the Resume transaction *Abort*(DISCONNECT) all method transactions TR-Invoke.req(Class 0, Disconnect) S-Disconnect.ind(USERREQ)	NULL
Disconnect		TR-Abort.req(DISCONNECT) the Resume transaction *Abort*(DISCONNECT) all method transactions S-Disconnect.ind(DISCONNECT)	NULL
S-Resume.res		*Disconnect* any other session for the peer address quadruplet. Bind session to new peer address quadruplet TR-Result.req(Reply) *Release* all method transactions in HOLDING state	RESUMING_2
Suspend		TR-Abort.req(SUSPEND) the Resume transaction *Abort*(SUSPEND) all method transactions S-Suspend.ind(SUSPEND)	SUSPENDED
TR-Invoke.ind	Class 2, Method	Start new method transaction (see method state table)	
	Class 2, Resume	TR-Invoke.res TR-Abort.req(RESUME) the old Resume transaction *Abort*(RESUME) all method transactions S-Suspend.ind(RESUME) S-Resume.ind	

(*Continues*)

SERVER SESSION RESUMING (CONT.)			
EVENT	**CONDITIONS**	**ACTION**	**NEXT STATE**
	Class 0, Suspend	TR-Abort.req(SUSPEND) the Resume transaction *Abort*(SUSPEND) all method transactions S-Suspend.ind(SUSPEND)	SUSPENDED
	Class 0, Disconnect	TR-Abort.req(DISCONNECT) the Resume transaction *Abort*(DISCONNECT) all method transactions S-Disconnect.ind(DISCONNECT)	NULL
TR-Abort.ind	Resume transaction	*Abort*(SUSPEND) all method transactions S-Suspend.ind(abort reason)	SUSPENDED

SERVER SESSION RESUMING_2			
EVENT	**CONDITIONS**	**ACTION**	**NEXT STATE**
S-Disconnect.req		TR-Abort.req(DISCONNECT) the Resume transaction *Abort*(DISCONNECT) all method and push transactions TR-Invoke.req(Class 0, Disconnect) S-Disconnect.ind(USERREQ)	NULL
Disconnect		TR-Abort.req(DISCONNECT) the Resume *Abort*(DISCONNECT) all method and push transactions S-Disconnect.ind(DISCONNECT)	NULL
S-MethodInvoke.res		See method state table	
S-MethodResult.req		See method state table	
S-Push.req		TR-Invoke.req(Class 0, Push)	
S-ConfirmedPush.req		Start new push transaction (see push state table)	
Suspend		TR-Abort.req(SUSPEND) the Resume transaction *Abort*(SUSPEND) all method and push transactions S-Suspend.ind(SUSPEND)	SUSPENDED
TR-Invoke.ind	Class 2, Method	Start new method transaction (see method state table) *Release* the new method transaction	RESUMING
	Class 2, Resume	TR-Invoke.res TR-Abort.req(RESUME) the old resume transaction *Abort*(RESUME) all method and push transactions	

		S-Suspend.ind(RESUME) S-Resume.ind	
	Class 0, Suspend	*Abort*(SUSPEND) all method and push transactions S-Suspend.ind(SUSPEND)	SUSPENDED
	Class 0, Disconnect	TR-Abort.req(DISCONNECT) the Resume *Abort*(DISCONNECT) all method and push transactions S-Disconnect.ind(DISCONNECT)	NULL
TR-Invoke.cnf	Push transaction	See push state table	
TR-Result.cnf	Resume transaction		CONNECTED
	Method transaction	See method state table	
TR-Abort.ind	Resume transaction	*Abort*(SUSPEND) all method and push transactions S-Suspend.ind(abort reason)	SUSPENDED
	Push transaction	See push state table	
	Method transaction	See method state table	

4.1.6.5 Server Method State Table

The following tables show the method states and event processing that occur on the server when using a transaction service:

SERVER METHOD NULL			
EVENT	**CONDITIONS**	**ACTION**	**NEXT STATE**
TR-Invoke.ind	Class 2, Method PDU, N_Methods == MOM	TR-Abort.req(MOREXCEEDED)	NULL
	Class 2, Method PDU	Increment N_Methods	HOLDING

SERVER METHOD HOLDING			
EVENT	**CONDITIONS**	**ACTION**	**NEXT STATE**
Release		S-MethodInvoke.ind	REQUESTING
Abort		Decrement N_Methods TR-Abort.req(abort reason) the method	NULL
TR-Abort.ind	Reason == DISCONNECT	*Disconnect* the session	
	Reason == SUSPEND	*Suspend* the session	
	Other	Decrement N_Methods	NULL

SERVER METHOD REQUESTING			
EVENT	**CONDITIONS**	**ACTION**	**NEXT STATE**
S-MethodInvoke.res		TR-Invoke.res	PROCESSING
S-MethodAbort.req		Decrement N_Methods TR-Abort.req(PEERREQ) the method S-MethodAbort.ind(USERREQ)	NULL
Abort		Decrement N_Methods TR-Abort.req(abort reason) the method S-MethodAbort.ind(abort reason)	NULL
TR-Abort.ind	Reason == DISCONNECT	*Disconnect* the session	
	Reason == SUSPEND	*Suspend* the session	
	Other	Decrement N_Methods S-MethodAbort.ind(abort reason)	NULL

SERVER METHOD PROCESSING			
EVENT	**CONDITIONS**	**ACTION**	**NEXT STATE**
S-MethodResult.req		TR-Result.req	REPLYING
S-MethodAbort.req		Decrement N_Methods TR-Abort.req(PEERREQ) the method S-MethodAbort.ind(USERREQ)	NULL
Abort		Decrement N_Methods TR-Abort.req(abort reason) the method S-MethodAbort.ind(abort reason)	NULL
TR-Abort.ind	Reason == DISCONNECT	*Disconnect* the session	
	Reason == SUSPEND	*Suspend* the session	
	Other	Decrement N_Methods S-MethodAbort.ind(abort reason)	NULL

SERVER METHOD REPLYING			
EVENT	**CONDITIONS**	**ACTION**	**NEXT STATE**
S-MethodAbort.req		Decrement N_Methods TR-Abort.req(PEERREQ) the method S-MethodAbort.ind(USERREQ)	NULL
Abort		Decrement N_Methods TR-Abort.req(abort reason) the method S-MethodAbort.ind(abort reason)	NULL

TR-Result.cnf		Decrement N_Methods S-MethodResult.cnf (Acknowledgment Headers = Exit Info) *Note:support for Acknowledgment Headers is optional*	NULL
TR-Abort.ind	Reason == DISCONNECT	*Disconnect* the session	
	Reason == SUSPEND	*Suspend* the session	
	Other	Decrement N_Methods S-MethodAbort.ind(abort reason)	NULL

4.1.6.6 Server Push State Table

The following tables show the push states and event processing that occur on the server when using a transaction service:

SERVER PUSH NULL			
EVENT	**CONDITIONS**	**ACTION**	**NEXT STATE**
S-ConfirmedPush.req		TR-Invoke.req(Class 1, Push)	PUSHING

SERVER PUSH PUSHING			
EVENT	**CONDITIONS**	**ACTION**	**NEXT STATE**
Abort		TR-Abort.req(abort reason) the push transaction S-PushAbort.ind(abort reason)	NULL
TR-Invoke.cnf		S-ConfirmedPush.cnf (Acknowledgment Headers = Exit Info) *Note:support for Acknowledgment Headers is optional*	NULL
TR-Abort.ind	Reason == DISCONNECT	*Disconnect* the session	
	Reason == SUSPEND	*Suspend* the session	
	Other	S-PushAbort.ind(abort reason)	NULL

4.2 Connectionless WSP/B

This section is written as if the session service provider is using the Transport SAP directly. However, this section also applies to the use of the Security SAP. There is a one-to-one mapping of connectionless transport primitives [WAPWDP] to security primitives. For example, T-DUnitdata.request maps directly to SEC-UnitData.request. To allow for this ambiguity, the layer prefixes ("T-D" or "SEC-") have been omitted from the primitive names.

The connectionless WSP/B protocol does not require state machines. Each primitive of the connectionless WSP/B service interface maps directly to sending a WSP/B PDU with the underlying Unitdata primitive as shown in the following table:

EVENT	CONDITION	ACTION
S-Unit-MethodInvoke.req		Unitdata.req(Method) *Note: "Method" means either the Get or Post PDU using the PDU type assigned to the particular method.*
S-Unit-MethodResult.req		Unitdata.req(Reply)
S-Unit-Push.req		Unitdata.req(Push)
T-DError.ind		Ignore
Unitdata.ind	Method PDU *Note: "Method" means either the Get or Post PDU using the PDU type assigned to the particular method.*	S-Unit-MethodInvoke.ind
	Reply PDU	S-Unit-MethodResult.ind
	Push PDU	S-Unit-MethodPush.ind

Protocol parameters, such as the Maximum Receive Unit and the persistent session headers in effect, are defined by mutual agreement between the service users. No particular mechanism for this is required, but the well-known port of the server MAY be used to imply the parameter settings.

5. WSP/B Data Unit Structure and Encoding

This section describes the structure of the data units used to exchange WSP/B data units between client and server.

5.1 Data Formats

The following data types are used in the data format definitions (see Table 14.11).

5.1.1 Primitive Data Types

Network octet order for multi-octet integer values is big-endian. In other words, the most significant octet is transmitted on the network first, followed subsequently by the less significant octets.

Table 14.11 Format Definition Data Types

DATA TYPE	DEFINITION
bit	1 bit of data
octet	8 bits of opaque data
uint8	8-bit unsigned integer
uint16	16-bit unsigned integer
uint32	32-bit unsigned integer
uintvar	variable length unsigned integer (see next section)

Network bit ordering for bit fields within an octet is big-endian. In other words, bit fields described first are placed in the most significant bits of the octet and are transmitted first, followed subsequently by the less significant bits.

5.1.2 Variable-Length Unsigned Integers

Many fields in the data unit formats are of variable length. Typically, there will be an associated field that specifies the size of the variable-length field. In order to keep the data unit formats as small as possible, a variable-length unsigned integer encoding is used to specify lengths. The larger the unsigned integer, the larger the size of its encoding.

Each octet of the variable-length unsigned integer is comprised of a single *Continue* bit and 7 bits of payload as shown in Figure 14.27.

To encode a large unsigned integer, split it into 7-bit fragments and place them in the payloads of multiple octets. The most significant bits are placed in the first octets with the least significant bits ending up in the last octet. All octets MUST set the *Continue* bit to 1 except the last octet, which MUST set the *Continue* bit to 0.

For example, the number 0x87A5 (1000 0111 1010 0101) is encoded in three octets as shown in Figure 14.28.

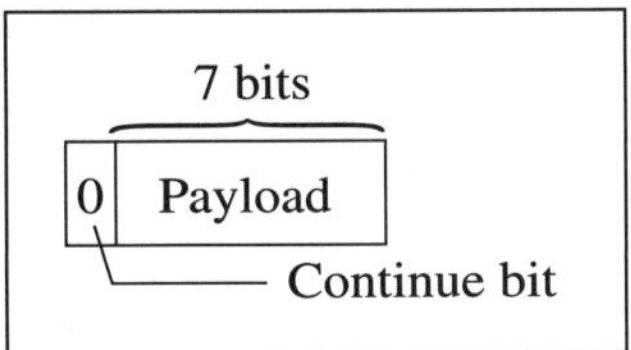

Figure 14.27 Variable-length integer octet.

1	0000010	1	0001111	0	0100101

Figure 14.28 Long field length.

The unsigned integer MUST be encoded in the smallest encoding possible. In other words, the encoded value MUST NOT start with an octet with the value 0x80.

In the data unit format descriptions, the data type *uintvar* will be used to indicate a variable length integer field. The maximum size of a *uintvar* is 32 bits. It will be encoded in no more than five octets.

5.2 Protocol Data Unit Structure

WSP/B generates WTP SDUs that contain a single WSP/B protocol data unit. Each PDU serves a particular function in the protocol and contains type-specific information.

5.2.1 PDU Common Fields

This section describes fields that are common across all or many PDUs (see Figure 14.29).

Every PDU starts with a conditional transaction identifier and a type identifier (see Table 14.12).

The *TID* field is used to associate requests with replies in the connectionless session service. The presence of the *TID* is conditional. It MUST be included in the connectionless WSP/B PDUs, and MUST NOT be present in the connection-mode PDUs. In connectionless WSP/B, the TID is passed to and from the session user as the "Transaction Id" or "Push Id" parameters of the session primitives.

The *Type* field specifies the type and function of the PDU. The type numbers for the various PDUs are defined in Table A1 in Appendix A. The rest of the PDU is type-specific information, referred to as the contents.

The following sections describe the format of the contents for each PDU type. In the interest of brevity, the PDU header has been omitted from the description of each PDU in the sections that follow.

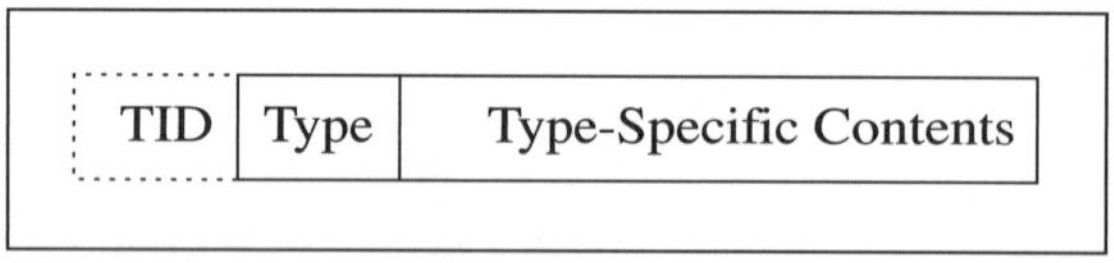

TID	Type	Type-Specific Contents

Figure 14.29 PDU structure.

Table 14.12 PDU Header Fields

NAME	TYPE	SOURCE
TID	uint8	S-Unit-MethodInvoke.req::Transaction Id *or* S-Unit-MethodResult.req::Transaction Id *or* S-Unit-Push.req::Push Id
Type	uint8	PDU type

5.2.2 Session Management Facility

5.2.2.1 Connect

The *Connect* PDU is sent to initiate the creation of a session (see Table 14.13).

The *Version* field identifies the version of the WSP/B protocol. This is used to determine the formats of this and all subsequent PDUs. The version number is encoded as follows: The major number of the version is stored in the high-order 4 bits, and the minor number is stored in the low-order 4 bits. This version number used for this specification is 1.0, i.e., 0x10.

The *CapabilitiesLen* field specifies the length of the *Capabilities* field.

The *HeadersLen* field specifies the length of the *Headers* field.

The *Capabilities* field contains encoded capability settings requested by the sender. Each capability has capability-specific parameters associated with it. For more information on the encoding of this field, see Section 5.3, *Capability Encoding*.

The *Headers* field contains headers sent from client to server that apply to the entire session.

5.2.2.2 ConnectReply

The *ConnectReply* PDU is sent in response to the *Connect* PDU (see Table 14.14).

The *ServerSessionId* contains the server session identifier. It is used to identify the session in subsequently sent PDUs used for session management. In particular, the client uses this session identifier if it wants to resume the session after a change in the underlying transport.

Table 14.13 Connect Fields

NAME	TYPE	SOURCE
Version	uint8	WSP/B protocol version
CapabilitiesLen	uintvar	Length of the *Capabilities* field
HeadersLen	uintvar	Length of the *Headers* field
Capabilities	*CapabilitiesLen* octets	S-Connect.req::Requested Capabilities
Headers	*HeadersLen* octets	S-Connect.req::Client Headers

Table 14.14 ConnectReply Fields

NAME	TYPE	SOURCE
ServerSessionId	Uintvar	Session_ID variable
CapabilitiesLen	Uintvar	Length of Capabilities field
HeadersLen	Uintvar	Length of the Headers field
Capabilities	*CapabilitiesLen* octets	S-Connect.res::Negotiated Capabilities
Headers	*HeadersLen* octets	S-Connect.res::Server Headers

The *CapabilitiesLen* field specifies the length of the *Capabilities* field.

The *HeadersLen* field specifies the length of the *Headers* field.

The *Capabilities* field contains zero or more capabilities accepted by the sender. For more information on capabilities, see Section 5.3, *Capability Encoding.*

The *Headers* field contains headers that apply to the entire session.

5.2.2.3 Redirect

The *Redirect* PDU may be returned in response to a Connect PDU, when the session establishment attempt is refused. It can be used to migrate clients from servers whose addresses have changed or to perform a crude form of load balancing at session creation time (see Table 14.15).

The *Flags* field indicates the nature of the redirect. Flags that are unassigned MUST be set to 0 by the server and MUST be ignored by the client. The flags are defined as follows:

FLAG BIT	DESCRIPTION
0x80	Permanent Redirect
0x40	Reuse Security Session

If the *Permanent Redirect* flag is set, the client SHOULD store the redirect addresses and use them to create all future sessions with the server. If the *Reuse Security Session* flag is set, the client can use the current security session when requesting a session from the server it is being redirected to.

The *Redirect Addresses* field contains one or more new addresses for the server. Subsequent Connect PDUs should be sent to these addresses instead of the server address, which cause the Redirect PDU to be sent. The length of the *Redirect Addresses* field is determined by the SDU size as reported from the underlying transport. Each redirect address is coded in the following format (see Table 14.16).

The *BearerType Included* and *PortNumber Included* fields indicate the inclusion of the *BearerType* and *PortNumber* fields, respectively. The *BearerType* and *PortNumber* SHOULD be excluded, if the session establishment attempt is redirected to the same type of bearer network and same destination port number as used for the initial Connect PDU.

The *AddressLen* field contains the length of the *Address* field.

The *BearerType* field indicates the type of bearer network to be used. The bearer type codes are defined in [WAPWDP].

Table 14.15 Redirect Fields

NAME	TYPE	SOURCE
Flags	uint8	S-Disconnect.req::Redirect Security *and* S-Disconnect.req::Reason
Redirect Addresses	multiple octets	S-Disconnect.req::Redirect Addresses

Table 14.16 AddressType

NAME	TYPE	PURPOSE
NetworkType Included	1 bit	Flag indicating inclusion of *NetworkType* field
PortNumber Included	1 bit	Flag indicating inclusion of *PortNumber* field
Address Len	6 bits	Length of the *Address* field
BearerType	uint8	Type of bearer network to use
PortNumber	uint16	Port number to use
Address	*AddressLen* octets	Bearer address to use

The *PortNumber* field contains the destination port number.

The *Address* field contains the bearer address to use. The *BearerType* implies also the bearer-dependent address format used to encode this field. The encoding shall use the native address transmission format defined in the applicable bearer specifications. If this format uses a number of bits, which is not a multiple of 8, the address shall be encoded as a big-endian multi-octet integer. The necessary number of 0 fill bits shall be included in the most significant octet so that the fill bits occupy the most significant bits. The used bearer address formats are defined in [WAPWDP] together with the bearer type codes.

5.2.2.4 Disconnect

The *Disconnect* PDU is sent to terminate a session (see Table 14.17).

The *ServerSessionId* contains the session identifier of the session to be disconnected.

5.2.2.5 Reply

The Reply PDU is used by the session creation facility, and it is defined in Section 5.2.3.3, *Reply*, later.

5.2.3 Method Invocation Facility

There are two PDUs used to invoke a method in the server: *Get* and *Post*, depending on the parameters required.

Methods defined in HTTP/1.1 [RFC2068] are assigned a specific PDU type number. PDU type numbers for methods not defined in HTTP/1.1 are established during capability negotiation. These methods use either the *Get* or *Post* PDU, depending on whether

Table 14.17 Disconnect Fields

NAME	TYPE	SOURCE
ServerSessionId	uintvar	Session_ID variable

the method includes request content or not. Methods using *Get* use PDU type numbers in the range 0x40–0x5F. Methods using *Post* use numbers in the range 0x60–0x7F.

5.2.3.1 Get

The *Get* PDU is used for the HTTP/1.1 GET, OPTIONS, HEAD, DELETE, and TRACE methods, as well as extension methods that do not send request content to the server (see Table 14.18).

The *URILen* field specifies the length of the *URI* field.

The *HeadersLen* field specifies the length of the *Headers* field.

The *URI* field contains the URI. If the URI is a normally stored as a null-terminated string, the implementation MUST NOT include the null in the field.

The *Headers* field contains the headers associated with the request.

5.2.3.2 Post

The *Post* PDU is used for the HTTP/1.1 POST and PUT methods, as well as extended methods that send request content to the server (see Table 14.19).

Table 14.18 Get Fields

NAME	TYPE	SOURCE
URILen	uintvar	Length of the *URI* field
HeadersLen	uintvar	Length of the *Headers* field
URI	*URILen* octets	S-MethodInvoke.req::Request URI *or* S-Unit-MethodInvoke.req::Request URI
Headers	*HeadersLen* octets	S-MethodInvoke.req::Request Headers *or* S-Unit-MethodInvoke.req::Request Headers

Table 14.19 Post Fields

NAME	TYPE	SOURCE
UriLen	uintvar	Length of the *URI* field
HeadersLen	uintvar	Length of the *ContentType* and *Headers* fields combined
Uri	*UriLen* octets	S-MethodInvoke.req::Request URI *or* S-Unit-MethodInvoke.req::Request URI
ContentType	multiple octets	S-MethodInvoke.req::Request Headers *or* S-Unit-MethodInvoke.req::Request Headers
Headers	(*HeadersLen* – length of *ContentType*) octets	S-MethodInvoke.req::Request Headers *or* S-Unit-MethodInvoke.req::Request Headers
Data	multiple octets	S-MethodInvoke.req::Request Body *or* S-Unit-MethodInvoke.req::Request Body

The *UriLen* field specifies the length of the URI field.

The *HeadersLen* field specifies the length of the *ContentType* and *Headers* fields combined.

The *URI* field contains the URI. If the URI is normally stored as a null-terminated string, the implementation MUST NOT include the null in the field.

The *ContentType* field contains the content type of the data. It conforms to the Content-Type value encoding specified in Section 5.4.2.24, *Content Type Field*, below.

The *Headers* field contains the headers associated with the request.

The *Data* field contains the data associated with the request. The length of the *Data* field is determined by the SDU size as provided to and reported from the underlying transport. The *Data* field starts immediately after the *Headers* field and ends at the end of the SDU.

5.2.3.3 Reply

Reply is the generic response PDU used to return information from the server in response to a request. Reply is used in the S-Connect primitive to indicate an error during session creation (see Table 14.20).

The *Status* field contains a result code of the attempt to understand and satisfy the request. The status codes have been defined by HTTP/1.1 [RFC2068] and have been mapped into single-octet values listed in Table A-3 in Assigned Numbers.

The *HeadersLen* field specifies the length of the *ContentType* and *Headers* fields combined.

The *ContentType* field contains the content type of the data. It conforms to the Content-Type value encoding specified in Section 5.4.2.24, *Content Type Field*.

The *Headers* field contains the reply headers.

Table 14.20 Reply Fields

NAME	TYPE	SOURCE
Status	uint8	S-MethodResult.req::Status *or* S-Disconnect.req::Reason *or* S-Unit-MethodResult.req::Status
HeadersLen	uintvar	Length of the ContentType and Headers fields combined
ContentType	multiple octets	S-MethodResult.req::Response Headers *or* S-Disconnect.req::Error Headers *or* S-Unit-MethodResult.req::Response Headers
Headers	(*HeadersLen* – length of *ContentType*) octets	S-MethodResult.req::Response Headers *or* S-Disconnect.req::Error Headers *or* S-Unit-MethodResult.req::Response Headers
Data	multiple octets	S-MethodResult.req::Response Body *or* S-Disconnect.req::Error Body *or* S-Unit-MethodResult.req::Response Body

The *Data* field contains the data returned from the server. The length of the *Data* field is determined by the SDU size as provided to and reported from the underlying transport. The *Data* field starts immediately after the *Headers* field and ends at the end of the SDU.

5.2.3.4 Acknowledgment Headers

Acknowledgment Headers is not an actual PDU; it may be carried by the Exit Info parameter of the TR-Result primitive. The service provider uses it to carry the data needed by the optional Acknowledgment Headers feature (see Table 14.21).

The *Headers* field contains information encoded in the manner defined in Section 5.4, *Header Encoding*. The size of the field is implied by the size of the transaction Exit Data.

5.2.4 Push and Confirmed Push Facilities

5.2.4.1 Push and ConfirmedPush

The Push and ConfirmedPush PDUs are used for sending unsolicited information from the server to the client. The formats of the two PDUs are the same; only the PDU type is different (see Table 14.22).

Table 14.21 Acknowledgment Headers Fields

NAME	TYPE	SOURCE
Headers	multiple octets	S-MethodResult.res::Acknowledgement Headers *or* S-ConfirmedPush.res::Acknowledgement Headers

Table 14.22 Push and ConfirmedPush Fields

NAME	TYPE	SOURCE
HeadersLen	uintvar	Length of the *ContentType* and *Headers* fields combined
ContentType	multiple octets	S-Push.req::Push Headers *or* S-ConfirmedPush.req::Push Headers *or* S-Unit-Push.req::Push Headers
Headers	(*HeadersLen* – length of *ContentType*) octets	S-Push.req::Push Headers *or* S-ConfirmedPush.req::Push Headers *or* S-Unit-Push.req::Push Headers
Data	multiple octets	S-Push.req::Push Body *or* S-ConfirmedPush.req::Push Body *or* S-Unit-Push.req::Push Body

The *HeadersLen* field specifies the length of the *ContentType* and *Headers* fields combined.

The *ContentType* field contains the content type of the data. It conforms to the Content-Type value encoding specified in Section 5.4.2.24, *Content Type Field*.

The *Headers* field contains the push headers.

The *Data* field contains the data pushed from the server. The length of the *Data* field is determined by the SDU size as provided to and reported from the underlying transport. The *Data* field starts immediately after the *Headers* field and ends at the end of the SDU.

5.2.4.2 Acknowledgment Headers

If the service provider implements the optional Acknowledgment Headers feature with the Confirmed Push facility, *Acknowledgment Headers* are used to carry the associated data.

5.2.5 Session Resume Facility

5.2.5.1 Suspend

The *Suspend* PDU is sent to suspend a session (see Table 14.23).

The *SessionId* field contains the session identifier of the session to be suspended.

5.2.5.2 Resume

The *Resume* PDU is sent to resume an existing session after a change in the underlying transport protocol (see Table 14.24).

The *SessionId* field contains the session identifier returned from the server when the session was originally created. The server looks up the session based on the session identifier. It then binds that session to the transaction service instance identified by the peer address quadruplet of the transaction that carried the PDU.

5.2.5.3 Reply

The Reply PDU is used by the session resume facility and it is defined in Section 5.2.3.3, *Reply*.

Table 14.23 Suspend Fields

NAME	TYPE	SOURCE
SessionId	Uintvar	Session_ID variable

Table 14.24 Resume Fields

NAME	TYPE	PURPOSE
SessionId	uintvar	Session_ID variable

5.3 Capability Encoding

Capabilities allow the client and server to negotiate characteristics and extended behaviors of the protocol. A general capability format is defined so capabilities that are not understood can be ignored.

A set of capability values is encoded as a sequence of capability structures described in the next section. If the sender wants to provide the receiver with a set of alternative values for a particular capability, one of which can be chosen, it sends multiple instances of the capability, each with different parameters and with the most preferred alternative first. A responder must not encode and send the value of a capability, unless the initiator is known to recognize it, as indicated by either the version number of the session protocol or by the initiator already having sent that capability during the session.

When the initiator of capability negotiation encodes a capability defined in Section 5.3.2, *Capability Definitions*, below, and the value is equal to the capability setting (default or negotiated) currently in effect, the capability structure MAY be omitted. In this case the responder MUST interpret this in the same way, as if it had received the explicitly encoded value. When the responder encodes a capability defined in Section 5.3.2, *Capability Definitions*, and the value is equal to the capability setting proposed by the initiator, the capability structure MAY be omitted; the initiator MUST interpret this in the same way, as if it had received the explicitly encoded value.

5.3.1 Capability Structure

The format of a capability is described using a table similar to the ones used in PDU definitions (see Table 14.25):

The *Length* field specifies the length of the *Identifier* and *Parameters* fields combined.

The *Identifier* field identifies the capability. The capability identifier values defined in this protocol version are listed in Table A-4 in Assigned Numbers. It is encoded in the same way as the header field names, using the *Field-name* BNF rule specified in Section 5.4.2.6, *Header*.

The *Parameters* field (if not empty) contains capability-specific parameters.

If a capability with an unknown *Identifier* field is received during capability negotiation, its value must be ignored. The responder must also reply with the same capability with an empty *Parameters* field, which indicates that the capability was not recognized and did not have any effect. As a consequence, the encodings for any provider-specific

Table 14.25 Capability Fields

NAME	TYPE	PURPOSE
Length	uintvar	Length of the *Identifier* and *Parameters* fields combined
Identifier	multiple octets	Capability identifier
Parameters	(*Length* – length of *Identifier*) octets	Capability-specific parameters

additional capabilities MUST BE chosen so that an empty *Parameters* field either is illegal (as for capabilities with integer values) or indicates that no extended functionality is enabled.

5.3.2 Capability Definitions

5.3.2.1 Service Data Unit Size

There are two Service Data Unit (SDU) size capabilities, one for the client and one for the server:

- Client-SDU-Size
- Server-SDU-Size

These capabilities share the same parameter format (see Table 14.26).

The *MaxSize* field specifies the maximum SDU size that can be received or will be sent by the client or server, depending on the context of the capability. A *MaxSize* of 0 means there is no limit to the SDU size.

When the client sends the Client-SDU-Size capability, it is indicating the maximum size SDU it can receive (i.e., the client MRU). When the server sends the Client-SDU-Size capability, it is indicating the maximum SDU size it will send.

When the client sends the Server-SDU-Size capability, it is indicating the maximum size SDU it will send. When the server sends the Server-SDU-Size capability, it is indicating the maximum SDU size it can receive (i.e., the server MRU).

The default SDU sizes are specified in Section 5.3.3, *Capability Defaults*. The default SDU size SHOULD be treated as an implementation minimum. Otherwise, a method request sent during session establishment would risk being aborted, since the server cannot indicate its true MRU until session has been established.

5.3.2.2 Protocol Options

The Protocol Options capability is used to enable extended, optional protocol functions (see Table 14.27).

When the client sends the Protocol Options capability to the server, the *Flags* field specifies the options the client will accept. When the server sends the Protocol Options capability back to the client, the *Flags* field specifies the options the server will perform. Although the *Flags* field may be multiple octets long, the currently defined flag bits fit

Table 14.26 SDU Size Capability Fields

NAME	TYPE	PURPOSE
MaxSize	uintvar	Maximum Size

Table 14.27 Protocol Options Capability Fields

NAME	TYPE	PURPOSE
Flags	Multiple octets	Option flags

into a single octet, and an implementation SHOULD send only one octet. All undefined bits must be set to 0, and the receiver MUST ignore them, including all additional trailing octets. As more flag bits are defined in the future, new octets can then be appended to the field.

A flag bit set to 1 indicates that the associated optional function is enabled; a flag bit cleared to 0 indicates that it is disabled. The flags are defined as follows:

FLAG BIT	DESCRIPTION
0x80	Confirmed Push Facility
0x40	Push Facility
0x20	Session Resume Facility
0x10	Acknowledgment Headers

When the client enables the Confirmed Push and/or Push facilities, it is advertising that it is able to and also wants to accept data pushes. If the client can receive data pushes, but the service provider in the server cannot send pushes, the appropriate push flags MUST be cleared when replying with the negotiated capabilities. If the service user in the server will not send any data pushes of a certain type, the appropriate push flag SHOULD be cleared in the reply. This will allow the client to free up any resources that would otherwise be dedicated to receiving data pushes.

When the client enables the Session Resume facility, it is advertising that it would like to suspend and resume the session. If the server is not able or willing to support the Session Resume facility, it MUST clear the Session Resume facility flags when replying with the negotiated capabilities.

When the client sets the Acknowledgment Headers flag, it is advertising whether or not it would like to send Acknowledgment headers. The server indicates with the Acknowledgment Headers flag in the reply, whether or not it is able to process Acknowledgment Headers. If the server is not able to process the headers, the client SHOULD not send them; if the client still sends them, the headers shall be ignored.

5.3.2.3 Maximum Outstanding Requests (MOR)

There are two MOR capabilities, one for methods and one for pushes:

- Method-MOR
- Push-MOR

The Method-MOR and Push-MOR capabilities, respectively, indicate the number of outstanding method or push transactions that may occur simultaneously (see Table 14.28).

Table 14.28 Maximum Outstanding Requests Capability Fields

NAME	TYPE	PURPOSE
MOR	uint8	Maximum Outstanding Requests

When the client is able to submit multiple outstanding method requests, it indicates the maximum number of simultaneous requests it will ever send in the Method-MOR capability. The server replies with the lesser of the client's Method-MOR and the number of method transactions the server can simultaneously process.

Similarly, when the client is able to process multiple outstanding push requests, it indicates the maximum number of simultaneous requests it can process in the Push-MOR capability. The server replies with the lesser of the client's Push-MOR and the maximum number of simultaneous push transactions the server will ever send.

5.3.2.4 Extended Methods

The Extended Methods capability declares the set of extended methods to be used during the session and assigns PDU types to them (see Table 14.29).

When sent from client to server in the Connect PDU, the capability-specific parameters for the Extended Methods capability contain zero or more *PDU Type* to *Method Name* assignments. The end of the list of assignments is determined from the end of the capability as specified in the capability length. Each capability assignment contains a *PDU Type* and a *Method Name*. The PDU types are assigned by the client from the range 0x50–0x5F for methods that use the Get PDU format, and the range 0x70–0x7F for methods that use the Post PDU format. The method name is a null terminated string.

When sent from server to client in the ConnectReply PDU, the capability-specific parameters for the Extended Methods capability contain the zero or more PDU type codes (without the method names) that the server accepts and can receive.

5.3.2.5 Header Code Pages

The Header Code Pages capability declares the set of header code pages to be used during the session and assigns page codes to them (see Table 14.30).

When sent from client to server in the Connect PDU, the capability-specific parameters for the Header Code Pages capability contain zero or more header page name to code assignments. The end of the list of assignments is determined from the end of the capability as specified in the capability length. Each capability assignment contains a *Page Code* and a *Page Name*. The *Page Name* is a null terminated string.

Table 14.29 Extended Methods Capability Field Entries

NAME	TYPE	PURPOSE
PDU Type	uint8	PDU Type for method
Method Name	Multiple octets	Null terminated method name

Table 14.30 Header Code Pages Capability Field Entries

NAME	TYPE	PURPOSE
Page Code	uint8	Code for header page
Page Name	Multiple octets	Name of header page

When sent from server to client in the ConnectReply PDU, the capability-specific parameters for the Header Code Pages capability contain the zero or more *Page Codes* (without the *Page Names*), that the server can and will use.

When the client sends this capability, it is indicating its desire to use the named header code pages. The response from the server indicates which of these pages actually shall be used during the remainder of the session. Once the use of an extension header code page has been negotiated, the headers belonging to it MUST be sent encoded using the binary syntax defined by the code page. If the server declines to use a particular header code page, the (application-specific) headers MUST be sent in textual format unless some other code page defines an encoding syntax for them.

If the server agrees to use a header code page, the *Page Code* selected by the client shall be used during the remainder of the session, when the header code page needs to be identified in a code page shift sequence.

5.3.2.6 Aliases

The Aliases capability declares a list of alternate addresses for the sender (see Table 14.31).

The *Addresses* field is encoded in the same format as the *Redirect Addresses* field in the Redirect PDU, described in Section 5.2.2.3. The addresses sent by a server may be used to facilitate a switch to an alternate bearer network when a session is resumed. The addresses sent by a client may be used to facilitate the use of the connectionless session service.

5.3.3 Capability Defaults

Unless otherwise specified for a specific bearer or well-known application port, the capability defaults are as follows:

NAME	SETTING
Aliases	*None*
Client SDU Size	1400 octets
Extended Methods	*None*
Header Code Pages	*None*
Protocol Options	0x00
Maximum Outstanding Method Requests	1
Maximum Outstanding Push Requests	1
Server SDU Size	1400 octets

Table 14.31 Aliases Capability Fields

NAME	TYPE	PURPOSE
Addresses	Multiple octets	Alternate addresses

5.4 Header Encoding

5.4.1 General

WSP/B header fields are included in WSP/B PDUs or in multipart data objects. The header fields contain general information, request information, response information, or entity information. Each header field consists of a field name followed by a field value (see Figure 14.30).

WSP/B defines a compact format for encoding header fields that is compatible with HTTP/1.1 header fields.

The following procedures are used to reduce the size of the headers:

- Well-known tokens are mapped to binary values.
- Date values, integer values, quality factors, and delta second values are coded in binary format.
- Redundant information is removed.

The encoding utilizes the fact that the first octet of the text strings in HTTP headers is typically in the range 32–126, except for some rare cases when a text string is initiated with an 8-bit character value (e.g., national characters). Ranges 0–31 and 127–255 can be used for binary values, quote characters, or length indicators of binary data. This makes it possible to mix binary data and text strings efficiently, which is an advantage when the generic parts of HTTP/1.1 headers shall be encoded.

5.4.1.1 Field Name

Field names with assigned integer encoding values MUST be encoded using the integer value. Field names without assigned integer values MUST be encoded as text. The representation of the integer encodings is made more compact by dividing them into *header code pages*. Each header code page encodes up to 128 identities of well-known field names, so that the integer encoding value is represented using a single octet. The most common well-known header names are defined in the default header code page, but additional encoding values can be made available by shifting between code pages.

The header code pages used during a session are identified with numeric codes. Header code page 1 is the default page and is always active at the beginning of a set of headers. A shift to a new code page is accomplished by sending a *shift sequence* between two header fields. The new header code page remains active until the end of the set of headers being decoded. This procedure applies to the header fields in each WSP/B PDUs, as well as to the header fields of each entity embedded in a multipart entity.

The default header code pages defines all HTTP/1.1 field names and WAP specific header fields. The numbers for header code pages are assigned in the following way:

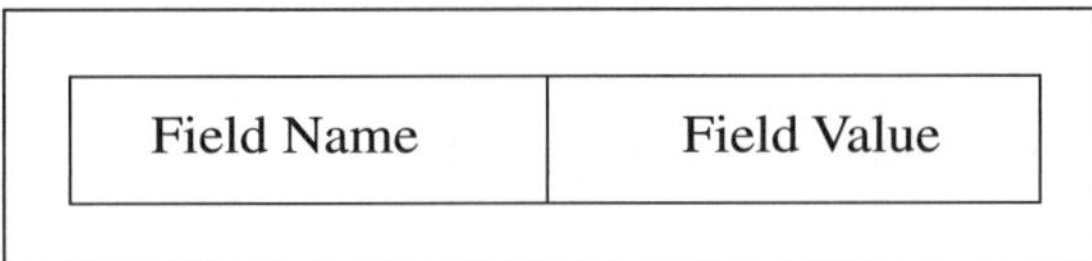

Figure 14.30 Header field comprised of field name and field value.

- 1, default header code page, including HTTP/1.1 and WAP specific headers
- 2–15, reserved for WAP-specific header code pages
- 16–127, reserved for application-specific code pages
- 128–255, reserved for future use

An application-specific header code page is identified by a textual name (string). However, when capability negotiation is used to agree on the set of extension header code pages, which shall be used during the session, each application-specific code page is also assigned a numeric identity from the range reserved for them. This identity remains in effect to the end of the session and MUST be used to identify the page in a shift sequence.

If capability negotiation leads to an agreement on the use of a header code page, then the application-specific field names MUST be sent using the well-known single-octet values defined by the page. If there is no agreement on the use of a header code page, the application-specific field names MUST be encoded using the *Token-text* rule.

For example, a sequence of well-known headers and application-specific header can be structured as follows:

```
<WSP header 1>
.
.
<WSP header n>
<Shift to application specific code page>
<Application specific header 1>
.
.
<Application specific header m>
```

5.4.1.2 Field Values

The syntax of encoded field values is defined by the field name. Well-known field values MUST be encoded using the compact binary formats defined by the header syntax; the textual values shall be used only if no other encoding is available. The WSP field values are encoded so that the length of the field value can always be determined, even if the detailed format of a specific field value is not known. This makes it possible to skip over individual header fields without interpreting their content. The header syntax in Section 5.4.2 is defined so that the first octet in all the field values can be interpreted as follows:

VALUE	INTERPRETATION OF FIRST OCTET
0–30	This octet is followed by the indicated number (0–30) of data octets.
31	This octet is followed by a **uintvar**, which indicates the number of data octets after it.
32–127	The value is a text string, terminated by a zero octet (NULL character).
128–255	It is an encoded 7-bit value; this header has no more data.

It is up to the application to define how application-specific field values shall be encoded, but the encodings MUST adhere to the general format described in the preceding table.

If there is a mutual agreement between server and client on the used extension header code pages, then there is also a mutual agreement on how application-specific field values defined by these code pages shall be encoded. In this case, the applicable field values MUST be encoded according to the syntax rules defined by these code pages.

If the client and server cannot agree on the use of a header code page during capability negotiation, application-specific field values MUST be encoded using the *Application-specific-value* rule.

5.4.1.3 Encoding of List Values

If the syntax defined by RFC2068 for a header field with a well-known field name permits a comma-separated list using 1#*rule*, the header MUST be converted into a sequence of headers. Each shall have the original field name and contain one of the values in the original list. The order of the headers shall be the same as the order of their values in the original list value. The encoding rule for the well-known header shall be applied only after this transformation.

5.4.2 Header Syntax

This section defines the syntax and semantics of all HTTP/1.1 header fields in WSP/B. The mechanisms specified in this document are described in augmented BNF similar to that used by [RFC2068].

The notation <Octet N> is used to represent a single octet with the value *N* in the decimal system. The notation <Any octet M-N> is used for a single octet with the value in the range from *M* to *N*, inclusive.

5.4.2.1 Basic Rules

The following rules are used through this specification to describe the basic parsing constructs. The rules for Token, TEXT, and OCTET have the same definition as per [RFC2068].

```
Text-string = [Quote] TEXT End-of-string
; If the first character in the TEXT is in the range of 128-255, a Quote
       character must precede it.
; Otherwise the Quote character must be omitted. The Quote is not part of
       the contents.
Token-text = Token End-of-string

Quoted-string = <Octet 34> TEXT End-of-string
;The TEXT encodes an RFC2068 Quoted-string with the enclosing quotation-
       marks <"> removed

Short-integer = OCTET
; Integers in range 0-127 shall be encoded as a one octet value with the
       most significant bit set
```

```
; to one (1xxx xxxx) and with the value in the remaining least significant
       bits.

Long-integer = Short-length Multi-octet-integer
; The Short-length indicates the length of the Multi-octet-integer

Multi-octet-integer = 1*30 OCTET
; The content octets shall be an unsigned integer value
; with the most significant octet encoded first (big-endian
       representation).
; The minimum number of octets must be used to encode the value.

Uintvar-integer = 1*5 OCTET
; The encoding is the same as the one defined for uintvar in Section 0.

Constrained-encoding = Token-text | Short-integer
; This encoding is used for token values, which have no well-known binary
       encoding, or when
; the assigned number of the well-known encoding is small enough to fit
       into Short-integer.

Quote = <Octet 127>
End-of-string = <Octet 0>
```

5.4.2.2 Length

The following rules are used to encode length indicators:

```
Value-length = Short-length | (Length-quote Length)
; Value length is used to indicate the length of the value to follow
Short-length = <Any octet 0-30>
Length-quote = <Octet 31>
Length = Uintvar-integer
```

5.4.2.3 Parameter Values

The following rules are used in encoding parameter values:

```
No-value = <Octet 0>
; Used to indicate that the parameter actually has no value,
; eg, as the parameter "bar" in ";foo=xxx; bar; baz=xyzzy".

Text-value = No-value | Token-text | Quoted-string

Integer-Value = Short-integer | Long-integer
Date-value = Long-integer
; The encoding of dates shall be done in number of seconds from
; 1970-01-01, 00:00:00 GMT.

Delta-seconds-value = Integer-value

Q-value = 1*2 OCTET
; The encoding is the same as in Uintvar-integer, but with restricted size.
       When quality factor 0
```

```
; and quality factors with one or two decimal digits are encoded, they
       shall be multiplied by 100
; and incremented by one, so that they encode as a one-octet value in range
       1-100,
; ie, 0.1 is encoded as 11 (0x0B) and 0.99 encoded as 100 (0x64). Three
       decimal quality
; factors shall be multiplied with 1000 and incremented by 100, and the
       result shall be encoded
; as a one-octet or two-octet uintvar, eg, 0.333 shall be encoded as 0x83
       0x31.
; Quality factor 1 is the default value and shall never be sent.

Version-value = Short-integer | Text-string
; The three most significant bits of the Short-integer value are
       interpreted to encode a major
; version number in the range 1-7, and the four least significant bits
       contain a minor version
; number in the range 0-14. If there is only a major version number, this
       is encoded by
; placing the value 15 in the four least significant bits. If the version
       to be encoded fits these
; constraints, a Short-integer must be used, otherwise a Text-string shall
       be used.

Uri-value = Text-string
; URI value should be encoded per [RFC2068], but service user may use a
       different format.
```

5.4.2.4 Parameter

The following rules are used to encode parameters:

```
Parameter = Typed-parameter | Untyped-parameter

Typed-parameter = Well-known-parameter-token Typed-value
; the actual expected type of the value is implied by the well-known
       parameter
Well-known-parameter-token = Integer-value
; the code values used for parameters are specified in the Assigned Numbers
       appendix
Typed-value = Compact-value | Text-value
; In addition to the expected type, there may be no value.
; If the value cannot be encoded using the expected type, it shall be
       encoded as text.

Compact-value = Integer-value |
                Date-value | Delta-seconds-value | Q-value | Version-value |
                Uri-value
Untyped-parameter = Token-text Untyped-value
; the type of the value is unknown, but it shall be encoded as an integer,
       if that is possible.

Untyped-value = Integer-value | Text-value
```

5.4.2.5 Authorization

The following common rules are used for authentication and authorization.

```
Credentials = ( Basic Basic-cookie ) | ( Authentication-scheme *Auth-param )
Basic = <Octet 128>
Basic-cookie = User-id Password
User-id = Text-string
Password = Text-string
; Note user identity and password shall not be base 64 encoded.
Authentication-scheme = Token-text
Auth-param = Parameter
Challenge = ( Basic Realm-value ) | ( Authentication-scheme Realm-value
        *Auth-param )
Realm-value = Text-string
; shall be encoded without the quote characters <"> in the corresponding
        RFC2068 Quoted-string
```

5.4.2.6 Header

The following rules are used to encode headers:

```
Header = Message-header | Shift-sequence
Shift-sequence = ( Shift-delimiter Page-identity ) | Short-cut-shift-delimiter
Shift-delimiter = <Octet 127>
Page-identity = <Any octet 1-255>
Short-cut-shift-delimiter = <Any octet 1-31>

Message-header = Well-known-header | Application-header

Well-known-header = Well-known-field-name Wap-value

Application-header = Token-text Application-specific-value

Field-name = Token-text | Well-known-field-name
Well-known-field-name = Short-integer
Application-specific-value = Text-string
Wap-value =
         Accept-value |
         Accept-charset-value |
         Accept-encoding-value |
         Accept-language-value |
         Accept-ranges-value |
         Age-value |
         Allow-value |
         Authorization-value |
         Cache-control-value |
         Connection-value |
         Content-base-value |
         Content-encoding-value |
```

```
        Content-language-value |
        Content-length-value |
        Content-location-value |
        Content-MD5-value |
        Content-range-value |
        Content-type-value |
        Date |
        Etag-value |
        Expires-value |
        From-value |
        Host-value |
        If-modified-since-value |
        If-match-value |
        If-none-match-value |
        If-range-value |
        If-unmodified-since-value |
        Location-value |
        Last-modified |
        Max-forwards-value |
        Pragma-value |
        Proxy-authenticate-value |
        Proxy-authorization-value |
        Public-value |
        Range-value |
        Referer-value |
        Retry-after-value |
        Server-value |
        Transfer-encoding-value |
        Upgrade-value |
        User-agent-value |
        Vary-value |
        Via-value |
        Warning |
        WWW-authenticate-value |
        Content-disposition-value
```

5.4.2.7 Accept Field

The following rules are used to encode accept values:

```
Accept-value = Constrained-media | Accept-general-form
Accept-general-form = Value-length Media-range [Accept-parameters]
Media-range = (Well-known-media | Token-text) *(Parameter)
Accept-parameters = Q-token Q-value *(Accept-extension)
Accept-extension = Parameter
Constrained-media = Constrained-encoding
Well-known-media = Integer-value
; Both are encoded using values from Content Type Assignments table in
        Assigned Numbers
Q-token = <Octet 128>
```

5.4.2.8 Accept Charset Field

The following rules are used to encode accept character set values:

```
Accept-charset-value = Constrained-charset | Accept-charset-general-form
Accept-charset-general-form = Value-length (Well-known-charset | Token-
       text) [Q-value]
Constrained-well-known-charset = Constrained-encoding
Well-known-charset = Integer-value
; Both are encoded using values from Character Set Assignments table in
       Assigned Numbers
```

5.4.2.9 Accept Encoding Field

The following rules are used to encode accept encoding values:

```
Accept-encoding-value = Content-encoding-value
```

5.4.2.10 Accept Language Field

The following rules are used to encode accept language values:

```
Accept-language-value = Constrained-language | Accept-language-general-form
Accept-language-general-form = Value-length (Well-known-language | Text-
       string) [Q-value]
Constrained-language = Any-language | Constrained-encoding
Well-known-language = Any-language | Integer-value
; Both are encoded using values from Character Set Assignments table in
       Assigned Numbers

Any-language = <Octet 128>
; Equivalent to the special RFC2068 language range "*"
```

5.4.2.11 Accept Ranges Field

The following rules are used to encode accept range values:

```
Accept-ranges-value = (None | Bytes | Token-text)
None = <Octet 128>
Bytes = <Octet 129>
```

5.4.2.12 Age Field

The following rule is used to encode age values:

```
Age-value = Delta-seconds-value
```

5.4.2.13 Allow Field

The following rules are used to encode allow values:

```
Allow-value = Well-known-method
Well-known-method = Short-integer
; Any well-known method or extended method in the range of 0x40-0x7F
```

5.4.2.14 Authorization Field

The following rule is used to encode authorization values:

```
Authorization-value = Value-length Credentials
```

5.4.2.15 Cache-Control Field

The following rules are used to encode cache control values:

```
Cache-control-value =      No-cache |
                           No-store |
                           Max-stale |
                           Only-if-cached |
                           Private |
                           Public |
                           No-transform |
                           Must-revalidate |
                           Proxy-revalidate |
                           Cache-extension |
                           Value-length Cache-directive
Cache-directive =  No-cache 1*(Field-name) |
                   Max-age Delta-second-value |
                   Max-stale Delta-second-value |
                   Min-fresh Delta-second-value |
                   Private 1*(Field-name) |
                   Cache-extension Parameter
No-cache = <Octet 128>
No-store = <Octet 129>
Max-age = <Octet 130>
Max-stale = <Octet 131>
Min-fresh = <Octet 132>
Only-if-cached = <Octet 133>
Public = <Octet 134>
Private = <Octet 135>
No-transform = <Octet 136>
Must-revalidate = <Octet 137>
Proxy-revalidate = <Octet 138>
Cache-extension = Token-text
```

5.4.2.16 Connection Field

The following rules are used to encode connection values:

```
Connection-value = (Close | Token-text)
Close = <Octet 128>
```

5.4.2.17 Content-Base Field

The following rule is used to encode content base values:

```
Content-base-value = Uri-value
```

5.4.2.18 Content Encoding Field

The following rules are used to encode content encoding values:

```
Content-encoding-value = (Gzip | Compress | Deflate | Token-text)
Gzip = <Octet 128>
Compress = <Octet 129>
Deflate = <Octet 130>
```

5.4.2.19 Content Language Field

The following rule is used to encode content language values:

```
Content-language-value = (Well-known-language | Token-text)
```

5.4.2.20 Content Length Field

The following rule is used to encode content length values. Normally the information in the content length header is redundant and MAY not be sent—the content length is available in the PDU or can be calculated when the Transport layer provides the PDU size.

If the PDU contains no entity body at all (response to HEAD), then the Content-Length SHOULD be encoded in the header fields so that the client can learn the size of the entity.

```
Content-length-value = Integer-value
```

5.4.2.21 Content Location Field

The following rule is used to encode content location values:

```
Content-location-value = Uri-value
```

5.4.2.22 Content MD5 Field

The following rules are used to encode content MD5 values:

```
Content-MD5-value = Value-length Digest
; 128-bit MD5 digest as per [RFC1864]. Note the digest shall not be
       base-64 encoded.
Digest = 16*16 OCTET
```

5.4.2.23 Content Range Field

The following rules are used to encode content range values. Last-byte-pos available in the HTTP/1.1 header is redundant. The content range length is available in the PDU or can be calculated when the Transport layer provides the PDU size. Last-byte-pos can be calculated by adding together First-byte-pos with size of content range.

```
Content-range = Value-length First-byte-pos Entity-length
First-byte-pos = Uintvar-integer
Entity-length = Uintvar-integer
```

5.4.2.24 Content Type Field

The following rules are used to encode content type values. The short form of the Content-type-value MUST only be used when the well-known media is in the range of 0–127 or a text string. In all other cases, the general form MUST be used.

```
Content-type-value = Constrained-media | Content-general-form
Content-general-form = Value-length Media-type
Media-type = (Well-known-media | Token-text) *(Parameter)
```

5.4.2.25 Date Field

The following rule is used to encode date values:

```
Date = Date-value
```

5.4.2.26 Etag Field

The following rule is used to encode entity tag values:

```
Etag-value = Text-string
; The value shall be encoded as per [RFC2068]
```

5.4.2.27 Expires Field

The following rule is used to encode expires values:

```
Expires-value = Date-value
```

5.4.2.28 From Field

The following rule is used to encode from values:

```
From-value = Text-string
; The value shall be encoded as an e-mail address as per [RFC822]
```

5.4.2.29 Host Field

The following rule is used to encode host values:

```
Host-value = Text-string
; The value shall be encoded as per [RFC2068]
```

5.4.2.30 If Modified Since Field

The following rule is used to encode if modified since values:

```
If-modified-since-value = Date-value
```

5.4.2.31 If Match Field

The following rule is used to encode if match values:

```
If-match-value = Text-string
; The value shall be encoded as per [RFC2068]
```

5.4.2.32 If None Match Field

The following rule is used to encode if none match values:

```
If-none-match-value = Text-string
; The value shall be encoded as per [RFC2068]
```

5.4.2.33 If Range Field

The following rule is used to encode if range values:

```
If-range = Text-string | Date-value
; The value shall be encoded as per [RFC2068]
```

5.4.2.34 If Unmodified Since Field

The following rule is used to encode if unmodified since values:

```
If-unmodified-since-value = Date-value
```

5.4.2.35 Last Modified Field

The following rule is used to encode last modified values:

```
Last-modified-value = Date-value
```

5.4.2.36 Location Field

The following rule is used to encode location values:

```
Location-value = Uri-value
```

5.4.2.37 Max Forwards Field

The following rule is used to encode max forwards values:

```
Max-forwards-value = Integer-value
```

5.4.2.38 Pragma Field

The following rule is used to encode pragma values:

```
Pragma-value = No-cache | Parameter
; The quoted text string shall be encoded as per [RFC2068]
```

5.4.2.39 Proxy-Authenticate

The following rules are used to encode proxy authenticate values:

```
Proxy-authenticate-value = Value-length Challenge
```

5.4.2.40 Proxy Authorization Field

The following rules are used to encode proxy authorization values:

```
Proxy-authorization-value = Value-length Credentials
```

5.4.2.41 Public Field

The following rule is used to encode public values:

```
Public-value = (Well-known-method | Token-text)
```

5.4.2.42 Range Field

The following rules are used to encode range values:

```
Range-value = Value-Length (Byte-range-spec | Suffix-byte-range-spec)
Byte-range-spec = Byte-range First-byte-pos [ Last-byte-Pos ]
Suffix-byte-range-spec = Suffix-byte-range Suffix-length
First-byte-pos = Uintvar-integer
Last-byte-pos = Uintvar-integer
Suffix-length = Uintvar-integer
Byte-range = <Octet 128>
Suffix-byte-range = <Octet 129>
```

5.4.2.43 Referer Field

The following rule is used to encode referer values:

```
Referer-value = Uri-value
```

5.4.2.44 Retry After Field

The following rules are used to encode retry after values:

```
Retry-after-value = Value-length (Retry-date-value | Retry-delta-seconds)
Retry-date-value = Absolute-time Date-value
Retry-delta-seconds = Relative-time Delta-seconds-value
Absolute-time = <Octet 128>
Relative-time = <Octet 129>
```

5.4.2.45 Server Field

The following rule is used to encode server values:

```
Server-value = Text-string
; The value shall be encoded as per [RFC2068]
```

5.4.2.46 Transfer Encoding Field

The following rules are used to encode transfer encoding values:

```
Transfer-encoding-values = Chunked | Token-text
Chunked = <Octet 128>
```

5.4.2.47 Upgrade Field

The following rule is used to encode upgrade values:

```
Upgrade-value = Text-string
; The value shall be encoded as per [RFC2068]
```

5.4.2.48 User Agent Field

The following rule is used to encode user agent values:

```
User-agent-value = Text-string
; The value shall be encoded as per [RFC2068]
```

5.4.2.49 Vary Field

The following rule is used to encode vary values:

```
Vary-value = Field-name
```

5.4.2.50 Via Field

The following rule is used to encode via values:

```
Via-value = Text-string
; The value shall be encoded as per [RFC2068]
```

5.4.2.51 Warning Field

The following rules are used to encode warning values. The warning code values are defined in [RFC2068].

```
Warning = Warn-code | Warning-value
Warning-value = Value-length Warn-code Warn-agent Warn-text
Warn-code = Short-integer
Warn-agent = Text-string
; The value shall be encoded as per [RFC2068]
Warn-text = Text-string
```

5.4.2.52 WWW Authenticate Field

The following rule is used to encode WWW authenticate values:

```
Proxy-authenticate-value = Value-length Challenge
```

5.4.2.53 Content-Disposition Field

The following rule is used to encode the content-disposition fields used when submitting form data:

```
Content-disposition-value = Value-length Disposition *(Parameter)
Disposition = Form-data | Attachment

Form-data = <Octet 128>
Attachment = <Octet 129>
```

5.5 Multipart Data

HTTP/1.1 has adopted the MIME multipart format to transport composite data objects (e.g., "multipart/mixed"). WSP/B defines a compact binary form of the MIME multipart entity. There is a straightforward translation of both the multipart entity and the

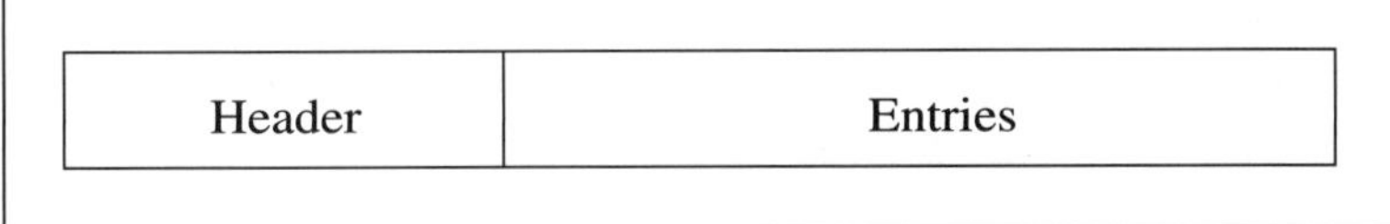

Figure 14.31 X-WAP.Multipart format.

content type. After translation, a "multipart/mixed" entity becomes an "x-wap.multipart/mixed" entity. Thus, all MIME "multipart/*" content types can be converted into "x-wap.multipart/*" content types. No information is lost in the translation.

5.5.1 X-WAP.Multipart Format (Figure 14.31)

The X-WAP.Multipart content type consists of a header followed by 0 or more entries.

5.5.2 Multipart Header

The multipart header format is shown in Table 14.32.

The *nEntries* field specifies the number of entries in the multipart entity.

5.5.3 Multipart Entry

The multipart entry format is shown in Table 14.33.

The *HeadersLen* field specifies the length of the *ContentType* and *Headers* fields combined.

Table 14.32 Multipart Header Fields

NAME	TYPE	PURPOSE
nEntries	uintvar	The number of entries in the multipart entity

Table 14.33 Multipart Entry Fields

NAME	TYPE	PURPOSE
HeadersLen	uintvar	Length of the *ContentType* and *Headers* fields combined
DataLen	uintvar	Length of the *Data* field
ContentType	multiple octets	The content type of the data
Headers	(*HeadersLen* – length of *ContentType*) octets	The headers
Data	DataLen octets	The data

The *DataLen* field specifies the length of the *Data* field in the multipart entry.

The *ContentType* field contains the content type of the data. It conforms to the Content-Type value encoding specified in Section 5.4.2.24, *Content Type Field*.

The *Headers* field contains the headers of the entry.

The *Data* field contains the data of the entry.

6. Definitions

For the purposes of this specification the following definitions apply.

Bearer Network. A bearer network is used to carry the messages of a Transport layer protocol—and ultimately also of the Session layer protocols—between physical devices. During the lifetime of a session, several bearer networks may be used.

Capability. Capability is a term introduced in Section 3.3.2, *Capabilities*, to refer to the Session layer protocol facilities and configuration parameters that a client or server supports.

Capability Negotiation. Capability negotiation is the mechanism defined in Section 3.3.2.1, *Capability Negotiation*, for agreeing on session functionality and protocol options. Session capabilities are negotiated during session establishment. Capability negotiation allows a server application to determine whether a client can support certain protocol facilities and configurations.

Client and Server. The terms *client* and *server* are used in order to map WSP to well-known and existing systems. A client is a device (or application) that initiates a request for a session. The server is a device that passively waits for session requests from client devices. The server can either accept the request or reject it.

An implementation of the WSP protocol may include only client or server functions in order to minimize the footprint. A client or server may only support a subset of the protocol facilities, indicating this during protocol capability negotiation.

Connectionless Session Service. Connectionless session service is an unreliable session service. In this mode, only the request primitive is available to service users, and only the indication primitive is available to the service provider.

Connection-Mode Session Service. Connection-mode session service (Section 3.3) is a reliable session service. In this mode, both request and response primitives are available to service users, and both indication and confirm primitives are available to the service provider.

Content. The entity body sent with a request or response is referred to as *content*. It is encoded in a format and encoding defined by the entity-header fields.

Content Negotiation. Content negotiation is the mechanism the server uses to select the appropriate type and encoding of content when servicing a request. The type and encoding of content in any response can be negotiated. Content negotiation allows a server application to decide whether a client can support a certain form of content.

Entity. An entity is the information transferred as the payload of a request or response. An entity consists of meta-information in the form of entity-header fields and content in the form of an entity-body.

Header. A header contains meta-information. Specifically, a session header contains general information about a session that remains constant over the lifetime of a session; an entity-header contains meta-information about a particular request, response, or entity body (content).

Layer Entity. In the OSI architecture, the active elements within a layer that participate in providing layer service are called *layer entities*.

Method. Method is the *type* of client request as defined by HTTP/1.1 (e.g., Get, Post, etc.). A WSP client uses methods and extended methods to invoke services on the server.

Null Terminated String. A sequence of nonzero octets followed by a zero octet.

Peer Address Quadruplet. Sessions are associated with a particular client address, client port, server address, and server port. This combination of four values is called the *peer address quadruplet* in the specification.

Proxy. An intermediary program that acts both as a server and a client for the purpose of making requests on behalf of other clients. Requests are serviced internally or by passing them on, with possible translation, to other servers.

Pull and Push Data Transfer. Push and pull are common vernacular in the Internet world to describe push transactions and method transactions, respectively. A server "pushes" data to a client by invoking the WSP/B push service, whereas a client "pulls" data from a server by invoking the WSP/B method service.

Session. A long-lived communication context established between two programs for the purpose of transactions and typed data transfer.

Session Service Access Point (S-SAP). Session Service Access Point is a conceptual point at which session service is provided to the upper layer.

Session Service Provider. A Session Service Provider is a layer entity that actively participates in providing the session service via an S-SAP.

Session Service User. A Session Service User is a layer entity that requests services from a Session Service Provider via an S-SAP.

Transaction. Three forms of transactions are specified herein. We do not use the term *transaction* to imply the semantics often associated with database transactions.

- A *method transaction* is a three-way request-response-acknowledge communication initiated by the client to invoke a method on the server.
- A *push transaction* is a two-way request-acknowledge communication initiated by the server to push data to the client.
- A *transport transaction* is a lower-level transaction primitive provided by a Transaction Service Provider.

7. Abbreviations

For the purposes of this specification the following abbreviations apply.

API	Application Programming Interface
A-SAP	Application Service Access Point
HTTP	Hypertext Transfer Protocol
ISO	International Organization for Standardization
MOM	Maximum Outstanding Method requests
MOP	Maximum Outstanding Push requests
MRU	Maximum Receive Unit
OSI	Open System Interconnection
PDU	Protocol Data Unit
S-SAP	Session Service Access Point
SDU	Service Data Unit
SEC-SAP	Security Service Access Point
T-SAP	Transport Service Access Point
TID	Transaction Identifier
TR-SAP	Transaction Service Access Point
WDP	Wireless Datagram Protocol
WSP	Wireless Session Protocol
WSP/B	Wireless Session Protocol—Browsing
WTP	Wireless Transaction Protocol

8. Documentation Conventions

This specification uses the same keywords as specified in RFC 2119 [RFC2119] for defining the significance of each particular requirement. These words are:

MUST. This word, or the terms "REQUIRED" or "SHALL," means that the definition is an absolute requirement of the specification.

MUST NOT. This phrase, or the phrase "SHALL NOT," means that the definition is an absolute prohibition of the specification.

SHOULD. This word, or the adjective "RECOMMENDED," means that there may exist valid reasons in particular circumstances to ignore a particular item, but the full implications must be understood and carefully weighed before choosing a different course.

SHOULD NOT. This phrase, or the phrase "NOT RECOMMENDED," means that there may exist valid reasons in particular circumstances when the particular behavior is acceptable or even useful, but the full implications should be understood and the case carefully weighed before implementing any behavior described with this label.

MAY. This word, or the adjective "OPTIONAL," means that an item is truly optional. One vendor may choose to include the item because a particular marketplace requires it or because the vendor feels that it enhances the product, while another vendor may omit the same item. An implementation that does not include a particular option MUST be prepared to interoperate with another implementation that does include the option, though perhaps with reduced functionality. In the same vein, an implementation that does include a particular option MUST be prepared to interoperate with another implementation that does not include the option (except, of course, for the feature the option provides).

9. Normative References

[WAPARCH] "WAP Architecture Specification," WAP Forum, 30-April-1998. URL: http://www.wapforum.org/

[WAPWDP] "Wireless Datagram Protocol Specification," WAP Forum, 30-April-1998. URL: http://www.wapforum.org/

[WAPWTP] "Wireless Transaction Protocol Specification," WAP Forum, 30-April-1998. URL: http://www.wapforum.org/

[RFC2119] "Key Words for Use in RFCs to Indicate Requirement Levels," Bradner, S., March 1997. URL: ftp://ftp.isi.edu/in-notes/rfc2119.txt.

[RFC2068] "Hypertext Transfer Protocol—HTTP/1.1," Fielding, R., et. al., January 1997. URL: ftp://ftp.isi.edu/in-notes/rfc2068.txt.

[RFC1521] "MIME (Multipurpose Internet Mail Extensions) Part One: Mechanisms for Specifying and Describing the Format of Internet Message Bodies," Borenstein, N., et. al., September 1993. URL: ftp://ftp.isi.edu/in-notes/rfc1521.txt.

[RFC2047] "MIME (Multipurpose Internet Mail Extensions) Part Three: Message Header Extensions for Non-ASCII Text," Moore, K., November 1996. URL: ftp://ftp.isi.edu/in-notes/rfc2047.txt.

[RFC822] "Standard for the Format of ARPA Internet Text Messages," Crocker, D., August 1982. URL: ftp://ftp.isi.edu/in-notes/rfc822.txt.

10. Informative References

[ISO7498] "Information Technology—Open Systems Interconnection—Basic Reference Model: The Basic Model," ISO/IEC 7498-1:1994.

[ISO10731] "Information Technology—Open Systems Interconnection—Basic Reference Model—Conventions for the Definition of OSI Services," ISO/IEC 10731:1994.

[RFC1630] "Universal Resource Identifiers in WWW, a Unifying Syntax for the Expression of Names and Addresses of Objects on the Network as used in the World Wide Web," Berners-Lee, T., June 1994. URL:ftp://ftp.isi.edu/in-notes/rfc1630.txt.

[RFC1738] "Uniform Resource Locators (URL)," Berners-Lee, T., et. al., December 1994. URL:ftp://ftp.isi.edu/in-notes/rfc1738.txt.

[RFC1808] "Relative Uniform Resource Locators," Fielding, R., June 1995. URL:ftp://ftp.isi.edu/in-notes/rfc1808.txt.

[RFC1864] "The Content-MD5 Header Field," Meyers, J. and Rose, M., October 1995. URL:ftp://ftp.isi.edu/in-notes/rfc1864.txt.

Appendix A: Assigned Numbers

This section contains tables of the WSP/B assigned numbers (see Tables A.1 through A.8). The WAP Architecture Group is responsible for administering the values.

The character set encodings are done using the MIBEnum values assigned by the IANA in the registry available in <URL:ftp://ftp.isi.edu/in-notes/iana/assignments/character-sets>. Table A.9 provides just a quick reference.

Table A.1 PDU Type Assignments

NAME	ASSIGNED NUMBER
Reserved	0x00
Connect	0x01
ConnectReply	0x02
Redirect	0x03
Reply	0x04
Disconnect	0x05
Push	0x06
ConfirmedPush	0x07
Suspend	0x08
Resume	0x09
Unassigned	0x10–0x3F
Get	0x40
Options (Get PDU)	0x41
Head (Get PDU)	0x42
Delete (Get PDU)	0x43
Trace (Get PDU)	0x44
Unassigned (Get PDU)	0x45-0x4F
Extended Method (Get PDU)	0x50-0x5F
Post	0x60
Put (Post PDU)	0x61
Unassigned (Post PDU)	0x62–0x6F
Extended Method (Post PDU)	0x70–0x7F
Reserved	0x80–0xFF

Table A.2 Abort Reason Code Assignments

NAME	DESCRIPTION	ASSIGNED NUMBER
PROTOERR	Protocol error, illegal PDU received	0xE0
DISCONNECT	Session has been disconnected	0xE1
SUSPEND	Session has been suspended	0xE2
RESUME	Session has been resumed	0xE3
CONGESTION	The peer is congested and can not process the SDU	0xE4
CONNECTERR	The session connect failed	0xE5
MRUEXCEEDED	The Maximum Receive Unit size was exceeded	0xE6
MOREXCEEDED	The Maximum Outstanding Requests was exceeded	0xE7
PEERREQ	Peer request	0xE8
NETERR	Network error	0xE9
USERREQ	User request	0xEA

Table A.3 Status Code Assignments

HTTP STATUS CODE	DESCRIPTION	ASSIGNED NUMBER
None	Reserved	0x00 to 0x0F
100	Continue	0x10
101	Switching protocols	0x11
200	OK, Success	0x20
201	Created	0x21
202	Accepted	0x22
203	Nonauthoritative information	0x23
204	No content	0x24
205	Reset content	0x25
206	Partial content	0x26

(Continues)

Table A.3 (*Continued*)

HTTP STATUS CODE	DESCRIPTION	ASSIGNED NUMBER
300	Multiple choices	0x30
301	Moved permanently	0x31
302	Moved temporarily	0x32
303	See other	0x33
304	Not modified	0x34
305	Use proxy	0x35
400	Bad Request—server could not understand request	0x40
401	Unauthorized	0x41
402	Payment required	0x42
403	Forbidden—operation is understood but refused	0x43
404	Not found	0x44
405	Method not allowed	0x45
406	Not acceptable	0x46
407	Proxy authentication required	0x47
408	Request timeout	0x48
409	Conflict	0x49
410	Gone	0x4A
411	Length required	0x4B
412	Precondition failed	0x4C
413	Requested entity too large	0x4D
414	Request-URI too large	0x4E
415	Unsupported media type	0x4F
500	Internal server error	0x60
501	Not implemented	0x61
502	Bad gateway	0x62
503	Service unavailable	0x63
504	Gateway timeout	0x64
505	HTTP version not supported	0x65

Table A.4 Capability Assignments

CAPABILITY	ASSIGNED NUMBER
Client-SDU-Size	0x00
Server-SDU-Size	0x01
Protocol options	0x02
Method-MOR	0x03
Push-MOR	0x04
Extended methods	0x05
Header code pages	0x06
Aliases	0x07
Unassigned	0x08 to 0x7F

Table A.5 Well-Known Parameter Assignments

TOKEN	ASSIGNED NUMBER	EXPECTED BNF RULE FOR VALUE
Q	0x00	Q-value
Charset	0x01	Well-known-charset
Level	0x02	Version-value
Type	0x03	Integer-value
Uaprof	0x04	Untyped-value
Name	0x05	Text-string
Filename	0x06	Text-string
Differences	0x07	Field-name
Padding	0x08	Short-integer

Table A.6 Header Field Name Assignments

NAME	ASSIGNED NUMBER	NAME	ASSIGNED NUMBER
Accept	0x00	If-Match	0x18
Accept-Charset	0x01	If-None-Match	0x19
Accept-Encoding	0x02	If-Range	0x1A
Accept-Language	0x03	If-Unmodified-Since	0x1B
Accept-Ranges	0x04	Location	0x1C
Age	0x05	Last-Modified	0x1D
Allow	0x06	Max-Forwards	0x1E
Authorization	0x07	Pragma	0x1F
Cache-Control	0x08	Proxy-Authenticate	0x20
Connection	0x09	Proxy-Authorization	0x21
Content-Base	0x0A	Public	0x22
Content-Encoding	0x0B	Range	0x23
Content-Language	0x0C	Referer	0x24
Content-Length	0x0D	Retry-After	0x25
Content-Location	0x0E	Server	0x26
Content-MD5	0x0F	Transfer-Encoding	0x27
Content-Range	0x10	Upgrade	0x28
Content-Type	0x11	User-Agent	0x29
Date	0x12	Vary	0x2A
Etag	0x13	Via	0x2B
Expires	0x14	Warning	0x2C
From	0x15	WWW-Authenticate	0x2D
Host	0x16	Content-Disposition	0x2E
If-Modified-Since	0x17		

Table A.7 Content Type Assignments

CONTENT-TYPE	ASSIGNED NUMBER
/	0x00
text/*	0x01
text/html	0x02
text/plain	0x03
text/x-hdml	0x04
text/x-ttml	0x05
text/x-vCalendar	0x06
text/x-vCard	0x07
text/x-wap.wml	0x08
text/x-wap.wmlscript	0x09
text/x-wap.wta-event	0x0A
multipart/*	0x0B
multipart/mixed	0x0C
multipart/form-data	0x0D
multipart/byteranges	0x0E
multipart/alternative	0x0F
application/*	0x10
application/java-vm	0x11
application/x-www-form-urlencoded	0x12
application/x-hdmlc	0x13
application/x-wap.wmlc	0x14
application/x-wap.wmlscriptc	0x15
application/x-wap.wta-eventc	0x16
application/x-wap.uaprof	0x17
application/x-wap.wtls-ca-certificate	0x18
application/x-wap.wtls-user-certificate	0x19
application/x-x509-ca-cert	0x1A
application/x-x509-user-cert	0x1B

(Continues)

Table A.7 *(Continued)*

CONTENT-TYPE	ASSIGNED NUMBER
image/*	0x1C
image/gif	0x1D
image/jpeg	0x1E
image/tiff	0x1F
image/png	0x20
image/x-wap.wbmp	0x21
x-wap.multipart/*	0x22
x-wap.multipart/mixed	0x23
x-wap.multipart/form-data	0x24
x-wap.multipart/byteranges	0x25
x-wap.multipart/alternative	0x26
Unassigned	0x27–0x7F

Table A.8 ISO 639 Language Assignments

LANGUAGE	SHORT	ASSIGNED NUMBER	LANGUAGE	SHORT	ASSIGNED NUMBER
Afar		0x01	Maori		0x47
Abkhazian		0x02	Macedonian	mk	0x48
Afrikaans	af	0x03	Malayalam		0x49
Amharic		0x04	Mongolian		0x4A
Arabic		0x05	Moldavian		0x4B
Assamese		0x06	Marathi		0x4C
Aymara		0x07	Malay		0x4D
Azerbaijani		0x08	Maltese		0x4E
Bashkir		0x09	Burmese		0x4F
Byelorussian	be	0x0A	Nauru		0x50
Bulgarian	bg	0x0B	Nepali		0x51
Bihari		0x0C	Dutch	nl	0x52
Bislama		0x0D	Norwegian	no	0x53

Table A.8 *(Continued)*

LANGUAGE	SHORT	ASSIGNED NUMBER	LANGUAGE	SHORT	ASSIGNED NUMBER
Bengali; Bangla		0x0E	Occitan		0x54
Tibetan		0x0F	(Afan) Oromo		0x55
Breton		0x10	Oriya		0x56
Catalan	ca	0x11	Punjabi		0x57
Corsican		0x12	Polish	po	0x58
Czech	cs	0x13	Pashto, Pushto		0x59
Welsh		0x14	Portuguese	pt	0x5A
Danish	da	0x15	Quechua		0x5B
German	de	0x16	Rhaeto-Romance		0x5C
Bhutani		0x17	Kirundi		0x5D
Greek	el	0x18	Romanian	ro	0x5E
English	en	0x19	Russian	ru	0x5F
Esperanto		0x1A	Kinyarwanda		0x60
Spanish	es	0x1B	Sanskrit		0x61
Estonian		0x1C	Sindhi		0x62
Basque	eu	0x1D	Sangho		0x63
Persian		0x1E	Serbo-Croatian		0x64
Finnish	fi	0x1F	Sinhalese		0x65
Fiji		0x20	Slovak	sk	0x66
Faeroese	fo	0x21	Slovenian	sl	0x67
French	fr	0x22	Samoan		0x68
Frisian		0x23	Shona		0x69
Irish	ga	0x24	Somali		0x6A
Scots Gaelic	gd	0x25	Albanian	sq	0x6B
Galician	gl	0x26	Serbian	sr	0x6C
Guarani		0x27	Siswati		0x6D
Gujarati		0x28	Sesotho		0x6E
Hausa		0x29	Sundanese		0x6F

(Continues)

Table A.8 (*Continued*)

LANGUAGE	SHORT	ASSIGNED NUMBER	LANGUAGE	SHORT	ASSIGNED NUMBER
Hebrew (formerly iw)		0x2A	Swedish	sv	0x70
Hindi		0x2B	Swahili		0x71
Croatian	hr	0x2C	Tamil		0x72
Hungarian	hu	0x2D	Telugu		0x73
Armenian		0x2E	Tajik		0x74
Interlingua		0x2F	Thai		0x75
Indonesian (formerly in)	id	0x30	Tigrinya		0x76
Interlingue		0x31	Turkmen		0x77
Inupiak		0x32	Tagalog		0x78
Icelandic	is	0x33	Setswana		0x79
Italian	it	0x34	Tonga		0x7A
Inuktitut		0x35	Turkish	tr	0x7B
Japanese	ja	0x36	Tsonga		0x7C
Javanese		0x37	Tatar		0x7D
Georgian		0x38	Twi		0x7E
Kazakh		0x39	Uighur		0x7F
Greenlandic		0x3A	Ukrainian	uk	0x81
Cambodian		0x3B	Urdu		0x82
Kannada		0x3C	Uzbek		0x83
Korean	ko	0x3D	Vietnamese		0x84
Kashmiri		0x3E	Volapuk		0x85
Kurdish		0x3F	Wolof		0x86
Kirghiz		0x40	Xhosa		0x87
Latin		0x41	Yiddish (formerly ji)		0x88
Lingala		0x42	Yoruba		0x89
Laothian		0x43	Zhuang		0x8A
Lithuanian		0x44	Chinese	zh	0x8B
Latvian, Lettish		0x45	Zulu		0x8C
Malagasy		0x46			

Table A.9 Character Set Assignment Examples

CHARACTER SET	ASSIGNED NUMBER	IANA MIBENUM VALUE
big5	0x07EA	2026
iso-10646-ucs-2	0x03E8	1000
iso-8859-1	0x04	4
iso-8859-2	0x05	5
iso-8859-3	0x06	6
iso-8859-4	0x07	7
iso-8859-5	0x08	8
iso-8859-6	0x09	9
iso-8859-7	0x0A	10
iso-8859-8	0x0B	11
iso-8859-9	0x0C	12
shift_JIS	0x11	17
us-ascii	0x03	3
utf-8	0x6A	106
gsm-default-alphabet	Not yet assigned	Not yet assigned

Appendix B: Header Encoding Examples

This section contains some illustrative examples for how header encoding shall be applied.

B.1 Header Values

The header values are given in HTTP/1.1 syntax together with the corresponding WSP/B header-encoded octet stream.

B.1.1 Encoding of Primitive Value

HTTP/1.1 header: Accept: application/x-wap.wmlc

Encoded header:

0x80 —Well-known field name "Accept" coded as a short integer

0x94 —Well-known media "application/x-wap.wmlc" coded as a short integer

B.1.2 Encoding of Structured Value

HTTP/1.1 header: Accept-Language: en;q=0.7

Encoded header:

0x83 —Well-known field name "Accept-Language"

0x02 —Value length, general encoding must be applied.

0x99 —Well-known language "English"

0x47 —Quality factor 0.7 (0.7 * 100 + 1 = 0x47)

B.1.3 Encoding of Well-Known List Value

HTTP/1.1 header: Accept-Language: en, sv

Encoded header:

0x83 —Well-known field name "Accept-Language"

0x99 —Well-known language "English"

0x83 —Well-known field name "Accept-Language"

0xF0 —Well-known language "Swedish"

B.1.4 Encoding of Date Value

HTTP/1.1 header: Date: Thu, 23 Apr 1998 13:41:37 GMT

Encoded header:

0x92 —Well-known field name "Date"

0x04 —Length of multi-octet integer

0x35 —4 date octets encoded as number of seconds from 1970-01-01,

0x3f —00:00:00 GMT. The most significant octet shall be first.

0x45 —

0x11 —

B.1.5 Encoding of Content Range

HTTP/1.1 header: Content-range: bytes 0-499/1025

Encoded header:

0x90 —Well-known field name "Content-range"

0x03 —Value length

0x00 —First octet position

0x88 —Entity length

0x01 —Entity length

B.1.6 Encoding of a New Unassigned Token

HTTP/1.1 header: Accept-ranges: new-range-unit

Encoded header:

0x84 —Well-known field name "Accept-ranges"

'n"e"w"-"r"a"n"g"e"-"u"i"n"t' 0x00—Token coded as a null terminated text string

B.1.7 Encoding of a New Unassigned Header Field Name

HTTP/1.1 header: X-New-header: foo

Encoded header:

'X' '-' 'N"e"w"-"h"e"a"d"e"r' 0x00 —Field name coded as a null terminated text string

'f"o"o' 0x00 —Field value coded as null terminated text string

B.1.8 Encoding of a New Unassigned List-Valued Header

HTTP/1.1 header: X-New-header: foo, bar

Encoded header:

'X' '-' 'N"e"w"-"h"e"a"d"e"r' 0x00—Field name coded as a null terminated text string

'f"o"o' ',' 'b' 'a' 'r' 0x00 —Field value coded as null terminated text string

B.2 Shift Header Code Pages

This section illustrates how header code pages can be shifted.

B.2.1 Shift Sequence

Shift to header code page 64

Encoded shift sequence:

0x7F —Shift delimiter

0x40 —Page identity

B.2.2 Shortcut

Shift to header code page 16

Encoded shift sequence:

0x10 —Short cut shift delimiter

Appendix C: Implementation Notes

The following implementation notes are provided to identify areas in which implementation choices may impact the performance and effectiveness of the WSP protocols. These notes provide guidance to implementers of the protocols.

C.1 Confirmed Push and Delayed Acknowledgments

One of the features of the Wireless Transaction Protocol is delayed acknowledgment of transactions, which may significantly reduce the number of messages sent over the bearer network. However, this feature may also result in poor throughput for push traffic, especially if the server waits for a confirmed push to be acknowledged before starting the next confirmed push transaction. Use of delayed acknowledgments will cause the push cycle to take at least one round-trip time plus the duration of the delayed acknowledgment timer. This effect will be even more pronounced when the bearer network has a long round-trip delay, since then WTP will typically use a larger delayed acknowledgment timer value.

The Session layer protocol does not address this issue because the WTP service interface does not include a means to effect the delayed acknowledgment timer. Rather, the control of that timer is a matter local to the implementation. If the performance implications are considered significant, an implementation should provide the service user with means to specify the largest acceptable acknowledgment delay for each push transaction. Forcing the delayed acknowledgment timer to always have a value that is small enough to provide good push throughput is not a good solution. This will prevent the remaining WTP message traffic associated with method requests from being optimized, and the number of messages sent over the air-interface will be doubled.

C.2 Handling of Race Conditions

Connection-mode WSP/B is layered on top of the service provided by the Wireless Transaction Protocol, which does not guarantee that transaction invocations and results arrive to the peer in the same order as in which the service user has submitted them. This results in certain race conditions, if method or push transactions are initiated while the session creation procedure has not yet been fully completed. In order to reduce protocol complexity, WSP/B does not attempt to handle all of these gracefully, but in many cases simply chooses to abort the transaction caught in the race condition. As a consequence, the reason for an aborted transaction may be reported to be DISCONNECT; in other words, nonexistent session, although the session actually exists and can be used. In such a case, the service user should simply retry the transaction request.

This policy was chosen since these race conditions were not considered frequent enough to make the cost of the additional protocol complexity worthwhile. However, if the problem is considered significant, it can still be alleviated using certain implementation strategies. First of all, if session management, method, and push transactions are initiated so close together that the race conditions are possible, then WTP concatenation procedures should be capable of combining the resulting PDUs into the same transport datagram. WTP should also handle the concatenation and separation in such a manner that the order of operations is preserved if the resulting PDUs are carried by the same datagram. This will ensure that the state machine of WSP/B will not need to react to primitives related to method and push transactions before it has had a chance to complete creation of the session.

If an implementation wants to prevent completely these kinds of race conditions, it can postpone the initiation of method and push transactions until the session creation process is fully complete—this is quite legal as far as the protocol peer is concerned. However, the resulting user experience may be considered unacceptably poor, if the used bearer has a very long round-trip time.

C.3 Optimizing Session Disconnection and Suspension

The protocol requires all pending method and push transactions to be aborted when a peer starts disconnecting or suspending a session. This may result in a burst of very short messages containing transaction abort PDUs being sent in addition to the actual Disconnect or Suspend PDU. However, all these PDUs are so short that typically it will be possible to concatenate them into a single transport datagram. An implementation should ensure that it is able to concatenate the PDUs at the WTP level at least in this special case, so that the impact on the network will be minimized.

C.4 Decoding the Header Encodings

WSP/B defines compact binary encodings for HTTP/1.1 headers. One method used to achieve this is the use of context information to define how a particular encoding is supposed to be interpreted, instead of encoding it explicitly. For instance, the header field name implies the format of the header field value. In a structured value, the position of each item implies its type, even if the binary encodings used to represent the values of different types may in fact be identical. The most obvious method, which an implementation can use to support this, is using a top-down strategy when parsing the header encoding.

C.5 Adding Well-known Parameters and Tokens

The header encoding defined by WSP/B imposes a strict syntax on the header field values. Within it, only such values that have been assigned well-known binary identities in advance can be encoded very compactly. If an application turns out to use token values extensively and especially parameters, which have not been foreseen, the overhead of the required textual encoding may eventually be considered prohibitive. If updating the WSP/B specification so that a new protocol version is produced is not a viable approach, then more efficient encodings can still be implemented within the WSP/B framework. The application may introduce an extension header code page, which redefines the syntax for the appropriate standard HTTP/1.1 header so that the needed new well-known values are recognized. The application peers can then use WSP/B capability negotiation to agree on using this new code page. Once this has been done, the application can modify its header processing so that the header defined on the new code page will be used instead of the standard header with the same name. The cost of shifting to the new code page should be only one extra octet, which should be more than offset by the more compact value encoding.

CHAPTER

15

Wireless Transaction Protocol Specification

1. Scope

A transaction protocol is defined to provide the services necessary for interactive "browsing" (request/response) applications. During a browsing session, the client requests information from a server, which MAY be fixed or mobile, and the server responds with the information. The request/response duo is referred to as a "transaction" in this document. The objective of the protocol is to reliably deliver the transaction while balancing the amount of reliability required for the application with the cost of delivering the reliability.

WTP runs on top a datagram service and optionally a security service. WTP has been defined as a lightweight transaction-oriented protocol that is suitable for implementation in "thin" clients (mobile stations) and operates efficiently over wireless datagram networks. The benefits of using WTP include:

- Improved reliability over datagram services. WTP relieves the upper layer from retransmissions and acknowledgments, which are necessary if datagram services are used.
- Improved efficiency over connection-oriented services. WTP has no explicit connection setup or teardown phases.
- WTP is message oriented and designed for services oriented toward transactions such as "browsing."

2. Protocol Overview

2.1 Protocol Features

The following list summarizes the features of WTP:

- Three classes of transaction service:
  - Class 0: Unreliable invoke message with no result message
  - Class 1: Reliable invoke message with no result message
  - Class 2: Reliable invoke message with exactly one reliable result message
- Reliability is achieved through the use of unique transaction identifiers, acknowledgments, duplicate removal, and retransmissions.
- No explicit connection setup or teardown phases. Explicit connection open and/or close imposes excessive overhead on the communication link.
- Optionally, user-to-user reliability. The WTP user confirms every received message.
- Optionally, the last acknowledgment of the transaction MAY contain out-of-band information related to the transaction; for example, performance measurements.
- Concatenation MAY be used, where applicable, to convey multiple Protocol Data Units in one Service Data Unit of the datagram transport.
- Message orientation. The basic unit of interchange is an entire message and not a stream of bytes.
- The protocol provides mechanisms to minimize the number of transactions being replayed as the result of duplicate packets.
- Abort of outstanding transaction, including flushing of unsent data both in client and server. The abort can be triggered by the user canceling a requested service.
- For reliable invoke messages, both success and failure is reported. If an invoke cannot be handled by the Responder, an abort message will be returned to the Initiator instead of the result.
- The protocol allows for asynchronous transactions. The Responder sends back the result as the data becomes available.

2.2 Transaction Classes

The following subsections describe the transaction classes of WTP. The WTP provider initiating a transaction is referred to as the *Initiator*. The WTP provider responding to a transaction is referred to as the *Responder*. The transaction class is set by the Initiator and indicated in the invoke message sent to the Responder. Transaction classes cannot be negotiated.

2.2.1 Class 0: Unreliable Invoke Message with No Result Message

Class 0 transactions provide an unreliable datagram service. It can be used by applications that require an "unreliable push" service. This class is intended to augment the transaction service with the capability for an application using WTP to occasionally send a datagram within the same context of an existing session using WTP. It is not intended as a primary means of sending datagrams. Applications requiring a datagram service as their primary means of data delivery SHOULD use WDP [WDP].

The basic behavior for Class 0 transactions is as follows: One invoke message is sent from the Initiator to the Responder. The Responder does not acknowledge the invoke message and the Initiator does not perform retransmissions. At the Initiator, the transaction ends when the invoke message has been sent. At the Responder, the transaction ends when the invoke has been received. The transaction is stateless and cannot be aborted.

2.2.2 Class 1: Reliable Invoke Message with No Result Message

Class 1 transactions provide a reliable datagram service. It can be used by applications that require a "reliable push" service.

The basic behavior for Class 1 transactions is as follows: One invoke message is sent from the Initiator to the Responder. The invoke message is acknowledged by the Responder. The Responder maintains state information for some time after the acknowledgment has been sent to handle possible retransmissions of the acknowledgment if it gets lost and/or the Initiator retransmits the invoke message. At the Initiator, the transaction ends when the acknowledgment has been received. The transaction can be aborted at any time.

If the User acknowledgment function is enabled, the WTP user at the Responder confirms the invoke message before the acknowledgment is sent to the Initiator.

2.2.3 Class 2: Reliable Invoke Message with One Reliable Result Message

Class 2 transactions provide the basic invoke/response transaction service. One WSP session MAY consist of several transactions of this type.

The basic behavior for Class 2 transactions is as follows: One invoke message is sent from the Initiator to the Responder. The Responder replies with exactly one result message that implicitly acknowledges the invoke message. If the Responder takes longer to service the invoke than the Responder's acknowledgment timer interval, the Responder MAY reply with a "hold on" acknowledgment before sending the result message. This prevents the Initiator from unnecessarily retransmitting the invoke message. The Responder sends the result message back to the Initiator. The result message is acknowledged by the Initiator. The Initiator maintains state information for some time after the acknowledgment has been sent. This is done in order to handle possible retransmissions of the acknowledgment if it gets lost and/or the Responder retransmits the result message. At the Responder the transaction ends when the acknowledgment has been received. The transaction can at any time be aborted.

If the User acknowledgment function is enabled, the WTP user at the Responder confirms the invoke message before the result is generated. The WTP user at the Initiator confirms the result message before the acknowledgment is sent to the Responder.

2.3 Relation to Other Protocols

This section describes how WTP relates to other WAP protocols. For a complete description of the WAP Architecture, refer to [WAP]. The following table illustrates where the services provided to the WTP user are located:

WTP USER (E.G., WSP)	
WTP	❒ Transaction handling ❒ Retransmissions, duplicate removal, acknowledgments ❒ Concatenation and separation
[WTLS]	❒ Optionally compression ❒ Optionally encryption ❒ Optionally authentication
Datagram Transport (e.g., WDP)	❒ Port number addressing ❒ Segmentation and reassembly (if provided) ❒ Error detection (if provided)
Bearer Network (e.g., IP, GSM SMS/USSD, IS-136 GUTS)	❒ Routing ❒ Device addressing (IP address, MSISDN) ❒ Segmentation and reassembly (if provided) ❒ Error detection (if provided)

WTP is specified to run over a datagram transport service. The WTP protocol data unit is located in the data portion of the datagram. Since datagrams are unreliable, WTP is required to perform retransmissions and send acknowledgment in order to provide a reliable service to the WTP user. WTP is also responsible for concatenation (if possible) of multiple protocol data units into one transport service data unit.

The datagram transport for WAP is defined in [WDP]. The datagram transport is required to route an incoming datagram to the correct WDP user. Normally, the WDP user is identified by a unique port number. Currently, no datagram port number has been allocated for WTP-WSP. The responsibility of WDP is to provide a datagram service to the WDP user, regardless of the capability of the bearer network type. Fortunately, datagram service is a common transport mechanism, and most bearer networks already provide such a service. For example, for IP-based, use UDP for this service.

The bearer network is responsible for routing datagrams to the destination device. Addressing is different depending on the type of bearer network (IP addresses or phone numbers). In addition, some networks are using dynamic allocation of addresses, and a server has to be involved to find the current address for a specific device. Network addresses within the WAP stack MAY include the bearer type and the address (e.g., IP; 123.456.789.123). The multiplexing of data to and from multiple bearer networks with different address spaces to the same WAP stack has not been specified. WAP has specified protocols above the datagram service boundary.

2.4 Security Considerations

WTP has no security mechanisms.

2.5 Management Entity

The WTP Management Entity is used as an interface between the WTP layer and the environment of the device. The WTP Management Entity provides information to the WTP layer about changes in the devices environment, which MAY impact the correct operation of WTP.

The WTP protocol is designed around an assumption that the environment in which it is operating is capable of transmitting and receiving data. For example, this assumption includes the following basic capabilities that MUST be provided by the mobile device:

- The mobile is within a coverage area applicable to the bearer service being invoked.
- The mobile has sufficient power and the power is on.
- Sufficient resources (processing and memory) within the mobile are available to WTP.
- The WTP protocol is correctly configured.
- The user is willing to receive/transmit data.

The WTP Management Entity monitors the state of the preceding services/capabilities of the mobile's environment and would notify the WTP layer if one or more of the assumed services were not available. For example, if the mobile roamed out of coverage for a bearer service, the Bearer Management Entity SHOULD report to the WTP Management Entity that transmission/reception over that bearer is no longer possible. In turn, the WTP Management Entity would indicate to the WTP layer to close all active connections over that bearer. Other examples such as low battery power would be handled in a similar way by the WTP Management Entity.

In addition to monitoring the state of the mobile environment, the WTP Management Entity MAY be used as the interface to the user for setting various configuration parameters used by WTP, such as device address. It could also be used to implement functions available to the user such as a "drop all data connections" feature. In general, the WTP Management Entity will deal with all issues related to initialization, configuration, dynamic reconfiguration, and resources as they pertain to the WTP layer.

Since the WTP Management Entity MUST interact with various components of a mobile device that are manufacturer specific, the design and implementation of the

WTP Management Entity is considered outside the scope of the WTP Specification and is an implementation issue.

2.6 Static WTP Conformance Clause

This static conformance clause defines a minimum set of WTP features that can be implemented to ensure that the implementation will be able to interoperate.

The features needed from WTP are dictated by the WTP user. In the case when WSP is the WTP user, it also depends on whether the WSP protocol operates as a client or as a server. In Table 15.1, Mandatory (M) and Optional (O) features of WTP are listed in the case when WSP is the user.

Table 15.1 WTP Static Conformance Clause when WSP Is the User

FUNCTION	TYPE	WSP CLIENT	WSP SERVER
Transaction Class 0	Initiate Respond	M M	M M
Transaction Class 1	Initiate Respond	M M	M M
Transaction Class 2	Initiate Respond	M O	O M
User acknowledgment		M	M
Concatenation		O	O
Separation		M	M
Retransmission until acknowledgment		M	M
Transaction abort		M	M
Version handling		M	M
Error handling		M	M
Information in last acknowledgment		M	M
Asynchronous transactions		O	O
Transaction identifier verification	Initiate Respond	O M	O M
Transport information items	Error Info Option PSN	M M O O	M M O O
Segmentation and reassembly with selective retransmission and packet groups		O	O

If the WTP provider is requested to execute a procedure it does not support, the transaction MUST be aborted with the an appropriate error code. For example, if a Responder that does not support Class 2 receives a Class 2 transaction, it aborts the transaction with the NOTIMPLEMENTEDCL2 abort code.

Segmentation and reassembly (SAR) and selective retransmission MAY be implemented in order to enhance the WTP service. If SAR is not implemented in WTP, this functionality should be provided by another layer in the stack. For example, in IS-136 the SSAR layer handles SAR; in an IP network IP [RFC791] handles SAR; and for GSM SMS/USSD, SAR is achieved by using SMS concatenation [GSM0340]. The motivation for implementing WTP SAR is the selective retransmission procedure, which MAY, if large messages are sent, improve the over-the-air efficiency of the protocol.

Whether WTP SAR is supported or not is indicated by the Initiator when the transaction is invoked. Table 15.2 shows how WTP Initiators and Responders SHOULD guarantee interoperability between WTP providers that have and those that have not implemented WTP SAR.

Note: If a Responder not supporting WTP SAR receives a nonsegmented message from an Initiator that supports WTP SAR, there is no need to abort the transaction. The Initiator will never be aware of the fact that the Responder does not support WTP SAR.

2.7 Other WTP Users

The intended use of this protocol is to provide WSP [WSP] with a reliable transaction service over an unreliable datagram service. However, the protocol can be used by other applications with similar communication needs.

Table 15.2 Interoperability between WTP Providers with and without WTP SAR

	INITIATOR	
RESPONDER	WTP SAR	NOT WTP SAR
WTP SAR	Full interoperability	Responder MUST NOT respond with a WTP segmented message
Not WTP SAR	Responder abort transaction with the abort code NOTIMPLEMENTEDSAR Initiator MUST resend the transaction without using WTP SAR	Full interoperability

3. Elements for Layer-to-Layer Communication

3.1 Notations Used

3.1.1 Definition of Service Primitives and Parameters

Communications between layers and between entities within the layer are accomplished by means of service primitives. Service primitives represent, in an abstract way, the logical exchange of information and control between the Transaction layer and adjacent layers. They do not specify or constrain implementations.

Service primitives consist of commands and their respective responses associated with the services requested of another layer. The general syntax of a primitive is

X - Generic name . Type (Parameters)

where X designates the layer providing the service. For this specification, X is

"TR" for the Transaction layer.

An example of a service primitive for the WTP layer would be TR-Invoke Request.

Service primitives are not the same as an Application Programming Interface (API) and are not meant to imply any specific method of implementing an API. Service primitives are an abstract means of illustrating the services provided by the protocol layer to the layer above. The mapping of these concepts to a real API and the semantics associated with a real API are an implementation issue and are beyond the scope of this specification.

3.1.2 Primitives Types

The primitives types defined in this specification are listed in the following table:

TYPE	ABBREVIATION	DESCRIPTION
Request	req	Used when a higher layer is requesting a service from the next lower layer.
Indication	ind	A layer providing a service uses this primitive type to notify the next higher layer of activities related to the peer (such as the invocation of the request primitive) or to the provider of the service (such as a protocol generated event).
Response	res	A layer uses the response primitive type to acknowledge receipt of the indication primitive type from the next lower layer.
Confirm	cnf	The layer providing the requested service uses the confirm primitive type to report that the activity has been completed successfully.

3.1.3 Service Parameter Tables

The service primitives are defined using tables indicating which parameters are possible and how they are used with the different primitive types. For example, a simple confirmed primitive might be defined using the following:

PRIMITIVE	TR-PRIMITIVE			
PARAMETER	*REQ*	*IND*	*RES*	*CNF*
Parameter 1	M	M(=)	-	-
Parameter 2	-	-	O	C(=)

In the preceding table, *Parameter 1* is always present in *TR-primitive.request* and corresponding *TR-primitive.indication*. *Parameter 2* MAY be specified in *TR-primitive .response,* and in that case it MUST be present and have the equivalent value also in the corresponding *TR-primitive.confirm*; otherwise, it MUST NOT be present.

If some primitive type is not possible, the column for it will be omitted. The entries used in the primitive type columns are defined in Table 15.3.

3.2 Requirements on the Underlying Layer

The WTP protocol is specified to run on top of a datagram service. The datagram service MUST handle the following functions:

- Port numbers to route the incoming datagram to the WTP layer
- Length information for the SDU passed up to the WTP layer

The datagram service MAY handle the following functions:

- Error detection. For example, by using a checksum.

Table 15.3 Parameter Usage Legend

M	Presence of the parameter is mandatory—it MUST be present.
C	Presence of the parameter is conditional depending on values of other parameters.
O	Presence of the parameter is a user option; it MAY be omitted.
P	Presence of the parameter is a service provider option; an implementation MAY not provide it.
ñ	The parameter is absent.
*	Presence of the parameter is determined by the lower layer protocol.
(=)	The value of the parameter is identical to the value of the corresponding parameter of the preceding service primitive.

In addition, Segmentation And Reassembly (SAR) is expected to be provided by the underlying layers. However, it is usually done at a layer below the datagram layer. For example, in an IP network, the IP protocol handles SAR.

3.3 Services Provided to Upper Layer

3.3.1 TR-Invoke

This primitive is used to initiate a new transaction.

PRIMITIVE	TR-INVOKE			
PARAMETER	***REQ***	***IND***	***RES***	***CNF***
Source Address	M	M (=)		
Source Port	M	M (=)		
Destination Address	M	M (=)		
Destination Port	M	M (=)		
Ack-Type	M	M (=)		
User Data	O	C (=)		
Class Type	M	M (=)		
Exit Info			O	C (=)
Handle	M	M	M	M

3.3.1.1 Source Address

The source address is the unique address of the device making a request to the WTP layer. The source address MAY be an MSISDN number, IP address, X.25 address, or other identifier.

3.3.1.2 Source Port

The source port number associated with the source address.

3.3.1.3 Destination Address

The destination address of the user data submitted to the WTP layer. The destination address MAY be an MSISDN number, IP address, X.25 address, or other identifier.

3.3.1.4 Destination Port

The destination port number associated with the destination address for the requested or existing transaction.

3.3.1.5 Ack-Type

This parameter is used to turn the User acknowledgment function on or off.

3.3.1.6 User Data

The user data carried by the WTP protocol. The unit of data submitted to or received from the WTP layer is also referred to as the *Service Data Unit*. This is the complete unit (message) of data that the higher layer has submitted to the WTP layer for transmission. The WTP layer will transmit the Service Data Unit and deliver it to its destination without any manipulation of its content.

3.3.1.7 Class Type

Indicates the WTP transaction class.

3.3.1.8 Exit Info

Additional user data to be sent to the originator on transaction completion.

3.3.1.9 Handle

The transaction handle is an index returned to the higher layer so the higher layer can identify the transaction and associate the data received with an active transaction. The TR-Handle uniquely identifies a transaction. TR-Handle is an alias for the source address, source port, destination address, and destination port of the transaction.

The TR-Handle has local significance only.

3.3.2 TR-Result

This primitive is used to send back a result of a previously initiated transaction.

PRIMITIVE	TR-RESULT			
PARAMETER	***REQ***	***IND***	***RES***	***CNF***
User Data	O	C (=)		
Exit Info			O	C (=)
Handle	M	M	M	M

3.3.3 TR-Abort

This primitive is used to abort an existing transaction.

PRIMITIVE	TR-ABORT	
PARAMETER	***REQ***	***IND***
Abort Code	O	C (=)
Handle	M	M

3.3.3.1 Abort Code

The abort code indicates the reason for the transaction being aborted. This can include abort codes generated by the WTP protocol and user-defined local abort codes.

4. Classes of Operation

4.1 Class 0 Transaction

4.1.1 Motivation

Class 0 is an unreliable datagram service. It can be used by WSP [WSP], for example, to make an unreliable "push" within a session using the same socket association.

This class is intended to augment the transaction service with the capability for an application using WTP to occasionally send a datagram within the same context of an existing session using WTP. It is not intended as a primary means of sending datagrams. Applications requiring a datagram service SHOULD use WDP as defined in [WDP].

4.1.2 Protocol Data Units

The following PDU is used:

1. Invoke PDU

4.1.3 Procedure

A Class 0 transaction is initiated by the WTP user by issuing the TR-Invoke request primitive with the Transaction Class parameter set to Class 0. The WTP provider sends the invoke message and becomes the Initiator of the transaction. The remote WTP provider receives the invoke message and becomes the Responder of the transaction. The Initiator does not wait for or expect a response. If the invoke message is received by the Responder, it is accepted immediately. There is no duplicate removal or verification procedure performed. However, the client MUST increment the TID counter between each transaction, but the server MUST NOT update its cached TID.

This transaction class MUST be supported by the WTP provider. The WTP provider MUST be able to act as both Initiator and Responder.

4.2 Class 1 Transaction

4.2.1 Motivation

The Class 1 transaction is a reliable invoke message without any result message. This type of transaction can be used by WSP [WSP] to realize a reliable "push" service.

4.2.2 Service Primitive Sequences

Table 15.4 describes legal service primitive sequences. A primitive listed in the column header MAY only be followed by primitives listed in the row headers that are marked with an "X".

Table 15.4 Primitive Sequence Table for Transaction Class 1

	TR-INVOKE				TR-ABORT	
	REQ	*IND*	*RES*	*CNF*	*REQ*	*IND*
TR-Invoke.req						
TR-Invoke.ind						
TR-Invoke.res		X				
TR-Invoke.cnf	X					
TR-Abort.req	X	X	X			
TR-Abort.ind	X	X	X			

4.2.3 Protocol Data Units

The following PDUs are used:

1. Invoke PDU
2. Ack PDU

4.2.4 Procedure

A Class 1 transaction is initiated by the WTP user by issuing the TR-Invoke request primitive with the Transaction Class parameter set to Class 1. The WTP provider sends the invoke message and becomes the Initiator of the transaction. The remote WTP provider receives the invoke message and becomes the Responder of the transaction. The Responder checks the Transaction Identifier and determines whether a verification has to be initiated. If not, it delivers the message to the user and returns the last acknowledgment to the Initiator. The Responder MUST keep state information in order to retransmit the last acknowledgment if it gets lost.

This transaction class MUST be supported by the WTP provider. The WTP provider MUST be able to act as both Initiator and Responder.

4.3 Class 2 Transaction

4.3.1 Motivation

The Class 2 transaction is the basic request/response transaction service. This is the most commonly used transaction service. For example, it is used by WSP [WSP] for method invocations.

4.3.2 Service Primitive Sequences

Table 15.5 describes legal service primitive sequences. A primitive listed in the column header MAY only be followed by primitives listed in the row header that are marked with an "X".

4.3.3 Protocol Data Units

The following PDUs are used:

1. Invoke PDU
2. Result PDU
3. Ack PDU
4. Abort PDU

4.3.4 Procedure

A Class 2 transaction is initiated by the WTP user by issuing the TR-Invoke request primitive with the Transaction Class parameter set to Class 2. The WTP provider sends the invoke message and becomes the Initiator of the transaction. The remote WTP provider receives the invoke message and becomes the Responder of the transaction. The Responder checks the Transaction Identifier and determines whether a verification has to be initiated. If not, it delivers the message to the WTP user and waits for the result. The Responder MAY send a hold on acknowledgment after a specified time.

Table 15.5 Primitive Sequence Table for Transaction Class 2

	TR-INVOKE				TR-RESULT				TR-ABORT	
	REQ	IND	RES	CNF	REQ	IND	RES	CNF	REQ	IND
TR-Invoke.req										
TR-Invoke.ind										
TR-Invoke.res		X								
TR-Invoke.cnf	X									
TR-Result.req		X*	X							
TR-Result.ind	X*			X						
TR-Result.res						X				
TR-Result.cnf					X					
TR-Abort.req	X	X	X	X	X	X	X			
TR-Abort.ind	X	X	X	X	X	X	X			

* = NOT valid if User acknowledgment is used.

The WTP user sends the result message by issuing the TR-Result request primitive. When the Initiator has received the result message it returns the last acknowledgment to the Responder. The Initiator MUST keep state information in order to retransmit the last acknowledgment if it gets lost.

If the Responder does not support this transaction class it returns an Abort PDU with the abort reason NOTIMPLEMENTEDCL2 as a response to the invoke message.

5. Protocol Features

5.1 Message Transfer

5.1.1 Description

WTP consists of two types of messages: *data messages* and *control messages*. Data messages carry user data. Control messages are used for acknowledgments, error reporting, and so forth, and do not carry user data. This section gives the reader an overall picture of how transactions are realized by WTP. The procedures to guarantee reliable message transfer are outlined. Special functions like concatenation and separation, retransmission until acknowledgment, transaction abort, user acknowledgment, and others are described in further detail in separate sections.

It is important to note that not all messages and functions are used by all transaction classes. Table 15.6 illustrates which messages are used for the different transaction classes.

Note 1: Only sent in the case when the user takes longer to service the invoke message than the Responder's acknowledgment timer interval.

Note 2: The Class 0 transaction is unreliable. No response is expected from the Responder and no verification is performed.

5.1.2 Service Primitives

The following service primitives are used during nominal WTP transactions. Their use is transaction-class dependent.

1. TR-Invoke
2. TR-Result

Table 15.6 Summary of WTP Message Transfer

MESSAGE/FUNCTION	CLASS 2	CLASS 1	CLASS 0
Invoke message	X	X	X (Note 2)
Verification	X	X	
Hold on acknowledgment	X (Note 1)		
Result message	X		
Last acknowledgment	X	X	

5.1.3 Transport Protocol Data Units

The following PDUs are used during nominal WTP transactions. It is important to note that not all PDUs are used in every transaction class.

1. Invoke PDU
2. Result PDU
3. Ack PDU

5.1.4 Timer Intervals and Counters

The following timer intervals and counters are used during a nominal WTP transaction. Their use is transaction-class dependent.

1. Retransmission interval
2. Retransmission counter
3. Acknowledgment interval
4. Wait timeout interval

The values and relations between timer intervals and counters MAY depend on the transaction class being used.

5.1.5 Procedure

A transaction takes place between two WTP providers. A WTP user initiates a transaction by issuing the TR-Invoke request primitive. The TCL parameter of the primitive indicates the transaction class: 0, 1, or 2. In WTP, the Initiator is the WTP provider initiating the transaction and the Responder is the WTP provider responding to the initiated transaction.

5.1.5.1 Invoke Message

The invoke message is always the first message of a transaction and it is sent using the Invoke PDU. The Initiator administers the Transaction Identifier (TID) by incrementing the TID by 1 for every initiated transaction. The TID is conveyed in every PDU belonging to the transaction. When the Invoke PDU has been sent, the Initiator starts the retransmission timer and waits for a response. When the Responder receives the Invoke PDU with a valid TID, it delivers the message to the user by generating the TR-Invoke indication primitive.

5.1.5.2 Verification

When the Responder has received and accepted the invoke message, it SHOULD cache the TID. This is done in order to filter out duplicate and old invoke messages that have lower or identical TID values (see Section 5.8, *Transaction Identifier*). If the Responder determines the TID in the Invoke PDU is invalid, the Responder can verify whether the invoke message is a new or delayed message. This is accomplished by sending an Ack

PDU, which initiates a three-way handshake towards the Initiator (see Section 8.5, *TID Verification*). In this case, the Responder MUST NOT deliver the data to the user until the three-way handshake is successfully completed. If the three-way handshake attempt fails, the transaction is aborted by the Initiator.

5.1.5.3 Hold On Acknowledgment

When the invoke message has been delivered to the WTP user, the acknowledgment timer is started. If the WTP user requires more time to service the invoke message than the acknowledgment timer interval, the Responder MAY or SHOULD or MUST send a "hold on" acknowledgment. This is done to prevent the Initiator from retransmitting the Invoke PDU. When the Initiator receives the Ack PDU, it stops retransmitting the Invoke PDU and generates the TR-Invoke confirm primitive.

5.1.5.4 Result Message

Upon assembling the data, the WTP user sends a result message by initiating the TR-Result request primitive. The result message is transmitted using the Result PDU. When the Result PDU has been sent, the Responder starts the retransmission timer and waits for a response. After the Result PDU is received by the Initiator, it generates the TR-Invoke confirm primitive if one has not already been issued and the forwards up the TR-Result indication primitive.

5.1.5.5 Last Acknowledgment

The last Ack PDU is sent when the last message of the transaction has been received. The sender of the acknowledgment MUST maintain state information required to handle a retransmission of the previous message. This can be done by using a wait timer or by keeping a transaction history that indicates the results of past transactions.

5.2 Retransmission Until Acknowledgment

5.2.1 Motivation

The retransmission until acknowledgment procedure is used to guarantee reliable transfer of data from one WTP provider to another in the event of packet loss. To minimize the number of packets sent over the air, WTP uses implicit acknowledgments wherever possible. An example of this is the use of the Result message to implicitly acknowledge the Invoke message.

5.2.2 Transport Protocol Data Units

The following PDUs are used:

1. Invoke PDU
2. Result PDU
3. Ack PDU

5.2.3 Timer Intervals and Counters

The following timer intervals and counters are used:

1. Retransmission interval
2. Retransmission counter

The values and relationships between timers and counters MAY depend on the transaction class being used. A detailed description of timers and counters is provided in Section 7.4.

5.2.4 Procedure

When a packet has been sent, the retransmission timer is started and the retransmission counter is set to 0. If a response has not been received when the retransmission timer expires, the retransmission counter is incremented by 1, the packet retransmitted, and the retransmission timer restarted. The WTP provider continues to retransmit until the number of retransmissions has exceeded the maximum retransmission value. If no acknowledgment has been received when the retransmission counter is fully incremented and the timer expires, the transaction is terminated and the local WTP user is informed.

The first time a PDU is transmitted, the retransmission indicator (RID) field in the header is clear. For all retransmissions, the RID field is set. Other than the RID field, the WTP provider MUST NOT change any fields in the PDU header.

The motivation for the retransmission indicator is for the receiver to detect messages that have been duplicated by the network. A WTP provider that receives two identical messages with the RID set to 0 can safely ignore the second message because it must have been duplicated by the network. Any subsequent retransmissions that have the RID flag set to 1 cannot be ignored by the receiver. Retransmitted messages that gets duplicated by the network must be treated as valid messages by the provider. The receiver in this situation can no longer distinguish between provider retransmissions and network duplicated packets. In this case, if the message is an Invoke PDU, there is a risk that the transaction will be replayed. To avoid such an error, the WTP provider should make a TID validation.

5.3 User Acknowledgment

5.3.1 Motivation

The User Acknowledgment function allows for the WTP user to confirm every message received by the WTP provider.

When this function is enabled, the WTP provider does not respond to a received message until after the WTP user has confirmed the indication service primitive (by issuing the response primitive). If the WTP user does not confirm the indication primitive after a specified time, the transaction is aborted by the provider. Note that this is a much stronger form of a confirmed service than the traditional definition [ISO8509]. The traditional definition of a confirmed service is that there is a confirmation from the service provider; however, there is not necessarily any relationship to a response from the peer service user. In WTP, when the User Acknowledgment function is used, the service provider requires a response from the service user for each indication. As a result, when the confirmation primitive is generated, there is a guarantee that there was a response from the peer service user.

This function is optional within WTP; however, WSP does utilize the User Acknowledgment feature. Therefore any implementation of WTP that will have WSP as the higher layer must implement it. WSP requires a feature that at the end of a request-response transaction, the server gets a positive indication that the client has processed the response. This is illustrated in Figure 15.1.

In this model, the *Acknowledgment* is used to convey the fact that the response was received and processed by the client application. It is important to note that the *Client* and the *Server* in the figure refer to the client and server *Application*, and not only the protocol stack.

When the User Acknowledgment function is used, the WSP-WTP primitive sequence for a Class 2 transaction becomes as illustrated in Figure 15.2.

The primitive sequence started by the *S-Reply.res* and *TR-Result.res* primitives realizes the *Complete* and *Confirm* primitives from Figure 15.1. If the application and/or the WSP for some reason does not issue these primitives, WTP aborts the transaction with the NORESPONSE reason. The abort is used by the WSP server as an indication that the result was not properly received or processed by the client.

The primitive sequence started by the *S-Method.res* and *TR-Invoke.res* primitives can be used by the client WSP to indicate to the application (and human user) that the invoke message has been received by the server WSP.

When this function is not used, WTP MAY acknowledge received messages independently of the WTP user. In Figure 15.2 this means that the response primitives MAY be ignored by the WTP provider. Put in other words, the WTP provider receives a message, returns an acknowledgment, and indicates to the user that a message has been received. If there is an error, the transaction will be aborted by the WTP provider. If the WTP user is alive but cannot process the message, it MAY abort the transaction with an appropriate abort reason.

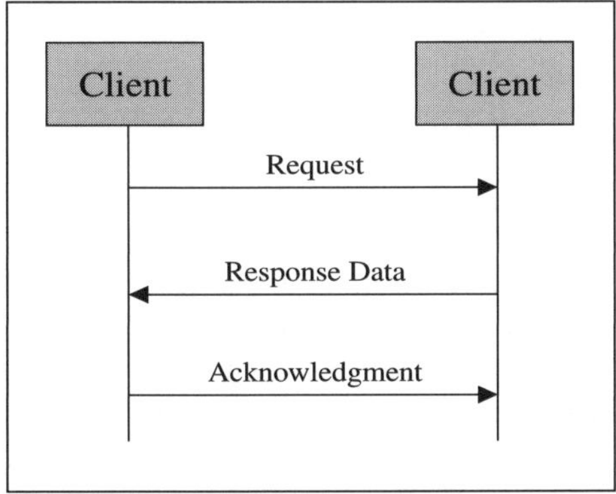

Figure 15.1 Generic WSP [WSP] transaction.

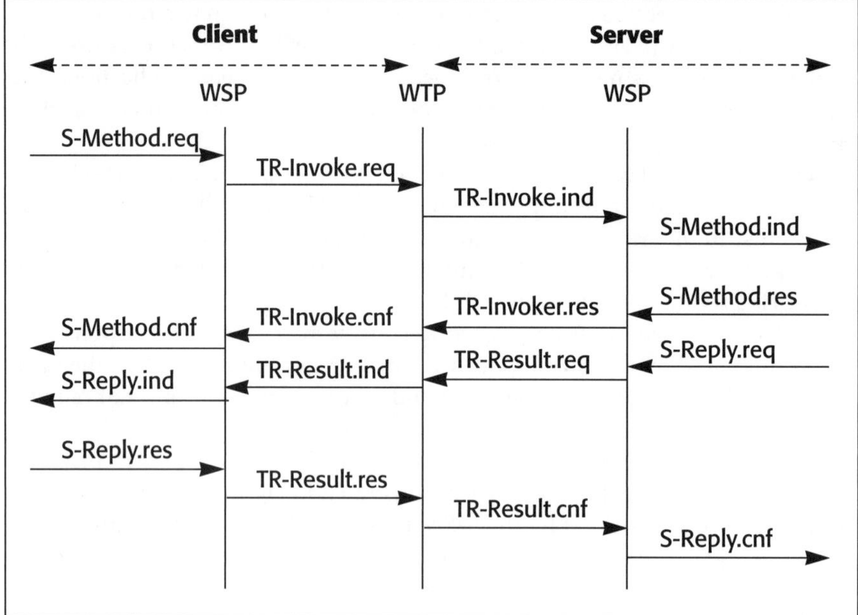

Figure 15.2 WSP-WTP primitive sequence for request-response.

This function is optional. It applies to transaction Classes 1 and 2.

Note: Even though the WTP user has issued a response primitive, there is no guarantee that it has interpreted the data and started processing. The WTP user MAY have only copied the data from one buffer to another, or issued the response primitive without any action taken at all. A WTP user can always abort a transaction if it discovers that the received data is corrupt or for some other reason not possible to process (see Section 5.7, *Transaction Abort*).

5.3.2 Protocol Data Units

The following PDUs are used:

1. Invoke PDU
2. Abort PDU

5.3.3 Procedure

The Initiator sets the U/P-flag in the Invoke PDU to indicate that User acknowledgment is required. A Responder not supporting this function aborts the transaction with the abort reason NOTIMPLEMENTEDUACK. The Initiator MAY then make the decision to reinitiate the transaction without the User acknowledgment function.

When the Responder receives the Invoke PDU with the U/P-flag set, it generates the TR-Invoke indication and starts the acknowledgment timer. To give the WTP user time to read the parameters in the indication primitive and issue the TR-Invoke response primitive, the value of the timer MAY have a higher value than the provider's acknowledgment timer (see Appendix A). The Responder MUST NOT return a response before the WTP user has issued the TR-Invoke response primitive. If the Initiator retransmits Invoke PDUs due to lack of acknowledgment, the Responder MUST silently discard the PDU and restart the acknowledgment timer. When the WTP user issues the TR-Invoke response primitive, the Responder is enabled to send the Ack PDU. If the TR-Invoke response primitive has not been issued after a specified time, the provider aborts the transaction with the abort reason NORESPONSE. If the WTP user issues the TR-Result request primitive, the result is sent instead of the acknowledgment. The Initiator receiving the Ack PDU generates the confirm primitive, which indicates that the remote WTP user has issued the corresponding response primitive.

For Class 2 transactions, if the Initiator has indicated that the User Acknowledgment function shall be used, it is valid for the entire transaction. This means that when the Initiator has received the result and generated the TR-Result indication primitive, it MUST wait for the TR-Result response primitive from the WTP user before the last acknowledgment can be sent. If the TR-Result response primitive has not been issued after a specified time, the provider aborts the transaction with the abort reason NORESPONSE. When the Responder receives the NORESPONSE abort, it generates the TR-Abort indication primitive, indicating to the WTP user that the transaction failed.

5.4 Information in Last Acknowledgment

5.4.1 Motivation

The WTP user is allowed to attach information in the last, and only the last, acknowledgment of a transaction. This function is meant for transporting small amounts of information related to the transaction. The information can be, for example, performance measurements collected in order to evaluate the user's perceived quality of service.

For Class 2 transactions, this function can be used by the Initiator to communicate some information back to the Responder. For a Class 1 transaction, this function can be used by the Responder to communicate some information to the Initiator.

5.4.2 Service Primitives

The following service primitives and parameters are used:

1. TR-Result.res (Class 2)
2. TR-Invoke.res (Class 1)

5.4.3 Protocol Data Units

The following PDU is used:

1. Ack PDU

5.4.4 Procedure

For a Class 2 transaction, information is attached to the last acknowledgment by issuing the TR-Result response primitive with the ExitInfo parameter.

For a Class 1 transaction, information is attached to the last acknowledgment by issuing the TR-Invoke response primitive with the ExitInfo parameter.

The exit information is transferred as a Transport Information Item (TPI) in the variable part of the Ack PDU header.

For Class 2 transactions, the ExitInfo parameter MUST NOT be included in the TR-Invoke response primitive, and the Info TPI MUST NOT be included in the Ack PDU that acknowledges the Invoke PDU.

5.5 Concatenation and Separation

5.5.1 Motivation

Concatenation is the procedure to convey multiple WTP Protocol Data Units (PDUs) in one Service Data Unit (SDU) of the bearer network. When concatenation is done, a special mapping of the WTP PDUs to the SDUs is used.

Separation is the procedure to extract multiple PDUs from one SDU. When the PDUs have been separated they are dispatched to the transactions.

Concatenation and separation is used to provide over-the-air efficiency, since fewer transmissions over the air are required.

5.5.2 Procedure

Concatenation can only be done for messages with the same address information (source and destination port, source and destination device address).

Concatenation of PDU from different transactions can be done at any time. For example, the last acknowledgment of one transaction can be concatenated with the invoke message of the next transaction. Concatenation and separation is performed outside the WTP state machine.

The exact implementation of concatenation is not specified. Only the structure to be used when multiple packets are concatenated is specified. Exactly how the packets are buffered and concatenated is an implementation issue.

5.6 Asynchronous Transactions

5.6.1 Motivation

The implementation of the WTP provider SHOULD be able to initiate multiple transactions before it receives the response to the first transaction. Multiple transactions SHOULD be handled asynchronously. For example, the responses to transaction number 1, 2, and 3 MAY arrive to the Initiator as 3, 1, and 2. The Responder SHOULD send back the result as soon as it is ready, independently of other transactions.

The maximum number of outstanding transactions at any moment is limited by the maximum number of Transaction Identifiers. The Transaction Identifier is 16 bits, but the high-order bit is used to indicate the direction of the message, so the maximum number of outstanding transactions is 2**15. The implementation environment will also set a limit to how many outstanding transactions it can handle simultaneously.

5.7 Transaction Abort

5.7.1 Motivation

An outstanding transaction can be aborted by the WTP user by issuing the TR-Abort request primitive. The user abort can be triggered by the application (e.g., input from human user) or it can be a negative result (e.g., the WTP user could not generate a result due to an error).

An outstanding transaction can also be aborted by the WTP provider due to a protocol error (e.g., reject the received data) or if a requested function is not implemented.

This function MUST be used with care. If the invoke message has already been sent, the response message MAY be on its way to the client and an abort will only increase network load.

5.7.2 Transport Protocol Data Units

The following PDU is used:

1. Abort PDU

5.7.3 Service Primitives

The following service primitive is used:

1. TR-Abort

5.7.4 Procedure

There are three special cases of the abort procedure:

A) The sending WTP provider has not yet sent the message; the provider MUST discard the message from its memory.

B) The sending WTP provider has sent the message to the peer or is in the process of sending the message; the provider MUST send the Abort PDU to the remote peer to discard all data associated with the transaction.

C) The receiving provider receives the Abort PDU; it generates the TR-Abort indication primitive and discards all transaction data.

When an Abort PDU is sent the reason for the abort is indicated in the abort reason field. There are two main types of aborts: User abort (USER) and Provider abort (PROVIDER). The user abort occurs when the WTP user has issued the TR-Abort request primitive. The provider abort occurs when there is an error in the WTP provider.

5.8 Transaction Identifier

5.8.1 Motivation

A transaction is uniquely identified by the socket pair (source address, source port, destination address, and destination port) and the Transaction Identifier (TID). The Initiator increments the TID by 1 for every initiated transaction. This means that TIDs 1, 2, and 3 can go to server A; TIDs 4, 5, and 6 to server B; and TIDs 7, 8, and 9 to server A.

The main use of the TID is to identify messages belonging to the same transaction. When a message is retransmitted, the TID is reused for the retransmitted messages. A Responder MAY choose to remember the TID after an invoke message has been accepted and force TID verification in order to avoid replaying transactions. Also, the Initiator increments the TID by 1 for each transaction. This information can be used by the Responder to filter out new invoke messages from old and duplicated invoke messages; a new invoke always has a higher TID value.

Since transactions can be initiated simultaneously from both directions on the same socket association, the high-order bit of the TID is used to indicate the direction of the transaction. The Initiator sets the high-order bit to 0 in the Invoke PDU. Thereafter, the high-order bit is always inverted in the received TID before it is added to the response packet. By setting the high-order bit of the TID field to 0 at the Initiator and 1 at the Responder, the Initiator can be guaranteed that the allocated TID will not collide with the remote entity.

The TID is 16 bits but the high-order bit is used to indicate the direction. This means that the TID space is 2**15. The TID is an unsigned integer.

5.8.2 Procedure at the Responder

5.8.2.1 Variables

If the Responder caches old TID values for each different Initiator, the old TID value is called LastTID. The TID in the received invoke message is called RcvTID.

5.8.2.2 Decisions When Receiving a New Invoke Message

When the Responder receives an invoke message, it takes one of the actions listed in Table 15.7 (depending on whether the Responder is caching old TID values or not), the characteristics of the underlying transport, and the outcome of the TID test (described in the following chapter).

Note 1: This is the case, for example, if a Security layer is located under WTP and can remove duplicates.

Note 2: This is not very efficient and SHOULD be avoided.

5.8.2.3 The TID Test

One method of validating the TID is to use a window mechanism. The Responder MAY cache the last valid TID (LastTID) from each different Initiator. When the Responder receives a new invoke message, it compares the TID in the invoke message (RcvTID) with the cached one. Let W be the size of the window. If W=2**14, it means that the boundary between two TID values occurs when they differ by 2**14; that is, half the TID space.

Table 15.7 Decisions When Receiving New Invoke Message

EVENT	CONDITION	ACTION
TID test Fail	Underlying transport service can guarantee there are no duplicates (Note 1).	Start transaction
	Underlying transport service CANNOT guarantee there are no duplicates.	Invoke TID verification
TID test Ok		LastTID = RcvTID Start transaction
TIDnew flag set		LastTID = 0 Invoke TID verification
No cache	Responder caches the TID for each Initiator for the Maximum Packet Lifetime (MPL) of the network and it has not been rebooted during this time period and lost the information. If the invoke was not a new one, the Responder would have had the latest TID in its cache.	Create new record for this Initiator LastTID = RcvTID Start transaction
	Responder does not cache TIDs (Note 2).	Invoke TID verification

Tables 15.8 and 15.9 show different results from the TID test. If the test succeeds, it is guaranteed that the received invoke message is new and not an old delayed one. This is under the assumption that all messages have a Maximum Packet Lifetime (MPL), and that after MPL seconds it is guaranteed that there are no duplicate messages present in the network (see Note). Furthermore, it is assumed that the TID is not incremented faster than 2**14 steps in 2*MPL.

Table 15.8 TID Test; RcvTID >= LastTID

<table>
<tr><th colspan="2">RCVTID >= LASTTID</th></tr>
<tr><th>| RCVTID - LASTTID |</th><th>TID TEST</th></tr>
<tr><td>0</td><td>Fail</td></tr>
<tr><td><= W</td><td>Ok</td></tr>
<tr><td>> W</td><td>Fail</td></tr>
</table>

Table 15.9 TID Test; RcvTID < LastTID

<table>
<tr><th colspan="2">RCVTID < LASTTID</th></tr>
<tr><th>| RCVTID - LASTTID |</th><th>TID TEST</th></tr>
<tr><td>< W</td><td>Fail</td></tr>
<tr><td>>= W</td><td>Ok</td></tr>
</table>

Note: For some network types, the average Maximum Packet Lifetime MAY have a very high variance. For example, in a store-and-forward network like GSM SMS, a short message MAY reside in the SMS-C for a very long time before it gets delivered to the destination. This fact MAY in some cases violate the correctness of the TID validation.

5.8.2.4 Reception of Out-of-Order Invoke Messages

Messages can arrive out of order. This means that even if the Initiator increments the TID by 1 for each transaction, a transaction with a lower TID value can arrive after a TID with a higher value. This MAY cause the TID test to fail and a TID verification to be started. This will not break the protocol; however, it will lead to degraded performance. One way to overcome this is to keep an array of TID values for past transactions. If the received TID is not in the array, it can be accepted without any TID verification. This solution improves performance but requires the Responder to maintain more information.

5.8.3 Procedure at the Initiator

5.8.3.1 Administration of TID

The Initiator is responsible for incrementing the TID by 1 for each transaction. This MUST NOT be done faster than 2**14 steps in 2*MPL.

5.8.3.2 Violating the Monotonic Property of the TID

There are cases when the Initiator MAY generate nonmonotonic TID values; that is, the next TID MAY be smaller than the previous:

1. The Initiator has crashed and rebooted and randomly picked a smaller TID value than the previous.
2. The TID values have wrapped around the finite space. This can happen if, for example, the Initiator sends a transaction to Responder A, then sends 2**14 transactions to Responder B, and finally returns to Responder A. The cached TID value at Responder A for this Initiator will now be smaller than current TID.

Neither of these two cases will break the protocol. However, TID verifications will be invoked and that will lead to lower efficiency.

In (1), if the Responder discards cached TID values after MPL seconds and the time to reboot takes longer than that, the Responder will accept the new TID value without a TID verification. We have assumed that it will take longer time than 2*MPL to increment the TID 2**14 steps. However, if the Responder caches the TID value longer than for MPL seconds, it will initiate a TID verification in this case.

The wraparound in (2) will be detected only if the Initiator caches the last sent TID to each Responder.

In both (1) and (2), excessive use of the TID verification mechanism SHOULD be avoided by setting the TIDnew flag in the Invoke PDU. This will invalidate the Responder's cached TID for the Initiator. When the Initiator uses the TIDnew flag, it MUST NOT initiate any subsequent transaction until the TID verification has been completed. The reason for this is that the TIDnew MAY be delayed in the network. If, during that time period, transactions with higher TID are initiated, duplicates from these will get erroneously accepted when Responder has updated its cache with the lower TID in the TIDnew packet.

5.9 Transaction Identifier Verification

5.9.1 Motivation

The transaction identifier verification procedure is a three-way handshake. A three-way handshake between an Initiator (I) and a Responder (R) has the following steps:

1. I → R This is the TID. (Invoke PDU)
2. I ← R Do you have an outstanding transaction with this TID? (Ack PDU)
3. I → R Yes/No! (Ack PDU / Abort PDU)

The TID verification procedure is necessary to guarantee that the same invoke message is not accepted and delivered to the WTP user more than once, due to old duplicate packets.

The invoke message MUST NOT be delivered to the user before the TID verification procedure is completed successfully.

5.9.2 Protocol Data Units

The following PDUs are used:

1. Invoke PDU
2. Ack PDU
3. Abort PDU

5.9.3 Procedure

In the event that the Responder has received an Invoke PDU from an Initiator and has decided to verify the TID using the rules for the Transaction Identifier procedure, the following process is used.

The Responder sends an Ack PDU with Tve flag set indicating that it has received an invoke message with this TID.

When the Initiator receives the Ack PDU from the Responder, it checks whether it has a corresponding outstanding transaction with this TID. In this case, the Initiator sends back an Ack PDU with TIDok flag set indicating that the TID is valid. This completes the three-way handshake. If the Initiator does not have a corresponding outstanding transaction, it MUST abort the transaction by sending an Abort PDU with the Abort reason INVALIDTID.

Depending on the outcome of the TID verification, WTP SHOULD take different actions. These are listed in Table 15.10.

The TIDnew flag is set in the invoke message and is used by the Initiator to invalidate the Responder's cache.

Table 15.10 Actions Depending on Result of TID Verification

RESULT OF TID VERIFICATION	CONDITION	ACTION
Valid TID	TIDnew == True	Start transaction LastTID = RcvTID
	TIDnew == False	Start transaction LastTID = LastTID
Invalid TID		Abort transaction

5.10 Transport Information Items (TPIs)

5.10.1 Motivation

The variable portion of the header in a WTP PDU MAY consist of Transport Information Items (TPIs). If not, the variable part of the header MUST be empty. The use of TPIs allows for future extensions of the protocol.

5.10.2 Procedure

All TPIs follow the general structure: TPI identity, TPI length, and TPI data; the length can be 0. Table 15.11 lists the currently defined TPIs and in which section they are explained.

All TPIs are optional except for the Error TPI, which is used to inform the sender if an unsupported or erroneous TPI was received. Consequently, a WTP provider MUST be able to recognize the general TPI structure in order to skip an unsupported TPI and report back to the sender.

When a WTP provider receives a TPI that is not supported, the WTP provider returns the Error TPI with the ErrorCode indicating "Unknown TPI" along with the identity of the unsupported TPI. When a WTP provider receives a supported TPI, but fails to understand the content of the TPI, the WTP provider returns the Error TPI with the ErrorCode indicating "Known TPI, unknown content," and the identity of the TPI and the first octet of the content are included as argument.

Table 15.11 WTP Transport Information Items (TPIs)

TRANSPORT INFORMATION ITEM	DESCRIBED IN SECTION
Error	"Transport Information Items (TPIs)"; Section 5.10
Info	"Information in Last Acknowledgment"
Option	"Transmission of Parameters"; Section 5.11
Packet Sequence Number	"Segmentation and Reassembly"; Section 5.14

5.11 Transmission of Parameters

5.11.1 Motivation

Protocol parameters can be transmitted between two WTP providers by using the Option TPI in the variable part of the PDU header.

No mandatory parameters have been defined.

Optional parameters used by the segmentation and reassembly function are listed in Section 5.14.

5.11.2 Procedure

A WTP provider MAY support only a subset of all parameters. The parameters are transported in the variable part of the PDU header by using the Option TPI. The first octet of the Option TPI identifies the parameter, and the following octets contain the value of the parameter. A WTP provider not supporting a parameter ignores it and returns the Error TPI.

5.12 Error Handling

5.12.1 Motivation

When an unrecoverable error is detected during the transaction, the transaction MUST be aborted. Currently, no recovery mechanisms have been defined.

5.12.2 Protocol Data Units

The following PDU is used:

1. Abort PDU

5.12.3 Procedure

When an error occurs in the WTP provider during a transaction, the transaction MUST be aborted with an appropriate Abort reason and the local WTP user informed.

5.13 Version Handling

5.13.1 Motivation

A WTP provider receiving an invoke message with a higher version number than what is supported MUST abort the transaction.

5.13.2 Protocol Data Units

The following PDUs and parameters are used:

1. Invoke PDU
2. Abort PDU

5.13.3 Procedure

The Initiator indicates its version in the version field of the Invoke PDU.

If the Responder does not support the version it MUST return an Abort PDU with the Abort Reason set to WTPVERSIONONE. This indicates that the WTP provider supports version 1 of the WTP protocol.

5.14 Segmentation and Reassembly (Optional)

5.14.1 Motivation

If the length of a message exceeds the MTU for the current bearer, the message can be segmented by WTP and sent in several packets. When a message is sent as a large number of small packets, the packets MAY be sent and acknowledged in groups. The sender can exercise flow control by changing the size of the packet groups depending on the characteristics of the network.

Selective retransmission allows for a receiver to request one or multiple lost packets. The alternative is for the sender to retransmit the entire message, which MAY include packets that have been successfully received. This function minimizes the number of packets sent by WTP.

This function is optional. If SAR is not implemented in WTP, this functionality has to be provided by another layer in the stack. For example, in IS-136, the SSAR layer handles SAR; in an IP network, IP [RFC791] handles SAR; and for GSM SMS/USSD, SAR is achieved by using SMS concatenation [GSM0340]. The motivation for implementing WTP SAR is the selective retransmission procedure, which MAY, if large messages are sent, improve the over-the-air efficiency of the protocol.

5.14.2 Procedure for Segmentation

For the sake of brevity, only the procedure to segment an invoke message is described here (segmentation of a result message is identical except for the names of the PDUs).

An invoke message that exceeds the MTU for the network is segmented into an ordered sequence of one Invoke PDU followed by one or more Segmented Invoke PDUs. The initial Invoke PDU has the implicit packet sequence number of 0, the following Segmented Invoke PDU has the packet sequence number 1, and all the following Segmented Invoke PDUs have packet sequence numbers that are 1 greater than the previous (n, n+1, n+2, etc.). The Invoke PDU has an "implicit" packet sequence number since this number is not included as a field in the header. The client indicates in the Invoke PDU if the invoke message is segmented by clearing the TTR flag. If the invoke message is segmented, the server counts the Invoke PDU as packet number 0 and waits for the following Segmented Invokes PDUs. The packet sequence number MUST NOT wrap. The packet sequence number field is 8 bits, and thus the maximum number of packets is 256.

5.14.3 Procedure for Packet Groups

The packets (Segmented Invoke PDUs and/or Segmented Result PDUs) are sent and acknowledged in groups. The sender MUST NOT send any new packets belonging to the same transaction until the previous packet group has been acknowledged; that is, packet groups are sent according to a stop-and-wait protocol. The sender determines the number of packets for each packet group. The size of a packet group SHOULD be decided with regards to the characteristics of the network and the device. No procedure for determining packet group size has been defined.

The packets in a packet group are sent in one batch. The last packet of the group has the GTR flag set. The last packet of the last packet group of the entire message has the TTR flag set. Since the first group is sent without knowing the status of the receiver, the number of packets SHOULD not be too large. When the receiver receives a packet that is not a GTR or TTR packet, it MUST store the packet and wait for a new one.

When the receiver receives a packet with the GTR flag set, it MUST check whether it has received all packets belonging to that packet group. If the complete packet group has been received, the receiver returns an Ack PDU with the PSN TPI containing the Packet Sequence Number of the GTR packet. If one or more packets are missing, the receiver returns a Nack PDU including the sequence number(s) of missing packet(s). The missing packets are retransmitted with the original Packet Sequence Numbers but with the Retransmission Indicator flag set. When the receiver has received the complete packet group, including those that were retransmitted, it acknowledges the GTR packet.

When the receiver has received a complete packet group and the last packet has the TTR flag set, it SHOULD be able to reassemble the complete message.

If the sender has not received an acknowledgment when the retransmission timer expires, only the GTR/TTR packet is retransmitted, not the entire packet group.

5.14.4 Procedure for Selective Retransmission

When a GTR or TTR packet has been received and one or more packets of the packet group are missing, the WTP provider returns the Nack PDU with the sequence number of the missing packet(s). For example, if the receiver has received packet numbers 2, 3, 5, and 7, and packet number 7 has the GTR flag set, it returns a Nack PDU with packet numbers 4 and 6, indicating missing packets. The packet sequence number of the missing packets are contained in the header part of the Nack PDU.

If the Nack PDU is received with the number of missing packets field set to 0, this means that the entire packet group shall be retransmitted.

The missing packets are retransmitted with the original Packet Sequence Numbers. When the sender has retransmitted the requested packets, it reverts to wait for the original acknowledgment (for the GTR or TTR packet).

When the receiver has received all packets it acknowledges the GTR or TTR packet according to the normal procedure, using the Ack PDU.

A WTP provider not supporting this function MUST retransmit the entire message when one or multiple packets are requested for retransmission.

6. Structure and Encoding of Protocol Data Units

6.1 General

A PDU contains an integer number of octets and consists of:

a) the header, comprising:
   1. the fixed part
   2. the variable part

b) the data, if present

The fixed part of the headers contains frequently used parameters and the PDU code. The length and the structure of the fixed part are defined by the PDU code. The PDU types listed in Table 15.12 are currently defined:

The variable part is used to define less frequently used parameters. Variable parameters are carried in Transport Information Items, TPI.

The very first bit of the fixed header indicates whether the PDU has a variable header or not. The length of the fixed header is given by the PDU type. The variable header consists of TPIs. Every TPI has a length field for its own length. The very first bit of each TPI indicates whether it is the last TPI or not.

Network octet order for the PDUs is big-endian; in other words, the most significant octet is transmitted on the network first followed subsequently by the less significant octets.

Network bit order for bit fields is big-endian; in other words, the left-most bit in the bit field is the most significant bit of the octet and is transmitted first, followed subsequently by less significant bits.

Note 1: If the first octet of a datagram is 0x00, it will be interpreted as if the datagram contains multiple concatenated PDUs. See Section 6.5.

Note 2: This PDU is only applicable if the optional Segmentation and Reassembly function is implemented.

Table 15.12 WTP PDU Types

PDU TYPE	PDU CODE
* NOT ALLOWED *	0x00 (Note 1)
Invoke	0x01
Result	0x02
Ack	0x03
Abort	0x04
Segmented Invoke	0x05 (Note 2)
Segmented Result	0x06 (Note 2)
Negative Ack	0x07 (Note 2)

6.2 Common Header Fields

6.2.1 Continue Flag, CON

As the first bit of the fixed portion of the header, the Continue Flag indicates the presence of any TPIs in the variable part. If the flag is set, there are one or more TPIs in the variable portion of the header. If the flag is clear, the variable part of the header is empty.

This flag is also used as the first bit of a TPI and indicates whether the TPI is the last of the variable header. If the flag is set, another TPI follows this TPI. If the flag is clear, the octet after this TPI is the first octet of the user data.

6.2.2 Group Trailer (GTR) and Transmission Trailer (TTR) Flags

When segmentation and reassembly is implemented, the TTR flag is used to indicate the last packet of the segmented message, and the GTR flag is used to indicate the last packet of a packet group (see Table 15.13).

The default setting SHOULD be GTR=1 and TTR=1; that is, WTP segmentation and reassembly not supported.

6.2.3 Packet Sequence Number

This is used by the PDUs belonging to the Segmentation and Reassembly function. This number indicates the position of the packet in the segmented message.

6.2.4 PDU Type

The PDU Type field indicates what type of WTP PDU the PDU is (Invoke, Ack, etc.). This provides information to the receiving WTP provider as to how the PDU data SHOULD be interpreted and what action is required.

6.2.5 Reserved, RES

All reserved bits are to be set to the value 0x00 unless otherwise specified.

Table 15.13 GTR/TTR Flag Combinations

GTR	TTR	DESCRIPTION
0	0	Not last packet
0	1	Last packet of message
1	0	Last packet of packet group
1	1	Segmentation and Reassembly NOT supported

6.2.6 *Retransmission Indicator, RID*

Enables the receiver to differentiate between packets duplicated by the network and packets retransmitted by the sender. In the original message, the RID is clear. When the message gets retransmitted, the RID is set.

6.2.7 *Transaction Identifier, TID*

The TID is used to associate a packet with a particular transaction.

6.3 Fixed Header Structure

6.3.1 *Invoke PDU (Table 15.14)*

6.3.1.1 Transaction Class, TCL

The Initiator indicates the desired transaction class in the invoke message (see Table 15.15).

6.3.1.2 TIDnew Flag

This is set when the Initiator has "wrapped" the TID value; that is, the next TID will be lower than the previous. When the Responder receives the Invoke PDU and the TID-new flag is set, it invalidates its cached TID value for this Initiator.

6.3.1.3 Version

The current version is 0x00.

Table 15.14 Structure of Invoke PDU

BIT/OCTET	7	6	5	4	3	2	1	0
1	CON	PDU Type = Invoke				GTR	TTR	RID
2 3	TID							
4	Version		TIDnew	U/P	RES	RES	TCL	

Table 15.15 Encoding of Class Field

CLASS	TCL
0	0x00
1	0x01
2	0x10

6.3.1.4 U/P Flag

When this flag is set it indicates that the Initiator requires a User acknowledgment from the server WTP user. This means that the WTP user confirms every received message.

When this flag is clear the WTP provider MAY respond to a message without a confirmation from the WTP user.

6.3.2 Result PDU (Table 15.16)

6.3.3 Acknowledgment PDU (Table 15.17)

6.3.3.1 Tve/Tok flag

In the direction from the responder to the initiator, the Tve (TID Verify) means: "Do you have an outstanding transaction with this TID?" In the opposite direction, the Tok (TID OK) flag means: "I have an outstanding transaction with this TID!"

6.3.4 Abort PDU (Table 15.18)

6.3.4.1 Abort Type and Abort Reasons

Currently the abort types listed in Table 15.19 are specified.

Table 15.16 Structure of Result PDU

BIT/OCTET	7	6	5	4	3	2	1	0
1	CON	PDU Type = Result				GTR	TTR	RID
2 3	TID							

Table 15.17 Structure of Ack PDU

BIT/OCTET	7	6	5	4	3	2	1	0
1	CON	PDU Type = Acknowledgment				Tve/Tok	RES	RID
2 3	TID							

Table 15.18 Structure of Abort PDU

BIT/OCTET	7	6	5	4	3	2	1	0
1	CON	PDU Type = Abort				Abort type		
2 3	TID							
4	Abort reason							

Table 15.19 WTP Abort Types

ABORT TYPE	CODE	DESCRIPTION
Provider (PROVIDER)	0x00	The abort was generated by the WTP provider itself. The abort reason is specified in the next section.
User (USER)	0x01	The abort was generated by the WTP user. The abort reason is provided to the WTP provider by the WTP user.

6.3.4.1.1 Abort Reasons from the WTP Provider The abort reasons in Table 15.20 are specified.

6.3.4.1.2 Abort Reasons from the WTP User The abort reasons from the WTP user are given to the local WTP provider in the T-TRAbort request primitive. The abort reason is specific to the WTP user. For example, if the WTP user is WSP, abort codes defined in [WSP] can be used.

Table 15.20 WTP Provider Abort Codes

ABORT REASON (PROVIDER)	CODE	DESCRIPTION
Unknown (UNKNOWN)	0x00	A generic error code indicating an unexpected error .
Protocol Error (PROTOERR)	0x01	The received PDU could not be interpreted. The structure MAY be wrong.
Invalid TID (INVALIDTID)	0x02	Only used by the Initiator as a negative result to the TID verification.
Not Implemented Class 2 (NOTIMPLEMENTEDCL2)	0x03	The transaction could not be completed since the Responder does not support Class 2 transactions.
Not Implemented SAR (NOTIMPLEMENTEDSAR)	0x04	The transaction could not be completed since the Responder does not support SAR.
Not Implemented User Acknowledgment (NOTIMPLEMENTEDUACK)	0x05	The transaction could not be completed since the Responder does not support User acknowledgments.
WTP Version 1 (WTPVERSIONONE)	0x06	Current version is 1. The initiator requested a different version that is not supported.
Capacity Temporarily Exceeded (CAPTEMPEXCEEDED)	0x07	Due to an overload situation the transaction cannot be completed.

6.3.5 Segmented Invoke PDU (Optional)

BIT/OCTET	7	6	5	4	3	2	1	0
1	CON	PDU Type = Segmented Invoke				GTR	TTR	RID
2 3	TID							
4	Packet Sequence Number							

6.3.6 Segmented Result PDU (Optional)

BIT/OCTET	7	6	5	4	3	2	1	0
1	CON	PDU Type = Segmented Result				GTR	TTR	RID
2 3	TID							
4	Packet Sequence Number							

6.3.7 Negative Acknowledgment PDU (Optional)

BIT/OCTET	7	6	5	4	3	2	1	0
1	CON	PDU Type = Negative Ack				Reserved	RID	
2 3	TID							
4	Number of Missing Packets = N							
5 ... 4+N	Packet Sequence Number(s) of Missing Packets							

6.3.7.1 Number of Missing Packets

Indicates the requested number of missing packets. If 0x00, this means that the entire packet group will be retransmitted.

6.3.7.2 Packet Sequence Number(s) of Missing Packets

List of packet sequence number for the request packets.

6.4 Transport Information Items

6.4.1 General

The variable part of the PDU can consist of one or several Transport Information Items, TPIs. The length field of a TPI can be 2 or 8 bits.

The long TPI (8-bits length) has the structure shown in Table 15.21.

The short TPI (2 bits length) is structured as shown in Table 15.22.

In the preceding tables, N=0..255 and M=0..3. The data field of the TPI MUST contain an integer number of octets. In theory the maximum length of a TPI is 255 octets; however, it is also limited by the MTU size of the bearer network and the number of, and length of, other TPIs in the same PDU header.

The TPIs listed in Table 15.23 are currently defined.

Note: This TPI is only applicable if the optional segmentation and reassembly function is implemented.

6.4.2 Error TPI

The Error TPI is returned to the sender of an erroneous or unsupported TPI. Currently the error codes listed in Table 15.24 have been defined.

Depending on the ErrorCode, the Error TPI can have different structures (see Tables 15.25 and 15.26).

Note that this TPI is mandated to support by a WTP provider. Consequently, the WTP provider MUST also be able to recognize the general structure of a TPI.

6.4.3 Info TPI

This TPI is used to piggyback a small amount of data in the variable part of the PDU header; the data can be performance measurements or statistical data.

Table 15.21 Long TPI Structure

BIT/OCTET	7	6	5	4	3	2	1	0
1	CON		TPI Identity			1	RES	RES
2				TPI Length = N				
3 ... 2+N				TPI Data				

Table 15.22 Short TPI Structure

BIT/OCTET	7	6	5	4	3	2	1	0
1	CON		TPI Identity			0	TPI Length = M	
2 ... 1+M				TPI Data				

Table 15.23 Encoding of TPIs

TPI	TPI IDENTITY	COMMENT
Error	0x00	
Info	0x01	
Option	0x02	
Packet Sequence Number (PSN)	0x03	Note 1

Table 15.24 Encoding of Error TPI

ERROR	CODE	ARGUMENT
Unknown TPI	0x01	TPI Identity of unknown TPI
Known TPI, unknown content	0x02	TPI Identity and first octet of content

Table 15.25 Structure of Error TPI (UNKNOWN)

BIT/OCTET	7	6	5	4	3	2	1	0
1	CON	TPI Identity				0	TPI Length = 0x01	
2	ErrorCode = 0x01				TPI Identity			

Table 15.26 Structure of Error TPI (KNOWN)

BIT/OCTET	7	6	5	4	3	2	1	0
1	CON	TPI Identity				0	TPI Length = 0x02	
2	ErrorCode = 0x02				TPI Identity			
3	First octet of TPI							

Table 15.27 Structure of Info TPI

BIT/OCTET	7	6	5	4	3	2	1	0
1	CON	TPI Identity				0	TPI Length = N	
2 ... 1+N	Information							

The structure of the Info TPI is illustrated in Table 15.27.

Table 15.27 shows the Info TPI as short TPI. If more information MUST be sent, the long TPI can be used.

Table 15.28 Encoding of Option TPI

OPTION	IDENTITY	DESCRIPTION	COMMENT
Maximum Receive Unit	0x01	This parameter is used by the Initiator to advertise the maximum unit of data in bytes that can be received in the result	Note 1
Total Message Size	0x02	This parameter can be sent in the first packet of a segmented message to inform the receiver about the total message size in bytes	Note 1
Delay Transmission Timer	0x03	This parameter can be sent in the Ack PDU when a packet group is acknowledged. The receiver MUST NOT send the next packet group until the specified time has elapsed. The time is in 1/10 seconds.	Note 1

Table 15.29 Structure of Option TPI

BIT/OCTET	7	6	5	4	3	2	1	0
1	CON		TPI Identity			0	TPI Length = N	
2				Option Identity				
3 ... 1+N				Option Value				

6.4.4 Option TPI

The Option TPI is used to transfer parameters between two WTP entities. The parameter carried in the Option TPI is valid for the lifetime of the transaction. The options listed in Table 15.28 are currently defined.

The structure of the Option TPI is illustrated in Table 15.29.

Note 1: This parameter is only applicable if the optional segmentation and reassembly function is implemented.

6.4.5 Packet Sequence Number TPI (Optional)

The Ack PDU does not have a Packet Sequence Number (PSN) field. When Segmentation and Reassembly is used, this TPI is attached to the variable part of the Ack PDU header. The PSN included in the Ack PDU is the PSN of the acknowledged packet (GTR or TTR packet).

BIT/OCTET	7	6	5	4	3	2	1	0
1	CON	TPI Identity = PSN TPI				0	Length = 0x01	
2	Packet Sequence Number							

6.5 Structure of Concatenated PDUs

One or more WTP Protocol Data Units (PDUs) MAY be contained in one datagram Service Data Unit (SDU). This is illustrated in the following figure:

Datagram Service Data Unit

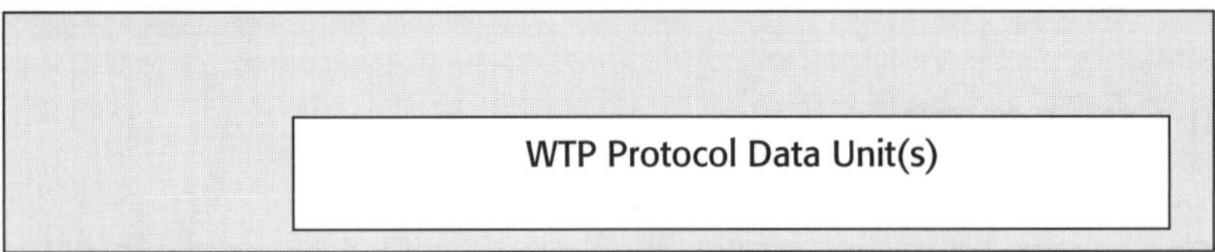

Table 15.30 represents a datagram SDU with one WTP PDU. The PDU including header and data is N octets.

Table 15.31 represents two WTP PDUs concatenated in the same SDU of the bearer network. The first PDU is N octets and the second is M octets.

The concatenation indicator is used to indicate that the SDU contains multiple WTP PDUs. The number of PDUs is limited only by the maximum size of the SDU.

Table 15.30 WTP PDU without Concatenation

BIT/OCTET	7	6	5	4	3	2	1	0
1 ... N	WTP PDU							

Table 15.31 Concatenated WTP PDUs

BIT/OCTET	7	6	5	4	3	2	1	0
1	Concatenation Indicator = 0x00							
2	0	WTP PDU Length = N						
3 ... N+2	WTP PDU							
N+3	0	WTP PDU Length = M						
N+4 ... N+M+3	WTP PDU							

The PDU Length field can be 7 or 15 bits. If the first bit in the PDU Length field is set, the length field is 15 bits; if not, it is 7 bits. This means that the PDU Length field takes up 8 or 16 bits depending on whether the first bit is set or not. In Table 15.31 the first bit is 0, and thus the length field is 7 bits.

7. State Tables

7.1 General

This chapter defines state tables for the core WTP protocol without the optional Segmentation and Reassembly function.

7.2 Event Processing

The WTP provider initiating a transaction is called the Initiator. The WTP provider responding to an initiated transaction is called the Responder. An implementation of the WTP protocol is not required to have both Initiator and Responder functionality. For example, if the WTP user is the WSP client protocol, the WTP provider MAY only support initiation of transactions; that is, no Responder functionality. See WTP conformance clause for details on what MUST be implemented in order to conform to the standard.

The interface to the next higher layer is defined by the WTP service primitives. The next lower layer is typically a datagram service and the only service primitives are the UnitData indication and requests. The request and response service primitives from the next higher layer together with indication primitive from the next lower layer are termed *events*. If multiple PDUs are concatenated in the SDU from the next lower layer, they MUST be separated and dispatched to the transactions. In addition to the external events, there will also be internal events such as timer expirations and errors.

An event is validated before it is processed. The tests listed in Table 15.32 are performed, and if no action is taken, the event is processed according to the state tables.

7.3 Actions

7.3.1 Timers

The following timer actions can be used in the state tables:

Start timer, <value>: Starts the timer with the specified interval value. If the timer is already running, it is restarted with the new value.

Stop timer: Stop the timer without generating an event.

7.3.2 Counters

The following counter actions can be used in the state tables:

Reset counter: Set the counter to 0.

Increment counter: Increment the counter with 1.

Table 15.32 Test of Incoming Events

TEST	ACTION
UnitData.ind on the Responder: Invoke PDU	Create a new transaction
UnitData.ind on the Initiator: Ack PDU with the TIDve flag set, no matching outstanding transaction	Send Abort PDU (INVALIDTID)
UnitData.ind: Ack PDU, Result PDU or Abort PDU, no matching outstanding transaction	Ignore
Illegal PDU type or erroneous header structure	Send Abort PDU (PROTOERR)
Buffer overflow or out-of-memory errors	Send Abort PDU (CAPTEMPEXCEED)
UnitData.ind on the Responder: Invoke PDU requesting Class 2 transaction and Class 2 is not supported	Send Abort PDU (NOTIMPLEMENTEDCL2)
UnitData.ind on the Responder: Invoke PDU using SAR and SAR is not supported	Send Abort PDU (NOTIMPLEMENTEDSAR)
UnitData.ind on the Responder: Invoke PDU requesting User acknowledgment and User acknowledgment is not supported	Send Abort PDU (NOTIMPLEMENTEDUACK)
UnitData.ind on the Responder: Invoke PDU with Version != 0x00	Send Abort PDU (WTPVERSIONONE)

7.3.3 Messages

The following message actions can be used in the state tables:

Queue (Time T): Queuing a PDU causes it to be queued for eventual delivery. The message MUST NOT be queued for longer time than T time units.

Send: Sending a PDU causes it and any queued PDUs to be sent immediately.

The queuing mechanism is used to concatenate messages from different transactions. This can be seen as a concatenation layer that operates below the transaction state machine. The realization of the concatenation layer is implementation dependent and not specified.

7.4 Timers, Counters, and Variables

7.4.1 Timers

The timers listed in Table 15.33 are used by WTP.

A timer can be started with different timer values depending on the type of transaction and the current state of the transaction. Timer values are grouped according to their purpose. This is shown in Table 15.34.

Table 15.33 WTP Timers

TIMER	DESCRIPTION
Transaction timer	Each transaction has a timer associated with it. The timer is used for the retry interval, acknowledgment interval, and wait timeout interval.

Table 15.34 WTP Timer Intervals

TIMER INTERVAL (NAME)	DESCRIPTION
Acknowledgment interval (A)	This sets a bound for the amount of time to wait before sending an acknowledgment.
Retry interval (R)	This sets a bound for the amount of time to wait before retransmitting a PDU.
Wait timeout interval (W)	This sets a bound for the amount of time to wait before state information about a transaction is released. Only Class 2 Initiator and Class 2 Responder

The Retry interval MAY be implemented as an array with the retransmission counter as an index, R[RCR]. An exponential back-off algorithm can be implemented by populating R[] with exponentially increasing values.

The value of a timer interval depends on the following parameters:

- The characteristics of the bearer network
- The transaction class
- The state of the transaction (which message is being retried or acknowledged)

Timer interval values for different bearer networks can be found in Appendix A of this chapter.

7.4.2 Counters

The counters listed in Table 15.35 are used by the WTP.

Table 15.35 WTP Counters

COUNTER (BAME)	DESCRIPTION
Retransmission Counter (RCR)	This set a bound for the maximum number of retransmissions of any PDU. The max value is defined as RCR_MAX.
Acknowledgment Expiration Counter (AEC)	This sets a bound for the maximum number of times the transaction timer, initialized with the acknowledgment interval, is allowed to expire and be restarted before the transaction is aborted. The max value is defined as AEC_MAX.

7.4.3 Variables

The variables listed in Table 15.36 are used by WTP at the Initiator and Responder.

The Uint16 type is an unsigned 16-bit integer. The BOOL type is an Boolean value that only can take the value of True or False.

Table 15.36 WTP Variables

WTP VARIABLES			
VARIABLES	**TYPE**	**DESCRIPTION**	
GenTID	Uint16	The TID to use for the next transaction. Incremented by 1 for every initiated transaction.	Global Only Initiator
SendTID	Uint16	The TID value to send in PDUs in this transaction.	One per transaction
RcvTID	Uint16	The TID values expected to receive in every PDU in this transaction. RcvTID = SendTID XOR 0x8000	One per transaction
LastTID	Uint16	The last received TID from a certain remote host.	One per remote host Only Responder
HoldOn	BOOL	True if HoldOn acknowledgment has been received.	One per Class 2 transaction
Uack	BOOL	True if User Acknowledgment has been requested for this transaction.	One per transaction

7.5 WTP Initiator

WTP INITIATOR NULL			
EVENT	**CONDITION**	**ACTION**	**NEXT STATE**
TR-Invoke.req	Class == 2 | 1	SendTID = GenTID Send Invoke PDU Reset RCR Start timer, R [RCR] Uack = False	RESULT WAIT
	Class == 2 | 1 UserAck	SendTID = GenTID Send Invoke PDU Reset RCR Start timer, R [RCR] Uack = True	
	Class == 0	SendTID = GenTID Send Invoke PDU	NULL

WTP INITIATOR RESULT WAIT			
EVENT	CONDITION	ACTION	NEXT STATE
TR-Abort.req		Abort transaction Send Abort PDU (USER)	NULL
RcvAck	Class == 2	Stop timer Generate T-TRInvoke.cnf HoldOn = True	RESULT WAIT
	Class == 1	Stop timer Generate T-TRInvoke.cnf	NULL
	TIDve Class == 2 | 1	Send Ack(TIDok) Increment RCR Start timer, R [RCR]	RESULT WAIT
RcvAbort		Abort transaction Generate TR-Abort.ind	NULL
TimerTO_R	RCR < MAX_RCR	Increment RCR Start timer, R [RCR] Send Invoke PDU	RESULT WAIT
	RCR == MAX_RCR	Abort transaction Generate TR-Abort.ind	NULL
RcvResult	Class == 2 HoldOn == True	Stop timer Generate TR-Result.ind Start timer, A	RESULT RESP WAIT
	Class == 2 HoldOn == False	Stop timer Generate TR-Invoke.cnf Generate TR-Result.ind Start timer, A	

WTP INITIATOR RESULT RESP WAIT			
EVENT	CONDITION	ACTION	NEXT STATE
TR-Result.res		Queue(A) Ack PDU Start timer, W	WAIT TIMEOUT
	ExitInfo	Queue(A) Ack PDU with Info TPI Start timer, W	
RcvAbort		Abort transaction Generate T-TRAbort.ind	NULL
TR-Abort.req		Abort transaction Send Abort PDU (USER)	
RcvResult		Ignore	RESULT RESP WAIT

TimerTO_A	AEC < AEC_MAX	Increment AEC Start timer, A	RESULT RESP WAIT
	AEC == AEC_MAX	Abort transaction Send Abort PDU (NORESPONSE)	NULL
	Uack == False	Queue(A) Ack PDU Start timer, W	WAIT TIMEOUT

WTP INITIATOR WAIT TIMEOUT			
EVENT	CONDITION	ACTION	NEXT STATE
RcvResult		Send Ack PDU	WAIT TIMEOUT
RcvAbort		Abort transaction Generate T-TRAbort.ind	NULL
TimerTO_W			
TR-Abort.req		Abort transaction Send Abort PDU (USER)	

7.6 WTP Responder

WTP RESPONDER LISTEN			
EVENT	CONDITION	ACTION	NEXT STATE
RcvInvoke	Class == 2 | 1 Valid TID U/P flag	Generate TR-Invoke.ind Start timer, A Uack = True	INVOKE RESP WAIT
	Class == 2 | 1 Valid TID	Generate TR-Invoke.ind Start timer, A Uack = False	
	Class == 0	Generate TR-Invoke.ind	LISTEN
Class == 2 | 1	Send Ack(TIDve) Invalid TID	TIDOK WAIT	

WTP RESPONDER TIDOK WAIT			
EVENT	CONDITION	ACTION	NEXT STATE
RcvAck	Class == 2 | 1 TIDok	Generate TR-Invoke.ind Start timer, A	INVOKE RESP WAIT
RcvAbort		Abort transaction	LISTEN

WTP RESPONDER INVOKE RESP WAIT			
EVENT	**CONDITION**	**ACTION**	**NEXT STATE**
TR-Invoke.res	Class == 1	Queue(A) Ack PDU with InfoTPI	WAIT TIMEOUT
	ExitInfo	Start timer,W	
	Class == 1	Queue(A) Ack PDU Start timer, W	
	Class == 2	Start timer, A	RESULT WAIT
TR-Abort.req		Abort transaction Send Abort PDU (USER)	LISTEN
RcvAbort		Generate TR-Abort.ind Abort transaction	LISTEN
RcvInvoke		Ignore	INVOKE RESP WAIT
TimerTO_A	AEC < AEC_MAX	Increment AEC Start timer, A	INVOKE RESP WAIT
	AEC == AEC_MAX	Abort transaction Send Abort PDU (NORESPONSE)	LISTEN
	Class == 1	Queue(A) Ack PDU	WAIT TIMEOUT
	Uack == False	Start timer, W	
	Class == 2	Send Ack PDU	RESULT WAIT
	Uack == False	Stop timer	

WTP RESPONDER RESULT WAIT			
EVENT	**CONDITION**	**ACTION**	**NEXT STATE**
TR-Result.req		Reset RCR Start timer, R[RCR] Send Result PDU	RESULT RESP WAIT
TR-Abort.req		Abort transaction Send Abort PDU (USER)	LISTEN
RcvAbort		Generate T-TRAbort.ind Abort transaction	LISTEN
TimerTO_A		Send Ack PDU Stop timer	RESULT WAIT

WTP RESPONDER RESULT RESP WAIT			
EVENT	**CONDITION**	**ACTION**	**NEXT STATE**
TR-Abort.req		Abort transaction Send Abort PDU (USER)	LISTEN
RcvAbort		Generate T-TRAbort.ind Abort transaction	LISTEN
RcvAck		Generate TR-Result.cnf	LISTEN
TimerTO_R	RCR < MAX_RCR	Increment RCR Send Result PDU Start timer, R [RCR]	RESULT RESP WAIT
	RCR == MAX_RCR	Generate T-TRAbort.ind Abort transaction	LISTEN

WTP RESPONDER WAIT TIMEOUT			
EVENT	**CONDITION**	**ACTION**	**NEXT STATE**
RcvInvoke		Send Ack PDU	WAIT TIMEOUT
RcvAbort		Abort transaction Generate T-TRAbort.ind	LISTEN
TimerTO_W			
TR-Abort.req		Abort transaction Send Abort PDU (USER)	

8. Examples of Protocol Operation

8.1 Introduction

The examples in this section attempt to illustrate and clarify how the protocol operates. For the sake of brevity, only header fields relevant for the specific examples are included in the diagrams. Each flag in the Flag field of the PDU header is indicated by one character. Table 15.37 shows the different characters that can appear in the examples.

Parameters like Abort reason and Error codes are written in clear text, and so are TPIs. For Transaction Identifiers, N* is N with the high-order bit set; if N = 0x0000, then N* = 0x8000.

Table 15.37 Abbreviations Used in the Examples

ABBREVIATION	MEANING
N	TIDnew flag is set
V	TIDve flag is set
O	TIDok flag is set
U	U/P flag is set
G	GTR flag is set
T	TTR flag is set
TG	Both TTR and GTR flags are set to indicate that SAR is not supported
RID = X	Re-transmission Indicator is X
TID = N	Transaction Identifier is N
c0	The TCL field indicates Class 0 transaction
c1	The TCL field indicates Class 1 transaction
c2	The TCL field indicates Class 2 transaction

8.2 Class 0 Transaction

8.2.1 Basic Transaction (Figure 15.3)

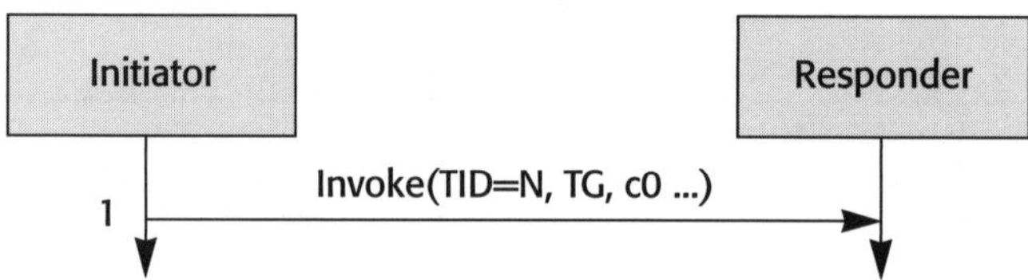

Figure 15.3 Basic Class 0 transaction.

1. The Initiator initiates a Class 0 transaction (c0).

8.3 Class 1 Transaction

8.3.1 Basic Transaction (Figure 15.4)

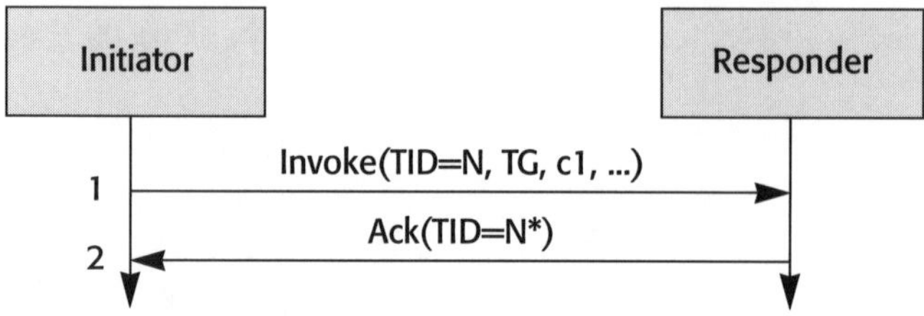

Figure 15.4 Basic Class 1 transaction.

1. The Initiator initiates a Class 1 transaction (c1).
2. The Responder acknowledges the received invoke message.

8.4 Class 2 Transaction

8.4.1 Basic Transaction (Figure 15.5)

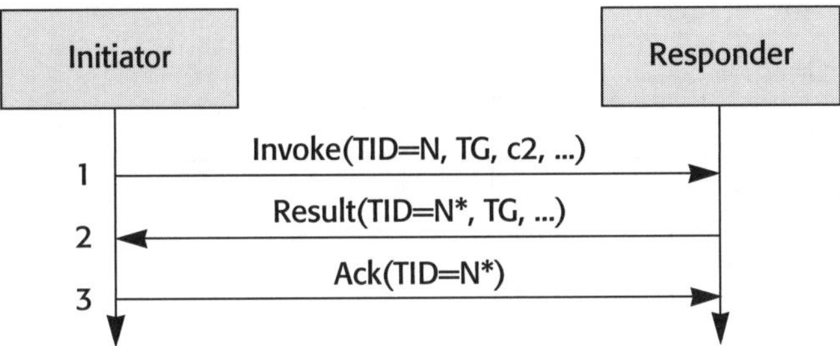

Figure 15.5 Basic Class 2 transaction.

1. The Initiator initiates a Class 2 transaction (c2).
2. The Responder waits for the invoke message to be processed and implicitly acknowledges the invoke message with the Result.
3. The Initiator acknowledges the received result message.

8.4.2 Transaction with "hold on" Acknowledgment (Figure 15.6)

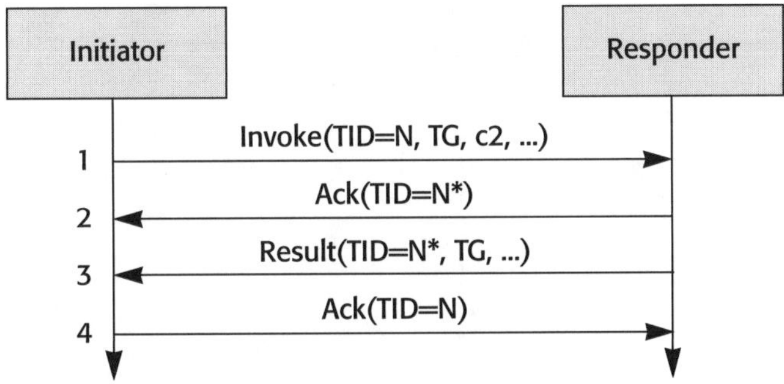

Figure 15.6 Class 2 transaction with "hold on" acknowledgment.

1. The Initiator initiates a Class 2 transaction (c2).
2. The Responder waits for the invoke message to be processed. The acknowledgment timer at the Responder expires and an "hold-on" acknowledgment is sent to prevent the Initiator from retransmitting the invoke message.
3. The result is sent to the Initiator.
4. The Initiator acknowledges the received result message.

8.5 Transaction Identifier Verification

8.5.1 Verification Succeeds (Figure 15.7)

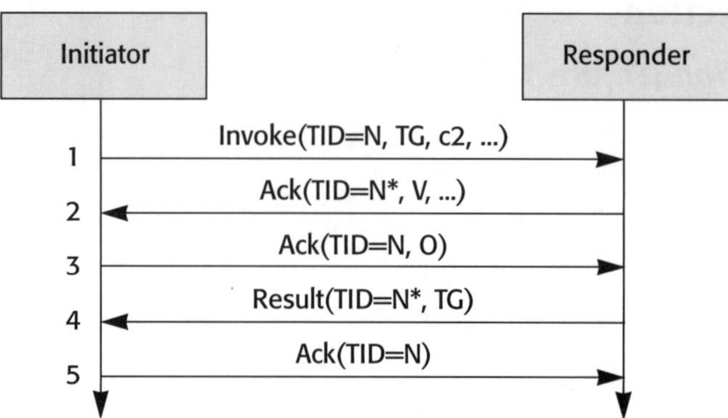

Figure 15.7 Verification succeeds.

The Responder receives a new invoke message and the TID test fails. This causes the Verification procedure to be invoked. The Responder returns an acknowledgment to the Initiator for a verification of whether it has an outstanding transaction with this TID. In this example, the Initiator has an outstanding transaction with the TID and acknowledges the verification.

8.5.2 Verification Fails (Figure 15.8)

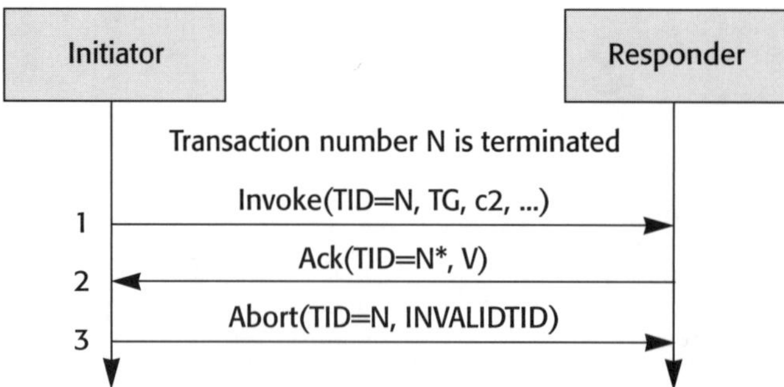

Figure 15.8 Verification fails.

The invoke message with TID=N is duplicated in the network, or has been delayed. When it arrives, transaction N has already been terminated and the Responder asks the Initiator to verify the transaction. The Initiator aborts the transaction by sending an Abort.

8.5.3 Transaction with Out-Of-Order Invoke

An invoke message is delayed in the network. When the message finally arrives to the Responder, the Responder has cached a higher TID value. The Responder initiates a Verification in order to check whether the Initiator still has an invoke message with TID=N outstanding (see Figure 15.9).

Note that the Responder must not replace its cached TID value (N+3) with the lower TID value (N). If the cached TID is moved backwards, old duplicates with higher TID values will erroneously get accepted.

8.6 Segmentation and Reassembly

Figure 15.10 illustrates a Class 2 transaction using segmentation. The Invoke is segmented and sent in five packets in two packet groups.

The Initiator starts off by sending the first three packets in one batch. The last packet has the GTR flag to trigger an acknowledgment from the Responder. Once the acknowledgment is received by the Initiator the last two packets of the message are sent. The final message has the TTR flag set. After some time, the Responder sends back the result to the Initiator. The Initiator acknowledges the result and the transaction is finished.

Note that the PSN TPI is used for the Packet Sequence Number in the Ack PDU.

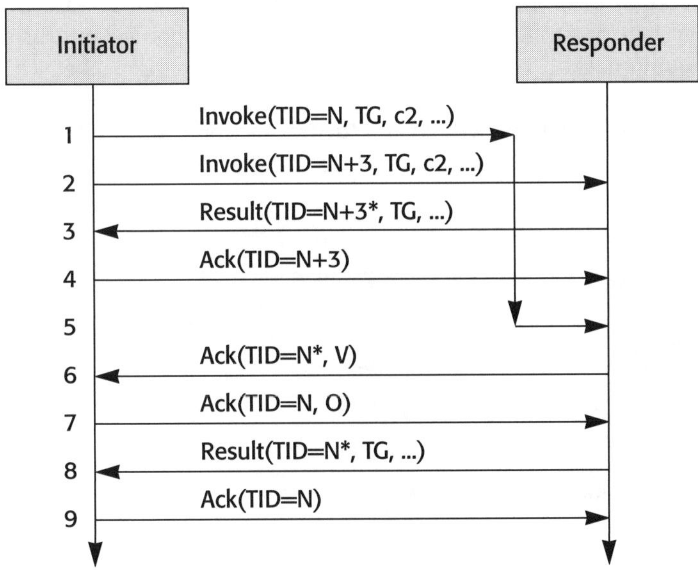

Figure 15.9 Delayed invoke message.

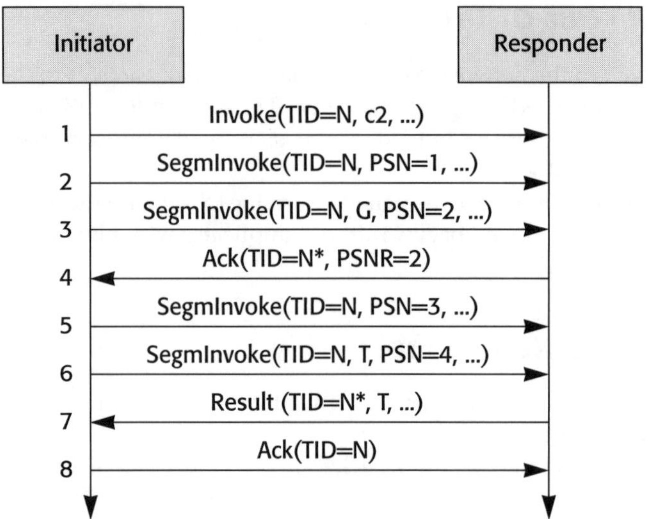

Figure 15.10 Segmentation of invoke message.

8.6.1 Selective Retransmission

Figure 15.11 illustrates a Class 1 transaction using segmentation. One of the packets in the first packet group is lost and the Responder has to request the packet to be retransmitted.

The Initiator starts off by sending the first three packets. The second packet is lost. When the Responder receives the packet with the GTR flag set, it attempts to reassemble the packet group but fails due to the one missing packet. The Responder returns a Nack to request the missing packet. The Initiator retransmits the missing packet. The retransmitted packet has the RID flag set. Once the missing packet has been received by the Responder, the message is acknowledged and the transaction is finished.

Note that the PSN TPI is used for the Packet Sequence Number in the Ack PDU.

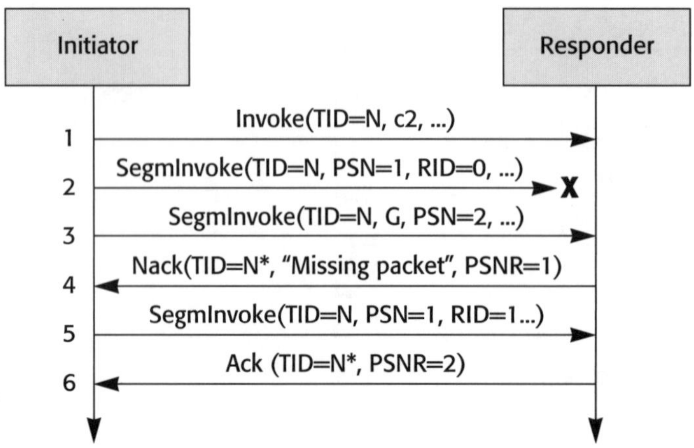

Figure 15.11 Selective retransmission.

9. Definitions

For the purpose of this document, the following definitions apply:

Device Address. The unique network address assigned to a device and following the format defined by an international standard such as E.164 for MSISDN addresses, X.121 for X.25 addresses, or RFC 791 for IPv4 addresses. An address uniquely identifies the sending and/or receiving device.

Initiator. The WTP provider initiating a transaction is referred to as the *Initiator*.

Mobile Device. Refers to a device, such as a phone, pager, or PDA, connected to the wireless network via a wireless link. While the term *mobile* implies the device is frequently moving, it MAY also include fixed or stationary wireless devices (i.e., wireless modems on electric meters) connected to a wireless network.

Network Type. Network type refers to any network that is classified by a common set of characteristics (i.e., air interface) and standards. Examples of network types include GSM, CDMA, IS-136, iDEN, FLEX, ReFLEX, and Mobitex. Each network type MAY contain multiple underlying bearer services.

Protocol Control Information (PCI). Information exchanged between WTP entities to coordinate their joint operation.

Protocol Data Unit (PDU). A unit of data specified in the WTP protocol and consisting of WTP protocol control information and possibly user data.

Responder. The WTP provider responding to a transaction is referred to as the *Responder*.

Service Data Unit (SDU). Unit of information from an upper-level protocol that defines a service request to a lower-layer protocol.

Service Primitive. An abstract, implementation-independent interaction between a WTP user and the WTP provider.

Transaction. The transaction is the unit of interaction between the Initiator and the Responder. A transaction begins with an invoke message generated by the Initiator. The Responder becomes involved with a transaction by receiving the invoke. In WTP several transaction classes have been defined. The invoke message identifies the type of transaction requested that defines the action required to complete the transaction.

User Data. The data transferred between two WTP entities on behalf of the upper-layer entities (e.g., Session layer) for whom the WTP entities are providing services.

WTP Provider. An abstract machine that models the behavior of the totality of the entities providing the WTP service as viewed by the user.

WTP User. An abstract representation of the totality of those entities in a single system that make use of the WTP service. Examples of WTP users include the WAP session protocol WSP or an application that runs directly onto WTP.

10. Abbreviations

For the purposes of this specification the following abbreviations apply:

API	Application Programming Interface
CDMA	Code Division Multiple Access
CDPD	Cellular Digital Packet Data
CSD	Circuit Switched Data
DBMS	Database Management System
DCS	Data Coding Scheme
ETSI	European Telecommunication Standardization Institute
GPRS	General Packet Radio Service
GSM	Global System for Mobile Communication
GTR	Group Trailer, indicates the end of packet group
GUTS	General UDP Transport Service
IE	Information Element
iDEN	Integrated Digital Enhanced Network
IP	Internet Protocol
LSB	Least Significant Bits
MPL	Maximum Packet Lifetime
MSISDN	Mobile Subscriber ISDN (Telephone number or address of device)
MS	Mobile Station
MSB	Most Significant Bits
PCI	Protocol Control Information
PCS	Personal Communication Services
PLMN	Public Land Mobile Network
R-Data	Relay Data
RTT	Round-Trip Time
SAR	Segmentation and Reassembly
SMSC	Short Message Service Center
SMS	Short Message Service
SPT	Server Processing Time
TIA/EIA	Telecommunications Industry Association/Electronic Industry Association
PDU	Protocol Data Unit
SAP	Service Access Point
SDU	Service Data Unit

TTR	Transmission Trailer
UDCP	USSD Dialogue Control Protocol
UDH	User-Data Header (see [GSM 03.40])
UDHL	User-Data Header Length (see [GSM 03.40])
UDL	User-Data Length (see [GSM 03.40])
UDP	Unreliable Datagram Protocol
USSD	Unstructured Supplementary Service Data
WAE	Wireless Application Environment
WAP	Wireless Application Protocol
WSP	Wireless Session Protocol
WTP	Wireless Transaction Protocol
WDP	Wireless Datagram Protocol

11. Requirements

This specification uses the following words for defining the significance of each particular requirement:

MUST. This word, or the terms "REQUIRED" or "SHALL," mean that the definition is an absolute requirement of the specification.

MUST NOT. This phrase, or the phrase "SHALL NOT," mean that the definition is an absolute prohibition of the specification.

SHOULD. This word, or the adjective "RECOMMENDED," mean that there MAY exist valid reasons in particular circumstances to ignore a particular item, but the full implications MUST be understood and carefully weighed before choosing a different course.

SHOULD NOT. This phrase, or the phrase "NOT RECOMMENDED," mean that there MAY exist valid reasons in particular circumstances when the particular behavior is acceptable or even useful, but the full implications SHOULD be understood and the case carefully weighed before implementing any behavior described with this label.

MAY. This word, or the adjective "OPTIONAL," mean that an item is truly optional. One vendor MAY choose to include the item because a particular marketplace requires it or because the vendor feels that it enhances the product, while another vendor MAY omit the same item. An implementation that does not include a particular option MUST be prepared to interoperate with another implementation that does include the option, though perhaps with reduced functionality. In the same vein, an implementation that does include a particular option MUST be prepared to interoperate with another implementation that does not include the option (except, of course, for the feature the option provides).

12. Normative References

[FLEX] FLEX Protocol Specification and FLEX Encoding and Decoding Requirements, Version G1.9, Document Number 68P81139B01, March 16, 1998, Motorola.

[FLEXSuite] FLEX Suite of Application Protocols, Version 1.0, Document Number 6881139B10, October 29, 1997, Motorola.

[GSM0260] ETSI European Digital Cellular Telecommunication Systems (phase 2+) : General Packet Radio Service (GPRS)—stage 1 (GSM 02.60).

[GSM0290] ETSI European Digital Cellular Telecommunication Systems (phase 2) : Unstructured Supplementary Service Data(USSD)—stage 1 (GSM 02.90).

[GSM0340] ETSI European Digital Cellular Telecommunication Systems (phase 2+) : Technical Realization of the Short Message Service (SMS) Point-to-Point (P) (GSM 03.40).

[GSM0360] ETSI European Digital Cellular Telecommunication Systems (phase 2+) : General Packet Radio Service (GPRS)—stage 2 (GSM 03.60).

[GSM0390] ETSI European Digital Cellular Telecommunication Systems (phase 2) : Unstructured Supplementary Service Data(USSD)—stage 2 (GSM 03.90).

[GSM0490] ETSI European Digital Cellular Telecommunication Systems (phase 2) : Unstructured Supplementary Service Data(USSD)—stage 3 (GSM 04.90).

[IS130] EIA/TIA IS-130.

[IS135] EIA/TIA IS-135.

[IS136] EIA/TIA IS-136.

[IS176] EIA/TIA IS-176—CDPD 1.1 specifications.

[IS637] TIA/EIA/IS-637: Short Message Services for Wideband Spread Spectrum Cellular Systems.

[ISO7498] ISO 7498 OSI Reference Model.

[ISO8509] ISO TR 8509 Service conventions.

[ReFLEX] ReFLEX25 Protocol Specification Document, Version 2.6, Document Number 68P81139B02-A, March 16, 1998, Motorola.

[RFC2119] S. Bradner "Key Words for use in RFCs to Indicate Requirement Levels," RFC2119.
URL: http://www.internic.net/rfc/rfc2119.txt

[TR45.3.6] General UDP Transport Teleservice (GUTS) ñ Stage III, TR45.3.6/97.12.15.

[WAE] "Wireless Application Environment Specification," WAP Forum.
URL: http://www.wapforum.org/

[WAPARCH] "Wireless Application Protocol Architecture Specification," WAP Forum.
URL: http://www.wapforum.org/

[WAPUD] "WAP and GSM USSD," WAP Forum.
URL: http://www.wapforum.org/

[WDP] "Wireless Datagram Protocol Specification," WAP Forum.
URL: http://www.wapforum.org/

[WSP] "Wireless Session Protocol Specification," WAP Forum.
URL: http://www.wapforum.org/

13. Informative References

[RFC768] J. Postel, "User Datagram Protocol," RFC768, August 1980.
URL: http://www.internic.net/rfc/rfc768.txt

[RFC791] J. Postel, "IP: Internet Protocol," RFC791.
URL: http://www.internic.net/rfc/rfc791.txt

Appendix A: Default Timer and Counter Values

The timers are initial estimates and have not yet been verified.

The timer values in the following tables are expressed in seconds. The counters are expressed in times an event happens.

GSM SMS

The maximum round-trip time is assumed to be 40 seconds (while a median round-trip time is about 10 seconds), and the timer values are thus suggested to be:

TIMER INTERVAL	TYPE	WITHOUT USER ACK.	WITH USER ACK.
Acknowledgment interval (A)	ACK_T	10	10
	S_ACK_T	0	5
	L_ACK_T	20	20
Retry interval (R)	TTR_T	60	60
	S_TTR_T	35	40
	L_TTR_T	70	70
	GTR_T	45	45
Wait timeout interval (W)	WAIT_T	300	300

COUNTER NAME	VALUE FOR STACK ACKS	VALUE FOR USER ACKS
Max Retransmissions	4	4
Max Ack Timer Expiration	4	4

GSM USSD

The maximum round-trip time is assumed to be 5 seconds, and the timer values are thus suggested to be:

TIMER INTERVAL	TYPE	WITHOUT USER ACK.	WITH USER ACK.
Acknowledgment interval (A)	ACK_T	10	10
	S_ACK_T	0	5
	L_ACK_T	10	10
Retry interval (R)	TTR_T	20	20
	S_TTR_T	14	14
	L_TTR_T	20	20
	GTR_T	10	10
Wait timeout interval (W)	WAIT_T	60	60

COUNTER NAME	VALUE FOR STACK ACKS	VALUE FOR USER ACKS
Max Retransmissions	4	4
Max Ack Timer Expiration	4	4

CDPD

The maximum round-trip time is assumed to be 3 seconds, and the timer values are thus suggested to be:

TIMER INTERVAL	TYPE	WITHOUT USER ACK.	WITH USER ACK.
Acknowledgment interval (A)	ACK_T	2	2
	S_ACK_T	0	2
	L_ACK_T	2	3
Retry interval (R)	TTR_T	3	3
	S_TTR_T	3	3
	L_TTR_T	3	3
	GTR_T	3	3
Wait timeout interval (W)	WAIT_T	30	30

COUNTER NAME	VALUE FOR STACK ACKS	VALUE FOR USER ACKS
Max Retransmissions	8	8
Max Ack Timer Expiration	6	6

Circuit Switched Data

The maximum round-trip time is assumed to be 3 seconds, and the timer values are thus suggested to be:

TIMER INTERVAL	TYPE	WITHOUT USER ACK.	WITH USER ACK.
Acknowledgment interval (A)	ACK_T	2	2
	S_ACK_T	0	1
	L_ACK_T	7	7
Retry interval (R)	TTR_T	5	5
	S_TTR_T	3	4
	L_TTR_T	10	10
	GTR_T	3	3
Wait timeout interval (W)	WAIT_T	40	40

COUNTER NAME	VALUE FOR STACK ACKS	VALUE FOR USER ACKS
Max Retransmissions	4	4
Max Ack Timer Expiration	4	4

Timer Usage

There are a number of timers with similar behavior but different values. These timers are defined to enable an optimal use of the available bandwidth. The following table shows what timer intervals shall be used for the different messages in a transaction:

MESSAGE TYPE	CLASS 2	CLASS 1
Invoke message	TTR_T	S_TTR_T
Hold on acknowledgment	ACK_T	-
Result message	L_TTR_T	-
Last acknowledgment	L_ACK_T	S_ACK_T
Last packet of packet group	GTR_T	GTR_T

For Class 0, no timer values are applicable.

Appendix B: PICS Proforma

The supplier of a protocol implementation that claims conformance to this Specification shall complete a copy of the PICS proforma provided in this appendix, including the information necessary to identify both the supplier and the implementation.

B.1 Introduction

The supplier of a protocol implementation which is claimed to conform to this Specification shall complete the following Protocol Implementation Conformance Statement (PICS) proforma.

A completed PICS proforma is the PICS for the implementation in question. The PICS is a statement of which capabilities and options of the protocol have been implemented. The PICS can have a number of uses, including:

- The protocol implementor, as a checklist to reduce the risk of failure to conform to the standard through oversight
- The supplier and acquirer—or potential acquirer—of the implementation, as a detailed indication of the capabilities of the implementation, stated relative to the common basis for understanding provided by the standard PICS proforma
- The user—or potential user—of the implementation, as a basis for initially checking the possibility of interworking with another implementation (note that while interworking can never be guaranteed, failure to interwork can often be predicted from incompatible PICSs)
- A protocol tester, as the basis for selecting appropriate tests against which to assess the claim for conformance of the implementation.

B.2 Abbreviations and Special Symbols

B.2.1 Status Symbols

M	Mandatory
O	Optional
O.<n>	Optional, but support of at least one of the group of options labeled by the same numeral <n> is required
X	Prohibited
<pred>:	Conditional-item symbol, including predicate identification (see Section B.3.4)
^	Logical negation, applied to a conditional item's predicate

B.2.2 Other Symbols

<r>	Receive aspects of an item
<s>	Send aspects of an item

B.3 Instructions for Completing the PICS Proforma

B.3.1 General Structure of the PICS Proforma

The first part of the PICS proforma—Implementation Identification and Protocol Summary—is to be completed as indicated with the information necessary to identify fully both the supplier and the implementation.

The main part of the PICS proforma is a fixed-format questionnaire divided into a number of major subclauses. These can be divided into further subclauses, each containing a group of individual items. Answers to the questionnaire items are to be provided in the right-most column, either by simply marking an answer to indicate a restricted choice (usually Yes or No) or by entering a value or a set or range of values.

Note: There are some items for which two or more choices from a set of possible answers can apply. All relevant choices are to be marked in these cases.

Each item is identified by an item reference in the first column; the second column contains the question to be answered; and the third column contains the reference or references to the material that specifies the item in the main body of this Specification. The remaining columns record the status of the item—whether support is mandatory, optional, prohibited, or conditional—and provide space for the answers (see also Section B.3.4).

A supplier may also provide further information, categorized as either Additional Information or Exception Information. When present, each kind of further information is to be provided in a further subclause of items labeled A<i> or X<i>, respectively, for cross-referencing purposes, where <i> is any unambiguous identification for the item (e.g., a number); there are no other restrictions on its format or presentation.

A completed PICS proforma, including any Additional Information and Exception Information, is the Protocol Implementation Conformance Statement for the implementation in question.

Note: Where an implementation is capable of being configured in more than one way, a single PICS may be able to describe all such configurations. However, the supplier has the choice of providing more than one PICS, each covering some subset of the implementation's configuration capabilities, in cases where this makes for easier and clearer presentation of the information.

B.3.2 Additional Information

Items of Additional Information allow a supplier to provide further information intended to assist in the interpretation of the PICS. It is not intended or expected that a large quantity will be supplied, and a PICS can be considered complete without any such information. Examples might be an outline of the ways in which a (single) implementation can be set up to operate in a variety of environments and configurations, or a brief rationale—based perhaps upon specific application needs—for the exclusion of features which, although optional, are nonetheless commonly present in implementations of this protocol.

References to items of Additional Information may be entered next to any answer in the questionnaire, and may be included in items of Exception Information.

B.3.3 Exception Information

It may occasionally happen that a supplier will wish to answer an item with mandatory or prohibited status (after any conditions have been applied) in a way that conflicts with the indicated requirement. No preprinted answer will be found in the support column for this; instead, the supplier shall write the missing answer into the Support column, together with an X<i> reference to an item of Exception Information, and shall provide the appropriate rationale in the Exception Information item itself.

An implementation for which an Exception Information item is required in this way does not conform to this Specification.

Note: A possible reason for the situation just described is that a defect in the standard has been reported, a correction for which is expected to change the requirement not met by the implementation.

B.3.4 Conditional Status

B.3.4.1 Conditional Items

The PICS proforma contains a number of conditional items. These are items for which the status—mandatory, optional, or prohibited—that applies is dependent upon whether or not certain other items are supported, or upon the values supported for other items.

In many cases, whether or not the item applies at all is conditional in this way, as well as the status when the item does apply.

Where a group of items is subject to the same condition for applicability, a separate preliminary question about the condition appears at the head of the group, with an instruction to skip to a later point in the questionnaire if the "Not Applicable" answer is selected. Otherwise, individual conditional items are indicated by one or more conditional symbols (on separate lines) in the status column.

A conditional symbol is of the form "<pred>:<x>", where "<pred>" is a predicate as described in Section B.3.4.2, and "<x>" is one of the status symbols M, O, O.<n>, or X.

If the value of the predicate in any line of a conditional item is true (see Section B.3.4.2), then the conditional item is applicable, and its status is that indicated by the status symbol following the predicate; the answer column is to be marked in the usual way. If the value of a predicate is false, the Not Applicable (N/A) answer is to be marked in the relevant line. Each line in a multiline conditional item should be marked; at most, one line will require an answer other than N/A.

B.3.4.2 Predicates

A predicate is one of the following:

a) An item reference for an item in the PICS proforma. The value of the predicate is true if the item is marked as supported, and is false otherwise.

b) A predicate name, for a predicate defined elsewhere in the PICS proforma (usually in the Major Capabilities section or at the end of the section containing the conditional item) (see next page).

c) The logical negation symbol "^" prefixed to an item reference or predicate name. The value of the predicate is true if the value of the predicate formed by omitting the "^" is false, and vice versa.

The definition for a predicate name is one of the following:

a) An item-reference, evaluated as at (a) above.
b) A relation containing a comparison operator (=, < , etc.) with at least one of its operands being an item reference for an item taking numerical values as its answer; the predicate is true if the relation holds when each item reference is replaced by the value entered in the Support column as an answer to the item referred to.
c) A Boolean expression constructed by combining simple predicates, as in (a) and (b), using the Boolean operators AND, OR, and NOT, and parentheses, in the usual way. The value of such a predicate is true if the Boolean expression evaluates to true when the simple predicates are interpreted as described above.

Each item whose reference is used in a predicate or predicate definition is indicated by an asterisk in the Item column.

B.4 Identification

B.4.1 Implementation Identification

Supplier	
Contact point for queries about the PICS	
Implementation name(s) and version(s)	
Other information necessary for full identification (e.g., name(s) and version(s) of machines and/or operating systems, system name(s))	

NOTES

1 Only the first three items are required for all implementations; other information may be completed as appropriate in meeting the requirement for full identification.
2 The terms *Name* and *Version* should be interpreted appropriately to correspond with a supplier's terminology (e.g., Type, Series, Model).

B.4.2 Protocol Summary

Identification of protocol specification	WAP Wireless Transaction Protocol
Identification of corrigenda and amendments of the PICS proforma	
Protocol version(s) supported	
Have any Exception Information items been required (see A.3.3)? YES ❐ NO ❐ (The answer YES means that the implementation does not conform to this Specification)	
Date of statement	

B.5 Wireless Transaction Protocol

B.5.1 Applicability

Clause B.5 is applicable to all implementations that claim conformance to this Specification.

B.5.5 Protocol Functions

B.5.5.1 Transaction Classes

ITEM	FUNCTION	REFERENCE	STATUS	SUPPORT
INCL0	Does the implementation support the initiation of Class 0 transactions?	0	M	YES NO
INCL1	Does the implementation support the initiation of Class 1 transactions?	0	M	YES NO
INCL2	Does the implementation support the initiation of Class 2 transactions?	0	O	YES NO
RECL1	Does the implementation support responding to Class 1 transactions?	0	M	YES NO
RECL2	Does the implementation support responding to Class 2 transactions?	0	O	YES NO

B.5.5.1 Protocol Features

ITEM	FUNCTION	REFERENCE	STATUS	SUPPORT	
UACK	Does the implementation support the user acknow-ledgment function?	0	O	YES	NO
CONC	Does the implementation support concatenation?	0	O	YES	NO
SEPA	Does the implementation support separation of concatenated PDUs?	0	M	YES	NO
RETR	Does the implementation support retransmission until acknowledgment?	0	M	YES	NO
TRAB	Does the implementation support transaction abort?	0	M	YES	NO
VERS	Does the implementation support version handling?	0	M	YES	NO
ERRO	Does the implementation support error handling?	0	M	YES	NO
VERI	Does the implementation support initiation of trans-action verification?	0	O	YES	NO
VERR	Does the implementation support responding to trans-action verification?	0	M	YES	NO
TPIE	Does the implementation support the Error TPI?	0	M	YES	NO
TPII	Does the implementation support the Info TPI?	0	M	YES	NO
TPIO	Does the implementation support the Option TPI?	0	O	YES	NO
TPIP	Does the implementation support the PSN TPI?	0	O	YES	NO
SAR	Does the implementation support segmentation and reassembly?	0	O	YES	NO

Appendix C: History and Contact Information

Document History		
Date	**Status**	**Comment**
29-April-1998	Specification	First version

Contact Information

http://www.wapforum.org.

technical-comments@wapforum.org

CHAPTER

16

Wireless Transport Layer Security Specification

1. Scope

The Wireless Application Protocol (WAP) is a result of continuous work to define an industrywide specification for developing applications that operate over wireless communication networks. The scope for the WAP Forum is to define a set of specifications to be used by service applications. The wireless market is growing very quickly, and reaching new customers and services. To enable operators and manufacturers to meet the challenges in advanced services, differentiation, and fast/flexible service creation, WAP Forum defines a set of protocols in Transport, Security, Transaction, Session, and Application layers. For additional information on the WAP architecture, please refer to *Wireless Application Protocol Architecture Specification* [WAPARCH].

The Security layer protocol in the WAP architecture is called the *Wireless Transport Layer Security*, WTLS. The WTLS layer operates above the Transport protocol layer. The WTLS layer is modular and it depends on the required security level of the given application whether it is used or not. WTLS provides the upper-level layer of WAP with a secure transport service interface that preserves the transport service interface below it. In addition, WTLS provides an interface for managing (e.g., creating and terminating) secure connections.

The primary goal of the WTLS layer is to provide privacy, data integrity, and authentication between two communicating applications. WTLS provides functionality similar to TLS 1.0 and incorporates new features such as datagram support, optimized handshake, and dynamic key refreshing. The WTLS protocol is optimized for low-bandwidth bearer networks with relatively long latency.

2. WTLS Architectural Overview

2.1 Reference Model

A model of layering the protocols in WAP is illustrated in Figure 16.1. The layering of WAP protocols and their functions is similar to that of the ISO OSI Reference Model [ISO7498] for upper layers. Layer Management Entities handle protocol initialization, configuration, and error conditions (such as loss of connectivity due to the mobile terminal roaming out of coverage) that are not handled by the protocol itself.

WTLS is designed to function on connection-oriented and/or datagram transport protocols. Security is assumed to be an optional layer above the Transport layer. The Security layer preserves the transport service interfaces. The session or application management entities are assumed to provide additional support required to manage (e.g., initiate and terminate) secure connections.

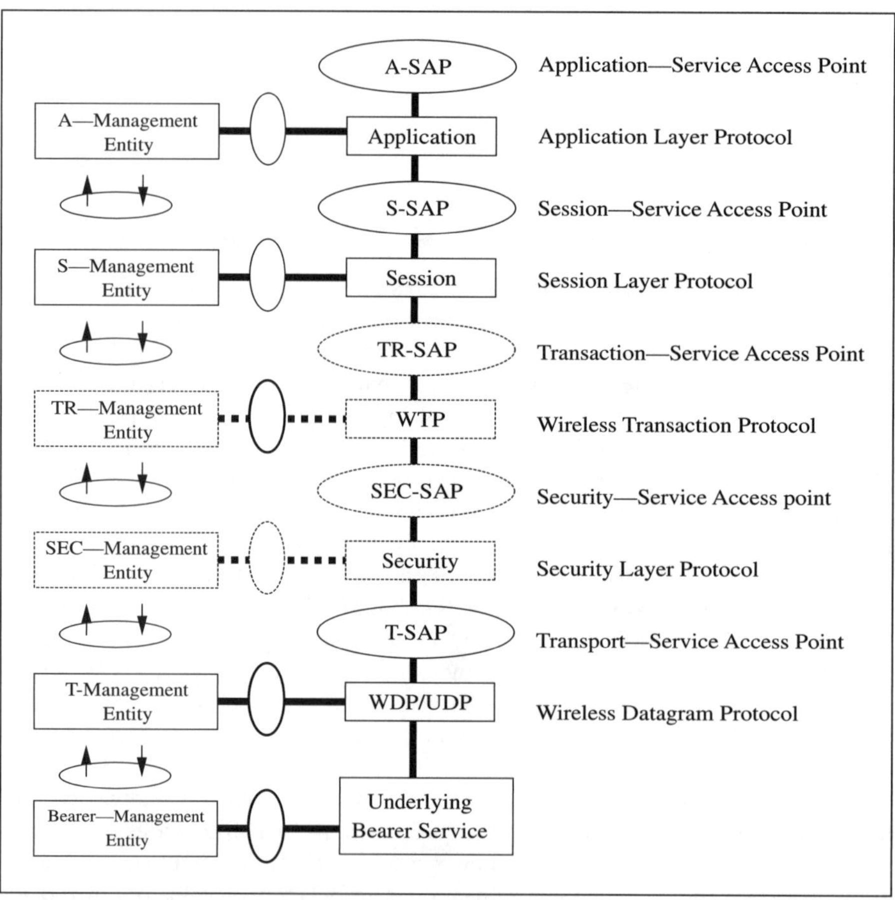

Figure 16.1 Wireless application protocol reference model.

3. WTLS Elements for Layer-to-Layer Communication

3.1 Notations Used

3.1.1 Definition of Service Primitives and Parameters

Communication between layers is accomplished by means of service primitives. Service primitives represent, in an abstract way, the logical exchange of information and control between the Security layer and adjacent layers.

Service primitives consist of commands and their respective responses associated with the services requested of another layer. The general syntax of a primitive is

X-Service.type (Parameters)

where X designates the layer providing the service. For this specification, X is "SEC" for the Security layer.

Service primitives are not the same as an Application Programming Interface (API) and are not meant to imply any specific method of implementing an API. Service primitives are an abstract means of illustrating the services provided by the Protocol layer to the layer above. The mapping of these concepts to a real API and the semantics associated with a real API are an implementation issue and are beyond the scope of this specification.

3.1.2 Time Sequence Charts

The behavior of service primitives is illustrated using time sequence charts, which are described in [ISO10731].

Figure 16.2 illustrates a simple nonconfirmed service, which is invoked using a request primitive and results in an indication primitive in the peer. The dashed line

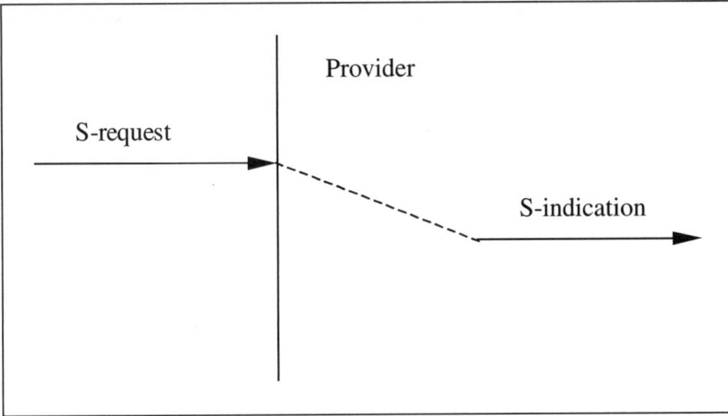

Figure 16.2 A nonconfirmed service.

represents propagation through the provider over a period of time indicated by the vertical difference between the two arrows representing the primitives.

3.1.3 Primitive Types

The primitives types defined in this specification are:

TYPE	ABBREVIATION	DESCRIPTION
request	req	Used when a higher layer is requesting a service from the next lower layer.
indication	ind	A layer providing a service uses this primitive type to notify the next higher layer of activities related to the request primitive type of the peer (such as the invocation of the request primitive) or to the provider of the service (such as a protocol generated event).
response	res	A layer uses the response primitive type to acknowledge receipt of the indication primitive type from the next lower layer.
confirm	cnf	The layer providing the requested service uses the confirm primitive type to report that the activity has been completed successfully.

3.1.4 Service Parameter Tables

The service primitives are defined using tables indicating which parameters are possible and how they are used with the different primitive types. For example, a simple confirmed primitive might be defined using the following:

PRIMITIVE	S-PRIMITIVE			
PARAMETER	REQ	IND	RES	CNF
Parameter 1	M	M(=)		
Parameter 2			O	C(=)

If some primitive type is not possible, the column for it will be omitted. The entries used in the primitive type columns are defined in the following table:

M Presence of the parameter is mandatory—it MUST be present.

C Presence of the parameter is conditional depending on values of other parameters.

O Presence of the parameter is a user option—it MAY be omitted.

P Presence of the parameter is a service provider option—an implementation MAY not provide it.

ñ The parameter is absent.

* Presence of the parameter is determined by the lower layer protocol.

(=) The value of the parameter is identical to the value of the corresponding parameter of the preceding service primitive.

In the preceding table, *Parameter 1* is always present in *S-primitive.request* and corresponding *S-primitive.indication*. *Parameter 2* MAY be specified in *S-primitive.response,* and in that case it MUST be present and have the equivalent value also in the corresponding *S-primitive.confirm;* otherwise, it MUST NOT be present.

3.2 WTLS Transport Service

3.2.1 Service Primitives

3.2.1.1 SEC-Unitdata

This primitive is used to exchange user data between the peers. SEC-Unitdata can only be invoked when there is an existing secure connection between the transport addresses of the peers.

PRIMITIVE	SEC-UNITDATA	
PARAMETER	***REQ***	***IND***
Source Address	M	M(=)
Source Port	M	M(=)
Destination Address	M	O(=)
Destination Port	M	O(=)
User Data	M	M(=)

Source Address identifies the originator.
Source Port identifies the port from which the message is sent.
Destination Address identifies the peer to which the user data is sent.
Destination Port identifies the port to which the message is sent.
User Data is the data to be transmitted.

3.3 WTLS Connection Management

3.3.1 Overview

WTLS Connection management allows a client to connect with a server and to agree on protocol options to be used. The secure connection establishment consists of several steps and either client or server can interrupt the negotiation at will (e.g., if the parameters proposed by the peer are not acceptable). The negotiation may include the security parameters (e.g., cryptographic algorithms and key lengths), key exchange, and authentication. Either the server or client service user can also terminate the connection at any time.

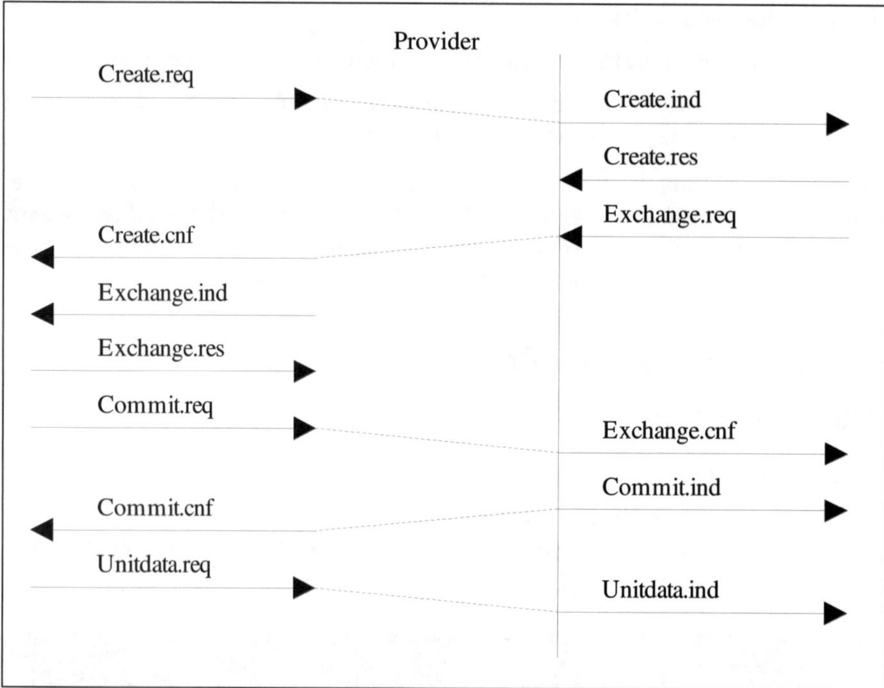

Figure 16.3 Full handshake.

The primitive sequence for establishing a secure session (full handshake) is shown in Figure 16.3.

The primitive sequence for establishing a secure session in an optimized or abbreviated way is shown in Figure 16.4.

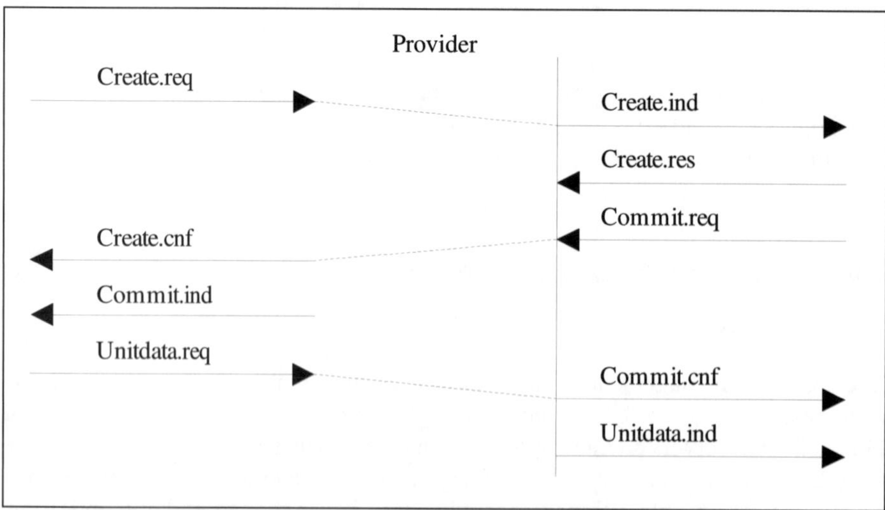

Figure 16.4 Abbreviated or optimized handshake.

3.3.2 Service Primitives

3.3.2.1 SEC-Create

This primitive is used to initiate a secure connection establishment.

PARAMETER / PRIMITIVE	SEC-CREATE REQ	IND	RES	CNF
Source Address	M	M(=)		
Source Port	M	M(=)	-	-
Destination Address	M	O(=)	-	-
Destination Port	M	O(=)		
Client Identities	O	C(=)	-	-
Proposed Key Exchange Suites	M	M(=)	-	-
Proposed Cipher Suites	M	M(=)	-	-
Proposed Compression Methods	M	M(=)	-	-
Sequence Number Mode	O	C(=)	M	M(=)
Key Refresh	O	C(=)	M	M(=)
Session Id	O	C(=)	M	M(=)
Selected Key Exchange Suite	-	-	M	M(=)
Selected Cipher Suite	-	-	M	M(=)
Selected Compression Method	-	-	M	M(=)
Server Certificate	-	-	O	C(=)

Source Address identifies the originator.

Source Port identifies the port from which the message is sent.

Destination Address identifies the peer to which the user data is sent.

Destination Port identifies the port to which the message is sent.

Client Identities identify the originator in a transport independent way. This parameter may be used by the server to look up the corresponding client certificate. Client can send several identities corresponding to different keys or certificates.

Proposed Key Exchange Suites include the key exchange suites proposed by the client.

Proposed Cipher Suites include the cipher suites proposed by the client.

Proposed Compression Methods include the compression methods proposed by the client.

Sequence Number Mode defines how sequence numbers are used in this secure connection.

Key Refresh defines how often the encryption and protection keys are refreshed within a secure connection.

Session Id identifies the secure session. It is unique per server.

Selected Key Exchange Suite identifies the key exchange suite selected by the server.

Selected Cipher Suite identifies the cipher suite selected by the server.
Selected Compression Method identifies the compression method chosen by the server.
Server Certificate is the public-key certificate of the server.

3.3.2.2 SEC-Exchange

This primitive is used in a secure connection creation if the server wishes to perform public-key authentication or key exchange with the client.

PRIMITIVE	SEC-EXCHANGE			
PARAMETER	REQ	IND	RES	CNF
Client Certificate	-	-	M	M(=)

Client Certificate is the public-key certificate of the client.

3.3.2.3 SEC-Commit

This primitive is initiated when the handshake is completed and either peer requests to switch into the newly negotiated connection state.

PRIMITIVE	SEC-COMMIT			
PARAMETER	REQ	IND	RES	CNF
-	-	-	-	-

3.3.2.4 SEC-Terminate

This primitive is used to terminate the connection.

PRIMITIVE	SEC-TERMINATE	
PARAMETER	REQ	IND
Alert Description	M	M(=)
Alert Level	M	M(=)

Alert Description identifies the reason that caused the termination.
Alert Level defines whether the session (fatal) or just a connection (critical) is terminated.

3.3.2.5 SEC-Exception

This primitive is used to inform the other end about warning level alerts.

PRIMITIVE	SEC-NOTIFY	
PARAMETER	REQ	IND
Alert Description	M	M(=)

Alert Description identifies what caused the warning.

3.3.2.6 SEC-Create-Request

This primitive is used by the server to request the client to initiate a new handshake.

PRIMITIVE PARAMETER	SEC-CREATE-REQUEST *REQ*	*IND*
Source Address	O	C(=)
Source Port	O	C(=)
Destination Address	O	C(=)
Destination Port	O	C(=)

Source Address identifies the originator.

Source Port identifies the port from which the message is sent.

Destination Address identifies the client to which the data is sent. This parameter is needed when the primitive is used in a NULL session state.

Destination Port identifies the port to which the data is sent.

3.3.3 Constraints on Using the Service Primitives

Tables 16.1–16.3 define the permitted primitive sequences on the service interface. The client and server have separate tables, since the service is asymmetric.

Only the permitted primitives are listed on the rows; the layer prefix is omitted for brevity. The table entries are interpreted as shown in Table 16.1.

4. WTLS State Tables

The following state tables define the actions of WTLS on a datagram transport service provider.

WTLS PDUs are identified in *italics*.

By default, all WTLS PDUs will be processed under the state that is currently in use.

If any PDUs other than the ones listed under Conditions are received, the receiver may generate an alert depending on the severity of the case.

Table 16.1 Table Entry Legend

ENTRY	DESCRIPTION
	The indication or confirm primitive cannot occur.
N/A	Invoking this primitive is an error. The appropriate action is a local implementation matter.
STATE_NAME	Primitive is permitted and moves the service interface view to the named state.

Table 16.2 Permitted Client Security Layer Primitives

CLIENT SEC-PRIMITIVE	SESSION STATES							
	NULL	CREATING	CREATED	EXCHANGE	COMMIT1	COMMIT2	OPENING	OPEN
Create.req	CREATING	N/A	N/A	N/A	N/A	N/A	N/A	CREATING
Commit.req	N/A	N/A	N/A	N/A	COMMIT2	N/A	N/A	N/A
Terminate.req	N/A	NULL	NULL	NULL	NULL	NULL	NULL	NULL
Exception.req	N/A	CREATING	CREATED	EXCHANGE	COMMIT1	COMMIT2	OPENING	OPEN
Unitdata.req	N/A	N/A	N/A	N/A	N/A	N/A	OPENING	OPEN
Exchange.res	N/A	N/A	N/A	COMMIT1	N/A	N/A	N/A	N/A
Exchange.ind			EXCHANGE					
Commit.ind			OPENING					
Terminate.ind		NULL				NULL	NULL	NULL
Exception.ind		CREATING				COMMIT2	OPEN	OPEN
Create-Request.ind	NULL						OPEN	OPEN
Unitdata.ind							OPEN	OPEN
Create.cnf		CREATED						
Commit.cnf						OPEN		

Table 16.3 Permitted Server Security Layer Primitives

SERVER SEC-PRIMITIVE	SESSION STATES						
	NULL	CREATING	CREATED	EXCHANGE	COMMIT	OPENING	OPEN
Exchange.req	N/A	N/A	EXCHANGE	N/A	N/A	N/A	N/A
Commit.req	N/A	N/A	COMMIT	N/A	N/A	N/A	N/A
Create-Request.req	NULL	N/A	N/A	N/A	N/A	N/A	OPEN
Terminate.req	N/A	NULL	NULL	NULL	NULL	NULL	NULL
Exception.req	N/A	CREATING	CREATED	EXCHANGE	COMMIT	OPENING	OPEN
Unitdata.req	N/A	N/A	N/A	N/A	N/A	N/A	OPEN
Create.res	N/A	CREATED	N/A	N/A	N/A	N/A	N/A
Commit.ind						OPEN	
Create.ind	CREATING			CREATING	CREATING		CREATING
Terminate.ind				NULL	NULL		NULL
Exception.ind	NULL			EXCHANGE	COMMIT		OPEN
Unitdata.ind							OPEN
Exchange.cnf				OPENING			
Commit.cnf					OPEN		

Although the state tables provided are helpful to understand the WTLS protocol, they are not the formal and complete definition. Those tables tend to be concise and readable so that certain levels of details are not reflected. It is therefore essential that the textual description of this specification is the unique and complete definition of the WTLS protocol.

4.1 Client State Tables

The following tables show the protocol states and event processing on the client:

CLIENT SECURE SESSION NULL			
EVENT	**CONDITIONS**	**ACTION**	**NEXT STATE**
SEC-Create.req		T-Unitdata.req (*ClientHello*) The sequence number is present during a handshake.	CREATING
T-Unitdata.ind	*HelloRequest*	SEC-Create-Request.ind The client may initiate a handshake with SEC-Create.req, initiate an *alert (no_renegotiation)*, or ignore the request.	NULL

CLIENT SECURE SESSION CREATING			
EVENT	**CONDITIONS**	**ACTION**	**NEXT STATE**
SEC-Terminate.req		T-Unitdata.req (*Alert (fatal or critical)*)	NULL
SEC-Exception.req		T-Unitdata.req (*Alert (warning)*)	CREATING
T-Unitdata.ind	*ServerHello* *Certificate** *ServerKeyExchange** *CertificateRequest** *ServerHelloDone*	SEC-Create.cnf SEC-Exchange.ind	EXCHANGE
	ServerHello *Certificate** *ChangeCipherSpec* *Finished*	SEC-Create.cnf SEC-Commit.ind The pending state is made current by *ChangeCipherSpec* so that *Finished* is processed under the new state and the sequence numbers are set to 0.	CREATED
	Alert (critical or fatal)	SEC-Terminate.ind	NULL
	Alert (warning)	SEC-Exception.ind	CREATING

Retransmission timer expires		T-Unitdata.req (*ClientHello*) The last buffer resent without incrementing the sequence number. The retransmission timer is cleared. The retransmission counter is incremented.	CREATING
Retransmission counter exceeds the maximum value		SEC-Terminate.ind	NULL

*) Whether these messages are present or not depends on the chosen key exchange method.

CLIENT SECURE SESSION EXCHANGE			
EVENT	**CONDITIONS**	**ACTION**	**NEXT STATE**
SEC-Exchange.res		Create a buffer with: *ClientKeyExchange** *CertificateVerify**	COMMIT1
SEC-Terminate.req		T-Unitdata (*Alert (critical or fatal)*)	NULL
SEC-Exception.req		T-Unitdata (*Alert (warning)*)	EXCHANGE

*) Whether these messages are present or not depends on the chosen key exchange method.

CLIENT SECURE SESSION COMMIT1			
EVENT	**CONDITIONS**	**ACTION**	**NEXT STATE**
SEC-Commit.req		Append to the buffer: *ChangeCipherSpec* *Finished* The pending state is made current by *ChangeCipherSpec* so that *Finished* is processed under the new negotiated state and the sequence number is set to 0. Send the buffer out with T-Unitdata.req.	COMMIT2
SEC-Terminate.req		T-Unitdata (*Alert (critical or fatal*)	NULL
SEC-Exception.req		T-Unitdata (*Alert (warning)*)	COMMIT1

CLIENT SECURE SESSION COMMIT2			
EVENT	**CONDITIONS**	**ACTION**	**NEXT STATE**
SEC-Terminate.req		T-Unitdata.req (*Alert (critical or fatal)*)	NULL
SEC-Exception.req		T-Unitdata (*Alert (warning)*)	COMMIT2
T-Unitdata.ind	*Alert (critical or fatal)*	SEC-Terminate.ind	NULL
	Alert (warning)	SEC-Exception.ind	COMMIT2
	Finished	SEC-Commit.cnf	OPEN
Retransmission timer expires	No response from the server is received.	T-Unitdata.req The last buffer is resent without incrementing the sequence number. The retransmission timer is cleared. The retransmission counter is incremented.	COMMIT2
Retransmission counter exceeds the maximum value.		SEC-Terminate.ind	NULL

CLIENT SECURE SESSION CREATED			
EVENT	**CONDITIONS**	**ACTION**	**NEXT STATE**
	Implementation may send *Finished* immediately with-out user data.	Create a buffer with: *Finished* Send it out with T-Unitdata.req.	OPENING
	Implementation may delay sending *Finished* and pre-pend it to user data (if any).	Create a buffer with: *Finished* Set up a Finished prepending timer.	OPENING
SEC-Terminate.req		T-Unitdata.req (*Alert (critical or fatal)*)	NULL
SEC-Exception.req		T-Unitdata.req (*Alert (warning)*)	CREATED

CLIENT SECURE SESSION OPENING			
EVENT	**CONDITIONS**	**ACTION**	**NEXT STATE**
SEC-Unitdata.req		Prepend buffer to user data and call T-Unitdata.req	OPENING
SEC-Terminate.req		T-Unitdata.req (*Alert (critical or fatal)*)	NULL
SEC-Exception.req		T-Unitdata.req (*Alert (warning)*)	OPENING
	Finished pre-pending timer is set	Prepend buffer to user data and call T-Unitdata.req. Remove the Finished prepending timer.	OPENING
Finished prepend-ing timer expires		Send buffer out with T-Unitdata.req.	OPENING
T-Unitdata.ind	User data is received	SEC-Unitdata.ind	OPEN
	Alert (duplicate_finished _received)		OPEN
	Alert (critical or fatal)	SEC-Terminate.ind	NULL
	Alert (warning)	SEC-Exception.ind	OPEN
	HelloRequest	SEC-Create-Request.ind The client may initiate a handshake with SEC-Create.req, initiate an *alert (no_renegotiation)*, or ignore the request.	OPEN

CLIENT SECURE SESSION OPEN			
EVENT	**CONDITIONS**	**ACTION**	**NEXT STATE**
SEC-Create.req		T-Unitdata.req (*ClientHello*)	CREATING
SEC-Terminate.req		T-Unitdata.req (*Alert (critical or fatal)*)	NULL

(Continues)

CLIENT SECURE SESSION OPEN (*CONT.*)			
EVENT	CONDITIONS	ACTION	NEXT STATE
SEC-Exception.req OPEN		T-Unitdata.req (*Alert (warning)*)	
SEC-Unitdata.req		T-Unitdata.req	OPEN
T-Unitdata.ind	User data received	SEC-Unitdata.ind	OPEN
	Alert (critical or fatal)	SEC-Terminate.ind	NULL
	Alert (warning)	SEC-Exception.ind	OPEN
	HelloRequest	SEC-Create-Request.ind The client may initiate a handshake with SEC-Create.req, initiate an *alert (no_renegotiation)*, or ignore the request.	OPEN

4.2 Server State Tables

The following tables show the protocol states and event processing on the client.

SERVER SECURE SESSION NULL			
EVENT	CONDITIONS	ACTION	NEXT STATE
SEC-Create-Request.req		T-Unitdata.req (*HelloRequest*) The rate at which HelloRequests are sent should be limited.	NULL
T-Unitdata.ind	*ClientHello*	SEC-Create.ind	CREATING
	Alert (no_renegotiation)	SEC-Exception.ind	NULL

SERVER SECURE SESSION CREATING			
EVENT	CONDITIONS	ACTION	NEXT STATE
SEC-Terminate.req		T-Unitdata.req (*Alert (critical or fatal)*)	NULL
SEC-Exception.req		T-Unitdata.req (*Alert (warning)*)	CREATING
SEC-Create.res		Create a buffer with: *ServerHello* *Certificate**	CREATED

*) Whether this message is present or not depends on the chosen key exchange method.

SERVER SECURE SESSION CREATED			
EVENT	**CONDITIONS**	**ACTION**	**NEXT STATE**
SEC-Exchange.req	Full handshake	Append to the buffer: *ServerKeyExchange** *CertificateRequest** *ServerHelloDone* Send it out with T-Unitdata.req.	EXCHANGE
SEC-Commit.req	Optimized or abbreviated handshake	Append to the buffer: *ChangeCipherSpec* *Finished* The pending state is made current by *ChangeCipherSpec* so that *Finished* is processed under the new negotiated state and sequence numbers are set to 0. Send the buffer out with T-Unitdata.req.	COMMIT
SEC-Terminate.req		T-Unitdata.req (*Alert (critical or fatal)*)	NULL
SEC-Exception.req		T-Unitdata.req (*Alert (warning)*)	CREATED

*) Whether these messages are present or not depends on the chosen key exchange method.

SERVER SECURE SESSION EXCHANGE			
EVENT	**CONDITIONS**	**ACTION**	**NEXT STATE**
SEC-Terminate.req		T-Unitdata.req (*Alert (critical or fatal)*)	NULL
SEC-Exception.req		T-Unitdata.req (*Alert (warning)*)	EXCHANGE
T-Unitdata.ind	*ClientHello* A record identical to the previous one is received	Resend last buffer with T-Unitdata.req.	EXCHANGE
	ClientHello A record not identical to the previous one is received	SEC-Create.ind	CREATING
	Alert (critical or fatal)	SEC-Terminate.ind	NULL
	Alert (warning)	SEC-Exception.ind	EXCHANGE
	*Certificate**	SEC-Exchange.cnf	OPENING

(Continues)

SERVER SECURE SESSION EXCHANGE (*CONT.*)			
EVENT	**CONDITIONS**	**ACTION**	**NEXT STATE**
	*ClientKeyExchange**	SEC-Commit.ind	
	*CertificateVerify** *ChangeCipherSpec* *Finished*	The pending state is made current after *ChangeCipherSpec* so that *Finished* is processed under the new negotiated state and sequence numbers are set to 0. Create a new buffer with: *Finished* Send it out with T-Unitdata.req.	

*) Whether these messages are present or not depends on the chosen key exchange method.

SERVER SECURE SESSION COMMIT			
EVENT	**CONDITIONS**	**ACTION**	**NEXT STATE**
SEC-Terminate.req		T-Unitdata.req (*Alert (critical or fatal)*)	NULL
SEC-Exception.req		T-Unitdata.req (*Alert (warning)*)	COMMIT
T-Unitdata.ind	*ClientHello* A record identical to the previous one is received.	Resend last buffer with T-Unitdata.req.	COMMIT
	ClientHello A record not identical to the previous one is received.	SEC-Create.ind	CREATING
	Alert (critical or fatal)	SEC-Terminate.ind	NULL
	Alert (warning)	SEC-Exception.ind	COMMIT
	Finished	SEC-Commit.cnf	OPEN
	Finished and user data	SEC-Commit.cnf SEC-Unitdata.ind	OPEN

SERVER SECURE SESSION OPENING			
EVENT	**CONDITIONS**	**ACTION**	**NEXT STATE**
SEC-Create-Request.req		T-Unitdata (*HelloRequest*)	OPENING

SEC-Terminate.req		T-Unitdata (*Alert (critical or fatal)*)	NULL
SEC-Exception.req		T-Unitdata.req (*Alert (warning)*)	OPENING
SEC-Unitdata.req		T-Unitdata.req	OPENING
T-Unitdata.ind	*ClientHello*	SEC-Create.ind	CREATING
	Alert (critical or fatal)	SEC-Terminate.ind	NULL
	Alert (warning)	SEC-Exception.ind	OPENING
	User data received	SEC-Unitdata.ind	OPEN
	*Certificate** *ClientKeyExchange** *CertificateVerify** *ChangeCipherSpec* *Finished* A group of records identical to the previous one is received.	Resend last buffer with T-Unitdata.req.	OPENING

SERVER SECURE SESSION OPEN			
EVENT	**CONDITIONS**	**ACTION**	**NEXT STATE**
SEC-Create-Request.req		T-Unitdata (*HelloRequest*)	OPEN
SEC-Terminate.req		T-Unitdata (*Alert (critical or fatal)*)	NULL
SEC-Exception.req		T-Unitdata.req (*Alert (warning)*)	OPEN
SEC-Unitdata.req		T-Unitdata.req	OPEN
T-Unitdata.ind	*ClientHello*	SEC-Create.ind	CREATING
	Alert (critical or fatal)	SEC-Terminate.ind	NULL
	Alert (warning)	SEC-Exception.ind	OPEN
	User data received	SEC-Unitdata.ind	OPEN
	Finished A record identical to the previous *Finished* is received.	T-Unitdata (*Alert (duplicate_finished_received)*)	OPEN
	Finished and user data. A record identical to the previous *Finished* is received.	SEC-Unitdata.ind T-Unitdata (*Alert (duplicate_finished_received)*)	OPEN

5. Presentation Language

This document deals with the formatting of data in an external representation similar to TLS. The following very basic and somewhat casually defined presentation language syntax will be used. The syntax draws from several sources in its structure. Although it resembles the programming language C in its syntax and XDR [XDR] in both its syntax and intent, it would be risky to draw too many parallels. The purpose of this presentation language is to document WTLS only, not to have general application beyond that particular point.

5.1 Basic Block Size

The representation of all data items is explicitly specified. The basic block size is 1 byte (i.e., 8 bits). Multiple byte data items are concatenations of bytes, from left to right, from top to bottom. From the byte stream a multibyte item (a numeric in the example) is formed (using C notation) by:

```
value = (byte[0] << 8*(n-1)) | (byte[1] << 8*(n-2)) | ... | byte[n-1];
```

This byte ordering for multibyte values is the commonplace network byte order or big endian format.

5.2 Miscellaneous

Comments begin with "/*" and end with "*/".

Optional components are denoted by enclosing them in "[[ ]]" double brackets.

Single byte entities containing uninterpreted data are of type opaque.

5.3 Vectors

A vector (single-dimensioned array) is a stream of homogeneous data elements. The size of the vector may be specified at documentation time or left unspecified until runtime. In either case, the length declares the number of bytes, not the number of elements, in the vector. The syntax for specifying a new type T' that is a fixed-length vector of type T is

```
T T'[n];
```

Here T' occupies n bytes in the data stream, where n is a multiple of the size of T. The length of the vector is not included in the encoded stream.

In the following example, Datum is defined to be 3 consecutive bytes that the protocol does not interpret, while Data is 3 consecutive Datum, consuming a total of 9 bytes.

```
opaque Datum[3];    /* three uninterpreted bytes */
Datum Data[9];      /* 3 consecutive 3 byte vectors */
```

Variable-length vectors are defined by specifying a subrange of legal lengths, inclusively, using the notation <floor..ceiling>. When encoded, the actual length precedes the vector's contents in the byte stream. The length will be in the form of a number consuming as many bytes as required to hold the vector's specified maximum (ceiling) length. A variable-length vector with an actual length field of 0 is referred to as an *empty vector*.

```
T T'<floor..ceiling>;
```

In the following example, mandatory is a vector that must contain between 300 and 400 bytes of type opaque. It can never be empty. The actual length field consumes 2 bytes, a uint16, sufficient to represent the value 400. On the other hand, longer can represent up to 800 bytes of data, or 400 uint16 elements, and it may be empty. Its encoding will include a 2-byte actual length field prepended to the vector. The length of an encoded vector must be an even multiple of the length of a single element (for example, a 17-byte vector of uint16 would be illegal).

```
opaque mandatory<300..400>;    /* length field is 2 bytes, cannot be
empty */
uint16 longer<0..800>;         /* zero to 400 16-bit unsigned integers */
```

The notation

```
A = B[first..last];
```

indicates that vector A is assigned to be the elements from first to last of B.

5.4 Numbers

The basic numeric data type is unsigned byte (uint8). All larger numeric data types are formed from fixed-length series of bytes that are concatenated and are also unsigned. The following numeric types are predefined:

```
uint8 uint16[2];
uint8 uint24[3];
uint8 uint32[4];
uint8 uint64[8];
```

All values, here and elsewhere in the specification, are stored in "network" or "big-endian" order; the uint32 represented by the hex bytes 01 02 03 04 is equivalent to the decimal value 16909060.

5.5 Enumerateds

An additional sparse data type is available called enum. A field of type enum can only assume the values declared in the definition. Each definition is a different type. Only enumerateds of the same type may be assigned or compared. Every element of an enumerated MUST be assigned a value, as demonstrated in the following example. Since the elements of the enumerated are not ordered, they can be assigned any unique value, in any order.

```
enum { e1(v1), e2(v2), … , en(vn), [[(n)]] } Te;
```

Enumerateds occupy as much space in the byte stream as would its maximal defined ordinal value. The following definition would cause 1 byte to be used to carry fields of type Color.

```
enum { red(3), blue(5), white(7) } Color;
```

One may optionally specify a value without its associated tag to force the width definition without defining a superfluous element. In the following example, Taste will consume 2 bytes in the data stream but can only assume the values 1, 2, or 4.

```
enum { sweet(1), sour(2), bitter(4), (32000) } Taste;
```

The names of the elements of an enumeration are scoped within the defined type. In the first example, a fully qualified reference to the second element of the enumeration would be Color.blue. Such qualification is not required if the target of the assignment is well specified.

```
Color color = Color.blue;   /* overspecified, legal */
Color color = blue;         /* correct, type implicit */
```

For enumerateds that are never converted to external representation, the numerical information may be omitted.

```
enum { low, medium, high } Amount;
```

5.6 Constructed Types

Structure types may be constructed from primitive types for convenience. Each specification declares a new, unique type. The syntax for definition is much like that of C.

```
struct {
  T1 f1;
  T2 f2;
  …
  Tn fn;
} [[T]];
```

The fields within a structure may be qualified using the type's name using a syntax much like that available for enumerateds. For example, T.f2 refers to the second field of the previous declaration. Structure definitions may be embedded.

5.6.1 Variants

Defined structures may have variants based on some knowledge that is available within the environment. The selector MUST be an enumerated type that defines the possible variants the structure defines. There MUST be a case arm for every element of the enumeration declared in the select, or a default arm for those elements missing. The body of the variant structure may be given a label for reference. The mechanism by which the variant is selected at runtime is not prescribed by the presentation language.

```
struct {
  T1 f1;
  T2 f2;
  ...
  Tn fn;
  Td fd;
  select (E) {
    case e1: Te1;
    case e2: Te2;
    ...
    case en: Ten;
    default: TeDefault;
  } [[fv]];
} [[Tv]];
```

For example:

```
enum { apple, orange } VariantTag;
struct {
  uint16 number;
  opaque string<0..10>;     /* variable length */
} V1;
struct {
  uint32 number;
  opaque string[10];        /* fixed length */
} V2;
struct {
  select (VariantTag) {     /* value of selector is implicit */
    case apple: V1;         /* VariantBody, tag = apple */
    case orange: V2;        /* VariantBody, tag = orange */
  } variant_body;
} VariantRecord;
```

Variant structures may be qualified (narrowed) by specifying a value for the selector prior to the type. For example, a

```
orange VariantRecord
```

is a narrowed type of VariantRecord containing a variant_body of type V2.

5.7 Cryptographic Attributes

The four cryptographic operations, digital signing, stream cipher encryption, block cipher encryption, and public key encryption, are designated digitally signed, stream-ciphered, block-ciphered, and public-key-encrypted, respectively. A field's cryptographic processing is specified by prepending an appropriate keyword designation before the field's type specification. Cryptographic keys are implied by the current session state.

In digital signing, one-way hash functions are used as input for a signing algorithm. A digitally signed element is encoded as an opaque vector <0..2^{16}-1>, where the length is specified by the signing algorithm and key.

In stream cipher encryption, the plaintext is exclusive-Ored with an identical amount of output generated from a cryptographically secure keyed pseudo-random number generator.

In block cipher encryption, every block of plaintext encrypts to a block of ciphertext. All block cipher encryption is done in CBC (Cipher Block Chaining) mode, and all items that are block-ciphered will be an exact multiple of the cipher block length.

In public-key encryption, a public key algorithm is used to encrypt data in such a way that it can be decrypted only with the matching private key. A public-key-encrypted element is encoded as an opaque vector <0..2^{16}-1>, where the length is specified by the signing algorithm and key.

In the following example, the contents of hash are used as input for the signing algorithm, then the entire structure is encrypted with a block cipher. The length of this structure in bytes would be exact multiple of the cipher block length.

```
block-ciphered struct {
  uint8 field1;
  uint8 field2;
  digitally-signed opaque hash[20];
} UserType;
```

5.8 Constants

Typed constants can be defined for purpose of specification by declaring a symbol of the desired type and assigning values to it. Under-specified types (opaque, variable-length vectors, and structures that contain opaque) cannot be assigned values. No fields of a multi-element structure or vector may be elided.

For example,

```
struct {
  uint8 f1;
  uint8 f2;
} Example1;

Example1 ex1 = {1, 4};       /* assigns f1 = 1, f2 = 4 */
```

5.9 String Constants

A string constant must be interpreted as a vector of bytes (uint8) with a fixed length. Strings are enclosed in quotation marks. Unlike in C, no terminating nulls are implied. ASCII coding must be used.

For example,

```
block = H(parameter, "key expansion");
  /* string length is 13 bytes (no terminating null) */
```

6. Record Protocol Specification

The WTLS Record Protocol is a layered protocol. The Record Protocol takes messages to be transmitted, optionally compresses the data, applies a MAC, encrypts, and transmits the result. Received data is decrypted, verified, and decompressed, then delivered to higher-level clients.

Four record protocol clients are described in this document: the change cipher spec protocol, the handshake protocol, the alert protocol, and the application data protocol. If a WTLS implementation receives a record type it does not understand, it should ignore it.

Several records can be concatenated into one transport SDU. For example, several handshake messages can be transmitted in one transport SDU. This is particularly useful with packet-oriented transports such as GSM short messages.

6.1 Connection State

A WTLS connection state is the operating environment of the WTLS Record Protocol. It specifies a compression algorithm, encryption algorithm, and MAC algorithm. In addition, the parameters for these algorithms are known: the MAC secret and the bulk encryption keys and IVs for the secure connection in both the read and the write directions.

Logically, there are always two connection states outstanding: the current state and the pending state. All records are processed under the current state. The security parameters for the pending state are set by the WTLS Handshake Protocol. The Handshake Protocol must make the pending state current. The pending state is then reinitialized to an empty state. The initial current state always specifies that no encryption, compression, or MAC will be used.

The security parameters for a WTLS connection state are set by providing the following values. Note that the following values are agreed on in a handshake procedure between a client and server when a secure session is negotiated.

These parameters are defined in the presentation language as:

```
enum { server(1), client(2) } ConnectionEnd;

uint8 BulkCipherAlgorithm;
```

```
enum { stream(1), block(2), (255) } CipherType;

enum { true, false } IsExportable;

uint8 MACAlgorithm;

enum { off(0), implicit(1), explicit(2), (255) } SequenceNumberMode;

uint8 CompressionMethod;

struct {
   ConnectionEnd        entity;
   BulkCipherAlgorithm bulk_cipher_algorithm;
   CipherType           cipher_type;
   uint8                key_size; /* bytes */

   uint8                iv_size; /* bytes */
   uint8                key_material_length; /* bytes */
   IsExportable         is_exportable;
   MACAlgorithm         mac_algorithm;
   uint8                mac_key_size; /* bytes */
   uint8                mac_size; /* bytes */
   opaque               master_secret[20];
   opaque               client_random[16];
   opaque               server_random[16];
   SequenceNumberMode   sequence_number_mode;
   uint8                key_refresh;
   CompressionMethod    compression_algorithm;
} SecurityParameters;
```

ITEM	DESCRIPTION
Connection End	Whether this entity is considered a client or a server in this secure session.
Bulk Cipher Algorithm	An algorithm to be used for bulk encryption. This specification includes the key size of this algorithm, how much of that key is secret, whether it is a block or stream cipher, the block size of the cipher (if appropriate), and whether it is considered as an "export cipher". Bulk cipher algorithms are listed in Appendix A of this chapter.
MAC Algorithm	An algorithm to be used for message authentication. This specification includes the size of the key used for MAC calculation and the size of the hash that is returned by the MAC algorithm. MAC algorithms are listed in Appendix A.
Compression Algorithm	The algorithm to compress data prior to encryption. This specification must include all information the algorithm requires to do compression.
Master Secret	A 20-byte secret shared between the two peers in the secure connection.

Client Random	A 16-byte value provided by the client.
Server Random	A 16-byte value provided by the server.
Sequence Number Mode	Which scheme is used to communicate sequence numbers in this secure connection: Implicit sequence numbering Sequence numbers will be used as an input to MAC calculations. This requires that a reliable transport protocol be used. Explicit sequence numbering The sequence number will be sent in plaintext with record layer messages and it is used as an input to MAC calculations. This option MUST be used when operating on a datagram transport protocol. Note that in this case, sequence numbers do not have to be in unbroken sequence, but they have to be sent in monotonic way (the sequence number of each sent record is greater than the previous one). If the verification fails, *bad_record_mac* alert is sent as normally. Off No sequence numbers will be used. This option is not recommended, and choosing it makes the system vulnerable for playback attacks. In this case, protection against such attacks must be provided by upper protocol layers.
Key Refresh	Defines how often some connection state parameters (encryption key, MAC secret, and IV) are updated. New keys are calculated at every $n = 2^{key\_refresh}$ messages; i.e., when the sequence number is 0, n, 2n, 3n, etc. For example, if 3 is chosen as a value for key_refresh, a new set of keys is generated for every eight (2^8) messages; i.e., messages with sequence numbers 0, 8, 16, etc. If 0 is chosen, a new key set is generated for each message (2^0).

Once the security parameters have been set and the keys have been generated, the connection states can be instantiated by making them the current states. These current states must be updated for each record processed. Each connection state includes the following elements:

ITEM	DESCRIPTION
Compression State	The current state of the compression algorithm. Note that a stateful compression cannot be used when operating on top of a datagram protocol. If a stateful compression is used, there are separate states for both directions.
Client write MAC secret	The secret used for MAC calculation/verification for records sent by the client. The secret must be updated according to the key refresh parameter.

ITEM	DESCRIPTION
Client write encryption key	The key used for encryption/decryption of records sent by the client. The key must be updated according to the key refresh parameter.
Client write IV	The base IV used to calculate a record level IV for block ciphers running in CBC mode for records sent by the client.
Client write sequence number	The sequence number used for records sent by the client. Sequence numbers are of type uint16 and may not exceed 2^{16}–1. When a new connection state is established, the sequence number of the first record is 0.
Server write MAC secret	The secret used for MAC calculation/verification for records sent by the server. The secret must be updated according to the key refresh parameter.
Server write encryption key	The key used for encryption/decryption of records sent by the server. The key must be updated according to the key refresh parameter.
Server write IV	The base IV used to calculate a record level IV for block ciphers running in CBC mode for records sent by the server.
Server write sequence number	The sequence number used for records sent by the server. Sequence numbers are of type uint16 and may not exceed 2^{16}–1. When a new connection state is established, the sequence number first record is 0.

6.2 Record Layer

The WTLS Record layer receives uninterpreted data from higher layers in nonempty blocks of size maximum of 2^{16}–1.

6.2.1 Fragmentation

Unlike in TLS, the Record layer does not fragment information blocks. It is assumed that the Transport layer takes care of the necessary fragmentation and reassembly.

```
enum {
   change_cipher_spec(1), alert(2), handshake(3),
    application_data(4), (15)
} ContentType;

enum { without(0), with(1) } SequenceNumberIndication;

enum { without(0), with(1) } FragmentLengthIndication;

struct {
   opaque record_type[1];
```

```
    select (SequenceNumberIndication) {
        case without: struct {};
        case with: uint16 sequence_number;
    }
    select (FragmentLengthIndication) {
        case without: struct {};
        case with: uint16 length;
    }   opaque fragment[WTLSPlaintext.length];
} WTLSPlaintext;
```

Description of WTLSPlaintext fields:

ITEM	DESCRIPTION
record_type	Defines the higher level protocol used to process the enclosed fragment. Contains also information about the existence of optional fields in the record and an indication about ciphering state.

	BITS	LENGTH	DESCRIPTION
	0–3	4 bits	Content type.
	4	1 bit	Reserved for future use.
	5	1 bit	Cipher spec indicator defines whether this record is transmitted under a cipher spec different from null: 0 = null cipher spec used. 1 = current, different from null, cipher spec is used. Null cipher spec means that no compression, MAC protection, or encryption is used. Its usage is restricted to handshake messages starting a new session and certain alerts sent in cleartext.
	6	1 bit	Sequence number field indicator defines whether the next byte in this record contains a sequence number field: 0 = no sequence number field. 1 = sequence number included. The sequence number field MUST be used with datagram transports (see Section 6.1 for explicit sequence numbering).
	7	1 bit	Record length field indicator defines whether the record contains a length field: 0 = no record length field. 1 = record length field included. In some circumstances, it is possible to avoid sending the record length in the record layer. This reduces the amount of overhead by 2 bytes per record. The requirements for leaving the field out are:

BITS	LENGTH	DESCRIPTION
		1. The receiver must be able to determine the size of the transport SDU. 2. This is the last (or the only) record in this transport SDU. If both requirements are met, each peer can decide per message whether they use the record length field or not. If possible, the record length field should be left out.
sequence_number		An optional sequence number of the record. Note that this field MUST be used with datagram transports.
length		The optional length (in bytes) of the following WTLSPlaintext.fragment. This field MUST be used if several records are concatenated into one transport SDU.
fragment		The application data. This data is transparent and treated as an independent block to be dealt with by the higher-level protocol specified by the type field.

Note: Data of different WTLS Record layer content types may be interleaved. Application data is generally of lower precedence for transmission than other content types.

6.2.2 Record Compression and Decompression

All records are compressed using the compression algorithm defined in the current connection state. There is always an active compression algorithm; however, initially it is defined as NULL. Note that a stateful compression algorithm cannot be used if WTLS is run on top of a datagram transport.

The compression algorithm translates a WTLSPlaintext structure into a WTLSCompressed structure. This means that the WTLSPlaintext.fragment is compressed and copied. Other fields (such as the fragment length) are updated if needed.

```
struct {
   opaque record_type[1];
   select (SequenceNumberIndication) {
       case without: struct {};
       case with: uint16 sequence_number;
   }
   select (FragmentLengthIndication) {
       case without: struct {};
       case with: uint16 length;
   }
   opaque fragment[WTLSCompressed.length];
} WTLSCompressed;
```

Description of WTLSCompressed fields:

ITEM	DESCRIPTION
record_type	As in Section 6.2.1.
sequence_number	As in Section 6.2.1.
length	The optional length (in bytes) of the following WTLSCompressed.fragment (See Section 6.2.1).
fragment	The compressed form of WTLSPlaintext.fragment.

6.2.3 Record Payload Protection

The encryption and MAC functions translate a WTLSCompressed structure into a WTLSCiphertext. The decryption functions reverse the process.

```
struct {
   opaque record_type[1];
   select (SequenceNumberIndication) {
       case without: struct {};
       case with: uint16 sequence_number;
   }
   select (FragmentLengthIndication) {
       case without: struct {};
       case with: uint16 length;
   }
   select (SecurityParameters.cipher_type) {
       case stream: GenericStreamCipher;
       case block: GenericBlockCipher;
   } fragment;
} WTLSCiphertext;
```

ITEM	DESCRIPTION
record_type	As in Section 6.2.1.
sequence_number	As in Section 6.2.1.
length	The optional length (in bytes) of the following WTLSCiphertext.fragment (See Section 6.2.1).
fragment	The encrypted form of WTLSCompressed.fragment.

6.2.3.1 Explicit Sequence Numbering

When explicit sequence numbering is used, record verification and decryption require special measures. Explicit sequence numbering MUST be used with a datagram transport protocol, meaning that records can be lost, duplicated, or received out of order.

The receiver MUST keep books about received records in order to discard duplicated records. This can be implemented using a sliding window. For example, a window size of 32 can be used. Using this window, the receiver can keep books on received messages with sequence numbers in the range

n–32 … n

where n is the current (expected) sequence number. Records with sequence numbers n–32 MUST be discarded.

When a handshake starts with plain text message exchanges, sequence numbers start from 0 and are incremented by 1 in each handshake message. When a handshake starts on a secure connection, the current sequence numbers for the secure connection are used for handshake messages and are incremented by 1 for each handshake message. They are set to 0 after ChangeCipherSpec message for either cases. In retransmissions, sequence numbers remain the same as in the original messages. When the sequence number exceeds 2^{16}–1, the secure connection MUST be closed.

In handshake messages, sequence numbers MUST be used (even on connection-oriented transports). After negotiation, sequence numbers are either used or not. Note that with datagram transport protocols, sequence numbers MUST always be used.

6.2.3.2 Null or Standard Stream Cipher

Stream ciphers (including BulkCipherAlgorithm NULL) convert WTLSCompressed .fragment structures to and from stream WTLSCiphertext.fragment structures.

```
stream-ciphered struct {
   opaque content[WTLSCompressed.length];
   opaque MAC[SecurityParameters.mac_size];
} GenericStreamCipher;
```

The MAC is generated as

```
HMAC_hash ( MAC_secret, seq_number + WTLSCompressed.record_type +
            WTLSCompressed.length + WTLSCompressed.fragment )
```

where "+" denotes concatenation. If WTLSCompressed.length is not available, the actual length of the compressed fragment should be used instead. If sequence numbers are not used at all, a value of 0 is assumed.

Note that no stream ciphers except BulkCipherAlgorithm NULL are defined in the current WTLS specification.

6.2.3.3 CBC Block Cipher

For block ciphers (such as RC5 and DES), the encryption and MAC functions convert WTLSCompressed.fragment structures to and from block WTLSCiphertext.fragment structures.

```
block-ciphered struct {
   opaque content[WTLSCompressed.length];
   opaque MAC[SecurityParameters.hash_size];
   uint8 padding[padding_length];
```

```
    uint8 padding_length;
} GenericBlockCipher;
```

The MAC is generated as described in Section 6.1.

ITEM	DESCRIPTION
padding	Padding that is added to force the length of the plaintext to be a multiple of the block cipher's block length. Each uint8 in the padding data vector MUST be filled with the padding length value.
padding_length	The padding length should be such that the total size of the GenericBlockCipher structure is a multiple of the cipher's block length. Legal values range from 0 to 255, inclusive.

The encrypted data length (WTLSCiphertext.length) is 1 more than the sum of WTLSCompressed.length, CipherSpec.hash_size, and padding_length.

Example: If the block length is 8 bytes, the content length (WTLSCompressed .length) is 59 bytes, and if 10 bytes of the MAC are used, the length before padding is 70 bytes. Since 70 mod 8 is 6, 2 bytes of padding are required.

7. Handshake Protocol Specification

The WTLS Handshake Protocol is composed of three subprotocols that are used to allow peers to agree upon security parameters for the record layer, authenticate themselves, instantiate negotiated security parameters, and report error conditions to each other.

The Handshake Protocol is responsible for negotiating a secure session, which consists of the following items:

ITEM	DESCRIPTION
Session Identifier	An arbitrary byte sequence chosen by the server to identify an active or resumable secure session.
Protocol Version	WTLS protocol version number.
Peer Certificate	Certificate of the peer. This element of the state may be null.
Compression Method	The algorithm used to compress data prior to encryption.
Cipher Spec	Specifies the bulk data encryption algorithm (such as null, RC5, DES, etc.) and a MAC algorithm (such as SHA-1). It also defines cryptographic attributes such as the mac_size.
Master Secret	20-byte secret shared between the client and server.

ITEM	DESCRIPTION
Sequence Number Mode	Which sequence numbering scheme (off, implicit, or explicit) is used in this secure connection.
Key Refresh	Defines how often some connection state values (encryption key, MAC secret, and IV) calculations are performed.
Is Resumable	A flag indicating whether the secure session can be used to initiate new secure connections.

These items are then used to create security parameters for use by the Record layer when protecting application data. Many secure connections can be instantiated using the same secure session through the resumption feature of the WTLS Handshake Protocol.

7.1 Change Cipher Spec Protocol

The change cipher spec protocol exists to signal transitions in ciphering strategies. The protocol consists of a single message, which is encrypted and compressed under the current (not the pending) connection state. The message consists of a single byte of value 1.

```
struct {
   enum { change_cipher_spec(1), (255) } type;
} ChangeCipherSpec;
```

The change cipher spec is sent either by the client or server to notify the other party that subsequent records will be protected under the newly negotiated CipherSpec and keys. In practice, it means that both peers should immediately make the pending state current. The change cipher spec message is sent during the handshake after the security parameters have been agreed upon, but before the verifying finished message is sent. Implementations MUST check that the change cipher spec message is sent or received before sending or receiving the verifying finished message, so that the finished and subsequent messages are protected under the newly negotiated CipherSpec and keys.

7.2 Alert Protocol

One of the content types supported by the WTLS Record layer is the alert type. Alert messages convey the severity of the message and a description of the alert.

Alert messages with a level of fatal result in the immediate termination of the secure connection. In this case, other connections using the secure session MAY continue, but the session identifier MUST be invalidated, preventing the failed secure session from being used to establish new secure connections.

Alert messages with a level of critical result in the immediate termination of the secure connection. Other connections using the secure session MAY continue, and the session identifier MAY be preserved to be used for establishing new secure connections.

An alert message is either sent as specified by the current connection state (i.e., compressed and encrypted) or under null cipher spec (i.e., without compression or encryption).

A 4-byte checksum is used in alerts. The checksum is calculated from the last record (i.e., WTLSCiphertext structure) received from the other party in the following way:

1. Pad the record with 0 bytes so that its length is modulo 4.
2. Divide the result into 4-byte blocks.
3. XOR these blocks together.

The receiver of the alert SHOULD verify that the checksum matches with the message earlier sent by him.

```
enum { warning(1), critical(2), fatal(3), (255) } AlertLevel;

enum {
   connection_close_notify(0),
   session_close_notify(1)
   no_connection(5),
   unexpected_message(10),
   bad_record_mac(20),
   decryption_failed(21),
   record_overflow(22),
   decompression_failure(30),
   handshake_failure(40),
   bad_certificate(42),
   unsupported_certificate(43),
   certificate_revoked(44),
   certificate_expired(45),
   certificate_unknown(46),
   illegal_parameter(47),
   unknown_ca(48),
   access_denied(49),
   decode_error(50),
   decrypt_error(51),
   unknown_key_id(52),
   disabled_key_id(53),
   key_exchange_disabled(54),
   session_not_ready(55),
   unknown_parameter_index(56),
   duplicate_finished_received(57),
   export_restriction(60),
   protocol_version(70),
   insufficient_security(71),
   internal_error(80),
   user_canceled(90),
   no_renegotiation(100), (255)
} AlertDescription;

struct {
   AlertLevel level;
   AlertDescription description;
   opaque checksum[4]
} Alert;
```

7.2.1 Closure Alerts

The client and the server must share knowledge that the secure connection is ending. Either party may initiate the exchange of closing messages.

ALERT	DESCRIPTION
connection_close_notify	This message notifies the recipient that the sender will not send any more messages using this connection state.
session_close_notify	This message notifies the recipient that the sender will not send any more messages using this connection state or the secure session.

Either party may initiate a close by sending a *connection_close_notify* or *session_close_notify* alert. Any data received after a closure alert is ignored. It is required that the other party responds with a *connection_close_notify* or *session_close_notify* alert of its own, respectively, and closes down the secure connection immediately, discarding any pending writes. In the case of a *session_close_notify*, the receiver MUST also invalidate the session identifier. It is not required for the initiator of the close to wait for the responding *connection_close_notify* or *session_close_notify* alert before closing the read side of the secure connection.

7.2.2 Error Alerts

Error handling in the WTLS Handshake protocol is very simple. When an error is detected, the detecting party sends a message to the other party. Upon transmission or receipt of a fatal alert message, both parties immediately close the secure connection. Servers and clients are required to forget any session identifiers, keys, and secrets associated with a failed secure connection. Upon transmission or receipt of a critical alert message, both parties immediately close the secure connection but MAY preserve the session identifiers and use that for establishing new secure connections. The following error alerts are defined:

ALERT	DESCRIPTION
no_connection	A message was received while there is no secure connection with the sender. This message is fatal or critical. The message is sent in cleartext.
unexpected_message	An inappropriate message was received. This alert SHOULD be fatal or critical.
bad_record_mac	This alert is returned if a record is received with an incorrect MAC. This message is generally a warning. The message is sent in cleartext.
decryption_failed	A WTLSCiphertext decrypted in an invalid way; either it wasn't a multiple of the block length or its padding values, when checked, weren't correct. This message is generally a warning. The message is sent in cleartext.

ALERT	DESCRIPTION
record_overflow	A WTLSCiphertext record was received which had a length more than allowed bytes, or a record decrypted to a WTLSCompressed record with more than allowed bytes. This message is generally a warning. The message is sent in cleartext.
decompression_failure	The decompression function received improper input (e.g., data that would expand to excessive length). This message is generally a warning. The message is sent in cleartext.
handshake_failure	Reception of a handshake_failure alert message indicates that the sender was unable to negotiate an acceptable set of security parameters given the options available. This is a fatal error.
bad_certificate	A certificate was corrupt, contained signatures that did not verify correctly, etc.
unsupported_certificate	A certificate was of an unsupported type.
certificate_revoked	A certificate was revoked by its signer. Note that certificate revocation is likely to be checked by servers only.
certificate_expired	A certificate has expired or is not currently valid.
certificate_unknown	Some other (unspecified) issue arose in processing the certificate, rendering it unacceptable.
illegal_parameter	A field in the handshake was out of range or inconsistent with other fields. This is always fatal.
unknown_ca	A valid certificate chain or partial chain was received, but the certificate was not accepted because the CA certificate could not be located or couldn't be matched with a known, trusted CA. This message is always fatal.
access_denied	A valid certificate was received, but when access control was applied, the sender decided not to proceed with negotiation. This message is always fatal.
decode_error	A message could not be decoded because some field was out of the specified range or the length of the message was incorrect. This message is fatal or critical.
decrypt_error	A handshake cryptographic operation failed, including being unable to correctly verify a signature, decrypt a key exchange, or validate a finished message. This message SHOULD be sent as fatal.
unknown_key_id	None of the client key_ids listed in ClientHello.client_key_ids is known or recognized to the server, or the client did not supply any items, if the server has the policy that requires recognition of client_key_ids. This is generally a fatal alert.

ALERT	DESCRIPTION
disabled_key_id	All the client_key_ids listed in ClientHello.client_key_ids are disabled administratively. This is generally a critical alert.
key_exchange_disabled	To protect the outcome of the anonymous key exchange from being overridden by the undesirable subsequent anonymous key exchanges, key exchange is administratively disabled.
session_not_ready	The secure session is not ready to resume new secure connections due to administrative reasons such as that the session is temporarily not available due to maintenance in the server. This is generally a critical alert.
unknown_parameter_index	The client has suggested a key exchange suite that could be supported by the server, but the server does not know the key exchange parameter index supplied. When receiving this alert, the client may initiate a new handshake and suggest another parameter index, supply the parameters explicitly, or let the server supply the parameters.
duplicate_finished_received	In an abbreviated or optimized handshake, the client has sent a second (resent) finished message. This message is generally a warning.
export_restriction	A negotiation not in compliance with export restrictions was detected. This message is always fatal.
protocol_version	The protocol version the client (or server) has attempted to negotiate is recognized, but not supported by the server (or client). (For example, old protocol versions might be avoided for security reasons). This message is always fatal.
insufficient_security	Returned instead of handshake_failure when a negotiation has failed specifically because the server requires ciphers more secure than those supported by the client. This message is always fatal.
internal_error	An internal error unrelated to the peer or the correctness of the protocol makes it impossible to continue (such as a memory allocation failure). This message is fatal or critical.
user_canceled	This handshake is being canceled for some reason unrelated to a protocol failure. If the user cancels an operation after the handshake is complete, just closing the secure connection by sending a *connection_close_notify* is more appropriate. This alert should be followed by a *connection_close_notify*. This message is generally a warning.
no_renegotiation	Sent by the client in response to a hello request or by the server in response to a client hello after initial handshaking. Either of these would normally lead to renegotiation. When that is not appropriate, the recipient SHOULD respond with this alert. At that point, the original requester can decide whether to proceed with the secure connection.

For all errors where an alert level is not explicitly specified, the sending party may determine at its discretion whether this is a fatal or critical error or a warning; if an alert with a level of warning or critical is received, the receiving party may decide at its discretion whether to treat this as a fatal error or not. However, all messages that are transmitted with a level of fatal MUST be treated as fatal messages.

Implementations MAY maintain a count of received alerts with a level of warning or critical, and treat them as fatal when a certain configurable limit is exceeded.

A fatal alert only terminates the session to be created and leaves the existing session intact if the handshaking is conducted on an existing secure session. However, there may be some cases in which closing the existing session is desirable. A *session_close_notify* MUST be sent to the peer if one of the parties decides to terminate the existing session immediately after a fatal alert is sent or received during a handshake that intends to create a new session. Under any other circumstances, a fatal alert is treated normally as described at the beginning of this section.

7.3 Handshake Protocol Overview

The cryptographic parameters of the secure session are produced by the WTLS Handshake Protocol, which operates on top of the WTLS Record layer. When a WTLS client and server first start communicating, they agree on a protocol version, select cryptographic algorithms, optionally authenticate each other, and use public-key encryption techniques to generate a shared secret.

The WTLS Handshake Protocol involves the following steps:

1. Exchange hello messages to agree on algorithms, exchange random values.
2. Exchange the necessary cryptographic parameters to allow the client and server to agree on a pre-master secret.
3. Exchange certificates and cryptographic information to allow the client and server to authenticate themselves.
4. Generate a master secret from the pre-master secret and exchanged random values.
5. Provide security parameters to the Record layer.
6. Allow the client and server to verify that their peer has calculated the same security parameters and that the handshake occurred without tampering by an attacker.

These goals are achieved by the handshake protocol, which can be summarized as follows: The client sends a client hello message to which the server must respond with a server hello message, or else a fatal error will occur and the secure connection will fail. The client hello and server hello are used to establish security enhancement capabilities between client and server. The client hello and server hello establish the following attributes: Protocol Version, Key Exchange Suite, Cipher Suite, Compression Method, Key Refresh, and Sequence Number Mode. Additionally, two random values are generated and exchanged: ClientHello.random and ServerHello.random.

The actual key exchange uses up to four messages: the server certificate, the server key exchange, the client certificate, and the client key exchange. New key exchange methods can be created by specifying a format for these messages and defining the use of the messages to allow the client and server to agree upon a shared secret. This secret should be quite long. For wireless environments, 20 bytes can be considered suitable.

Following the hello messages, the server will send its certificate, if it is to be authenticated. Additionally, a server key exchange message may be sent, if it is required (e.g., the server does not have a certificate, or if its certificate is for signing only). The server may request a certificate from the client (or get the certificate from some certificate distribution service), if that is appropriate to the key exchange suite selected. Now the server will send the server hello done message, indicating that the hello-message phase of the handshake is complete. (The previous handshake messages are combined in one lower-layer message.) The server will then wait for a client response. If the server has sent a certificate request message, the client must send the certificate message. The client key exchange message is now sent if the client certificate does not contain enough data for key exchange or if it is not sent at all. The content of that message will depend on the public key algorithm selected between the client hello and the server hello. If the client is to be authenticated using a certificate with a signing capability (e.g., RSA), a digitally signed certificate verify message is sent to explicitly verify the certificate.

At this point, a change cipher spec message is sent by the client, and the client copies the pending CipherSpec into the current CipherSpec. The client then immediately sends the finished message under the new algorithms, keys, and secrets. From now on, the CipherSpec indicator is set to 1 in the messages. When the server receives the change CipherSpec message it also copies the pending CipherSpec into the current CipherSpec. In response, the server will send its own finished message under the new CipherSpec. At this point, the handshake is complete and the client and server may begin to exchange application layer data (see Figure 16.5).

When the client and server decide to resume a previous secure session instead of negotiating new security parameters, the message flow is as follows: The client sends a ClientHello using the Session ID of the secure session to be resumed. The server then

```
Client                                            Server


ClientHello                --------->
                                                  ServerHello
                                                  Certificate*
                                                  ServerKeyExchange*
                                                  CertificateRequest*
                           <---------             ServerHelloDone
Certificate*
ClientKeyExchange*
CertificateVerify*
[ChangeCipherSpec]
Finished                   --------->
                           <---------             Finished

Application Data           <-------->             Application Data
```

Figure 16.5 Message flow for a full handshake.

* Indicates optional or situation-dependent messages that are not always sent.

checks its secure session cache for a match. If a match is found, and the server is willing to reestablish the secure connection under the specified secure session, it will send a ServerHello with the same Session ID value. At this point, the server must send a change CipherSpec message and proceed directly to the finished message to which the client should response with its own finished message. Once the reestablishment is complete, the client and server may begin to exchange Application layer data. (See Figure 16.6.) If a Session ID match is not found, the server generates a new session ID and the TLS client and server perform a full handshake.

Note that many simultaneous secure connections can be instantiated under one secure session. Each secure connection established from the same secure session shares some parameters with the others (e.g., master secret).

The shared-secret handshake means that the new secure session is based on a shared secret already implanted in both ends (e.g., physically). In this case, the shared-secret KeyExchangeSuite is requested by the client. The message flow is similar to the abbreviated handshake in Figure 16.6.

Another variation is that the server, after receiving the ClientHello, can retrieve the client's certificate using a certificate distribution service or from its own sources. In a Diffie-Hellman-type key exchange method, assuming the Diffie-Hellman parameters are provided in the certificates, the server can calculate the pre-master secret and master secret at this point. In this case, the server sends its certificate, a ChangeCipherSpec, and a Finished message. See Figure 16.7.

```
Client                                          Server

ClientHello               -------->
                                                ServerHello
                                                [ChangeCipherSpec]
                          <--------             Finished
Finished
Application Data          -------->

Application Data          <------->             Application Data
```

Figure 16.6 Message flow for an abbreviated handshake.

```
Client                                          Server

ClientHello               -------->
                                                ServerHello
                                                Certificate
                                                [ChangeCipherSpec]
                          <--------             Finished
Finished
Application Data          -------->

Application Data          <------->             Application Data
```

Figure 16.7 Message flow for an optimized full handshake.

7.4 Handshake Reliability over Datagrams

In the datagram environment, handshake messages may be lost, out of order, or duplicated. To make the handshake reliable over datagrams, WTLS requires that the handshake messages going in the same direction must be concatenated in a single transport Service Data Unit (SDU) for transmission, that the client retransmits the handshake messages if necessary, and that the server MUST appropriately respond to the retransmitted messages from the client.

The handshake may consist of multiple messages to be delivered in one direction before any responses are required from the other end. Those messages must be concatenated into a single transport SDU for transmission or retransmission to guarantee that all the messages in the same SDU arrive in order. For instance, ServerHello, ChangeCipherSpec, and Finished messages can be sent in a single transport SDU for the abbreviated handshake. The maximum size of SDU for the underlying Transport Service layer must be sufficient to contain all those messages.

For the full handshake, the client must retransmit ClientHello and Finished messages if the expected response messages are not received from the server for a predefined timeout period. Note that the whole transport SDU that contains the Finished message must be retransmitted. After the number of retransmissions exceeds the maximum predefined retransmission counter, the client terminates the handshake. Those predefined time-out and counter values may be obtained from the WTP stack through the management entity if the WTP stack is present above the WTLS stack.

For the optimized and abbreviated handshakes, like the full handshake, the client retransmits ClientHello, if necessary. In addition, the client must also prepend Finished message with the Application Data message until an Application Data message from the server is received and decrypted successfully, or a *duplicated_finished_received* alert (warning) is received from the server. However, the first Finished message can be either sent alone or prepend with the Application Data message, if any.

For the full handshake, the server MUST retransmit the transport SDU that contains the ServerHello message upon receiving a duplicated ClientHello message. However, if the ClientHello is new, the server MUST start a new handshake and SEC-Create.ind service primitive MUST be generated. The server MUST also retransmit the transport SDU that contains the Finished message upon receiving a duplicated Finished message from the client.

For the optimized and abbreviated handshakes, the server behaves the same as that in the full handshake for handling the duplicated or new ClientHello messages. In addition, the server MUST ignore duplicated Finished message and keep the committed secure connection intact. If the server has no Application Data to send to the client, it SHOULD send *duplicated_finished_received* alert (warning).

7.5 Handshake Protocol

The WTLS Handshake Protocol is one of the defined higher-level clients of the WTLS Record Protocol. This protocol is used to negotiate the secure attributes of a secure session. Handshake messages are supplied to the WTLS Record layer, where they are encapsulated within one or more WTLSPlaintext structures, which are processed and transmitted as specified by the current active connection state.

```
enum {
   hello_request(0), client_hello(1), server_hello(2),
   certificate(11), server_key_exchange(12),
   certificate_request(13), server_hello_done(14),
   certificate_verify(15), client_key_exchange(16),
   finished(20), (255)
} HandshakeType;
struct {
   HandshakeType msg_type; /* handshake type */
   uint16 length;          /* bytes in message */
   select (msg_type) {
       case hello_request:        HelloRequest;
       case client_hello:         ClientHello;
       case server_hello:         ServerHello;
       case certificate:          Certificate;
       case server_key_exchange   ServerKeyExchange;
       case certificate_request:  CertificateRequest;
       case server_hello_done:    ServerHelloDone;
       case certificate_verify:   CertificateVerify;
       case client_key_exchange:  ClientKeyExchange;
       case finished:             Finished;
   } body;
} Handshake;
```

The handshake protocol messages are presented in the order they must be sent; sending handshake messages in an unexpected order results in a fatal error. Unneeded handshake messages can be omitted, however. Note one exception to the ordering: The Certificate message is used twice in the handshake (from server to client, then from client to server) but described only in its first position. The one message that is not bound by these ordering rules is the Hello Request message, which can be sent at any time but should be ignored by the client if it arrives in the middle of a handshake.

7.5.1 Hello Messages

The hello phase messages are used to agree on used security parameters between the client and server. When a new secure session begins, the connection state (encryption, hash, and compression algorithms) is initialized to null. The CipherSpec indicator is set to 0 in the records.

7.5.1.1 Hello Request

When this message will be sent:

The hello request message may be sent by the server at any time.

Meaning of this message:

Hello request is a simple notification that the client should begin the negotiation process anew by sending a client hello message when convenient. This message will be ignored by the client if the client is currently negotiating a secure session. This message MAY be ignored by the client if it does not wish to make a new handshake, or the client may, if it wishes, respond with a *no_renegotiation* alert.

Since handshake messages are intended to have transmission precedence over application data, it is expected that the negotiation will begin before no more than a few records are received from the client. If the server sends a hello request but does not receive a client hello in response, it MAY close the secure connection with a fatal alert.

After sending a hello request, servers should not repeat the request until the subsequent handshake negotiation is complete. However, if the client does not respond in a reasonable time, the message MAY be sent again.

Structure of this message:

```
struct { } HelloRequest;
```

Note: This message must not be included in the message hashes that are maintained throughout the handshake and used in the finished messages and the certificate verify message.

7.5.1.2 Client Hello

When this message will be sent:

When a client first connects to a server it is required to send the client hello as its first message. The client can also send a client hello in response to a hello request or on its own initiative in order to renegotiate the security parameters in an existing secure connection.

Structure of this message:

The key exchange list contains the cryptographic key exchange algorithms supported by the client in decreasing order of preference. In addition, each entry defines the certificate or public key the client wishes to use. The server will select one or, if no acceptable choices are presented, return a *handshake_failure* alert and close the secure connection. The trusted authorities list with a similar format identifies the trusted certificates known by the client.

```
struct {
   uint32 gmt_unix_time;
   opaque random_bytes[12];
} Random;
```

ITEM	DESCRIPTION
gmt_unix_time	The current time and date in standard Unix 32-bit format (seconds since the midnight starting Jan 1, 1970, GMT) according to the sender's internal clock. Clocks are not required to be set correctly by the basic WTLS Protocol (so, if client has no date and time available it can place null here); higher-level or application protocols may define additional requirements.
random_bytes	12 bytes generated by a secure random number generator. This value will be used later in the protocol.

```
uint8 KeyExchangeSuite;    /* Key exchange suite selector */

struct {
   uint8 dh_e;
   opaque dh_p<1..2^16-1>;
   opaque dh_g<1..2^16-1>;
} DHParameters;
```

ITEM	DESCRIPTION
dh_e	The exponent length in bytes. The value 0 indicates that the default length is used (i.e., the same length as the prime).
dh_p	The prime modulus used for the Diffie-Hellman operation.
dh_g	The generator used for the Diffie-Hellman operation.

```
enum { ec_prime_p(1), ec_characteristic_two(2), (255) } ECFieldID;

enum { ec_basis_onb, ec_basis_trinomial, ec_basis_pentanomial }
ECBasisType;

struct {
   opaque a <1..2^8-1>;
   opaque b <1..2^8-1>;
   opaque seed <0..2^8-1>;
} ECCurve;
```

ITEM	DESCRIPTION
a, b	These parameters specify the coefficients of the elliptic curve. Each value shall be the octet string representation of a field element following the conversion routine in [X9.62], Section 4.3.1.
seed:	This is an optional parameter used to derive the coefficients of a randomly generated elliptic curve.

```
struct {
   opaque point <1..2^8-1>;
} ECPoint;
```

ITEM	DESCRIPTION
point	This is the octet string representation of an elliptic curve point following the conversion routine in [X9.62], Section 4.4.2.a. The representation format is defined following the definition in [X9.62], Section 4.4.

```
struct {
   ECFieldID   field;
   select (field) {
```

```
        case ec_prime_p: opaque prime_p <1..2^8-1>;
        case ec_characteristic_two:
            uint16      m;
            ECBasisType basis;
            select (basis) {
                case ec_basis_onb:
                    struct { };
                case ec_trinomial:
                    opaque k <1..2^8-1>;
                case ec_pentanomial:
                    opaque k1 <1..2^8-1>;
                    opaque k2 <1..2^8-1>;
                    opaque k3 <1..2^8-1>;
            };
        };
        ECCurve     curve;
        ECPoint     base;
        opaque      order <1..2^8-1>;
        opaque      cofactor <1..2^8-1>;
    } ECParameters;
```

ITEM	DESCRIPTION
field	This identifies the finite field over which the elliptic curve is defined.
prime_p	This is the odd prime defining the field F_p.
m	This is the degree of the characteristic-two field F_{2^m}.
k	The exponent k for the trinomical basis representation $x^m + x^k + 1$.
k1, k2, k3	The exponents for the pentanomial representation $x^m + x^{k3} + x^{k2} + x^{k1} + 1$.
Curve	Specifies the coefficients a and b of the elliptic curve E.
base	The base point P on the elliptic curve.
order	The order n of the base point. The order of a point P is the smallest possible integer n such that nP = 0 (the point at infinity).
cofactor	The integer h = #E(Fq)/n, where #E(Fq) represents the number of points on the elliptic curve E defined over the field Fq.

```
uint8 ParameterIndex;

enum { rsa, diffie_hellman, elliptic_curve } PublicKeyAlgorithm;

struct {
   select (PublicKeyAlgorithm) {
       case rsa: struct {};
       case diffie_hellman: DHParameters params;
       case elliptic_curve: ECParameters params;
   }
```

```
} ParameterSet;

struct {
   ParameterIndex parameter_index;
   select (parameter_index) {
       case 255: ParameterSet parameter_set;
       default: struct {};
   }
} ParameterSpecifier;
```

ITEM	DESCRIPTION
parameter_index	Indicates parameters relevant for this key exchange suite. 0 = not applicable, or specified elsewhere. 1–254 = assigned number of a parameter set, defined in Appendix A. 255 = explicit parameters are present in the next field.
parameter_set	Explicit parameters; e.g., Diffie-Hellman or ECDH parameters. Implementations SHOULD use parameter indexes instead of explicit parameters.

```
enum { null(0), text(1), binary(2), key_hash_sha(254), x509_name(255)}
   IdentifierType;

uint16 CharacterSet;

struct {
   IdentifierType identifier_type;
   select (identifier_type) {
       case null: struct {};
       case text:
           CharacterSet character_set;
           opaque name<1.. 2^8-1>;
       case binary: opaque identifier<1..2^8-1>;
       case key_hash_sha: opaque key_hash[20];
       case x509_name: opaque distinguished_name<1..2^8-1>;
} Identifier;
```

ITEM	DESCRIPTION
identifier_type	Type of identifier used. 0 = no identity supplied. 1 = textual name with character set. 2 = binary identity. 254 = SHA-1 hash of the public key. 255 = X.509 distinguished name.
character_set	Maps to IANA defined character set.
name	Textual name.

ITEM	DESCRIPTION
identifier	Binary identifier.
key_hash	Hash calculated over the public key of the key pair which the client intends to use in the handshake to prove its identity.
distinguished_name	X.509 distinguished name.

```
struct {
   KeyExchangeSuite key_exchange_suite;
   ParameterSpecifier parameter_specifier;
   Identifier identifier;
} KeyExchangeId;
```

ITEM	DESCRIPTION
key_exchange_suite	Assigned number of the key exchange suite, defined in Appendix A.
parameter_specifier	Specifies parameters relevant for this key exchange suite. Value 0 of a parameter index for a key exchange suite using parameters indicates that the server MUST supply parameters
identifier	Identifies the client in a relevant way for the key exchange suite. The server can use this information to fetch a client certificate from a database.

The CipherSuite list, passed from the client to the server in the client hello message, contains the combinations of symmetric cryptographic algorithms supported by the client in order of the client's preference (favorite choice first). Each CipherSuite defines a bulk encryption algorithm (including secret key length) and a MAC algorithm. The server will select a cipher suite or, if no acceptable choices are presented, return a *handshake_failure* alert and close the secure connection.

```
struct {
   BulkCipherAlgorithm bulk_cipher_algorithm;
   MACAlgorithm        mac_algorithm;
} CipherSuite
```

ITEM	DESCRIPTION
bulk_cipher_algorithm	Assigned number of the bulk cipher algorithm, defined in Appendix A.
mac_algorithm	Assigned number of the MAC algorithm, defined in Appendix A.

```
opaque SessionID<0..8>;
```

The client hello includes a list of compression algorithms supported by the client, ordered according to the client's preference.

```
uint8 CompressionMethod;

struct {
   uint8 client_version;
   Random random;
   SessionID session_id;
   KeyExchangeId client_key_ids<3..2^16-1>;
   KeyExchangeId trusted_key_ids<0..2^16-1>;
   CipherSuite cipher_suites<2..2^8-1>;
   CompressionMethod compression_methods<1..2^8-1>;
   SequenceNumberMode sequence_number_mode;
   uint8 key_refresh;
} ClientHello;
```

ITEM	DESCRIPTION
client_version	The version of the WTLS protocol by which the client wishes to communicate during this secure session. This should be the latest (highest valued) version supported by the client. For this version of the specification, the version will be 1.
random	A client-generated random structure.
session_id	The ID of a secure session the client wishes to use for this secure connection. This field should be empty if no session_id is available or the client wishes to generate new security parameters.
client_key_ids	A list of cryptographic key exchange options and identities supported by the client, with the client's first preference first.
trusted_key_ids	A list of trusted certificates known by the client, with the client's first preference first.
cipher_suites	This is a list of the cryptographic options supported by the client, with the client's first preference first.
compression_methods	This is a list of the compression methods supported by the client, sorted by client preference. This vector MUST contain, and all implementations MUST support, CompressionMethod NULL. Thus, a client and server will always be able to agree on a compression method.
sequence_number_mode	This value indicates how sequence numbering should be used in Record layer messages.
key_refresh	Defines how often some connection state parameters (encryption key, MAC secret, and IV) are updated.

After sending the client hello message, the client waits for a server hello message. Any other handshake message returned by the server except for a hello request is treated as a critical or fatal error.

When the client has an existing session_id and is initiating an abbreviated handshake, it MAY omit key exchange related items (client_key_ids, trusted_key_ids) from the client hello message. In this case, if the server is not willing to resume the session and is not able to continue with a full handshake, it MUST return an *unknown_key_id* alert.

7.5.1.3 Server Hello

When this message will be sent:

The server will send this message in response to a client hello message when it was able to find an acceptable set of algorithms. If it cannot find such a match, it must respond with a *handshake_failure* alert.

Structure of this message:

```
struct {
   uint8 server_version;
   Random random;
   SessionID session_id;
   uint8 client_key_id;
   CipherSuite cipher_suite;
   CompressionMethod compression_method;
   SequenceNumberMode sequence_number_mode;
   uint8 key_refresh;
} ServerHello;
```

ITEM	DESCRIPTION
server_version	This field will contain the lower of that suggested by the client in the client hello and the highest supported by the server. For this version of the specification, the version is 1.
random	This structure is generated by the server and must be different from (and independent of) ClientHello.random.
session_id	This is the identity of the secure session corresponding to this secure connection. If the ClientHello.session_id was nonempty, the server will look in its secure session cache for a match. If a match is found and the server is willing to establish the new secure connection using the specified secure session, the server will respond with the same value as was supplied by the client. This indicates a resumed secure session and dictates that the parties must proceed directly to the finished messages. Otherwise, this field will contain a different value identifying the new secure session. The server MAY return an empty session_id to indicate that the secure session will not be cached and therefore cannot be resumed. If a secure session is resumed, it must be using the same cipher suite it was originally negotiated with.

client_key_id	The number of the key exchange suite selected by the server from the list in ClientHello.client_key_ids. For example, value 1 indicates that the first entry was selected.
cipher_suite	The single cipher suite selected by the server from the list in ClientHello.cipher_suites.
compression_method	The single compression algorithm selected by the server from the list in ClientHello.compression_methods.
sequence_number_ mode	If the client suggested usage of sequence numbers, then the server MUST confirm the value. If the client did not suggest usage, the server can confirm that choice or indicate that sequence numbering should be used. So, if any party wishes to use sequence numbers then they have to be used.
key_refresh	This value indicates how many bits of the sequence number the server wishes to use to trigger key refresh. The value can be equal to what the client suggested or less. So, lower choice is used resulting in more frequent key refresh and thus higher security.

7.5.2 Server Certificate

When this message will be sent:

If sent this message must always immediately follow the server hello message.

Meaning of this message:

The certificate type must be appropriate for the selected key exchange suite's algorithm. It can a X.509v3 certificate [X509] or a WTLS certificate that is optimized for size. Other certificate types may be added in the future. It must contain a key that matches the key exchange method, as follows. Unless otherwise specified, the signing algorithm for the certificate must be the same as the algorithm for the key carried in the certificate. Unless otherwise specified, the public key may be of any length.

As KeyExchangeSuites that specify new key exchange methods are specified for the WTLS Protocol, they will imply certificate format and the required encoded keying information.

Structure of this message:

```
enum { WTLSCert(1), X509Cert(2), (255) } CertificateFormat;

opaque ASN1Cert<1..2^16-1>;

enum {      anonymous(0), ecdsa_sha(1), rsa_sha(2), (255)}
SignatureAlgorithm;

enum { rsa(2), ecdh(3), ecdsa(4), (255) } PublicKeyType;

ECPoint ECPublicKey;
```

ITEM	DESCRIPTION
ECPublicKey	The EC public key W = sG [P1363].

```
struct {
   opaque rsa_exponent<1..2^16-1>;
   opaque rsa_modulus<1..2^16-1>;
} RSAPublicKey;
```

ITEM	DESCRIPTION
rsa_exponent	The exponent of the server's RSA key.
rsa_modulus	The modulus of the server's RSA key.

```
struct {
   select (PublicKeyType) {
       case ecdh: ECPublicKey;
       case ecdsa: ECPublicKey;
       case rsa: RSAPublicKey;
} PublicKey;

struct {
   uint8 certificate_version;
   SignatureAlgorithm signature_algorithm;
   Identifier issuer;
   uint32 valid_not_before;
   uint32 valid_not_after;
   Identifier subject;
   PublicKeyType public_key_type;
   ParameterSpecifier parameter_specifier;
   PublicKey public_key;
} ToBeSignedCertificate;
```

ITEM	DESCRIPTION
certificate_version	Version of the certificate. For this specification, the version is 1.
signature_algorithm	Algorithm used to sign the certificate.
issuer	Issuer of the certificate. Defines who signed the certificate. Certificates are usually signed by Certification Authorities (CA).
valid_not_before	Beginning of the validity period of the certificate, expressed in standard Unix 32-bit format (seconds since the midnight starting Jan 1, 1970, GMT).
valid_not_after	End of the validity period of the certificate, expressed in standard Unix 32-bit format (seconds since the midnight starting Jan 1, 1970, GMT).

subject	Owner of the key, associated with the public key being certified.
public_key_type	Type (algorithm) of the public key.
parameter_specifier	Specifies parameter relevant for the public key.
public_key	Public key that is being certified.

The hash value and the signature is calculated from ToBeSignedCertificate using the algorithms defined in CertificateSignatureAlgorithm.

```
select( SignatureAlgorithm )
{
   case anonymous: { };
   case ecdsa_sha:
       digitally-signed struct {
           opaque sha_hash[20]; /* SHA-1 hash of data to be signed */
       }
   case rsa_sha:
       digitally-signed struct {
           opaque sha_hash[20]; /* SHA-1 hash of data to be signed */
       }
} Signature;

struct {
   ToBeSignedCertificate to_be_signed_certificate;
   Signature signature;
} WTLSCertificate;

struct {
   CertificateFormat certificate_format;
   select (certificate_format)     {
       case X.509:  ASN1Cert;
       case WTLSCert:   WTLSCertificate;
   }
} Certificate;

struct {
   Certificate certificate_list<0..2^16-1>;
} Certificates;
```

ITEM	DESCRIPTION
certificate_list	This is a sequence (chain) of certificates. The sender's certificate MUST come first in the list. Each following certificate MUST directly certify the one preceding it. Because certificate validation requires that root keys must be distributed independently, the self-signed certificate that specifies the root certificate authority is omitted from the chain, under the assumption that the remote end must already possess it in order to validate it in any case.

The same message type and structure will be used for the client's response to a certificate request message. Note that a client may send no certificates if it does not have an appropriate certificate to send in response to the server's authentication request.

To optimize the traffic and client processing, the chain should have minimal length. For server certificates, it is possible to have only one certificate: the server certificate certified by a CA public key of which is distributed independently.

Client certificate chain is likely to contain several certificates. However, this is acceptable because this chain is processed by the server. Also, the server may get the client certificate from a certificate distribution service.

In a certificate chain, all certificates must use algorithms appropriate for the selected key exchange suite. For example:

- For RSA, all certificates carry RSA keys signed with RSA.
- For ECDH_ECDSA, the first certificate contains an ECDH key signed with ECDSA, and the following certificates carry ECDSA keys signed with ECDSA.

7.5.3 Server Key Exchange Message

When this message will be sent:

This message will be sent immediately after the server certificate message (or the server hello message, if this is an anonymous negotiation).

The server key exchange message is sent by the server only when the server certificate message (if sent) does not contain enough data to allow the client to exchange a pre-master secret. This is true for the following key exchange methods:

- ECDH_anon
- RSA_anon
- DH_anon

The server key exchange message MUST NOT be sent for the following key exchange methods:

- ECDH_ECDSA (fixed parameters)
- RSA

Meaning of this message:

This message conveys cryptographic information to allow the client to communicate the pre-master secret: either an RSA public key to encrypt a secret with, or EC Diffie-Hellman parameters with which the client can complete a key exchange (with the result being the pre-master secret). As additional Key Exchange Suites are defined for WTLS that include new key exchange algorithms, the server key exchange message will be sent if and only if the certificate type associated with the key exchange algorithm does not provide enough information for the client to exchange a pre-master secret.

Structure of this message:

```
enum { rsa, rsa_anon, dh_anon, ecdh_anon } KeyExchangeAlgorithm;

struct {
   opaque dh_Y<1..2^16-1>;
} DHPublicKey;
```

ITEM	DESCRIPTION
dh_Y	The Diffie-Hellman public value (Y).

```
struct {
   ParameterSpecifier parameter_specifier;
   select (KeyExchangeAlgorithm) {
       case rsa_anon:
           RSAPublicKey params;
       case diffie_hellman_anon:
           DHPublicKey params;
       case ec_diffie_hellman_anon:
           ECPublicKey params;
   };
} ServerKeyExchange;
```

ITEM	DESCRIPTION
parameter_specifier	Specifies parameters relevant for this key exchange suite. Value 0 of a parameter index for a key exchange suite using parameters indicates that the server is willing to use those parameters indicated by the client. If the client has not indicated parameters, then the server MUST indicate them.
params	The server's key exchange parameters (RSA, ECDH, or DH public key).

7.5.4 Certificate Request

When this message will be sent:

A server can optionally request a certificate from the client, if appropriate for the selected cipher suite. This message, if sent, will immediately follow the Server Certificate message and Server Key Exchange message (if sent).

Structure of this message:

```
struct {
   KeyExchangeId trusted_authorities<0..2^16-1>;
} CertificateRequest;
```

ITEM	DESCRIPTION
trusted_authorities	A list of the names and types of acceptable certificate authorities. These names may specify a desired ID for a root CA or for a subordinate CA; thus, this message can be used both to describe known roots and a desired authorization space. If no authorities are sent, the client may send any certificate.

7.5.5 Server Hello Done

When this message will be sent:

The server hello done message is sent by the server to indicate the end of the server hello and associated messages. After sending this message the server will wait for a client response.

Meaning of this message:

This message means that the server is done sending messages to support the key exchange, and the client can proceed with its phase of the key exchange.

Upon receipt of the server hello done message the client should verify that the server provided a valid certificate if required and check that the server hello parameters are acceptable.

Structure of this message:

```
struct { } ServerHelloDone;
```

7.5.6 Client Certificate

When this message will be sent:

This message from the client can be sent after receiving a server hello done message. This message is only sent if the server requests a certificate. If no suitable certificate is available, the client must send a certificate message containing no certificates. If client authentication is required by the server for the handshake to continue, it MAY respond with a fatal *handshake_failure* alert. Client certificates are sent using the Certificate structure defined previously for server certificates.

7.5.7 Client Key Exchange Message

When this message will be sent:

This message will immediately follow the client certificate message, if it is sent. Otherwise, it will be the first message sent by the client after it receives the server hello done message.

Meaning of this message:

With this message, the pre-master secret is set, either through direct transmission of the RSA-encrypted secret, or by the transmission of EC Diffie-Hellman public key which will allow each side to agree upon the same pre-master secret. When the key exchange method is ECDH, client certification has been requested, and the client was able to respond with a certificate that contained EC Diffie-Hellman parameters which matched those specified by the server in its certificate, this message is omitted.

Structure of this message:

The structure of the message depends on which key exchange method has been selected.

```
struct {
   select (KeyExchangeAlgorithm) {
       case rsa: RSAEncryptedSecret param;;
       case rsa_anon: RSAEncryptedSecret param;
       case dh_anon: DHPublicKey param; /* client public value*
       case ecdh_anon: ECPublicKey param; /* client public value */
   } exchange_keys;
} ClientKeyExchange;
```

7.5.7.1 RSA Encrypted Secret Message

Meaning of this message:

If RSA is being used for key agreement and authentication, the client generates a 20-byte secret, encrypts it using the public key from the server's certificate, and sends the result in an encrypted secret message.

Structure of this message:

```
struct {
   uint8 client_version;
   opaque random[19];
} Secret;
```

ITEM	DESCRIPTION
client_version	The latest (newest) version supported by the client. This is used to detect version rollback attacks. Upon receiving the secret, the server should check that this value matches the value transmitted by the client in the client hello message.
random	19 securely generated random bytes.

```
struct {
   public-key-encrypted Secret secret;
} EncryptedSecret;
```

ITEM	DESCRIPTION
secret	This random value is generated by the client. This value appended with the public key is used as the pre-master secret, which is used to generate the master secret.

7.5.7.2 Client EC Diffie-Hellman Public Value

Meaning of this message:

This message conveys the client's EC Diffie-Hellman public key if it was not already included in the client's certificate. This structure is a variant of the client key exchange message, not a message in itself.

7.5.7.3 Client Diffie-Hellman Public Value

Meaning of this message:

This message conveys the client's Diffie-Hellman public key if it was not already included in the client's certificate. This structure is a variant of the client key exchange message, not a message in itself.

7.5.8 Certificate Verify

When this message will be sent:

This message is used to provide explicit verification of a client certificate. This message is only sent by the client following a client certificate that has signing capability (i.e., RSA certificates). When sent, it will immediately follow the client key exchange message.

Structure of this message:

```
struct {
   Signature signature;
} CertificateVerify;
```

ITEM	DESCRIPTION
signature	The hash value to be signed is calculated as follows: H(handshake_messages); Here handshake_messages refers to all handshake messages sent or received starting at client hello up to but not including this message, in the order they were sent by the client or by the server, including the data visible at the handshake layer; i.e., also the type and length fields of the handshake messages. This is the concatenation of all the Handshake structures (as defined in Section 7.3) exchanged this far. The hash algorithm used is the one agreed upon during the handshake.

7.5.9 Finished

When this message will be sent:

A finished message is always sent at the end of the handshake to verify that the key exchange and authentication processes were successful. Both ends must change finished messages immediately after a change cipher spec message.

Meaning of this message:

The finished message is the first protected with the just-negotiated algorithms, keys, and secrets. Recipients of finished messages MUST verify that the contents are correct. Once a side has sent its Finished message and received and validated the Finished message from its peer, it may begin to send and receive application data over the secure connection.

Structure of this message:

```
struct {
   opaque verify_data[12];
} Finished;
```

ITEM	DESCRIPTION
verify_data	The value is calculated as follows: PRF(master_secret, finished_label, H(handshake_messages)) [0..11]; finished_label For Finished messages sent by the client, the string "client finished". For Finished messages sent by the server, the string "server finished". handshake_messages All of the data from all handshake messages up to but not including this message, in the order they were sent by the client or by the server. This is only data visible at the handshake layer and does not include Record layer headers. This is the concatenation of all the Handshake structures (as defined in Section 7.3) exchanged thus far.

It is a critical or fatal error if a finished message is not preceded by a ChangeCipherSpec message at the appropriate point in the handshake.

The value handshake_messages includes all handshake messages starting at client hello up to, but not including, this finished message. The handshake_messages for the finished message sent by the client will be different from that for the finished message sent by the server, because the one that is sent second will include the prior one.

Note: ChangeCipherSpec messages, alerts, and any other record types are not handshake messages and are not included in the hash computations. Also, Hello Request messages are omitted from handshake hashes.

8. Cryptographic Computations

8.1 Computing the Master Secret

In order to begin message protection, the WTLS Record Protocol requires specification of a suite of algorithms, a master secret, and the client and server random values. The encryption and MAC algorithms are determined by the cipher_suite selected by the server and revealed in the server hello message. The key exchange and authentication algorithms are determined by the key_exchange_suite also revealed in the server hello. The compression algorithm is negotiated in the hello messages, and the random values are exchanged in the hello messages. All that remains is to calculate the master secret.

For all key exchange methods, the same algorithm is used to convert the pre_master_secret into the master_secret. The pre_master_secret SHOULD be deleted from memory once the master_secret has been computed.

```
master_secret = PRF( pre_master_secret, "master secret",
                     ClientHello.random + ServerHello.random ) [0..19];
```

The master secret is always exactly 20 bytes in length. The length of the pre_master_secret will vary depending on key exchange method.

8.1.1 RSA Encryption Scheme

When RSA is used for server authentication and key exchange, a 20-byte secret value is generated by the client, encrypted under the server's public key, and sent to the server. The server uses its private key to decrypt the secret value . The pre_master_secret is the secret value appended with the server's public key. Both parties then convert the pre_master_secret into the master_secret, as specified earlier.

In RSA signing, a 20-byte structure of SHA-1 [SHA] hash is signed (encrypted with the private key), using PKCS #1 [PKCS1] block type 1.

RSA public key encryption is performed using PKCS #1 block type 2.

8.1.2 Diffie-Hellman

The conventional Diffie-Hellman computation is performed. The negotiated key (Z) is used as the pre_master_secret and is converted into the master_secret, as specified earlier.

8.1.3 EC Diffie-Hellman

The EC Diffie-Hellman computation is performed. The negotiated key (Z) is used as the pre_master_secret and is converted into the master_secret, as specified earlier.

Elliptic curve calculations are performed according to [P1363].

EC parameters may be transmitted explicitly or using an algorithm definition which specifies predefined parameters (see Appendix A).

EC points are represented according to [P1363] Elliptic Curve Point to Octet String Primitive (EC2OSP). Implementations SHOULD use point compression.

ECDSA signature and verification is performed according to [P1363] Elliptic Curve Signature Scheme with Appendix (ECSSA) using:

- EMSA-hash with SHA-1, for calculating the hash of the data to be signed
- The Elliptic Curve Signature Primitive, DSA version (ECSP-DSA) for signature, and the Elliptic Curve Verification Primitive, DSA version (ECVP-DSA) for verification
- Output format for ECSSA, for output of the signature as an octet string

ECDH calculation of the key Z is performed according to [P1363]:

- Using the Elliptic Curve Secret Value Derivation Primitive, Diffie-Hellman version (ECSVDP-DH), for generating a shared secret value z as a field element
- Converting the shared secret value z to an octet string Z using Field Element to Octet String Conversion Primitive (FE2OSP)

8.1.4 Session Resume

In a session resume, the master_secret is not recalculated. This means that a resumed session uses the same master_secret as the previous one.

Note that although the same master_secret is used, new ClientHello.random and ServerHello.random values are exchanged in the abbreviated handshake. These randoms are taken into account in key block generation, meaning that each secure connection starts up with different key material.

8.2 Key Calculation

A connection state is the operating environment of the Record Protocol. An algorithm is required to generate the connection state (encryption keys, IVs, and MAC secrets) from the secure session parameters provided by the handshake protocol.

A new connection state is calculated in the following way:

The master secret is hashed into a sequence of secure bytes, which are assigned to the MAC secrets, encryption keys, and IVs. To generate the key material, compute:

```
key_block = PRF (SecurityParameters.master_secret,
                 expansion_label, seq_num +
                 SecurityParameters.server_random +
                 SecurityParameters.client_random);
```

until the needed amount of output has been generated.

A new key block generation takes place at intervals of the sequence number, corresponding to key refresh frequency. The sequence number used in the calculation is the first one that mandates key refresh.

Different values of expansion_label are used for client write keys and server write keys. So, the key_block generated with "client expansion" as expansion_label, is partitioned as follows:

```
client_write_MAC_secret[SecurityParameters.hash_size]
client_write encryption_key[SecurityParameters.key_material]
client_write IV[SecurityParameters.IV_size]
```

The key_block generated with "server expansion" as expansion_label is partitioned as follows:

```
server_write_MAC_secret[SecurityParameters.hash_size]
server_write encryption_key[SecurityParameters.key_material]
server_write IV[SecurityParameters.IV_size]
```

In WTLS many connection state parameters can be recalculated during a secure connection. This feature is called the *key refresh.* It is performed in order to minimize the need for new handshakes. In the key refresh, the values of MAC secret, encryption key, and IV will change due to the sequence number. The frequency of these updates depends on the key refresh parameter. For example, the key refresh may be performed for every four records. The seq_num parameters used in the preceding calculation is the sequence number of the record that triggers key refresh. If sequence numbering is not used at all, the sequence numbers are equal to 0 in all calculations.

Exportable encryption algorithms (for which SecurityParameters.is_exportable is true) require additional processing as follows to derive their final write keys:

```
final_client_write_encryption_key =
   PRF(SecurityParameters.client_write_encryption_key, "client write key",
   SecurityParameters.client_random + SecurityParameters.server_random);

final_server_write_encryption_key =
   PRF(SecurityParameters.server_write_encryption_key, "server write key",
   SecurityParameters.client_random + SecurityParameters.server_random);
```

Exportable encryption algorithms derive their IVs solely from the random values from the hello messages.

```
iv_block = PRF("", "IV block", seq_num +
   SecurityParameters.client_random + SecurityParameters.server_random);
```

The iv_block is partitioned into two initialization vectors as thekey_block was:

```
client_write_IV[SecurityParameters.IV_size]
server_write_IV[SecurityParameters.IV_size]
```

Note that the PRF is used without a secret in this case. This just means that the secret has a length of 0 bytes and contributes nothing to the hashing in the PRF.

For CBC mode block ciphers, the IV for each record is calculated in the following way,

```
record_IV = IV XOR S
```

where IV is the original IV (client_write_IV or server_write_IV) and S is obtained by concatenating the 2-byte sequence number of the record needed a number of times to obtain as many bytes as in IV. It is also possible that an encryption algorithm supports using a sequence number as input. Then the record sequence number is used as the algorithm sequence number.

8.3 HMAC and the Pseudo-Random Function

A number of operations in the WTLS record and handshake layer require a keyed MAC; this is a secure digest of some data protected by a secret.

In addition, a construction is required to do expansion of secrets into blocks of data for the purposes of key generation or validation. This pseudo-random function (PRF) takes as input a secret, a seed, and an identifying label and produces an output of arbitrary length.

8.3.1 MAC Calculation

HMAC [HMAC] can be used with a variety of different hash algorithms. For example, SHA-1 [SHA] or MD5 [MD5] could be used. The cryptographic hash function is denoted by H. In addition, a secret key K is required. We assume H to be a cryptographic hash function where data is hashed by iterating a basic compression function on blocks of data. We denote by B the byte-length of such blocks (B=64 for all the preceding examples of hash functions), and by L the byte-length of hash outputs (L=16 for MD5, L=20 for SHA-1). The authentication key K can be of any length up to B, the block length of the hash function. Applications that use keys longer than B bytes will first hash the key using H and then use the resultant L byte string as the actual key to HMAC. In any case, the minimal recommended length for K is L bytes (as the hash output length).

We define two fixed and different strings ipad and opad as follows (the "i" and "o" are mnemonics for inner and outer):

```
ipad = the byte 0x36 repeated B times
opad = the byte 0x5C repeated B times.
```

To compute HMAC over the data we perform:

```
H( K XOR opad + H( K XOR ipad + data ) )
```

where + indicates concatenation.

Namely,

1. Append 0s to the end of K to create a B byte string (e.g., if K is of length 20 bytes and B=64, then K will be appended with 44 0 bytes 0x00).
2. XOR (bitwise exclusive-OR) the B byte string computed in step (1) with ipad.
3. Append the data to the B byte string resulting from step (2).
4. Apply H to the data generated in step (3).

5. XOR (bitwise exclusive-OR) the B byte string computed in step (1) with opad.
6. Append the H result from step (4) to the B byte string resulting from step (5).
7. Apply H to the data generated in step (6) and output the result.

8.3.2 Pseudo-Random Function

In the TLS standard, two hash algorithms were used in order to make the PRF as secure as possible. In order to save resources, WTLS can be implemented using only one hash algorithm. Which hash algorithm is actually used is agreed during the handshake as a part of the cipher spec.

First, we define a data expansion function, P_hash(secret, data) using a single hash function to expand a secret and seed into an arbitrary quantity of output

```
P_hash( secret, seed ) = HMAC_hash( secret, A(1) + seed ) +
                         HMAC_hash( secret, A(2) + seed ) +
                         HMAC_hash( secret, A(3) + seed ) + ...
```

where + indicates concatenation.

```
A(0) = seed
A(i) = HMAC_hash( secret, A(i-1) )
```

P_hash can be iterated as many times as is necessary to produce the required quantity of data. For example, if P_SHA was being used to create 64 bytes of data, it would have to be iterated five times (through A(4)), creating 80 bytes of output data; the last 16 bytes of the final iteration would then be discarded, leaving 64 bytes of output data.

Then,

```
PRF( secret, label, seed ) = P_hash( secret, label + seed )
```

9. Definitions

For the purposes of this specification the following definitions apply:

Abbreviated Handshake. A creation of a new *connection state* based on an existing *secure session*. See also *Session Resume*.

Connection State. The operating environment of the *record protocol*. The connection state includes all parameters that are needed for the cryptographic operations (encryption/decryption and MAC calculation/verification). Each *secure connection* has a connection state

Datagram Transport. A transport service that does not guarantee that the sent transport SDUs are not lost, duplicated, or delivered out of order.

Handshake. The procedure of agreeing on the protocol options to be used between a client and a server. It includes the negotiation of security parameters (e.g., algorithms and key lengths), key exchange, and authentication. Handshaking occurs in the beginning of each secure connection.

Handshake Protocol. The protocol that carries out the *handshake.*

Full Handshake. A creation of a new *secure session* between two peers. The full handshake includes the parameter negotiation and the exchange of public-key information between the client and server.

Optimized Handshake. A creation of a new *secure session* between two peers. Unlike in the *full handshake*, the server looks up the client certificate from its own source without requesting it over the air from the client.

Record. A protocol data unit (PDU) in the *record protocol* layer.

Record Protocol. The record protocol takes messages to be transmitted, optionally compresses the data, applies a MAC, encrypts and transmits the result. Received data is decrypted, verified, decompressed, and then delivered to higher-level clients. There are four record protocol clients described in this document: the handshake protocol, the alert protocol, the ChangeCipherSpec protocol, and the application data protocol.

Secure Connection. The WTLS connection that has a *connection state*. Each secure connection is identified by the transport addresses of the communicating peers.

Secure Session. The secure session that is negotiated on a handshake. The items that are negotiated (e.g., session identifier, algorithms, and master secret) are used for creating *secure connections*. Each secure session is identified by a session ID allocated by the server.

Session Resume. A new *secure connection* can be established based on a previously negotiated *secure session*. So if there is an existing secure session, it is not necessary to perform the full handshake and cryptographic calculations again. For example, a secure connection may be terminated and resumed later. Many secure connections can be established using the same secure session through the resumption feature of the WTLS *handshake protocol*.

Shared Secret Authentication. An authentication method based on a shared secret. This method works without public-key algorithms but requires that the pre-master secret is implanted or entered manually into both client and server. The shared secret is sensitive information and, therefore, a secure channel is needed for the distribution.

10. Abbreviations

For the purposes of this specification the following abbreviations apply:

API	Application Programming Interface
CA	Certification Authority
CBC	Cipher Block Chaining
DH	Diffie-Hellman
EC	Elliptic Curve
ECC	Elliptic Curve Cryptography

ECDH	Elliptic Curve Diffie-Hellman
ECDSA	Elliptic Curve Digital Signature Algorithm
IV	Initialization Vector
MAC	Message Authentication Code
ME	Management Entity
OSI	Open System Interconnection
PDU	Protocol Data Unit
PRF	Pseudo-Random Function
SAP	Service Access Point
SDU	Service Data Unit
SHA-1	Secure Hash Algorithm
SMS	Short Message Service
SSL	Secure Sockets Layer
TLS	Transport Layer Security
WAP	Wireless Application Protocol
WDP	Wireless Datagram Protocol
WSP	Wireless Session Protocol
WTLS	Wireless Transport Layer Security
WTP	Wireless Transaction Protocol

11. Document Conventions

This specification uses the same keywords as specified in RFC 2119 [RFC2119] for defining the significance of each particular requirement. These words are:

MUST. This word, or the terms "REQUIRED" or "SHALL," mean that the definition is an absolute requirement of the specification.

MUST NOT. This phrase, or the phrase "SHALL NOT," means that the definition is an absolute prohibition of the specification.

SHOULD. This word, or the adjective "RECOMMENDED," means that there may exist valid reasons in particular circumstances to ignore a particular item, but the full implications must be understood and carefully weighed before choosing a different course.

SHOULD NOT. This phrase, or the phrase "NOT RECOMMENDED," means that there may exist valid reasons in particular circumstances when the particular behavior is acceptable or even useful, but the full implications should be understood and the case carefully weighed before implementing any behavior described with this label.

MAY. This word, or the adjective "OPTIONAL," means that an item is truly optional. One vendor may choose to include the item because a particular marketplace requires it or because the vendor feels that it enhances the product while another vendor may omit the same item. An implementation that does not include a particular option MUST be prepared to interoperate with another implementation that does include the option, though perhaps with reduced functionality. In the same vein, an implementation that does include a particular option MUST be prepared to interoperate with another implementation that does not include the option (except, of course, for the feature the option provides).

12. Normative References

[WAPARCH] "WAP Architecture Specification," WAP Forum, 30-April-1998.
URL: http://www.wapforum.org/

[WAPWDP] "Wireless Datagram Protocol Specification," WAP Forum, 30-April-1998.
URL: http://www.wapforum.org/

[WAPWTP] "Wireless Transaction Protocol Specification," WAP Forum, 30-April-1998.
URL: http://www.wapforum.org/

[RFC2119] "Key Words for Use in RFCs to Indicate Requirement Levels," Bradner, S., March 1997.
URL: ftp://ftp.isi.edu/in-notes/rfc2119

[TLS] "The TLS Protocol," Dierks, T. and Allen, C., November 1997.
URL: ftp://ftp.ietf.org/internet-drafts/draft-ietf-tls-protocol-05.txt

[RFC2068] "Hypertext Transfer Protocol—HTTP/1.1," Fielding, R., et. al., January 1997.
URL: ftp://ftp.isi.edu/in-notes/rfc2068

[HMAC] "HMAC: Keyed-Hashing for Message Authentication," Krawczyk, H., Bellare, M., and Canetti, R., RFC 2104, February 1997.
URL: ftp://ftp.isi.edu/in-notes/rfc2104.txt

[SHA] "Secure Hash Standard," NIST FIPS PUB 180-1, National Institute of Standards and Technology, U.S. Department of Commerce, DRAFT, May 1994.

[X509] "The Directory—Authentication Framework," CCITT, Recommendation X.509, 1988.

[3DES] "Hellman Presents No Shortcut Solutions To DES," Tuchman, W., IEEE Spectrum, v. 16, n. 7, July 1979, pp. 40–41.

[DES] "American National Standard for Information Systems-Data Link Encryption," ANSI X3.106, American National Standards Institute, 1983.

[DH1] "New Directions in Cryptography," Diffie, W. and Hellman M. E., IEEE Transactions on Information Theory, V. IT-22, n. 6, Jun 1977, pp. 74–84.

[DSS] "Digital Signature Standard," NIST FIPS PUB 186, National Institute of Standards and Technology, U.S. Department of Commerce, May 1994.

[IDEA] "On the Design and Security of Block Ciphers," Lai, X., ETH Series in Information Processing, v. 1, Konstanz: Hartung-Gorre Verlag, 1992.

[MD5] "The MD5 Message Digest Algorithm," Rivest, R., RFC 2104, April 1992.
URL: ftp://ftp.isi.edu/in-notes/rfc2104.txt

[PKCS1] "PKCS #1: RSA Encryption Standard," version 1.5, RSA Laboratories, November 1993.

[RSA] "A Method for Obtaining Digital Signatures and Public-Key Cryptosystems," Rivest, R., Shamir, A., and Adleman L. M., Communications of the ACM, v. 21, n. 2, Feb 1978, pp. 120–126.

[RC5] "The RC5, RC5-CBC, RC5-CBC-Pad, and RC5-CTS Algorithms," Baldwin, R. and Rivest R., RFC 2040, October 1996.
URL: ftp://ftp.isi.edu/in-notes/rfc2040.txt

[P1363] "Standard Specifications For Public Key Cryptography," IEEE P1363 / D1a (Draft Version 1a), February 1998.
URL: http://grouper.ieee.org/groups/1363/

[X9.62] "The Elliptic Curve Digital Signature Algorithm (ECDSA)," ANSI X9.62 Working Draft, November 1997.

13. Informative References

[WAPWSP] "Wireless Session Protocol Specification," WAP Forum, 30-April-1998.
URL: http://www.wapforum.org/

[GSM03.40] "European Digital Cellular Telecommunication System (phase 2+): Technical Realization of Short Message Service (SMS) Point-to-Point (P)," ETSI.

[XDR] "XDR: External Data Representation Standard," Srinivansan, R., RFC-1832:, August 1995.
URL: ftp://ftp.isi.edu/in-notes/rfc1832.txt

[ISO7498] "Information Technology—Open Systems Interconnection—Basic Reference Model: The Basic Model," ISO/IEC 7498-1:1994.

[ISO10731] "Information Technology—Open Systems Interconnection—Basic Reference Model—Conventions for the Definition of OSI Services," ISO/IEC 10731:1994.

14. Acknowledgments

WTLS is derived from [TLS]. TLS is based on the SSL 3.0 specification.

Appendix A: Algorithm Definitions

Table A.1 The Available Key Exchange Suites

KEY EXCHANGE SUITE	ASSIGNED NUMBER	DESCRIPTION	KEY SIZE LIMIT (BITS)
NULL	0	No key exchange is done. A 0 length pre-master secret is used. Master secret and Finished messages are used for error checking purposes only.	N/A
SHARED_SECRET	1	Symmetric-key based handshake. Parties share a secret key that is used as the pre-master key as such.	None
DH_anon	2	Diffie-Hellman key exchange without authentication. Parties send each other (temporary) DH public keys. Each party calculates the pre-master secret based on one's own private key and counterpart's public key.	None
DH_anon_512	3	As DH_anon, but with a limited length DH key.	512
DH_anon_768	4	As DH_anon, but with a limited length DH key.	768
RSA_anon	5	RSA key exchange without authentication. The server sends its RSA public key. The client generates a secret value, encrypts it with the server's public key, and sends it to the server. The pre-master secret is the secret value appended with the server's public key.	None
RSA_anon_512	6	As RSA_anon, but with a limited-length server public key.	512
RSA_anon_768	7	As RSA_anon, but with a limited-length server public key.	768
RSA	8	RSA key exchange with RSA-based certificates. The server sends a certificate that contains its RSA public key. The server certificate is signed with RSA by a third party trusted by the client. The client extracts server's public key from received certificate, generates a secret value, encrypts it with the server's	None

(Continues)

Table A.1 *(Continued)*

KEY EXCHANGE SUITE	ASSIGNED NUMBER	DESCRIPTION	KEY SIZE LIMIT (BITS)
RSA *(cont.)*	8	public key, and sends it to the server. The pre-master secret is the secret value appended with the server's public key. If the client is to be authenticated it signs some data (messages send during the handshake) with its RSA private key and sends its certificate and the signed data.	none
RSA_512	9	As RSA, but with a limited length of certified server public key.	512
RSA_768	10	As RSA, but with a limited length of certified server public key.	768
ECDH_anon	11	EC Diffie-Hellman key exchange without authentication. Parties send each other (temporary) ECDH public keys. Each party calculates the pre-master secret based on one's own private key and counterpart's public key.	None
ECDH_anon_113	12	As ECDH_anon, but with a limited-length ECDH key.	113
ECDH_anon_131	13	As ECDH_anon, but with a limited-length ECDH key.	131
ECDH_ECDSA	14	EC Diffie-Hellman key exchange with ECDSA-based certificates. The server sends a certificate that contains its ECDH public key. The server certificate is signed with ECDSA by a third party trusted by the client. Depending whether the client is to be authenticated or not, it sends its certificate containing its ECDH public key signed with ECDSA by a third party trusted by the server, or just its (temporary) ECDH public key. Each party calculates the premaster secret based on one's own private key and counterpart's public key received as such or contained in a certificate.	None

Note that regarding to some key exchange suites, export restrictions may apply.

Table A.2 The Available Bulk Encryption Algorithms

CIPHER	ASSIGNED NUMBER	IS EXPORTABLE	TYPE	KEY MATERIAL (BYTES)	EXPANDED KEY MATERIAL (BYTES)	EFFECTIVE KEY BITS (BITS)	IV SIZE (BYTES)	BLOCK SIZE (BYTES)
NULL	0	True	Stream	0	0	0	0	N/A
RC5_CBC_40	1	True	Block	5	16	40	8	8
RC5_CBC_56	2	True	Block	7	16	56	8	8
RC5_CBC	3	False	Block	16	16	128	8	8
DES_CBC_40	4	True	Block	5	8	40	8	8
DES_CBC	5	False	Block	8	8	56	8	8
3DES_CBC_EDE	6	False	Block	24	24	168	8	8
IDEA_CBC_40	7	True	Block	5	16	40	8	8
IDEA_CBC_56	8	True	Block	7	16	56	8	8
IDEA_CBC	9	False	Block	16	16	128	8	8

FIELD	DESCRIPTION
IsExportable	Encryption algorithms for which IsExportable is true have a limited effective key length in order to comply with certain export regulations. For them, an additional key expansion is performed and the initialization vector is derived in a special way. This specification does not imply whether it is actually legal to export these algorithms (or illegal to export algorithms for which IsExportable is false) from one specific country to another.
Type	Indicates whether this is a stream cipher of a block cipher running in CBC mode.
Key Material	The number of bytes from the key_block that are used for generating the write keys.
Expanded Key Material	The number of bytes in the write keys.
Effective Key Bits	How much entropy material is in the key material being fed into the encryption routines.
IV Size	How much data needs to be generated for the initialization vector. Zero for stream ciphers; equal to the block size for block ciphers.
Block Size	The amount of data a block cipher enciphers in one chunk; a block cipher running in CBC mode can only encrypt a multiple of its block size.

RC5 [RC5] is a family of block cipher algorithms. RC5 implementations can be designated as RC5-w/r/b, where w is the word size in bits (and also the half of the block size), r is the number of rounds, and b is the length of the key in bytes. Using this notation, the cipher RC5_CBC is RC5-32/16/16. The cipher RC5_CBC_40 is implemented as an export cipher, using 5 bytes as key material and expanding that to 16 bytes, and then applying RC5-32/12/16. The cipher RC5_CBC_56 is implemented as an export cipher, using 7 bytes as key material and expanding that to 16 bytes, and then applying RC5-32/12/16.

Data Encryption Standard (DES) is a very widely used symmetric encryption algorithm. DES is a block cipher with a 56-bit key and an 8-byte block size. Note that in WTLS, for key generation purposes, DES is treated as having an 8-byte key length (64 bits), but it still only provides 56 bits of protection. DES can also be operated in a mode where three independent keys and three encryptions are used for each block of data; this uses 168 bits of key (24 bytes in the WTLS key generation method) and provides the equivalent of 112 bits of security. [DES], [3DES]

IDEA is a 64-bit block cipher designed by Xuejia Lai and James Massey. [IDEA]

FIELD	DESCRIPTION
Key Size	The number of bytes used as the HMAC key.
Hash Size	The number of bytes used in the MAC.

Table A.3 The Available Keyed MAC Algorithms

HASH FUNCTION	ASSIGNED NUMBER	DESCRIPTION	KEY SIZE (BYTES)	HASH SIZE (BYTES)
SHA_0	0	No keyed MAC is calculated. Note than in other than keyed MAC operations (e.g., PRF) the full-length SHA-1 is used.	0	0
SHA_40	1	The keyed MAC is calculated using SHA-1 but only the first 5 bytes of the output are used. Note that in other than keyed MAC operations (e.g., PRF) the full-length SHA-1 is used.	20	5
SHA_80	2	The keyed MAC is calculated using SHA-1 but only the first half of the output (10 bytes) is used. Note that in other than keyed MAC operations (e.g., PRF) the full-length SHA-1 is used.	20	10
SHA	3	The keyed MAC is calculated using SHA-1.	20	20
SHA_XOR_40	4	A 5-byte XOR checksum. The input data is first divided into the multiple blocks of 5 bytes. Then all blocks are XOR'ed one after another. If the last block is less than 5 bytes, it is padded with 0x00. SHA is much stronger than XOR for generating MACs, although there were no significant attacks reported on XOR MACs, which must be encrypted and is only used for CBC mode block ciphers. XOR is only intended for some devices with very limited CPU resources. Warning: With exportable grade of encryption (e.g., RC5_40), XOR cannot provide as strong message integrity protection as SHA can. It is recommended that the security consequence should be carefully evaluated before XOR MAC is adopted in those environments. In other than MAC operations for message integrity (e.g., PRF) the full-length SHA-1 is used.	0	5
MD5_40	5	The keyed MAC is calculated using MD5 but only the first 5 bytes of the output are used. Note than in other than keyed MAC operations (e.g., PRF), the full-length MD5 is used.	16	5
MD5_80	6	The keyed MAC is calculated using MD5 but only the first 10 bytes of the are used. Note than in other than keyed MAC operations (e.g., PRF) the full-length MD5 is used.	16	10
MD5	7	The keyed MAC is calculated using MD5.	16	16

Table A.4 The Available Compression Algorithms

COMPRESSION ALGORITHM	ASSIGNED NUMBER	DESCRIPTION
NULL	0	No compression.

Table A.5 Elliptic Curve Parameters For Selected Curves

PARAMETER	VALUE
Assigned number	1
Field size	113
Elliptic curve E	$y^2 + x y = x^3 + a x^2 + b$ over $F(2^{113})$
Curve parameter a	1
Curve parameter b	1
Generating point G	01667979A40BA497E5D5C270780617, 00F44B4AF1ECC2630E08785CEBCC15
The order of G	00FFFFFFFFFFFFFFFDBF91AF6DEA73
The cofactor k	2
Assigned number	2
Field size	131
Elliptic curve E	$y^2 + x y = x^3 + a x^2 + b$ over $F(2^{131})$
Curve parameter a	0
Curve parameter b	1
Generating point G	043A891E4FD64F01E60F8831C3D7E195B22FF19BEE, 04035AB7114A900F460549987F48C3B1F00B5A1D58
The order of G	0200000000000000004D4FDD5703A3F269
The cofactor k	4
Assigned number	3
Field size	163
Elliptic curve E	$y^2 + x y = x^3 + a x^2 + b$ over $F(2^{163})$
Curve parameter a	1
Curve parameter b	1
Generating point G	02FE13C0537BBC11ACAA07D793DE4E6D5E5C94EEE8, 0289070FB05D38FF58321F2E800536D538CCDAA3D9
The order of G	04000000000000000000020108A2E0CC0D99F8A5EF
The cofactor k	2

Table A.6 Predefined Diffie-Hellman Parameters

PARAMETER	VALUE
Assigned number	1
Exponent bits	160
Prime modulus (512 bits)	FAF30C63D171E54A8131CD331D7C8D6C 8AED41B0354E1A29D8DAD03E2E67FF8E 00053A07FD28A1EE6AF199FD70330EA8 C4C602B86EDFBF47FD1D7BFB6456BD57
Generator (512 bits)	E7734EBBCF50893C760181B2AA2DB0AC F2D5B6E775EE88BAFC7AA5A6BB20A64E B9F54301141F90291B7B375135394504 81C9F9CB2BA3E67B4580E2153FD22B80
Assigned number	2
Exponent bits	160
Prime modulus (768 bits)	85DB5DB185090AED3BDB3BABFCB46669F9563E681EDB4359 9241FEF6AA9B5DF9EFE39C0CB7994A04F2BD8F57B5B22AF7 5E360526216420BCA08FCDF98FF6417DCFDD1C40E4FFB183 260E3B28EF0B31A3633788C988B1BC6734A81B31A28CD6FB
Generator (760 bits)	1B15C3C57263B0DD1A9D996768B88370ED458D7B0081A220 054EFDD23B9CD8298B719FD3B67CB093817332D033642D21 130F83D9CB2CC5ACDD36E6E6DDB2410AB30311CDBEE9222C CFE644443B0C7204F2D12F7A3719C8866A20A0E778EBBA

Appendix B: Implementation Notes

The following implementation notes are provided to identify areas where implementation choices may impact the security, performance, and effectiveness of the WTLS protocols. The implementation notes provide guidance to implementers of the protocols.

B.1 Negotiating Null CipherSpec

Null CipherSpec can be negotiated to be used in a session. The NULL key exchange suite may be used for that purpose, so that no key exchange actually takes place. The master secret is calculated with a 0-length pre-master secret. The message flow is like in the abbreviated handshake.

Implementations MUST be careful when accepting a null CipherSpec since it offers no security.

B.2 Anonymous Handshakes

Completely anonymous sessions can be established using RSA or Diffie-Hellman for key exchange. With anonymous RSA, the client generates a secret value and encrypts it with the server's uncertified public key extracted from the server key exchange message. The result is sent in a client key exchange message. Since eavesdroppers do not know the server's private key, it will be unfeasible for them to decode the secret value. (The pre_master_secret is this value appended with server's public key.)

With Diffie-Hellman, the server's public value is contained in the server key exchange message and the client's is sent in the client key exchange message. Eavesdroppers who do not know the private values are not able to find the Diffie-Hellman result (i.e., the pre_master_secret).

Warning: Completely anonymous handshakes (i.e., where neither the client nor the server is authenticated) only provide protection against passive eavesdropping. The active eavesdroppers, or the active man-in-the-middle attackers may replace the finished messages with their own during the handshaking process for creating sessions. However, there are known methods that may effectively defeat those active attacks in environments where those attacks are a concern; for instance, server authentication, or using an independent tamper-proof channel to verify that the finished messages were not replaced by the attacker. When the handshaking process is complete and authenticated or verified, the established sessions should be secure and protected against both passive and active man-in-the-middle attacks or eavesdroppers.

B.3 Key Refresh

The passive key refresh mechanism of WTLS makes it possible to update keys in a secure connection without handshaking.

Key refresh makes cryptoanalysis less attractive for an attacker because keys will be invalidated regularly and the material that can be gained is limited. This is particularly useful in environments, where export-restricted encryption is used and handshaking is expensive (i.e., connections with long lifetimes are desirable).

The frequency of key refresh is agreed on during the handshake. This parameter defines how many messages are sent before key refresh is triggered. For example, key refresh may be triggered after each four messages.

In key refresh, a new key block is generated using the master secret as a source of entropy and the message sequence number as an additional parameter (along with other parameters) in the pseudo-random function. The generated key block is used for message protection keys: MAC keys, encryption keys, and initialization vectors.

Note that key refresh can always be done also by performing/forcing a new handshake.

B.4 Denial-of-Service Attacks

Since WTLS operates on top of datagrams, the implementation should pay special attention to preventing denial-of-service attacks. It should take into account that in some networks transport addresses may be forged relatively easy.

In order to make denial-of-service attacks harder to accomplish, it may not be possible for an attacker to break up an existing connection/session by sending a single message in plaintext from a forged address.

In addition, the server should be careful in accepting new connection requests in plaintext within an existing secure connection. Note that the server cannot just ignore them because, for example, ClientHello in plain text may be sent by a client whose connection state was lost. Special care must be taken with arbitrated and optimized handshakes in which the server switches the pending state current immediately after responding to ClientHello message. In such a case, the old active state should be kept intact until the new handshake is accomplished. In other words, the server should not discard the old active state until the client responds with Finished and the handshake is completed successfully. The old active state should be restored to the current state if it is evidenced that the handshake started is invalid.

For the same reason, when a client receives a plaintext ServerHello on its secure connection, it should not cause the existing secure connection broken because of the unexpected message. It should keep the existing secure connection and send the *unexpected_message* as a warning.

Appendix C: Implementation Classes

WTLS implementations may have support for various features. This appendix defines classes guiding implementors to select these features (see Table C.1). A class may have mandatory (M) or optional (O) support for a certain feature. Certain features are not yet defined in the current version of the specification.

The current version of the WTLS specification covers all features in Class 1.

Table C.1 WTLS Classes

FEATURE	CLASS 1	CLASS 2	CLASS 3
Public-key exchange	M	M	M
Server certificates	O	M	M
Client certificates	O	O	M
Shared-secret handshake	O	O	O
Compression	–	O	O
Encryption	M	M	M
MAC	M	M	M
Smart card interface	–	O	O

Appendix D: Requirements for the WTLS Protocol

The common requirements set by wireless mobile networks are described below.

ITEM	DESCRIPTION
Datagram transport protocol	Both datagram- and connection-oriented Transport layer protocols must be supported. It must be possible to cope with, for example, lost, duplicated, or out-of-order datagrams without breaking the connection state.
Slow interactions	The protocol must take into account that round-trip times with some bearers (e.g., SMS [GSM03.40]) can be long. For example, sending a query and receiving a response might require more than 10 seconds. This must be taken into account in the protocol design.
Low transfer rate	The slowness of some bearers is a major constraint. Therefore, the amount of overhead must be kept to the minimum. For example, with SMS the effective transfer rate may be lower than 100 bit/s.
Limited processing power	The processing power of many mobile terminals is quite limited. This must be taken into account when cryptographic algorithms are chosen.
Limited memory capacity	The memory capacity of most mobile terminals is very modest. Therefore, the number of cryptographic algorithms must be minimized and small-sized algorithms must be chosen. Especially the RAM requirements must be as low as possible.
Restrictions on exporting and using cryptography	International restrictions and rules for using, exporting, and importing cryptography must be taken into account. This means that it must be possible to achieve the best permitted security level according to the legislation of each area. For example, in many cases, strong authentication can be used although strong encryption is prohibited.

CHAPTER

17

Wireless Datagram Protocol Specification

1. Scope

The Transport layer protocol in the WAP architecture consists of the Wireless Transaction Protocol (WTP) and the Wireless Datagram Protocol (WDP). The WDP layer operates above the data-capable bearer services supported by the various network types. As a general datagram service, WDP offers a consistent service to the upper-layer protocols (Security, Transaction, and Session) of WAP and communicates transparently over one of the available bearer services.

The protocols in the WAP family are designed for use over narrowband bearers in wireless telecommunications networks.

Since the WDP protocols provide a common interface to the upper-layer protocols (Security, Transaction, and Session layers), they are able to function independently of the underlying wireless network. This is accomplished by adapting the Transport layer to specific features of the underlying bearer.

2. WDP Architectural Overview

The WDP protocol operates above the data capable bearer services supported by multiple network types. WDP offers a consistent service to the upper-layer protocols (Security, Transaction, and Session) of WAP and communicates transparently over one of the available bearer services.

2.1 Reference Model

The model of protocol architecture for the Wireless Datagram Protocol is given in Figure 17.1.

The services offered by WDP include application addressing by port numbers, optional segmentation and reassembly, and optional error detection. The services allow for applications to operate transparently over different available bearer services.

The model of protocol architecture for the Wireless Transport Protocol is given in Figure 17.2.

WDP offers a consistent service at the Transport Service Access Point to the upper-layer protocol of WAP. This consistency of service allows for applications to operate transparently over different available bearer services. The varying heights of each of the bearer services shown in Figure 17.2 illustrate the difference in functions provided

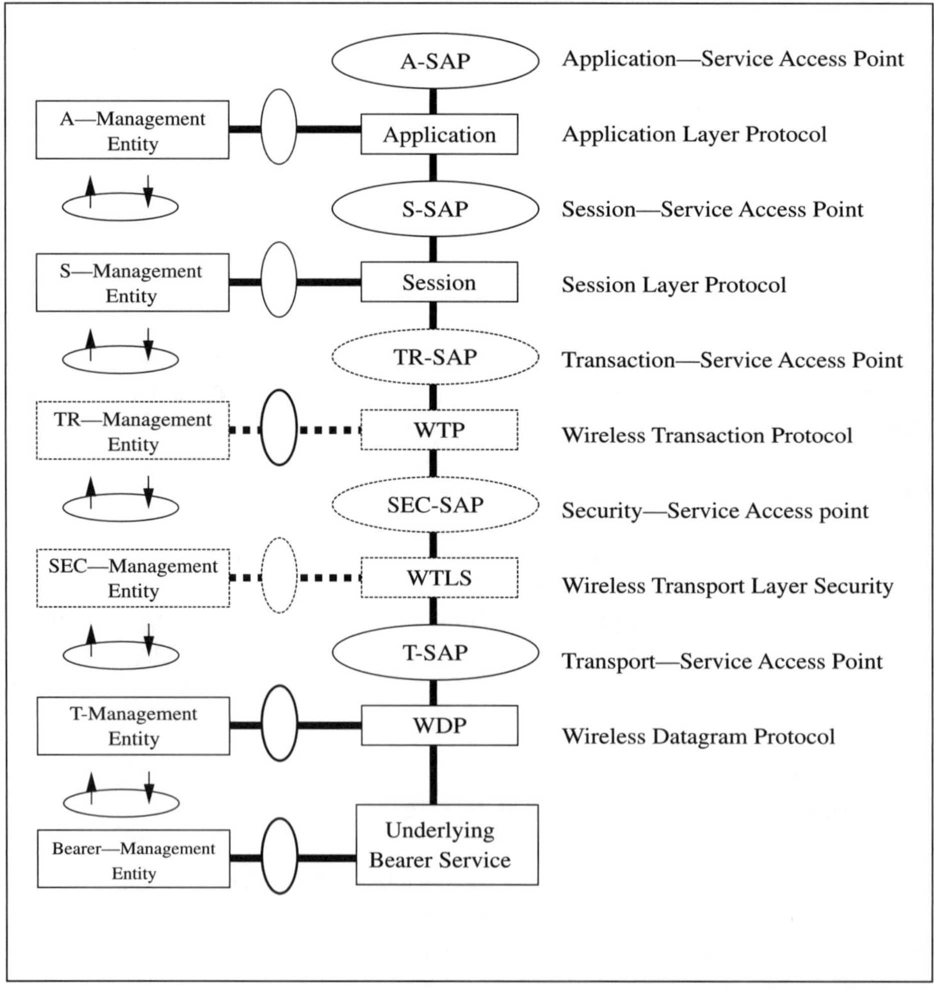

Figure 17.1 Wireless datagram protocol architecture.

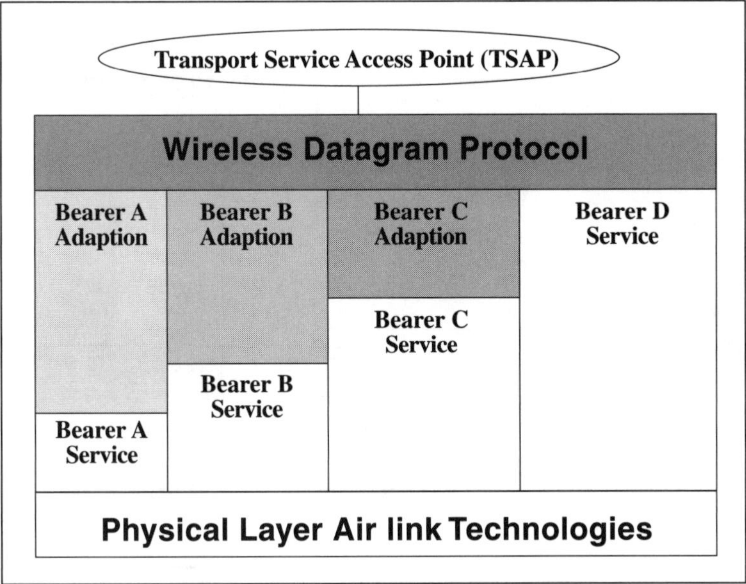

Figure 17.2 Wireless Transport protocol architecture.

by the bearers and thus the difference in WDP protocol necessary to operate over those bearers to maintain the same service offering at the Transport Service Access Point is accomplished by a bearer adaptation.

WDP can be mapped onto different bearers, with different characteristics. In order to optimize the protocol with respect to memory usage and radio transmission efficiency, the protocol performance over each bearer may vary. However, the WDP service and service primitives will remain the same, providing a consistent interface to the higher layers.

2.2 General Description of the WDP Protocol

The WDP layer operates above the data-capable bearer services supported by the various network types. As a general datagram service, WDP offers a consistent service to the upper-layer protocols (Security, Transaction, and Session) of WAP and communicates transparently over one of the available bearer services.

WDP supports several simultaneous communication instances from a higher layer over a single underlying WDP bearer service. The port number identifies the higher-layer entity above WDP. This may be another protocol layer such as the Wireless Transaction Protocol (WTP) or the Wireless Session Protocol (WSP) or an application such as electronic mail. By reusing the elements of the underlying bearers, WDP can be implemented to support multiple bearers and yet be optimized for efficient operation within the limited resources of a mobile device.

Figure 17.3 shows a general model of the WAP protocol architecture and how WDP fits into that architecture.

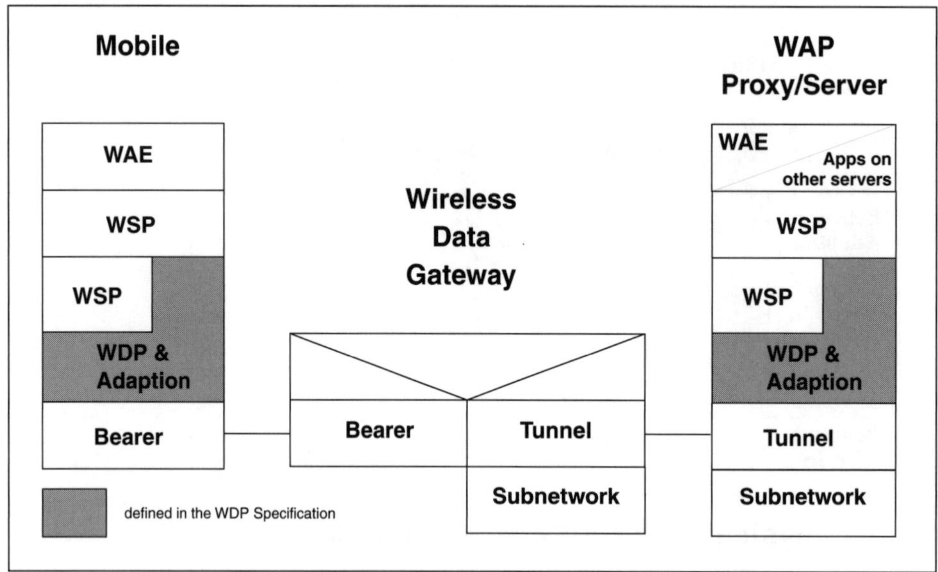

Figure 17.3 General WDP architecture.

In Figure 17.3 the shaded areas are the layers of protocol to which the WDP Specification is specifically applicable. At the mobile, the WDP protocol consists of the common WDP elements shown by the layer labeled WDP. The Adaptation layer is the layer of the WDP protocol that maps the WDP protocol functions directly onto a specific bearer. The Adaptation layer is different for each bearer and deals with the specific capabilities and characteristics of that bearer service. The Bearer layer is the bearer service such as GSM SMS, USSD, IS-136 R-Data, or CDMA Packet Data. At the Gateway the Adaptation layer terminates and passes the WDP packets on to a WAP Proxy/Server via a Tunneling protocol, which is the interface between the Gateway that supports the bearer service and the WAP Proxy/Server. For example, if the bearer were GSM SMS, the Gateway would be a GSM SMSC and would support a specific protocol (the Tunneling protocol) to interface the SMSC to other servers. The subnetwork is any common networking technology that can be used to connect two communicating devices; examples are wide area networks based on TCP/IP or X.25, or LANs operating TCP/IP over Ethernet. The WAP Proxy/Server may offer application content or may act as a gateway between the wireless WTP protocol suites and the wired Internet.

2.2.1 WDP Management Entity

The WDP Management Entity is used as an interface between the WDP layer and the environment of the device. The WDP Management Entity provides information to the WDP layer about changes in the devices environment that may impact the correct operation of WDP.

The WDP protocol is designed around an assumption that the operating environment is capable of transmitting and receiving data.

For example, this assumption includes the following basic capabilities that must be provided by the mobile:

- The mobile is within a coverage area applicable to the bearer service being invoked.
- The mobile has sufficient power and the power is on.
- Sufficient resources (processing and memory) within the mobile are available to WDP.
- The WDP protocol is correctly configured.
- The user is willing to receive/transmit data.

The WDP Management Entity would monitor the state of the preceding services/ capabilities of the mobile's environment and would notify the WDP layer if one or more of the assumed services were not available.

For example, if the mobile roamed out of coverage for a bearer service, the Bearer Management Entity should report to the WDP Management Entity that transmission/reception over that bearer is no longer possible. In turn, the WDP Management Entity would indicate to the WDP layer to close all active connections over that bearer. Other examples such as low battery power would be handled in a similar way by the WDP Management Entity.

In addition to monitoring the state of the mobile environment, the WDP Management Entity may be used as the interface to the user for setting various configuration parameters used by WDP, such as device address. It could also be used to implement functions available to the user, such as a "drop all data connections" feature. In general, the WDP Management Entity will deal with all issues related to initialization, configuration, dynamic reconfiguration, and resources, as they pertain to the WDP layer.

Since the WDP Management Entity must interact with various components of a device that are manufacturer specific, the design and implementation of the WDP Management Entity is considered outside the scope of the WDP Specification and is an implementation issue.

2.2.2 Processing Errors of WDP Datagrams

Processing errors can happen when WDP datagrams are sent from a WDP provider to another. For example, a Wireless Data Gateway may not be able to send the datagram to the WAP Gateway, or there is no application listening to the destination port, or the receiver might not have enough buffer space to receive a large message.

The Wireless Control Message Protocol (WCMP) provides an efficient error-handling mechanism for WDP, resulting in improved performance for WAP protocols and applications. Therefore, the WCMP protocol SHOULD be implemented. See the [WCMP] specification.

2.3 WDP Static Conformance Clause

This static conformance clause defines a minimum set of WDP features that can be implemented to ensure that implementations from multiple vendors will be able to interoperate.

Table 17.1 WDP Static Conformance Clause for Non-IP Bearer Operation.

FUNCTION	OPERATION	WDP OVER A NON-IP BEARER	NOTES
Source Port Number	Send Receive	M M	
Destination Port Number	Send Receive	M M	
Segmentation and Reassembly (SAR)	Send Receive	O O	The provider must be able to recognize SAR upon receive, where applicable for the bearer.
Text Header	Send Receive	O O	
T-DUnitdata Service Primitive	Request Indication	M M	
T-Derror Service Primitive	Indication	O	

The WDP protocol operates over various bearer services. Each bearer service for which WDP is specified supports a datagram service. It is this datagram service that WDP uses to support the abstract service primitives defined in this specification. For bearer services supporting IP, the WDP protocol MUST be UDP. For bearer services not supporting IP, the WDP protocol defined in this specification MUST be used. In Table 17.1 Mandatory (M) and Optional (O) features of WDP when operating over a bearer not supporting IP are listed.

2.4 WDP Bearer Dependent Profiles

Figures 17.4 and 17.5 illustrate the protocol profiles for operating WDP between a mobile device and server over a specific RF technology, and a specific bearer within that technology.

2.4.1 WDP over GSM

2.4.1.1 GSM SMS Profile

Figure 17.4 illustrates the protocol profile for the WDP layer when operating over the SMS bearer service.

2.4.1.2 GSM USSD Profile

Figure 17.5 illustrates the protocol profile for the WTP layer when operating over the USSD bearer service.

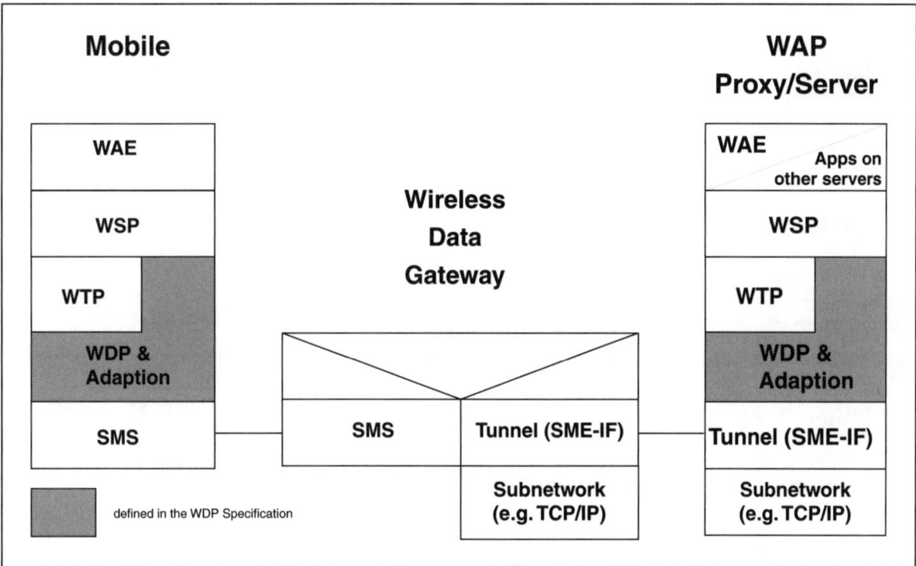

Figure 17.4 WDP over a GSM SMS.

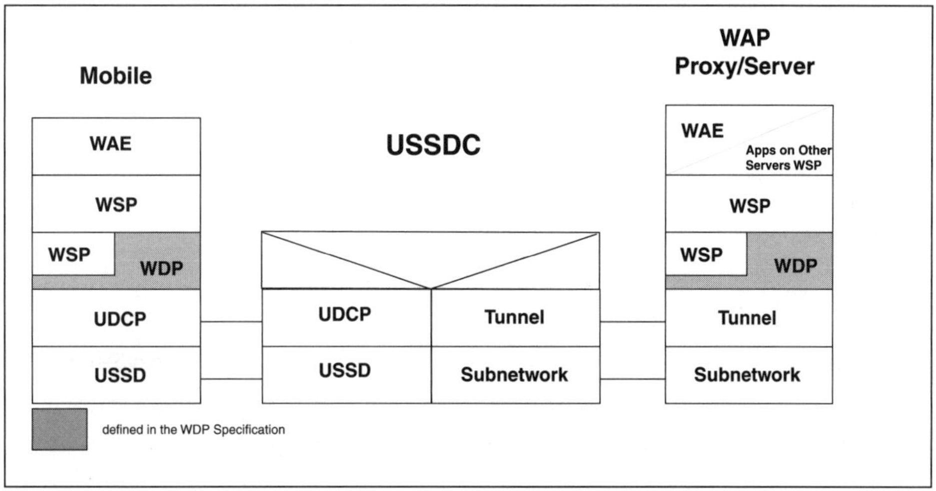

Figure 17.5 USSD Profile.

The USSD Dialog Control Protocol (UDCP) is responsible for managing the half duplex USSD dialog and providing the upper layer with the address to the WAP Proxy/Server.

2.4.1.3 GSM Circuit-Switched Data

Figure 17.6 illustrates the protocol profile for the WDP layer when operating over a Circuit-Switched Data connection. The IWF provides nontransparent CSD services and is not present in transparent circuit data calls. The Remote Access Server (RAS) or the

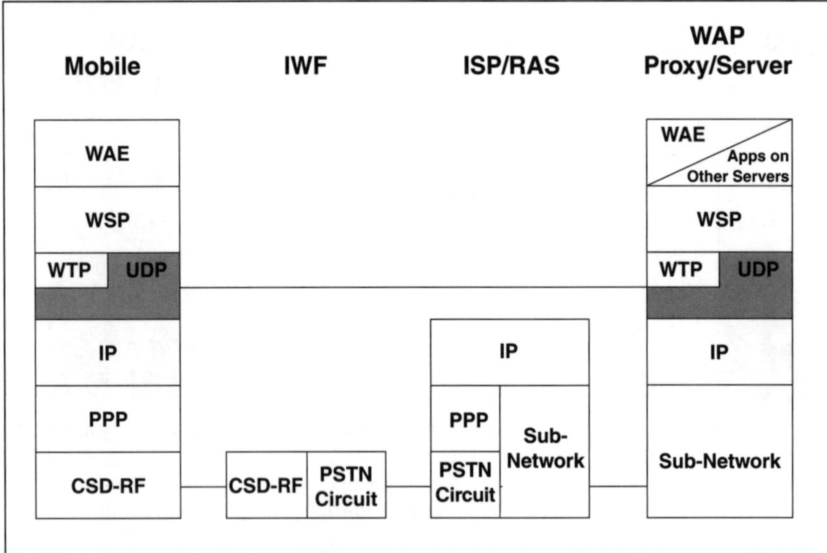

Figure 17.6 WDP over GSM circuit-switched data channel.

Internet Service Provider (ISP) provides connectivity to the Internet network so that the mobile and WAP Proxy/Server can address each other. The WAP Proxy/Server can terminate the WAE or serve as a proxy to other applications on the Internet.

2.4.1.4 GSM GPRS Profile

Figure 17.7 illustrates the protocol profile for the WDP layer when operating over the GPRS bearer service. GPRS supports IP to the mobile; therefore, UDP/IP will provide datagram services.

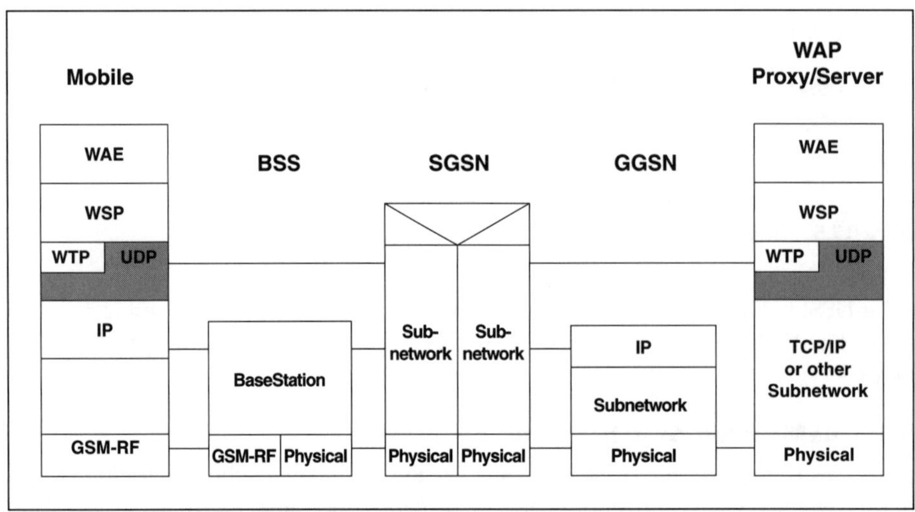

Figure 17.7 WDP over GSM GPRS.

2.4.2 WDP over IS-136

The WDP layer operates above the data-capable bearer services supported by IS-136.

2.4.2.1 IS-136 R-Data Profile

Figure 17.8 illustrates the protocol profile for the WDP layer when operating over the IS-136 GUTS and R-Data bearer service. For efficiency, WDP can be supported directly on GUTS. A GUTS protocol discriminator would be needed for this purpose. The IS-136 Teleservice Server interface protocol is Subnetwork dependent and not specified in the WAP specifications.

2.4.2.2 IS-136 Circuit-Switched Data Profile

Figure 17.9 illustrates the protocol profile for the WDP layer when operating over an IS-136 Circuit-Switched Data connection. A remote access or an Internet Service Provider (ISP) provides connectivity to a WAP Proxy/Server. The WAP Proxy/Server can terminate the WAE or serve as a proxy to other applications on the Internet.

2.4.2.3 IS-136 Packet Data Profile

Figure 17.10 illustrates the protocol profile for the WDP layer when operating over the IS-136 Packet Data bearer service. IS-136 Packet Data supports IP to the mobile; therefore, UDP/IP will provide the datagram services.

2.4.3 WDP over CDPD

Figure 17.11 illustrates the protocol profile for the WDP layer when operating over the CDPD bearer service. CDPD supports IP to the mobile; therefore, UDP/IP will provide the datagram services.

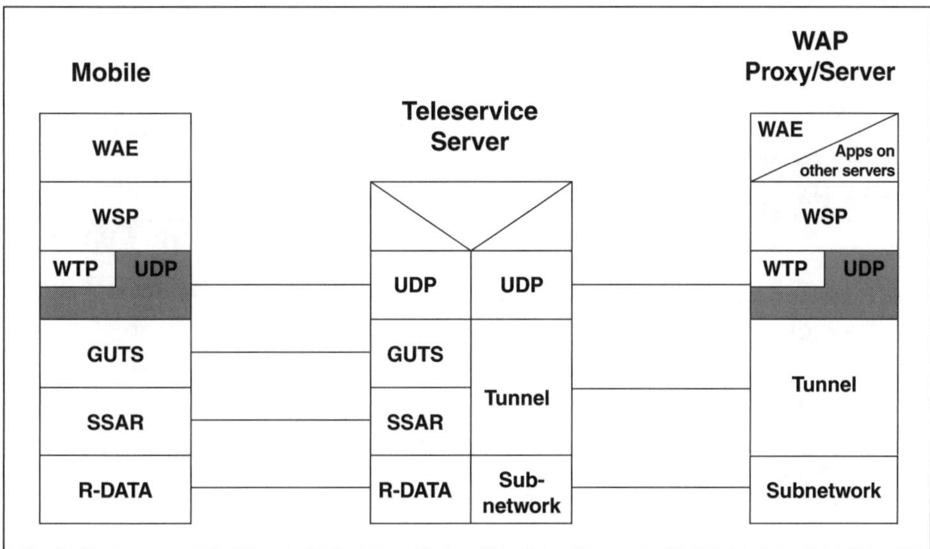

Figure 17.8 WDP over IS-136 R-Data.

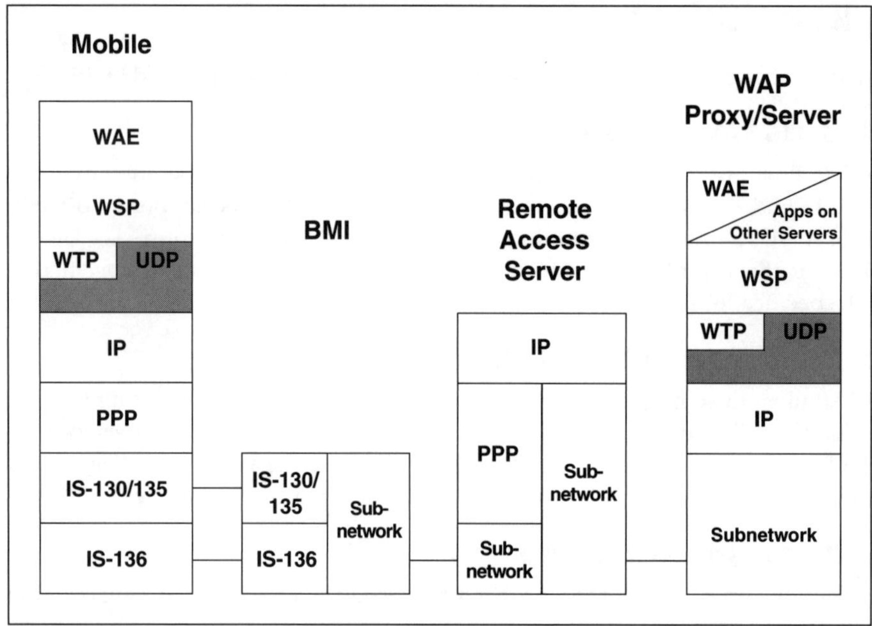

Figure 17.9 WDP over IS-136 Circuit-Switched Data.

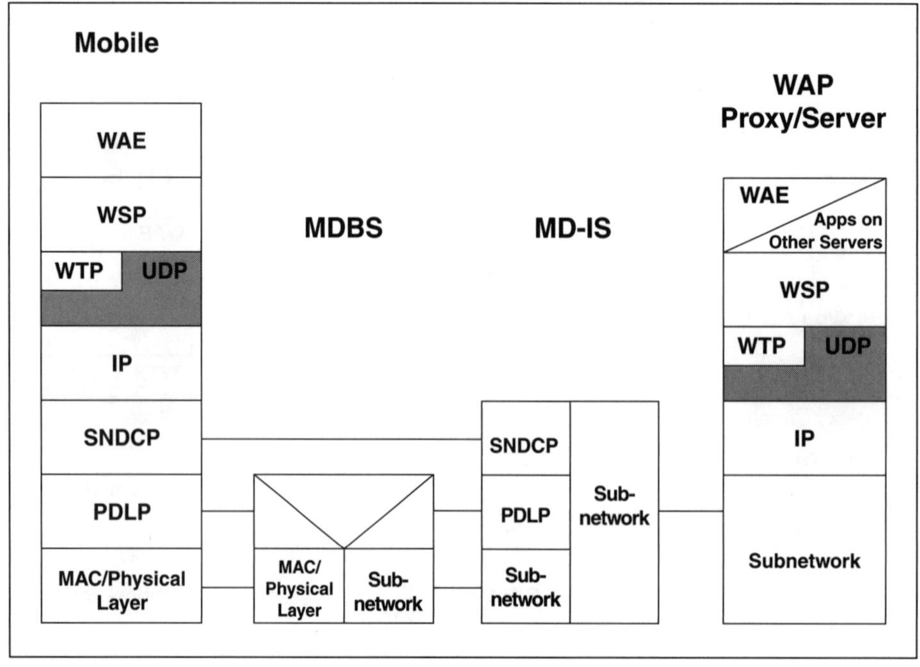

Figure 17.10 WDP over IS-136 Packet Data.

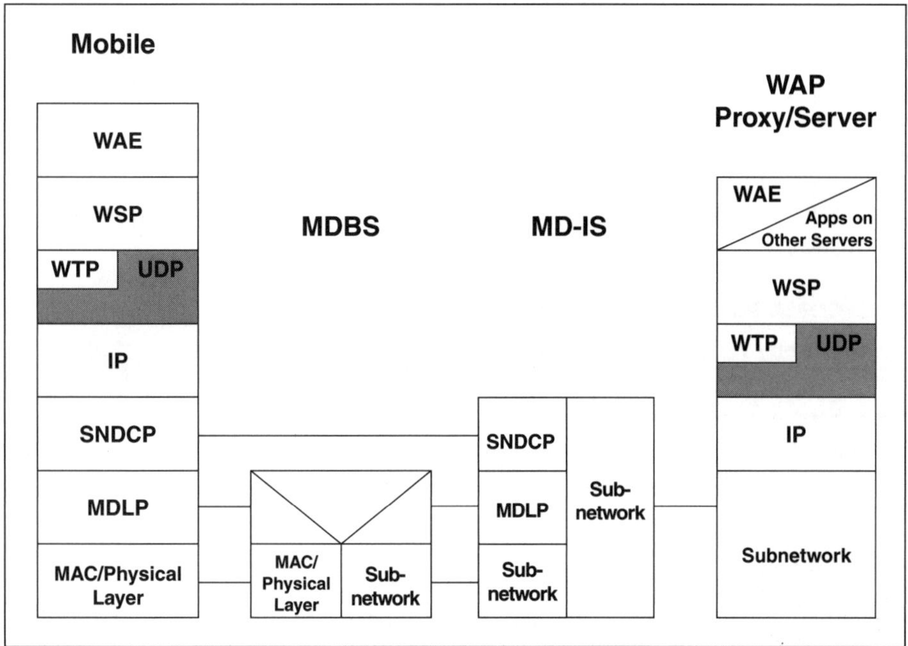

Figure 17.11 WDP over CDPD.

2.4.4 WDP over CDMA

The WDP layer operates above the data capable bearer services supported by CDMA. Figure 17.12 identifies the CDMA bearer services presented in this specification.

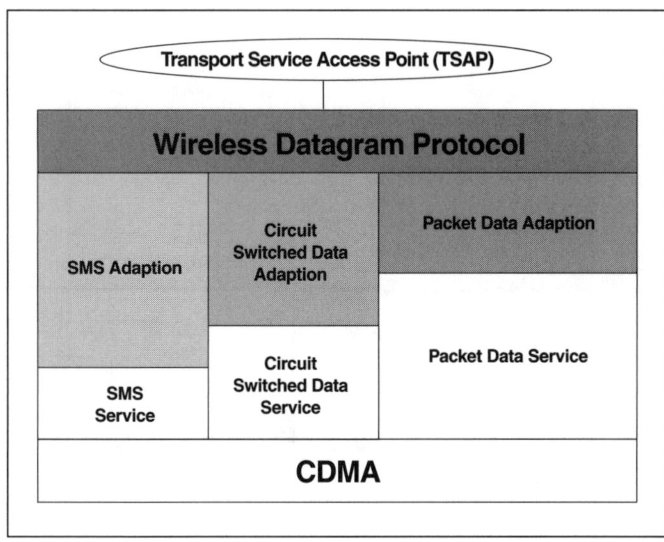

Figure 17.12 WDP over CDMA bearer services.

2.4.4.1 CDMA Circuit-Switched Data Profile

Figure 17.13 illustrates the protocol profile for the WDP layer when operating over the CDMA Circuit-Switched bearer service. The Internet Service Provider (ISP) provides connectivity to the Internet network so that the mobile and WAP Proxy/Server can address each other. The WAP Proxy/Server can terminate the WAE or serve as a proxy to other applications on the Internet. The CDMA Circuit-Switched Data protocol consists of TCP, IP, PPP, and RLP layers as defined in IS-707 specification over IS-95 air interface.

2.4.4.2 CDMA Packet Data Profile

To be defined by WDP CDMA Ad Hoc Group.

2.4.4.3 CDMA SMS

WDP over CDMA SMS will be defined in a companion document [WAP over CDMA SMS] that is currently being developed, to be released at a later date.

2.4.5 WDP over PDC (Japan)

The WDP layer operates above the data-capable bearer services supported by PDC. Figure 17.14 identifies the PDC bearer services presented in this specification.

The SMS bearer service for PDC is not a part of the specification. Operators have their proprietary solutions. It is therefore left to the operators and applicable vendors to define WDP interface for each proprietary SMS bearer service.

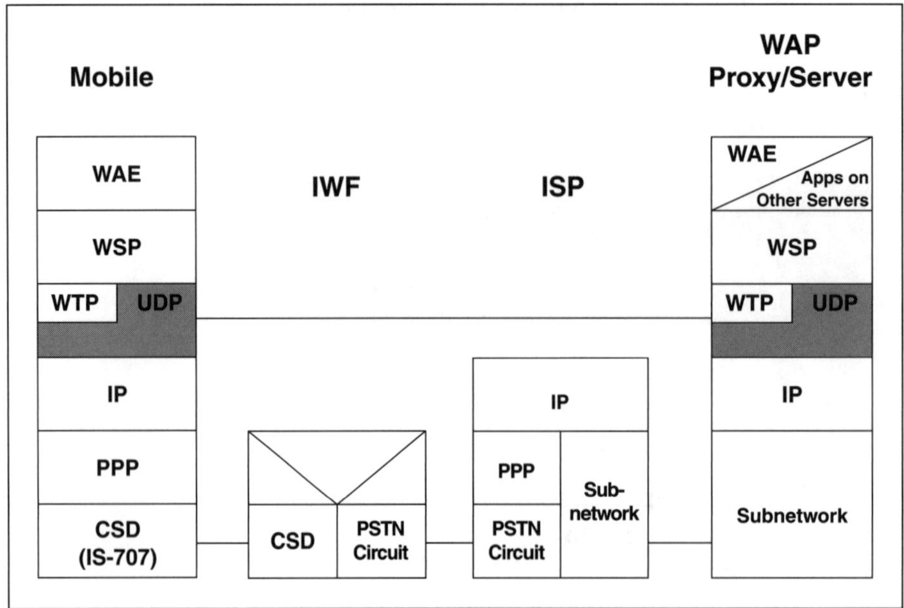

Figure 17.13 WDP over CDMA circuit-switched data channel.

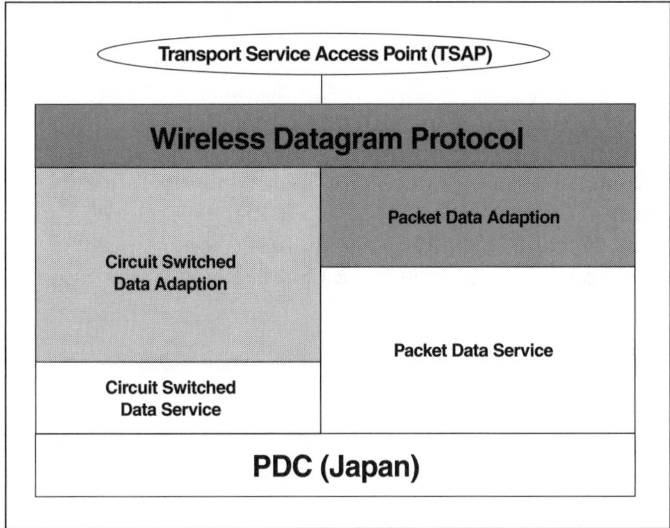

Figure 17.14 WTP over PDC bearer services.

2.4.5.1 PDC Circuit-Switched Data

Figure 17.15 illustrates the protocol profile for the WTP layer when operating over a Circuit-Switched Data connection. The IWU provides CSD services. The Internet Service Provider (ISP) provides Internet connectivity to the Internet network so that the mobile and the WAP Proxy/Server can address each other. WTP over UDP and

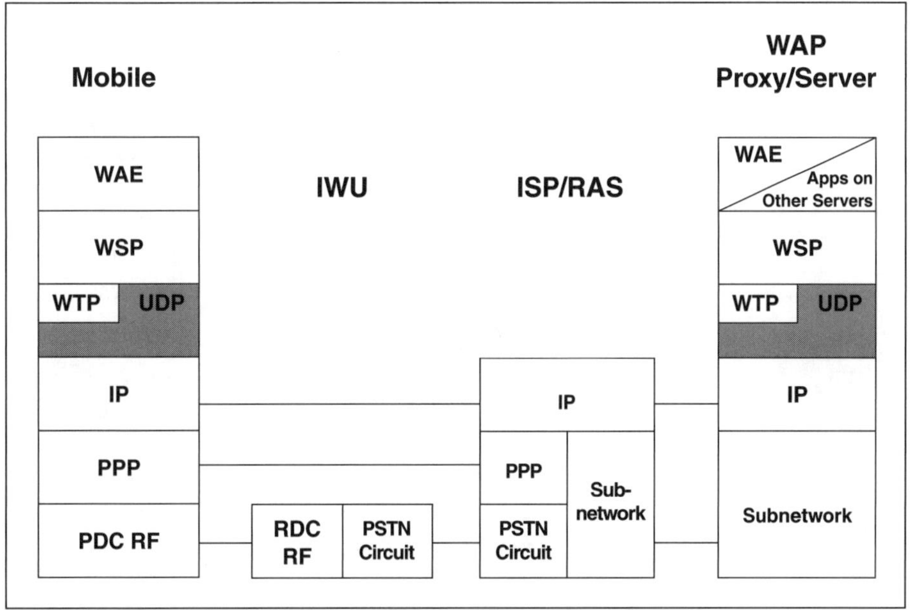

Figure 17.15 WDP over PDC circuit-switched data channel.

UDP/IP provide transaction-oriented and datagram services, respectively, to WSP. The WAP Proxy/Server can terminate the WAE or serve as a proxy to other applications on the Internet.

2.4.5.2 PDC Packet Data Profile

Figure 17.16 illustrates the protocol profile for the WDP layer when operating over a PDC Packet Data bearer service. PDC Packet Data supports IP to the mobile. WTP over UDP and UDP/IP provide transaction-oriented and datagram services, respectively, to WTP. The WAP Proxy/Server can terminate the WAE or serve as a proxy to other applications on the Internet.

2.4.6 WDP Profile Over iDEN

iDEN provides three data services: Short Message Service, Circuit Switched, and iDEN Packet Data. Both the Circuit Switched and Packet Data services provide IP connectivity to the mobile device. Therefore, the datagram protocol used for iDEN's data bearer services is UDP. This section provides a high-level protocol architecture description of these two bearer services.

2.4.6.1 iDEN Short Message Service

The SMS service adaptation of WDP has not yet been defined.

2.4.6.2 iDEN Circuit-Switched Data

Figure 17.17 illustrates the protocol profile for the datagram layer when operating over an iDEN Circuit-Switched Data connection. The IWF provides nontransparent Circuit Switched Data services for all CSD calls within iDEN. The iDEN CSD service is very

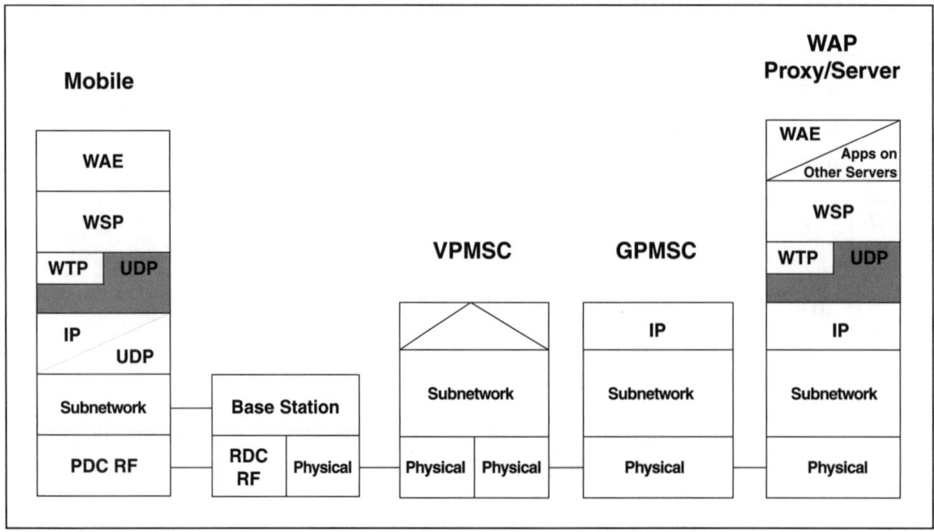

Figure 17.16 WDP over PDC packet data channel.

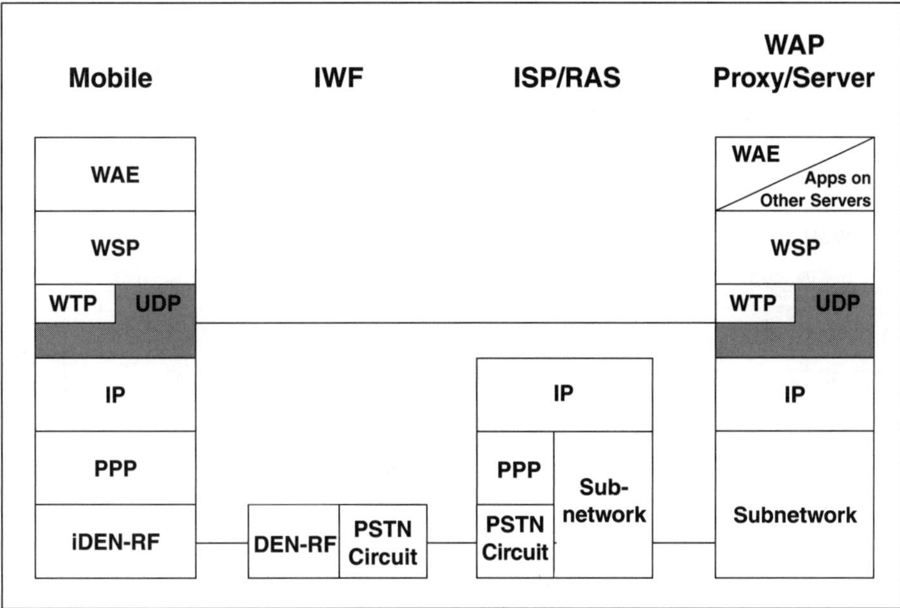

Figure 17.17 WDP over iDEN Circuit-Switched Data channel.

similar to the GSM CSD service. The Remote Access Server (RAS) or the Internet Service Provider (ISP) provides connectivity to the Internet network so that the mobile and WAP proxy server can address each other. The WAP Proxy/Server can terminate the WAE or serve as a proxy to other applications on the Internet.

2.4.6.3 iDEN Packet Data

Figure 17.18 illustrates the protocol profile for the WTP layer when operating over the iDEN Packet Data bearer service. The iDEN packet data network utilizes the IETF defined mobile IP tunneling protocol to route data to the mobile device. A Home Agent router on the mobile's home network forwards datagrams to an iDEN Mobile Data Gateway. The MDG acts as a mobile IP Foreign Agent that transfers IP between the wired IP network and the wireless device via the iDEN RF protocols.

2.4.7 WDP over FLEX and ReFLEX

Figure 17.19 illustrates the protocol profile for the WDP layer when operating over the FLEX and ReFLEX paging protocols. The profile for FLEX and ReFLEX requires a generic messaging network protocol for connecting the WAP Proxy/Server to the FLEX or ReFLEX network. WDP packets are transferred between the mobile and the paging network through the use of the FLEX Suite of Application Enabling protocols. Optionally, the FLEX Suite protocols may be carried to the WAP Proxy/Server, depending on the desired functionality. The WAP Proxy/Server can terminate the WAE or serve as a proxy to other applications on the Internet or other networks.

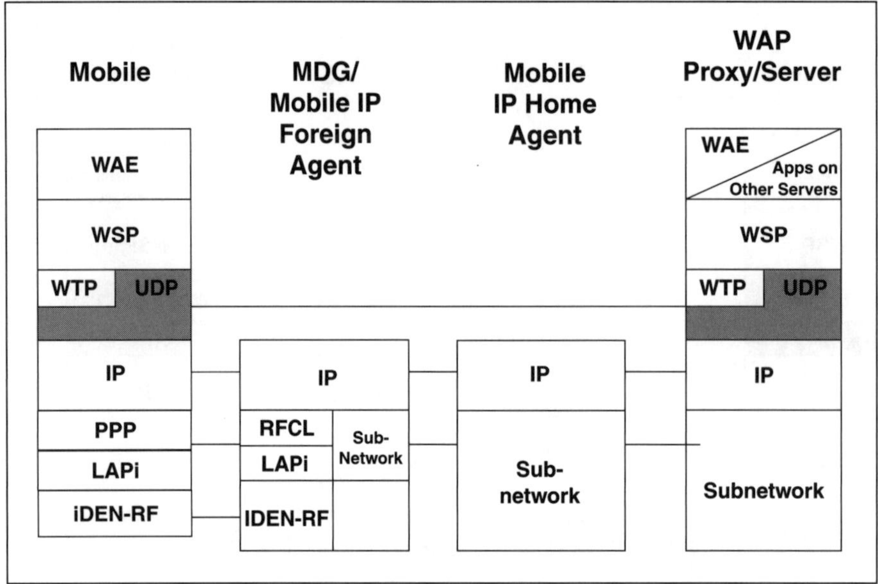

Figure 17.18 WTP over iDEN packet data.

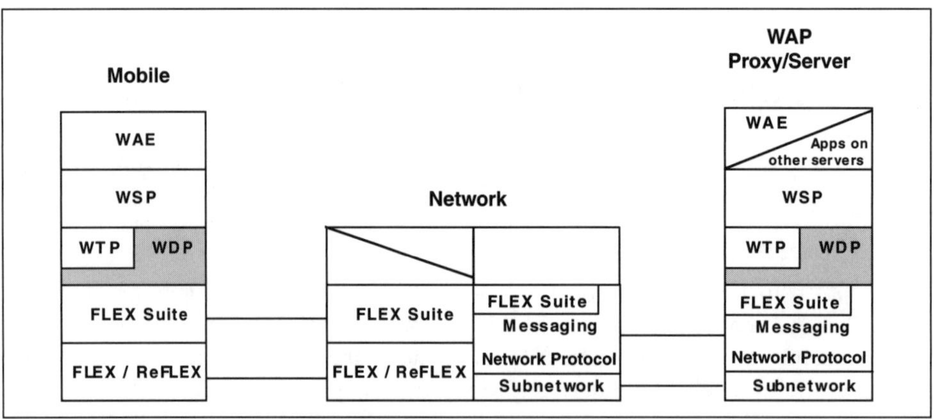

Figure 17.19 FLEX and ReFLEX profile.

3. Elements for Layer-to-Layer Communication

3.1 Service Primitive Notation

Communications between layers and between entities within the Transport layer are accomplished by means of service primitives. Service primitives represent, in an abstract way, the logical exchange of information and control between the Transport layer and adjacent layers. They do not specify or constrain implementations.

Service primitives consist of commands and their respective responses associated with the services requested of another layer. The general syntax of a primitive is

X - Generic name . Type (Parameters)

where X designates the layer providing the service. For this specification, X is

"T" for the Transport Layer

An example of a service primitive for the WDP layer would be T-DUnitdata Request.

Service primitives are not the same as an Application Programming Interface (API) and are not meant to imply any specific method of implementing an API. Service primitives are an abstract means of illustrating the services provided by the Protocol layer to the layer above. The mapping of these concepts to a real API and the semantics associated with a real API are an implementation issue and are beyond the scope of this specification.

3.2 Service Primitives Types

The primitives types defined in this specification are discussed in the following sections.

3.2.1 Request (.Req)

The Request primitive type is used when a higher layer is requesting a service from the next lower layer.

3.2.2 Indication (.Ind)

The Indication primitive type is used by a layer providing a service to notify the next higher layer of activities related to the Request primitive type of the peer.

3.2.3 Response (.Res)

The Response primitive type is used by a layer to acknowledge receipt, from the next lower layer, of the Indication primitive type.

3.2.4 Confirm (.Cnf)

The Confirm primitive type is used by the layer providing the requested service to confirm that the activity has been completed (successfully or unsuccessfully).

3.3 WDP Service Primitives

3.3.1 General

The following notation is used in the description of the service primitives:

ABBREVIATION	MEANING
M	Presence of the parameter is mandatory.
C	Presence of the parameter is conditional.
O	Presence of the parameter is a user option.
*	Presence of the parameter is determined by the lower-layer protocol.
blank	The parameter is absent.
(=)	The value of the parameter is identical to the value of the corresponding parameter of the preceding primitive.

The WDP protocol uses a single service primitive T-DUnitdata. WDP may also receive a T-DError primitive if the requested transmission cannot be executed by the WDP protocol layer.

3.3.1.1 T-DUnitdata

T-DUnitdata is the primitive used to transmit data as a datagram. T-DUnitdata does not require an existing connection to be established. A T-DUnitdata.Req can be sent to the WDP layer at any time.

PRIMITIVE	T-DUNITDATA			
PARAMETER	*REQ*	*IND*	*RES*	*CNF*
Source Address	M	M(=)		
Source Port	M	M(=)		
Destination Address	M	O(=)		
Destination Port	M	O(=)		
User Data	M	M(=)		

3.3.1.1.1 Destination Address The destination address of the user data submitted to the WDP layer. The destination address may be an MSISDN number, IP address, X.25 address, or other identifier.

3.3.1.1.2 Destination Port The application address associated with the destination address for the requested communication instance.

3.3.1.1.3 Source Address The source address is the unique address of the device making a request to the WDP layer. The source address may be an MSISDN number, IP address, X.25 address, or other identifier.

3.3.1.1.4 Source Port The application address associated with the source address of the requesting communication instance.

3.3.1.1.5 User Data The user data carried by the WDP protocol. The unit of data submitted to or received from the WDP layer is also referred to as the Service Data Unit. This is the complete unit (message, packet, package) of data which the higher layer has submitted to the WDP layer for transmission. The WDP layer will transmit the Service Data Unit and deliver it to its destination without any manipulation of its content.

3.3.1.2 T-DError

The T-DError primitive is used to provide information to the higher layer when an error occurs that may impact the requested service. A T-DError Indication may be issued by the WDP layer only after the higher layer has made a request to the WDP layer, such as by issuing a T-DUnitdata Request. The T-DError primitive is used when the WDP layer is unable to complete the requested service due to a local problem. It is not used to inform the upper layer of networking errors external to the device/server.

An example would be if the upper layer issues a D-Unitdata Request containing an SDU that is larger than the maximum size SDU allowed by the specific WDP implementation. In this case, a T-DError Indication would be returned to the upper layer with an error code indicating the SDU size is too large.

PRIMITIVE	T-ERROR			
PARAMETER	*REQ*	*IND*	*RES*	*CNF*
Source Address		O		
Source Port		O		
Destination Address		O		
Destination Port		O		
Error Code		M		

3.3.1.2.1 Error Code An error return code carried by the D-Error primitive to the higher layer. The error codes are of local significance only.

4. WDP Protocol Description

4.1 Introduction

In order to implement the WDP datagram protocol, the following fields are necessary:

- Destination Port.
- Source Port.
- If the underlying bearer does not provide Segmentation and Reassembly, the feature is implemented by the WDP provider in a bearer dependent way.

4.2 Mapping of WDP for IP

The User Datagram Protocol (UDP) is adopted as the WDP protocol definition for any wireless bearer network where IP is used as a routing protocol. UDP provides port based addressing and IP provides the segmentation and reassembly in a connectionless datagram service. There is no value in defining a new datagram protocol to operate over IP when the ubiquitous User Datagram Protocol (UDP) will provide the same mechanisms and functions, and is already very widely implemented. Therefore, in all cases where the IP protocol is available over a bearer service, the WDP Datagram service offered for that bearer will be UDP. UDP is fully specified in RFC 768 while the IP networking layer is defined in RFC 791.

4.3 Mapping of WDP for GSM SMS and GSM USSD

WDP bearers in the Global System for Mobile Communications (GSM) include GSM Short Message Service (GSM SMS) and GSM Unstructured Supplementary Service Data (GSM USSD).

WDP for GSM supports mandatory binary and optional text-based headers. GSM USSD Phase 2 supports binary headers, GSM SMS Phase 2 supports both binary and text-based headers, and GSM SMS Phase 1 supports text-based headers.

Each packet (segment) used in the WDP protocol is identified by a User Data Header Information Element Identifier defining a port number structure located in the header of the packet. This Information Element Identifier for GSM SMS or USSD has a similar function to the Protocol Identifier in a IP-based network. The construct enables the WDP protocol to coexist with other features of the legacy bearer network.

4.3.1 Header Formats

4.3.1.1 Binary Header Format

For GSM SMS and GSM USSD, the WDP headers structure is defined using the User Data Header (UDH) framework as defined in GSM 03.40. See Appendix A of this chapter for more information.

4.3.2 Segmentation and Reassembly

The WDP segmentation is implemented as specified in GSM 03.40.

Two segmentation formats, the short format and the long format, have been defined. The difference between the two formats is only the range of the Datagram Reference Number. A format with only 8 bits for reference number is good enough for mobile originated communication, but in high volume applications originated at a fixed server, the reference number wraps around very quickly. The larger reference number range significantly lessens the risk of overlapping reference numbers and thus incorrect reassembly.

Mobile stations MAY use the 8-bit reference number header for sending messages, but fixed devices MUST use the 16-bit reference number (unless it is known to the device that the receiver supports only 8-bit reference numbers). Each implementation of the WDP MUST support reception of both 8- and 16-bit reference numbers, but a mobile implementation can be restricted to sending capability of only 8-bit reference numbers.

4.3.2.1 Fragmentation Information Element (short)

The Fragmentation Information Element Identifier is defined in GSM 03.40.

4.3.2.2 Fragmentation Information Element (long)

The Long Fragmentation Information Element Identifier is an octet with the hex value XX.

The Long Information Element Data octets shall be coded as shown in Figure 17.20.

An Information Element (IE) identifier is to be applied and obtained from ETSI.

4.3.2.3 Port Address Information Element

The Information Element Identifier is defined in GSM 03.40.

4.3.3 Mapping of WDP to GSM SMS Phase 1 Text-Based Headers

The text-based headers are designed as an optional method for environments that support only reduced character sets; for example, not 8-bit binary headers. This is the case for GSM phase 1 SMS, but can also be used as a generic mechanism in similar environments. See Figures 17.21 and 17.22.

Octet 1–2	Datagram reference number	This octet shall contain a modulo 0xFFFF counter indicating the reference number for a particular datagram. This reference number shall remain constant for every segment which makes up a particular datagram.
Octet 3	Maximum number of segments in the datagram.	This octet shall contain a value in the range 1 to 255, indicating the totalnumber of segments within the datagram. The value shall remain constant for every segment that makes up the datagram. If the value is 0, then the receiving entity shall ignore the whole Information Element.
Octet 4	Sequence number of the current segment	This octet shall contain a value in the range 1 to 255, indicating the sequence number of a particular segment within the datagram. The value shall start at 1 and increment by 1 for every segment sent within the datagram. If the value is 0 or the value is greater than the value in octet 2, then the receiving entity shall ignore the whole Information Element.

Figure 17.20 Segmentation and Reassembly Information Element using 16-bit reference number.

```
<WDP -text-socket-header> ::=
          <WDP-keyword> <WDP-port-information> [<WDP-other-header> ] <WDP
          delimiter>
  <WDP-delimiter> ::= <space>
  <WDP-keyword> ::= "//SCK"
  <WDP-port-information> ::=
          <WDP-short-destination-address> |
          <WDP-short-destination-address> <WDP-short-source-address> |
          <WDP-short-destination-address> <WDP-short-source-address> <WDP-SAR-  information> |
          "L" <WDP-long-destination-address> |
          "L" <WDP-long-destination-address> <WDP-long-source-address> |
          "L" <WDP-long-destination-address> <WDP-long-source-address> <WDP-SAR- information>
  <WDP-other-header> ::= <header-expansions-starting-with-// >
  <WDP-short-destination-address> ::= <common-hex-digit> <common-hex-digit>
          ; Destination WDP port in ASCII coded hexadecimal [00..FF, or 00..FFFF]. When the
           truncated port presentation is used (only destination port), then the source port
           of the message is defaulted to be the same as the destination port.'
  <WDP-short-source-address> ::= <common-hex-digit> <common-hex-digit>
          ; Source WDP port in ASCII coded hexadecimal [00..FF], i.e., decimal [0..255].'
  <WDP-long-destination-address> ::=
          <common-hex-digit> <common-hex-digit> <common-hex-digit> <common-hex-digit>
          ; Destination WDP port in ASCII coded hexadecimal [0000..FFFF] , i.e., decimal
           [0..65535].'
  <WDP-long-source-address> ::=
          <common-hex-digit> <common-hex-digit> <common-hex-digit> <common-hex-digit>
          ; Source WDP port in ASCII coded hexadecimal [0000..FFFF] , i.e., decimal
           [0..65535].
  <WDP-SAR-information> ::=
          <WDP-SAR-reference> <WDP-SAR-total-segments> <WDP-SAR-current-    segment>
  <WDP-SAR-reference> ::= <common-hex-digit> <common-hex-digit>
          ; Concatenated message reference number in ASCII coded hexadecimal [00..FF], i.e.,
           decimal [0..255].'
  <WDP-SAR-total-segments> ::= <common-hex-digit> <common-hex-digit>
          ; 'Concatenated message total segment count in ASCII coded hexadecimal [01..FF],
           i.e., decimal [1..255].'
  <WDP-SAR-current-segment> ::= <common-hex-digit> <common-hex-digit>
          ; 'Concatenated message segment index in ASCII coded hexadecimal [01..FF], i.e.,
           decimal [1..255].'
```

Figure 17.21 Definition of WDP headers in text format.

No protocol indication at a higher level is needed to indicate the presence of protocol information in the data part of the message. The first characters "//SCK" identify the WDP datagram addressing scheme to the receiving device. The header can be presented in various lengths, from 2 bytes (only destination port) to 15 bytes (containing full WDP information), in addition to the 5 bytes of "//SCK".

7	6	5	4	3	2	1	0
"/"							
"/"							
"S"							
"C"							
"K"							
"L"							
Destination port (High hex)							
Destination Port (Low hex)							
Originator Port (High hex)							
Originator Port (Low hex)							
Reference Number (High hex)							
reference number (Low hex)							
Total number of *segments* (High hex)							
Total number of *segments* (Low hex)							
Segment count (High hex)							
Segment count (Low hex)							
1-n 7-bit characters of user data							

Figure 17.22 Example of a WDP header for compatibility with legacy GSM networks.

The text-based header is always terminated with a space (" ") character. This allows for future enhancements to the protocol.

Devices not supporting the concatenation should *not* put dummy values into the header, as they can be misinterpreted and consume valuable bandwidth. Instead, they shall truncate the header and omit the Segmentation and Reassembly part of the header

4.3.4 Mapping of WDP to GSM USSD

GSM USSD adaptation layer is specified in the WAP WDP Implementation Companion document. See [WAPGSMUD].

4.4 Mapping of WDP for IS-136 GUTS/R-Data

IS-136 GUTS is used to support UDP datagrams on IS-136 R-Data. GUTS adds a 1-octet protocol discriminator and message type to the UDP header. Port address information is assumed to be carried within the UDP header. Segmentation and reassembly can be optionally provided by the IS-136 Simplified Segmentation and Reassembly (SSAR) layer between GUTS and R-Data. IP address and routing information is specified within the R-Data layer when using GUTS.

4.5 Mapping of WDP to CDPD

To be defined.

4.6 Mapping of WDP to CDMA

To be defined.

4.7 Mapping of WDP to PDC

To be defined.

4.8 Mapping of WDP to iDEN

To be defined.

4.9 Mapping of WDP to FLEX and ReFLEX

To be defined.

5. Definitions

For the purposes of this specification the following definitions apply:

Cellular Digital Packet Data (CDPD). CDPD is an AMPS overlay packet radio service.

CSD. Circuit-Switched Data provides a point-to-point connection between the device and the network. This service is typically available in cellular and PCS networks.

Device. An entity that is capable of sending and/or receiving packets of information via a wireless network and has an unique device address. See [WAP] for further information.

Device Address. The address of a device is its unique network address assigned by a carrier and following the format defined by an international standard such as E.164 for MSISDN addresses, X.121 for X.25 addresses, or RFC 791 for IPv4 addresses. An address uniquely identifies the sending and/or receiving device.

FLEX. A one-way paging protocol developed to optimize channel efficiency, battery life, and cost per bit for transmitting messages over a wide geographical area.

FLEX Suite of Application Enabling Protocols. A suite of protocols and features that enable applications on FLEX and ReFLEX networks. The FLEX Suite protocols operate at the layer above the FLEX and/or ReFLEX protocol layers.

GPRS. General Packet Radio Service as defined in GSM 02.60 and 03.60. GPRS provide a packet data service overlay to GSM networks.

iDEN. Integrated Digital Enhanced Network.

iDEN Circuit Switched Data. iDEN Circuit-Switched Data provides a point-to-point connection between the device and the network.

iDEN Packet Data. iDEN Packet Data provides a packet data radio service to the iDEN system. This packet data service utilizes mobile IP as the mechanism to enable mobile devices to roam within iDEN.

IS-136 General UDP Transport Service (GUTS). GUTS is a general-purpose application data delivery service. GUTS utilizes the Internet Standard User Datagram Protocol (UDP) to specify the intended application or port.

IS-136 Packet Data. IS-136 Packet Data provides a packet data radio service in IS-136.

IS-136 R-DATA. IS-136 R-Data is a two-way narrowband transport mechanism that is supported on the digital control channel (DCCH) and digital traffic channel (DTC). R-Data can be used to carry GUTS messages or other teleservices messages such as the Cellular Messaging Teleservice (CMT). It is by nature similar to a datagram service.

Maximum Packet Lifetime, MPL. MPL is fixed by the used carrier (the network system).

Network Type. Network type refers to any network, which is classified by a common set of characteristics (i.e., air interface) and standards. Examples of network types include GSM, CDMA, IS-136, iDEN, FLEX, and Mobitex. Each network type may contain multiple underlying bearer services suitable for transporting WDP.

Packet. A packet is a set of bytes being transmitted over the network as an undivided entity. Each packet contains a header, which describes the context of the packet, its position in the packet group, its position in the transmission, and other pertinent information. The WDP header is positioned into the packet according to the features of the underlying bearer.

Port. Ports are used as a subaddressing mechanism inside a device. A port number identifies the higher-layer entity (such as a protocol or application) directly above the WDP layer.

ReFLEX. A two-way paging protocol developed to enable the efficient delivery of messages and content over the air in both the outbound (system to pager) and inbound (pager to system) directions.

SMS. Point-to-Point Short Message Service is a narrow-bandwidth data transport mechanism typically available in cellular and PCS networks.

Transmission. Transmission is a collection of one or more packets from a source to a destination.

Underlying Bearer. An underlying bearer is a data transport mechanism used to carry the WDP protocols between two devices. Examples of underlying bearers include CDPD, GSM SMS, GSM USSD, GSM CSD, GSM GPRS, IS-136 GUTS, CSD, and Packet Data. During a data exchange between two devices, more than one underlying bearer may be used.

USSD. Unstructured Supplementary Service Data is a narrow-bandwidth transport mechanism. USSD is a GSM supplementary service. It uses the signaling channels as a bearer, and is half-duplex (only one of the parties are allowed to send at any one moment). It is by nature similar to circuit switched data service.

6. General Concepts

This section describes the industry terminology related to the specifications.

Client and Server. The terms *client* and *server* are used in order to map the WAP environment to well-known and existing systems. A client is a device (or application) that initiates requests for data. The server is a device that passively waits for data requests from client devices or actively pushes data to client devices. The server can either accept the request or reject it.

A device can simultaneously act both as client and server for different applications, or even in the context of one application. An application can serve a number of clients (as a server), but act as a client towards another server.

7. Abbreviations

For the purposes of this specification, the following abbreviations apply:

API	Application Programming Interface
BMI	Base Station, MSC, Interworking Function (IWF)
BSD	Berkeley Software Distribution
CDMA	Code Division Multiple Access
CDPD	Cellular Digital Packet Data
CSD	Circuit Switched Data
DBMS	Database Management System
DCS	Data Coding Scheme
ETSI	European Telecommunication Standardization Institute
GPRS	General Packet Radio Service
GSM	Global System for Mobile Communication
GTR	Group Trailer, indicates the end of packet group
GUTS	General UDP Transport Service
HLR	Home Location Register
iDEN	Integrated Digital Enhanced Network
IE	Information Element
IP	Internet Protocol
LAPi	Link Access Protocol iDEN
LSB	Least significant bits

MAC	Medium Access Control
MAP	Mobile Application Part
MDBS	Mobile Data Base Station
MDG	Mobile Data Gateway
MD-IS	Mobile Data—Intermediate System
MDLP	Mobile Data Link Protocol
MGL	Maximum Group Length
MMI	Man Machine Interface
MPL	Maximum Packet Lifetime (constant)
MPS	Maximum Packet Size
MSISDN	Mobile Subscriber ISDN (Telephone number or address of device)
MS	Mobile Station
MSB	Most significant bits
MSC	Mobile Switching Centre
MSS	Maximum Segment Size
PCI	Protocol Control Information
PCS	Personal Communication Services
PDLP	Packet Data Link Protocol
PLMN	Public Land Mobile Network
PPP	Point-to-Point Protocol
R-Data	Relay Data
RFCL	Radio Frequency Convergence Layer
RTT	Round-Trip Time
SAR	Segmentation and Reassembly
SMSC	Short Message Service Centre
SMS	Short Message Service
SNDCP	SubNetwork Dependent Convergence Protocol
SPT	Server Processing Time
SS7	Signaling System 7
SSAR	Simplified Segmentation and Reassembly
TCAP	Transaction Capability Application Part
TCP/IP	Transmission Control Protocol/Internet Protocol
TDMA	Time Division Multiple Access
TIA/EIA	Telecommunications Industry Association/Electronic Industry Association
TSAP	Transport Service Access Point

TTR	Transmission Trailer, indicates the end of transmission
UDH	User-Data Header (see GSM 03.40)
UDHL	User-Data Header Length
UDL	User-Data Length
UDP	User Datagram Protocol
UDCP	USSD Dialog Control Protocol
USSD	Unstructured Supplementary Service Data
VLR	Visitor Location Registry
VPLMN	Visitor Public Land Mobile Network
WAE	Wireless Application Environment
WAP	Wireless Application Protocol
WDP	Wireless Datagram Protocol
WSP	Wireless Session Protocol
WTP	Wireless Transaction Protocol

8. Requirements

This specification uses the following words for defining the significance of each particular requirement:

MUST. This word, or the terms "REQUIRED" or "SHALL," means that the definition is an absolute requirement of the specification.

MUST NOT. This phrase, or the phrase "SHALL NOT," means that the definition is an absolute prohibition of the specification.

SHOULD. This word, or the adjective "RECOMMENDED," means that there may exist valid reasons in particular circumstances to ignore a particular item, but the full implications must be understood and carefully weighed before choosing a different course.

SHOULD NOT. This phrase, or the phrase "NOT RECOMMENDED," means that there may exist valid reasons in particular circumstances when the particular behavior is acceptable or even useful, but the full implications should be understood and the case carefully weighed before implementing any behavior described with this label.

MAY. This word, or the adjective "OPTIONAL," means that an item is truly optional. One vendor may choose to include the item because a particular marketplace requires it or because the vendor feels that it enhances the product, while another vendor may omit the same item. An implementation that does not include a particular option MUST be prepared to interoperate with another implementation that does include the option, though perhaps with reduced functionality. In the same vein, an implementation that does include a particular option MUST be prepared to interoperate with another implementation that does not include the option (except, of course, for the feature the option provides).

9. Security Considerations

WDP has no authentication mechanisms.

10. Normative References

[FLEX] FLEX™ Protocol Specification and FLEX™ Encoding and Decoding Requirements, Version G1.9, Document Number 68P81139B01, March 16, 1998, Motorola.

[FLEXSuite] FLEX™ Suite of Application Protocols, Version 1.0, Document Number 6881139B10, October 29, 1997, Motorola.

[GSM0260] ETSI European Digital Cellular Telecommunication Systems (phase 2+) : General Packet Radio Service (GPRS)—stage 1 (GSM 02.60).

[GSM0290] ETSI European Digital Cellular Telecommunication Systems (phase 2) : Unstructured Supplementary Service Data (USSD)—stage 1 (GSM 02.90).

[GSM0340] ETSI European Digital Cellular Telecommunication Systems (phase 2+) : Technical Realization of the Short Message Service (SMS) Point-to-Point (P) (GSM 03.40).

[GSM0360] ETSI European Digital Cellular Telecommunication Systems (phase 2+) : General Packet Radio Service (GPRS)—stage 2 (GSM 03.60).

[GSM0390] ETSI European Digital Cellular Telecommunication Systems (phase 2) : Unstructured Supplementary Service Data (USSD)—stage 2 (GSM 03.90).

[GSM0490] ETSI European Digital Cellular Telecommunication Systems (phase 2) : Unstructured Supplementary Service Data (USSD)—stage 3 (GSM 04.90).

[iDEN] iDEN™ Technical Overview, Motorola Document Number 68P81095E55-A.

[IS130] EIA/TIA IS-130.

[IS135] EIA/TIA IS-135.

[IS136] EIA/TIA IS-136.

[IS637] TIA/EIA/IS-637: Short Message Services for Wideband Spread Spectrum Cellular Systems.

[IS732] EIA/TIA/IS-732 Cellular Digital Packet Data.

[IS07498] ISO 7498 OSI Reference Model.

[ReFLEX] ReFLEX25 Protocol Specification Document, Version 2.6, Document Number 68P81139B02-A, March 16, 1998, Motorola.

[RFC2119] S. Bradner "Key Words for use in RFCs to Indicate Requirement Levels," RFC2119.

[TR45.3.6] General UDP Transport Teleservice (GUTS)—Stage III, TR45.3.6/97.12.15.

[WAE] WAP Wireless Application Group, Wireless Application Environment Specification 30-April-1998.
URL: http://www.wapforum.org/

[WAPARCH] WAP Architecture Working Group "Wireless Application Protocol Architecture Specification," version 1.0.
URL: http://www.wapforum.org/

[WAPGSMUD] WAP and GSM USSD 30-April-1998.
URL: http://www.wapforum.org/

[WCMP] WAP Wireless Transport Group, Wireless Control Message Protocol Specification 30-April-1998.
URL: http://www.wapforum.org/

[WTPGOAL] WAP WTP Working Group "Wireless Transport Protocol Goals Document" version 0.01; document number 112597.
URL: http://www.wapforum.org/

[WTPREQ] WAP WTP Working Group "Wireless Transport Protocol Requirements Document" version 0.02; document number 112597.
URL: http://www.wapforum.org/

[WSP] WAP Wireless Session Group, Wireless Session Protocol Specification 30-April-1998.
URL: http://www.wapforum.org/

[WTLS] WAP Wireless Session Group, Wireless Transport Layer Security Specification 30-April-1998.
URL: http://www.wapforum.org/

[WTP] WAP Wireless Transport Group, Wireless Transaction Protocol Specification 30-April-1998.
URL: http://www.wapforum.org/

11. Informative References

[RFC768] J. Postel, "User Datagram Protocol," RFC768, August 1980.

[RFC791] J. Postel, "IP: Internet Protocol," RFC791.

[RFC793] J. Postel, "Transmission Control Protocol," RFC793, September 1981.

[RFC2188] M. Banan (Neda), M. Taylor (AT&T), J. Cheng (AT&T), "Efficient Short Remote Operations Protocol Specification Version 1.2," RFC2188, September 1997.

[TCP/Ipill3] W. Richard Stevens, "TCP/IP Illustrated, Volume 3," Addison-Wesley Publishing Company Inc., 1996, ISBN 0-201-63495-3.

Appendix A: PICS Proforma

The supplier of a protocol implementation that claims conformance to this Specification shall complete a copy of the PICS proforma provided in this appendix, including the information necessary to identify both the supplier and the implementation.

A.1 Introduction

The supplier of a protocol implementation which is claimed to conform to this Specification shall complete the following Protocol Implementation Conformance Statement (PICS) proforma.

A completed PICS proforma is the PICS for the implementation in question. The PICS is a statement of which capabilities and options of the protocol have been implemented. The PICS can have a number of uses, including:

- The protocol implementor, as a checklist to reduce the risk of failure to conform to the standard through oversight.
- The supplier and acquirer—or potential acquirer—of the implementation, as a detailed indication of the capabilities of the implementation, stated relative to the common basis for understanding provided by the standard PICS proforma.
- The user—or potential user—of the implementation, as a basis for initially checking the possibility of interworking with another implementation (note that, while interworking can never be guaranteed, failure to interwork can often be predicted from incompatible PICSs).
- A protocol tester, as the basis for selecting appropriate tests against which to assess the claim for conformance of the implementation.

A.2 Abbreviations and Special Symbols

A.2.1 Status Symbols

M	Mandatory
O	Optional
O.<n>	Optional, but support of at least one of the group of options labeled by the same numeral <n> is required
X	Prohibited
<pred>:	Conditional-item symbol, including predicate identification (see A.3.4)
^	Logical negation, applied to a conditional item's predicate

A.2.2 Other Symbols

<r>	Receive aspects of an item
<s>	Send aspects of an item

A.3 Instructions for Completing the PICS Proforma

A.3.1 General Structure of the PICS Proforma

The first part of the PICS proforma—Implementation Identification and Protocol Summary—is to be completed as indicated with the information necessary to identify fully both the supplier and the implementation.

The main part of the PICS proforma is a fixed-format questionnaire divided into a number of major subclauses; these can be divided into further subclauses, each containing a group of individual items. Answers to the questionnaire items are to be provided in the right-most column, either by simply marking an answer to indicate a restricted choice (usually Yes or No), or by entering a value or a set or range of values.

Note: There are some items for which two or more choices from a set of possible answers can apply. All relevant choices are to be marked in these cases.

Each item is identified by an item reference in the first column; the second column contains the question to be answered; and the third column contains the reference or references to the material that specifies the item in the main body of this Specification. The remaining columns record the status of the item—whether support is mandatory, optional, prohibited, or conditional—and provide space for the answers (see also A.3.4).

A supplier may also provide further information, categorized as either Additional Information or Exception Information. When present, each kind of further information is to be provided in a further subclause of items labeled A<i> or X<i>, respectively, for cross-referencing purposes, where <i> is any unambiguous identification for the item (e.g., a number); there are no other restrictions on its format or presentation.

A completed PICS proforma, including any Additional Information and Exception Information, is the Protocol Implementation Conformance Statement for the implementation in question.

Note: Where an implementation is capable of being configured in more than one way, a single PICS may be able to describe all such configurations. However, the supplier has the choice of providing more than one PICS, each covering some subset of the implementation's configuration capabilities, in cases where this makes for easier and clearer presentation of the information.

A.3.2 Additional Information

Items of Additional Information allow a supplier to provide further information intended to assist in the interpretation of the PICS. It is not intended or expected that a large quantity will be supplied, and a PICS can be considered complete without any such information. Examples might be an outline of the ways in which a (single) implementation can be set up to operate in a variety of environments and configurations, or a brief rationale—based perhaps upon specific application needs—for the exclusion of features which, although optional, are nonetheless commonly present in implementations of this protocol.

References to items of Additional Information may be entered next to any answer in the questionnaire, and may be included in items of Exception Information.

A.3.3 Exception Information

It may occasionally happen that a supplier will wish to answer an item with mandatory or prohibited status (after any conditions have been applied) in a way that conflicts with the indicated requirement. No preprinted answer will be found in the support column for this; instead, the supplier shall write the missing answer into the Support column, together with an X<i> reference to an item of Exception Information, and shall provide the appropriate rationale in the Exception Information item itself.

An implementation for which an Exception Information item is required in this way does not conform to this Specification.

Note: A possible reason for the situation just described is that a defect in the standard has been reported, a correction for which is expected to change the requirement not met by the implementation.

A.3.4 Conditional Status

A.3.4.1 Conditional Items

The PICS proforma contains a number of conditional items. These are items for which the status—mandatory, optional, or prohibited—that applies is dependent upon whether or not certain other items are supported, or upon the values supported for other items.

In many cases, whether or not the item applies at all is conditional in this way, as well as the status when the item does apply.

Where a group of items is subject to the same condition for applicability, a separate preliminary question about the condition appears at the head of the group, with an instruction to skip to a later point in the questionnaire if the "Not Applicable" answer is selected. Otherwise, individual conditional items are indicated by one or more conditional symbols (on separate lines) in the status column.

A conditional symbol is of the form "<pred>:<x>", where "<pred>" is a predicate as described in A.3.4.2, and "<x>" is one of the status symbols M, O, O.<n>, or X.

If the value of the predicate in any line of a conditional item is true (see A.3.4.2), then the conditional item is applicable, and its status is indicated by the status symbol following the predicate; the answer column is to be marked in the usual way. If the value of a predicate is false, the Not Applicable (N/A) answer is to be marked in the relevant line. Each line in a multiline conditional item should be marked; at most, one line will require an answer other than N/A.

A.3.4.2 Predicates

A predicate is one of the following:

a) An item-reference for an item in the PICS proforma. The value of the predicate is true if the item is marked as supported and is false otherwise.
b) A predicate name, for a predicate defined elsewhere in the PICS proforma (usually in the Major Capabilities section or at the end of the section containing the conditional item).
c) The logical negation symbol "^" prefixed to an item-reference or predicate name. The value of the predicate is true if the value of the predicate formed by omitting the "^" is false, and vice versa.

The definition for a predicate name is one of the following:

a) An item-reference, evaluated as at (a) above.
b) A relation containing a comparison operator (=, < , etc.) with at least one of its operands being an item-reference for an item taking numerical values as its answer. The predicate is true if the relation holds when each item-reference is replaced by the value entered in the Support column as an answer to the item referred to.
c) A Boolean expression constructed by combining simple predicates, as in (a) and (b), using the boolean operators AND, OR, and NOT, and parentheses, in the usual way. The value of such a predicate is true if the boolean expression evaluates to true when the simple predicates are interpreted.

Each item whose reference is used in a predicate or predicate definition is indicated by an asterisk in the Item column.

A.4 Identification

A.4.1 Implementation Identification

Supplier	
Contact point for queries about the PICS	
Implementation name(s) and version(s)	
Other information necessary for full identification (e.g., name(s) and version(s) of machines and/or operating systems, system name(s))	

NOTES

1 Only the first three items are required for all implementations; other information may be completed as appropriate in meeting the requirement for full identification.

2 The terms Name and Version should be interpreted appropriately to correspond with a supplier's terminology (e.g., Type, Series, Model).

A.4.2 Protocol Summary

Identification of protocol specification	WAP Wireless Transaction Protocol
Identification of corrigenda and amendments of the PICS proforma	
Protocol version(s) supported	
Have any Exception Information items been required (see A.3.3)? YES ❐ NO ❐ (The answer YES means that the implementation does not conform to this Specification)	
Date of statement	

A.5 Wireless Datagram Protocol

A.5.1 Applicability

Clause A.5 is applicable to all implementations that claim conformance to this Specification.

A.5.2 Cellular Technology / Network Type

ITEM	DESCRIPTION	REFERENCE	STATUS	SUPPORT
RFCDMA	Does the implementation operate with CDMA technology?	TIA/EIA/IS-95	O.1	YES NO
RFCDPD	Does the implementation operate with CDPD technology?	TIA/EIA/IS-732	O.1	YES NO
RFFLEX	Does the implementation operate with FLEX technology?	Motorola Doc# 68P81139B02-A	O.1	YES NO
RFGSM	Does the implementation operate with GSM technology?	ETSI GSM	O.1	YES NO
RFIS136	Does the implementation operate with IS-136 (TDMA) technology?	TIA/EIA/IS-136	O.1	YES NO
RFiDEN	Does the implementation operate with iDEN technology?	Motorola Doc# 68P81095E55-A	O.1	YES NO
RFPDC	Does the implementation operate with PDC technology?	O.1	YES NO	
RFPHS	Does the implementation operate with PHS technology?	O.1	YES NO	

A.5.3 Bearer Services Supported

ITEM	DESCRIPTION	REFERENCE	STATUS	SUPPORT
BCDMA-SMS	Does the implementation operate with CDMA SMS bearer service?	TIA/EIA/IS-637	RFCDMA:O.1	YES NO
BCDMA-PKT	Does the implementation operate with CDMA Packet bearer service?	TIA/EIA/IS-707	RFCDMA:O.1	YES NO

(Continues)

(Continued)

ITEM	DESCRIPTION	REFERENCE	STATUS	SUPPORT	
BCDMA-CSD	Does the implementation operate with CDMA Circuit-Switched bearer service?	TIA/EIA/IS-707	RFCDMA:O.1	YES	NO
BCDPD-PKT	Does the implementation operate with CDPD Packet service?	TIA/EIA/IS-732	RFCDPD:O.2	YES	NO
BCDPD-CSD	Does the implementation operate with Circuit-Switched CDPD service?	TIA/EIA/ IS-732-1024	RFCDPD:O.2	YES	NO
BFLEX	Does the implementation operate with FLEX service?	Motorola Doc# 68P81139B01	RFFLEX:M	YES	NO
BGSM-SMS	Does the implementation operate with GSM SMS bearer service?	ETSI GSM 03.40	RFGSM:O.3	YES	NO
BGSM-USSD	Does the implementation operate with GSM USSD bearer service?	ETSI GSM 03.90	RFGSM:O.3	YES	NO
BGSM-GPRS	Does the implementation operate with GSM GPRS bearer service?	ETSI GSM 03.60	RFGSM:O.3	YES	NO
BGSM-CSD	Does the implementation operate with GSM Circuit-Switched bearer service?	ETSI GSM	RFGSM:O.3	YES	NO
BIS136-RDAT	Does the implementation operate with IS-136 R-Data service?	TIA/EIA/IS-136	RFIS136:O.4	YES	NO
BIS136-PKT	Does the implementation operate with IS-136 Packet Data service?	TIA/EIA/IS-136	RFIS136:O.4	YES	NO
BIS136-CSD	Does the implementation operate with IS-136 Circuit-Switched Data service?	TIA/EIA/IS-136	RFIS136:O.4	YES	NO
BiDEN	Does the implementation operate with iDEN service?	Motorola Doc# 68P81095E55-A	RFiDEN:M	YES	NO
BPDC-PKT	Does the implementation operate with PDC Packet Data service?		RFPDC:O.5	YES	NO
BPDC-CSD	Does the implementation operate with PDC Circuit-Switched Data service?		RFPDC:O.5	YES	NO
BPHS	Does the implementation operate with PHS service?		RFPHS:O.6	YES	NO

A.5.4 Network and Application Addressing

ITEM	DESCRIPTION	REFERENCE	STATUS	SUPPORT	
NA-E164	Does the implementation use E.164 addresses?	ITU E.164	O.1	YES	NO
NA-X25	Does the implementation use X.25 addresses?	ITU X.25	O.1	YES	NO
NA-IPV4	Does the implementation use IPv4 addresses?	RFC 791	O.1 BCDMA-PKT:M BCDPD-PKT:M BCDPD-CSD:M BGSM-GPRS:M BGSM-CSD:M BiDEN:M	YES	NO
NA-OTH	Does the implementation use a proprietary addressing scheme?	Not Applicable	O.1	YES[1]	NO
AA-DPORT	Does the implementation support Destination Port application addressing?		M	YES	NO
AA-SPORT	Does the implementation support Source Port | application addressing?		M	YES	NO

Note 1: If a proprietary addressing scheme is used, supply a reference document here, or describe the addressing scheme in a separate attachment to this PICS.

A.5.5 Protocol Functions

ITEM	FUNCTION	REFERENCE	STATUS	SUPPORT	
ASPUDR	Does the implementation support the abstract service primitive functions for T-DUnitdata.Req?		M	YES	NO
ASPUDI	Does the implementation support the abstract service primitive functions for T-DUnitdata.Ind?		M	YES	NO
ASPERR	Does the implementation support the abstract service primitive functions for T-DError.Ind?		O	YES	NO

A.5.6 Network Type and Bearer Specific Features

This section of the PICS will cover issues specific to a network type and bearer service within that network type.

A.5.6.1 GSM SMS Specific Features

ITEM	FUNCTION	REFERENCE	STATUS	SUPPORT
GSM-SMS01	Does the implementation support GSM SMS Phase 1 text headers?		BGSM-SMS:O	YES NO
GSM-SMS02	Does the implementation support GSM SMS long fragmentation information element?		BGSM-SMS:M	YES NO
GSM-SMS03	Does the implementation support GSM SMS short fragmentation information element?		BGSM-SMS:O	YES NO

A.5.6.2 GSM USSD Specific Features

ITEM	FUNCTION	REFERENCE	STATUS	SUPPORT
GSM-USSD01			BGSM-USSD	

A.5.6.3 GSM GPRS Specific Features

ITEM	FUNCTION	REFERENCE	STATUS	SUPPORT
GSM-GPRS01			BGSM-GPRS	

A.5.6.4 GSM Circuit Switched Data Specific Features

ITEM	FUNCTION	REFERENCE	STATUS	SUPPORT
GSM-CSD01			BGSM-CSD	

Appendix B: Mapping WDP over GSM SMS and USSD

This appendix describes additional information on mapping WDP over GSM SMS and USSD.

B.1 Binary Header Format

For GSM SMS and GSM USSD, the WDP headers structure is defined using the User Data Header (UDH) framework as defined in GSM 03.40 (see Figure B.1).

The 'Length-of-Information-Element' fields shall be the integer representation of the number of octets within its associated 'Information-Element-Data' field that follows and shall not include itself in its count value.

The 'Length-of-User-Data-Header' field shall be the integer representation of the number of octets within the 'User-Data-Header' information fields that follow and shall not include itself in its count.

Byte order of integers is most significant byte first. In case the information word of the payload data is different from an octet, then the binary header is padded with bits to the start position of an information word (GSM uses a 7-bit alphabet) in most cases. Thus the header is compatible with legacy devices not supporting the WDP Datagram protocol.

FIELD	LENGTH
Length of User Data Header	1 octet
Information Element Identifier 'A'	1 octet
Length of Information-Element 'A'	1 octet
Information-Element 'A' Data	1 to 'n' octets
Information-Element-Identifier 'B'	1 octet
Length of Information-Element 'B'	1 octet
Information-Element 'B' Data	1 to 'n' octets
... ...	
Information-Element-Identifier 'n'	1 octet
Length of Information-Element 'n'	1 octet
Information-Element 'n' Data	1 to 'n' octets

Figure B.1 The generic User Data Header structure in GSM SMS and GSM USSD.

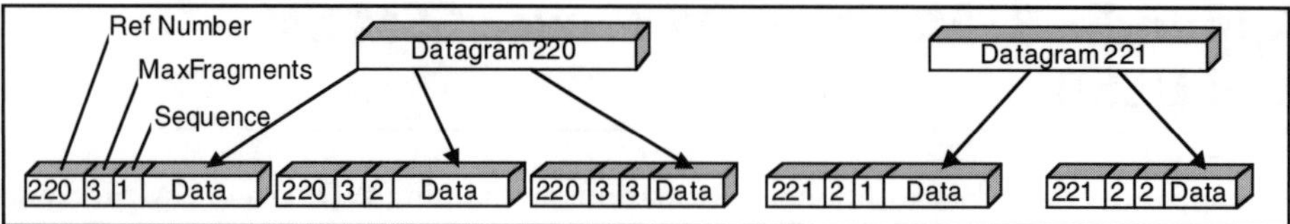

Figure B.2 Segmentation.

B.2 Segmentation and Reassembly

Figure B.2 shows how a typical datagram will be segmented to be transported. It only shows the segmentation logic (i.e., the Adaptation layer). A reference number is used to distinguish between different datagrams. The Segmentation and Reassembly mechanism uses a sequence number and a maxsize number to define the order and the completeness of the message.

The header of a packet contains the following segmentation information:

1. Reference number for WDP packet (0–255, or 0–65535)
2. Total number of segments in datagram (max 255)
3. Segment number (1-255)

The maximum length of a segmented datagram using this scheme is dependent on the packet size. In GSM SMS the maximum network packet size is 140 bytes, and in GSM USSD the maximum network packet size is 160 bytes

<table>
<tr><th>7</th><th>6</th><th>5</th><th>4</th><th>3</th><th>2</th><th>1</th><th>0</th></tr>
<tr><td colspan="8">Length of total User Data Header (all Information</td></tr>
<tr><td colspan="8">Elements)</td></tr>
<tr><td colspan="8">UDH IE identifier: Port numbers (5)</td></tr>
<tr><td colspan="8">UDH port number IE length (4)</td></tr>
<tr><td colspan="8">Destination Port (High)</td></tr>
<tr><td colspan="8">Destination Port (Low)</td></tr>
<tr><td colspan="8">Originator Port (High)</td></tr>
<tr><td colspan="8">Originator Port (Low)</td></tr>
<tr><td colspan="8">UDH IE identifier: SAR (0)</td></tr>
<tr><td colspan="8">UDH SAR IE length (3)</td></tr>
<tr><td colspan="8">Datagram Reference number</td></tr>
<tr><td colspan="8">Total number of segments in Datagram</td></tr>
<tr><td colspan="8">Segment count</td></tr>
<tr><td colspan="8">Padding Bits if User Data uses 7 bit alphabet</td></tr>
<tr><td colspan="8">1 - n bytes of User Data</td></tr>
<tr><td></td><td></td><td></td><td></td><td></td><td></td><td></td><td></td></tr>
</table>

Figure B.3 A complete datagram header with 8-bit reference for WDP in GSM SMS.

7	6	5	4	3	2	1	0
Length of total User Data Header (all Information Elements)							
UDH IE identifier: Port numbers (5)							
UDH port number IE length (4)							
Destination Port (High)							
Destination Port (Low)							
Originator Port (High)							
Originator Port (Low)							
Padding Bits if User Data uses 7 bit alphabet							
1 - n bytes of User Data							

Figure B.4 A datagram header without SAR for WDP in GSM SMS.

The sequence (reference and segment) number may be used to resolve problems with duplicate, dropped, and out-of-order packet delivery. The sequence number can be regarded as a counter that is incremented for each packet.

Reassembly is performed using a list of received packets. As packets arrive, they are inserted in order into the list, and then the list is checked for a complete datagram (all packets received, matching sequence numbers, and originator address). If an entire datagram exists it can be delivered to the upper layer.

B.3 Combined Use of Headers

Figures B.3 and B.4 illustrate the use of the User Data Header framework and the various Information Elements defined for WDP. A datagram always contains the port numbers for application-level routing, and optionally (if segmentation and reassembly is needed) contains also the adaptation layer.

Figure B.3 shows the complete datagram header using GSM phase 2 backward compatible headers.

Figure B.4 shows a datagram whose content fits into one bearer network package. In this case, no Segmentation and Reassembly header is present. This is possible since the UDH framework is modular.

Appendix C: Port Number Definitions

WAP is in the process of registering ports for applications in the WAP space. However, at the moment no applications to IANA have yet been made and ports from the Dynamic/Private range are defined. These temporary ports will be changed when ports from the registered range are approved. See Table C.1.

Table C.1 Temporary WAP port numbers.

PORT NUMBER	APPLICATION/PROTOCOL
49152	Connectionless WAP Browser Proxy Server *Protocol: WSP/Datagram*
49153	Secure Connectionless WAP Browser Proxy Server *Protocol: WSP/WTLS/Datagram*
49154	WAP Browser Proxy Server *Protocol: WSP/WTP/Datagram*
49155	Secure WAP Browser Proxy Server *Protocol: WSP/WTP/WTLS/Datagram*
49156	vCard Receiver *Protocol: vCard/Datagram*
49157	Secure vCard Receiver *Protocol: vCard/WTLS/Datagram*
49158	vCalendar Receiver *Protocol: vCalendar/Datagram*
49159	Secure vCalendar Receiver *Protocol: vCalendar/WTLS/Datagram*

The WAP protocols defined in the initial specifications are:

- Wireless Session Protocol (WSP/B) with and without security. The Wireless Session Protocol has two modes: a connection-oriented mode and a connectionless mode, and thus four ports are reserved. The connection-oriented mode uses [WTP] for transaction support.
- vCard for use for push of "phone book items" (with and without security) to an application in either a mobile client or a fixed server. The vCalendar structure is placed as the userdata of the UDP/WDP datagram.
- vCalendar for push of calendar events (with and without security) to a calendar application in either a mobile client or a fixed server. The vCalendar structure is placed as the userdata of the UDP/WDP datagram.

The security protocol for the preceding secure ports is WTLS.

Appendix D: Bearer Type Assignments

Table D.1 lists the bearer type code assignments.

Table D.1 Bearer Type Codes

BEARER	ASSIGNED NUMBER
IPv4	0x00
IPv6	0x01
GSM USSD	0x02
GSM SMS	0x03
IS-136 R-Data	0x04

Appendix E: History and Contact Information

Document History		
Date	**Status**	**Comment**
30-Jan-1998	Draft	Draft Version of the Specification for public review
30-Apr-1998	Final	Version 1.0 of the Specification

Contact Information

http://www.wapforum.org.

technical-comments@wapforum.org

CHAPTER

18

Wireless Control Message Protocol Specification

1. Scope

The Transport layer protocol in the WAP architecture consists of the Wireless Transaction Protocol (WTP) and the Wireless Datagram Protocol (WDP). The WDP layer operates above the data-capable bearer services supported by the various network types. As a general datagram service, WDP offers a consistent service to the upper-layer protocols (Security, Transaction, and Session) of WAP and communicates transparently over one of the available bearer services.

This document specifies the error reporting mechanism for WDP datagrams, the Wireless Control Message Protocol (WCMP). WCMP contains control messages that resemble the Internet Control Message Protocol (ICMP) [RFC 792] [RFC 1885] messages. WCMP can also be used for diagnostics and informational purposes.

2. WCMP Architectural Overview

Figure 18.1 shows a general model of the WAP protocol architecture and how WCMP fits into that architecture.

The Transport layer protocol in the WAP architecture is the Wireless Datagram Protocol (WDP). The WDP protocol operates above the data-capable bearer services supported by multiple network types. WDP offers a consistent but unreliable service to the upper-level protocols of WAP and communicates transparently over one of the available bearer services.

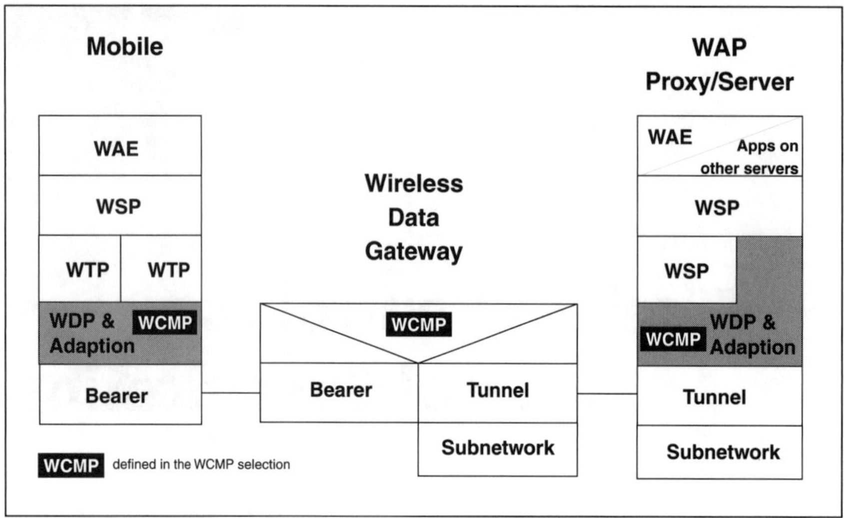

Figure 18.1 WCMP in the WAParchitecture.

WCMP is used by WDP nodes and Wireless Data Gateways to report errors encountered in processing datagrams. WCMP can also be used for informational and diagnostic purposes.

3. WCMP Protocol Description

3.1 General

The Wireless Control Message Protocol (WCMP) is used in environments that do not provide an IP bearer. WCMP is used by WDP nodes and Wireless Data Gateways to report errors encountered in processing datagrams. WCMP messages are usually generated by the WDP layer, the management entity, or a higher-layer protocol. WCMP can also be used for informational and diagnostic purposes.

A WCMP error message MUST NOT be generated in response to another WCMP error message. To report an error related to a fragmented datagram, more than one WCMP message MUST NOT be sent. Additionally, one WCMP MUST fit to a single bearer-level fragment.

The Wireless Control Message Protocol (WCMP) provides an efficient error-handling mechanism for WDP, resulting in improved performance for WAP protocols and applications.

3.2 Static WCMP Conformance Clause

This static conformance clause defines a minimum set of WCMP features that can be implemented to ensure that the implementation will be able to interoperate.

WCMP MESSAGE	WCMP TYPE	WCMP CODE	MANDATORY/ OPTIONAL		NOTE
Destination Unreachable	**51**				
• No route to destination		0	WDP Node	N/A	
			Wireless Data Gw	O	
• Communication administratively prohibited		1	WDP Node	N/A	
			Wireless Data Gw	O	
• Address unreachable		3	WDP Node	N/A	
			Wireless Data Gw	O	
• Port unreachable		4	WDP Node	M	
			Wireless Data Gw	N/A	
Parameter Problem	**54**				
• Erroneous header field		0	WDP Node	O	
			Wireless Data Gw	O	
Message Too Big	**60**	0	WDP Node	M	
			Wireless Data Gw	N/A	
Reassembly Failure	**61**				
• Reassembly time exceeded		1	WDP Node	O	
			Wireless Data Gw	N/A	
• Buffer overflow		2	WDP Node	O	
			Wireless Data Gw	N/A	
Echo Request	**178**	0	WDP Node	O	
			Wireless Data Gw	N/A	
Echo Reply	**179**	0	WDP Node	M	1)
			Wireless Data Gw	N/A	

Note 1: WCMP implementations MAY impose restrictions on the quantity of Echo Reply messages generated to protect, for example, from network overload or denial-of-service attacks.

3.3 WCMP in IP Networks

In IP-based networks, the functionality of the WCMP is implemented by using the Internet Control Message Protocol (ICMP). ICMP is defined in [RFC 792] for IPv4 and [RFC 1885] for IPv6.

At the time of publication, the known IP-based bearer networks that will use ICMP are GSM CSD, GSM GPRS, TDMA CSD, CDPD, CDMA CSD, iDEN CSD, iDEN Packet Data, and CDMA Packet Data.

3.4 WCMP in Non-IP Networks

3.4.1 WCMP in GSM SMS

For GSM SMS, the User Data Header (UDH) framework as defined in GSM 03.40 is used. The WCMP messages are carried in the UDH in an Information Element. A new WCMP Information Element Identifier (IEI) must be reserved for this purpose from ETSI.

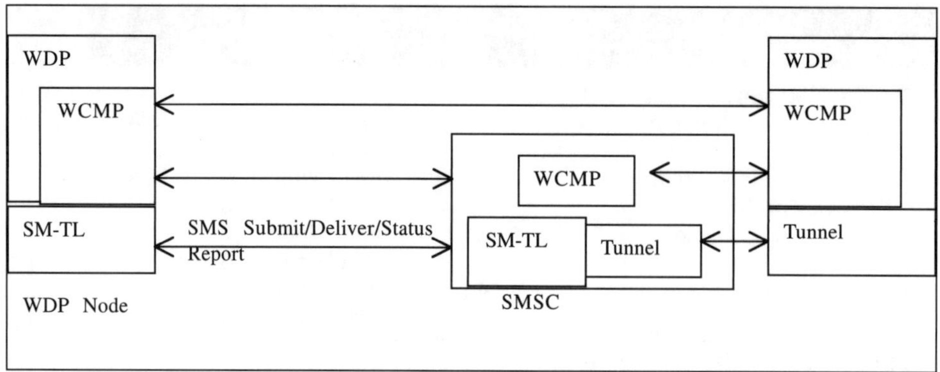

Figure 18.2 Error reporting protocols for WDP and the Short Message Transfer layer.

The WDP datagram protocol operates on top of the SMS Transfer layer and has a need to report errors unique to the datagram layer, end to end. This is done by using WCMP. Error messages supported by WCMP deal, for example, with erroneous port numbers, failures when reassembling a segmented message, and parameter errors in the WDP header. These datagram-related errors occur above the SMS Transfer layer.

Failures to transfer or process a short message at the SMS Transfer layer are reported using the SMS-SUBMIT-REPORT, SMS-DELIVER-REPORT, and SMS-STATUS-REPORT protocol data units. These messages may trigger the SMSC to generate WCMP messages if needed (see Figure 18.2).

The complete list of SMS Transfer layer failure causes can be found in [GSM0340].

3.4.2 WCMP in GSM USSD

For GSM USSD, the User Data Header (UDH) framework as defined in GSM 03.40 is used. The WCMP messages are carried in the UDH in an Information Element. A new WCMP Information Element Identifier (IEI) must be reserved for this purpose from ETSI.

3.4.3 WCMP in FLEX and ReFLEX

To be defined.

3.4.4 WCMP in CDMA SMS

To be defined.

3.4.5 WCMP in iDEN SMS

To be defined.

3.4.6 WCMP in TDMA R-data

To be defined.

3.5 WCMP Messages

3.5.1 General Message Structure

Network bit order for bit fields is big-endian. In other words, the left-most bit in the bit field is the most significant bit of the octet and is transmitted first followed subsequently by less significant bits. In 2-byte fields, the first byte is the high-order byte (see Figure 18.3).

Different WCMP messages are identified by the Type and Code fields. The Type field indicates the type of the message. Its value determines the format of the remaining data. The Code field depends on the message type and defines the format of the Data Fields.

WCMP messages are grouped into two classes, error messages and informational messages. Error messages have message types from 0 to 127, and informational messages have message types from 128 to 191. Types 192–255 are reserved for future purposes.

WCMP Type values are different from ICMP Type values. WCMP Type values have been selected by adding 50 to the respective ICMP Type. WCMP Codes are the same than in ICMP (see Figure 18.4).

BIT/OCTET	7	6	5	4	3	2	1	0
1	Type of Control Message							
2	Code of Control Message							
3 - N	Data Fields for WCMP (0–N octets)							

Figure 18.3 General format of a WCMP message.

MESSAGE DESCRIPTION	WCMP MSGTYPE	WCMP CODE
Destination Unreachable	**51**	
• No route to destination		0
• Communication administratively prohibited		1
• Address unreachable		3
• Port unreachable		4
Parameter Problem	**54**	
• Erroneous header field		0
Message Too Big	**60**	0
Reassembly Failure	**61**	
• Reassembly time exceeded		1
• Buffer Overflow		2
Echo Request	**178**	0
Echo Reply	**179**	0

Figure 18.4 Types and codes for WCMP messages.

3.5.2 Address Information Formats

The following Address Information field format MUST be used in the WCMP messages:

BIT/OCTET	7	6	5	4	3	2	1	0
1	Address Type = GSM							
2	Address Length							
3 – N	Address Data							

If the Address Type is GSM, the Address Data MUST be coded using the semi-octet representation defined in GSM 03.40.

BIT/OCTET	7	6	5	4	3	2	1	0
1	Address Type = IPv4							
2	Address Length							
3	32-Bit IP Address							
4								
5								
6								

BIT/OCTET	7	6	5	4	3	2	1	0
1	Address Type = IPv6							
2	Address Length							
3	1–32 Bits of IP Address							
4								
5								
6								
7	33–64 Bits of IP Address							
8								
9								
10								

BIT/OCTET	7	6	5	4	3	2	1	0
11	65–96 Bits of IP Address							
12								
13								
14								
15	97–128 Bits of IP Address							
16								
17								
18								

If the Address Type is IPv4 or IPv6, the address MUST be coded with the most significant bit first.

BIT/OCTET	7	6	5	4	3	2	1	0
1	Address Type = FLEX							
2	Address Length							
3–N	Address Data							

BIT/OCTET	7	6	5	4	3	2	1	0
1	Address Type = ReFLEX							
2	Address Length							
3	R	I	30-Bit ReFLEX Address					
4								
5								
6								

If the Address Type is FLEX, the Address Data MUST be coded according to [FLEX], Section 6.12, FLEX Capcodes.

If the Address Type is ReFLEX, the Address Data MUST be coded according to [ReFLEX]. The I-bit identifies whether the address is a personal or information services address. The R-bit (reserved) should be set to 0.

The assigned Address Type values for different bearers are specified in [WDP].

3.5.3 WCMP Messages

3.5.3.1 Destination Unreachable

BIT/OCTET	7	6	5	4	3	2	1	0
1	Type of Control Message							
2	Code of Control Message							
3	Destination Port of Original Datagram							
4								
5	Originator Port of Original Datagram							
6								
7–N	Address Information							

Description

A Destination Unreachable message SHOULD be generated by the receiving WDP node in response to a packet that cannot be delivered to its destination for reasons other than congestion. When the reason is "Port Unreachable," the WDP node MUST send a Destination Unreachable message.

A Destination Unreachable message SHOULD be generated by Wireless Data Gateways (e.g., SMSC, USSDC) when it cannot route the datagram to a WAP Gateway.

A WCMP message MUST NOT be generated if a packet is dropped due to congestion.

Type 51

Code

0 If the reason for the failure to deliver is lack of a matching entry in the forwarding node's routing table (e.g., in the SMSC or USSDC), the Code field is set to 0 (No Route To Destination).

1 If the reason for the failure to deliver is administrative prohibition (e.g., a node acts as a "firewall filter"), the Code field is set to 1 (Communication Administratively Prohibited).

3 If there is another reason for the failure to deliver, (e.g., inability to resolve the WDP destination address into a corresponding link or device address, or a link-specific problem of some sort), then the Code field is set to 3 (Address unreachable).

4 If the transport protocol (e.g., WDP) does not have a listener for a particular port, the destination node MUST send a Destination Unreachable message with Code 4 (Port Unreachable).

Address Information

The Address is the Destination Address of the original datagram.

3.5.3.2 Parameter Problem

BIT/OCTET	7	6	5	4	3	2	1	0
1	Type of Control Message							
2	Code of Control Message							
3–N	Address Information							
N + 1	Index (Value 0–64)							
N + 2–N + 65	Data from the Original Datagram (64 octets)							

Description

If a WDP node processing a packet finds a problem with a field in the WDP header such that it cannot complete processing the packet, it MUST discard the packet and SHOULD send a WCMP Parameter Problem message to the packet's source.

Type 54

Code 0—erroneous header field encountered

Address Information

The Address is the Destination Address of the original datagram.

Index

Index to point to the octet in the original datagram that caused the problem. When the index cannot point to that octet, it MUST be set to 0.

Data from the Original Datagram

Sixty-four octets from the beginning of the original datagram.

3.5.3.3 Message Too Big

BIT/OCTET	7	6	5	4	3	2	1	0
1	Type of Control Message							
2	Code of Control Message							
3	Destination Port of Original Datagram							
4								
5	Originator Port of Original Datagram							
6								
7–N	Address Information							
N + 1	Maximum Message Size in Octets							
N + 2								

Description

The Message Too Big message MUST be used to inform the sending party about buffer size limitations of the receiver. It MUST be used when the first datagram of a segmented message is received and there is not enough buffer space for the whole message.

Type 60

Code 0

Address Information

The Address is the Destination Address of the original datagram.

3.5.3.4 Reassembly Failure

BIT/OCTET	7	6	5	4	3	2	1	0
1	Type of Control Message							
2	Code of Control Message							
3	Destination Port of Original Datagram							
4								
5	Originator Port of Original Datagram							
6								
7–N	Address Information							

Description

If a node reassembling a fragmented datagram cannot complete the reassembly, it MAY send a Reassembly Failure message. The node SHOULD discard the datagram.

If the first fragment of a segmented message is not available, the Reassembly Failure message SHOULD NOT be sent; however, all fragments for the given message SHOULD be silently discarded.

Type 61

Code
1 Fragment reassembly time exceeded
2 Buffer overflow

Address Information

The Address is the Destination Address of the original datagram.

3.5.3.5 WCMP Echo Request/Reply

BIT/OCTET	7	6	5	4	3	2	1	0
1	Type of Control Message							
2	Code of Control Message							
3	Identifier Number							

BIT/OCTET	7	6	5	4	3	2	1	0
4								
5	Sequence Number							
6								
7–N	Data							

Description

A WDP node MUST implement a WCMP Echo function that receives Echo Requests and sends corresponding Echo Replies. A node SHOULD also implement an application-layer interface for sending Echo Requests and receiving Echo Replies, for diagnostic purposes.

The data received in the WCMP Echo Request message MUST be returned entirely and unmodified in the WCMP Echo Reply message, unless the Echo Reply would exceed the MTU of the path back to the Echo requester, in which case the data is truncated to fit that path MTU.

Type 178 Echo Request
179 Echo Reply

Code 0

Identifier Number

The Identifier Number is used as an aid to match Echo Replies to this Echo Request. May be 0.

Sequence Number

The Sequence Number is used as an aid to match Echo Replies to this Echo Request. May be 0.

Data

The Data can be 0 or more octets of arbitrary data.

4. Abbreviations

For the purposes of this specification the following abbreviations apply.

ETSI	European Telecommunication Standardization Institute
IE	Information Element
IP	Internet Protocol
LSB	Least significant bits
MSISDN	Mobile Subscriber ISDN (Telephone number or address of device)
MS	Mobile Station
MSB	Most significant bits
SMSC	Short Message Service Centre

SMS	Short Message Service
TCP/IP	Transmission Control Protocol/Internet Protocol
UDH	User-Data Header (see GSM 03.40)
UDP	Unreliable Datagram Protocol
USSD	Unstructured Supplementary Service Data
USSDC	Unstructured Supplementary Service Data Centre
WAE	Wireless Application Environment
WAP	Wireless Application Protocol
WDP	Wireless Datagram Protocol
WSP	Wireless Session Protocol
WTP	Wireless Transaction Protocol

5. Terminology

This specification uses the following words for defining the significance of each particular requirement:

MUST. This word, or the terms "REQUIRED" or "SHALL," mean that the definition is an absolute requirement of the specification.

MUST NOT. This phrase, or the phrase "SHALL NOT," mean that the definition is an absolute prohibition of the specification.

SHOULD. This word, or the adjective "RECOMMENDED," mean that there may exist valid reasons in particular circumstances to ignore a particular item, but the full implications must be understood and carefully weighed before choosing a different course.

SHOULD NOT. This phrase, or the phrase "NOT RECOMMENDED," mean that there may exist valid reasons in particular circumstances when the particular behavior is acceptable or even useful, but the full implications should be understood and the case carefully weighed before implementing any behavior described with this label.

MAY. This word, or the adjective "OPTIONAL," mean that an item is truly optional. One vendor may choose to include the item because a particular marketplace requires it, or because the vendor feels that it enhances the product, while another vendor may omit the same item. An implementation that does not include a particular option MUST be prepared to interoperate with another implementation that does include the option, though perhaps with reduced functionality. In the same vein, an implementation that does include a particular option MUST be prepared to interoperate with another implementation that does not include the option (except, of course, for the feature the option provides).

6. Normative References

[FLEX] FLEX Protocol Specification Document, version 1.9, Motorola.

[FLEXSuite] FLEX Suite of Application Enabling Protocols, version 1.0, Motorola.

[GSM0290] ETSI European Digital Cellular Telecommunication Systems (phase 2) : Unstructured Supplementary Service Data (USSD)—stage 1 (GSM 02.90).

[GSM0390] ETSI European Digital Cellular Telecommunication Systems (phase 2) : Unstructured Supplementary Service Data (USSD)—stage 2 (GSM 03.90).

[GSM0490] ETSI European Digital Cellular Telecommunication Systems (phase 2) : Unstructured Supplementary Service Data (USSD)—stage 3 (GSM 04.90).

[GSM0340] ETSI European Digital Cellular Telecommunication Systems (phase 2+) : Technical realization of the Short Message Service (SMS) Point-to-Point (P) (GSM 03.40).

[GSM0260] ETSI European Digital Cellular Telecommunication Systems (phase 2+) : General Packet Radio Service (GPRS)—stage 1 (GSM 02.60).

[GSM0360] ETSI European Digital Cellular Telecommunication Systems (phase 2+) : General Packet Radio Service (GPRS)—stage 2 (GSM 03.60).

[GUTS] General UDP Transport Teleservice (GUTS)—Stage III, TR45.3.6/97.12.15.

[IS136] EIA/TIA IS-136.

[IS130] EIA/TIA IS-130.

[IS135] EIA/TIA IS-135.

[IS176] EIA/TIA IS-176 - CDPD 1.1 specifications.

[IS637] TIA/EIA/IS-637: Short Message Services for Wideband Spread Spectrum Cellular Systems.

[IS07498] ISO 7498 OSI Reference Model.

[ReFLEX] ReFLEX25 Protocol Specification Document, version 2.6, Motorola.

[RFC768] J. Postel, "User Datagram Protocol," RFC768, August 1980.

[RFC791] J. Postel, "IP: Internet Protocol," RFC791.

[RFC792] J. Postel, "Internet Control Message Protocol," RFC792, September 1981.

[RFC793] J. Postel, "Transmission Control Protocol," RFC793, September 1981.

[RFC1885] A. Conta, S. Deering, "Internet Control Message Protocol (ICMPv6) for the Internet Protocol Version 6," RFC1885, December 1995.

[RFC2188] M. Banan (Neda), M. Taylor (AT&T), J. Cheng, (AT&T) "Efficient Short Remote Operations Protocol Specification Version 1.2," RFC2188, September 1997.

[TCP/Ipill3] W. Richard Stevens, "TCP/IP Illustrated, Volume 3," Addison-Wesley Publishing Company Inc., 1996, ISBN 0-201-63495-3.

[WAE] WAP Wireless Application Group, Wireless Application Environment Specification 30-April-1998.

[WAP] WAP Architecture Working Group "Wireless Application Protocol Architecture Specification," version 1.0.

[WDP] WAP Wireless Transport Group, Wireless Datagram Protocol Specification, 30-April-1998.

[WTP] WAP Wireless Transport Group, Wireless Transaction Protocol Specification, 30-April-1998.

Appendix A: History and Contact Information

Document History		
Date	**Status**	**Comment**
30-Apr-1998	Draft Specification	First version
12-June-1998	Specification	First version

Contact Information

http://www.wapforum.org.

technical.comments@wapforum.org

CHAPTER

19

WAP over GSM USSD Specification

1. Scope

This document describes the mapping of WAP onto GSM Unstructured Supplementary Service Data (USSD) phase 2. The document includes a brief description of GSM USSD. For a complete description refer to [GSM0290], [GSM0390], and [GSM0490].

The GSM USSD service lacks some fundamental services needed in order to use it as a bearer of the WAP protocols, and other applications with similar communication need. For example, the GSM USSD service is half-duplex and does not carry a destination address (only the MSISDN of the mobile phone). The USSD Dialog Control Protocol (UDCP) has been defined in order to overcome these limitations. UDCP is specified in this document. The UDCP protocol is not part of the GSM Specifications from ETSI.

2. General Description of USSD

2.1 Introduction

The GSM standard includes a wide range of supplementary services (Call Barring, Call Forwarding, etc.). The services may be managed by entering text strings. For example, entering the text string "**21*1234567# SEND" will divert all incoming calls to the number 1234567. However, most MS manufacturers provide more user-friendly methods to do this.

Normally when standard GSM supplementary services are managed from the MS, structured, functional signaling is available. For example, if the user activates the supplementary service Call Forwarding the MS recognizes this and invokes a standard signaling procedure towards the network. This is because the Call Forwarding supplementary service is part of the GSM standard.

The supplementary services were introduced in stages into the GSM standard. To support old mobiles and Operator Specific Services, OSS, the container mechanism Unstructured Supplementary Service Data, USSD, was introduced into the GSM standard. The USSD operation can be used towards the network when the MS does not recognize the text string entered by the user. Further standardization allowed the network to send USSD operations toward the MS, as well as combining mobile and network initiated operations in order to exchange data in a dialog manner. Since the content of the operations sent from the network ends up on the MS display, and operations sent from the MS can be routed to an operator-provided application in the network, USSD can be used as a transparent pipe through the GSM network.

The two most important features of USSD are:

- It can be used by operators to provide operator-specific services using a similar transport mechanism as when standard GSM supplementary services are used.
- It can be used as a transparent bearer through the GSM network.

2.2 The USSD Standard

2.2.1 USSD Phase 1

Network-initiated operations are not supported, only mobile-initiated. This means that the MS can send a request to the network and receive a response. There is no dialog mechanism.

2.2.2 USSD Phase 2

This is the present status of the standard. A dialog is established between the mobile and the network node. Multiple subsequent USSD operations can be sent within the dialog.

2.2.3 USSD Phase 2+ Enhanced USSD

The following USSD enhancements are considered by ETSI:

- Extending the usage of the DCS to distinguish between MMI-mode (DCS= '0000 1111') and bearer mode (DCS='01xx xxxx').
- In bearer mode: The DCS may indicate message classes; Immediate display, ME-specific, SIM-specific, and TE-specific.
- In bearer mode: replacing the alphanumerical Service Code with a binary coded Network Element Identifier to be used when routing USSD through the network.
- In bearer mode: adapting the User Data Header concept from SMS. See [GSM0340].
- Support for multiple dialogs.

2.3 USSD Characteristics and Parameters

2.3.1 General

The following subsections describe USSD specific characteristics and parameters.

USSD phase 2 is used as the baseline in the descriptions.

2.3.2 The USSD Dialog

There are two types of USSD dialogs: mobile- and network initiated.

2.3.2.1 Mobile-Initiated Dialog

The mobile-initiated dialog is shown in Figure 19.1. The MS initiates the dialog by invoking the ProcessUSSDRequest operation. The network can respond by either invoking a USSDRequest operation or release the dialog by returning the result to the

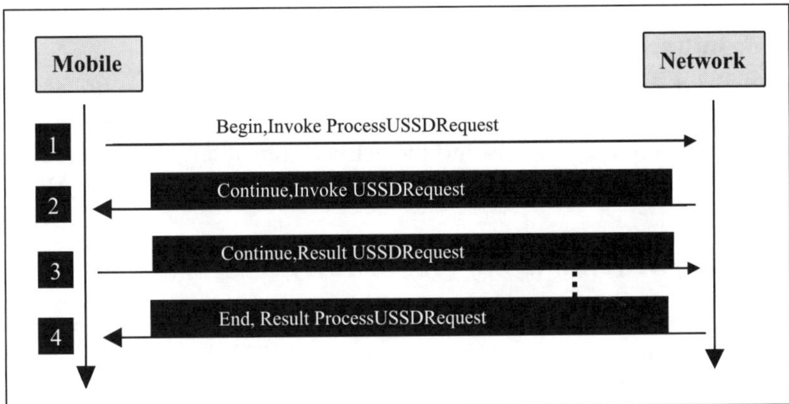

Figure 19.1 Mobile-initiated USSD dialog.

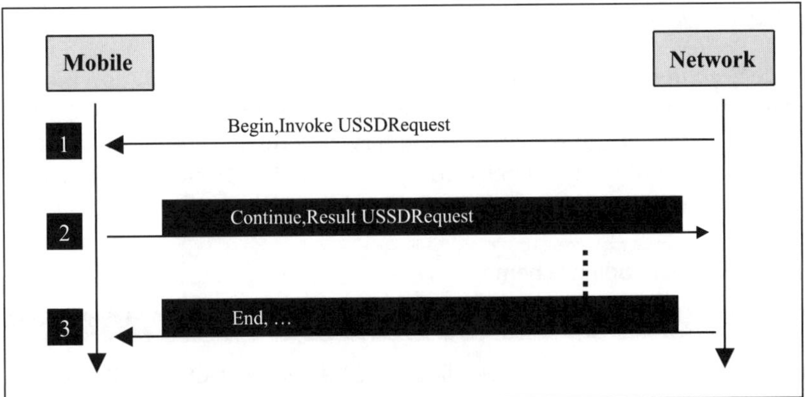

Figure 19.2 Network-initiated USSD dialog.

Table 19.1 Data Coding Scheme

OPERATION	DCS SETTING AS SPECIFIED IN [GSM0290] AND CODED ACCORDING TO [GSM0338]
Mobile-initiated operation	"Language unspecified' and 'SMS default alphabet". DCS = 0000 1111
Mobile-initiated operation response	Not specified.
Network-initiated operation	Not specified.
Network-initiated operation response	"Language unspecified' and 'SMS default alphabet". DCS = 0000 1111

received ProcessUSSDRequest operation. Both the MS and the network can at any time release the dialog by sending a RELEASE COMPLETE Radio Layer 3 message (END in TCAP).

2.3.2.2 Network-Initiated Dialog

The network-initiated dialog is shown in Figure 19.2. The network initiates the dialog by invoking the USSDRequest operation. The MS responds by returning the result to the USSDRequest operation. Both the MS and the network can at any time release the dialog by sending a RELEASE COMPLETE Radio Layer 3 message (END in TCAP).

2.3.3 *Data Coding Scheme (DCS) (Table 19.1)*

A USSD operation has two parameters: the DCS and the USSD string. The DCS specifies the data coding scheme used in the USSD string. [GSM 0290] specifies the setting of the DCS for certain operations.

According to [GSM 0390] the network should reject the operation with an error if the DCS violates the standard setting.

2.3.4 *Service Code (SC)*

The service code is an in-heritage from the initially intended use of USSD as a mechanism to manage operator-specific supplementary services (according to the MMI string format "*#SC*<data>#", in which SC is the service code).

The service code is part of the first USSD string sent from the MS and acts as a leader that guides the string to the end node (MSC, VLR, or HLR, depending on the value of

Table 19.2 Usage of Data Coding Scheme

USSD DIALOG	DCS
Network initiated	According to Cell Broadcast DCS in [GSM0338]
Mobile initiated	0x0F

the service code). Once a dialog is established between the MS and the application, a transparent pipe is opened through the network, thus the service code is not needed during the remaining part of the dialog.

This procedure as well as the allocation of service codes is standardized. [GSM0290] identifies two types of service codes: VPLMN and HPLMN service codes. HPLMN service codes always route the USSD string to the HLR, while VPLMN service codes route the string to the MSC/VLR. To be able to use USSD from outside the GSM network, a USSD application located in the HLR has to relay the USSD string to an external node. The application has to provide the function:

F(service code) -> External Node Address

If the end application (the one that provides the service the user requested) is not located in the external node, the USSD string (extracted from the USSD operation and wrapped into another protocol) has to be passed on to the node that hosts the end application.

2.3.5 USSD Timers

To supervise USSD dialogs and to avoid hanging dialogs there are timers in the network. The timers are specified in [GSM 0902].

2.3.5.1 ProcessUSSDRequest Invoke Timer

The timer is started when the Invoke ProcessUSSDRequest is received by the network (the MS has initiated a dialog). The timer runs until the Result ProcessUSSDRequest is sent to the MS (the dialog is released).

This timer limits the total length of the dialog. The value of the timer is between 1 and 10 minutes.

2.3.5.2 USSDRequest Invoke Timer

The timer is started when invoke USSDRequest is sent from the network and runs until the result USSDRequest is received.

This timer sets a restriction to the MS application processing time. For some applications this may include getting a response from the user. The value of the timer is between 1 and 10 minutes.

2.3.6 Multiple Dialogs

In the USSD GSM phase 2 specification, only one dialog between an MS and the network is allowed. If the MS receives a dialog initiation in parallel to a currently ongoing dialog, the new operation will be rejected with the "USSD Busy" error.

Once the dialog is established between the MS and an end node in the GSM network, another dialog cannot be established in parallel. This means that a fix host that cannot be reached via the end node to which the dialog is established cannot be reached at all without first aborting the established dialog, and then establishing a new dialog towards a different node from which the terminal can be reached.

2.3.7 Addressing Aspects

USSD was designed for dialogs between the MS and a USSD application in the MSC, VLR, or HLR. The MSISDN is transported in the dialog part of the TCAP message. For example, when a mobile-initiated dialog is established toward an application in the HLR, the MSISDN and the HLR address are included.

For a mobile-initiated dialog the USSD application in the HLR is probably not the end application. The USSD application in the HLR will only work as a relay, and pass USSD operations between the GSM network and the external node.

2.3.8 Length of USSD String

According to the USSD GSM specification [GSM 02.90], the Invoke USSDRequest (Network→MS) and the Invoke ProcessUSSDRequest (MS→Network) can have USSD strings with a length of 160 octets. In addition, the length of the USSD string is restricted to the capabilities of the lower signaling layers (TCAP), which can be configured differently in different networks.

3. WAP and GSM USSD

3.1 Introduction

WAP requires a full duplex datagram service from the bearer network. Unfortunately, GSM USSD does not provide such a service. Instead, GSM USSD provides a two-way-alternate interactive service designed to convey short text strings between the mobile phone and a node in the GSM network. This section identifies the necessary parameter configurations and additional functionality that is needed in order to use GSM phase 2 USSD as a bearer of the WAP protocols. Note that other applications with a similar communication need as the WAP protocols (that is, a datagram service) may also benefit from using GSM phase 2 USSD as a bearer.

3.2 USSD Dialog Control Protocol (UDCP)

The USSD dialog provides a two-way-alternate interactive service to the user. This means that only the entity (mobile phone or network node) with the turn may send, and its correspondent is permitted only to receive. To be able to use the USSD dialog as a full duplex service, a special protocol has to be specified that deals with the management of the dialog. The protocol has to hide the two-way-alternate characteristics of the USSD dialog to the upper layer and allow the upper layer to use USSD as a full duplex service onto which datagrams can be sent and received.

The protocol designed to hide the complexity of the USSD dialog is the USSD Dialog Control Protocol (UDCP). UDCP is mapped directly onto the USSD protocol and is located in the mobile and the end node in the GSM network. The end points of UDCP are identical to the end points of the USSD dialog.

The UDCP protocol is specified in Chapter 4. The UDCP protocol is NOT part of the ETSI GSM Specifications.

3.3 Data Coding Scheme (DCS)

A USSD operation consists of the Data Coding Scheme (DCS) and the USSD String.

According to [GSM0290], all mobile originating operations the DCS MUST have the value "Language unspecified" and "Default alphabet". According to [GSM0338] the DCS "Language unspecified" and "Default alphabet" should be coded as 0x0F.

For network-originated operations the DCS value is a matter for the network operator [GSM0290]. The network should ignore the value of the DCS [GSM0390]. By using the SMS Cell-Broadcast encoding [GSM0338] the DCS can indicate "Message class: Mobile Entity". This will terminate the network-initiated USSD dialog in the ME. See Table 19.2.

3.4 Service Code (SC)

The service code identifies the USSD network node and is an operator-specific parameter, just like the SMS-Center address. The user has to manually enter the service code when invoking a service, or it could be entered once as a "Setting" in an application in the MS. When the service code is sent in the USSD string it has to have the format as defined in [GSM0290]; for example, in the string "*#SC* n number of characters #", SC is the service code.

The service code is only sent in the first operation of the dialog and is there for routing purposes.

3.5 USSD Operation Timers

The Invoke USSDRequest timer will expire in the network if no Result USSDRequest message is received within the time set by the timer. As long as data is sent in the dialog (USSD operations are continuously sent between the mobile and the network) this timer will not expire. During long idle periods the dialog will be terminated by UDCP in order to free radio resources. This means that the Invoke USSDRequest timer can be ignored by UDCP.

The Invoke ProcessUSSDRequest timer limits the total length of a mobile-initiated dialog. When the timer expires, the dialog will be released regardless of whether data is sent in the dialog or not. If this happens, UDCP MAY try to reestablish the dialog.

3.6 Multiple Dialogs

A mobile can have no more than one USSD dialog established at any time. This means that once a USSD dialog has been established between a mobile and the network, no more USSD dialogs can be established. However, datagrams sent over the USSD dialog may belong to different applications. An application is identified by the port number in the datagram header.

Note that if datagrams from different applications are sent over the same USSD dialog, they must all go through the same USSD network node; a USSD dialog can only be established between one mobile and exactly one USSD network node. It is not possible to set up a second USSD dialog from a different USSD network node towards the same mobile.

3.7 Addressing Aspects

The service code is used by the mobile to address the USSD network node towards which the USSD dialog is established. The GSM network uses the service code to identify the USSD network node. Formats for service codes are standardized by the ETSI and can be found in [GSM0290].

The MSISDN of the mobile phone is carried by underlying layers (the GSM network) between the mobile and the USSD Gateway.

An external network node (WAP Gateway) may be connected to the USSD network node. The address to the external node must be included in the USSD string. The address field must contain an address type (for example, IP-address, MSISDN, etc.) and the address itself. An address field for this purpose is included in the UDCP protocol header.

Instead of using a specific address for the external node, the service code to the USSD network node can be mapped to a specific external node. In this case, the address field in the UDCP protocol header is omitted. For example, a network operator can decide that all USSD dialogs established with the service code "*#138" should be associated with a specific WAP Gateway.

3.8 Length of the USSD String (Table 19.3)

In [GSM 0902] 160 octets is stated as the maximum length for the USSD string. Due to underlying signaling layers, the maximum length of the USSD string depending on the message is limited.

3.9 The USSD String

When USSD is used as a full duplex datagram transport mechanism, the same structure of the message that is used for the GSM short message (SMS) is used in the USSD string.

In GSM SMS, the User Data field may comprise just the short message itself or a Header in addition to the short message. The User Data Header (UDH) is defined in [GSM 0340]. The UDH consists of one or several Information Elements (IE). An Infor-

Table 19.3 Length of USSD String

USSD OPERATION	MAX LENGTH [OCTETS]
"Begin, Invoke ProcessUSSDRequest"	133
"End, Result ProcessUSSDRequest"	160
First "Continue, Invoke USSDRequest" in mobile initiated dialog	154
"Begin, Invoke USSDRequest"	144
First "Continue, Result USSDRequest" in network initiated dialog	154
Other messages	160

Table 19.4 Structure of Information Element as Defined in [GSM0340]

FIELD IN INFORMATION ELEMENT	DESCRIPTION
Information Element Identifier (IEI)—1 octet	Identifier from [GSM0340]
Information Element Length (IEL)—1 octet	Length of IE Data
Information Element Data (IED)—1 to n octets	IE Data

mation Element has three fields: identifier, length, and data. Information Element identities are standardized by the ETSI to avoid conflicting identities; for example, the Port Number IE and the Fragmentation IE in order to realize a datagram service [WDP]. If a mobile receives an Information Element it does not recognize, the Element will be discarded. Table 19.4 represents the generic structure of an IE.

3.9.1 UDCP Information Element

When UDCP is used, an Information Element is included in the User Data Header. The Information Element contains the UDCP header.

Currently, no Information Element Identifier has been allocated by ETSI.

3.9.2 Encoding of the USSD String

This encoding of the USSD string is different depending on the USSD operation.

INVOKE PROCESSUSSDREQUEST (MS TO NETWORK)								
BIT/OCTET	**7**	**6**	**5**	**4**	**3**	**2**	**1**	**0**
1	"*NNN#"							
...	(Service Code according to [GSM0290] ; identifies USSD network-node)							
5								
6	User Data Length (UDL) = 1+M+N							
7	User Data Header Length (UDHL) = N							
8	Information Element (s)							
...	(N octets)							

INVOKE PROCESSUSSDREQUEST (MS TO NETWORK)								
BIT/OCTET	**7**	**6**	**5**	**4**	**3**	**2**	**1**	**0**
7+N								
8+N	User Data							
...	(M octets)							
7+N+M								

The shaded bytes are coded according to the GSM SMS 7-bit alphabet. The "*NNN#" is the Service Code and MUST comply to [GSM0290].

RESULT USSDREQUEST (MS TO NETWORK)								
BIT/OCTET	**7**	**6**	**5**	**4**	**3**	**2**	**1**	**0**
1	User Data Length (UDL) = 1+M+N							
2	User Data Header Length (UDHL) = N							
3	Information Element (s)							
...	(N octets)							
2+N								
3+N	User Data							
...	(M octets)							
2+N+M								

INVOKE USSDREQUEST (NETWORK TO MS) AND RESULT PROCESSUSSDREQUEST (NETWORK TO MS)								
BIT/OCTET	**7**	**6**	**5**	**4**	**3**	**2**	**1**	**0**
1	Network Element Identifier							
2	User Data Length (UDL) = 1+M+N							
3	User Data Header Length (UDHL) = N							
4	Information Element (s)							
...	(N octets)							
3+N								
4+N	User Data							
...	(M octets)							
3+N+M								

The Network Element Identifier (NEI) identifies the sending USSD Node in the network. The value of the NEI is configured by the network operator.

4. USSD Dialog Control Protocol

4.1 Goals and Requirements

The USSD Dialog Control Protocol (UDCP) is defined in this section. The goals and requirements for the protocol are the following:

1. In the USSD string it must be possible to include an address to an external node. The address should indicate source/destination of the data in the USSD string; for example, address to a WAP Gateway.
2. The address in (1) can be of different types. IP address and MSISDN should be possible to use.
3. The USSD dialog should remain established as long as there is data to be sent, or a timer expires. Terminating and establishing the dialog between each data transmission should be avoided.
4. It should be possible to use the USSD dialog as a full-duplex service. The half-duplex complexity should be hidden from the user.
5. It should be possible to reestablish the dialog after failure.
6. The end points of UDCP should be identical to the end points of the USSD dialog.

4.2 Architectural Overview

UDCP is located in the GSM mobile device and the USSD network node in the GSM network. Although UDCP may convey the address to an external node (e.g., WAP Gateway) UDCP is terminated in the USSD network node. This is illustrated in Figure 19.3.

In the mobile, the UDCP listens for incoming USSD dialogs. When a USSD dialogs is established to the mobile, the UDCP provider locates the UDCP Information Element (IE) in the User Data Header and extracts the data portion. The data portion of the UDCP IE contains the UDCP PDU. If no UDCP IE can be found, the UDCP provider MUST ignore the USSD dialog. Note that this doesn't mean that the USSD dialog must be ignored by other applications in the phone.

Typically the UDCP user is WDP. The protocol includes the Port Number IE in the UDH. If segmentation and reassembly are necessary, the Fragmentation IE is also included in the UDH. See [WDP].

4.3 Static UDCP Conformance Clause

This static conformance clause defines a minimum set of UDCP features that can be implemented to ensure that the implementation will be able to interoperate.

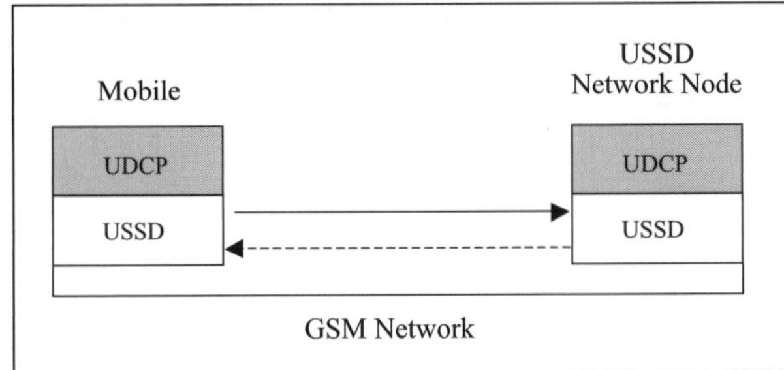

Figure 19.3 USSD and UDCP architecture.

FUNCTION	TYPE	MANDATORY/ OPTIONAL
Data transfer	Addressing with service code only Addressing with service code and external node address	M O
Error Handling		M
Dialog Release	Issued by User Due to USSD network timer expiration Idle dialog	M O O

4.4 Addressing

UDCP has been designed to handle two types of network architectures and addressing principles:

A. The Service Code of the USSD Dialog is used to address both the USSD Node and the External Node.

B. The Service Code of the USSD Dialog is used to address the USSD Node. An additional address is used to address the External Node.

In (A), once the dialog has been established, the USSD Node functions as a relay and passes data between the mobile and the External Node. The mobile can use the USSD dialog to communicate only with the External Node identified by the Service Code. If the mobile wants to send data to another External Node, it first has to terminate the existing USSD dialog and establish a new one.

In Figure 19.4 the Service Code of the USSD Dialog is mapped to the External Node. For example, *#138 may be mapped to the WAP Gateway. The Service Code is only sent in the first operation of the USSD dialog. Data in all subsequent operations of the USSD dialog is passed to the External Node identified by *#138.

In (B), the address to the External Node is included in the UDCP header by using a special PDU for this purpose. The address to the External Node is sent in every USSD operation as part of the UDCP header. This makes it possible to use the same USSD dialog for conversations with multiple External Node. However, this has a price, and the additional overhead is required to send, for example, a 32-bit IP address in every USSD operation.

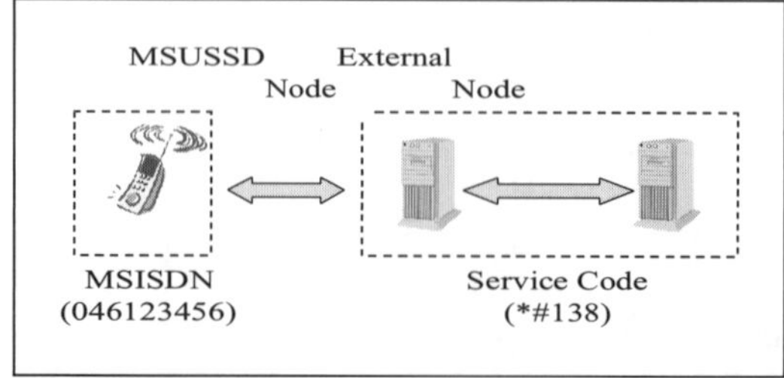

Figure 19.4 USSD Node and External Node both addressed by the same Service Code.

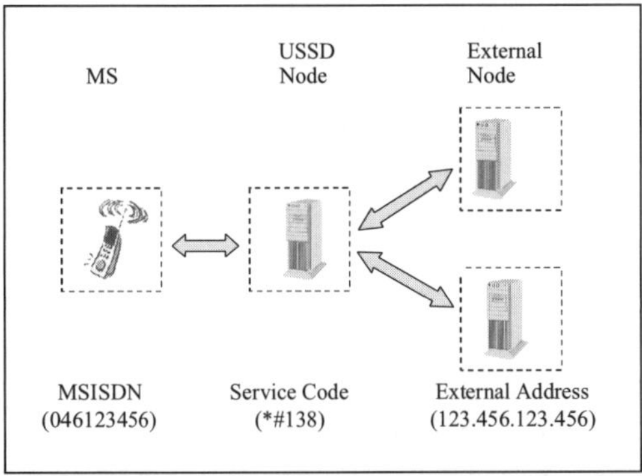

Figure 19.5 USSD Node addressed by Service Code and External Node addressed by an IP Address.

In Figure 19.5, the mobile may communicate with several External Nodes over the same USSD dialog. For example, the first operation of the USSD dialog may contain data destined for the External Node with the IP address 123.456.123.456. The following operation may contain data destined for a different External Node with a different address.

The two addressing principles MUST NOT be used mixed within the same USSD dialog. If a USSD dialog is established and the UDCP header does not include any External Address, all data in all subsequent operations in that dialog MUST be passed to the External Node identified by the Service Code of the dialog.

4.5 UDCP Service Primitives

4.5.1 Introduction

This section defines the interface of UDCP to the next higher layer. The interface is defined using abstract service primitives.

4.5.2 UDCP-Data

This service is used to transfer data between the mobile and the USSD Node.

PRIMITIVE	UDCP-DATA			
PARAMETER	***REQ***	***IND***	***RES***	***CNF***
Service Code (mobile only)	M			
Address to External Node	O	C (=)		
Address to Mobile Phone	M	M(=)		
User Data	M	M(=)		

Service Code (mobile only) The Service Code is sent in the first operation of the mobile initiated USSD dialog. It is used by the GSM network to route the USSD operation to the correct USSD Node. Once the USSD Node has been located, a dialog is established and the Service Code is no longer necessary.

Address to External Node In the mobile, if the destination application is located in an external node, the Address is the address to that node. If the destination application is in the USSD network node or the Service Code is the sole address, this parameter can be omitted.

In the network, if the source application is located in an external node, the Address is the address to that node. If the source application is in the USSD network node or the Service Code is the sole address, this parameter can be omitted.

Address to Mobile Phone This is the MSISDN to the mobile phone.

User Data The user data transported in the USSD string. This consists of two parts: Information Elements (IE) for the User Data Header and the message itself.

4.5.3 UDCP-Error

This service is used if there is an error; for example, if the USSD service is not available from the network, or the USSD dialog is terminated due to lack of radio coverage and cannot be reestablished.

PRIMITIVE	UDCP-ERROR			
PARAMETER	*REQ*	*IND*	*RES*	*CNF*
Error Code		M		

Error Code Error codes conveyed between UDCP providers are defined in the next chapter.

4.5.4 UDCP-Release

This service is used by the user to release the USSD dialog:

PRIMITIVE	UDCP-ERROR			
PARAMETER	*REQ*	*IND*	*RES*	*CNF*
Release Code	O	C(=)		

Release Code Release codes conveyed between UDCP providers are defined in the next chapter.

4.6 Data Transfer

4.6.1 Motivation

Data transfer is the procedure to transfer data over the USSD dialog between a mobile and a network node in full-duplex mode.

4.6.2 Procedure at the Mobile

The UDCP user sends data by issuing the UDCP-Data request primitive. If an address to an External Node is included, the Data_Long PDU is used for the dialog. If not, the Data PDU is used. See separate chapter on Addressing.

If the UDCP user is WDP [WDP], the user data will consist of the port number and the fragmentation Information Elements and the WDP user data.

The transmission mode of USSD dialog is two-way alternate. During the time when the remote entity has the turn to send, the local UDCP user may initiate UDCP-Data request primitives. In that case, data has to be buffered up until the local UDCP provider has the turn to send.

If the UDCP provider has more data to send than it can send in one USSD operation, it should set the More To Send (MTS) flag in the Data PDU. This indicates to the remote UDCP provider that it immediately should return an operation in order to enable for the sender to send the rest of the data. When the local UDCP provider has no more data to send, it clears the MTS flag. When a UDCP provider receives a PDU with the MTS flag set, and it has no data to send, it MUST return the Receive Ready PDU. The Receive Ready PDU is a dummy PDU sent only to give the token to the remote entity.

4.7 Error Handling

4.7.1 Motivation

If an error occurs that does not lead to a USSD dialog release, the peer should be informed by returning the Error PDU with an appropriate error code.

If an error occurs that does lead to a USSD dialog releasing, the UDCP provider MAY reestablish the dialog automatically.

4.7.2 Procedure

If an error occurs that cannot be mapped to any existing error code, the UDCP provider MUST return the Error PDU with the error code set to UNKNOWN.

If the UDCP provider receives a USSD string that it is unable to interpret, it MUST return the Error PDU with the error code set to PROTOERROR.

If the UDCP provider receives a UDCP PDU with a version number different from 0x00, it MUST return the Error PDU with the error code set to UDCPVERSIONZERO to indicate that the supported version is 0x00.

If the UDCP provider receives the UDCP Data_Long PDU and only supports service code addressing, it MUST return the Error PDU with the error code set to EXTADDRNOTSUPP.

4.8 USSD Dialog Release

4.8.1 Motivation

Before UDCP releases the USSD dialog it informs the remote UDCP provider.

4.8.2 Procedure

The dialog release procedure may be triggered by different events. Depending on the event that triggered the release, different release codes are used.

The UDCP user has issued the UDCP-Release request primitive. Release code = USER.

The UDCP provider MAY monitor the USSD network timers in the network [GSM0902]. Before any of the timers expire, the dialog can be released and reestablished. This will refresh the timers, and the GSM network will not abort the dialog due to a timer expiration. Release code = UTIMEOUT.

The UDCP provider MAY keep the dialog established for some time after the last Data PDU is sent. This can be done by counting the number of subsequent RR PDUs. When the number of RR PDUs has reached a specified value, the dialog is released. Release code = UIDLE.

The procedure to gracefully release the USSD dialog is different depending on the type of USSD dialog: mobile or network originated.

Mobile-initiated dialog. If the mobile releases the dialog, it sends the Release Dialog PDU in the Response USSDRequest operation. The network should respond by sending the Release Dialog PDU in the Response ProcessUSSDRequest operation and terminate the dialog. If the network releases the dialog, it sends the Release Dialog PDU in the Response ProcessUSSDRequest operation, and the dialog is terminated.

Network-initiated dialog. If the mobile releases the dialog, it sends the Release Dialog PDU in the Response USSDRequest operation, and the dialog is terminated. If the network releases the dialog, it sends the Release Dialog PDU in the Request USSDRequest operation. The mobile should respond by sending the Release Dialog PDU in the Response USSDRequest operation and terminate the dialog.

4.9 Timers and Counters

4.9.1 Idle Timer (IT)

If a Receive Ready PDU is received and there is no data to be sent, the receiver waits IT seconds before returning a response.

Recommended value : 2–10 seconds

4.9.2 Number of RR (NumOfRR)

This counter counts the number of received subsequent RR PDUs. When the value reaches its maximum, MaxNumOfRR, the dialog is released.

Recommended value of MaxNumOfRR : 1–5

4.10 Protocol Data Units

4.10.1 Data PDU

The Data PDU is used to send data between the Mobile and the USSD network node. This is used when the USSD network node can be identified by the Service Code (sent in the first USSD operation of the USSD dialog).

BIT/OCTET	7	6	5	4	3	2	1	0
1	PDUtype = 0x00			RES	Version	MTS	RES	RES

4.10.2 Data_Long PDU

The Data_Long PDU is a special Data PDU used to send data between a Mobile and a node external to the GSM network. In this case, the Service Code identifies the USSD network node. In the USSD network node the data is extracted and relayed to an external node. The address to the external node is included in the Data_Long PDU.

BIT/OCTET	7	6	5	4	3	2	1	0
1	PDUtype = 0x01			RES	Version	MTS	RES	RES
2	Address Type				Address Length = N			
3 ... 2+N	Address Data							

4.10.3 Receive Ready (RR) PDU

This is a dummy PDU sent only to overcome the two-way alternate mode of the USSD dialog.

BIT/OCTET	7	6	5	4	3	2	1	0
1	PDUtype = 0x02			RES	Version	RES	RES	RES

4.10.4 Error PDU

The Error PDU is used to indicate an error to the peer.

BIT/OCTET	7	6	5	4	3	2	1	0
1	PDUtype = 0x03			RES	Version	Error Reason		

4.10.5 Release Dialog (RD) PDU

This is used by UDCP to indicate to the remote provider that the dialog will be released.

BIT/OCTET	7	6	5	4	3	2	1	0
1	PDUtype = 0x04			RES	Version	Release Code		

4.11 Header Fields

4.11.1 More to Send Flag (MTS)

The sender sets the More To Send flag to indicate that it has more data to send. The receiver must return an operation to enable the sender to send the rest of the data. If the receiver has no data to send, it should send the Receive Ready PDU.

If the flag is clear it indicates that the sender has no data to send. This is used to poll the remote entity.

4.11.2 Address Field

In the network-to-mobile direction the Address field holds the source address, and in the opposite direction it holds the destination address. This address corresponds to the destination/source address field in an SMS message, see [GSM 0340].

Encoding of the Address Type is specified in [WDP].

4.11.3 Version Flag

The current version number is 0x00.

4.11.4 Error Code

The following error codes have been defined:

ERROR	CODE	DESCRIPTION
Unknown (UNKNOWN)	0x00	A generic error code indicating an unexpected error.
Protocol error (PROTOERR)	0x01	The received PDU could not be interpreted. The structure may be wrong.
UDCP Version Zero (UDCPVERSIONZERO)	0x02	Current version is 0.
External Addressing Not Supported (EXTADDRNOTSUPP)	0x03	The Data_Long PDU was received but the provider does not support addressing of external node.

4.11.5 Release Code

The following release codes have been defined:

ERROR	CODE	DESCRIPTION
Unknown (UNKNOWN)	0x00	A generic error release code.
USSD Timer Expiration (UTIMEOUT)	0x01	The dialog is released by the UDCP provider to refresh a USSD network timer that otherwise would terminate the dialog at expiration.

Idle USSD Dialog (UIDLE)	0x02	The dialog is released by the UDCP provider since the dialog has been idle for longer time than specified as the maximum idle time at the provider.
User abort (USER)	0x03	The UDCP user triggered the abort by issuing the UDCP-Release request primitive.

5. UDCP State Tables

5.1 Event Processing

The interface to the next higher layer is defined by the UDCP service primitives. When the UDCP user issues a primitive, the corresponding event is generated. The next lower layer is the USSD service of the GSM phase 2 network. The following GSM phase 2 USSD operations are used by the UDCP state tables (see Table 19.5).

For a complete description of how the USSD operations are used and how the USSD dialog is initiated and terminated, see [GSM0290], [GSM0390], and [GSM0490]. When a USSD operation has been received, the USSD String is extracted, the UDCP control information analyzed, and an event is generated depending on the PDU type. For example, *RcvData* means that a Data PDU (or Data_Long PDU) has been received.

An event is validated before it is processed. The tests listed in Table 19.6 are performed, and if no action is taken, the event is processed according to the state tables.

Table 19.5 GSM Phase 2 Operation Used in the State Tables

GSM PHASE 2 USSD OPERATION	DESCRIPTION
USSDRequest	Initiates a dialog from the network. Used to invoke operations from the network within an established dialog.
ProcessUSSDRequest	Initiates a dialog from the mobile.

Table 19.6 Test of Events

TEST	ACTION
UDCP-Data.req and size of UserData > max size of USSD string	Generate UDCP-Error.ind
Illegal PDU type or erroneous structure	Send Error (PROTOERR)
Received PDU with version != 0x00	Send Error (UDCPVERSIONZERO)
Received Data_Long PDU without support for addressing to external node	Send Error (EXTADDRNOTSUPP)
Any other event not handled by the state tables	Ignore

5.2 Actions

5.2.1 Timers

The following timer actions can be used in the state tables:

Start timer, <value>. Starts the timer with the specified interval value. If the timer is already running, it is restarted with the new value.

Stop timer. Stops the timer without generating an event.

5.2.2 Counters

The following counter actions can be used in the state tables:

<counter>++. Add 1 to the counter value.

5.2.3 Messages

The following message actions can be used in the state tables:

USSDRequest. At the mobile this action sends the Invoke ProcessUSSDRequest. In the network this action sends the Invoke USSDRequest.

USSDResponse. At the mobile this action sends the Result USSDRequest. In the network this action sends the Result ProcessUSSDRequest.

5.2.4 Output Buffer

The UDCP provider manages an output buffer to queue outgoing messages. The buffer has the following methods:

Empty(). Returns True if the buffer is empty. Returns False if the buffer is not empty.

Length(). Returns the number of messages in the buffer. The maximum number of messages in the queue is MAX_BUF.

Queue(). Adds another message to the queue.

Dequeue(). Dequeues a message. The message is removed from the queue.

5.2.5 USSD Dialog

The following USSD Dialog actions can be used in the state tables:

Release Dialog. Release the USSD dialog. How this action is executed is implementation dependent.

Initiate Dialog. Initiate the USSD dialog. How this action is executed is implementation dependent.

5.2.6 States

The following states are used in the state tables:

IDLE. In this state there is no USSD dialog established.

LISTEN. In this state there is no USSD dialog established. The provider is listening for an incoming USSD dialog invocation.

WAIT NETWORK. The UDCP provider in the mobile is waiting for a USSD operation to be sent from the network.

WAIT MOBILE. The UDCP provider in the network is waiting for a USSD operation to the sent from the mobile.

WAIT USER. The UDCP provider is waiting for the local user to issue a service primitive. The Idle Timer is running.

5.3 Mobile-Initiated USSD Dialog

5.3.1 Mobile

UDCP MOBILE IDLE MOBILE-INITIATED DIALOG			
EVENT	**CONDITION**	**ACTION**	**NEXT STATE**
UDCP-Data.req		Initiate Dialog Send USSDRequest (Data PDU) ReleaseDlg = False NumOfRR = 0	WAIT NETWORK
UDCP-Release.req		Initiate Dialog Send USSDRequest (RD PDU) NumOfRR = 0	

UDCP MOBILE WAIT NETWORK MOBILE-INITIATED DIALOG			
EVENT	**CONDITION**	**ACTION**	**NEXT STATE**
RcvData	MTS == True	Generate UDCP-Data.ind Send USSDResponse (RR PDU) NumOfRR = 0	WAIT NETWORK
	MTS == False	Generate UDCP-Data.ind Start timer, IT NumOfRR = 0	WAIT USER
	!OutBuf.Empty()	Generate UDCP-Data.ind SendPDU = OutBuf.Dequeue() SendPDU.MTS = OutBuf.Empty() Send USSDResponse (SendPDU) NumOfRR = 0	WAIT NETWORK
	ReleaseDlg == True	Send USSDResponse (RD PDU) NumOfRR = 0	WAIT NETWORK

UDCP MOBILE WAIT NETWORK MOBILE-INITIATED DIALOG (*CONT.*)			
EVENT	**CONDITION**	**ACTION**	**NEXT STATE**
RcvRR	!OutBuf.Empty()	SendPDU = OutBuf.Dequeue() SendPDU.MTS = OutBuf.Empty() Send USSDResponse (SendPDU) NumOfRR = 0	WAIT NETWORK
	NumOfRR < MaxNumOfRR	Start timer, IT NumOfRR++	WAIT USER
	NumOfRR == MaxNumOfRR	Send USSDResponse (RD PDU)	WAIT NETWORK
	ReleaseDlg == True	Send USSDResponse (RD PDU)	WAIT NETWORK
RcvRD		Release Dialog	IDLE
UDCP-Data.req	OutBuf.Length() < MAX_BUF	OutBuf.Queue(Data PDU) NumOfRR = 0	WAIT NETWORK
	OutBuf.Length() == MAX_BUF	Generate UDCP-Error.ind (BUFFEROVERFLOW) NumOfRR = 0	
UDCP-Release.req	ReleaseDlg = True		

UDCP MOBILE WAIT USER MOBILE-INITIATED DIALOG			
EVENT	**CONDITION**	**ACTION**	**NEXT STATE**
UDCP-Data.req		Send USSDResponse (Data PDU)	WAIT NETWORK
TimerTO		Send USSDResponse (RR PDU)	
UDCP-Release.req		Send USSDResponse (RD PDU)	

5.3.2 Network

UDCP NETWORK LISTEN MOBILE-INITIATED DIALOG			
EVENT	**CONDITION**	**ACTION**	**NEXT STATE**
RcvData	MTS == True	Generate UDCP-Data.ind Send USSDRequest (RR PDU) ReleaseDlg = False NumOfRR = 0	WAIT MOBILE
	MTS == False	Generate UDCP-Data.ind Start timer, IT ReleaseDlg = False NumOfRR = 0	WAIT USER
RcvRD		Send USSDResponse (RD PDU) Release Dialog	LISTEN

UDCP NETWORK WAIT MOBILE MOBILE-INITIATED DIALOG			
EVENT	**CONDITION**	**ACTION**	**NEXT STATE**
RcvData	MTS == True	Generate UDCP-Data.ind Send USSDRequest (RR PDU) NumOfRR = 0	WAIT MOBILE
	MTS == False	Generate UDCP-Data.ind Start timer, IT NumOfRR = 0	WAIT USER
	!OutBuf.Empty()	Generate UDCP-Data.ind SendPDU = OutBuf.Dequeue() SendPDU.MTS = OutBuf.Empty() Send USSDRequest (SendPDU) NumOfRR = 0	WAIT MOBILE
	ReleaseDlg == True	Send USSDResponse (RD PDU) NumOfRR = 0	LISTEN
RcvRD		Send USSDResponse (RD PDU)	LISTEN
RcvRR	!OutBuf.Empty()	SendPDU = OutBuf.Dequeue() SendPDU.MTS = OutBuf.Empty() Send USSDRequest (SendPDU) NumOfRR = 0	WAIT MOBILE
	NumOfRR < MaxNumOfRR	start timer, IT NumOfRR++	WAIT USER
	NumOfRR == MaxNumOfRR	Send USSDResponse (RD PDU) Release Dialog	LISTEN
	ReleaseDlg == True	Send USSDResponse (RD PDU) Release Dialog	LISTEN
UDCP-Data.req	OutBuf.Length() < MAX_BUF	OutBuf.Queue(Data PDU) NumOfRR = 0	WAIT MOBILE
	OutBuf.Length() == MAX_BUF	Generate UDCP-Error.ind (BUFFEROVERFLOW) NumOfRR = 0	
UDCP-Release.req		ReleaseDlg = True	WAIT MOBILE

UDCP NETWORK WAIT USER MOBILE-INITIATED DIALOG			
EVENT	**CONDITION**	**ACTION**	**NEXT STATE**
UDCP-Data.req		Send USSDRequest (Data PDU)	WAIT MOBILE
TimerTO		Send USSDRequest (RR PDU)	
UDCP-Release.req		Send USSDResponse (RD PDU)	

5.4 Network-Initiated USSD Dialog

5.4.1 Mobile

UDCP MOBILE LISTEN NETWORK-INITIATED DIALOG			
EVENT	**CONDITION**	**ACTION**	**NEXT STATE**
RcvData	MTS == True	Generate UDCP-Data.ind Send USSDResponse (RR PDU) ReleaseDlg = False NumOfRR = 0	WAIT NETWORK
	MTS == False	Generate UDCP-Data.ind Start timer, IT ReleaseDlg = False NumOfRR = 0	WAIT USER
RcvRD		Send USSDResponse (RD PDU) Release Dialog	LISTEN

UDCP MOBILE WAIT NETWORK NETWORK-INITIATED DIALOG			
EVENT	**CONDITION**	**ACTION**	**NEXT STATE**
RcvData	MTS == True	Generate UDCP-Data.ind Send USSDResponse (RR PDU) NumOfRR = 0	WAIT NETWORK
	MTS == False	Generate UDCP-Data.ind Start timer, IT NumOfRR = 0	WAIT USER
	!OutBuf.Empty()	Generate UDCP-Data.ind SendPDU = OutBuf.Dequeue() SendPDU.MTS = OutBuf.Empty() Send USSDResponse (SendPDU) NumOfRR = 0	WAIT NETWORK
	ReleaseDlg == True	Send USSDResponse (RD PDU) Release Dialog	LISTEN
UDCP-Data.req	OutBuf.Length() < MAX_BUF	OutBuf.Queue(Data PDU) NumOfRR = 0	WAIT NETWORK
	OutBuf.Length() == MAX_BUF	Generate UDCP-Error.ind (BUFFEROVERFLOW) NumOfRR = 0	

UDCP MOBILE WAIT NETWORK NETWORK-INITIATED DIALOG (*CONT.*)			
EVENT	**CONDITION**	**ACTION**	**NEXT STATE**
RcvRR	!OutBuf.Empty()	SendPDU = OutBuf.Dequeue() SendPDU.MTS = OutBuf.Empty() Send USSDResponse (SendPDU) NumOfRR = 0	WAIT NETWORK
	NumOfRR < MaxNumOfRR	Start timer, IT NumOfRR++	WAIT USER
	NumOfRR == MaxNumOfRR	Send USSDResponse (RD PDU) Release Dialog	LISTEN
	ReleaseDlg == True	Send USSDResponse (RD PDU) Release Dialog	LISTEN
RcvRD		Send USSDResponse (RD PDU) Release Dialog	LISTEN
UDCP-Release.req		ReleaseDlg = True	WAIT NETWORK

UDCP MOBILE WAIT USER NETWORK-INITIATED DIALOG			
EVENT	**CONDITION**	**ACTION**	**NEXT STATE**
UDCP-Data.req		Send USSDResponse (Data PDU)	WAIT NETWORK
TimerTO		Send USSDResponse (RR PDU)	
UDCP-Release.req		Send USSDResponse (RD PDU) Release Dialog	

5.4.2 Network

UDCP NETWORK IDLE NETWORK-INITIATED DIALOG			
EVENT	**CONDITION**	**ACTION**	**NEXT STATE**
UDCP-Data.req		Initiate Dialog Send USSDRequest (Data PDU) ReleaseDlg = False NumOfRR = 0	WAIT MOBILE
UDCP-Release.req		Initiate Dialog Send USSDRequest (RD PDU)	

UDCP NETWORK WAIT MOBILE NETWORK-INITIATED DIALOG			
EVENT	**CONDITION**	**ACTION**	**NEXT STATE**
RcvData	MTS == True	Generate UDCP-Data.ind Send USSDRequest (RR PDU) NumOfRR = 0	WAIT MOBILE
	MTS == False	Generate UDCP-Data.ind Start timer, IT NumOfRR = 0	WAIT USER
	!OutBuf.Empty()	Generate UDCP-Data.ind SendPDU = OutBuf.Dequeue() SendPDU.MTS = OutBuf.Empty() Send USSDRequest (SendPDU) NumOfRR = 0	WAIT MOBILE
	ReleaseDlg == True	Send USSDRequest (RD PDU) NumOfRR = 0	WAIT MOBILE
RcvRR	!OutBuf.Empty()	SendPDU = OutBuf.Dequeue() SendPDU.MTS = OutBuf.Empty() Send USSDResponse (SendPDU) NumOfRR = 0	WAIT MOBILE
	NumOfRR < MaxNumOfRR	Start timer, IT NumOfRR++	WAIT USER
	NumOfRR == MaxNumOfRR	Send USSDRequest (RD PDU)	WAIT MOBILE
	ReleaseDlg == True	Send USSDRequest (RD PDU)	WAIT MOBILE
UDCP-Data.req	OutBuf.Length() < MAX_BUF	OutBuf.Queue(Data PDU) NumOfRR = 0	WAIT MOBILE
	OutBuf.Length() == MAX_BUF	Generate UDCP-Error.ind (BUFFEROVERFLOW) NumOfRR = 0	
UDCP-Release.req		ReleaseDlg = True	WAIT MOBILE
RcvRD		Release Dialog	IDLE

UDCP NETWORK WAIT USER NETWORK-INITIATED DIALOG			
EVENT	**CONDITION**	**ACTION**	**NEXT STATE**
UDCP-Data.req		Send USSDRequest (Data PDU)	WAIT MOBILE
IdleTimerTO		Send USSDRequest (RR PDU)	
UDCP-Release.req		Send USSDRequest (RD PDU)	

5.5 Example of WDP and UDCP

Figure 19.6 illustrates how the WDP protocol interworks with the UDCP protocol. Two datagrams, WDP SDU(1) and WDP SDU(2), are sent from the mobile to the network.

The WDP provider starts off by sending two subsequent datagrams to the UDCP provider. The UDCP provider establishes a USSD dialog to the USSD Node identified by the Service Code. The Service Code is provided to the UDCP provider from WDP as a parameter of the service primitive. In the first operation the MTS flag is set (not indicated in the figure) in the Data PDU. When the USSD Node receives the PDU with the MTS flag, it immediately returns the dummy RR PDU to allow for the mobile to send another USSD operation. Recall that the USSD dialog is half-duplex; the mobile cannot send the next operation before the network has returned an operation. Once the dummy RR PDU has been received by the mobile, the next Data PDU is sent with the last WDP SDU. This time the MTS is not set, since the mobile has no more data to send. When the USSD Node receives the Data PDU with the MTS flag clear, it waits for a period of time specified by the Idle Timer, after that it sends the RR PDU to poll the remote entity. After having received MaxNumOfRR number of RR PDUs, the USSD Node sends the RD PDU to release the dialog. The value of MaxNumOfRR is an implementation issue. In this example MaxNumOfRR =1.

6. Definitions

For the purpose of this specification the following definitions apply:

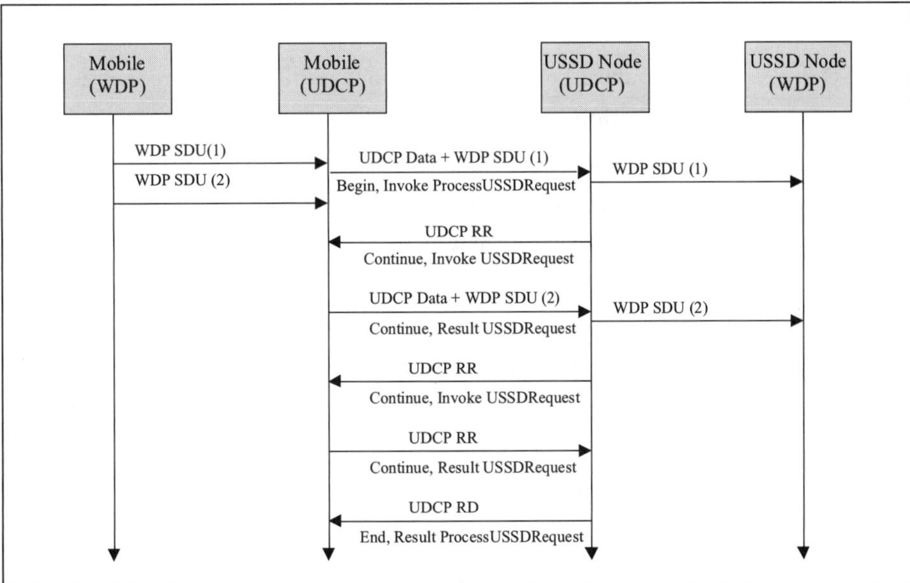

Figure 19.6 Example of WDP and UDCP interworking.

External Node. A node external to the GSM network. For example, a WAP Gateway.

Message. A general name for any PDU type.

Protocol Control Information (PCI). Information exchanged between two protocol entities to coordinate their joint operation.

Protocol Data Unit (PDU). A unit of data consisting of protocol control information and possibly user data.

Service Data Unit (SDU). An amount of data handed down to the lower layer and whose identity is preserved from one end of a connection to the other.

Service Primitive. An abstract, implementation-independent interaction between a user and the provider.

USSD Node. A node in the GSM network able to receive and initiate USSD dialogs. The network node may be connected to the MSC, VLR, or HLR. See [GSM0290].

USSD String. A parameter of the USSD operation. See [GSM0902].

USSD Operation. Operation in the GSM network used to send and receive USSD strings. See [GSM0902].

7. Abbreviations

For the purposes of this specification the following abbreviations apply:

DCS	Data Coding Scheme
ETSI	European Telecommunication Standardization Institute
GSM	Global System for Mobile Communication
IE	Information Element
MSISDN	Mobile Subscriber ISDN (Telephone number or address of device)
MS	Mobile Station
MSB	Most significant bits
NEI	Network Element Identifier
PCI	Protocol Control Information
PLMN	Public Land Mobile Network
RTT	Round-Trip Time
SAR	Segmentation and Reassembly
SMS	Short Message Service
PDU	Protocol Data Unit
SAP	Service Access Point
SDU	Service Data Unit
TCAP	Transaction Capability Application Part
UDCP	USSD Dialog Control Protocol
UDH	User-Data Header (see [GSM 03.40])

UDHL	User-Data Header Length (see [GSM 03.40])
UDL	User-Data Length (see [GSM 03.40])
USSD	Unstructured Supplementary Service Data
WAE	Wireless Application Environment
WAP	Wireless Application Protocol
WSP	Wireless Session Protocol
WTP	Wireless Transaction Protocol
WDP	Wireless Datagram Protocol

8. Requirements

This specification uses the following words for defining the significance of each particular requirement:

MUST. This word, or the terms "REQUIRED" or "SHALL," means that the definition is an absolute requirement of the specification.

MUST NOT. This phrase, or the phrase "SHALL NOT," means that the definition is an absolute prohibition of the specification.

SHOULD. This word, or the adjective "RECOMMENDED," means that there may exist valid reasons in particular circumstances to ignore a particular item, but the full implications must be understood and carefully weighed before choosing a different course.

SHOULD NOT. This phrase, or the phrase "NOT RECOMMENDED," means that there may exist valid reasons in particular circumstances when the particular behavior is acceptable or even useful, but the full implications should be understood and the case carefully weighed before implementing any behavior described with this label.

MAY. This word, or the adjective "OPTIONAL," means that an item is truly optional. One vendor may choose to include the item because a particular marketplace requires it or because the vendor feels that it enhances the product while another vendor may omit the same item. An implementation that does not include a particular option MUST be prepared to interoperate with another implementation that does include the option, though perhaps with reduced functionality. In the same vein, an implementation that does include a particular option MUST be prepared to interoperate with another implementation that does not include the option. (except, of course, for the feature the option provides.)

9. Normative References

[GSM0290] ETSI European Digital Cellular Telecommunication Systems (phase 2) : Unstructured Supplementary Service Data (USSD)—stage 1 (GSM 02.90).

[GSM0338] ETSI European Digital Cellular Telecommunication Systems (phase 2+) : Alphabets and language-specific information (GSM 03.38).

[GSM0340] ETSI European Digital Cellular Telecommunication Systems (phase 2+) : Technical realization of the Short Message Service (SMS) Point-to-Point (P) (GSM 03.40 version 5.6.x).

[GSM0390] ETSI European Digital Cellular Telecommunication Systems (phase 2) : Unstructured Supplementary Service Data (USSD)—stage 2 (GSM 03.90).

[GSM0490] ETSI European Digital Cellular Telecommunication Systems (phase 2) : Unstructured Supplementary Service Data (USSD)—stage 3 (GSM 04.90).

[GSM0902] ETSI European Digital Cellular Telecommunication Systems (phase 2) : Mobile Application Part (MAP) specification (GSM 09.02).

[ISO7498] ISO 7498 OSI Reference Model.

[ISO8509] ISO TR 8509 Service conventions.

[RFC2119] S. Bradner "Key Words for Use in RFCs to Indicate Requirement Levels," RFC2119.
URL: http://www.internic.net/rfc/rfc2119.txt

[WTP] "Wireless Transaction Protocol," WAP Forum, 1998.
URL: http://www.wapforum.org/

[WDP] "Wireless Datagram Protocol Specification," WAP Forum, 1998.
URL: http://www.wapforum.org/

[WSP] "Wireless Session Protocol Specification," WAP Forum, 1998.
URL: http://www.wapforum.org/

Appendix A: PICS Proforma

The supplier of a protocol implementation that claims conformance to this Specification shall complete a copy of the PICS proforma provided in this appendix, including the information necessary to identify both the supplier and the implementation.

A.1 Introduction

The supplier of a protocol implementation which is claimed to conform to this Specification shall complete the following Protocol Implementation Conformance Statement (PICS) proforma.

A completed PICS proforma is the PICS for the implementation in question. The PICS is a statement of which capabilities and options of the protocol have been implemented. The PICS can have a number of uses, including use by

- The protocol implementor, as a checklist to reduce the risk of failure to conform to the standard through oversight
- The supplier and acquirer—or potential acquirer—of the implementation, as a detailed indication of the capabilities of the implementation, stated relative to the common basis for understanding provided by the standard PICS proforma

- The user—or potential user—of the implementation, as a basis for initially checking the possibility of interworking with another implementation (note that, while interworking can never be guaranteed, failure to interwork can often be predicted from incompatible PICSs)
- A protocol tester, as the basis for selecting appropriate tests against which to assess the claim for conformance of the implementation

A.2 Abbreviations and Special Symbols

A.2.1 Status Symbols

M	Mandatory
O	Optional
O.<n>	Optional, but support of at least one of the group of options labeled by the same numeral <n> is required.
X	Prohibited
<pred>:	Conditional-item symbol, including predicate identification (see Section A.3.4)
^	Logical negation, applied to a conditional item's predicate

A.2.2 Other Symbols

<r>	Receive aspects of an item
<s>	Send aspects of an item

A.3 Instructions for Completing the PICS Proforma

A.3.1 General Structure of the PICS Proforma

The first part of the PICS proforma—Implementation Identification and Protocol Summary—is to be completed as indicated with the information necessary to identify fully both the supplier and the implementation.

The main part of the PICS proforma is a fixed-format questionnaire divided into a number of major subclauses; these can be divided into further subclauses, each containing a group of individual items. Answers to the questionnaire items are to be provided in the right most column, either by simply marking an answer to indicate a restricted choice (usually Yes or No), or by entering a value or a set or range of values.

Note: There are some items for which two or more choices from a set of possible answers can apply. All relevant choices are to be marked in these cases.

Each item is identified by an item reference in the first column; the second column contains the question to be answered; and the third column contains the reference or references to the material that specifies the item in the main body of this Specification. The remaining columns record the status of the item—whether support is mandatory, optional, prohibited, or conditional—and provide space for the answers (see also Section B.3.4).

A supplier may also provide further information, categorized as either Additional Information or Exception Information. When present, each kind of further information is to be provided in a further subclause of items labeled A<i> or X<i>, respectively, for cross-referencing purposes, where <i> is any unambiguous identification for the item (e.g., a number); there are no other restrictions on its format or presentation.

A completed PICS proforma, including any Additional Information and Exception Information, is the Protocol Implementation Conformance Statement for the implementation in question.

Note: Where an implementation is capable of being configured in more than one way, a single PICS may be able to describe all such configurations. However, the supplier has the choice of providing more than one PICS, each covering some subset of the implementation's configuration capabilities, in cases where this makes for easier and clearer presentation of the information.

A.3.2 Additional Information

Items of Additional Information allow a supplier to provide further information intended to assist in the interpretation of the PICS. It is not intended or expected that a large quantity will be supplied, and a PICS can be considered complete without any such information. Examples might be an outline of the ways in which a (single) implementation can be set up to operate in a variety of environments and configurations, or a brief rationale—based perhaps upon specific application needs—for the exclusion of features which, although optional, are nonetheless commonly present in implementations of this protocol.

References to items of Additional Information may be entered next to any answer in the questionnaire, and may be included in items of Exception Information.

A.3.3 Exception Information

It may occasionally happen that a supplier will wish to answer an item with mandatory or prohibited status (after any conditions have been applied) in a way that conflicts with the indicated requirement. No preprinted answer will be found in the support column for this; instead, the supplier shall write the missing answer into the Support column, together with an X<i> reference to an item of Exception Information, and shall provide the appropriate rationale in the Exception Information item itself.

An implementation for which an Exception Information item is required in this way does not conform to this Specification.

Note: A possible reason for the situation just described is that a defect in the standard has been reported, a correction for which is expected to change the requirement not met by the implementation.

A.3.4 Conditional Status

A.3.4.1 Conditional Items

The PICS proforma contains a number of conditional items. These are items for which the status—mandatory, optional, or prohibited—that applies is dependent upon whether or not certain other items are supported, or upon the values supported for other items.

In many cases, whether or not the item applies at all is conditional in this way, as well as the status when the item does apply.

Where a group of items is subject to the same condition for applicability, a separate preliminary question about the condition appears at the head of the group, with an instruction to skip to a later point in the questionnaire if the "Not Applicable" answer is selected. Otherwise, individual conditional items are indicated by one or more conditional symbols (on separate lines) in the status column.

A conditional symbol is of the form "<pred>:<x>", where "<pred>" is a predicate as described in Section A.3.4.2, and "<x>" is one of the status symbols M, O, O.<n>, or X.

If the value of the predicate in any line of a conditional item is true (see Section A.3.4.2), then the conditional item is applicable, and its status is that indicated by the status symbol following the predicate; the answer column is to be marked in the usual way. If the value of a predicate is false, the Not Applicable (N/A) answer is to be marked in the relevant line. Each line in a multiline conditional item should be marked: at most one line will require an answer other than N/A.

A.3.4.2 Predicates

A predicate is one of the following:

a) An item-reference for an item in the PICS proforma: The value of the predicate is true if the item is marked as supported, and is false otherwise.
b) A predicate name, for a predicate defined elsewhere in the PICS proforma (usually in the Major Capabilities section or at the end of the section containing the conditional item).
c) The logical negation symbol "^" prefixed to an item-reference or predicate name: The value of the predicate is true if the value of the predicate formed by omitting the "^" is false, and vice versa.

The definition for a predicate name is one of the following

a) An item-reference, evaluated as at (a) above.
b) A relation containing a comparison operator (=, < , etc.) with at least one of its operands being an item-reference for an item taking numerical values as its answer. The predicate is true if the relation holds when each item-reference is replaced by the value entered in the Support column as an answer to the item referred to.
c) A Boolean expression constructed by combining simple predicates, as in (a) and (b), using the Boolean operators AND, OR, and NOT, and parentheses, in the usual way. The value of such a predicate is true if the Boolean expression evaluates to true when the simple predicates are interpreted as described.

Each item whose reference is used in a predicate or predicate definition is indicated by an asterisk in the Item column.

A.4 Identification

A.4.1 Implementation Identification

Supplier	
Contact point for queries about the PICS	
Implementation name(s) and version(s)	
Other information necessary for full identification (e.g., name(s) and version(s) of machines and/or operating systems, system name(s))	

NOTES

1 Only the first three items are required for all implementations; other information may be completed as appropriate in meeting the requirement for full identification.

2 The terms Name and Version should be interpreted appropriately to correspond with a supplier's terminology (e.g., Type, Series, Model).

A.4.2 Protocol Summary

Identification of protocol specification	WAP USSD Dialog Control Protocol
Identification of corrigenda and amendments of the PICS proforma	
Protocol version(s) supported	
Have any Exception Information items been required? (see Section A.3.3) (The answer YES means that the implementation does not conform to this Specification.)	YES ❐ NO ❐
Date of statement	

A.5 USSD Dialog Control Protocol

A.5.1 Applicability

Clause A.5 is applicable to all implementations that claim conformance to this Specification.

A.5.5 Protocol Functions

ITEM	FUNCTION	REFERENCE	STATUS	SUPPORT	
ADSC	Does the implementation support addressing using the service code?	4.6	M	YES	NO
ADSCEX	Does the implementation support addressing using the service code and an external address?	4.6	O	YES	NO
ERRO	Does the implementation support error handling?	4.7	M	YES	NO
DRUS	Does the implementation support dialog release issued by the user?	4.8	M	YES	NO
DRNT	Does the implementation support dialog release to refresh USSD network timers?	4.8	O	YES	NO
DRID	Does the implementation support dialog release due to an idle dialog?	4.8	O	YES	NO

Appendix B: History and Contact Information

Document History		
Date	Status	Comment
29-April-1998	Specification	First version

Contact Information

http://www.wapforum.org.

technical-comments@wapforum.org

Index

CUSTOMER NOTE: IF THIS BOOK IS ACCOMPANIED BY SOFTWARE, PLEASE READ THE FOLLOWING BEFORE OPENING THE PACKAGE.

To use this CD-ROM, your system must meet the following requirements:

Macintosh:
Apple Macintosh with a 68040 Processor (or later) or a PowerPC
Minimum of 13 MB Free Memory
Apple System Software 7.5 or later

Windows (32-bit):
486 processor or higher (Pentium recommended)
Win95, Win98 or NT 3.51 or higher
Win95: 12 MB RAM; Win98 or NT: 16 MB RAM
3 MB free disk space for compact install; 15 MB disk space for normal install

Windows (16-bit):
386 processor or higher (486 recommended)
Windows 3.1 or higher
Minimum 8 MB RAM (12 MB recommended)
3 MB free disk space for compact install; 15 MB disk space for normal install